MW01014025

STECK-VAUGHN

HISTORY *of Our* WORLD

People, Places, and Ideas™

Henry Billings

www.steck-vaughn.com

About the Author

Henry Billings received his B.A. from the University of Massachusetts and his M.A.T. in World History from Salem State College. He has more than 16 years experience as a classroom teacher. He is the author of several Social Studies textbooks on topics ranging from Economics to History to Geography.

Content Reviewer

Jonathan Lee, Ph.D.
Assistant Professor of History
San Antonio College

Educational Reviewer

Roberta L. Frenkel
Director of English Language Arts and Social Studies, District 3
Scarsdale, New York

Acknowledgments

Editorial Director: Diane Schnell
Associate Editor: Terra G. Tarango
Associate Editor: Victoria Davis
Associate Director of Design: Joyce Spicer
Senior Designer: Joan Cunningham
Project Assistant: April Litz
Production Manager: Mychael Ferris-Pacheco
Production Coordinator: Susan Tyson Fogarasi
Image Services Coordinator: Ted Krause
Senior Technical Advisor: Alan Klemp
Electronic Production Specialists: David Hanshaw, John-Paxton Gremillion, Scott Melcer, Marc Watson
Electronic Production Artist: Perla Arce
Senior Photo Researcher: Alyx Kellington
Director of New Media: Sammi Frye
Website Producer: Linda LeFan

Credits

Illustrations: Leslie Evans p. 11 (icon), 14 (globe icon), 22, 43 (icon), 82 (icon), 106, 118, 125, 147 (icon), 152, 180, 194, 202 (icon), 242, 243 (icon), 265 (icon), 288, 319, 320 (icon), 328 (icon), 336, 366, 368 (icon), 403 (icon), 420 (icon), 434, 452, 453 (icon), 484 (icon), 525 (icon); David Chapman p.19 (Egyptian children), p.137 (Great Wall detail), p. 148 (Feudalism in Western Europe), p.236 (Feudalism in Japan)

Cartography: Maps.com / MAGELLAN Geographix

Voices in History Excerpts: p. 28 Adapted from "Tutankhamun: Anatomy of an Excavation. Howard Carter's Personal Diaries, November 26, 1922." Copyright Griffith Institute, Oxford. Reprinted by permission; p. 200 From "The Creation," www.jaguar-sun.com/popolvuh.html by Jeeni Criscenzo. ©1999 by Jeeni Criscenzo. Reprinted by permission; p. 526 United Nations Resolution Press Release on the World Summit on the Information Society, Addressing the "Digital Divide" and Harnessing Development Potential of ICTs, Geneva, January 9, 2002, spoken by Secretary General Kofi Annan. Reprinted by permission.

Web Site Development: Maximize Learning

Photo Credits: Cv-c ©Lee & Lee Communications/Art Resource, NY; cv-d ©Werner Forman/Art Resource, NY; cv-e © Bettmann/CORBIS; cv-f ©The Art Archive; cv-h Courtesy of NASA; cv-i ©Adelman/Cohen/Getty Images; page iii(a) ©Douglas Mazonowicz/Art Resource, NY; iii(b) ©Araldo de Luca/CORBIS; iii(c) ©SuperStock; iii(d) ©Stock Montage; iii(e) ©Asian Art & Archaeology, Inc./CORBIS; iv(a) ©The British Museum; iv(b) ©Holton Collection/SuperStock; iv© ©The Metropolitan Museum of Art, The Harry G.C. Packard Collection of Asian Art, Gift of Harry G.C. Packard and Purchase, Fletcher, Rogers, Harris Brisbane Dick and Louis V. Bell Funds, Joseph Pulitzer Bequest and The Annenberg Fund, Inc. Gift, 1975; iv(d) ©Werner Forman/Art Resource, NY; iv(e) ©Danny Lehman/CORBIS; v(a) ©Burstein Collection/CORBIS; v(b) ©Sandro Vannini/CORBIS; v(c) ©Werner Forman/Art Resource, NY; v(d) ©Hulton Archive/Getty Images; v(e) ©Historical Picture Archive/CORBIS; vi(c) ©Museo Nacional de la Mascara San Luis Potosi Mexico/Mireille Vautier/The Art Archive; vi(d) ©Réunion des Musées Nationaux/Art Resource, NY; vi(e) ©CORBIS; vi(f) ©The Art Archive; vii(a) ©AP/Wide World; vii(b) ©CORBIS; vii(c) ©Roman Soumar/CORBIS; vii(d) ©AFP/CORBIS; vii(e) ©David Turnley/CORBIS; vii(f) ©Ken Lucas/Visuals Unlimited, Inc.; p.2c ©Mireille Vautier/The Art Archive; p.2e ©Erich Lessing/Art Resource, NY; p.3a ©Giovanni Dagli Orti/CORBIS; p.3b ©CORBIS; p.3c ©Werner Forman/Art Resource, NY; p.7b ©SuperStock; p.8 ©Gianni Tortoli/Photo Researchers; p.9a ©Archivo Iconografico, S.A./CORBIS; p.9b ©Bettmann/CORBIS; p.11a ©Jonathan Blair/ CORBIS; p.11 ©Jack Unruh/National Geographic Image Collection; p.12a ©Douglas Mazonowicz/Art Resource, NY; p.12b ©Jim Mann Taylor; p.12c ©Mireille Vautier/The Art Archive; p.13 ©Robert Frerck/Odyssey/Chicago; p.16a ©Christie's Images/SuperStock; p.16b ©Michele Burgess/SuperStock; p.18a ©Musee De Grenoble/SuperStock; p.19b ©Erich Lessing/Art Resource, NY; p.20 ©Jonathan Blair/CORBIS; p.21a ©Egyptian National Museum, Cairo, Egypt/SuperStock; p.21b ©The British Museum; p.23a © Staffan Widstrand/CORBIS; p.23b ©Gian Berto Vanni/CORBIS; p.24a ©Archivo Iconografico, S.A./CORBIS; p.24b ©Sandro Vannini/CORBIS; p.24c ©Roger Wood/CORBIS; p.25 ©Araldo de Luca/CORBIS; p.29a ©The Granger Collection; p.30a ©Werner Forman/Art Resource, NY; p.30b ©David Lees/CORBIS; p.31a ©British Museum, London/The Bridgeman Art Library; p.31b,c ©Gianni Dagli Orti/CORBIS; p.33 ©Brown Brothers; p.34a ©United Design; p.34b ©Archivo Iconografico, S.A./CORBIS; p.35b ©Stock Montage; p.37 ©The Granger Collection; p.40a ©Asian Art & Archaeology, Inc./CORBIS; p.41a ©Eye Ubiquitous/CORBIS; p.41b ©Christie's Images/CORBIS; p.42a ©Craig Lovell/CORBIS; p.42b ©Royal Ontario Museum/CORBIS; p.43 ©Giraudon/Art Resource, NY; p.44 ©Asian Art & Archaeology, Inc./CORBIS; p.45a ©Boltin Picture Library; p.46b ©CORBIS; p.47a ©Diego Lezama Orezzoli/CORBIS; p.47b ©Archivo Iconografico, S.A./CORBIS; p.48a ©Arvind Garg/CORBIS; p.49 ©Archivo Iconografico, S.A./CORBIS; p.53a ©Werner Forman Archive/Art Resource, NY;

continued on page 580

ISBN 0-7398-6087-9

Printed and bound in the United States.
1 2 3 4 5 6 7 8 9 VHP 07 06 05 04 03

Contents

Voices
In History

People In History

Did You Know?

Charts, Graphs, and Diagrams

Maps

Using *History of Our World: People, Places, and Ideas*

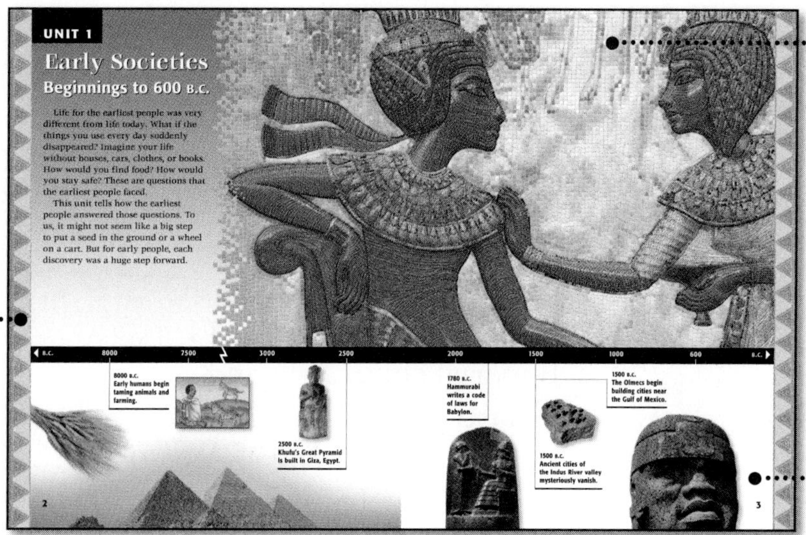

UNIT 1

Early Societies

Beginnings to 600 B.C.

Life for the earliest people was very different from life today. What if the things you use every day suddenly disappeared? Imagine your life without houses, cars, clothes, or books. How would you find food? How would you stay safe? These are questions that the earliest people faced.

This unit tells how the earliest people answered those questions. To us, it might not seem like a big step to put a seed in the ground or a wheel on a cart. But for early people, each discovery was a huge step forward.

B.C. 8000 7500 3000 2500 2000 1500 1000 600 B.C.

8000 B.C. Early humans begin taming animals and farming.

2500 B.C. Khufu's Great Pyramid is built in Giza, Egypt.

1780 B.C. Hammurabi writes a code of laws for Babylon.

1500 B.C. Ancient cities of the Indus River valley mysteriously vanish.

1500 B.C. The Olmecs begin building cities near the Gulf of Mexico.

2 3

Unit Opener

Each unit opens with a text introduction and a large image. Read the text and look at the image. See if they tell you anything about world history.

Unit Timeline

The timeline shows the years discussed in the unit. Read the entries and study the images to see what you'd like to learn more about.

Unit Borders

Each unit has a different border on the edge of the page. Use the borders to quickly identify what unit you're in.

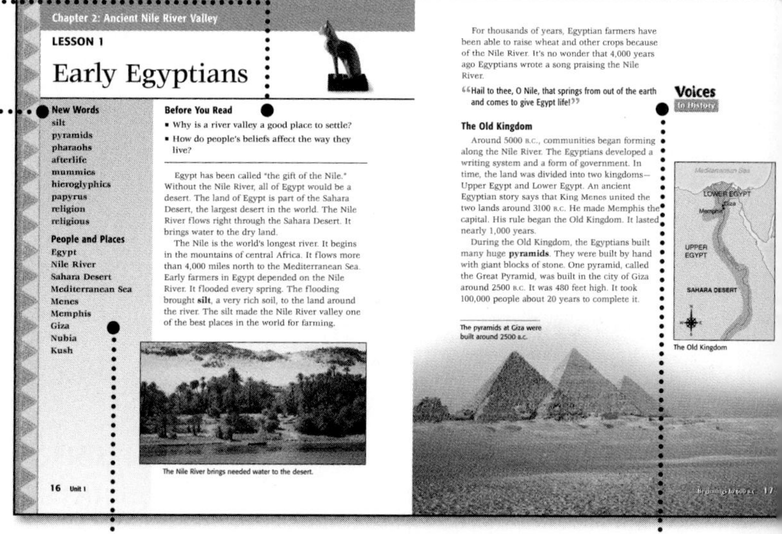

Chapter 2: Ancient Nile River Valley

LESSON 1

Early Egyptians

New Words
silt
pyramids
pharaohs
afterlife
mummies
hieroglyphics
papyrus
religion
religious

People and Places
Egypt
Nile River
Sahara Desert
Mediterranean Sea
Menes
Memphis
Giza
Nubia
Kush

Before You Read
- Why is a river valley a good place to settle?
- How do people's beliefs affect the way they live?

Egypt has been called "the gift of the Nile." Without the Nile River, all of Egypt would be a desert. The land of Egypt is part of the Sahara Desert, the largest desert in the world. The Nile River flows right through the Sahara Desert. It brings water to the dry land.

The Nile is the world's longest river. It begins in the mountains of central Africa. It flows more than 4,000 miles north to the Mediterranean Sea. Early farmers in Egypt depended on the Nile River. It flooded every spring. The flooding brought **silt**, a very rich soil, to the land around the river. The silt made the Nile River valley one of the best places in the world for farming.

The Nile River brings needed water to the desert.

16 Unit 1

For thousands of years, Egyptian farmers have been able to raise wheat and other crops because of the Nile River. It's no wonder that 4,000 years ago Egyptians wrote a song praising the Nile River.

Voices In History

"Hail to thee, O Nile, that springs from out of the earth and comes to give Egypt life!"

The Old Kingdom

Around 5000 B.C., communities began forming along the Nile River. The Egyptians developed a writing system and a form of government. In time, the land was divided into two kingdoms—Upper Egypt and Lower Egypt. An ancient Egyptian story says that King Menes united the two lands around 3100 B.C. He made Memphis the capital. His rule began the Old Kingdom. It lasted nearly 1,000 years.

During the Old Kingdom, the Egyptians built many huge **pyramids**. They were built by hand with giant blocks of stone. One pyramid, called the Great Pyramid, was built in the city of Giza around 2500 B.C. It was 480 feet high. It took 100,000 people about 20 years to complete it.

The pyramids at Giza were built around 2500 B.C.

The Old Kingdom

17

Before You Read

Read these questions before beginning a lesson. Use what you've learned from earlier lessons or past experiences to answer them.

New Words

These are the new words that appear in each lesson. These words are defined in the Glossary. Be sure you know their meanings before you begin reading.

People and Places

People and places are listed here the first time they are discussed. As you read, look for these people and places.

Voices in History

These primary sources appear throughout the text. Read these to learn about history in the words of those who lived it.

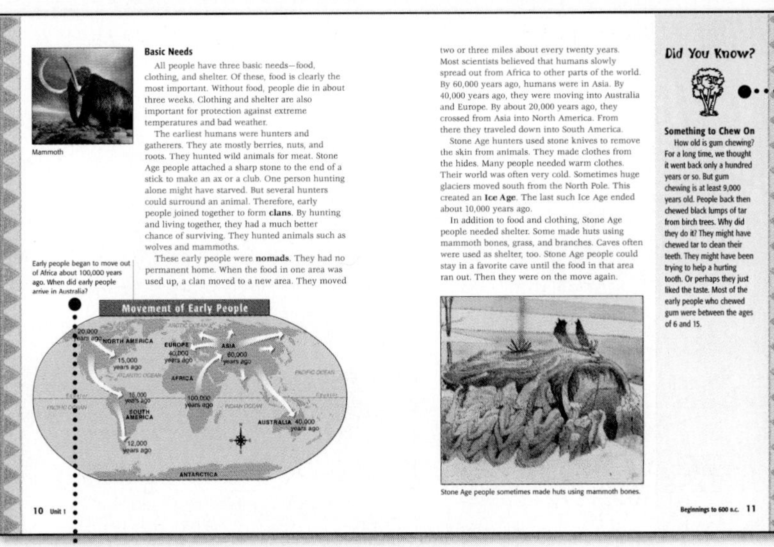

Basic Needs

Mammoth

All people have three basic needs—food, clothing, and shelter. Of these, food is clearly the most important. Without food, people die in about three weeks. Clothing and shelter are also important for protection against extreme temperatures and bad weather.

The earliest humans were hunters and gatherers. They ate mostly berries, nuts, and roots. They hunted wild animals for meat. Stone Age people attached a sharp stone to the end of a stick to make an ax or a club. One person hunting alone might have starved. But several hunters could surround an animal. Therefore, early people joined together to form **clans**. By hunting and living together, they had a much better chance of surviving. They hunted animals such as wolves and mammoths.

These early people were **nomads**. They had no permanent home. When the food in one area was used up, a clan moved to a new area. They moved two or three miles about every twenty years. Most scientists believed that humans slowly spread out from Africa to other parts of the world. By 60,000 years ago, humans were in Asia. By 40,000 years ago, they were moving into Australia and Europe. By about 20,000 years ago, they crossed from Asia into North America. From there they traveled down into South America.

Stone Age hunters used stone knives to remove the skin from animals. They made clothes from the hides. Many people needed warm clothes. Their world was often very cold. Sometimes huge glaciers moved south from the North Pole. This created an **Ice Age**. The last such Ice Age ended about 10,000 years ago.

In addition to food and clothing, Stone Age people needed shelter. Some made huts using mammoth bones, grass, and branches. Caves often were used as shelter, too. Stone Age people could stay in a favorite cave until the food in that area ran out. Then they were on the move again.

Early people began to move out of Africa about 100,000 years ago. When did early people arrive in Australia?

Movement of Early People

Stone Age people sometimes made huts using mammoth bones.

Did You Know?

Something to Chew On

How old is gum chewing? For a long time, we thought it went back only a hundred years or so. But gum chewing is at least 9,000 years old. People back then chewed black lumps of tar from birch trees. Why did they do it? They might have chewed tar to clean their teeth. They might have been trying to help a hurting tooth. Or perhaps they just liked the taste. Most of the early people who chewed gum were between the ages of 6 and 15.

10 Unit 1

Beginnings to 600 B.C. 11

Did You Know?

This special feature occurs two times in each unit. Read these to learn fun and interesting information related to the lesson.

Map Questions

Map questions appear next to some maps. Study the map to answer each question.

Using What You've Learned

After each chapter, you'll have a chance to show what you've learned. Read the questions and answer them carefully.

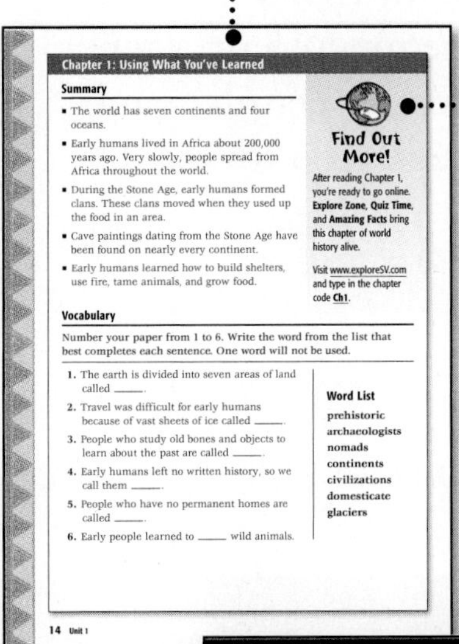

Chapter 1: Using What You've Learned

Summary

- The world has seven continents and four oceans.
- Early humans lived in Africa about 200,000 years ago. Very slowly, people spread from Africa throughout the world.
- During the Stone Age, early humans formed clans. These clans moved when they used up the food in an area.
- Cave paintings dating from the Stone Age have been found on nearly every continent.
- Early humans learned how to build shelters, use fire, tame animals, and grow food.

Find Out More!

After reading Chapter 1, you're ready to go online. **Explore Zone**, **Quiz Time**, and **Amazing Facts** bring this chapter of world history alive.

Visit www.exploreSV.com and type in the chapter code **Ch1**.

Vocabulary

Number your paper from 1 to 6. Write the word from the list that best completes each sentence. One word will not be used.

1. The earth is divided into seven areas of land called _____.
2. Travel was difficult for early humans because of vast sheets of ice called _____.
3. People who study old bones and objects to learn about the past are called _____.
4. Early humans left no written history, so we call them _____.
5. People who have no permanent homes are called _____.
6. Early people learned to _____ wild animals.

Word List
prehistoric
archaeologists
nomads
continents
civilizations
domesticate
glaciers

14 Unit 1

Find Out More!

After reading a chapter, you can visit that chapter online to find out more.

People in History

Read these biographies to better understand some interesting people in world history.

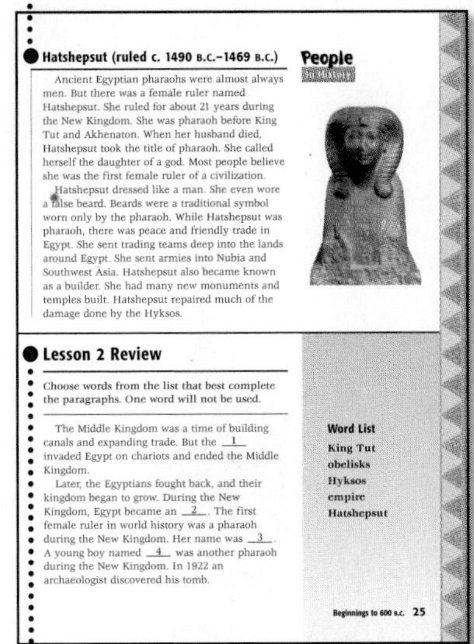

Hatshepsut (ruled c. 1490 B.C.–1469 B.C.)

People in History

Ancient Egyptian pharaohs were almost always men. But there was a female ruler named Hatshepsut. She ruled for about 21 years during the New Kingdom. She was pharaoh before King Tut and Akhenaton. When her husband died, Hatshepsut took the title of pharaoh. She called herself the daughter of a god. Most people believe she was the first female ruler of a civilization.

Hatshepsut dressed like a man. She even wore a false beard. Beards were a traditional symbol worn only by the pharaoh. While Hatshepsut was pharaoh, there was peace and friendly trade in Egypt. She sent trading teams deep into the lands around Egypt. She sent armies into Nubia and Southwest Asia. Hatshepsut also became known as a builder. She had many new monuments and temples built. Hatshepsut repaired much of the damage done by the Hyksos.

Lesson 2 Review

Choose words from the list that best complete the paragraphs. One word will not be used.

The Middle Kingdom was a time of building canals and expanding trade. But the __1__ invaded Egypt on chariots and ended the Middle Kingdom.

Later, the Egyptians fought back, and their kingdom began to grow. During the New Kingdom, Egypt became an __2__. The first female ruler in world history was a pharaoh during the New Kingdom. Her name was __3__. A young boy named __4__ was another pharaoh during the New Kingdom. In 1922 an archaeologist discovered his tomb.

Word List
King Tut
obelisks
Hyksos
empire
Hatshepsut

Beginnings to 600 B.C. 25

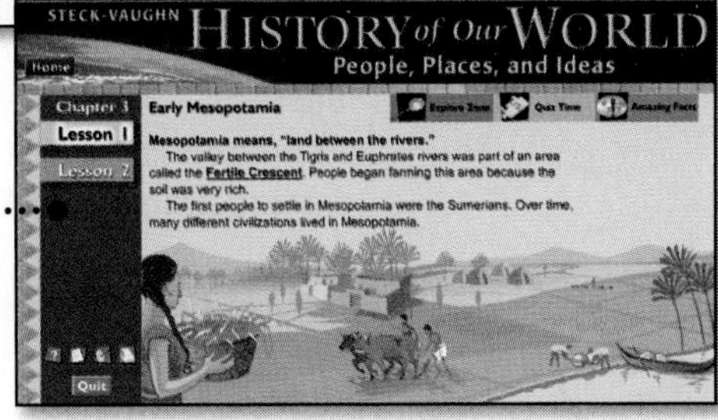

STECK-VAUGHN HISTORY of Our WORLD
People, Places, and Ideas
Home
Chapter 3
Lesson 1
Lesson 2
Early Mesopotamia
Explore Zone
Quiz Time
Amazing Facts
Mesopotamia means, "land between the rivers."
The valley between the Tigris and Euphrates rivers was part of an area called the Fertile Crescent. People began farming this area because the soil was very rich.
The first people to settle in Mesopotamia were the Sumerians. Over time, many different civilizations lived in Mesopotamia.
Quit

Lesson Review

Each lesson ends with a summary. Choose words from the Word List to complete the Lesson Review.

Steck-Vaughn Online

The Steck-Vaughn *History of Our World: People, Places, and Ideas* website brings the chapters of your textbook to life.

UNIT 1

Early Societies

Beginnings to 600 B.C.

Life for the earliest people was very different from life today. What if the things you use every day suddenly disappeared? Imagine your life without houses, cars, clothes, or books. How would you find food? How would you stay safe? These are questions that the earliest people faced.

This unit tells how the earliest people answered those questions. To us, it might not seem like a big step to put a seed in the ground or a wheel on a cart. But for early people, each discovery was a huge step forward.

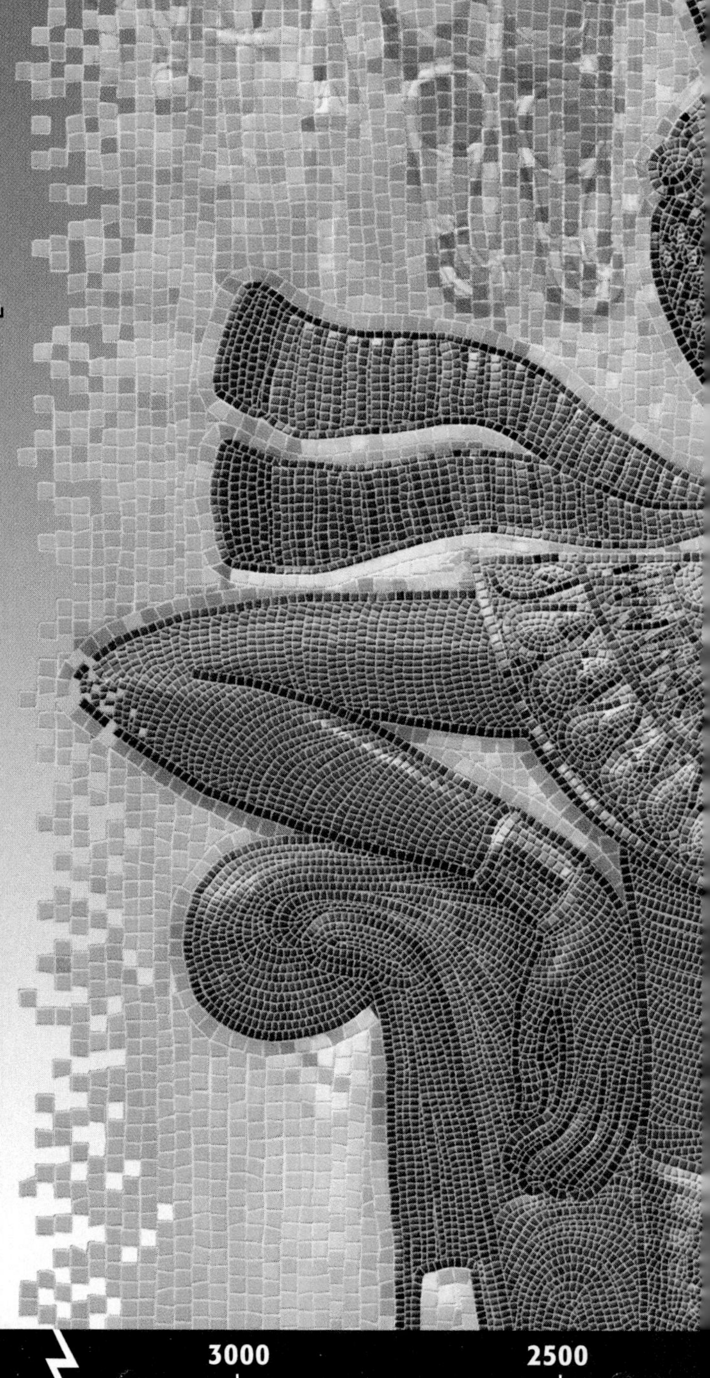

B.C. | 8000 | 7500 | 3000 | 2500

8000 B.C.
Early humans begin taming animals and farming.

2500 B.C.
Khufu's Great Pyramid is built in Giza, Egypt.

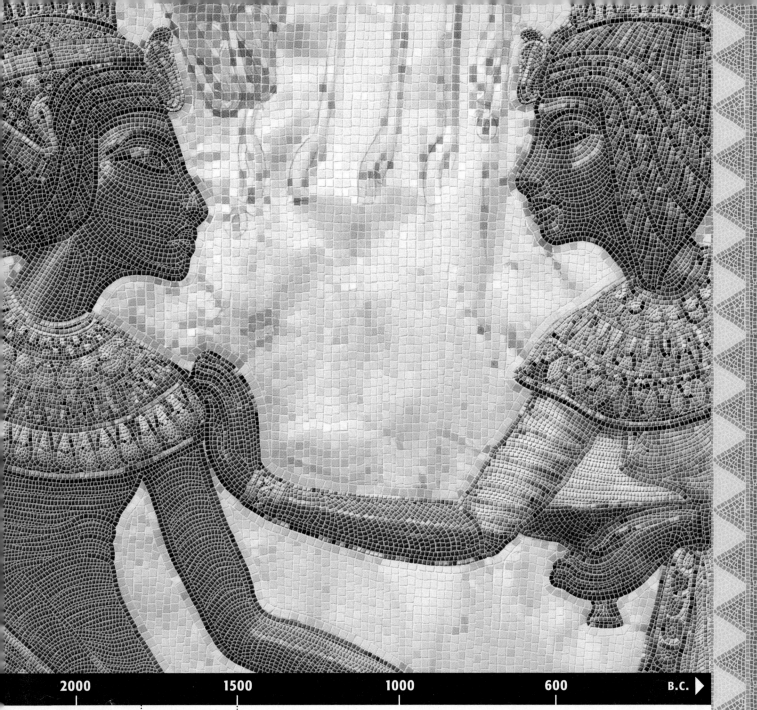

2000 | 1500 | 1000 | 600 | B.C.

1780 B.C.
Hammurabi writes a code of laws for Babylon.

1500 B.C.
Ancient cities of the Indus River valley mysteriously vanish.

1500 B.C.
The Olmecs begin building cities near the Gulf of Mexico.

LESSON 1

History's Stage

New Words
continents
glaciers
climate
archaeologists

People and Places
Earth
Pacific Ocean
Atlantic Ocean
Indian Ocean
Arctic Ocean
Asia
Africa
North America
South America
Antarctica
Europe
Australia
United States

Before You Read

- Do you think of the world as big or little?
- What could make a place difficult to live in?

People sometimes say the world gets smaller every day. In one sense, that is true. Planes fly halfway around the world in less than a day. You can see live sports or news on television from places thousands of miles away. You can send e-mail messages in an instant to someone across an ocean. So these days the world can indeed seem to be a pretty small place.

A Big Place, Too

On the other hand, the world really is a big place. It is almost 25,000 miles around. If you rode a bike at ten miles per hour for eight hours a day, it would take you nearly a year to go that distance. But you couldn't ride that far in a straight line without running into water.

This photo of Earth was taken from space.

Oceans and Continents of the World

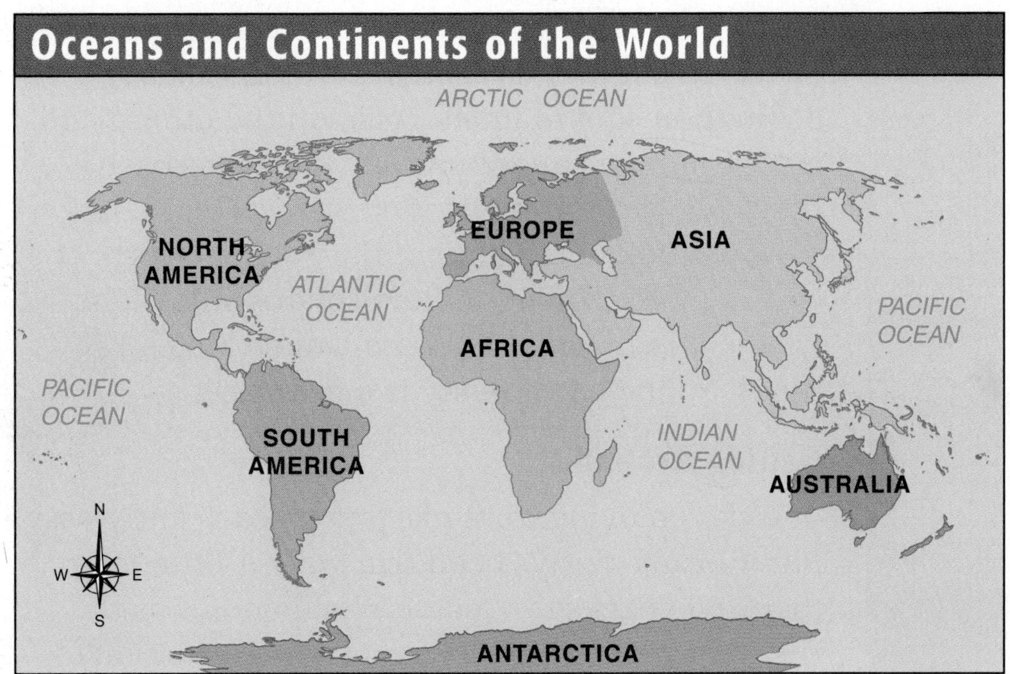

Earth has seven continents and four oceans. On which continent do you live?

About two thirds of Earth is covered by water. The world has many seas, bays, lakes, and rivers. But most of Earth's water is in its four great oceans. The biggest—by far—is the Pacific Ocean. It is nearly twice the size of the second largest, the Atlantic Ocean. The Indian Ocean is the third largest. The mostly ice-covered Arctic Ocean is the smallest.

Look at the world map above. There are no boundary lines between oceans. That is because the oceans are all connected. It is possible to sail through all four oceans and never see land.

The Land

The earth is divided into seven great areas of land, or **continents**. The largest continent is Asia. The second largest is Africa. North America is the third largest. The other four continents in order of size are South America, Antarctica, Europe, and Australia. Look again at the world map. Notice that some continents are joined together. Asia, Europe, and Africa are linked together. North America and South America are joined, too. Only Australia and Antarctica are separate from all the others.

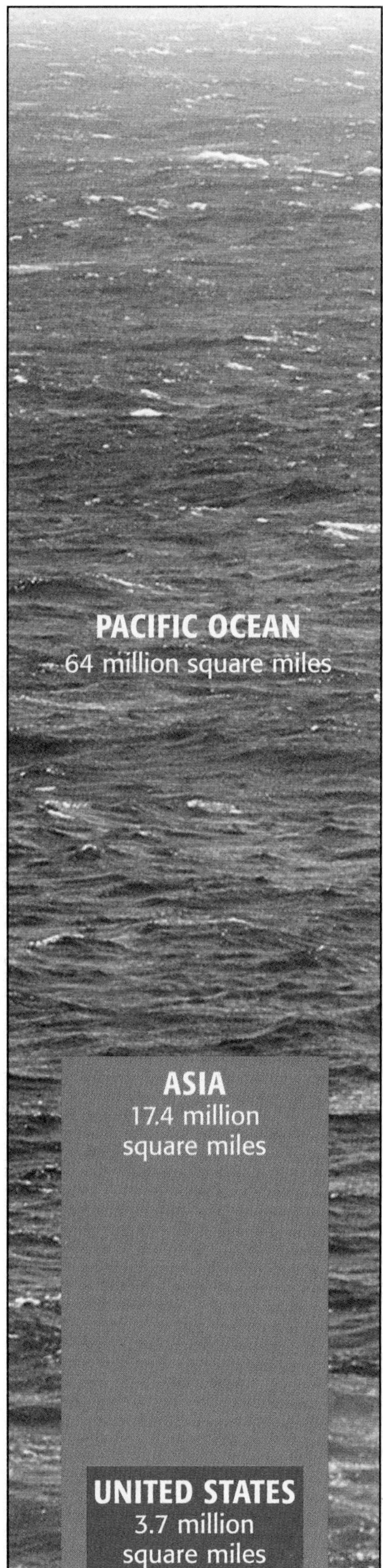

Relative Sizes of the Pacific Ocean, Asia, and the United States

How big are these continents? The United States, including Alaska and Hawaii, is about 3.7 million square miles. Asia, on the other hand, is 17.4 million square miles. Asia is nearly five times bigger than the United States.

Now think once more of the Pacific Ocean. It covers more than 64 million square miles. The Pacific Ocean could hold the United States 17 times. So the earth really is a big place.

Getting Around

Today, moving from place to place is fairly easy. But it hasn't always been that way. A little more than 200 years ago, George Washington was the first president of the United States. He couldn't get on a plane or e-mail his wife, Martha. For him, nothing moved faster than a running horse or a sailing ship.

But it was even harder hundreds of thousands of years before George Washington. Most scientists believe that modern humans began to live in Africa about 200,000 years ago. If these early humans wanted to go somewhere, they had to walk. However, they had no world maps showing them where they were or where they were going.

At least George Washington had maps. He knew about Asia and Africa and the Indian Ocean. Washington had some idea of the size of the world. As these early humans traveled, they couldn't know whether they were one mile or one thousand miles away from an ocean.

Geography and History

The early humans didn't divide the earth into seven continents and four oceans. But they did use the land and water every day. They got everything they needed from the earth. But it wasn't always easy. Huge lakes, seas, and oceans were problems. Early humans had to travel around large bodies of water because they had no ships. Mountains were another problem. The huge Himalayas in Asia and the Alps in Europe could not be crossed easily.

There were other travel problems. The lack of water and the heat made it dangerous to cross a desert. Spring floods made many rivers impossible to cross. **Glaciers**, or vast sheets of ice, also blocked travel.

Snow-covered mountains

In addition, the **climate** of the earth affected the lives of the early humans. Different places on the earth have different kinds of climates. People living in cold climates had to dress differently from those living in warm climates. Also, climates have changed over time. For example, most of the northern part of Africa is now the largest desert in the world. But 10,000 years ago, the same region had many large lakes and plenty of rain.

Humans also used the land to help them. The land provided early people with stones for tools and caves for shelter. Rivers gave them drinking water. Over time, people learned to live in many kinds of climates. Humans began to find ways to travel over mountains and across oceans.

Northern Africa today

Northern Africa might have looked like this 10,000 years ago.

The Story Begins

The geography of Earth provides a stage for people to live their lives. The story of the people living on Earth over time is what we call world history. This story begins about 200,000 years ago. That is when most scientists believe modern humans were living on the earth.

There are many parts of the story that are still a mystery. **Archaeologists** are people who study the past by digging up old bones and objects. Archaeologists can tell us a lot about how people lived long ago. But there will always be questions. We know that the early humans learned to live on the land. They passed their knowledge to their children. And humans have been learning ever since.

Archaeologists carefully dig objects out of the earth.

Lesson 1 Review

Choose words from the list that best complete the paragraphs. One word will not be used.

Word List

glaciers
maps
continents
archaeologists
oceans

Today we can be in touch with the rest of the world by just turning on a television or sending an e-mail. In one way, the world is small. But it is also a large place, with four huge __1__ and seven large __2__.

The earliest humans had to move from place to place to find food. Mountains and __3__ were two things that made it hard for these people to travel. Today we learn about the past from __4__ who study old bones and objects.

LESSON 2

Beginnings to 6000 B.C.

Before You Read

- What do people need in order to live?
- Why do people live in groups?

The early humans lived in a time that we call the **Stone Age**. The Stone Age lasted until around 5,500 years ago, or 3500 B.C. During this time, people made tools and weapons out of stone.

The Stone Age people didn't know how to write. They kept no diaries, exchanged no letters, and wrote no books. These early humans left no written history. That is why we call them **prehistoric**.

New Words

Stone Age
prehistoric
clans
nomads
Ice Age
domesticate
civilizations

People and Places

North Pole

This painting shows a prehistoric man making a stone tool.

Mammoth

Basic Needs

All people have three basic needs—food, clothing, and shelter. Of these, food is clearly the most important. Without food, people die in about three weeks. Clothing and shelter are also important for protection against extreme temperatures and bad weather.

The earliest humans were hunters and gatherers. They ate mostly berries, nuts, and roots. They hunted wild animals for meat. Stone Age people attached a sharp stone to the end of a stick to make an ax or a club. One person hunting alone might have starved. But several hunters could surround an animal. Therefore, early people joined together to form **clans**. By hunting and living together, they had a much better chance of surviving. They hunted animals such as wolves and mammoths.

These early people were **nomads**. They had no permanent home. When the food in one area was used up, a clan moved to a new area. They moved

Early people began to move out of Africa about 100,000 years ago. When did early people arrive in Australia?

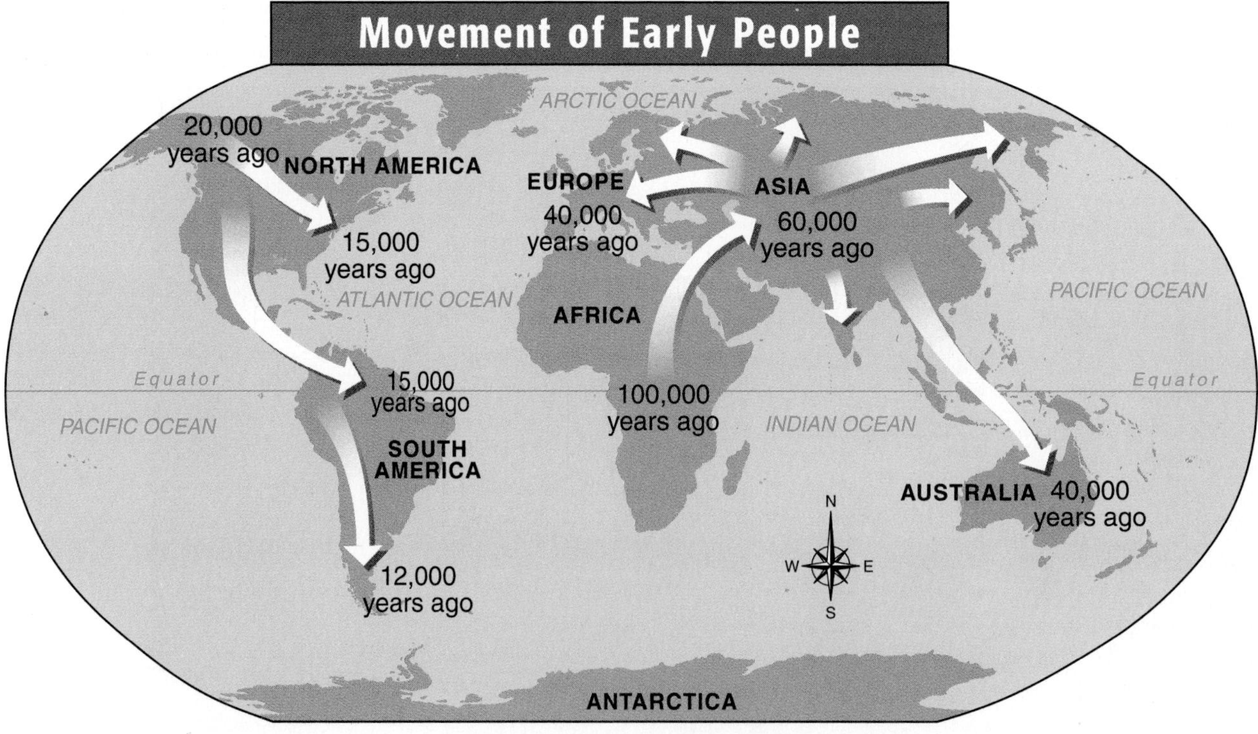

two or three miles about every twenty years. Most scientists believed that humans slowly spread out from Africa to other parts of the world. By 60,000 years ago, humans were in Asia. By 40,000 years ago, they were moving into Australia and Europe. By about 20,000 years ago, they crossed from Asia into North America. From there they traveled down into South America.

Stone Age hunters used stone knives to remove the skin from animals. They made clothes from the hides. Many people needed warm clothes. Their world was often very cold. Sometimes huge glaciers moved south from the North Pole. This created an **Ice Age**. The last such Ice Age ended about 10,000 years ago.

In addition to food and clothing, Stone Age people needed shelter. Some made huts using mammoth bones, grass, and branches. Caves often were used as shelter, too. Stone Age people could stay in a favorite cave until the food in that area ran out. Then they were on the move again.

Stone Age people sometimes made huts using mammoth bones.

Did You Know?

Something to Chew On

How old is gum chewing? For a long time, we thought it went back only a hundred years or so. But gum chewing is at least 9,000 years old. People back then chewed black lumps of tar from birch trees. Why did they do it? They might have chewed tar to clean their teeth. They might have been trying to help a hurting tooth. Or perhaps they just liked the taste. Most of the early people who chewed gum were between the ages of 6 and 15.

This horse was painted on the wall of a cave in France.

Cave painting in Africa

Some Stone Age people painted on the walls of caves. They used paintbrushes made with animal hair. For paint, they mixed animal fat with minerals. These Stone Age artists painted pictures of animals such as bison, deer, and horses. Some of the paintings are 30,000 years old. Cave paintings have been found in Africa, Europe, Asia, South America, and North America.

A Few Good Ideas

Early in the Stone Age, people learned to make fire. At first they used fire only to keep warm. Later they learned to use it for cooking.

Much later, around 10,000 years ago, some of the hunters and gatherers began raising animals. They learned to **domesticate**, or tame, wild animals. They tamed dogs, sheep, pigs, goats, and cattle. With domesticated animals, they had meat whenever they needed it. But they still had to move when the animals ate all the grass in an area.

Dogs and other animals were tamed around 8000 B.C.

Early humans also found they could plant a seed in the earth and grow food. It took thousands of years to develop the skills of farming. But farming was one of the greatest discoveries ever. The new plants provided more seeds to plant.

First Civilizations

After learning to farm, humans could settle in one place and stay there. They didn't have to hunt animals. They didn't have to gather wild roots, berries, and nuts. With more food available, communities began to grow.

Farmers needed a steady supply of water for their crops. So most early communities grew along the banks of rivers. By around 6000 B.C., some communities had grown into large **civilizations**. This means they had a language and a government. They had clear rules for living.

Several great civilizations developed in different parts of the world around the same time. You will learn about each of these in the following chapters.

The first civilizations might have had rooms like this.

Lesson 2 Review

Choose words from the list that best complete the paragraphs. One word will not be used.

Life for early humans was hard. Finding food was difficult. These __1__ had to move many times just to find food. They wore animal hides to keep warm and lived in huts and __2__.

In time, Stone Age people learned how to __3__ wild animals. They also learned how to farm. With a steady supply of food, they could settle in one place. Their communities grew large. They developed languages and governments. The communities became __4__.

Word List

civilizations
prehistoric
caves
nomads
domesticate

Chapter 1: Using What You've Learned

Summary

- The world has seven continents and four oceans.
- Early humans lived in Africa about 200,000 years ago. Very slowly, people spread from Africa throughout the world.
- During the Stone Age, early humans formed clans. These clans moved when they used up the food in an area.
- Cave paintings dating from the Stone Age have been found on nearly every continent.
- Early humans learned how to build shelters, use fire, tame animals, and grow food.

Find Out More!

After reading Chapter 1, you're ready to go online. **Explore Zone**, **Quiz Time**, and **Amazing Facts** bring this chapter of world history alive.

Visit www.exploreSV.com and type in the chapter code **Ch1**.

Vocabulary

Number your paper from 1 to 6. Write the word from the list that best completes each sentence. One word will not be used.

1. The earth is divided into seven areas of land called ______.
2. Travel was difficult for early humans because of vast sheets of ice called ______.
3. People who study old bones and objects to learn about the past are called ______.
4. Early humans left no written history, so we call them ______.
5. People who have no permanent homes are called ______.
6. Early people learned to ______ wild animals.

Word List

prehistoric
archaeologists
nomads
continents
civilizations
domesticate
glaciers

Comprehension

Number your paper from 1 to 5. Write one or more sentences to answer each question below.

1. How are Earth's largest bodies of water and great areas of land divided?
2. What are two things that made travel difficult for early humans?
3. How did climate affect the lives of early humans?
4. How did early people get food?
5. What did early people use for clothing?

Critical Thinking

Categories Number your paper from 1 to 4. Read the words in each group below. Think about how they are alike. Write the best title for each group.

Early Humans **Civilizations** **Continents** **Needs**

1. Africa
   North America
   Asia
2. food
   shelter
   clothing
3. hunters and gatherers
   nomads
   clans
4. language
   government
   rules for living

Writing

Write a paragraph explaining how early people lived and why they lived in groups.

LESSON 1

Early Egyptians

New Words
silt
pyramids
pharaohs
afterlife
mummies
hieroglyphics
papyrus
religion
religious

People and Places
Egypt
Nile River
Sahara Desert
Mediterranean Sea
Menes
Memphis
Giza
Nubia
Kush

Before You Read
- Why is a river valley a good place to settle?
- How do people's beliefs affect the way they live?

Egypt has been called "the gift of the Nile." Without the Nile River, all of Egypt would be a desert. The land of Egypt is part of the Sahara Desert, the largest desert in the world. The Nile River flows right through the Sahara Desert. It brings water to the dry land.

The Nile is the world's longest river. It begins in the mountains of central Africa. It flows more than 4,000 miles north to the Mediterranean Sea. Early farmers in Egypt depended on the Nile River. It flooded every spring. The flooding brought **silt**, a very rich soil, to the land around the river. The silt made the Nile River valley one of the best places in the world for farming.

The Nile River brings needed water to the desert.

For thousands of years, Egyptian farmers have been able to raise wheat and other crops because of the Nile River. It's no wonder that 4,000 years ago Egyptians wrote a song praising the Nile River.

"Hail to thee, O Nile, that springs from out of the earth and comes to give Egypt life!"

Voices In History

The Old Kingdom

Around 5000 B.C., communities began forming along the Nile River. The Egyptians developed a writing system and a form of government. In time, the land was divided into two kingdoms—Upper Egypt and Lower Egypt. An ancient Egyptian story says that King Menes united the two lands around 3100 B.C. He made Memphis the capital. His rule began the Old Kingdom. It lasted nearly 1,000 years.

During the Old Kingdom, the Egyptians built many huge **pyramids**. They were built by hand with giant blocks of stone. One pyramid, called the Great Pyramid, was built in the city of Giza around 2500 B.C. It was 480 feet high. It took 100,000 people about 20 years to complete it.

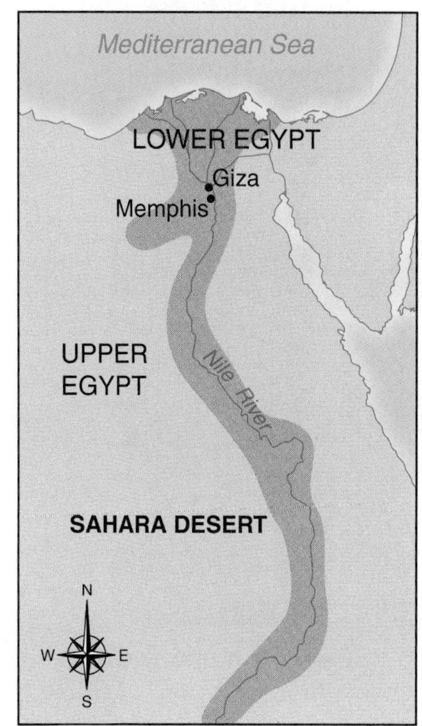

The Old Kingdom

The pyramids at Giza were built around 2500 B.C.

Egyptian mummy case

Pharaohs, or Egyptian rulers, were buried in the pyramids. Other wealthy people could also be buried in pyramids. The pyramids were important because Egyptians believed in an **afterlife**. They believed that after people died, they had another life. Clothing and jewelry often were placed inside the pyramids. The Egyptians believed the dead person would use these things in the afterlife.

Even the body itself was prepared for life after death. Egyptians who had enough money could have their bodies made into **mummies**. Their bodies would be preserved to last thousands of years. The process to turn a body into a mummy took about 70 days. Sometimes Egyptians even made animals into mummies.

Egyptians also improved their writing. They used a system of picture writing called **hieroglyphics**. Not every Egyptian knew how to use hieroglyphics. Only certain people were taught how to read and write. These same people also learned math. They collected taxes and kept important records for the Egyptian civilization.

Egyptians also found many uses for a plant called **papyrus**. The plant grew along the banks of the Nile River. Egyptians built boats with it. They used it to make baskets, shoes, and rope. They even made a special kind of paper using papyrus.

The Egyptians used a system of picture writing called hieroglyphics.

Ancient Egyptian children enjoyed playing games.

Egyptian Way of Life

The Egyptian **religion** had many gods. One of the most important gods was the sun god. After the gods, the pharaoh was the head of Egyptian society. Egyptians believed that a pharaoh was the child of a god. As the child of a god, the pharaoh had total rule over Egypt. A pharaoh's power was not questioned.

There were many jobs in ancient Egypt. Some people worked in government. Others made crafts. Still others were farmers or slaves. Egyptians worked from sunrise to sunset. Many did not work on **religious** holidays.

Women were usually in charge of the house. Children enjoyed playing many games. Some Egyptian games, such as tug-of-war and leapfrog, are still played today.

The pharaoh Khufu was buried in the Great Pyramid at Giza.

Nubia

Nubia formed around the same time as Egypt. Nubia was in an area south of Egypt where the land was very hot and dry. The Nubians, like the Egyptians, could not have survived without water from the Nile River.

The Nubians and the Egyptians traded with each other and shared ideas. For example, the Nubians built pyramids, but their pyramids were smaller and steeper than the Egyptian pyramids.

Nubian pyramids

The Nubians were well known for their beautiful pottery. They traded their pottery and other goods with Egyptians and other people. Nubia became an important trading area. It had trade routes connecting it with areas in Africa and Asia.

At times, Nubia and Egypt fought each other. Egyptians thought controlling the trade routes in Nubia would make them richer. Toward the end of the Old Kingdom, Egyptians took over northern Nubia. The Egyptians called the area Kush.

Lesson 1 Review

Choose words from the list that best complete the paragraphs. One word will not be used.

Word List

papyrus
pottery
pyramids
hieroglyphics
Nile River

Two civilizations developed along the Nile River. One was Egypt. The other was Nubia. Without the __1__, neither of them would have existed.

The Egyptians of the Old Kingdom built giant __2__. Pharaohs were buried inside them. The ancient Egyptians developed a form of writing called __3__.

The Nubian civilization developed south of Egypt. The Nubians made beautiful __4__. In addition, Nubia had valuable trade routes.

LESSON 2

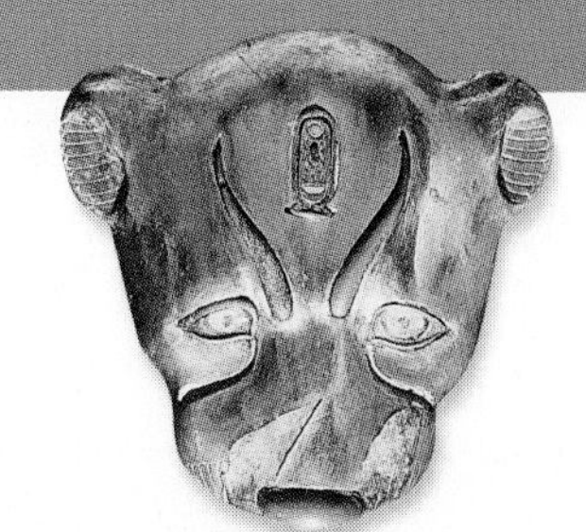

Egypt Becomes an Empire

Before You Read

- How do groups of people gain power over other groups?
- Why do people build temples and statues?

Around 2500 B.C., Egypt's Old Kingdom began to weaken. Pharaohs lost power. Government officials quarreled with one another. A war broke out. By 2100 B.C., the Old Kingdom had ended. There was no steady government because various kings were fighting for power. Each one wanted to rule Egypt.

Around 2050 B.C., the Middle Kingdom began. New rulers took over Egypt and moved the capital to Thebes.

New Words

invaded
chariots
empire
obelisks
tomb

People and Places

Thebes
Red Sea
Hyksos
Akhenaton
Nefertiti
King Tut
Howard Carter
Hatshepsut

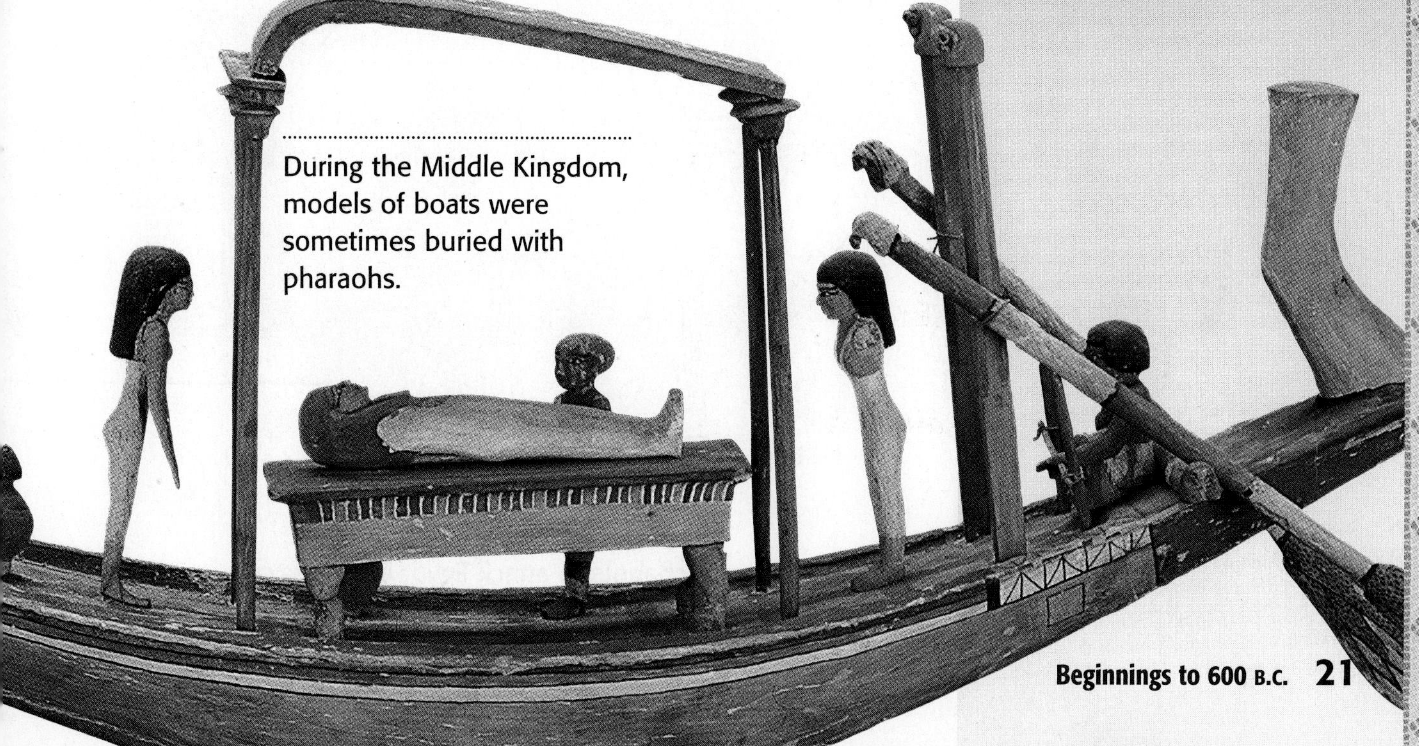

During the Middle Kingdom, models of boats were sometimes buried with pharaohs.

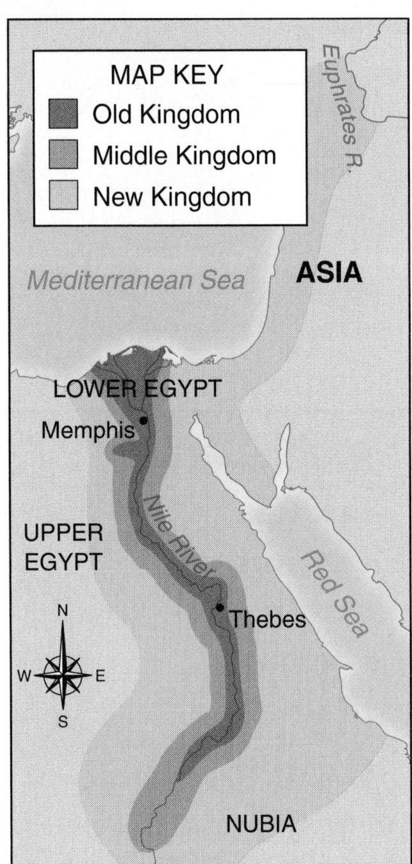

Ancient Egypt

The Middle Kingdom

Egyptians of the Middle Kingdom focused on art and writing. They didn't build as many pyramids as in the Old Kingdom. Instead, they built canals to drain swamps. This made even more land available for farming.

They also built a canal connecting the Nile River with trade routes near the Red Sea. This improved trade during the Middle Kingdom. Egyptians were able to get various kinds of wood from areas in Southwest Asia. This wood was used to build boats and furniture.

The Middle Kingdom lasted only a few hundred years. Around 1700 B.C., warriors called Hyksos **invaded**, or attacked, Egypt. They came from Asia on **chariots** pulled by horses. Each chariot carried two warriors. One man controlled the horse. The other carried a spear or a bow and arrow. The Egyptians were surprised by the chariots. They had always fought on foot.

The people of Kush joined with the Hyksos against the Egyptians. The Hyksos easily beat the Egyptians. For the first time, outsiders ruled the lands of Egypt.

The Hyksos used chariots to attack Egypt in 1700 B.C.

The New Kingdom

The Hyksos ruled with great force. They burned cities and destroyed temples. The Hyksos were cruel to many Egyptians. But such force didn't work for long. The Egyptians fought back. They used chariots against the Hyksos. Around 1539 B.C., they drove out the Hyksos. The Egyptians set up a new government known as the New Kingdom. It lasted 500 years.

The New Kingdom was really an **empire**. An empire exists when one group of people rules over another. The Egyptians had an army for the first time. This army took control of lands far beyond the Nile River, including parts of Asia. Egypt became the strongest and richest nation in the world. Thebes, the capital, became one of the most powerful cities.

Egyptian obelisk

Egyptians of the New Kingdom built great temples and statues. The temples were both religious places and schools. Egyptians built **obelisks** that were carved from single stones. The obelisks were built to honor the gods.

Around 1372 B.C., Akhenaton became pharaoh. He and his wife, Nefertiti, believed that the sun god was the only god. They tried to get all Egyptians to stop believing in the other gods.

Egyptians of the New Kingdom built massive temples.

Akhenaton offers gifts to the sun god.

Akhenaton began building new temples for the sun god. They were open and let in sunlight. Art from the New Kingdom often shows the pharaoh and his family offering gifts to the sun.

After Akhenaton died, a nine-year-old boy became pharaoh. This boy was Tutankhamen, or King Tut. He only ruled for about nine years. He is remembered because of the treasures that were found in his **tomb**. Many tombs of pharaohs were robbed over the years. But King Tut's tomb was hidden beneath another tomb. No one knew about it until 1922. That is when Howard Carter, an archaeologist, found it. He wrote about going inside the tomb.

Voices In History

> **"The scene grew clearer, and we could pick out individual objects. First . . . were three great . . . couches, their sides carved in the form of . . . animals . . . ."**

Some New Kingdom pharaohs were wealthy. But they began losing power during the New Kingdom. By 1075 B.C., Egypt was weak. The people of Kush later took over Egypt for around 50 years. Then, invaders from the north and east took over all the lands of the Egyptian New Kingdom. These invaders were the Assyrians.

These objects were found in King Tut's tomb. The chest plate (above) is shaped like a beetle. The decorated box (right) was King Tut's war chest.

Hatshepsut (ruled c. 1490 B.C.–1469 B.C.)

People In History

Ancient Egyptian pharaohs were almost always men. But there was a female ruler named Hatshepsut. She ruled for about 21 years during the New Kingdom. She was pharaoh before King Tut and Akhenaton. When her husband died, Hatshepsut took the title of pharaoh. She called herself the daughter of a god. Most people believe she was the first female ruler of a civilization.

Hatshepsut dressed like a man. She even wore a false beard. Beards were a traditional symbol worn only by the pharaoh. While Hatshepsut was pharaoh, there was peace and friendly trade in Egypt. She sent trading teams deep into the lands around Egypt. She sent armies into Nubia and Southwest Asia. Hatshepsut also became known as a builder. She had many new monuments and temples built. Hatshepsut repaired much of the damage done by the Hyksos.

Lesson 2 Review

Choose words from the list that best complete the paragraphs. One word will not be used.

The Middle Kingdom was a time of building canals and expanding trade. But the __1__ invaded Egypt on chariots and ended the Middle Kingdom.

Later, the Egyptians fought back, and their kingdom began to grow. During the New Kingdom, Egypt became an __2__. The first female ruler in world history was a pharaoh during the New Kingdom. Her name was __3__. A young boy named __4__ was another pharaoh during the New Kingdom. In 1922 an archaeologist discovered his tomb.

Word List

King Tut
obelisks
Hyksos
empire
Hatshepsut

Chapter 2: Using What You've Learned

Summary

- The Egyptians and Nubians built civilizations along the Nile River around 5000 B.C.
- The Old Kingdom of Egypt began in 3100 B.C. when Menes united Upper and Lower Egypt.
- Nubia, also known as Kush, became an important trading center.
- Egypt's Middle Kingdom began around 2050 B.C. and ended when the Hyksos invaded around 1700 B.C.
- The New Kingdom began about 1539 B.C. when the Egyptians drove out the Hyksos.
- Hatshepsut, Akhenaton, and King Tut were some New Kingdom rulers.

Find Out More!

After reading Chapter 2, you're ready to go online. **Explore Zone**, **Quiz Time**, and **Amazing Facts** bring this chapter of world history alive.

Visit www.exploreSV.com and type in the chapter code **Ch2**.

Vocabulary

Number your paper from 1 to 6. Finish the sentences from Group A with words from Group B. Write the letter of the correct answer.

Group A

1. The _____ from the flooding of the Nile River was good for growing crops.
2. Rulers of Egypt were buried in _____.
3. Egyptians used a system of picture writing called _____.
4. A belief in one or many gods is called a _____.
5. The Hyksos used _____ to defeat the Egyptians.
6. The Egyptians built an _____ by taking control of other lands.

Group B

a. hieroglyphics

b. empire

c. chariots

d. pyramids

e. silt

f. religion

Comprehension

Number your paper from 1 to 5. Read each sentence below. Then write the name of the person or people who might have said each sentence. One name from the list will not be used.

1. "I united Upper Egypt and Lower Egypt."
2. "We made beautiful pottery and had trade routes in Africa and Asia."
3. "I am the pharaoh who built temples for the sun god."
4. "I am known for the treasures found in my tomb."
5. "I might have been the first female ruler of a civilization."

Word List

Akhenaton
Menes
Hyksos
Hatshepsut
Nubians
King Tut

Critical Thinking

Cause and Effect Number your paper from 1 to 4. Read the causes in the left column. Then choose the correct effect from the right column. Write the letter of the correct effect.

Cause

1. The Egyptians needed more land for farming, so
2. Ancient Egyptians believed in life after death, so
3. Egyptians believed the pharaoh was a child of a god, so
4. Egyptians of the New Kingdom wanted to honor the gods, so

Effect

a. they left food and clothing in tombs.
b. they built canals to drain swamps.
c. they built temples and obelisks.
d. a pharaoh's power was not questioned.

Writing

Write a paragraph describing the many ways Egyptians used papyrus.

Skill Builder: Using Primary Sources

Primary sources can tell us about the lives of people who lived at different times. Primary sources can be written, like letters, diaries, and newspapers. Primary sources can also be objects, like clothing, tools, and household items.

We know what life was like in ancient Egypt from objects that archaeologists have found. In 1922, archaeologist Howard Carter discovered the tomb of King Tut. You read a description of his discovery on page 24. Now read more of his description.

accustomed
used to

interior
inside

gilded
covered in gold

ornamental caskets
large decorated boxes

Howard Carter's Diary

"It was some time before [we] could see. The hot air escaping caused the candle to flicker, but as soon as [our] eyes became ***accustomed*** *to the . . . light, the* ***interior*** *of the chamber gradually [appeared] before [us], with its strange and wonderful [group] of . . . beautiful objects heaped upon one another . . . . [There were] two strange . . . [statues] of a King, . . .* ***gilded*** *couches in strange forms, . . .* ***ornamental caskets****, . . . stools of all shapes and design, of both common and rare materials; and, lastly . . . overturned parts of chariots [shining] with gold . . . . We questioned one another as to the meaning of it all."*

Number your paper from 1 to 5. Write 1 to 2 sentences to answer each question.

1. What are many of the items Carter described made of?
2. What household items did Carter find in the tomb?
3. What object in the tomb shows how King Tut might have traveled?
4. How might Carter have known this was a pharaoh's tomb?
5. Why do you think Carter wrote about this experience?

LESSON 1

Early Mesopotamia

Before You Read

- Why did early people settle in river valleys?
- How are laws important to a civilization?

In the last chapter, you read about the Nile River and how important it was to the people who settled near it. In Southwest Asia, two other rivers were important. They were the Tigris and Euphrates rivers. Together they formed a valley called Mesopotamia, or "land between the rivers."

Mesopotamia was part of the **Fertile Crescent**. Its soil was very good for farming. The Fertile Crescent extended from the Mediterranean Sea to the Persian Gulf.

Civilizations were developing in Mesopotamia around the same time they were forming in Egypt. Around 5000 B.C., settlers began building cities in a part of Mesopotamia called Sumer.

The Fertile Crescent

New Words

Fertile Crescent
dikes
ziggurats
city-states
stylus
cuneiform
Code of Hammurabi

People and Places

Tigris River
Euphrates River
Mesopotamia
Persian Gulf
Sumer
Sargon
Akkad
Hammurabi
Babylon
Hittites
Phoenicians
Assyrians

The Sumerians

Unlike the Nile River, the Tigris and Euphrates rivers did not flood at the same time every year. When the rivers did flood, the Sumerians were surprised. The floods washed away their crops and their houses. The Sumerians built canals to control the flooding waters. They also built **dikes**, or mounds of dirt, to hold back flooding waters. Using the rich soil of the river valley, the Sumerians became excellent farmers.

Small Sumerian statue

Mesopotamia had few trees or stones for building. But there was plenty of clay. Sumerians made bricks from clay and let them dry in the sun. They used the bricks to build homes and temples. Their temples were called **ziggurats**. The ziggurats were built as special places for the gods. Sumerians believed they had to make the gods happy in order to have good crops.

Many Sumerian cities grew into **city-states**, independent cities surrounded by farming villages. A ziggurat was usually at the center of the city. A wall surrounded the city. There were farms and villages outside the wall. The wall protected the city from invaders. Each city-state had its own ruler. Sumerians believed that the ruler had the support of the local god. But unlike in Egypt, the ruler was not considered an actual child of a god.

The ziggurat was usually at the center of a Sumerian city-state.

Sumerian Inventions

Sumerian cart

The Sumerians found a good way to use the wheel. They connected wheels to a cart. Then they used donkeys to pull the cart. This simple invention changed how people and things traveled from one place to another. The Sumerians also invented a sail for boats. The sail made water travel easier.

Like the Egyptians, the Sumerians created a form of writing. They did not have paper. Instead they used soft clay tablets. Writers used a pointed stick called a **stylus** to make their marks. The tablets were then dried in the sun to make them hard. The Sumerians used a type of writing called **cuneiform**.

Sumerian clay tablet

By putting cuneiform symbols together, the Sumerians wrote stories, poems, and songs. They kept records of the goods they traded. They wrote down the names of cities and leaders. In this way, the Sumerians wrote their history.

Akkadians and Babylonians

Around 2340 B.C., a man named Sargon attacked and defeated the lands of Sumer. He led his soldiers in battles until all of Mesopotamia was united under his rule. Sargon built a new capital city called Akkad. Sargon saw how much the Sumerians had done. He adopted many of their ways. For example, the Akkadians began to use cuneiform writing. Sargon and the kings who followed him stayed in power for about 200 years.

This stone marker shows Hammurabi standing in front of the sun god. The Code of Hammurabi is carved below.

Next, the Babylonians gained control of Mesopotamia. Hammurabi became king of Babylon around 1792 B.C. He is remembered most for having all the Babylonian laws written down around 1780 B.C. Hammurabi knew the laws of the Sumerians and Akkadians. He changed them a little and made them a part of Babylonian laws. Hammurabi's collection of more than 250 laws is known as the **Code of Hammurabi**.

The code did not treat all people equally. Some had more rights than others. Still, the code told people what they could and could not do. Anyone who broke a law knew the punishment.

Voices In History

"If anyone steals the property of a temple or of the court, he shall be put to death, and also the one who receives the stolen thing from him shall be put to death."

Other Fertile Crescent People

There were other people who lived in the Fertile Crescent. The Hittites ruled lands in the northern part of the Fertile Crescent. The Hittites knew how to make iron tools and weapons.

Another group, the Phoenicians, lived on the western edge of the Fertile Crescent. They set up colonies along the Mediterranean Sea around 1000 B.C. They built boats and sailed as traders. The Phoenicians spread their traditions to the people in the colonies. At first, the Phoenicians sailed only during the day. Later they learned to study the stars to find their way at night.

Several groups of people ruled lands in or near the Fertile Crescent. Which group ruled the largest area?

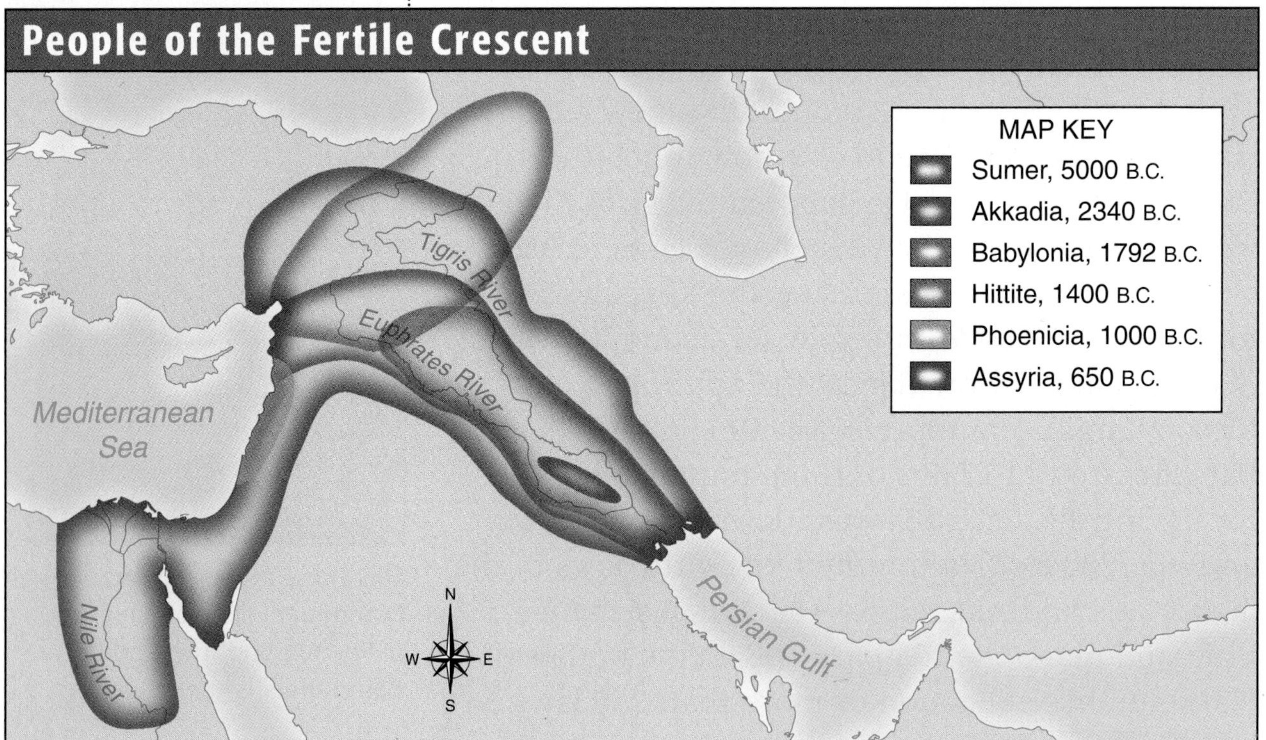

The Phoenicians developed a simple alphabet. The Sumerians had used hundreds of letters. That made cuneiform hard to use. The Phoenicians used just 22 letters. Today many languages are based on the Phoenician alphabet.

Many groups ruled parts of the Fertile Crescent. The Assyrians came to power around 800 B.C. They expanded their control over the next 150 years. By 650 B.C., they ruled all the land of the Fertile Crescent and the Nile River.

The Assyrian Empire was a combination of all the groups of people who lived in the Fertile Crescent and Egypt. The people spoke many different languages. The Assyrian Empire controlled this large area by being cruel. The Assyrians often took people away from their homes and moved them to a different part of the empire. When the empire ended around 600 B.C., many people celebrated.

The Phoenicians traded with other groups.

Lesson 1 Review

Choose words from the list that best complete the paragraphs. One word will not be used.

The land between the Tigris and Euphrates rivers was called Mesopotamia. It formed part of the Fertile Crescent. The __1__ developed the first civilization in this region. The Sumerians developed __2__. They wrote using cuneiform.

Other civilizations lived in the Fertile Crescent. Hammurabi is most remembered for his __3__ of laws. The Phoenicians learned to study the stars and sail at night. In time, the __4__ took over all the land of the Fertile Crescent and the Nile River.

Word List

Sumerians
Assyrians
Sargon
city-states
code

LESSON 2

The Hebrews

New Words
Torah
covenant
Promised Land
Exodus
Ten Commandments
Judaism
contact

People and Places
Hebrews
Abraham
Canaan
Moses
Sinai Desert
Mount Sinai
Israel
Philistines
David
Goliath
Jerusalem
Solomon
Judah

Before You Read
- Did early people believe in one or many gods?
- Why are strong leaders important to a group of people?

Most of the early civilizations of the Fertile Crescent have disappeared. There are no longer any Sumerians or Akkadians. There are no Babylonians or Hittites today. The Phoenicians and Assyrians are gone, too.

The Hebrews are different. They survived. Jewish people today trace their history back to the Hebrews. Their laws are written in a group of five books called the **Torah**. The Torah is part of the Bible. Their story began in Mesopotamia around 4,000 years ago.

Abraham, the first leader of the Hebrews, traveled with his family to Canaan.

Hebrew Beginnings

Like the Egyptians and the Sumerians, most early civilizations believed in many different gods. But the Torah tells of a man named Abraham who believed in only one God. He was the first leader of the Hebrews.

Jewish people believe that God spoke to Abraham and asked him to leave his home. Abraham and his family traveled west out of Mesopotamia. Around 2000 B.C., they came to a land called Canaan. There, Jewish people believe, God promised the Hebrews a home of their own. In return, the Hebrews promised to believe in God alone. This agreement was called a **covenant**. The Hebrews believed that Canaan was their **Promised Land**.

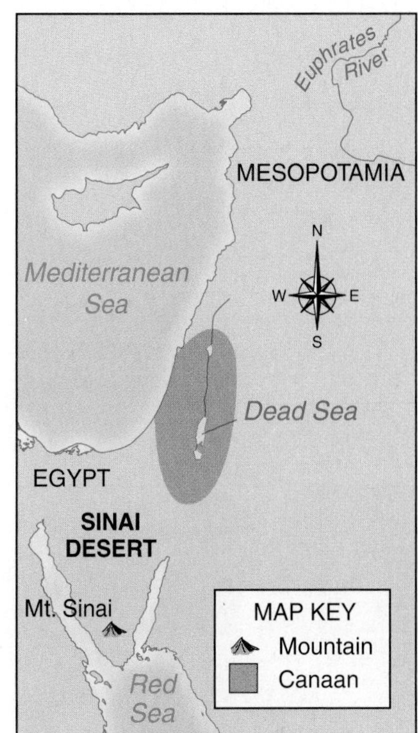

The Land of Canaan

But Canaan was very dry. The Hebrews could not grow enough food. So, around 1800 B.C., they traveled south to Egypt. The Egyptians at first welcomed them, but later forced them to work as slaves. Centuries passed. Around 1290 B.C., the Torah says that Moses became the Hebrew leader. He led the Hebrews out of Egypt. This story is told in a part of the Torah called **Exodus**. The word *exodus* means "road out."

Moses led the Hebrew people out of Egypt.

For years the Hebrews wandered in the Sinai Desert. They were going back to Canaan, the Promised Land. The Torah says that one day Moses went to the top of Mount Sinai. There, God gave him the **Ten Commandments**. These laws told the Hebrews how to behave.

Voices In History

"Respect your father and mother . . . . You shall have no gods other than me . . . . You shall not kill . . . . You shall not steal . . . ."

David and Goliath

Return to Canaan

At last, the Hebrews reached Canaan. They set up a new kingdom called Israel. But there were many other people living in the area. The Hebrews had to fight to win back their Promised Land. One group, the Philistines, had a strong army. A famous Hebrew story tells of a boy named David who defeated a Philistine named Goliath. Goliath was a giant man. He challenged any Hebrew to fight him. Only David was brave enough to accept. David beat Goliath by hurling a stone from a slingshot. David became a Hebrew king. He made Jerusalem the capital of Israel.

When David died, his son Solomon became king. King Solomon built a beautiful temple in Jerusalem. When Solomon died, the kingdom was divided. Hebrew people in the north formed the Kingdom of Israel. Hebrew people in the south set up the Kingdom of Judah. **Judaism**, the name of the Jewish religion, comes from Judah.

This division weakened the Hebrews. They fought one another for many years. Then neighboring kingdoms invaded. These new forces were too strong for the divided Hebrews. One group of outsiders, the Assyrians, took over Israel and Judah. As you have read, the Assyrians controlled all the lands of the Fertile Crescent and the Nile River until around 600 B.C.

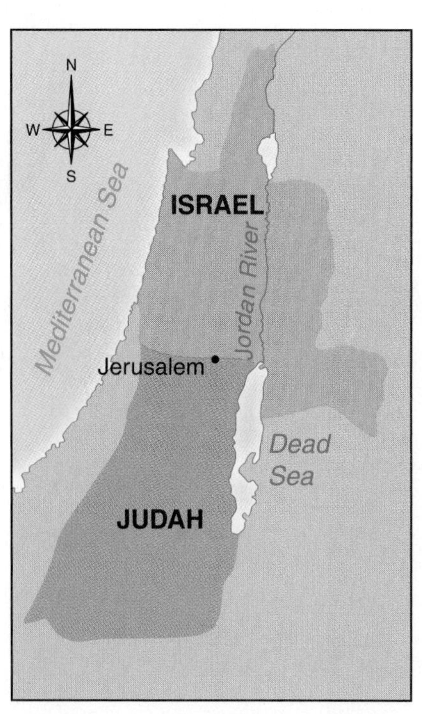

Kingdoms of Israel and Judah

King Solomon (ruled c. 977 B.C.–937 B.C.)

People In History

King Solomon was known for being very wise. As king of Israel, he sometimes acted as a judge. When the people of Israel had questions, they often would seek his advice. King Solomon was also a poet. He wrote a book called the Song of Solomon. This book is in the Bible.

But Solomon is best known for his temple. It was made with beautiful white stone from Jerusalem. Jewish people today pray at the western wall of Solomon's temple.

During Solomon's rule, Israel had **contact** with many parts of the world. Solomon sent ships across the Mediterranean Sea to trade with people of other lands. He brought the traditions and religions of other people into the kingdom of Israel. Some people did not like the new traditions and religions. This weakened Solomon's rule. This was one reason why the kingdom became divided after Solomon's death.

Lesson 2 Review

Choose words from the list that best complete the paragraphs. One word will not be used.

Word List

Commandments
Goliath
Moses
Solomon
Torah

The Hebrews, now called the Jewish people, have survived 4,000 years. Their laws are written in the __1__. Unlike other early civilizations, the Hebrews believed in only one God. Abraham made a covenant with God.

While in Egypt, the Hebrews became slaves. __2__ led them out of Egypt. On Mount Sinai, he received the Ten __3__. The Hebrews had to fight to win back their Promised Land. One of the great Hebrew kings was David. Another king, __4__, built a beautiful temple in Jerusalem.

Chapter 3: Using What You've Learned

Summary

- The Sumerians built the first civilization in the Fertile Crescent.
- The Akkadians, Babylonians, Hittites, Phoenicians, Hebrews, and Assyrians also lived in the Fertile Crescent.
- Hammurabi collected the Babylonian laws into the Code of Hammurabi.
- Abraham and Moses were Hebrew leaders. The Hebrews believed in one God.
- After Solomon died, the Hebrew kingdom split in two.

Find Out More!

After reading Chapter 3, you're ready to go online. **Explore Zone**, **Quiz Time**, and **Amazing Facts** bring this chapter of world history alive.

Visit www.exploreSV.com and type in the chapter code **Ch3**.

Vocabulary

Number your paper from 1 to 5. Write the letter of the correct answer.

1. Sumerians built **dikes** _____.
   a. to protect cities from invaders
   b. to hold back flooding waters
   c. to live in
   d. to honor their gods

2. Sumerians built **ziggurats** as special places for _____.
   a. animals
   b. farmers
   c. gods
   d. boats

3. The Hebrews believed that their **Promised Land** was _____.
   a. Canaan
   b. Thebes
   c. Assyria
   d. Mesopotamia

4. **Exodus** is the story of _____ leading the Hebrews out of Egypt.
   a. Sargon
   b. Moses
   c. Goliath
   d. David

5. The **Ten Commandments** were laws about how to _____.
   a. trade goods
   b. behave
   c. dress
   d. grow crops

Comprehension

Number your paper from 1 to 4. Write **True** for each sentence that is true. Write **False** for each sentence that is false.

1. The Code of Hammurabi treated all people equally.
2. The Hittites only made tools and weapons out of stone.
3. Today many languages are based on the Phoenician alphabet.
4. The Torah contains Hebrew laws.

Critical Thinking

Conclusions Number your paper from 1 to 4. Read each pair of sentences below. Then look for a conclusion that follows from these sentences. Write the letter of the correct conclusion.

1. Mesopotamia had few trees or stones.
   Mesopotamia had plenty of clay.
2. The Sumerians developed a cart with wheels.
   The Sumerians invented a sail for boats.
3. Hammurabi wrote down the Babylonian laws.
   These laws told people what they could and could not do.
4. After King Solomon died, the Hebrew kingdom divided in two.
   The Hebrew kingdoms of Israel and Judah fought one another.

Conclusions

a. The Sumerians changed how people and things traveled.

b. The people of Babylon knew whether they had broken the law.

c. The Sumerians made bricks from clay to build homes and temples.

d. The Hebrews were weakened.

Writing

Write a paragraph describing a what Sumerian city-state might have looked like.

LESSON 1

Early China

New Words
legends
historians
dynasty
bronze
millet
oracle bones
Mandate of Heaven

People and Places
Huang He
Yangshao
Longshan
Shang
Yin
Zhou

Before You Read
- What physical features might separate a place from the rest of the world?
- How do people try to tell the future?

The Chinese built their first civilization on a river, the Huang He, in northern China. The early Chinese knew nothing of the Egyptians or the Sumerians. They were separated from other people. The Pacific Ocean was to the east. Deserts and high mountains surrounded the rest of China. Like the Egyptians and the Sumerians, the Chinese learned to use the river to help them.

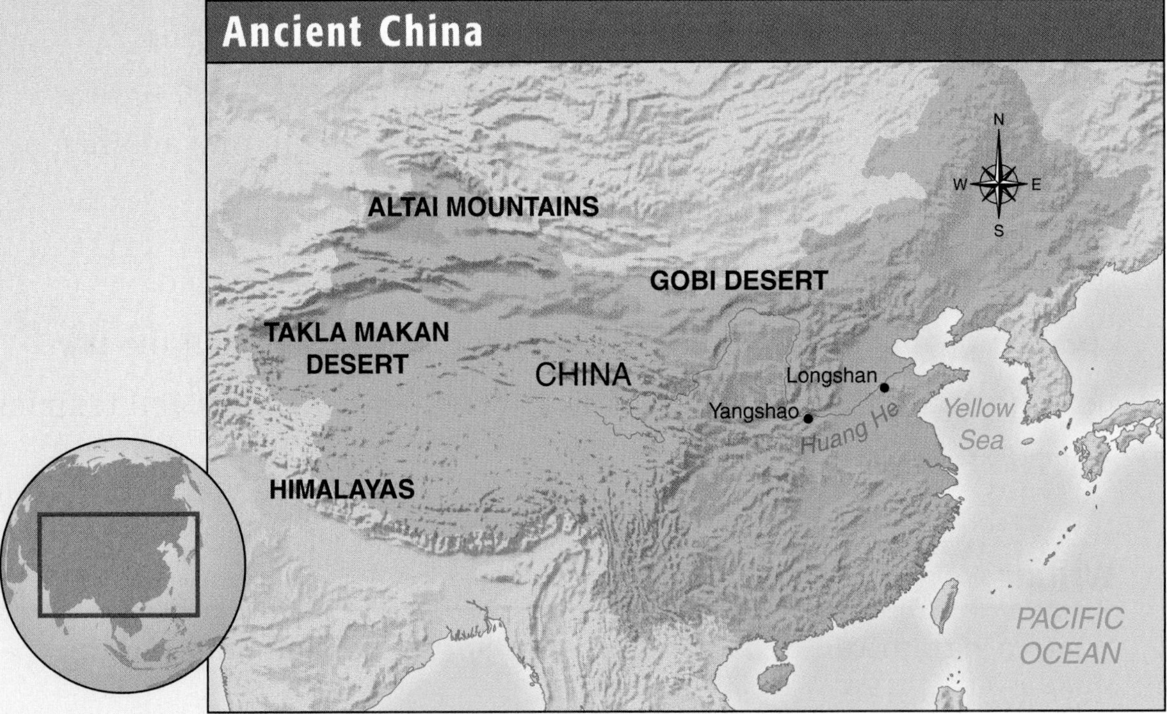

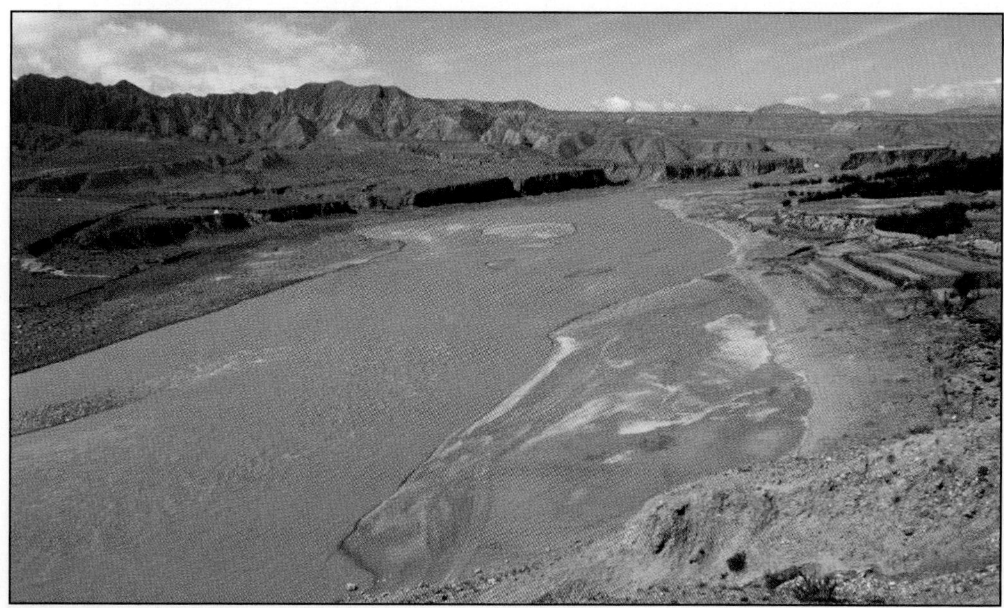

The Huang He runs through northern China.

First Cities

Chinese civilization probably began after civilizations in Egypt and Sumer. Still, Chinese civilization is very old. Early farming villages appeared in the area around 5000 B.C. The story of early China is mixed with **legends**. Until recently, many **historians** didn't believe the legends. But archaeologists have shown that many of the old stories are true. They have done this by digging up old cities, tools, and bones.

The earliest Chinese cities were Yangshao and Longshan. Most people in these cities were farmers along the Huang He. The Huang He is not deep, and the land around it is flat. So the river often flooded. The farmers needed the water, but they faced the same problem the Sumerians did. The floods often washed away whole villages. That is why the Huang He was called "China's Sorrow."

Yangshao pottery

Early Chinese people made pottery. The people of Yangshao used local clay. When they baked it, the clay turned red. The Longshan people lived farther down the river. They used a different kind of clay. They became famous for black pottery.

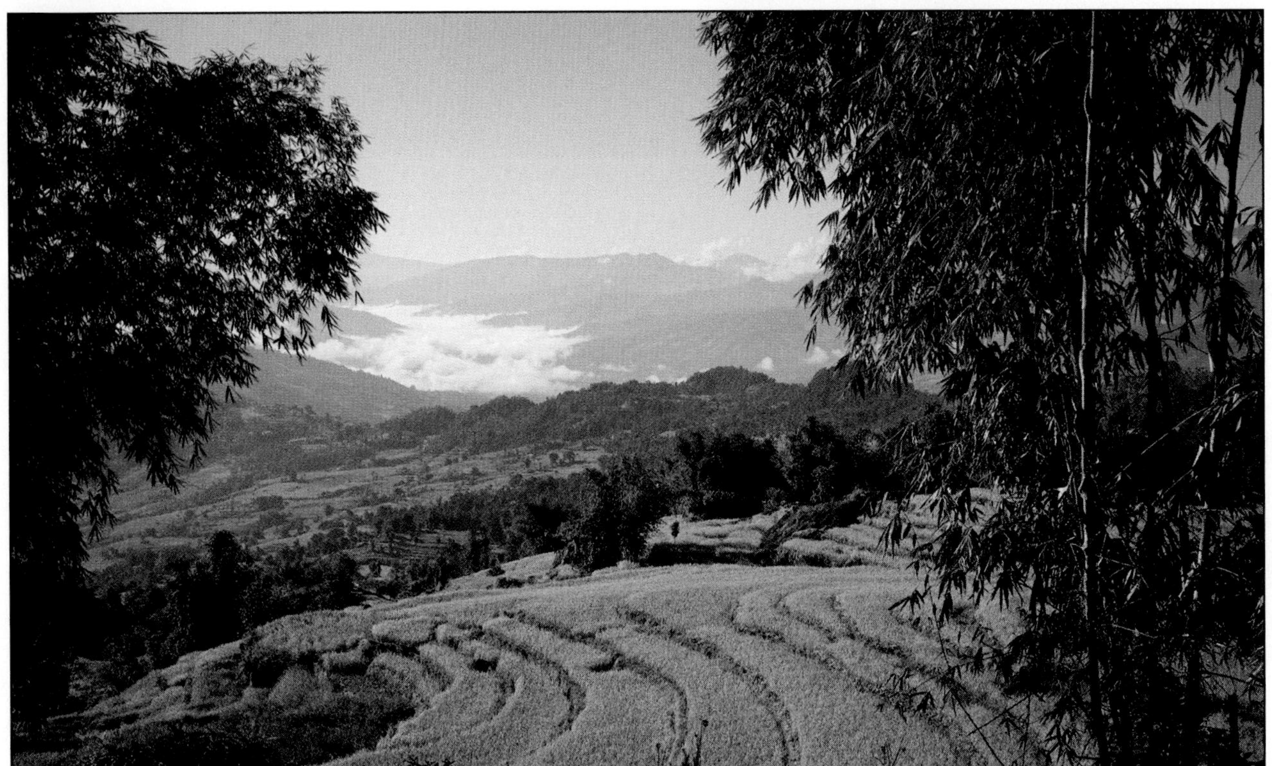

Farmers still plant large fields of millet.

The Shang

The Shang civilization was more advanced than the cities of Yangshao and Longshan. It was actually a **dynasty**, or family of kings. The Shang came to power around 1750 B.C. Tang was the first leader of this dynasty. He was a good ruler who treated people kindly.

Oracle bone

Archeologists have dug up many objects from Yin, the capital city of the Shang Dynasty. They have discovered beautiful objects made from **bronze**. Bronze is a hard metal made by mixing copper and tin. The Shang made bronze cooking pots. They made bronze containers to hold wine. They also made tools and weapons from bronze. The Shang grew wheat and **millet** in the fields of the Huang He valley. They also raised pigs, sheep, and other animals.

The Shang created picture writing. It had thousands of symbols. One purpose of this writing was to tell the future. A person scratched the symbols on an animal bone or a turtle shell to ask a question. The question might have been, "Will the king have a son?" or, "Will I have a good day hunting?"

Then the bone or shell was heated in a fire. The answer to the question depended on how the bone or shell broke. That is why the bones were called **oracle bones**. An oracle is someone who tells the future.

Like the Egyptians, the Shang built places to bury their kings. The kings were buried with things they might need in the next life.

The Zhou

The Shang lost power in 1027 B.C. The Zhou invaded from the west and set up a new dynasty. The Zhou Dynasty stayed in control for 200 years.

The Chinese believed their gods put the ruling family in power. Whoever held power had the right to do so. The Chinese called this special right the **Mandate of Heaven**. The people understood that a certain dynasty had the will, or mandate, of heaven. Just being in power proved it.

Emperors of the Zhou Dynasty often traveled in chariots such as this.

Did You Know?

All in the Family

In ancient China, the family was more important than the individual. That was true for both rich and poor families. If a boy or girl did something wrong, the whole family was punished. Parents chose husbands and wives for their children.

The family was almost holy. In fact, many ancient Chinese people prayed to their relatives who had died long ago.

This symbol represented the Mandate of Heaven.

But a dynasty could lose the Mandate of Heaven. If the kingdom experienced hard times, the people might think the gods no longer favored the ruling family. If the people thought a ruling family lost the Mandate of Heaven, they would no longer support the ruling family.

The Zhou rulers acted as if all the land and all the people belonged to them. They gave land and people to relatives and army leaders. In this way the Zhou created a lot of little kingdoms. These kingdoms had to obey the Zhou king. They also had to pay money to the king and supply him with soldiers in times of war. For more than 200 years, the Zhou kept the Mandate of Heaven.

Then, in 771 B.C., they lost this mandate. Many leaders of the little kingdoms didn't like the harsh rule of the Zhou. Also, the Zhou fought too many wars. That angered even more people. At last, an outside army invaded Zhou lands and killed their king. However, this was not the end of the Zhou. A new king moved further east and set up the Eastern Zhou Dynasty.

Lesson 1 Review

Choose words from the list that best complete the paragraphs. One word will not be used.

Word List

Mandate of Heaven
legends
Sorrow
shallow
oracle bones

Chinese civilization began on the Huang He in northern China. Archeologists have helped us learn more about these early people. The Huang He often flooded because it was __1__. Because of these floods, the river was called "China's __2__."

The early Chinese civilizations made pottery. The Shang made bronze objects and used __3__ to tell the future. The Zhou replaced the Shang but later lost the __4__.

LESSON 2

Indus River Civilizations

Before You Read

- Why is it hard to know about early civilizations?
- How are most early civilizations alike?

Not long after the Egyptians and the Sumerians, the Harappa and Mohenjo-Daro civilizations began in the Indus River valley. The Indus River is located in the modern country of Pakistan, near India. It starts high in the mountains. In the spring, the snow melts in the mountains and floods the Indus River.

Four Ancient Civilizations

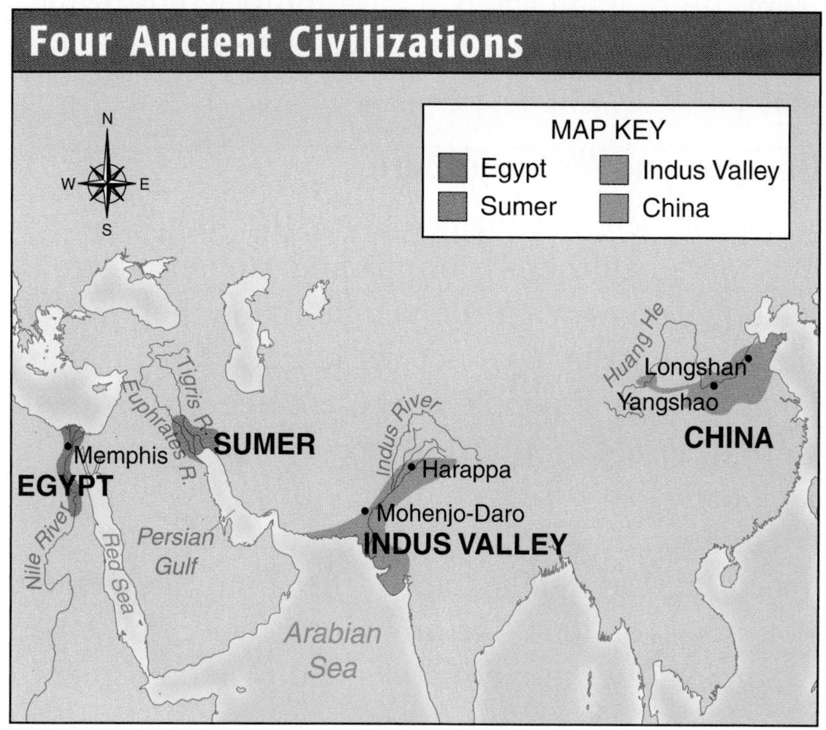

New Words

subcontinent
monsoon
citadel
granary
Vedas
castes
Brahman
untouchables

People and Places

Harappa
Mohenjo-Daro
Indus River
Himalayas
Hindu Kush
Aryans

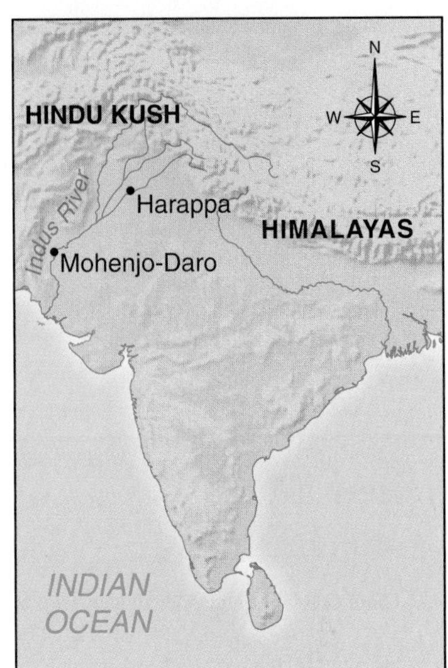

Ancient India

The Harappa and Mohenjo-Daro civilizations started around 2500 B.C. and lasted more than 1,000 years. Then they vanished. Like some other early civilizations, they were lost to history for a very long time. But archaeologists continue to discover more and more about the early people of the Indus River valley.

Geography and Climate

The modern country of India is sometimes called a **subcontinent**. India is a huge piece of land shaped like a triangle. The southern tip extends out into the Indian Ocean. To the north are two large mountain ranges. One is the Himalayas. The world's highest mountains are found there. The Himalayas separate India from China. The other mountain range is the Hindu Kush.

Except in the high mountains, the climate of India is mild. India has two seasons, dry and wet. From October to early June, the dry **monsoon** winds blow into India from Asia. From late June to September, the wet monsoon winds blow up from the Indian Ocean. These moist winds bring heavy rains. The word *monsoon* refers to both dry and wet winds.

Ancient Indian game

Harappa and Mohenjo-Daro

Two large cities formed along the Indus River. Today we call them Harappa and Mohenjo-Daro. We don't know what the people living there called them. Scientists have not yet learned to read the language of the people in these cities. Both cities were deserted around 1500 B.C. In 1922, archaeologists discovered the cities.

Harappa and Mohenjo-Daro were 400 miles apart. But they looked about the same. They did not, however, look like any other ancient city. For example, other ancient cities had twisting streets.

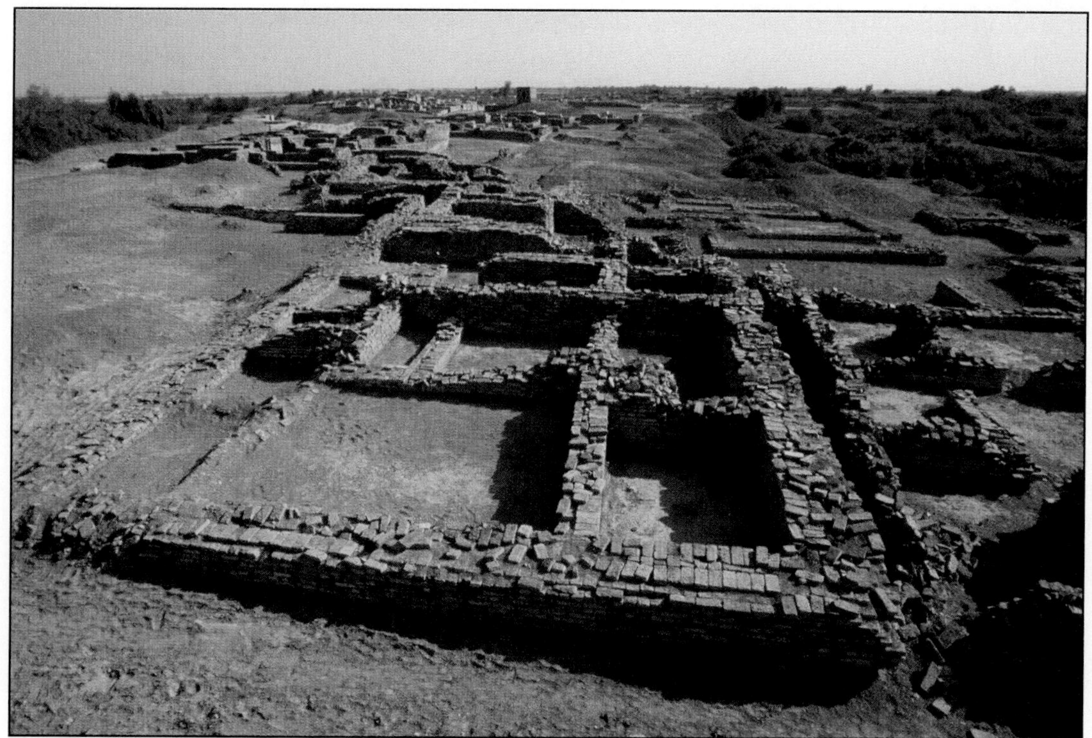
The ruins of Mohenjo-Daro are located in modern-day Pakistan.

In Harappa and Mohenjo-Daro the streets were straight and laid out in blocks. This shows that someone had a clear plan for how to build a city. The streets were wide and paved with bricks.

Most city people in Harappa and Mohenjo-Daro crafted goods. Shops inside the cities sold pottery and jewelry. Some sold cotton goods. Some crafts were traded with civilizations far away. Archaeologists have found crafts from the Indus River valley in the cities of Mesopotamia.

Most of the houses in the Indus River valley looked exactly alike. They were made with mud bricks, which were baked in ovens. Baking made the bricks harder and stronger than the sun-dried mud bricks of Sumer. The bricks in Harappa and Mohenjo-Daro were exactly the same size. The houses had no windows facing the street. The windows faced an open yard, which let sun and light into the house. Many homes had baths. Pipes along the streets drained the bath water out of the house.

Necklace from Mohenjo-Daro

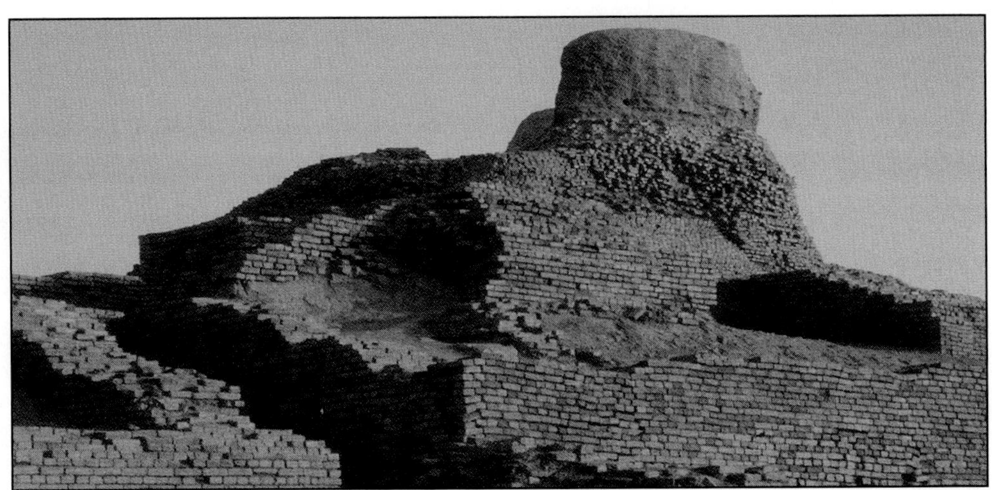

These ruins are from Mohenjo-Daro.

Harappa and Mohenjo-Daro had no temples. They did, however, have a large **citadel**, or fort. The citadel at Mohenjo-Daro was five stories high and had many rooms. Next to the citadel was a **granary**. This was where extra grain was kept. When there was not enough food, the people took the extra grain out of the granary.

Mysterious End and New Beginning

Around 1500 B.C., both cities were deserted. What caused this? Was it a flood? Was it an earthquake? Did the climate suddenly change? No one knows for sure.

About the same time, a group of warriors arrived from western and central Asia. They were called Aryans. Aryan means "noble one." These people brought the horse and the chariot to the Indus River valley. They also brought the Aryan language and religion throughout the Indian subcontinent. The Aryans mixed with the local people to produce a new way of life.

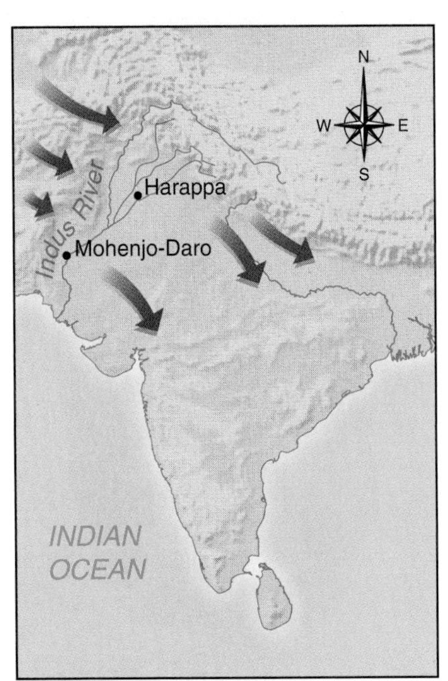

Aryan Movement into India

Aryan Beliefs

At first, Aryans passed down their religious beliefs by word of mouth. Later they wrote down their religious stories and poems in a collection of books. It took hundreds of years to finish them. These books are called the **Vedas**.

The oldest book is the Rig-Veda. One part tells how people were born into different classes, or **castes**. At the top was the priest, or **Brahman**. Then came the warrior. Next came the trader, or merchant. The bottom person was the worker.

Below the caste system were a group called the **untouchables**. These people were thought to be dirty and not pure. They had to do the worst jobs in the city. They had to pick up garbage and clean the dirty streets.

Another part of the Rig-Veda teaches people not to be greedy. It encourages them to give food to the hungry.

A Brahman

> "When the needy [man] comes . . . begging for bread to eat, [he who] hardens his heart against him . . . [will find no one] to comfort him."

Lesson 2 Review

Choose words from the list that best complete the paragraphs. One word will not be used.

India is often called a __1__. Civilizations there developed along the Indus River. The city of __2__ had organized streets. The people there also made pottery, jewelry, and cotton crafts.

Harappa and Mohenjo-Daro came to an end around 1500 B.C. No one knows why. The __3__ were the next group to enter the region. They came from western and central Asia. They wrote religious books called the Vedas. The Vedas taught that everyone belonged in a certain caste. The highest caste was the __4__. Below all the castes were the untouchables.

Word List

Harappa
citadel
subcontinent
Aryans
Brahman

Chapter 4: Using What You've Learned

Summary

- China was separated from other civilizations by deserts, mountains, and the Pacific Ocean.
- Early Chinese civilization began along the Huang He. Yangshao and Longshan were two early Chinese cities.
- The Shang Dynasty came to power around 1750 B.C. The Zhou Dynasty ruled by the Mandate of Heaven.
- India is surrounded by two mountain ranges and the Indian Ocean.
- Harappa and Mohenjo-Daro were two cities on the Indus River.
- The Aryans brought their language and religion to India around 1500 B.C.

Find Out More!

After reading Chapter 4, you're ready to go online. **Explore Zone, Quiz Time,** and **Amazing Facts** bring this chapter of world history alive.

Visit www.exploreSV.com and type in the chapter code **Ch4**.

Vocabulary

Number your paper from 1 to 6. Write the word or words from the list that best complete the paragraphs. One word will not be used.

The history of early Chinese civilization is mixed with __1__. Archaeologists now know about the history of China from objects they have found. Some of these objects are made from __2__, a hard metal made by mixing copper and tin. The Chinese believed their gods put the ruling family in power. This special right was called the __3__.

India is sometimes called a __4__ because it is a huge piece of land. The ancient Indian cities of Harappa and Mohenjo-Daro had __5__, or forts. Each city also had a __6__ where grain was kept.

Word List

legends
granary
bronze
Mandate of Heaven
citadels
millet
subcontinent

Comprehension

Number your paper from 1 to 4. Write the letter of the correct answer.

1. Where did the Chinese build their first civilization?
   a. along the Huang He
   b. on a subcontinent
   c. in a desert
   d. in high mountains

2. Who took power away from the Shang Dynasty in China?
   a. Aryans
   b. Zhou
   c. Tang
   d. Philistines

3. Where did the early civilizations of India begin?
   a. in Longshan
   b. in the Himalayas
   c. in the Indus River valley
   d. in the Hindu Kush

4. Which group of people were in the highest caste?
   a. warriors
   b. Brahmans
   c. untouchables
   d. workers

Critical Thinking

Fact or Opinion Number your paper from 1 to 5. For each fact, write **Fact**. Write **Opinion** for each opinion. You should find three sentences that are opinions.

1. Early farming villages appeared in China around 5000 B.C.
2. Archaeologists find Yangshao more interesting than Longshan.
3. Harappa was the best city of all early civilizations.
4. The people of Mohenjo-Daro traded with civilizations far away.
5. The Vedas contain the most beautiful ancient stories and poems.

Writing

Write a paragraph explaining how the Shang used oracle bones to try to tell the future.

Skill Builder: Reading a Timeline

A **timeline** shows the order in which events happened. A timeline also helps us see how much time there was between events. Dates tell us when events in history happened.

We say that events happened before or after the birth of a man called Jesus. Jesus was a religious leader you will read about in Chapter 9. Events that happened before Jesus' birth are marked **B.C.** Events that happened after Jesus' birth are marked **A.D.** When counting years before Jesus' birth, the highest number tells the oldest event. When counting years after Jesus' birth, the lowest number tells the oldest event. Read the timeline from left to right.

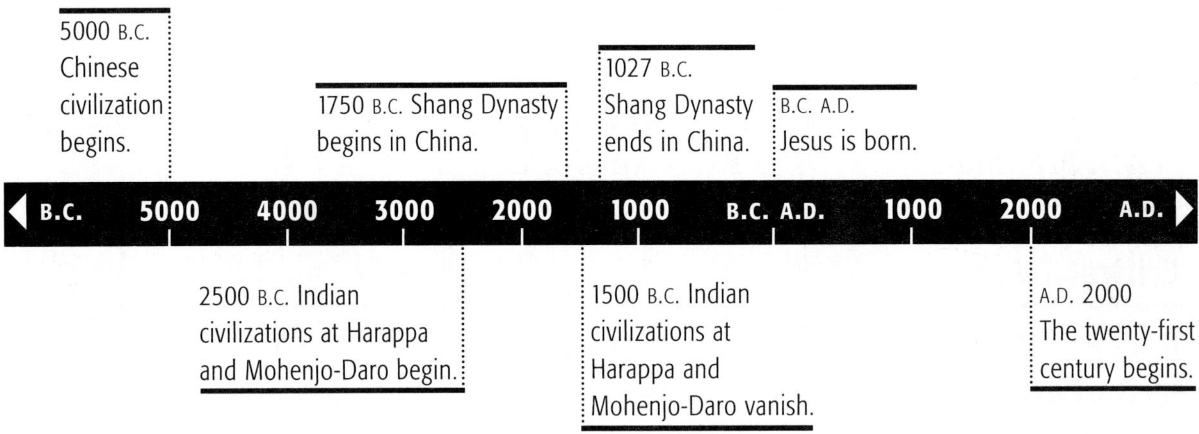

Number your paper from 1 to 5. Answer each question with a complete sentence.

1. Did the events in ancient China and ancient India happen before or after Jesus' birth?
2. Which is older: 1500 B.C. or 2500 B.C.?
3. Did China or India have the first civilization?
4. In what year did the Harappa and Mohenjo-Daro civilizations vanish?
5. Between which dates did the Shang Dynasty rule?

LESSON 1

The First Americans

Before You Read

- How did early people get to the Americas?
- Why would a nomad become a settler?

You might have heard that Christopher Columbus reached the Americas in 1492. But he wasn't the first person to see the Americas. The first people arrived thousands of years earlier. Today these people are called Native Americans. We don't know exactly when they first arrived. Many scientists think it was around 13,000 B.C. Others think it was as early as 30,000 B.C.

Crossing the Bering Strait

The first people in the Americas crossed the Bering Strait from Asia into North America. A **strait** is a thin body of water. It connects two larger bodies of water. Today, the Bering Strait connects the Pacific Ocean with the Arctic Ocean. It is 60 miles of open water.

New Words

strait
land bridge
migration
maize
population

People and Places

Americas
Native Americans
Bering Strait
Central America
Mexico

Ice floats in the cold water of the Bering Strait.

Early humans crossed the Bering Strait between Asia and North America.

During an Ice Age, the Pacific and Arctic oceans were 300 feet lower than they are now. Much of the water was trapped in glaciers. During that time, there was no water in what is now the Bering Strait. It was dry land. It served as a **land bridge** between Asia and North America.

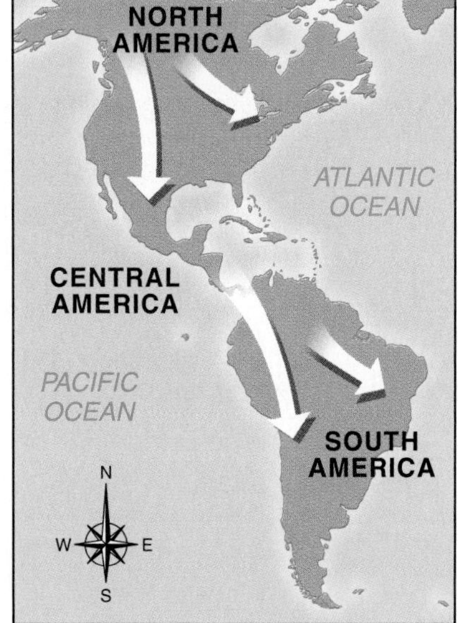

Migration into the Americas

Like all of the earliest humans, the people who used the land bridge were nomads. They were traveling from Asia, looking for animals to hunt and plants to eat. They took only what they could carry. They didn't make clay pots or build temples. They left few clues about their lives.

Over thousands of years, the nomads spread out to the south and east. This is called a **migration**. They lived in small groups. Some groups stayed in North America. Others kept moving. Some settled in Central America. Others kept going until they reached South America.

First Farming

The men hunted most of the time. Like other Stone Age people, the early Americans hunted using sharp spears made from stones. They hunted mammoths and other animals. The women and children gathered berries, nuts, and seeds.

Around 8000 B.C., the climate changed. The mammoth and other large animals did not survive. Hunters could only hunt smaller animals such as foxes, deer, and rabbits.

Some people began to put seeds into the ground. These Americans began farming in the area we call Mexico. They began farming around the same time as people in Egypt, Mesopotamia, China, and the Indus River valley. The early Americans planted beans, potatoes, squash, pumpkins, and peppers.

The most important crop was corn. The Americans called it **maize**. They learned how to mix wild maize with other grasses. They could grind the corn to use it in cooking.

Farming gave the Americans a steady food supply, which allowed the **population** to grow. Villages developed and grew. A steady food supply allowed for the building of cities and the beginning of civilization in the Americas.

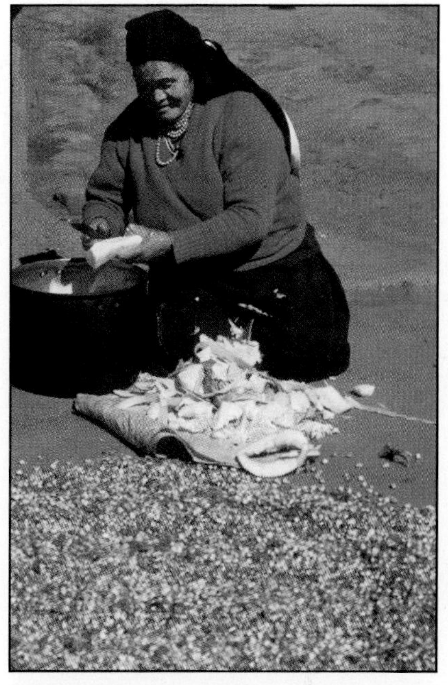

Corn is still a common food in Central America.

Lesson 1 Review

Choose words from the list that best complete the paragraphs. One word will not be used.

Word List
maize
population
nomads
Mexico
Bering Strait

People came to North America many thousands of years ago. They walked from Asia across the __1__. There was a land bridge between Asia and North America. These early Americans were __2__ who moved from place to place.

Early Americans hunted for food and gathered plants. The first farms developed in the modern country of __3__. An important crop was __4__. Farming gave the early Americans a steady food supply. American civilizations soon followed.

LESSON 2

Early American Civilizations

New Words
basalt
calendar
shamans
jaguar

People and Places
Olmecs
Caral
Gulf of Mexico
La Venta
Peru
Supe River

Before You Read

- How do scientists learn about early people?
- How are games important to people?

For a long time, no one knew about the early American civilizations. Many of their cities and objects were buried under deep grasses and hard clay. One group, the Olmecs, lived in the area that is now Mexico. In South America, an old city named Caral was discovered only recently. Both early American civilizations are some of the most mysterious of the ancient world.

The Olmecs

The Olmec civilization began about 1500 B.C. Like all early civilizations, it developed in an area that supported farming. The Olmecs settled along the Gulf of Mexico and built large religious centers. One such center was La Venta.

The Olmecs built huge statues of heads.

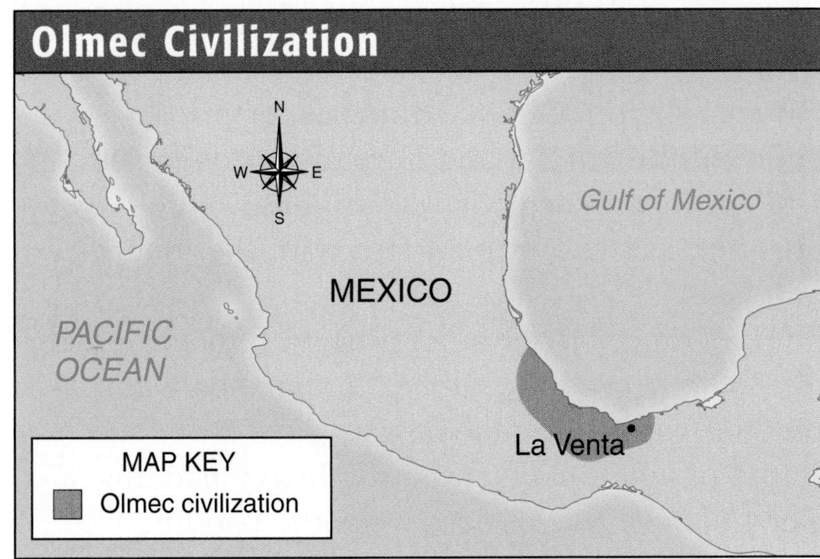

The Olmecs settled in modern-day Mexico. Along what body of water did they settle?

The Olmecs are most famous for their huge statues of heads. The heads were probably those of kings. They ranged in height from 5 feet to 11 feet. They weighed as much as 20 tons. The Olmecs made the heads out of a volcanic rock called **basalt**. But there was no basalt where the Olmecs lived. They had to bring the rock from as far as 80 miles away. How they did that is a mystery.

They might have carved the heads and then hauled them over land. But that would have been difficult since the Olmecs didn't use wheels. They also didn't use animals to pull heavy loads. Maybe the Olmecs floated the basalt heads on rafts down rivers. Then they could have placed the carved heads on land. But how would they have gotten them up the hills? No one really knows.

The Olmecs might have floated their statues on rafts.

Life for the Olmecs

The Olmecs built farms and made pottery. They studied the stars and made a **calendar**. They knew mathematics. They developed a writing system, too. The Olmecs used hieroglyphics. The Olmec hieroglyphics were very different from Egyptian hieroglyphics. Scientists have learned only recently what some of the Olmec pictures mean. One stone tells of a leader who could turn himself into an animal.

This statue has both human and jaguar features.

Animals played a big role in the lives of the Olmec people. They were even a part of the Olmec religion. Olmec **shamans**, or priests, believed the animal and human worlds mixed. One of the Olmec gods was a **jaguar**. Olmec art often shows a human face with the mouth of a jaguar.

The Olmecs lived in an area with lots of rubber trees. They used the rubber to make balls for outdoor games. Archaeologists have found a statue of a ball player wearing heavy padding. They believe the Olmecs wore the padding for protection when playing ball games.

Early Americans playing an outdoor ball game

The Olmecs disappeared around 300 B.C. No one knows why this civilization disappeared. It is another mystery. But many of the arts and skills of the Olmecs were passed on to the civilizations that followed.

Discovery in South America

Archaeologists continue to learn more about ancient civilizations. They used to think that the Olmecs were the oldest civilization in the Americas. But in 2001, they announced that an older city had been found in Peru. This city is called Caral.

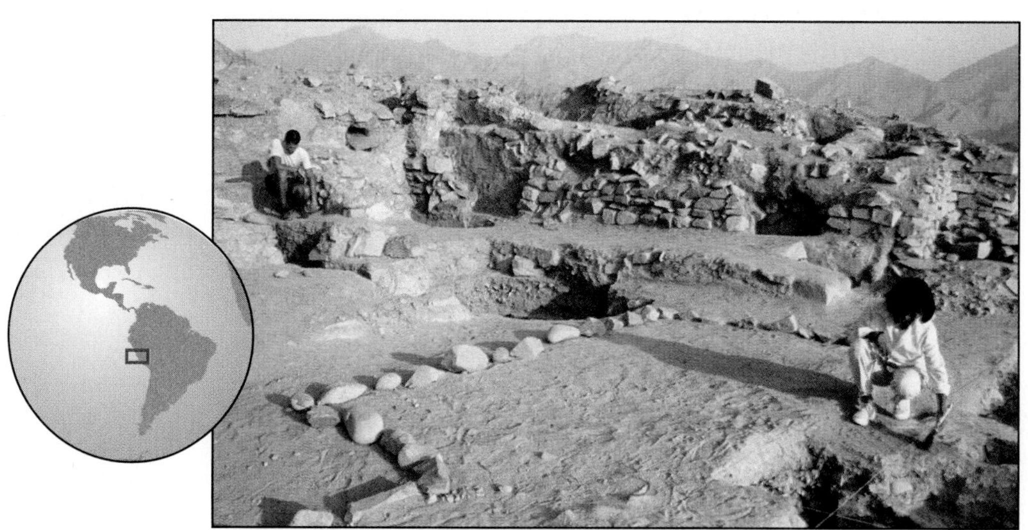

Archaeologists are still learning about the ancient city of Caral in Peru.

Caral was in the Supe River valley not far from the Pacific Ocean. It dates back to 2627 B.C., which means it is 1,100 years older than any Olmec city.

For its time, Caral was a large city. As many as 10,000 people might have lived there. Caral had six great pyramids. The people in Caral were building pyramids around the same time as people in the Old Kingdom of Egypt. But the pyramids in Caral were not as tall as those in Egypt. The biggest pyramid in Caral was 60 feet high and 500 feet long. The people of Caral built the pyramids with stones and mud. They did all this without using wheels or metal tools.

Fish hung up to dry

The people of Caral grew a few vegetables. They ate a lot of fish. They also used dried fish as money. They traded with people who lived in small fishing villages on the coast. One thing they traded was cotton. The villagers used the cotton to make fishing nets.

Lesson 2 Review

Choose words from the list that best complete the paragraphs. One word will not be used.

The Olmec civilization was located in modern-day __1__. It dates back to 1500 B.C. The Olmecs are known for their huge statues of heads. These heads were made from __2__. The Olmecs made fine pottery and developed their own calendar and writing system. Their shamans believed the human and animal worlds were mixed.

The oldest known city in the Americas is Caral, located in __3__. It dates back to 2627 B.C. The people there built pyramids. Their pyramids were built with stones and __4__. The people of Caral ate vegetables and fish.

Word List

basalt
Peru
rafts
Mexico
mud

Chapter 5: Using What You've Learned

Summary

- The first people to come to the Americas were nomads. They crossed a land bridge from Asia to Alaska, where the Bering Strait is today.
- Over thousands of years, these nomads spread out across North America and South America. In time, they settled and learned to farm.
- The Olmecs built a civilization in ancient Mexico about 3,500 years ago. They are known for building giant stone heads. They also developed a calendar and played ball games.
- In 2001, archaeologists learned that the city of Caral in Peru is the oldest known civilization in the Americas.

Find Out More!

After reading Chapter 5, you're ready to go online. **Explore Zone**, **Quiz Time**, and **Amazing Facts** bring this chapter of world history alive.

Visit www.exploreSV.com and type in the chapter code **Ch5**.

Vocabulary

Number your paper from 1 to 6. Write the word or words from the list that best complete each sentence. One word will not be used.

1. A thin body of water that connects two larger bodies of water is called a _____.
2. Early people came to the Americas across a _____.
3. People moving across a large area is called a _____.
4. The most important crop for early farmers in ancient Mexico was _____.
5. The Olmecs studied the stars and developed a _____.
6. Olmec priests were called _____.

Word List

shamans
calendar
maize
basalt
land bridge
migration
strait

Comprehension

Number your paper from 1 to 5. Write the word from the list that best completes the paragraph. One word will not be used.

The first people in the Americas crossed the Bering Strait. A __1__ is a thin body of water that connects two larger bodies of water. The early people who came to North America from Asia were __2__ who traveled looking for food. The early Americans hunted __3__. Around 8000 B.C., some Americans began to farm in the area now called __4__. Archaeologists think that the city called Caral is the oldest __5__ in the Americas.

Word List

civilization
domesticate
strait
nomads
mammoths
Mexico

Critical Thinking

Main Idea Number your paper from 1 to 4. Write the sentence that is the main idea in each group.

1. Many scientists think people came to the Americas in 13,000 B.C.
Some think people came to the Americas in 30,000 B.C.
We don't know exactly when people first arrived in the Americas.

2. Farming gave early people in the Americas a steady food supply.
More people began to live in villages and cities.
A steady food supply helped villages and cities in the Americas grow.

3. La Venta was an important early Olmec religious center.
Two of the earliest civilizations in the Americas were La Venta and Caral.
Caral, an old city in South America, was found just recently.

4. One of the Olmec gods was a jaguar.
Animals played an important part in the lives of the Olmecs.
Olmec art often shows animals such as the jaguar.

Writing

Write a paragraph describing a day in the life of a person living in an Olmec civilization.

UNIT 2

Vast Empires and World Religions

600 B.C.–A.D. 500

These years in history are marked by new ideas. Some people changed the way they thought about government. Others made discoveries in science and medicine. Still others began practicing new religions.

This unit tells about the rise and fall of some of the world's greatest empires. These empires gained vast lands from 600 B.C. to A.D. 500. Each empire helped shape our modern world. They gave us modern religions and modern languages. They brought us closer to the way of life we know today.

B.C. 600 500 400 300 200 100

500 B.C.
The city of Monte Albán is built on a mountaintop in Central America.

338 B.C.
Alexander the Great starts his journey to rule the world.

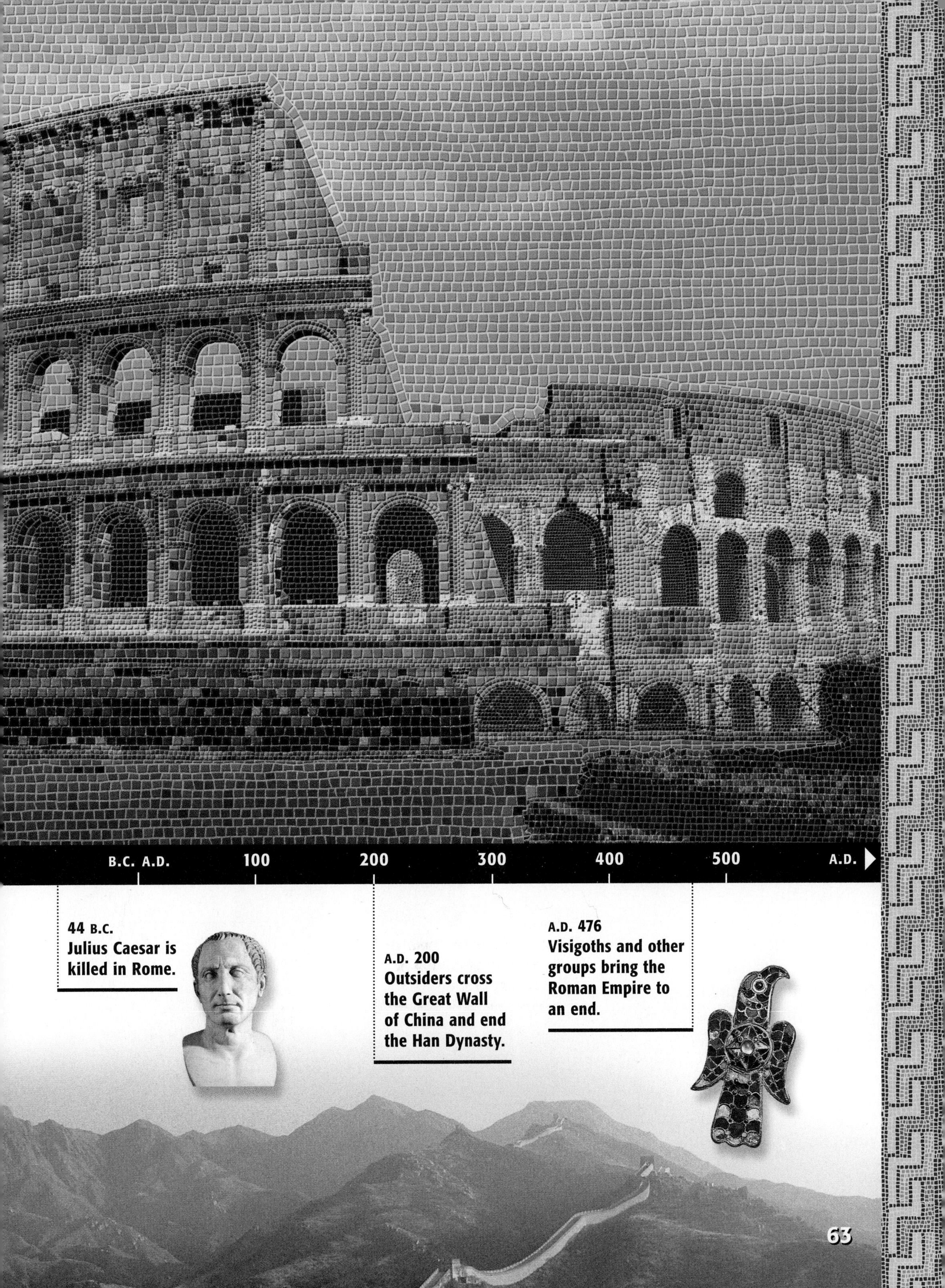

44 B.C.
Julius Caesar is killed in Rome.

A.D. 200
Outsiders cross the Great Wall of China and end the Han Dynasty.

A.D. 476
Visigoths and other groups bring the Roman Empire to an end.

LESSON 1

Africa After the New Kingdom

New Words

culture
iron ore
caravans
resources
artifacts
terracotta

People and Places

Kerma
Napata
Meroe
Sudan
Ezana
Axum
Ethiopia
Nok
West Africa
Nigeria

Before You Read

- Why do we study civilizations that have ended?
- Why are trade routes important to a civilization?

You have read how some early civilizations came to an end. Some were taken over by nearby civilizations. Others fell because the people fought one another for power.

Even when civilizations fall, however, they remain important. People today can enjoy the art, writings, and buildings of civilizations from long ago. People also can learn from the mistakes of past civilizations. That is one reason to study history—to learn from the past.

Students look at King Tut's mummy case in the Egyptian Museum.

This Egyptian art was created during Kushite rule.

Kush Rule Over Egypt

The Egyptian pharaohs began losing power during the New Kingdom. As the pharaohs lost power, Egypt became weak. It could no longer control the lands of Kush, to the South.

The trouble in the New Kingdom gave the people of Kush a chance to rule themselves. About 1100 B.C., they moved their capital from Kerma to a city further south called Napata. The Kush people thought of themselves as Egyptians. They shared much of Egyptian **culture**. They had the same gods. The Kushites even called their leaders pharaohs.

Kush got stronger while Egypt got weaker. Around 710 B.C., a Kushite pharaoh took over much of Egypt. Kushite pharaohs ruled Egypt for almost 50 years. They learned Egyptian hieroglyphics and repaired Egyptian temples.

Kushite rule of Egypt came to an end in 671 B.C. The Assyrians, who had already taken control of Mesopotamia, invaded Egypt. The Assyrians defeated the Kushites. The Assyrians used powerful iron weapons. They had learned how to use iron from the Hittites.

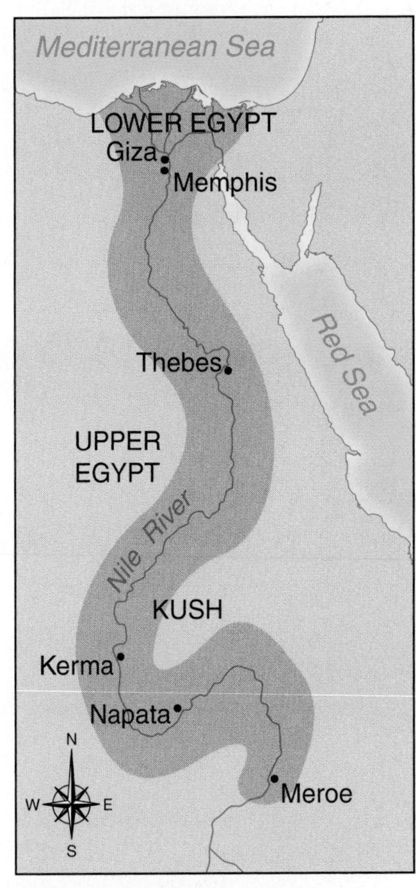

Area Controlled by Kingdom of Kush, 710 B.C.–671 B.C.

The Kushite civilization did not end when the Assyrians took over Egypt. The Kushite people moved their capital even further south to a city called Meroe. There they began building a new kingdom.

New Capital at Meroe

Meroitic bowl

The Kingdom of Kush was located in the area of modern-day Sudan. The city of Meroe was at a meeting point for many of the old Nubian trade routes. Meroe became a leading trading center. It was such an important city that this time in African history is called the Meroitic Period. The Meroitic Period lasted from about 270 B.C. to A.D. 330.

The Kushite people learned how to make iron from the Assyrians. They found that there was a great amount of **iron ore** in Meroe. During the Meroitic Period, Meroe became the East African leader in iron making.

Caravans, or groups of people traveling through the desert, stopped in Meroe. Some came from Southwest Asia and India. Others came from areas in western and southern Africa. The groups came to trade gold, spices, and other goods and **resources**.

These iron tools were made by the people of Meroe.

The Kushite people kept many of their old Egyptian ways. But Meroe was far away from Egypt. So the Kush also developed a culture of their own. For example, the Meroitic women were much more involved in government than Egyptian women were. Some Meroitic carvings even show women holding swords in battle.

Meroitic silver with jewels

The Rise of Axum

Meroe was a strong trading center when trading was done by land. But around A.D. 200, people began building ports along the Red Sea. Many traders used the sea routes instead of land routes.

Around A.D. 300, Ezana, the king of Axum, invaded the Kush kingdom. Axum was a kingdom on the Red Sea. Axum was located in the part of eastern Africa that is Ethiopia today. When Ezana defeated the Kushites, Axum took the place of Meroe as a leading trading center.

The people of Axum grew rich. As a trading center, people in Axum learned about the many changes happening in the world. Meroe, on the other hand, lost its importance as Axum grew. By A.D. 500, the Kushite culture had disappeared.

Around A.D. 200, people began trading across the Red Sea. Which kingdom was located along the Red Sea?

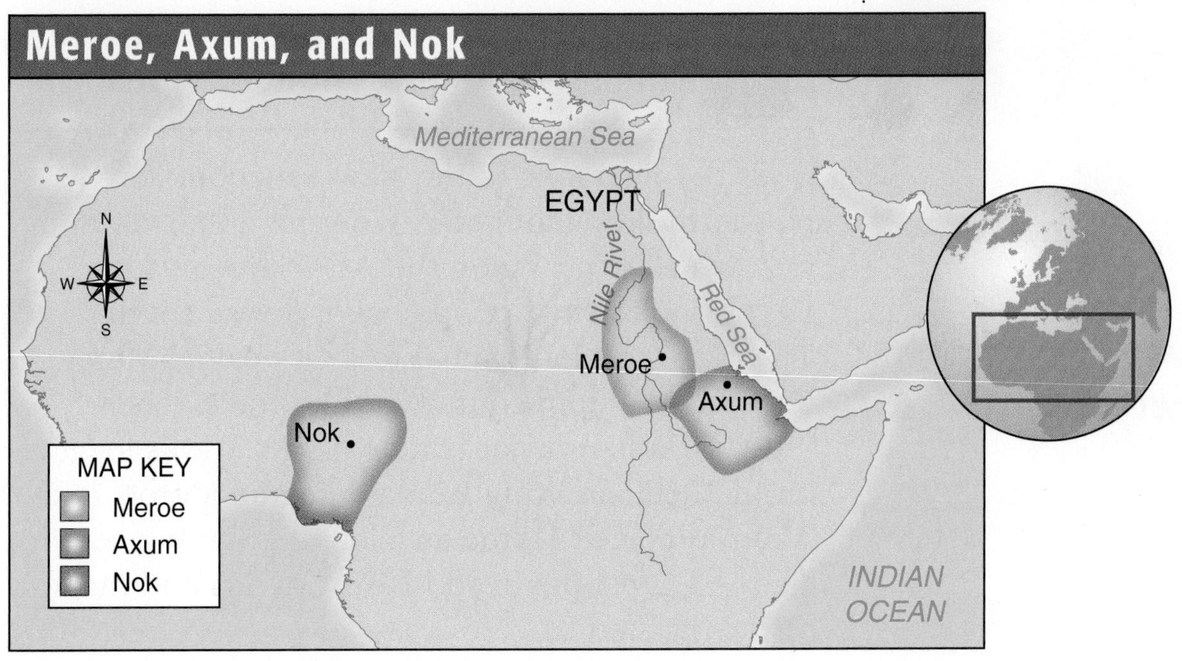

The Nok People

Nok terracotta statue

There were other civilizations in Africa, but scientists today know little about them. The Nok civilization was in West Africa in what is now Nigeria. The Nok people lived sometime between 900 B.C. and A.D. 200. Very little is known about this group. Scientists don't even know what they called themselves. The name *Nok* comes from the present-day Nigerian town of Nok. That is where many of the Nok **artifacts** have been found.

The Nok people probably knew how to work with iron and tin. They also knew how to bake clay with sand to make **terracotta**. The Nok people shaped this clay to make statues. The most famous Nok artifacts are terracotta statues that show human faces.

Lesson 1 Review

Choose words from the list that best complete the paragraphs. One word will not be used.

Word List

caravans
Nok
Kush
Nigeria
Ethiopia

As the pharaohs of the New Kingdom lost power, the Kingdom of __1__ grew in power and took over Egypt. When the Assyrians invaded Egypt, the Kushite people were forced south. They moved their capital to a city called Meroe. Many __2__ stopped in Meroe to trade goods.

Axum was in what is now __3__. It was located on the Red Sea. King Ezana defeated Meroe, and Axum replaced Meroe as a leading trading center. The __4__ people lived in West Africa and made terracotta statues.

LESSON 2

Central America

Before You Read

- Why did early civilizations want to please their gods?
- How did they try to please their gods?

A city called Monte Albán began in Central America around 500 B.C. Another city called Teotihuacán formed north of Monte Albán around 200 B.C. These two cities had much in common. They both had pyramids and temples. They both had great **plazas**, or big open areas. Both cities continued to grow for several centuries. Both cities began to disappear around A.D. 700.

Monte Albán

A group called the Zapotec built the city of Monte Albán. They built it on flat land at the top of a mountain. The city looked over the area now called the Oaxaca Valley. The Zapotec stayed in the city for around 1,200 years.

New Words

plazas
bas-reliefs
terraces
sacrifice
peninsula
slash-and-burn

People and Places

Monte Albán
Teotihuacán
Zapotec
Oaxaca Valley
Maya
Yucatan Peninsula

The ruins of Monte Albán are in modern-day Mexico.

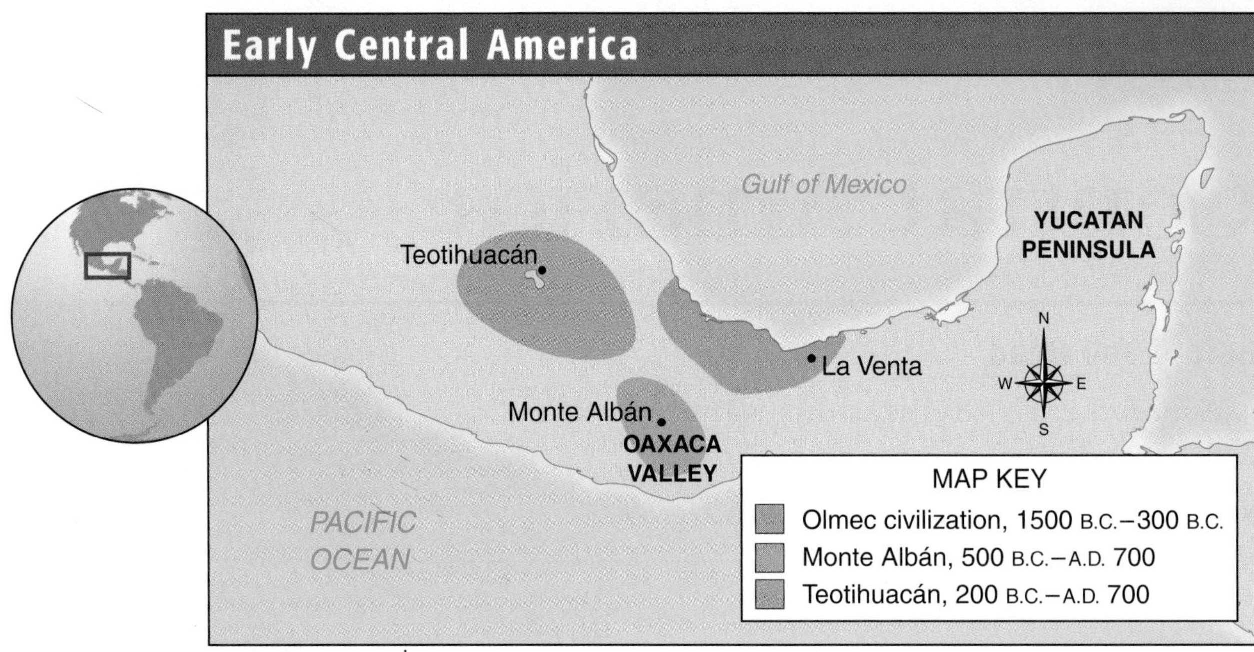

Early Central America was home to some of the first American civilizations. Which civilization began around 500 B.C.?

A huge plaza filled the center of Monte Albán. Temples, homes, and tombs surrounded the plaza. The king's palace was also there. There was even a courtyard where they played ball games.

One place was the Building of the Dancers. The name comes from the **bas-reliefs**, or carvings made on a flat surface. The bas-reliefs show human figures in twisted shapes. A long time ago, someone called the figures dancers. Today, scientists don't know whether the figures really were dancers. The human figures look very similar to those in Olmec art. The people of Monte Albán probably traded with the Olmecs.

Bas-relief from the Building of the Dancers

Monte Albán was high and dry. It was not a good place to grow crops. Zapotec farmers went to the valley below to grow corn, squash, and beans. The valley farmers grew enough food each year to feed the 17,500 people in the city.

The Zapotec left the city of Monte Albán around A.D. 700. No one knows why. There might have been a climate change. The soil might have stopped producing crops. Perhaps there was a disease or war that destroyed the city.

Teotihuacán

Teotihuacán was built about 200 miles northwest of Monte Albán. It was a huge city that covered more than seven square miles. By A.D. 400, more than 100,000 people lived there.

Teotihuacán means "City of the Gods." The people of Teotihuacán believed in many gods. These included gods of the sun, rain, corn, and fire. The people believed these gods controlled the crops. They worked hard to please the gods so that the land would produce good crops.

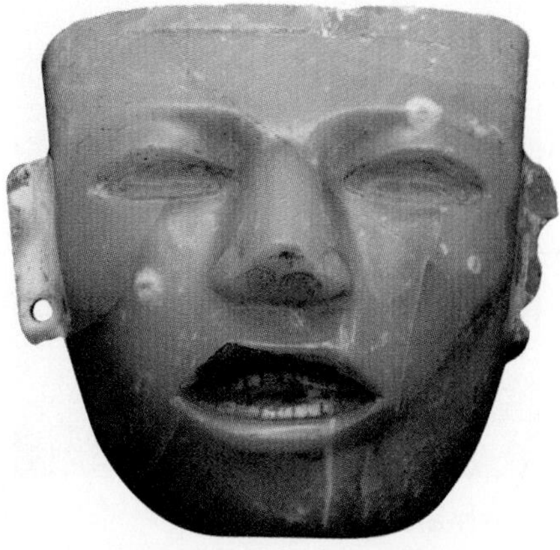

Mask from Teotihuacán

The city of Teotihuacán had a large plaza and wide streets. One two-mile road was called the Avenue of the Dead. It was lined with pyramids, temples, and palaces.

One pyramid was the Pyramid of the Sun. It had five **terraces**, or levels, and was 216 feet high. It was one of the largest pyramids in the world.

The people of Teotihuacán believed that one way to please the gods was to offer human **sacrifice**. This killing of people was not done to be cruel. The people felt that without human sacrifice, the gods would die. Then all the crops would fail, and all the people would die.

Around A.D. 650, invaders attacked Teotihuacán and burned the city. Who attacked the city and why they did so remain a mystery.

The Pyramid of the Sun was the largest building in Teotihuacán.

Slash-and-burn farming

Early Maya

Around 200 B.C., people called the Maya settled in an area now called the Yucatan Peninsula. A **peninsula** is a large piece of land that is mostly surrounded by water. The Maya had good farming methods. They used a **slash-and-burn** method to clear lands for farming. They cut down the plants and burned the fields. This kept the soil rich for long periods of time. Also, fields in lower areas sometimes had large puddles of standing water. So, the early Maya built raised fields. This kept their crops from rotting.

These farming methods helped the Maya become wealthy. They started building stone temples to honor their gods. By A.D. 250, many Mayan villages had grown into organized cities with massive temples. This was the beginning of one of the most remarkable civilizations of Central America.

Lesson 2 Review

Choose words from the list that best complete the paragraphs. One word will not be used.

Word List

Sun
bas-reliefs
sacrifice
slash-and-burn
Teotihuacán

Monte Albán was an ancient city in Central America. It is known for its __1__. These carvings show human figures in twisted shapes.

The largest city in Central America at this time was __2__. It had as many as 100,000 people. The people of Teotihuacán honored many gods. They felt they needed to please the gods in order to stay alive. The Pyramid of the __3__ had five terraces. It was one of the tallest pyramids in the world.

Another civilization, the Maya, began to grow. They used a __4__ method for farming and built raised fields.

Chapter 6: Using What You've Learned

Summary

- Meroe, the last capital of the Kingdom of Kush, was an important trading center.
- Ezana of Axum defeated the Kush kingdom around A.D. 300. Axum became the main trading center in Africa.
- The Nok lived in West Africa between 900 B.C. and A.D. 200. Very little is known about the Nok culture.
- Monte Albán and Teotihuacán were two large cities in early Central America. Both cities had temples and pyramids. Both cities began to disappear around A.D. 700.

Find Out More!

After reading Chapter 6, you're ready to go online. **Explore Zone**, **Quiz Time**, and **Amazing Facts** bring this chapter of world history alive.

Visit www.exploreSV.com and type in the chapter code **Ch6**.

Vocabulary

Number your paper from 1 to 5. Finish the sentences from Group A with words from Group B. Write the letter of the correct answer.

Group A

1. The _____ of the Kush people was like that of the Egyptians.
2. Meroe was a trading center where _____ stopped to trade gold, spices, and other goods.
3. The Nok people made _____ by baking clay with sand.
4. Cities in ancient Central America had big open areas called _____.
5. The Pyramid of the Sun had five_____, or levels.

Group B

a. terracotta
b. caravans
c. terraces
d. plazas
e. culture

Comprehension

Number your paper from 1 to 5. Write one or more sentences to answer each question below.

1. What did the Assyrians use to defeat Egypt?
2. Why did Axum become a leading trading center?
3. What are two things the cities of Monte Albán and Teotihuacán had in common?
4. What are two possible reasons that the Zapotec left Monte Albán?
5. Why did the people of Teotihuacán work hard to please their gods?

Critical Thinking

Categories Number your paper from 1 to 5. Read the words in each group below. Think about how they are alike. Write the best title for each group.

Monte Albán **Meroe** **Nok** **Teotihuacán** **Axum**

1. Kushite capital
   iron-making center
   early trading center
2. port on Red Sea
   King Ezana
   located in what is
   Ethiopia today
3. civilization in West Africa
   little is known about
   made terracotta statues
4. built by Zapotec
   Building of the Dancers
   built on the top of a mountain
5. "City of the Gods"
   Avenue of the Dead
   Pyramid of the Sun

Writing

Write a paragraph describing how the Egyptian and the Kushite cultures were alike and how they were different.

Skill Builder: Using a Map Key and Map Directions

Map Key Sometimes a map uses colors or symbols to show important things on the map. A **map key** tells what the colors or symbols mean. Study the map key on the map below.

Number your paper from 1 to 3. Write the answers to the questions.

1. What symbol is used to show a river? Name a river shown on the map.
2. What is the symbol for a city? Name a city shown on the map.
3. What color is used to show where the Olmecs lived?

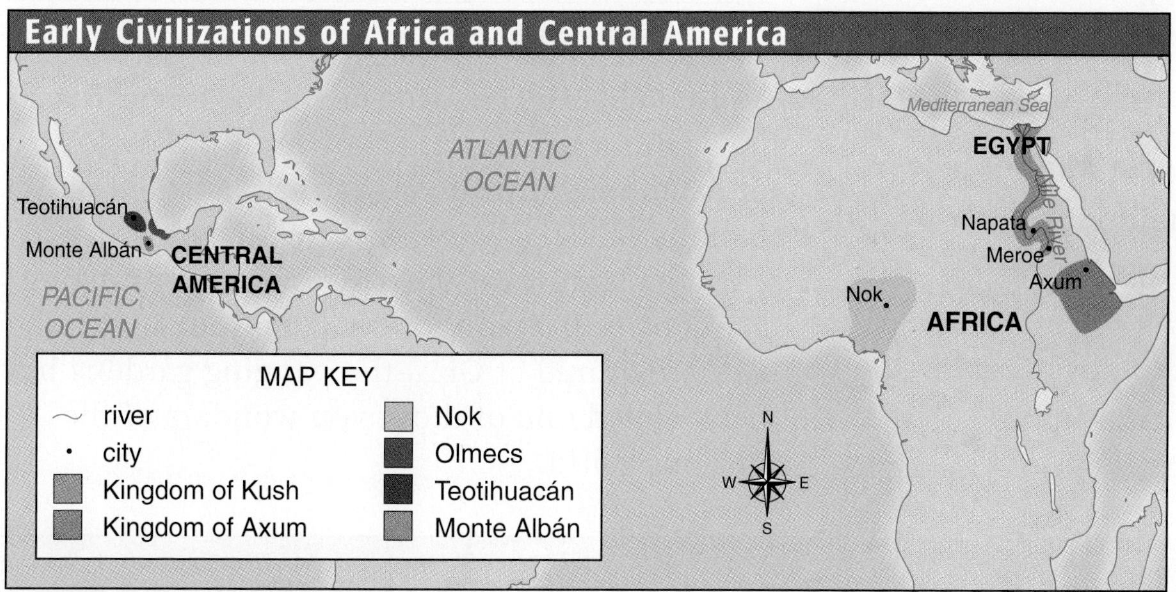

Map Directions The four main directions are **north**, **south**, **west**, and **east**. Maps use a **compass rose** to show these directions. The compass rose shortens the directions to **N**, **S**, **W**, and **E**.

Number your paper from 1 to 4. Write **north**, **south**, **west**, or **east** to complete each sentence.

1. The Kingdom of Kush is _____ of the Mediterranean Sea.
2. The Olmecs lived _____ of Teotihuacán.
3. Meroe is _____ of Axum.
4. Central America is _____ of Africa.

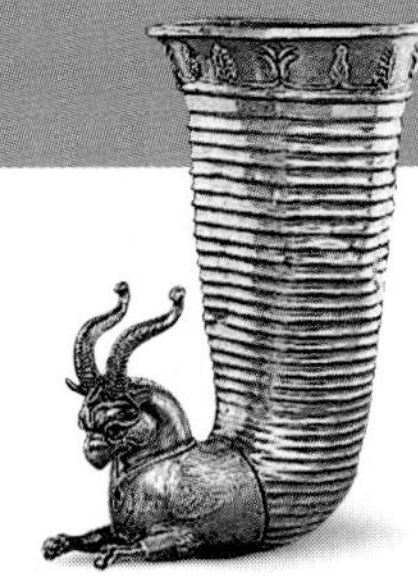

LESSON 1

The Persian Empire

New Words

conquered
tolerance
tribute
provinces
daric
Zoroastrianism
revolt

People and Places

Chaldeans
Nebuchadnezzar
Persians
Cyrus the Great
Darius I
Sardis
Aegean Sea
Susa
Zoroaster
Greece
Marathon
Athens
Xerxes

Before You Read

- Why might a large empire be difficult to hold together?
- How might a smaller army defeat a larger army?

The harsh rule of the Assyrian Empire ended around 600 B.C. The Chaldeans took over the lands of Mesopotamia. They rebuilt the old city of Babylon and made it their capital. The most famous Chaldean king was Nebuchadnezzar.

Nebuchadnezzar built the beautiful Hanging Gardens of Babylon for his wife. Along with the Great Pyramid at Giza, the hanging gardens have been called one of the seven wonders of the ancient world.

The Hanging Gardens of Babylon

Like the Assyrians, the Chaldeans were harsh rulers. But in 539 B.C., the Persians attacked Babylon and ended the Chaldean Empire.

Cyrus the Great returned objects to the Jewish temple.

The Persian Empire

The Persians came from lands in what is today the country of Iran. From about 600 B.C. to 500 B.C., they **conquered** a huge area of land. The first king of the Persians was Cyrus the Great.

Cyrus the Great practiced **tolerance**. He told his soldiers not to harm the people they conquered and not to burn their temples. He also was kind to the Jews. The Chaldeans had attacked Judah and forced the Jews to work as slaves in Babylon. Cyrus let them go back to their homes. He allowed conquered people to keep their customs. They could keep their religions and their languages. In return, the people paid **tribute**, or a kind of tax, to the king.

Controlling the Empire

In 522 B.C., Darius I became the leader of the Persians. Darius was a strong king. He rewarded his friends and punished his enemies. This is shown by the words carved into the side of a cliff in Persia.

“The man who was loyal, him I rewarded well, [but he] who was evil, him I punished well.”

The Persian Empire stretched from Egypt to India. Darius needed to find a way to control such a large empire. He divided his empire into **provinces**. He put a noble in charge of each province. He gave the nobles a lot of power. But he didn't trust them completely. He sent spies to each province to watch over the nobles. The spies were called the “Eyes and Ears of the King.”

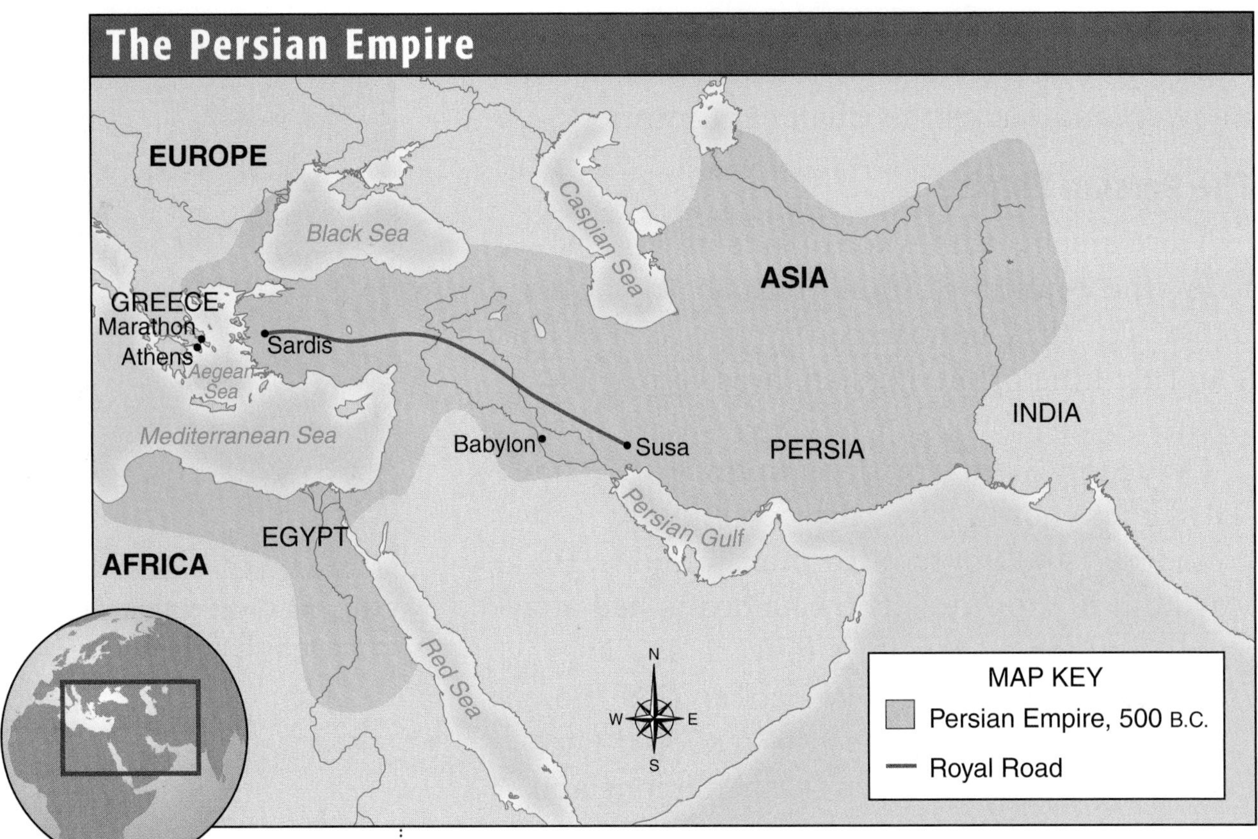

The Persian Empire controlled lands in Europe, Africa, and Asia. Which two cities did the Royal Road connect?

It took many months to get a message from one end of the empire to the other. To solve this problem, the Persians built roads. The longest was the Royal Road. It went from Sardis, near the Aegean Sea, to Susa, near the Persian Gulf. It was nearly 1,700 miles long.

The Persians used horses to travel on the Royal Road. A rider would run a horse as fast and as far as the horse could go. Then the rider chose a new horse and rode off again. The Royal Road had 111 stops for riders to change horses. Before using the system of horses, it took traders three months to travel the Royal Road. But with the horses, a message could reach the king in one week.

Persian daric

People traveling along the Persian roads would sometimes have to pay taxes. The Persians developed a money system based on a gold coin called the **daric**. The Persian daric became the coin used by traders from Southwest Asia, Egypt, and Europe.

Religion in Persia

Like other ancient people, the Persians had many gods. But around 600 B.C., a new religious leader appeared in Persia. His Greek name was Zoroaster. His religion became known as **Zoroastrianism**.

Zoroaster told people there were two gods in the world. The highest god, Ahura Mazda, stood for goodness and light. The lesser god, Ahriman, stood for evil and darkness. Zoroaster also taught that there was life after death. Good people were rewarded. Bad people were punished. The teachings of Zoroaster spread. His ideas about good and evil were adopted by other religions.

Ahura Mazda

The Persian Wars

Most of the time, the Persians enjoyed one victory after another. But they could not conquer the people of Greece. The Greeks had little land and a much smaller population. But they had strong fighters.

The Persian Wars started when Greek city-states within the Persian Empire refused to pay tribute to Darius, the Persian king. Greek city-states outside the Persian Empire helped in a **revolt** against Darius. The Persian army was able to stop the revolt. But Darius wanted to punish the Greeks.

The Greeks and the Persians fought in the Persian Wars.

In 490 B.C., Darius sent an army into the town of Marathon, Greece. The Persians had more men than the Greeks. But the Greeks did not give up.

The Greeks fought well and defeated the Persian army. According to legend, a runner raced 26 miles from Marathon to the Greek city-state of Athens with the news. This is why today we use the word *marathon* to describe a very long race.

In 480 B.C., Xerxes, the son of Darius, attacked the Greeks again. He sent a huge army and navy to Greece. The Persians captured Athens. But the Greeks fought hard. They defeated Xerxes and sent him back to Persia. The Greeks prevented the Persians from taking any more land. By around 350 B.C., the Persian Empire had lost most of its power.

Persian guards

Lesson 1 Review

Choose words from the list that best complete the paragraphs. One word will not be used.

Word List

Cyrus
Greeks
Marathon
Zoroaster
Darius

The Chaldeans ruled after the Assyrians. They were followed by the Persians. The first Persian king was __1__. He was known for his tolerance. He let people keep their customs. Another king, __2__, divided the Persian Empire into provinces. He put nobles in charge of the provinces.

The Persians built roads to improve travel. __3__ introduced the Persians to new religious ideas. The Persians tried to defeat the __4__ in 490 B.C. and 480 B.C., but they failed. The Persian Empire lost power over the next century and lost control of its vast lands.

LESSON 2

Ancient Greece

Before You Read

- How were most early civilizations ruled?
- Why did early civilizations need strong armies?

Greece is on a peninsula that extends into the Mediterranean Sea. Some of the first civilizations in Europe began in Greece. The Greeks, like the Phoenicians, were a **maritime** people. Their way of life depended on the sea.

Greece had many mountains and few rivers. The soil of Greece was rocky and poor. The Greeks could not grow enough food. So they became traders and developed colonies. Their way of life spread to their many colonies.

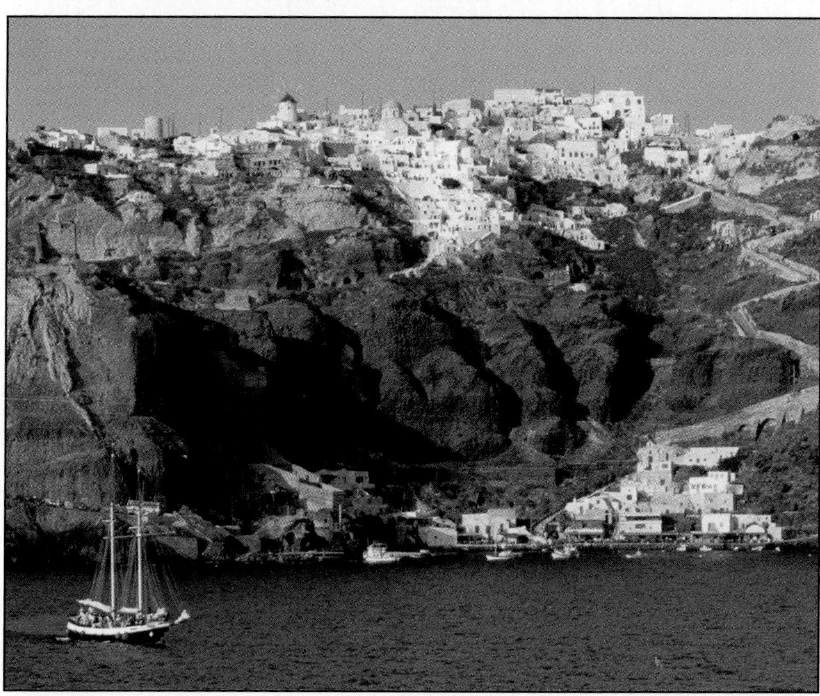

This Greek city was built on the rocky soil of an erupted volcano.

New Words

maritime
myth
epic
democracy
philosophy

People and Places

Minoans
Crete
Mycenaeans
Troy
Homer
Sparta
Socrates
Plato
Aristotle
Pericles
Macedonia
Alexander the Great

Did You Know?

Dressing Up

Ancient Greeks liked to look good. They often wore clothes with symbols from their own city-state. Some of their clothes were dyed with bright colors. But white was also popular. The Greeks often added a jeweled ring or hair pin. As a final touch, they also wore perfume made from boiled flowers and herbs.

Early Greek Civilizations

The first Greek civilization, the Minoan, began on the island of Crete. Around 1500 B.C., the Minoans were destroyed by a volcano. For a long time, people didn't know if the Minoans really existed. People thought the Minoan civilization was just a **myth**, or legend. Then archaeologists found the ruins of the Minoan civilization.

The Mycenaean civilization followed the Minoans. Around 1200 B.C., the Mycenaeans attacked Troy, a city across the Aegean Sea. Homer, a Greek poet, told the story of this battle in two **epic**, or long story, poems. The poems are called the *Iliad* and the *Odyssey*.

Athens and Sparta

By around 500 B.C., Athens and Sparta were the most famous city-states of ancient Greece. The Athenians and the Spartans had much in common. They spoke the same language and believed in the same gods. They both enjoyed sports.

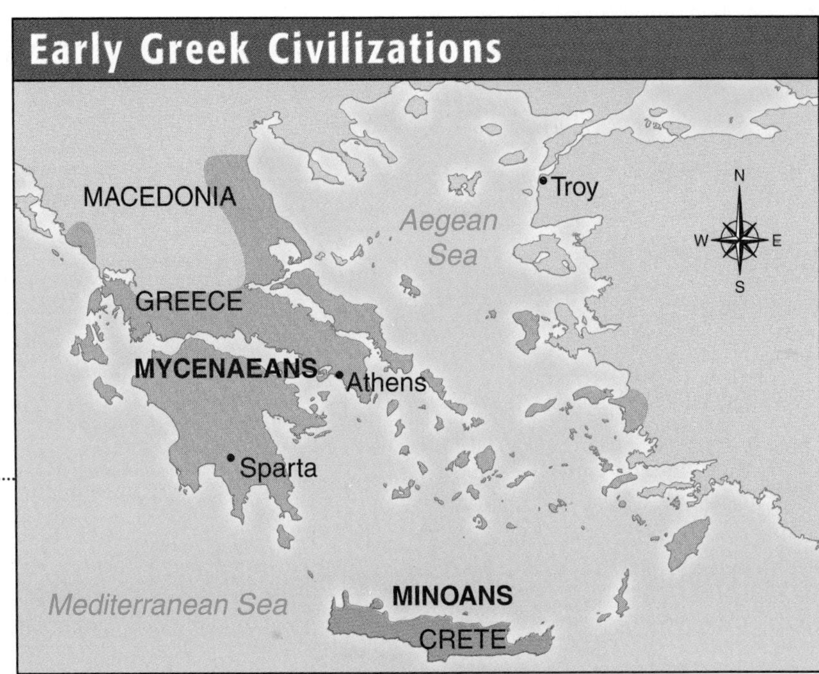

The Minoans and the Mycenaeans are the oldest known Greek civilizations. On what island did the Minoans live?

The Greeks built huge outdoor theaters.

In other ways, Athens and Sparta were not alike. Athens had a direct **democracy**. The people ruled themselves. They could vote on issues facing the city. The Athenians enjoyed going to the theater. They also went dancing.

Athens was famous for **philosophy**. A philosopher is someone who likes to think and learn about life and its values. Socrates was a Greek philosopher who gained wisdom by asking many questions. Two other well-known philosophers from Greece were Plato and Aristotle.

Life in Sparta was different. Spartans did not have the same freedoms that the Athenians had. In Sparta, everyday life was centered around the army. Boys were taken from their homes at the age of seven. From then on they were taught to be warriors. They learned some reading and writing. But the main goal was to build their strength. The young boys lived under harsh rules.

Spartan soldier

The Peloponnesian War

During the Persian Wars, Athens and Sparta joined together against the Persians. But by 431 B.C., Athens and Sparta both wanted to rule Greece. That year, Sparta attacked Athens, beginning the Peloponnesian War.

The leader of Athens was Pericles. He gave a speech praising the city of Athens, as well as those who died in battle.

Voices In History

"Such is the city for whose sake these men . . . fought and died. They could not bear the thought that [Athens] might be taken from them."

The Peloponnesian War lasted 27 years. Athens had a strong navy. Sparta had a strong army. In the end, Sparta won the war and gained control of Greece.

Alexander the Great

Macedonia was a kingdom north of the Greek city-states. It adopted much of the Greek culture. Around 357 B.C., King Phillip II of Macedonia began to take over the Greek city-states. He then planned to attack Persia. But Phillip was killed

Alexander the Great led his army from Macedonia and conquered the Persian Empire. Where did Alexander end his journey?

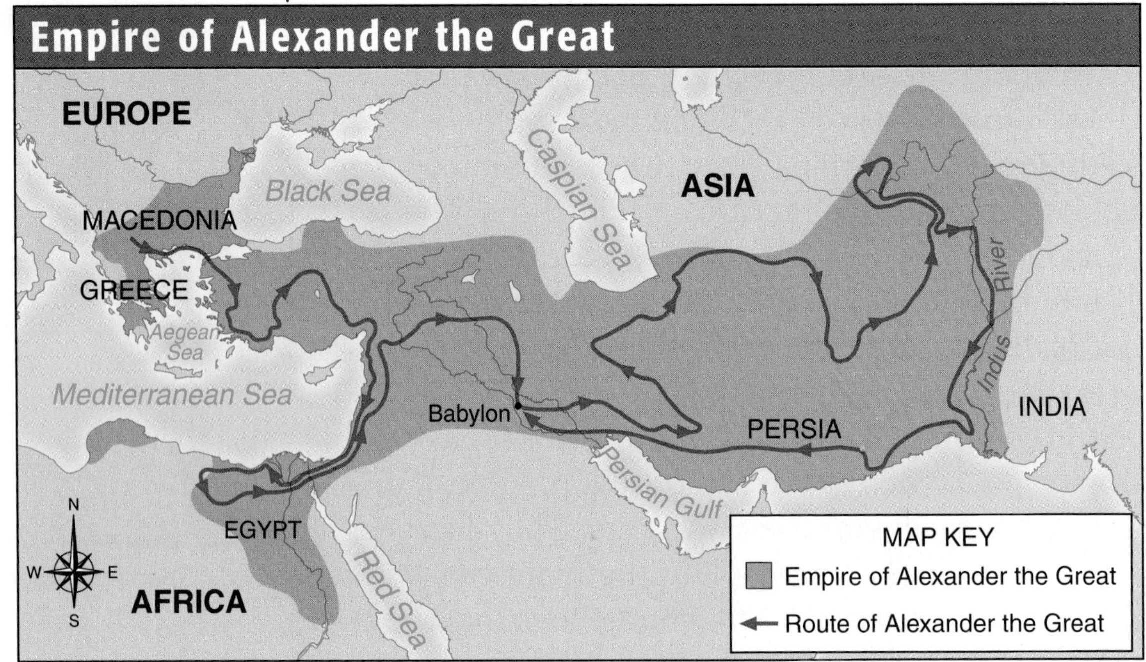

before he could attack. In 338 B.C., Phillip's 20-year-old son, Alexander, decided to carry out his father's plan. Alexander wanted more than Greece and Persia. He wanted to conquer the world.

Alexander first gained complete control of Greece. He then crossed into Asia and won battles in the western Persian Empire. Then he took control of Egypt. From there, he traveled east, conquering the rest of Persia. He continued all the way to the Indus River. But his tired army refused to go any further. Alexander and his army left India and headed home. In just over ten years, Alexander conquered and ruled one of the largest empires the world had ever seen. He died in Babylon three years later.

Without Alexander, the empire fell apart. But Greek culture spread throughout the vast lands. Many people admired the Greeks. They wanted to be like them. Greek culture remained strong for 300 years, until the rise of Rome.

Alexander the Great

Lesson 2 Review

Choose words from the list that best complete the paragraphs. One word will not be used.

The Minoans and the __1__ were early Greek civilizations. Later, Athens and Sparta were two powerful city-states. The Athenians had a direct __2__. They had much more freedom than the Spartans had.

After fighting the Persians, Athens and Sparta fought each other in the __3__ War. Sparta won and ruled Greece. Later, Alexander the Great conquered and ruled a huge empire. Greek __4__ spread and remained strong for 300 years.

Word List

culture
philosophy
Mycenaeans
democracy
Peloponnesian

Summary

- Cyrus the Great and Darius I were two early Persian kings. The Greeks defeated the Persians twice in the Persian Wars.
- Two early Greek civilizations were the Minoan and the Mycenaean.
- The Athenians enjoyed philosophy and art, while the Spartans trained for war.
- Sparta and Athens fought each other in the Peloponnesian War. Sparta won and took control of Greece.
- Alexander the Great built a huge empire. After his death, Greek culture continued to spread.

Find Out More!

After reading Chapter 7, you're ready to go online. **Explore Zone**, **Quiz Time**, and **Amazing Facts** bring this chapter of world history alive.

Visit www.exploreSV.com and type in the chapter code **Ch7**.

Vocabulary

Number your paper from 1 to 5. Write the letter of the correct answer.

1. Cyrus practiced **tolerance**. He let conquered people _____.
   a. keep their customs
   b. play sports
   c. pay taxes
   d. vote for their leaders

2. **Tribute** is a kind of _____.
   a. body of water
   b. running race
   c. statue
   d. tax

3. The Persian _____ was based on the **daric**.
   a. number system
   b. writing system
   c. land system
   d. money system

4. An **epic** is a _____.
   a. trade route
   b. long story poem
   c. big open area
   d. method to clear lands

5. In a **democracy**, _____ rule themselves.
   a. the people
   b. warriors
   c. pharaohs
   d. shamans

Comprehension

Number your paper from 1 to 5. Read each sentence below. Then write the name of the person or people who might have said each sentence. One name from the list will not be used.

1. "I was the Chaldean king who built the Hanging Gardens of Babylon."
2. "My ideas about good and evil were adopted by other religions."
3. "Our civilization was destroyed by a volcano around 1500 B.C."
4. "My long poems, the *Iliad* and the *Odyssey*, told about the Mycenaean's attack on Troy."
5. "I was a Greek philosopher who gained wisdom by asking questions."

Word List

Socrates
Zoroaster
Darius
Homer
Minoans
Nebuchadnezzar

Critical Thinking

Points of View Number your paper from 1 to 5. Read each sentence below. Write **Sparta** if the point of view is from someone in Sparta. If the point of view is from someone in Athens, write **Athens**.

1. Every-day life should center around the army.
2. People should rule themselves and vote on issues about the city.
3. People should go to the theater.
4. It is important for boys to build their strength.
5. People should think and learn about life and its values.

Writing

Write a paragraph that explains at least three ways that Cyrus practiced tolerance toward the people he conquered.

LESSON 1

Early Roman Republic

New Words

republic
representatives
consuls
senate
dictator
patricians
plebeians
tribunes

People and Places

Italy
Po River
Tiber River
Etruscans
Latins
Rome
Carthage
Hannibal
Alps

Before You Read

- How might people take part in government?
- Why might early civilizations have wanted to control the Mediterranean Sea?

Like Greece, Italy is on a peninsula. The Italian Peninsula is shaped like a boot. Also like Greece, Italy has many mountains. Unlike Greece, however, Italy has two large rivers. The Po River is in the north. The Tiber River is in the center. Italy also has much more land that can be used for farming.

In ancient times, different people settled on and around the Italian Peninsula. Phoenicians set up colonies in the area. The Greeks built more than 50 city-states, passing their culture on to the local people. The Greeks taught the local people to grow grapes and olives. They showed them how to build with stone. They also shared the Greek alphabet. This was the beginning of the Latin language.

Some letters of the Greek alphabet look like letters in today's English language.

The Early Roman Republic

A group of people called the Etruscans settled in northern Italy around 800 B.C. No one knows exactly where they came from. They began to expand their territory. Around 600 B.C., the Etruscans conquered the Latins who lived in the central part of the peninsula. One Latin village was called Rome. The Etruscans drained the marshes near Rome. This gave them more land on which to build. Under Etruscan rule, Rome grew into a city.

The Etruscan kings were often cruel. In 509 B.C., the Romans rebelled. They sent the Etruscan king out of Rome and set up a new kind of government. They called the new government a **republic**. It was similar to the government in Athens because the people could vote.

But Athens had a direct democracy. The people voted on each issue. Rome, however, set up an indirect democracy. The people voted for leaders. The leaders then voted on different issues. The leaders were called **representatives** because they represented the people. Different forms of representative government are still used today in the United States and other countries.

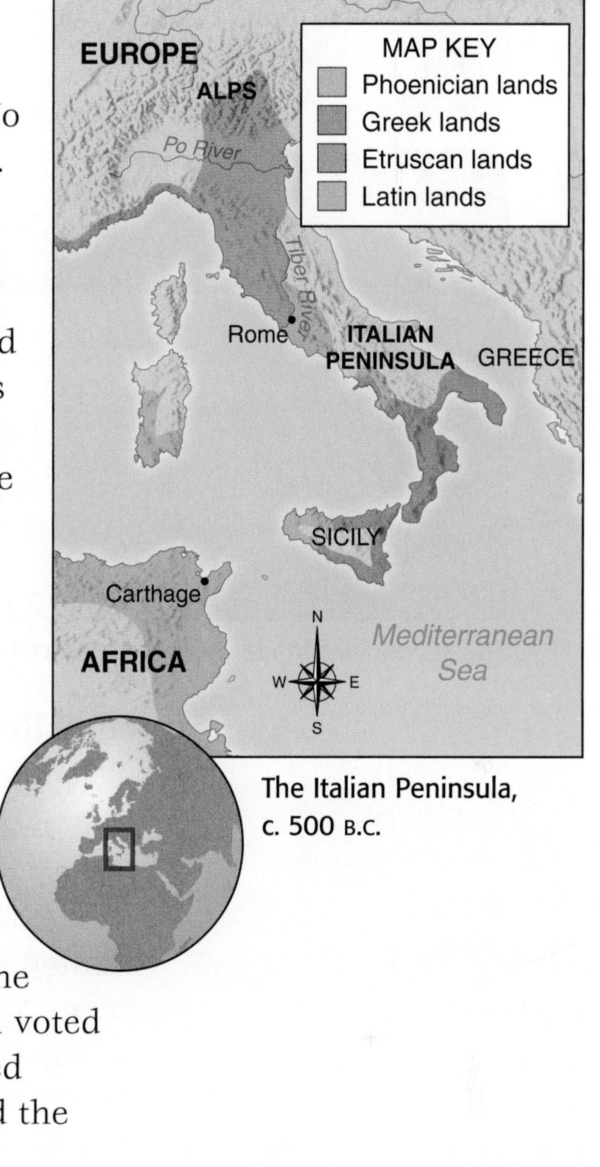

The Italian Peninsula, c. 500 B.C.

An Etruscan husband and wife

The senate was made up of 300 patrician men.

Early Roman Government

The new Roman government had two leaders. They were called **consuls**. They had the power of a king, but only if they agreed with each other. Each consul had the power to stop what the other wanted to do. Also, the consuls served for just one year. This kept them from becoming too powerful.

The consuls were advised by a **senate**. The senate was made up of 300 men. They helped the consuls make decisions. In times of war, the senate could choose a **dictator**. A dictator is a leader with absolute power. But even the dictator could hold power for only six months.

Roman plebeians

Roman citizens were divided into two classes. Wealthy people who owned land were called **patricians**. The farmers and other common people were called **plebeians**.

The Plebeians Gain Power

Plebeians had little power. Only patricians could be consuls. Only patricians could serve in the senate. Often the plebeians didn't even know what the laws were. The plebeians fought for change. They wanted the laws to be put in writing.

In 450 B.C., the laws were written down on tablets called the Twelve Tables. They were hung up for everyone to see. One of the laws made it clear that plebeians and patricians were not equal.

"Marriages should not take place between plebeians and patricians."

Once the plebeians learned the laws, they began demanding changes. Over time, plebeians gained more rights and had laws changed. They even demanded representatives of their own. They were allowed to vote for their own leaders. Those leaders were called **tribunes**. The plebeians even helped make a law that said one of the two consuls had to be a plebeian.

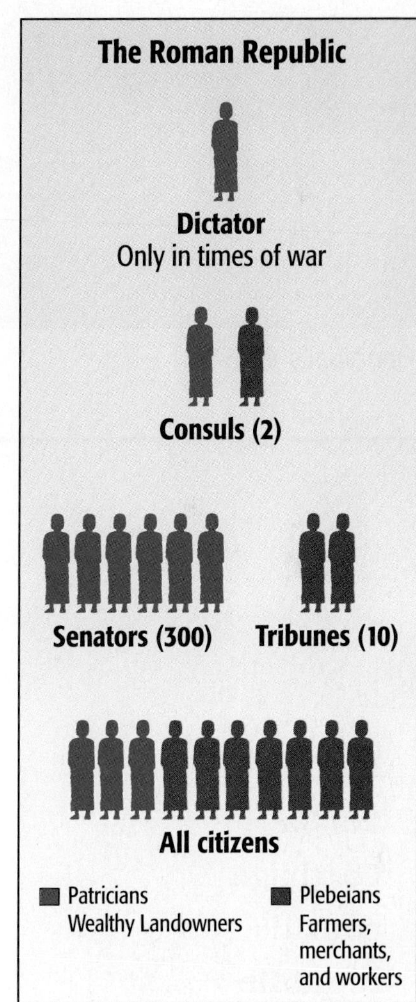

Life in the Roman Republic

In Roman homes, the father was in charge. No one in the home could question him. The family's possessions belonged to the father alone. In the early years of the republic, when the father died, his possessions went to his oldest son.

Women took care of the home and cared for the children. In poorer families, the wife might have worked in a shop or a field with her husband.

Boys and girls of the patrician class went to school together. Girls often married by the age of 13. Boys stayed in school longer and usually did not marry until the age of 20.

The Growth of the Roman Republic

The Romans were skilled soldiers. Their strong army took control of the entire Italian peninsula by about 270 B.C. Rome's next goal was to control trade in the Mediterranean Sea.

However, the people of Carthage, a city on the northern coast of Africa, also wanted this control. Carthage went to war against Rome in 264 B.C. This was the first of three wars known as the Punic Wars.

After 23 years of fighting, Rome won the first war. Then in 218 B.C., Hannibal led the army of Carthage over the Alps. His army included elephants that each carried around 15 soldiers. The Romans were taken by surprise. They didn't think any army could get through the mountains. Then the Romans attacked Carthage, forcing Hannibal to return home. Rome won the second Punic War in 202 B.C.

Hannibal's army

The third Punic War began in 149 B.C. Roman soldiers attacked Carthage. They surrounded the city and cut off the food supply. The Romans burned the city of Carthage to the ground. By the end of the Punic Wars, Rome controlled Greece, northern Africa, and other lands around the Mediterranean Sea.

Lesson 1 Review

Choose words from the list that best complete the paragraph. One word will not be used.

Word List

Persia
Carthage
consuls
republic
plebeians

The Etruscans conquered the Latins and controlled Rome for about 100 years. In 509 B.C., the Romans set up a __1__. Two __2__ ruled the new government. They were advised by a group of 300 men called the senate. The new form of government was a representative government. The __3__ were not a part of government in the beginning. In time, they gained more rights. The Romans took control of the Italian Peninsula. They then went to war three times with the city of __4__. Rome won all three of the Punic Wars.

LESSON 2

From Republic to Empire

Before You Read

- What makes a good leader?
- What problems might come from two people ruling the same republic?

After Carthage fell, Rome ruled the Mediterranean Sea. With all its new lands, Rome grew rich. Some Romans grew richer than others. There was trouble in the government. The patricians wanted more power. They tried to limit the role of the plebeians. Army generals fought for control of Rome. At last, one general won. His name was Julius Caesar.

Roman Lands, 509 B.C.–44 B.C.

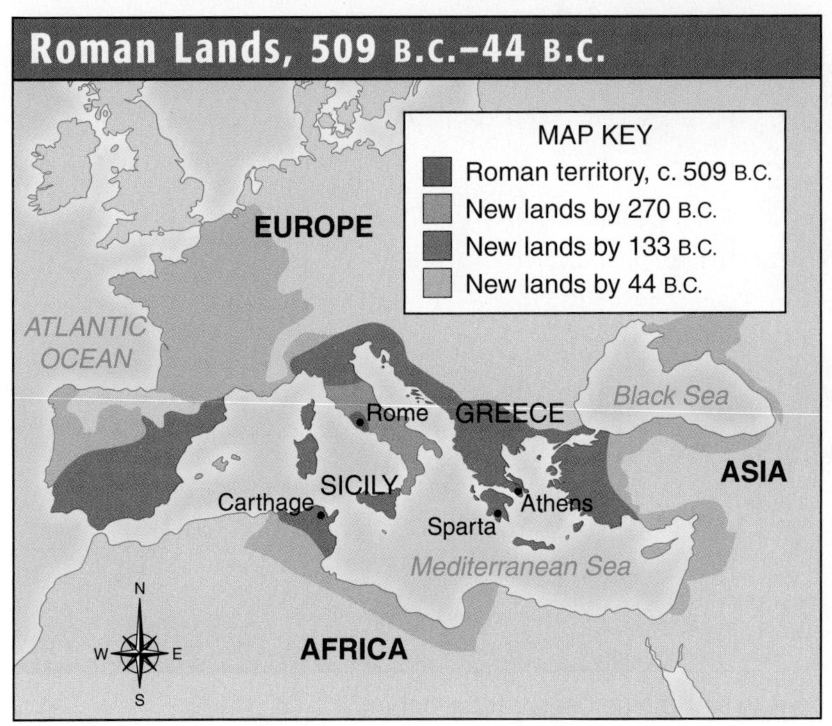

New Words

senators
triumvirate
emperor

People and Places

Julius Caesar
Marcus Brutus
Octavian
Lepidus
Mark Antony
Cleopatra
Actium
Augustus

The Life and Death of Julius Caesar

Julius Caesar

Caesar was a powerful general. He won many battles. After one easy victory, he wrote back to Rome, *"Veni, vidi, vici."* In English, that means, "I came, I saw, I conquered."

Many Romans loved Julius Caesar. He replaced bad officials with good ones. He allowed people in conquered lands to become Roman citizens. Caesar tried to give Romans a government that was fair. He also had plans to help the poor and to offer free land to farmers. In 44 B.C., the senate changed the Roman law and made Caesar a dictator for life, not just six months.

But Caesar had some enemies in Rome. They feared Caesar would make himself king. They didn't want to see an end to the republic. On March 15, 44 B.C., a group of **senators** stabbed Caesar to death. One of the killers, Marcus Brutus, was an old friend of Caesar.

This painting shows Marcus Brutus about to stab Julius Caesar from behind.

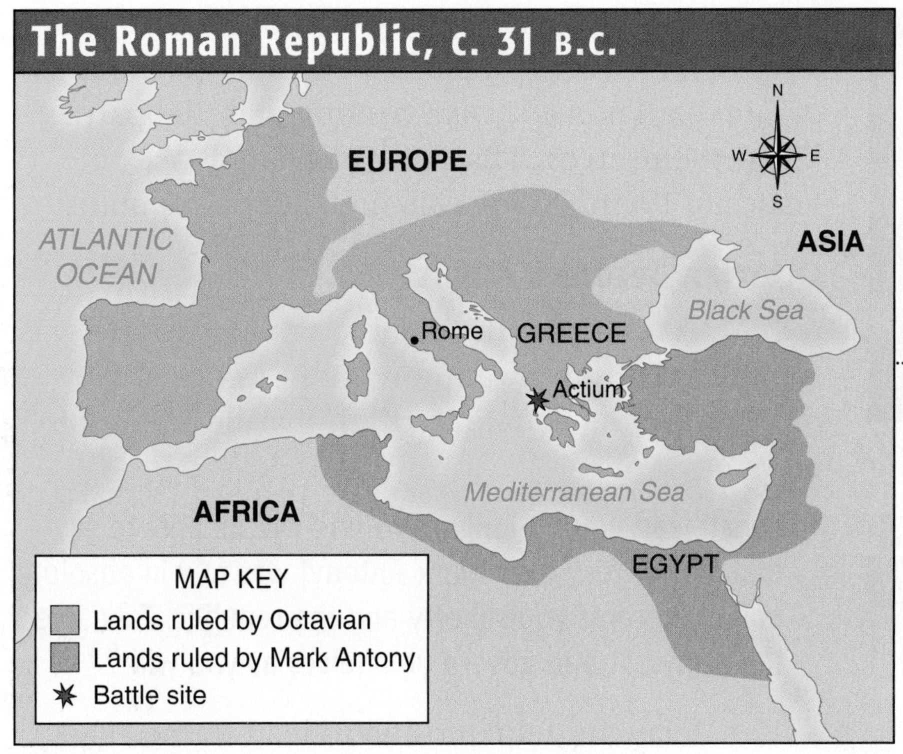

This map shows the Roman Republic divided between Octavian and Mark Antony. The city of Rome was under whose rule?

The Struggle for Control

Caesar's death led to more trouble. Who would take his place? At first, three men worked together to rule Rome. They formed a **triumvirate**, or group of three rulers. One of these men was Caesar's adopted son, Octavian. The other two were the generals Lepidus and Mark Antony.

The three men divided up Rome's lands. Lepidus took lands in Africa. Octavian controlled the West, including Rome. Mark Antony ruled the East, including Egypt. Then Lepidus decided to give up his lands. For ten years, Octavian and Mark Antony shared control of the republic.

In the western half of the republic, Octavian increased his power. In the eastern half, Mark Antony was spending much time in Egypt. He had fallen in love with Cleopatra, the queen of Egypt. Octavian did not approve. He told the senate that Antony was giving Roman lands to Cleopatra. Octavian declared war against Mark Antony and Cleopatra.

Mark Antony

Octavian

In 31 B.C., Octavian's navy beat the Egyptian navy. The battle took place at Actium off the coast of Greece. The next year, Antony and Cleopatra killed themselves. That left Octavian as the sole leader of Rome. Rome was no longer a republic.

Octavian Becomes Augustus

In 27 B.C., Octavian spoke to the senate. He was humble. He didn't want any more fighting. He didn't want the senate to think that he wanted to be king.

"I shall lead you no longer. No one will be able to say that [the victory over Mark Antony] was to win absolute power. Receive your liberty and the republic. Take over the army . . . and govern yourselves as you will."

But Octavian did continue to lead Rome. The senators were grateful to him and trusted him. In fact, they made Octavian an **emperor**.

Octavian became the ruler of the Roman Empire. The senate also gave him the name *Augustus*, which means "respected one." For 41 years, Augustus ruled Rome. This period became known as "The Age of Augustus."

Like Caesar, Augustus did many good things. He chose honest people for leaders. He improved the schools and raised the pay for teachers. He put people to work making Rome a better place.

Rome became a better place under Augustus.

Cleopatra (69 B.C.–30 B.C.)

People In History

Cleopatra was the queen of Egypt, but she was actually Greek. How was that possible? Earlier, Alexander the Great made a Greek family the rulers of Egypt. Cleopatra came from that family. She became queen in 51 B.C. Julius Caesar fell in love with Cleopatra. They had one child together.

Later, Mark Antony fell in love with Cleopatra. They had three children. Their story is one of the most famous love stories in history. It is also a sad story. After being defeated by Octavian, Antony heard a false story that Cleopatra had died. He was filled with sorrow and killed himself by falling on his sword. Cleopatra also killed herself. She allowed a deadly snake to bite her.

Lesson 2 Review

Choose words from the list that best complete the paragraphs. One word will not be used.

In 44 B.C., the Roman senate named __1__ a dictator for life. He made some good changes and had plans to do more. But on March 15, he was killed. After a while, two men took control of the Roman Empire. __2__ ruled Roman lands in the West while Mark Antony ruled Roman lands in the East.

Mark Antony fell in love with Cleopatra, the queen of Egypt. This led to a war between Octavian and Antony. Octavian won a battle off the coast of __3__. The Roman senate made Octavian an emperor. After that, he became known as __4__. Under his long rule, Romans had honest leaders and better schools.

Word List

Greece
Octavian
Egypt
Julius Caesar
Augustus

Chapter 8: Using What You've Learned

Summary

- The Latins and the Etruscans lived on the Italian Peninsula.
- Early Romans had a republic. Citizens voted for their own leaders.
- There were two groups of Roman citizens. The patricians owned land. The plebeians were workers.
- Rome defeated Carthage in the Punic Wars and won control over the lands surrounding the Mediterranean Sea.
- In 44 B.C., the Roman senate named Julius Caesar dictator for life. He was killed the same year.
- The senate made Octavian emperor in 27 B.C. He became known as Augustus.

Find Out More!

After reading Chapter 8, you're ready to go online. **Explore Zone**, **Quiz Time**, and **Amazing Facts** bring this chapter of world history alive.

Visit www.exploreSV.com and type in the chapter code **Ch8**.

Vocabulary

Number your paper from 1 to 5. Finish the sentences from Group A with words from Group B. Write the letter of the correct answer.

Group A

1. The Roman people voted for leaders called _____.
2. In the Roman Republic, wealthy people who owned land were called _____.
3. Farmers and other common people in the Roman Republic were called _____.
4. After Caesar's death, a group of three rulers called the _____ ruled Rome together.
5. Rome became an empire when the senate made Octavian _____.

Group B

a. patricians

b. triumvirate

c. representatives

d. emperor

e. plebeians

Comprehension

Number your paper from 1 to 5. Write the word from the list that best completes each sentence. One word will not be used.

1. The leaders of the Roman government were advised by a ______.
2. The plebeians voted for their own leaders, or ______.
3. ______ led the army of Carthage over the Alps.
4. After Caesar's death, ______ ruled the East, including Egypt.
5. Rome under Octavian's rule is known as "The Age of ______."

Word List

Cleopatra
senate
Augustus
tribunes
Hannibal
Mark Antony

Critical Thinking

Sequencing Number your paper from 1 to 5. Write the sentences below in the correct order.

The Punic Wars began in 264 B.C.

In 450 B.C., the Roman laws were written down on tablets called the Twelve Tables.

Octavian became the emperor of Rome.

A group of senators stabbed Caesar to death.

The Etruscans conquered Rome around 600 B.C.

Writing

Do you think Augustus was a good ruler? Write a paragraph to explain your answer.

Skill Builder: Reading a Chart

A **chart** lists a group of facts. Charts help you learn facts quickly. Read the chart below to learn about the Punic Wars.

The Punic Wars			
Punic War	**Dates Fought**	**Reason Fought**	**Results of War**
First Punic War	264 B.C.–241 B.C.	Rome and Carthage wanted control of the Mediterranean Sea.	▪ Romans won the war and gained Sicily. ▪ Carthage paid Rome for damages.
Second Punic War	218 B.C.–202 B.C.	Carthage and Rome wanted to control lands in Spain.	▪ Rome defeated Hannibal and gained land in Spain. ▪ Rome also received money and ships from Carthage.
Third Punic War	149 B.C.–146 B.C.	Carthage fought against the agreement resulting from the Second Punic War.	▪ Rome won and gained control of the Mediterranean Sea. ▪ Carthage was destroyed.

Number your paper from 1 to 5. Write the letter of the correct answer.

1. To read the names of the wars, read the chart from ______.
   a. left to right **b.** top to bottom **c.** the middle
2. To learn about the First Punic War, read the chart from ______.
   a. left to right **b.** top to bottom **c.** bottom to top
3. The ______ was the shortest Punic War.
   a. First Punic War **b.** Second Punic War **c.** Third Punic War
4. The ______ was fought to control lands in Spain.
   a. First Punic War **b.** Second Punic War **c.** Third Punic War
5. One result of the Third Punic War was that Rome ______.
   a. gained Sicily **b.** defeated Hannibal **c.** destroyed Carthage

LESSON 1

Life in the Roman Empire

Before You Read

- What kinds of forces could have stopped the Roman Empire from growing?
- What might a nation need to have a long period of peace?

New Words

Pax Romana
aqueducts
gladiators

People and Places

Germania
Rhine River
Danube River
Black Sea
Pompeii
Mount Vesuvius
Pliny the Younger

You have read how Rome grew from a village to a city. You also have learned how Rome became a republic. The Roman Republic lasted for almost 500 years. In 27 B.C., Augustus became the emperor of Rome. The Roman Republic was over. But the Roman Empire was only beginning. The Roman Empire also lasted about 500 years.

This image shows citizens of the Roman Empire.

Rome During the Pax Romana

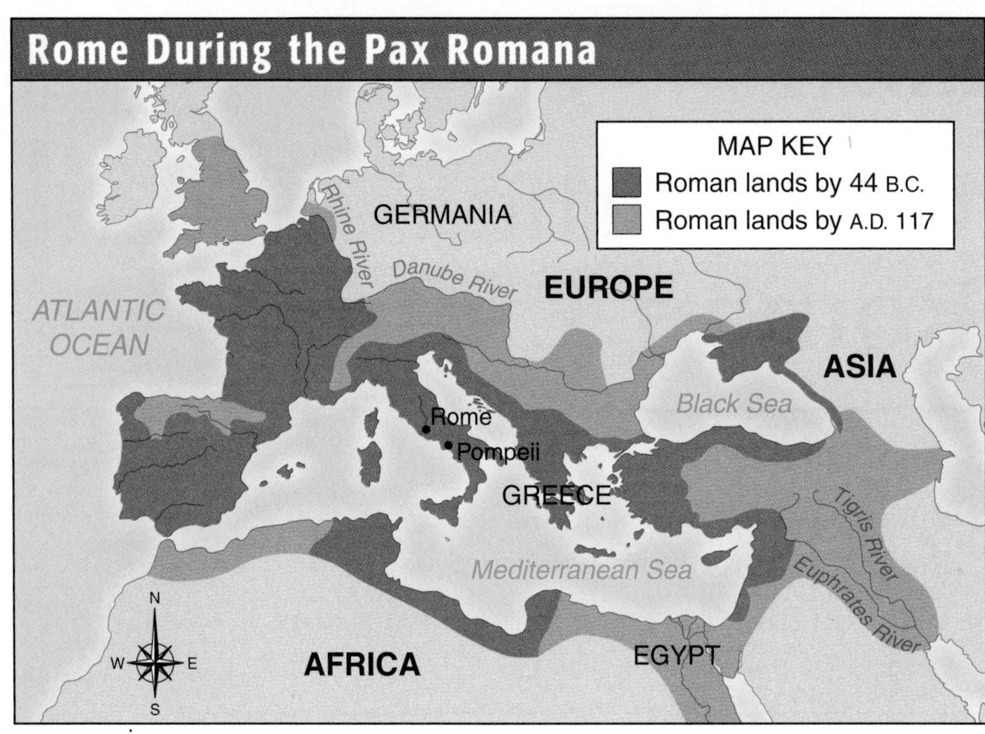

Rome controlled a vast empire during the Pax Romana. What large sea was in the middle of the empire?

Extending the Empire

Augustus increased the size of the Roman Empire. However, he had trouble extending into the area called Germania. The Germans forced the Romans back to the Rhine River in A.D. 9. The river remained the border for 300 years.

The Romans controlled the lands south of the Danube River. They extended their control around the Black Sea to the Euphrates River. The Romans also controlled lands in northern Africa. Within these borders, the Romans had full control. The Roman Empire was divided into provinces. Each province had its own governor.

The rule of Augustus began a peaceful time for Rome. Romans enjoyed good government and open trade. This time in Roman history is called the **Pax Romana**, or the "peace of Rome." It lasted from 27 B.C. to A.D. 180.

Augustus died in A.D. 14. He was 76 years old. He had made many good changes. He had united the Roman people. Some people thought he was a god, and they even built temples to honor him.

Enjoying Life in Ancient Rome

Ancient Rome was an exciting city. There was always something to do. There was horse racing at a place called Circus Maximus. This was a huge race track. It could hold up to 250,000 people. At night, theaters in Rome offered plays and music.

Circus Maximus

Then there was the Roman Forum. This was where the senate met. People came to the Forum to talk and to hear the latest news. In some ways, the Forum was like a mall today. It had shops offering goods from all over the empire. It had food stalls. Entertainers sang, danced, and even charmed snakes in the Forum.

Rome had more than 100 public baths. Building a new bath was one way an emperor could please the Roman people. The baths were open to the rich and the poor. Men and women bathed in them. People even had a choice of water temperature.

At the baths, people could exercise. They could read books. They could walk through gardens of flowers and herbs.

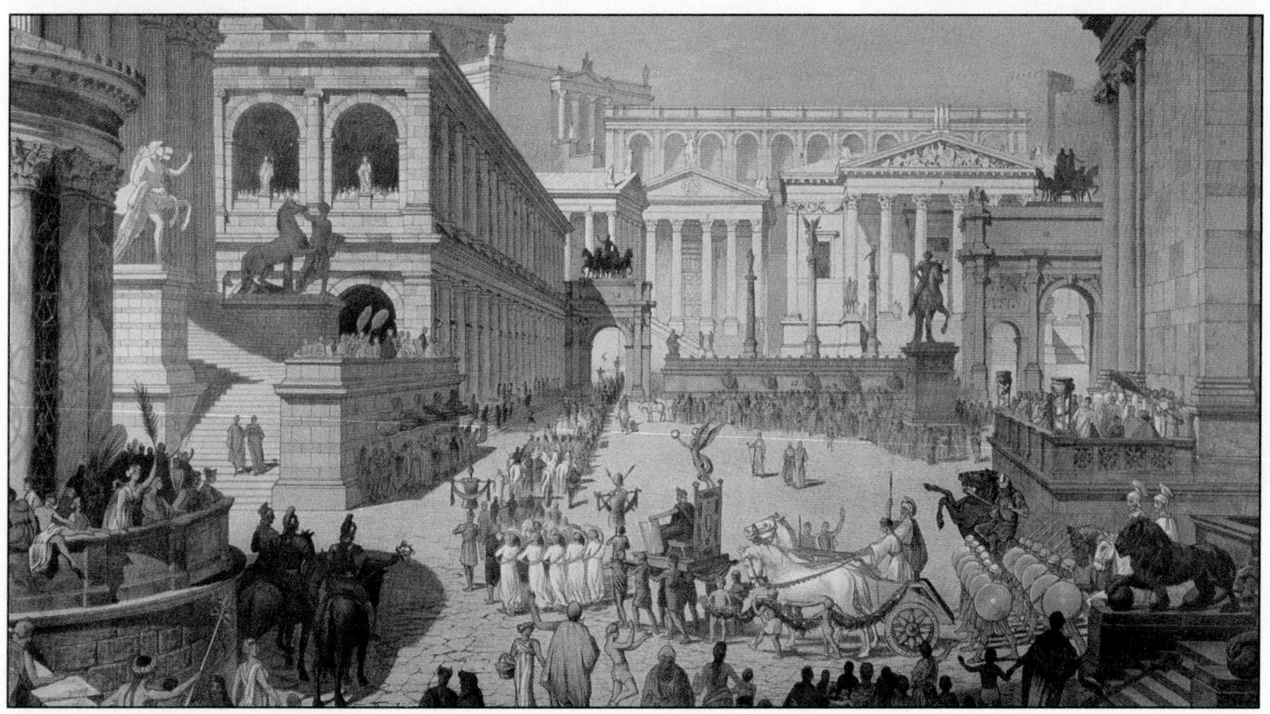

The Forum was a busy place in ancient Rome.

Roman bath

Fresh water for the baths came into Rome through **aqueducts**. Many of these were arched channels built high above the ground. The water ran downhill to Rome. Many aqueducts still exist today even though they are 2,000 years old.

The Colosseum

The Colosseum was built in Rome. It was made with stone and concrete. The oval-shaped Colosseum held as many as 50,000 people. In the Colosseum, the Romans watched people battle wild animals, such as lions, bears, and leopards, to the death.

Sometimes, people came to see warriors kill one another. These warriors were known as **gladiators**. They were usually slaves or prisoners of war.

Sometimes, the Romans flooded the Colosseum with water. Then they would have battles using ships. Like the aqueducts, much of the Colosseum is still standing.

Roman aqueduct

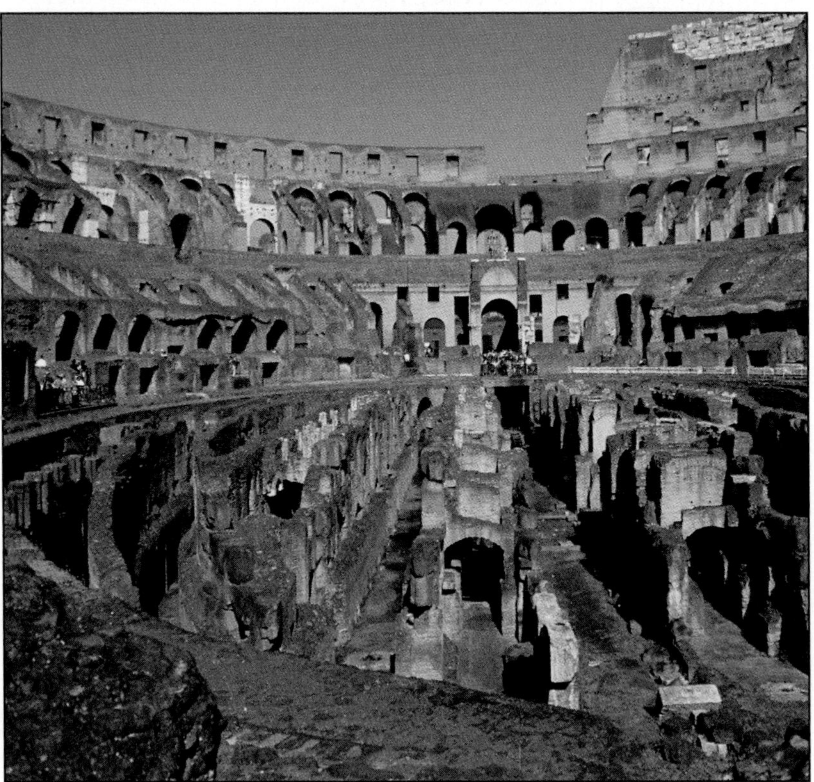

Today, visitors can see what is left of the Roman Colosseum.

Life and Death in Pompeii

Many cities in the Roman Empire wanted to be like Rome. One such city was Pompeii. Pompeii was a busy town with 20,000 people. Traders bought and sold such items as wine, cloth, fruits, and oil. Pompeii had its own forum. It had its own gladiator games. It had ten temples and a theater with 20,000 seats.

Mount Vesuvius destroyed the city of Pompeii.

Mount Vesuvius stood six miles away from Pompeii. On August 24, A.D. 79, this volcano erupted. For two days, white ashes and hot rocks fell on the city. The whole city, along with about 2,000 people, was buried in the ash. Pliny the Younger saw it from a safe distance and wrote about what he saw.

Voices In History

> "You could hear women [praying], children crying, men shouting . . . . Many believed that there were no gods any longer. This was one unending night for the world."

Lesson 1 Review

Choose words from the list that best complete the paragraphs. One word will not be used.

Word List
- aqueducts
- Germans
- gladiators
- Pompeii
- Pax Romana

The Roman Empire ruled many lands. Augustus tried to extend the empire. But his forces were defeated by the __1__. Still, his rule started a time of peace called the __2__. It lasted for about 200 years.

Romans liked to be entertained. They had race tracks and public baths. Fresh water flowed to the baths through __3__. The Roman Colosseum held up to 50,000 people. One Roman city, __4__, was destroyed by a volcano, Mount Vesuvius, in A.D. 79. About 2,000 people died.

LESSON 2

Religion in Rome

New Words

Christianity
Messiah
Gospels
crucified
disciples
resurrection
Edict of Milan
edict

People and Places

Jesus
Bethlehem
Judea
Nazareth
Paul
Constantine
Theodosius
Byzantium
Constantinople
Western Roman Empire
Eastern Roman Empire

Before You Read

- Why might some people be scared by a new religion?
- How do religions spread?

Religion was an important part of life in Rome. The Romans, like most ancient people, believed in many gods. Jupiter was the most powerful Roman god. Some other gods were Mars, Venus, and Cupid. Romans also believed in the Roman emperor as a god.

The Romans punished Christians and others who believed in someone or something higher than the Roman gods or the Roman emperor. So, some new religions began in secret. People were interested in these religions because they offered hope for a better life in the next world. One of these religions, **Christianity**, grew and spread throughout the world.

Jupiter was the main Roman god.

Christianity Begins

Jesus

Christianity grew out of Judaism. The Hebrew Bible told that a **Messiah**, or chosen one, would come to the Jews. He would bring them peace and freedom. Some Jews believed that a man named Jesus was that Messiah. They became known as Christians.

Followers of Jesus wrote about his life in four books called the **Gospels**. The Gospels and other books were added to the Hebrew Bible to make the Christian Bible. According to the Bible, Jesus was born in Bethlehem in the province of Judea. He grew up in the town of Nazareth. As he grew older, people said he was teaching new ideas and performing miracles. Jesus said he was the son of God. He taught that God loved all people.

Some people were concerned about Jesus. Some Jews thought Jesus was not the Messiah. They were angry that he claimed to be the son of God. The Romans also were worried. They thought people might be more loyal to Jesus than to the empire.

In A.D. 33, the Romans **crucified** Jesus by nailing him to a cross and leaving him there to die. The Gospels say that three days later Jesus rose from the dead and appeared to his **disciples**. The story of the **resurrection** became an important message of Christianity.

This famous painting is called "The Last Supper." It shows Jesus and his disciples the night before Jesus was crucified.

Emperor Constantine

The Spread of Christianity

A Jewish Roman citizen named Paul helped spread Christianity throughout the Roman Empire. Paul never actually met Jesus. At first, he was against Christianity. Then, the Bible says, he saw and spoke to the resurrected Jesus. After that, he began to teach about Jesus. For 30 years, Paul traveled from city to city spreading Christianity.

The Christians believed in only one God. They refused to believe that the Roman gods were the highest power. This angered some Roman emperors. Some Roman emperors ordered the killing of Christians.

For nearly 300 years, Christians lived in fear. But their religion continued to grow. In A.D. 313, life changed for Christians in Rome. Emperor Constantine had a vision before going to battle. He saw the Christian sign of the cross. When he won the battle, he said it was because of the Christian God. He became a Christian.

Constantine then issued the **Edict of Milan**, which made it legal to be a Christian. An **edict** is an order. Around A.D. 392, an emperor named Theodosius made Christianity the official religion of the Roman Empire.

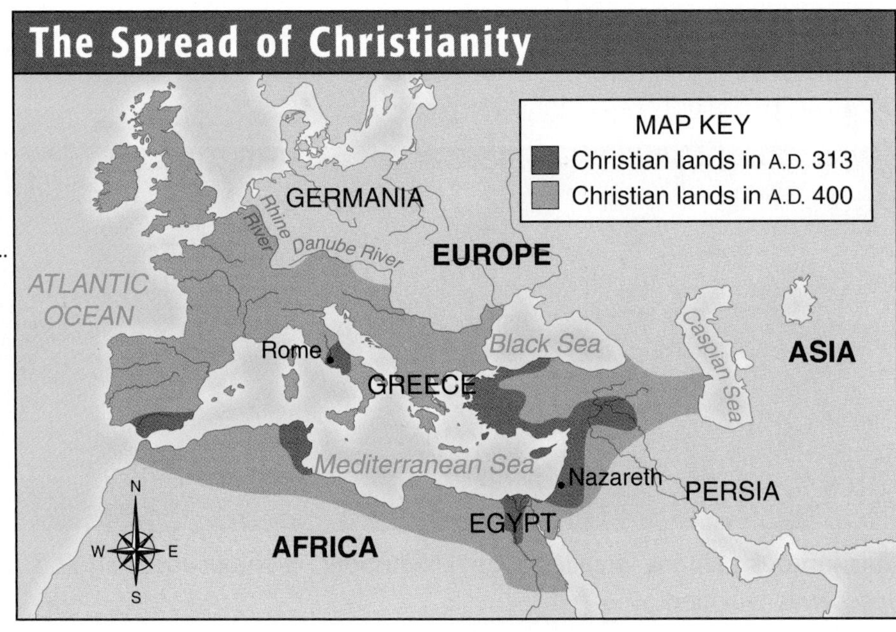

This map shows Christian lands before and after the Edict of Milan in A.D. 313. Did the Edict of Milan help or hurt the spread of Christianity?

East and West

Constantine moved from Rome to a Greek town called Byzantium. Later, Byzantium became known as the city of Constantine, or Constantinople.

The Roman Empire then had two capitals. Rome was in the West, while Constantinople was in the East. After A.D. 395, the Roman Empire had two emperors as well. One ruled the Western Roman Empire; one ruled the Eastern Roman Empire. In time, the Christian church also split in two. The Roman church stayed in Rome. The Greek, or Eastern, church was based in the city of Constantinople. Christianity spread throughout the Roman Empire and beyond. Today, there are around 1.9 billion Christians in the world.

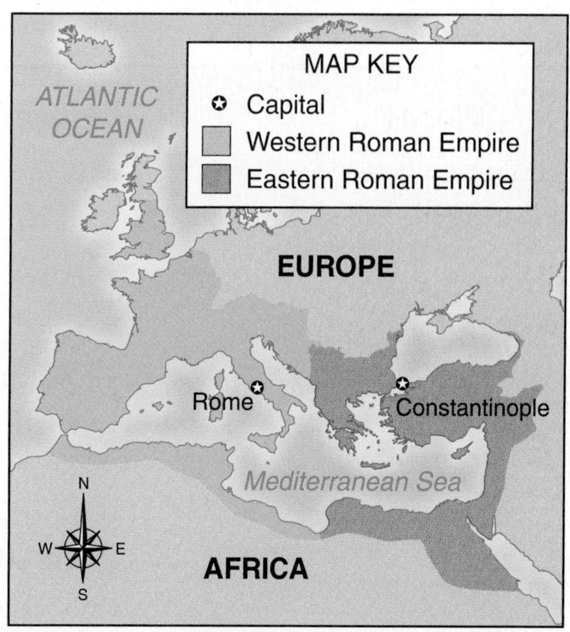

The Two Roman Empires

Lesson 2 Review

Choose words from the list that best complete the paragraphs. One word will not be used.

The Romans believed in many gods. The most powerful of their gods was __1__. Christianity began under the rule of Augustus. Some Jews believed that Jesus was the __2__. Jesus taught that God loved all people. In A.D. 33, the Romans crucified Jesus.

Christians refused to worship the Roman gods. Many emperors ordered the killing of Christians. But Emperor __3__ changed that. He made it legal to be a Christian. He moved his capital to __4__ in the East. The Roman Empire split in two.

Word List

Byzantium
Jupiter
Constantine
Gospels
Messiah

LESSON 3

The Fall of Rome

New Words
bribes
looted
pope
sanctuary
invasions

People and Places
Huns
Visigoths
Angles
Saxons
Franks
Vandals
Valens
Edward Gibbons

Before You Read
- What qualities of a leader might cause the fall of an empire?
- How might religion cause an empire to fall?

When Emperor Constantine moved to Byzantium, he knew the Roman Empire was not as strong as it once was. But it was just the beginning of a slow fall. In A.D. 476, about 150 years after Constantine, German invaders defeated the last Roman emperor in the West. They put a German king in his place. This is known as the fall of Rome.

Outside Trouble

Before the fall of Rome, the Germans had been trying to cross the northern border of the empire.

The city of Rome was destroyed by German invaders.

Invasions into Rome

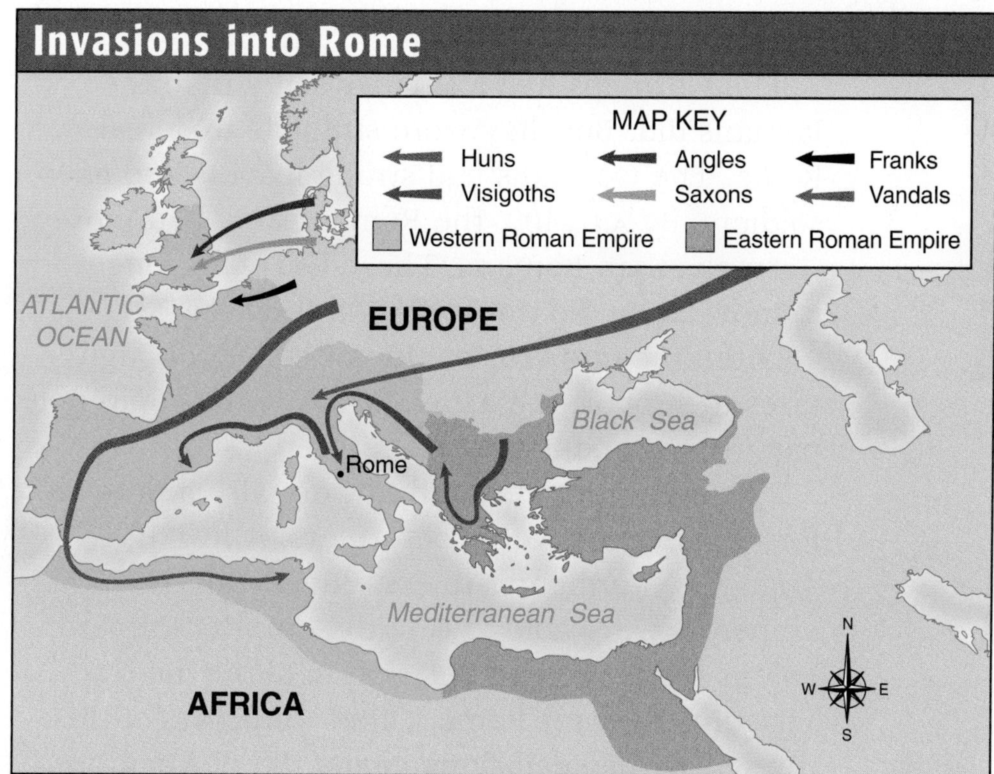

Several German tribes invaded the Western Roman Empire. Which tribe invaded the city of Rome?

Roman emperors sent armies to defeat the Germans. Sometimes, they won. Other times, they lost. At times, there was peace.

In the fourth century, a group called the Huns was moving toward the Roman Empire. They were from central Asia. The fierce Huns conquered Germans in eastern Europe. The Visigoths, a German tribe, begged Rome for help. The Romans allowed the Visigoths to come inside Roman borders and settle on empty land. The Visigoths had to promise to leave their weapons behind.

But some Romans charged the Visigoths high prices for the land. Some Romans also took **bribes**, or money, to let the Visigoths keep their weapons.

Soon, fighting broke out. In A.D. 378, the Visigoths beat the Romans. The defeat left Rome very weak. Four other German groups crossed the border into the Roman Empire. They were the Angles, Saxons, Franks, and Vandals. These groups invaded different parts of the empire. In A.D. 410, the Visigoths **looted**, or robbed, the city of Rome.

Attila the Hun

Roman soldier

Inside Trouble

The Germans had a smaller army than the Romans did. But they were still able to defeat Rome. The Germans had strong leaders and good soldiers. By A.D. 400, the Roman army had more Germans than Romans. These Germans fought for money. They did not feel loyal to Rome.

Often the emperor could not collect enough taxes to support the army. When Rome could not pay, the Germans soldiers refused to fight.

The emperors themselves were also a problem for Rome. Some were good rulers. A few, like Augustus, were great rulers. But not all the emperors were able to rule the empire. Emperor Valens made the bad decision to allow the Visigoths to enter Rome. Other emperors of this time made bad decisions. Many did not practice tolerance. In 1776, Edward Gibbons wrote a history of the fall of the Roman Empire. He wrote about how some of the Roman emperors were weak and dishonest.

Voices In History

"The [emperors], if they were stripped of their purple [robes] . . . would immediately sink to the lowest rank of society."

The fierce Huns conquered lands in eastern Europe.

The Growing Power of the Church

Meanwhile, the power of the western Christian church grew. The **pope**, who was head of this church, helped the poor and the weak. People who were in trouble could find safety in any church. This protection was called **sanctuary**. The pope set up church courts. He began to collect taxes. The pope controlled the army and even made repairs to the aqueducts. The growing power of the church took some power away from the Roman emperors.

The German **invasions**, weak emperors, and the growing power of the church all led to the fall of Rome. In A.D. 476, the last Roman emperor in the West was replaced by a German king. By A.D. 500, the Western Roman Empire had split into several German kingdoms.

The pope gained power during the 400s.

Lesson 3 Review

Choose words from the list that best complete the paragraphs. One word will not be used.

In the fourth century, the __1__ attacked the Germans in eastern Europe. Rome offered protection to one of these German groups, the Visigoths. But the Visigoths did not leave their __2__ behind. Once inside the empire, the Visigoths looted the city of Rome.

Germans fought in the Roman army. They had no loyalty to Rome. They fought for __3__. The Roman Empire failed to support its army. Too many emperors were weak. Also, the __4__ gained more and more power. All of this led to the fall of Rome in A.D. 476.

Word List

sanctuary
weapons
Huns
money
pope

Chapter 9: Using What You've Learned

Summary

- The Roman Empire was divided into provinces. Each province had its own governor.
- The period when the Roman Empire was most peaceful is called the Pax Romana.
- A volcano buried the city of Pompeii in A.D. 79, killing 2,000 people.
- Christianity was started by Jews who believed that Jesus was their Messiah. In A.D. 392, Christianity became the official religion of the Roman Empire.
- The Roman Empire fell in A.D. 476, when German invaders defeated the last Roman emperor in the West.

Find Out More!

After reading Chapter 9, you're ready to go online. **Explore Zone**, **Quiz Time**, and **Amazing Facts** bring this chapter of world history alive.

Visit www.exploreSV.com and type in the chapter code **Ch9**.

Vocabulary

Number your paper from 1 to 6. Write the word from the list that best completes each analogy. One word will not be used.

1. Roads are to people and goods as _____ are to water.
2. Judaism was to Hebrews as _____ was to Romans.
3. The Vedas were to Aryans as the _____ were to Christians.
4. Visigoths were to eastern Europe as _____ were to Asia.
5. An emperor is to an empire as a _____ is to the church.
6. Shelter is to a house as _____ is to a church.

Word List

Gospels
aqueducts
Christianity
pope
Huns
sanctuary
gladiators

Comprehension

Number your paper from 1 to 5. Write **True** for each sentence that is true. Write **False** for each sentence that is false.

1. The rule of Augustus began a peaceful time in Roman history called the Pax Romana.
2. In some ways, the Roman Forum was like a mall today.
3. Christians believed in many gods, including Jupiter, Mars, and Venus.
4. The Romans did not allow the Visigoths to come inside Roman borders.
5. The pope was the head of the western Christian church.

Critical Thinking

Cause and Effect Number your paper from 1 to 4. Read the causes in the left column. Then choose the correct effect from the right column. Write the letter of the correct effect.

Cause

1. Mount Vesuvius was six miles away from Pompeii, so _____
2. The Romans thought Jesus might take over the empire, so _____
3. In A.D. 378, the Visigoths beat the Romans, so _____
4. The pope began to collect taxes and control the Roman army, so _____

Effect

a. the power of the western Christian church grew.

b. it was easier for other German groups to invade Rome.

c. they crucified him.

d. Pompeii was buried in ash when Mount Vesuvius erupted.

Writing

Write a paragraph describing a day in the life of a person living during the Pax Romana.

LESSON 1

Indian Empires

New Words

assassinate
Buddhism
Hinduism
gravity
ahimsa

People and Places

Chandragupta Maurya
Pataliputra
Ganges River
Asoka
Gupta
Faxian
H.G. Wells

Before You Read

- Why might an emperor be nervous?
- What happens during the Golden Age of an empire?

In 327 B.C., Alexander the Great arrived at the Indus River. Alexander's army fought battles against the people there. His army conquered a part of India. But the army grew tired. They wanted to return home to Greece. Alexander and his army turned around in 326 B.C.

Alexander left some Greeks behind, however. They ruled the conquered lands in India. The Indian people feared more Greeks might come back to conquer all of India. They needed a strong empire of their own to protect them.

Alexander the Great arrived in India in 327 B.C.

Mauryan Empire

It wasn't long before India had such an empire. A new leader came to power in 322 B.C. He was Chandragupta Maurya. He united the many smaller kingdoms in India. Chandragupta built a huge army. Some say he had as many as 700,000 men and 9,000 elephants. His army defeated the Greeks that had stayed in India. The Mauryan Empire became the first empire in India.

The Mauryan Empire was divided into three provinces. The capital was Pataliputra in the Ganges River valley. Pataliputra was a rich and beautiful city. Merchants sold jewelry, silk, and leather there. Emperor Chandragupta built a massive palace. He planted various trees and plants. Beautiful parrots were brought to live among the trees.

Chandragupta was a nervous emperor. He lived in fear that someone would **assassinate**, or kill, him. He did not trust men. So, he had female soldiers watch over him. He had servants taste his food before he would eat it. He even slept in a different place every night.

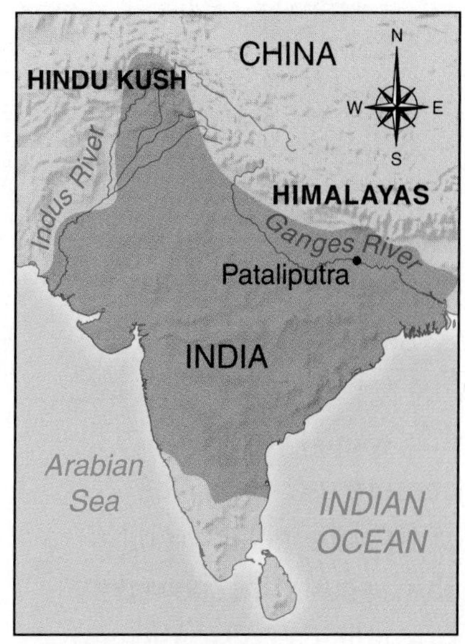

The Mauryan Empire, c. 320 B.C.–232 B.C.

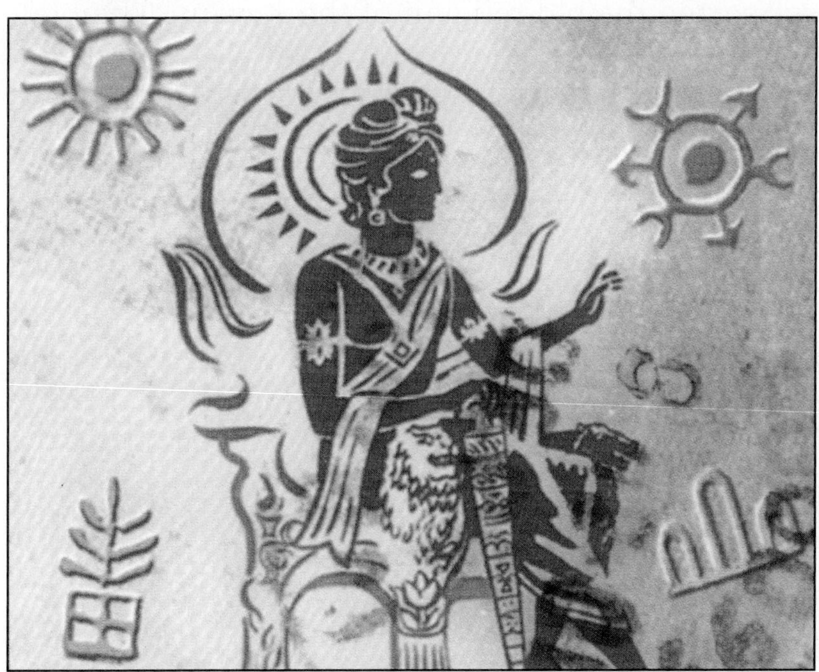

Chandragupta Maurya began the first empire in India.

Did You Know?

Fun and Games

Ancient Indians were the first to play cards. The cards they used didn't look like the ones we use today. The cards were made of cloth. The highest card showed a king riding a horse. The next highest card showed a general riding a horse. The rest of the cards showed a number of horses from one to ten. Today, there are 52 cards in a deck. In ancient India, they had 144 cards. Can you imagine shuffling 144 cloth cards?

In 273 B.C., Asoka, the grandson of Chandragupta, became the third ruler of the Mauryan Empire. Asoka was a fierce warrior who won many bloody victories. But after one battle, he realized that killing was wrong. He spent the rest of his life encouraging peace. He began to follow the teachings of **Buddhism**. Asoka began to spread Buddhism throughout the empire.

Gupta Empire

Asoka died in 232 B.C. His sons fought for control of the empire. Invaders attacked the northern provinces, and the Mauryan Empire fell apart by 180 B.C.

Once more, India became a land of small kingdoms. Over the next 500 years, the invaders became part of Indian society. The Indian people were good at bringing new people into their culture. They were able to live peacefully with many different people.

The Gupta Empire started around A.D. 320 and lasted more than 200 years. Like the Mauryan Empire, the Gupta Empire was centered in the Ganges River valley. The new emperors supported the old religion of the Aryans. They felt

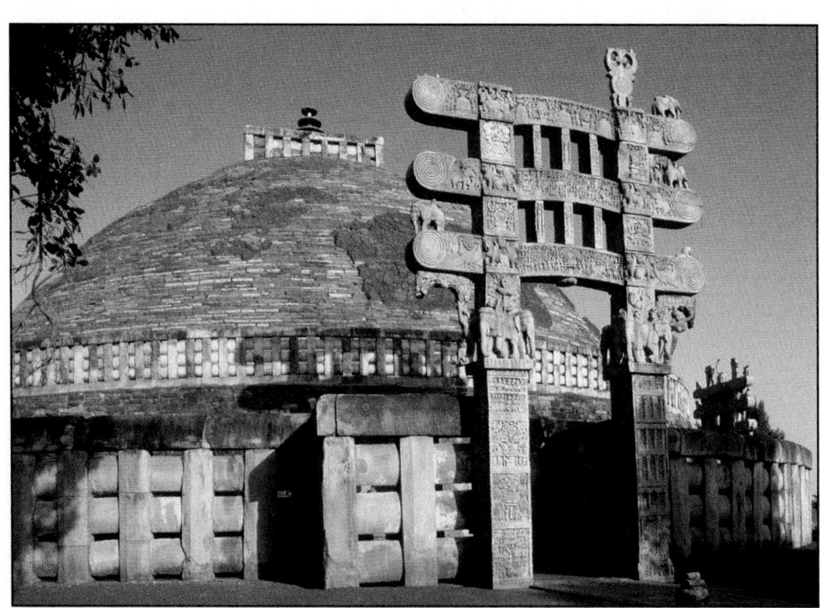

This monument was built to honor Asoka.

it was India's true religion. The religion became known as **Hinduism**.

Statue of the Buddha

The Golden Age of the Gupta

The Gupta Empire is known as the Golden Age of India. Before, the Indian artists mostly copied the Greeks. But during the Gupta Empire, they developed their own style. Using stone, metal, and clay, they made images of gods. Indians also created a famous peaceful image of the Buddha. It shows him sitting down with his eyes closed. His legs are crossed and his hands are at his chest.

During the Gupta Empire, Indians developed a number system using the numbers 1 through 9 and zero. Along with the Maya in Mexico, they were one of the first people to use the zero.

Chinese traveling monk

Indian scientists studied the stars and the movement of planets. They knew the true size of the moon. They learned about **gravity**. They learned these things more than 1,000 years before Europeans did. Indian doctors made many medical discoveries during this Golden Age. They learned to heal broken bones and to prevent diseases. Traders spread the Indian ideas of science and medicine to areas around the world.

Faxian, a Chinese monk, traveled to India in A.D. 400. He wrote about the people.

"The people are . . . happy beyond comparison. When people of other countries come to [India], they . . . supply them with what they need."

The Gupta Empire ended slowly. The Huns who invaded Rome also invaded India. In A.D. 480, just after the fall of Rome, the Huns took over northern India. By A.D. 500, the Huns had conquered western India. Fifty years later, the Gupta controlled no more land. But their science, mathematics, and art from the Golden Age have lived on.

People In History

Asoka (c. 299 B.C.–232 B.C.)

When Asoka became emperor, he fought for more land. But after a particularly bloody battle, Asoka turned against war. Why did Asoka suddenly change his mind about killing? It was because he learned the teachings of the Buddha.

Asoka began doing everything he could to preserve life. He believed in **ahimsa**, or never hurting others. Asoka said he was sorry for the deaths he had caused. He built hospitals. He stopped the killing of animals. He told his people to be kind. He sent people throughout India to teach about Buddhism. Asoka had a huge round stone monument built to honor the Buddha.

The author H.G. Wells wrote about Asoka in 1920. He said that of all the kings in history, "the name of Asoka shines, and shines almost alone, a star."

Lesson 1 Review

Choose words from the list that best complete the paragraphs. One word will not be used.

Word List

Golden Age
ahimsa
Huns
Ganges River
Asoka

The Mauryan Empire began in 322 B.C. Its first leader was Chandragupta Maurya. He lived in fear that someone would assassinate him. Another Mauryan emperor, __1__, changed his life after a terrible battle. From then on, he spent his life doing good.

Both the Mauyran and the Gupta empires were centered in the __2__ valley. The Guptas were in power during the __3__ of India. They made discoveries in math, science, and medicine. The Gupta Empire ended after the __4__ invaded India.

LESSON 2

Religion in India

Before You Read

- How do people use religion to explain suffering?
- What are some major world religions?

In Chapter 4, you read how the Aryans brought their ideas of the Brahmans and the caste system to the Indian subcontinent. You also learned about the holy books called the Vedas. These Aryan beliefs became known as Hinduism. Followers of Hinduism are called Hindus.

You read a little about Buddhism, too. You learned how its teachings changed the life of Asoka. Buddhism also changed the lives of many other people. Both Hinduism and Buddhism are still practiced today.

New Words

reincarnation
reborn
rebirth
enlightenment
Four Noble Truths
Eightfold Path
nirvana

People and Places

Siddartha Gautama

This Buddhist temple is called the Marble Temple.

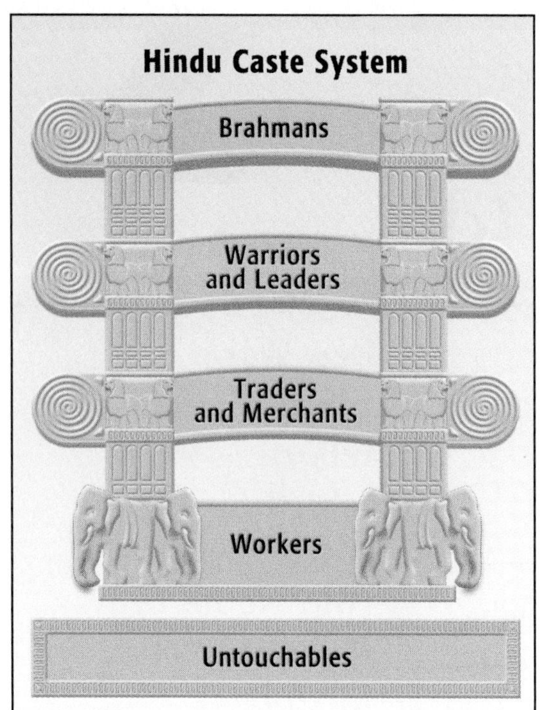

Hinduism and the Caste System

The Aryans brought the idea that people were divided into castes. The caste system became a part of Hinduism. Brahmans, or priests, were in the top caste. The second caste was the warriors and leaders. Traders and merchants made up the third caste. The lowest caste was for workers. Some people did not fit in any of these castes. They were called outcastes. They became known as untouchables.

People were born into the caste of their parents. They stayed in that caste until death. A member of one caste could not marry someone from another caste.

Life and Death

In Hinduism, there is a way to enter a higher caste, even for untouchables. Hindus believe in **reincarnation**. They believe that after death, a person's soul is born again in a new body. If a person lives a good life, he or she will be **reborn** into a higher caste. If a person lives a bad life, he or she will be reborn into a lower caste. Some

A Hindu god is shown holding up a mountain.

people could be reborn as animals. Hindus believe that animals have human souls. That is why most Hindus do not kill animals.

This pattern of birth, death, and **rebirth** continues. A person may live many lives. The pattern only ends when a person lives a perfect life. Then the soul is not reborn. Instead, it becomes part of one great spirit.

Vishnu

Hinduism has many gods. The three most important are Brahma, Vishnu, and Shiva. Brahma created the world. Vishnu preserves life. Shiva is the destroyer.

No one person started Hinduism. It developed over many years. It spread throughout India. However, around 500 B.C., many people became interested in a different religion—Buddhism.

The Life of Buddha

Buddhism began with the teachings of a man known as the Buddha. But Buddha was not his real name. He was born Siddartha Gautama around 567 B.C. in northern India. He was a prince. His father wanted to protect Siddartha from the sadness of the world. So, the father kept Siddartha inside the palace.

Siddartha Gautama cuts his hair with a sword.

When Siddartha was 30 years old, he left the palace for the first time. He wanted to see the real world. Siddartha was shocked by what he saw. He saw a dead body. He saw a sick man. He saw a beggar. Everywhere he looked, he saw suffering.

Siddartha wanted to know what caused all this pain. He left the palace for good. He threw out his silk robes and put on beggar's clothes. He ate very little food. He nearly starved to death. He wandered around India and read many books. He studied the holy Vedas. But still he found no answers.

Buddha reaches a state of peace.

Then one day he decided not to move until he found the secret of life. After many days of sitting under a tree, **enlightenment** came at last. He felt he saw the truth for the first time. He became known as the Buddha, or the "Enlightened One."

The Beliefs of Buddhism

The Buddha spent the rest of his life as a teacher. He taught what he called the **Four Noble Truths**: (1) Life is full of pain and suffering. (2) Pain is caused by greedy desire. (3) Pain will end when we stop being greedy. (4) This can be done by living the right way.

To live right, the Buddha said that people must follow the **Eightfold Path**. The first step in the path is to have the right beliefs or views about life. The next step is to have the right wishes and thoughts. The next three steps are to act, speak, and work in the right way. The final three steps are to always try, to always be mindful, and to stay calm.

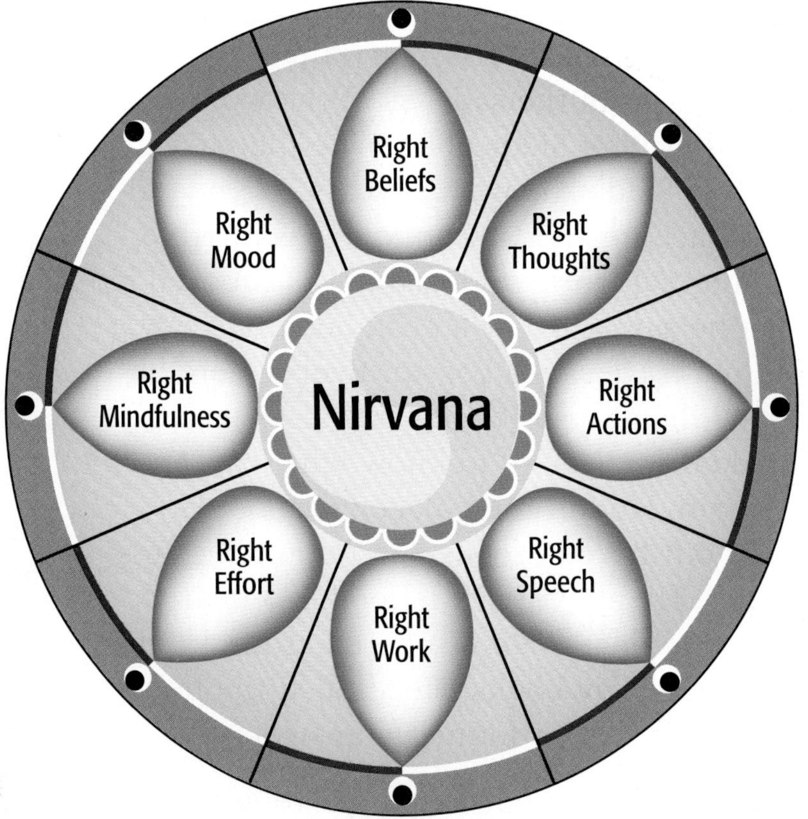

The Eightfold Path

If a person follows the eight steps of the path, the person enters **nirvana**. This is a state of mind where there is no desire or greed. There is only true peace.

This flower is a symbol of Buddhism.

The Spread of Indian Religions

Buddhism spread over much of India. Some people saw it as a challenge to Hinduism. The Buddha said that the caste system was wrong. He thought all people should be treated equally.

Over time, both Hinduism and Buddhism grew. Hinduism became the major religion of the Indian subcontinent. Today, Hinduism has about 750 million followers.

Buddhism faded in India. But it spread to other areas in Asia, including Japan, China, and Southeast Asia. Today, Buddhism is practiced by about 335 million people.

Lesson 2 Review

Choose words from the list that best complete the paragraphs. One word will not be used.

The Aryans brought the caste system to the Indian subcontinent. There were four major castes. Those below the caste system became known as __1__. The Aryan caste system became a part of Hinduism. Hindus believe in __2__. That means that when people die, their souls are reborn.

The __3__ first saw the outside world at the age of 30. He was shocked by the suffering he saw. He wanted to find out why there was so much pain in the world. In time, __4__ came to him. The Buddha taught the Four Noble Truths and the Eightfold Path. Today, both Hinduism and Buddhism are important world religions.

Word List

nirvana
untouchables
enlightenment
reincarnation
Buddha

LESSON 3

Chinese Empires

New Words
civil war
peasants
examination system
bureaucracy
porcelain
Silk Road

People and Places
Shi Huangdi
Qin
Han

Before You Read
- How do people get government jobs?
- How can trade help spread ideas?

In Chapter 4, you learned that in 771 B.C., the Zhou Dynasty fell. The new Eastern Zhou period began. This was a weak dynasty because no one had real control. A series of wars broke out. This time often is called the period of the Warring States. Large kingdoms fought one another for control of China.

At last, in 256 B.C., the Eastern Zhou fell. But fighting continued. Then in 221 B.C., one kingdom won control and united China. Shi Huangdi ruled the Qin Dynasty. The dynasty lasted just 15 years.

Different kingdoms fought for control of China during the period of the Warring States.

The Qin Dynasty

Shi Huangdi won new lands. He made the laws the same for all of China. Shi Huangdi had everyone use the same weights and measures. He built fine roads and further developed the Chinese language. Shi Huangdi also linked a series of walls on the western border into one long wall. This became known as the Great Wall of China. It was meant to protect China from any enemy who might attack from northern or western areas.

Shi Huangdi was a cruel leader. He felt books might put bad ideas into people's heads. So, he burned all the books he could find. He also had people killed for the smallest reasons. If a general was late for a meeting, Shi Huangdi had him killed.

Shi Huangdi's cruelty led to **civil war**. In 210 B.C., Shi Huangdi died. He was buried in a huge tomb that was cut into the side of a mountain. It had taken thousands of **peasants** many years of hard work to build the tomb.

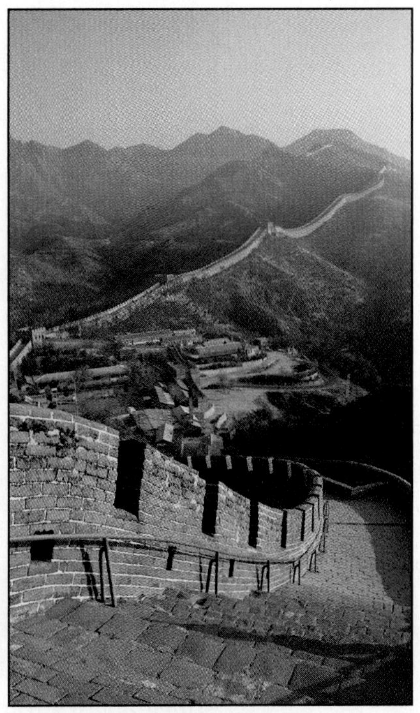

The Great Wall of China

Shi Huangdi ordered the burning of books during the Qin Dynasty.

Shi Huangdi's tomb is guarded by thousands of life-size clay soldiers.

Shi Huangdi had about 7,500 life-size clay soldiers buried with him. Each one was at least six feet tall. Each one had a different look on his face. The civil war continued after Shi Huangdi's death. Four years later, the Qin Dynasty fell.

The Han and Good Government

Chinese officials taking tests

The Han Dynasty took control in 206 B.C. This dynasty lasted more than 400 years. Han emperors were more gentle than Shi Huangdi. They gave nobles back some of their power. Peasants did not have to work as hard.

The Han changed how the government worked. They did not give jobs to their friends or family. Instead, the Han set up an **examination system**. A person had to pass a difficult test to become a government official. Students went to special schools to prepare for the test.

By 206 B.C., China was a huge country of about 60 million people. China had many more people than any other country at the time. Who would manage all this land and all these people? Who would keep the peace? China needed a large

bureaucracy, or many well-trained officials. All the dynasties that followed the Han used the examination system. Those who passed the tests became a part of the bureaucracy. Future dynasties continued using the examination system until the 1900s.

Han statue of a tower

Han Inventions

The Han invented many new things. They made a new and better plow. They also wrote the first dictionary and the first history of China. The Han were the first to use water mills to grind rice into flour. They put a special coating on pottery to make **porcelain**. Centuries later, when Europeans saw the porcelain, they liked it. Because of where it came from, they called it "china."

The Han were the first Chinese empire to trade with Southwest Asia and Europe. They developed a famous trade route called the **Silk Road**. This road ran through deserts and mountains. It stretched all the way from China to the Mediterranean Sea. The Chinese sold silk, spices, and furs. The Silk Road was the first major link between Asia and Europe. Ideas and goods were shared across the continents.

The Silk Road was built during the Han Dynasty. What mountain range did it cross?

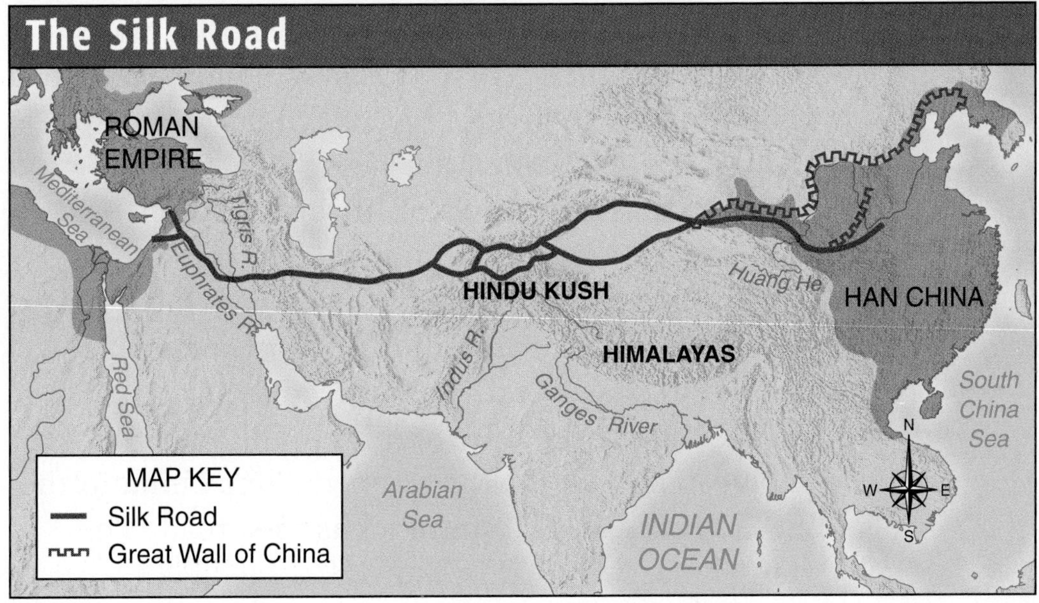

The Fall of the Han Dynasty

The inventions of the Han did not always help the poor people. The gap between the rich people and the poor people grew wide.

The Chinese made silk using the threads of silkworms.

Around A.D. 200, outside groups, including the Huns, attacked China. They broke through the Great Wall of China. The Han Dynasty began to lose power. The emperors were too weak to keep the country together. In A.D. 220, the Han Dynasty came to an end. Without a steady government, the flow of ideas slowed. China went from a time of much invention to a time of little or no invention. This lasted about 350 years.

Lesson 3 Review

Choose words from the list that best complete the paragraphs. One word will not be used.

Word List

Mediterranean Sea
cruel
protection
Europe
bureaucracy

The Qin Dynasty lasted only a short time. Shi Huangdi did many good things. He built the Great Wall of China to give __1__ to China. As a ruler, though, he was known for being __2__. Shi Huangdi had thousands of life-size soldiers buried with him in a mountain tomb.

The Han Dynasty lasted more than 400 years. To become a government official, a person needed to pass a test. China needed a __3__ because it was so large and had millions of people. The Silk Road stretched from China to the __4__. It allowed Chinese ideas to spread. The Han Dynasty ended in A.D. 220.

LESSON 4

Religion in China

Before You Read

- Why might a ruler want to burn religious books?
- What lessons can be learned from nature?

New Words
yin and yang
Confucianism
sage
Daoism

People and Places
Kong Fuzi
Confucius

During the Chinese period of the Warring States, several new ideas developed. This is considered one of the best times in Chinese philosophy. People needed to make sense out of the troubled time. One important idea to come out of this time was the idea of the **yin and yang**. Yin was darkness and weakness. Yang was brightness and strength. The Chinese believed that when yin and yang were balanced, there would be peace.

Yin and yang symbol

The yin and yang symbol is popular in Chinese art.

The Beginning of Confucianism

Another idea from this time became a major philosophy—**Confucianism**. A man named Kong Fuzi was born during the time of the Warring States, around 550 B.C. Today, we know this **sage**, or wise teacher, as Confucius.

Confucius

Few people listened to the ideas of Confucius during his lifetime. But over time, his ideas became more popular. Teachers continued spreading his ideas. The Qin Dynasty did not approve of Confucianism. Shi Huangdi had hundreds of teachers killed. He ordered all books on Confucianism burned. But some people hid many of these books. In this way, the ideas of Confucius were saved.

The Ideas of Confucius

What did Confucius teach? Why would his ideas upset a ruler such as Shi Huangdi? Confucius lived in a time of many wars. He wanted law and order. He thought that keeping the peace was the highest goal of government.

Confucius said that the best rulers were fair and just. They first learned to rule themselves. Good rulers, Confucius said, should be like fathers are to their families. They should be loving and set a good example.

"When a [leader's] personal conduct is correct, his government [works well] without the issuing of orders. If his personal conduct is not correct, he may issue orders but they will not be followed."

Confucius did not write any books. His followers collected his sayings and wrote them down. The most famous book of sayings is called the *Analects*. Confucius taught about how people should behave. He said that society would be at peace if people behaved in the right way. People should treat others the way they want to be treated.

Confucius put a high value on family life. In China, most families were large. They included the grandparents as well as the parents. There were clear rules to follow. If everyone followed these rules, the family would have peace and good fortune. Confucius believed the same was true of the government. Countries needed strong leaders in order to keep harmony and peace.

Confucius with students

Confucianism continued to grow even though the Qin Dynasty did not approve of it. During the Han Dynasty, Confucianism became the official philosophy of China.

Daoism

The Han also supported a religion called **Daoism**. Daoism began around 500 B.C., also during the period of the Warring States. The book of Daoism is called the *Dao de Jing*. Daoism teaches people to follow the way of nature. In other words, people should look to nature to see how to live.

For example, think of a river. How does the water behave? The water follows the easiest route. It moves around rocks. It always heads for the lowest point. Over time, the river is powerful enough to wear away the hardest rocks.

Daoism teaches people to follow the way of nature.

Daoist charm

Daoism teaches that people should follow that example. They shouldn't work too hard. They should not worry about having power. They should not worry about getting rich. Instead, people should be patient. Good things will come if they move through life the way water moves in a river.

Both Confucianism and Daoism became important in China. Confucianism appealed to those looking for clear rules. Daoism was followed by people wanting more freedom and fewer rules.

Hinduism, Buddhism, Confucianism, and Daoism all have survived over the centuries. They are sometimes called Eastern religions because they began in Asia. These religions are still practiced mostly in Asia. But people in all parts of the world have been affected by these teachings.

Lesson 4 Review

Choose words from the list that best complete the paragraphs. One word will not be used.

Word List

nature
Qin
Han
peace
Asia

Confucius thought the highest goal of government was to keep the __1__. He said the best rulers were fair and just. Centuries after Confucius died, his ideas became more popular. Under the __2__ Dynasty, Confucianism became the official philosophy of China.

Daoism began around 500 B.C. It taught that people should look to __3__ to see how to act. Hinduism, Buddhism, Confucianism, and Daoism all began in __4__. They are still practiced today by people all over the world.

Chapter 10: Using What You've Learned

Summary

- The Mauryan empire of India began in 322 B.C. in the Ganges River valley. The Gupta empire began around A.D. 320. The Gupta empire was the Golden Age of India.
- Hinduism and Buddhism began in India. Hinduism has many gods and a caste system. Buddhism teaches people to seek peace.
- During the Han Dynasty, the Chinese improved government and invented many things. They also expanded trade.
- Confucianism and Daoism began around 500 B.C. Confucianism teaches people to be fair and just. Daoism teaches people to follow nature.

Find Out More!

After reading Chapter 10, you're ready to go online. **Explore Zone**, **Quiz Time**, and **Amazing Facts** bring this chapter of world history alive.

Visit www.exploreSV.com and type in the chapter code **Ch10**.

Vocabulary

Number your paper from 1 to 6. Write the word or words from the list that best complete the paragraphs. One word will not be used.

Around 273 B.C. in India, Asoka began to follow the religious teachings of __1__. This religion says that to live right, people must follow the __2__. If a person follows these steps, the person enters a state of mind called __3__. Asoka believed in __4__, or never hurting others.

The Gupta Empire supported __5__, a religion based on the beliefs of the Aryans. The followers of this religion were divided into castes. A person could be __6__ into a higher caste if he or she lived a good life.

Word List

Eightfold Path
ahimsa
gravity
nirvana
reborn
Hinduism
Buddhism

Comprehension

Number your paper from 1 to 4. Write the word or words from the list that best complete each sentence. One word will not be used.

1. During the Qin Dynasty, the _____ was linked together to protect China.
2. The Han used a _____ to manage their large kingdom.
3. The trade route called the _____ linked Asia and Europe.
4. The Chinese believed that balancing _____ created peace.

Word List

yin and yang
Great Wall
porcelain
Silk Road
bureaucracy

Critical Thinking

Conclusions Number your paper from 1 to 3. Read each pair of sentences below. Then look for a conclusion that follows from these sentences. Write the letter of the correct conclusion.

1. The Huns invaded Rome.
   They also took over northern and western India.
2. Shi Huangdi burned books about Confucianism.
   He also killed hundreds of teachers of Confucianism.
3. Asoka did everything he could to preserve life.
   He built hospitals and stopped the killing of animals.

Conclusions

a. Asoka believed in ahimsa, or never hurting others.

b. The Qin Dynasty did not approve of Confucianism.

c. The Huns conquered large areas of land in Europe and Asia.

Writing

Write a short paragraph explaining why the Gupta Empire is known as the Golden Age of India.

Skill Builder: Reading a Diagram

A **diagram** is a picture that helps you understand information. The diagram on this page helps you understand the Great Wall of China.

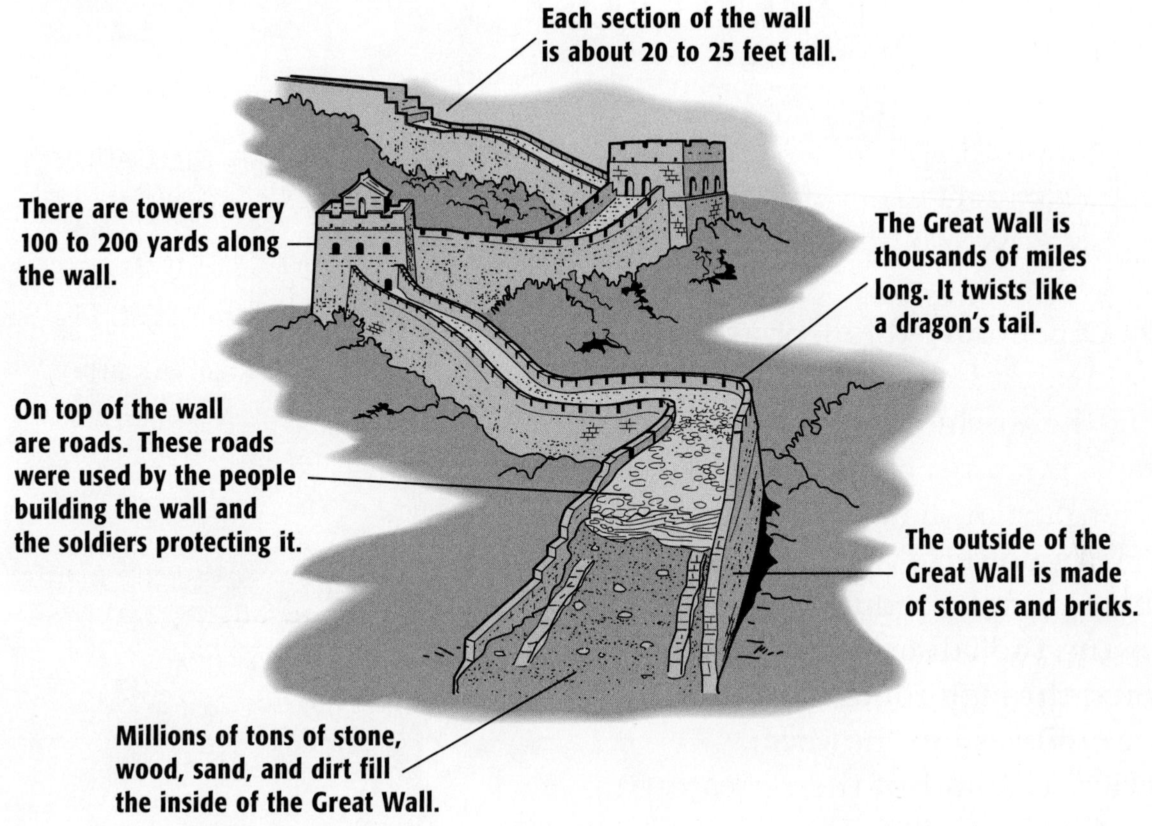

Each section of the wall is about 20 to 25 feet tall.
There are towers every 100 to 200 yards along the wall.
The Great Wall is thousands of miles long. It twists like a dragon's tail.
On top of the wall are roads. These roads were used by the people building the wall and the soldiers protecting it.
The outside of the Great Wall is made of stones and bricks.
Millions of tons of stone, wood, sand, and dirt fill the inside of the Great Wall.

Number your paper from 1 to 5. Write the word or number that best completes each sentence.

25	200	roads	thousands	millions

1. The Great Wall twists like the tail of a dragon for _____ of miles.
2. There are towers every 100 to _____ yards along the wall.
3. The inside of the Great Wall is filled with _____ of tons of stone, wood, sand, and dirt.
4. Each section of the wall is about 20 to _____ feet tall.
5. There are _____ on top of the wall.

UNIT 3

Rise and Fall of Civilizations

500–1000

Every early civilization had a story of its own. As you have seen, some made a brief appearance and then faded. Others stayed longer and affected future generations. Civilizations in one part of the world might have struggled. At the same time, civilizations in another part of the world might have been very powerful.

This unit tells about the 500 years following the fall of Rome. Europe suffered through some hard times. Other civilizations, however, experienced some of their greatest years. Civilizations in Asia, for example, took giant steps forward in art, science, and medicine.

A.D. 500 600 700

A.D. 500
The Byzantine Empire and the Sassanid Dynasty become two of the most powerful kingdoms.

A.D. 609
A six-year-old boy named Pacal becomes king of a Mayan city.

A.D. 700
The Soninke people rule Ghana in West Africa and control the gold trade.

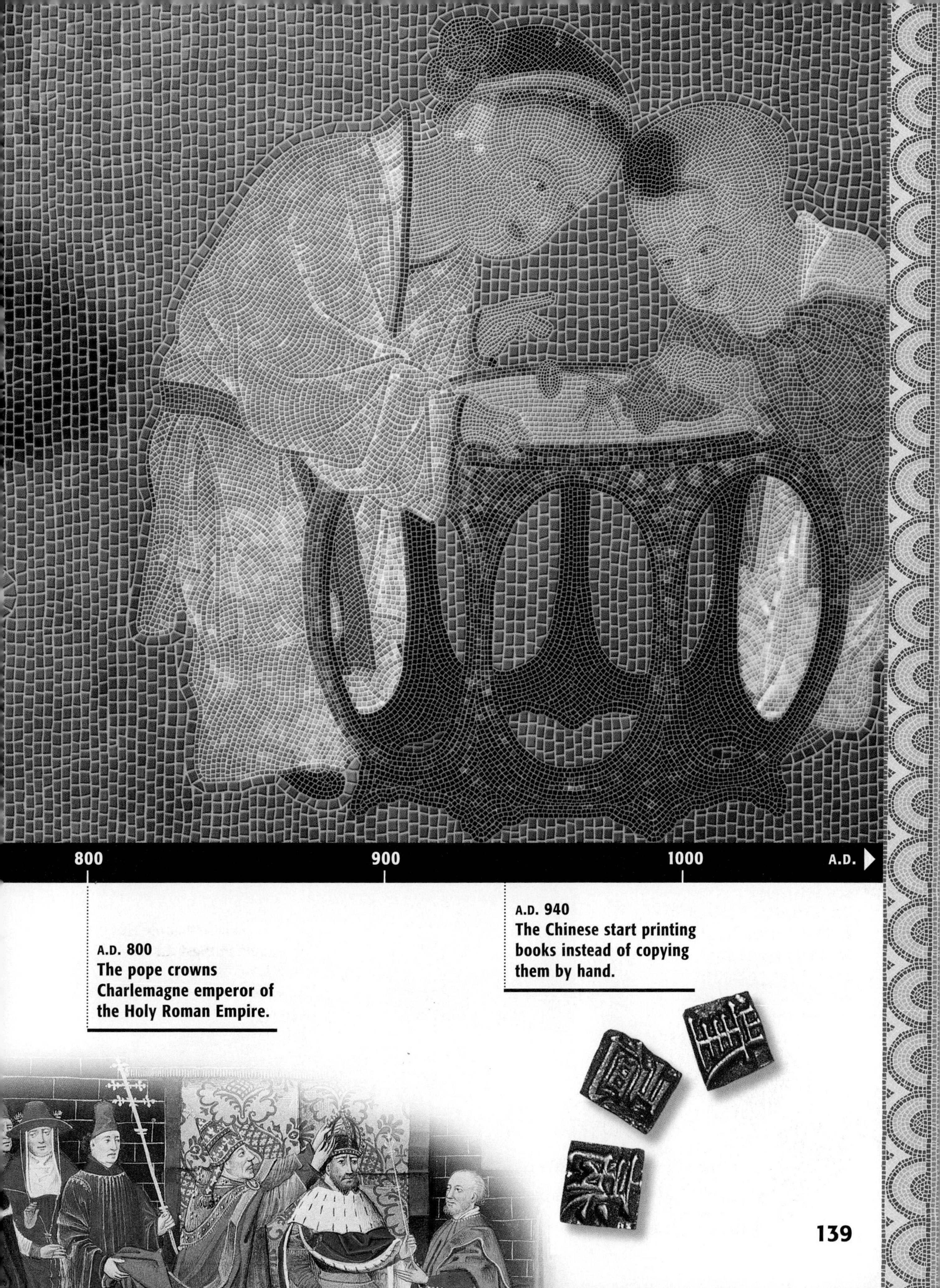

A.D. 800
The pope crowns Charlemagne emperor of the Holy Roman Empire.

A.D. 940
The Chinese start printing books instead of copying them by hand.

LESSON 1

After the Fall of Rome

New Words

Middle Ages
barbarians
mayor of the palace
Islam
Muslims
Papal States
Vikings
sagas

People and Places

Clovis
Merovingians
Charles Martel
Arabs
Tours
Pepin
Carolingians
Lombards
France
Normans
Normandy

Before You Read

- How might the church help a ruler?
- How might invaders affect the culture of the people they invade?

The Western Roman Empire fell in A.D. 476. For the next 500 years, no strong kingdom or empire ruled the area. The German invaders set up several kingdoms. Europe entered the **Middle Ages**. For Europe, this was a time between the ancient world and the modern world.

The Germans were very different from Romans. They wore rough clothes and animal skins. They carried weapons and fought often. They did not write books or build temples or paint pictures. Romans called them **barbarians**.

Barbarians were fierce warriors.

Clovis became a Christian in 496.

Merovingians

The Franks were one group of barbarians. A 15-year-old boy named Clovis became king of the Franks in 481. For ten years, he went to war with neighboring barbarians. He conquered lands and became the first king of the Merovingian Dynasty.

In 496, Clovis became a Christian. He forced all his followers to become Christians, too. The church leaders then supported Clovis and allowed the Merovingian kings to continue as rulers of the kingdom.

The Merovingians stayed in power for about 275 years. Most of the kings were weak. They became known as the "do-nothing kings." Power shifted to the king's officials. The most powerful official was the **mayor of the palace**.

In 732, Charles Martel was the mayor of the palace. That year, he led his army against Arab attackers. These Arabs practiced a new religion called **Islam**. Charles Martel defeated the **Muslims**, or believers of Islam, at the Battle of Tours. The church then supported Charles Martel instead of the Merovingian king.

Charles Martel defeated the Muslims at the Battle of Tours.

Pepin

Charles Martel held the power of a king without the title. His son Pepin changed that. Pepin wanted to take the title of king away from the powerless Merovingians. He asked the pope to choose either him or the Merovingian king to be the ruler. The pope chose Pepin. The Merovingian Dynasty ended in 751 when Pepin was crowned the new king of the Franks.

Carolingians

Pepin's rule began the Carolingian Dynasty. The Carolingians and the church worked closely together. Since the pope chose Pepin to be king, Pepin felt loyal to the pope.

Shortly after becoming king, Pepin sent an army of Franks to defeat the Lombards, a German group who had invaded Rome. Pepin gave the pope the captured Lombard lands. These lands became known as the **Papal States**, or states of the pope.

Trouble from the North

Few Europeans knew much about the clans living in far northern Europe. These clans lived in lands that are now Norway, Sweden, and Denmark. In 793, these **Vikings**, or "Northmen," began attacking the rest of Europe.

Vikings sailed from northern Europe in long, fast ships.

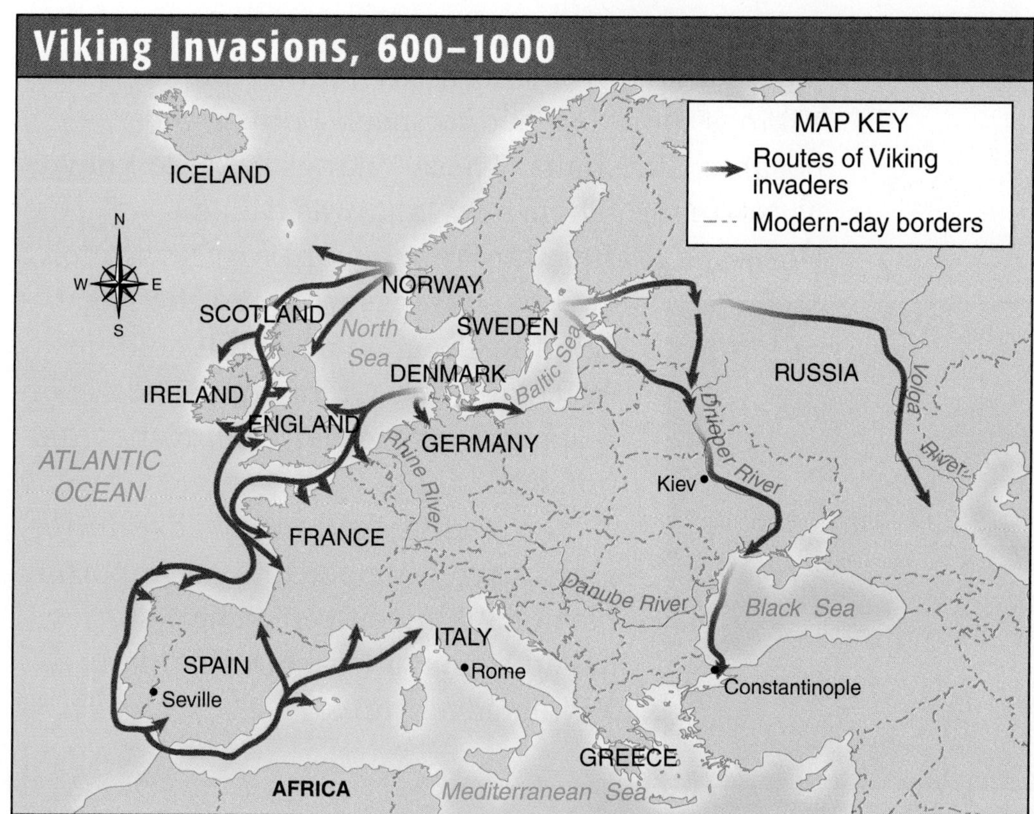

The Vikings began their invasions from what is now Norway, Sweden, and Denmark. What sea did they cross to reach England?

Europeans became very afraid of the Vikings. The Vikings had fast ships. Using sails and long oars, they could cross the open seas or sail up rivers. They were skilled sailors. First, the Vikings attacked lands in the modern-day countries of England, Scotland, and Ireland. Later, they moved south and east, attacking areas in France, Italy, Spain, and Russia.

The Vikings attacked churches to steal gold and silver. They burned many churches to the ground. The Vikings often went to the same place more than once. They wanted to make sure they hadn't left anything valuable behind.

Viking Settlers

Ruled by small German kingdoms, the Europeans could not stop the strong Vikings. Over time, the Vikings began to settle in the areas that they had invaded.

A Viking

In 911, one king gave some Vikings a huge piece of land in modern-day France. Many Vikings there learned to speak French and became Christians. These Vikings became known as Normans. Their new land was called Normandy, after the French word for "Northmen."

Viking carving

Other Vikings explored the North Atlantic Ocean. They built colonies in Iceland and Greenland. They even reached North America, but they did not settle there.

The Vikings had many adventures, and storytelling became an important part of Viking culture. Their stories, called **sagas**, told about the many Viking adventures.

Lesson 1 Review

Choose words from the list that best complete the paragraphs. One word will not be used.

Word List

Lombards
Tours
sagas
Vikings
Franks

Clovis was king of the __1__. In 496, he became a Christian. He conquered lands and began the Merovingian Dynasty. In 732, Charles Martel won the Battle of __2__. His son, Pepin, ended the rule of the Merovingians when the pope chose him to be king. Pepin later gave the pope land that he captured in Italy.

The __3__ came from northern Europe. They were skilled sailors with fast ships. Some of them settled in France and became known as Normans. They told __4__ about their many adventures.

LESSON 2

Life in the Early Middle Ages

Before You Read

- Why might a time be called the "Dark Ages"?
- How could a ruler offer protection to the people of the kingdom?

The early Middle Ages in western Europe are sometimes called the **Dark Ages**. The Roman Empire was gone. There was no central government. Roads and bridges were not repaired. Schools closed. Trade slowed down, too. Most merchants didn't want to travel in Europe during this time. They worried that robbers or invaders might attack them. People left the cities and moved to the country.

Many people moved to the country during western Europe's early Middle Ages.

New Words

Dark Ages
feudalism
fief
lord
vassal
manor
serfs
monasteries
convents

People and Places

Charlemagne
Gaul
Leo III
Holy Roman Empire

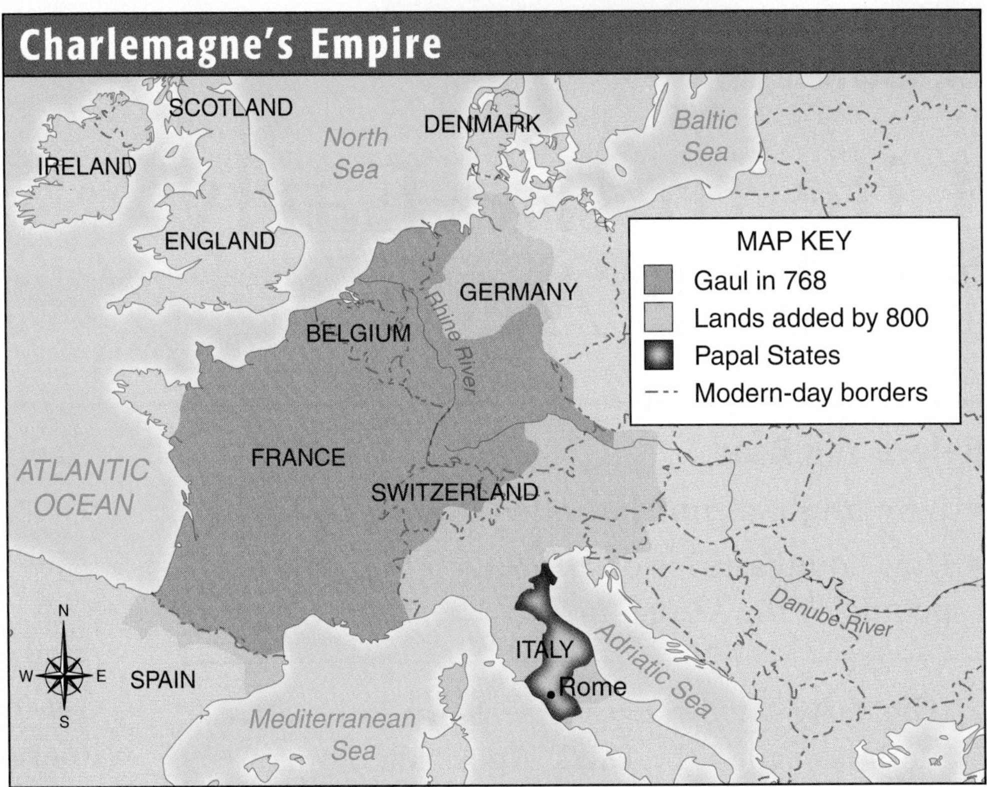

Charlemagne ruled much of western Europe. Did Charlemagne gain control of much of the Papal States before or after 768?

Charlemagne

One man tried to bring Europe together again. Charles the Great, or Charlemagne, was the son of Pepin. In 768, Charlemagne became king of the Franks. He ruled an empire called Gaul. His empire covered all of modern-day France and parts of Germany, Belgium, and Switzerland. Charlemagne added lands to his kingdom. By 800, he had gained control over much of western Europe, including the Papal States.

The poem *The Song of Roland* celebrates the greatness of Charlemagne. No one knows who wrote the poem. The opening lines tell of Charlemagne's victories in Spain.

Voices In History

"Charles the King, our Lord and [emperor]
Full seven years [he traveled] in Spain,
Conquered the land, and won the [West],
Now no [fort] against him [does] remain,
No city walls are left for him to gain."

Charlemagne tried to bring Europe out of the Dark Ages. Although he did not know how to write, he knew the importance of education. He opened new schools and hired the best teachers. He supported artists and writers.

The Holy Roman Empire

Charlemagne also worked closely with the church to spread Christianity. On Christmas Day in the year 800, Pope Leo III crowned Charlemagne and declared him emperor of the Holy Roman Empire. Three hundred years after the fall of Rome, the idea of a Roman Empire still existed. When Pope Leo crowned Charlemagne, it suggested that the pope had more power than the emperor. This was only the beginning of a long struggle. For centuries, popes and rulers in Europe would fight over who had the most power.

Charlemagne died in 814. His three grandsons divided up the land, but they could not stop invaders such as the Vikings from taking over many parts of the empire. Europe once again became a land of small kingdoms.

Pope Leo III crowned Charlemagne as emperor of the Holy Roman Empire.

Did You Know?

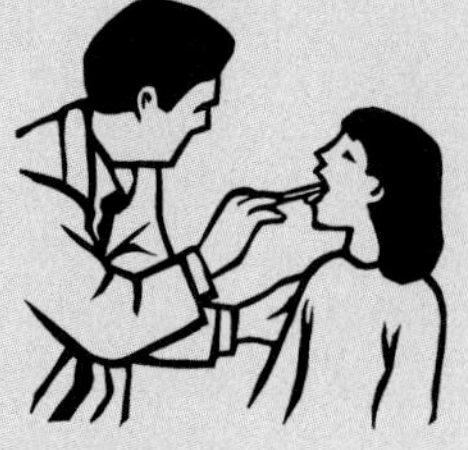

Say "Ahhhh"

It's never fun to be sick. But it was really tough in Europe's Dark Ages. People thought diseases were caused by evil spirits. To get rid of a fever, people were told to swallow spiders wrapped in raisins. To stop an aching tooth, they had to touch a dead man's tooth. For stomach problems, they tied an eel skin around their knee. If their leg was bothering them, the leg might have been cut open so that evil spirits would pour out along with the blood.

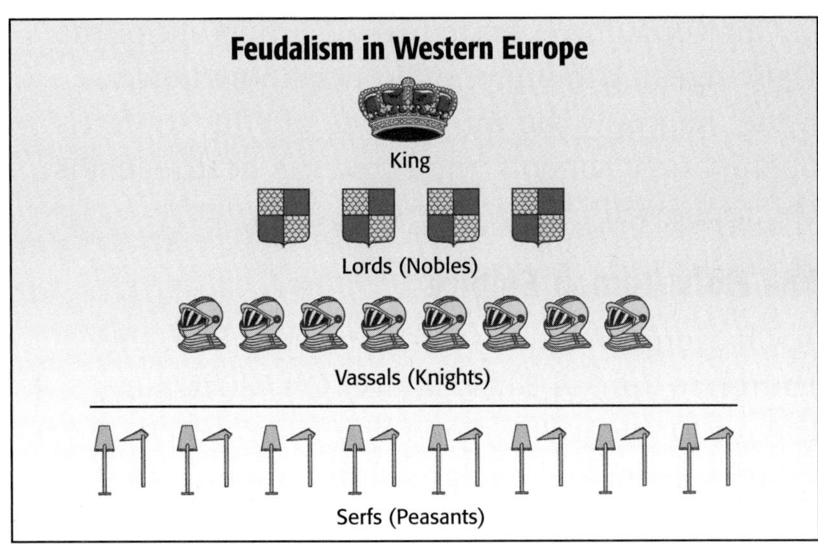

Feudalism

Charlemagne's death ended any hope for a strong central government. The local kings needed to protect the people. Wealthy nobles could offer that protection by providing knights and soldiers. The knights and soldiers served the nobles in exchange for land. This began the system of **feudalism**.

In feudalism, nobles gave each knight a **fief**, or large piece of land. In return, the knights promised to be loyal to the noble. Under this system, the noble who gave the land was a **lord**. The knight who received the land was a **vassal**. It was possible for a lord to be a vassal to an even more powerful lord.

Serfs often worked in the fields of a manor.

Life on the Manor

The fief that the lord ruled over was his **manor**. The manor usually included peasants who farmed the land. The peasants, or **serfs**, were bound to the land. They had to work on the manor where they were born.

Serfs grew all the food for themselves, the lord, and the lord's family. They cut down trees to make lumber. They chopped wood for fires. They raised animals for meat and wool. Serfs made almost everything the manor needed.

Religion and Culture

Life in the Middle Ages centered around the church. There were even religious communities. Men sometimes joined **monasteries** and became monks. Women sometimes joined **convents** and became nuns. These people lived for God alone and promised never to marry. They spent their days working, reading the Bible, and praying.

The power of the church affected culture, too. Most art from this time was about religion. Music was written for church services. Plays were written about Bible stories. Monks began decorating religious books with colorful paintings. They often painted pictures inside the first letter of a story.

This religious work is decorated with colorful paintings.

Lesson 2 Review

Choose words from the list that best complete the paragraphs. One word will not be used.

The early Middle Ages are sometimes called the __1__. It was a time of invasions and no central government. In 768, __2__ became king of the Franks. In 800, Pope Leo III crowned him emperor of the Holy Roman Empire.

After Charlemagne's death, Europe was ruled by local kings. The system of __3__ developed. A knight who promised to fight for a lord was a __4__. Serfs lived on a lord's manor. They worked the land and provided food for the lord and the lord's family.

The culture and art of the Middle Ages was centered on the church. Some people joined religious communities.

Word List

Charlemagne
feudalism
noble
vassal
Dark Ages

LESSON 3

Eastern Europe

New Words

Justinian Code
mosaics
icons
Catholic Church
Orthodox Church

People and Places

Byzantine Empire
Justinian
Theodora
Russia
Kiev
Kievan Russia
Zoe
Romanus III
Michael IV
Michael V

Before You Read

- Why might one culture want to copy another?
- What might cause one church to separate into two churches?

The fall of the Western Roman Empire in A.D. 476 sent western Europe into the Dark Ages. But the Eastern Roman Empire continued another one thousand years. It became known as the Byzantine Empire. The Byzantines wanted to gain back the glory of the Roman Empire. They built aqueducts, roads, and beautiful churches in the capital city of Constantinople. One church still stands today—the Hagia Sophia. When it was built, it was the world's largest and most magnificent church.

Hagia Sophia was the largest building in Constantinople.

The inside of Hagia Sophia is richly decorated.

The Byzantine Empire

In 527, Emperor Justinian set out to make the Byzantine Empire as mighty as the ancient Roman Empire. He conquered lands in the West, including Athens, Rome, and Carthage. He took the Roman laws and made them easier to understand. This new set of laws became known as the **Justinian Code**.

Justinian's wife, Theodora, played a large role in Justinian's government. She helped him choose army officials. She encouraged Justinian to make laws that were fair to women. One law allowed parents to leave property to their daughters. Before this change, they could only leave property to their sons.

The Byzantine Empire became known for its art. The Byzantine people filled churches with paintings and **mosaics**, or pictures made from small pieces of colored stone or glass.

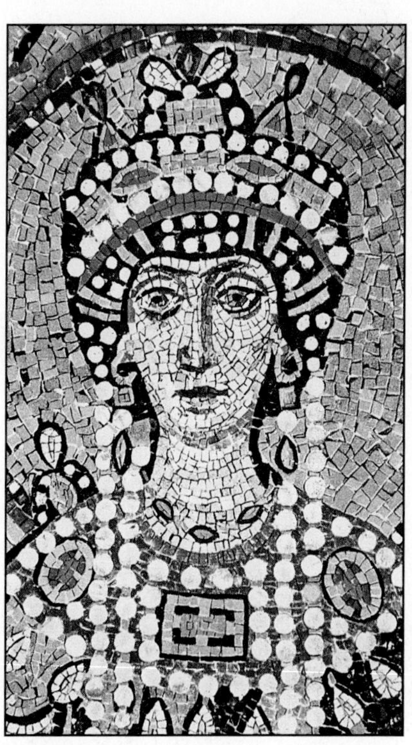

This mosaic shows Theodora.

Constantinople was the largest city in Europe. The city dazzled visitors. Most people had never seen so many markets or so many beautiful buildings. One man wrote of the city, "We knew not whether we were in heaven or on Earth."

One Religion, Two Churches

After 476, there was little communication between the two capital cities, Rome and Constantinople. The church in the East developed different ideas from the church in the West.

One difference involved **icons**. In the West, few people could read or write. The church used icons so people could learn Bible stories. In the East, church leaders felt it was wrong to pray to icons. They ordered that all the icons be destroyed. The two churches did not agree on other issues. By 1054, they had split into two separate groups. The **Catholic Church** was based in Rome. The **Orthodox Church** was based in Constantinople.

Church leaders in the East ordered that all icons be destroyed.

Beginning of Russia

The Vikings invaded the lands of Russia during the 800s. Together with the local people, the Vikings captured Kiev and other cities. The new lands became known as Kievan Russia.

There were many trade routes between Russia and the Byzantine Empire. The Russians began to copy the Byzantine style of writing and painting. They also copied the customs of the Byzantines.

Many trade routes between Kievan Russia and the Byzantine Empire followed rivers. Which river ran from Kiev to the Black Sea?

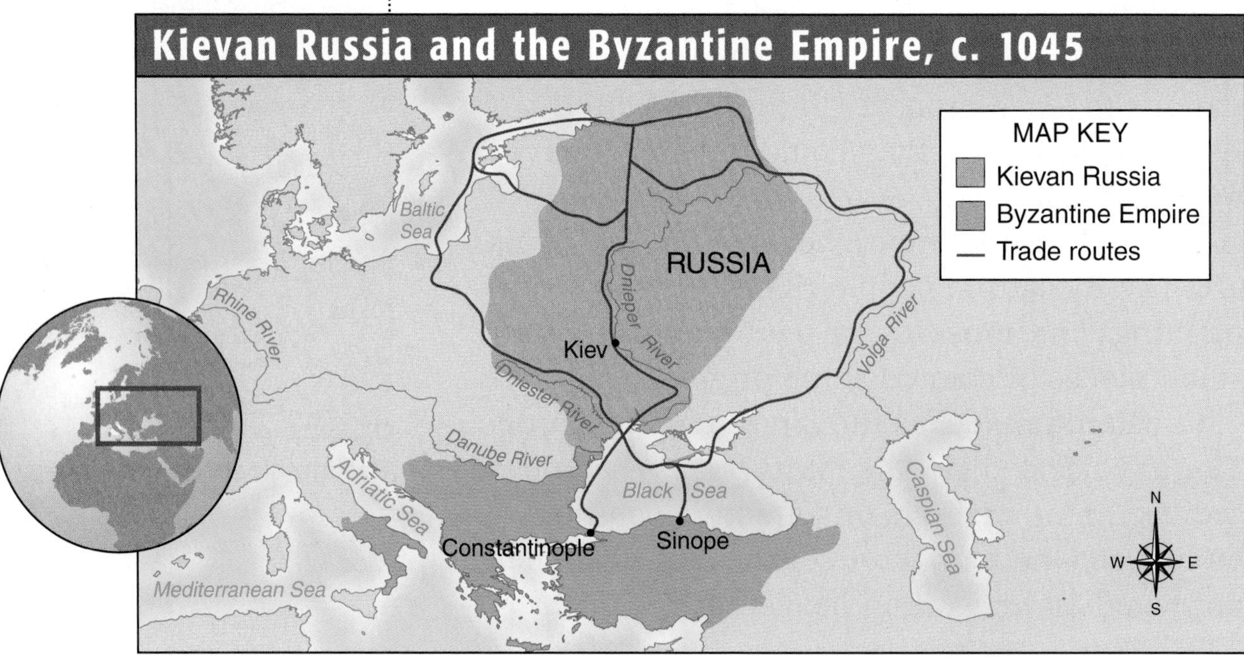

Empress Zoe (978–1050)

People **In History**

In 1028, the Byzantine emperor was dying. He had no sons. His 50-year-old daughter, Zoe, was in line to take over the throne. The emperor didn't think Zoe could successfully rule the empire. So he arranged for her to marry Romanus III.

Zoe didn't love Romanus, and Romanus didn't love Zoe. After six years, Zoe had Romanus killed. She then married the man she did love—Michael IV.

When Michael died in 1041, his nephew, Michael V, ruled with Zoe. Michael V did not want to share power with Zoe. He tried to send her to a convent. But the Byzantine people rose up against him. They brought Empress Zoe back to power. For a few months, Zoe ruled with her sister. Then she married a third husband. Together, Zoe, her sister, and her husband ruled the Byzantine Empire until Zoe's death in 1050.

Lesson 3 Review

Choose words from the list that best complete the paragraphs. One word will not be used.

Word List

Justinian
Byzantine
Orthodox
Catholic
Russian

The Western Roman Empire fell in 476. But the Eastern Roman Empire continued. It became known as the __1__ Empire. Under the rule of __2__, the empire gained back some western lands.

There was little communication between Rome and Constantinople. Church leaders argued over the use of icons and other issues. The church split in two. The church in the West became known as the __3__ Church. The church in the East became known as the __4__ Church.

Chapter 11: Using What You've Learned

Summary

- The period when western Europe was between the ancient and modern worlds is called the early Middle Ages, or "Dark Ages."
- Vikings invaded western Europe in 793. Some Vikings settled in France. Others continued to explore the North Atlantic Ocean.
- The Merovingians ruled western Europe for 275 years. The Merovingian Dynasty ended in 751 when Pepin became king of the Franks.
- Charlemagne tried to improve education and art. He also tried to spread Christianity.
- The Eastern Roman Empire became known as the Byzantine Empire. The Byzantine Empire produced beautiful churches and art.

Find Out More!

After reading Chapter 11, you're ready to go online. **Explore Zone**, **Quiz Time**, and **Amazing Facts** bring this chapter of world history alive.

Visit www.exploreSV.com and type in the chapter code **Ch11**.

Vocabulary

Number your paper from 1 to 5. Write the word or words from the list that best complete each analogy. One word will not be used.

1. Hot is to cold as _____ were to the Romans.
2. Epics were to the Greeks as _____ were to the Vikings.
3. The Code of Hammurabi was to the Babylonians as the _____ was to the Byzantines.
4. Bas-reliefs were to the Zapotecs as _____ were to the Byzantines.
5. The Catholic Church was to the Western Roman Empire as the _____ was to the Eastern Roman Empire.

Word List

mosaics
vassals
sagas
Orthodox Church
Justinian Code
barbarians

Comprehension

Number your paper from 1 to 4. Write the letter of the correct answer.

1. Who was the first king of the Merovingians?

a. Leo III **c.** Clovis
b. Charles Martel **d.** Pepin

2. Who tried to bring Europe out of the Dark Ages?

a. Empress Zoe **c.** Theodora
b. Charlemagne **d.** Romanus III

3. What did culture in the Middle Ages center around?

a. the church **c.** the theater
b. education **d.** trade

4. What city was the capital of the Byzantine Empire?

a. Normandy **c.** Rome
b. Kiev **d.** Constantinople

Critical Thinking

Fact or Opinion Number your paper from 1 to 6. For each fact, write **Fact**. Write **Opinion** for each opinion. You should find two sentences that are opinions.

1. Charles Martel defeated the Muslims at the Battle of Tours.

2. Pepin should not have given the Papal States to the pope.

3. The Vikings who settled in France were called Normans.

4. *The Song of Roland* is the best poem about Charlemagne.

5. Justinian wanted his empire to be like the Roman Empire.

6. The Byzantine people brought Empress Zoe back to power.

Writing

Write a paragraph explaining why western Europe's Middle Ages are sometimes called the Dark Ages.

LESSON 1

The Rise of Islam

New Words

bedouins
Allah
idols
hijrah
Kaaba
Qur'an
Five Pillars of Islam
prophet
fast
hajj
mosques

People and Places

Arabian Peninsula
Arabia
Mecca
Muhammad
Medina
Palestine
Syria

Before You Read

- What do some religions have in common?
- Why do people often oppose new religions?

The Arabian Peninsula, or Arabia, is in Southwest Asia. The peninsula is almost entirely desert. Some people lived in this area as **bedouins**, or nomads. Others settled in the few places with water. But for most of early history, very few people lived in Arabia.

Trade routes connected Arabia with both Africa and the rest of Asia. The Arabian city of Mecca became a trade center. The leader of Islam, Muhammad, was born in Mecca around 570.

Bedouins use camels for travel in the deserts of Arabia.

This caravan is traveling to Mecca.

The Life of Muhammad

Muhammad became a caravan manager. Meeting people along the trade routes, Muhammad probably heard the teachings of Judaism and Christianity.

Muslims believe that one day Muhammad went to a cave to pray. There, the angel Gabriel appeared. Gabriel told Muhammad he was to be the messenger of **Allah**. Gabriel also told Muhammad that there was only one God. The angel said that all people were equal. All people should share their wealth with the poor.

Map of Mecca

Muhammad started to teach this message. At first, few people listened. The people of Mecca had many gods. They did not like hearing that there was only one God. Merchants made money by selling **idols**, or statues of gods. They feared they would lose money if people believed in only one God. Some people in Mecca even wanted Muhammad killed.

A page from the Qur'an

In A.D. 622, Muhammad left Mecca. He went to the Arabian city of Medina, where people accepted him. This journey from Mecca to Medina is called the **hijrah**, which means a "journey from danger." It marks the first year of the Islamic calendar, just as the birth of Jesus marks the first year of the Christian calendar.

The people of Medina were more open to Muhammad's message. In 630, he returned to Mecca with an army. After several years of fighting, the people of Mecca accepted Islam. Muhammad went to the **Kaaba**. This was a temple where many idols were stored. He destroyed the idols. Two years later, in 632, Muhammad died.

The Beliefs of Islam

Muslims believe that Gabriel spoke to Muhammad many times. Muhammad wrote down the words of Allah as spoken through Gabriel. These writings became the **Qur'an**, or holy book of Islam.

The Qur'an states the five duties of all Muslims. These are called the **Five Pillars of Islam**. The

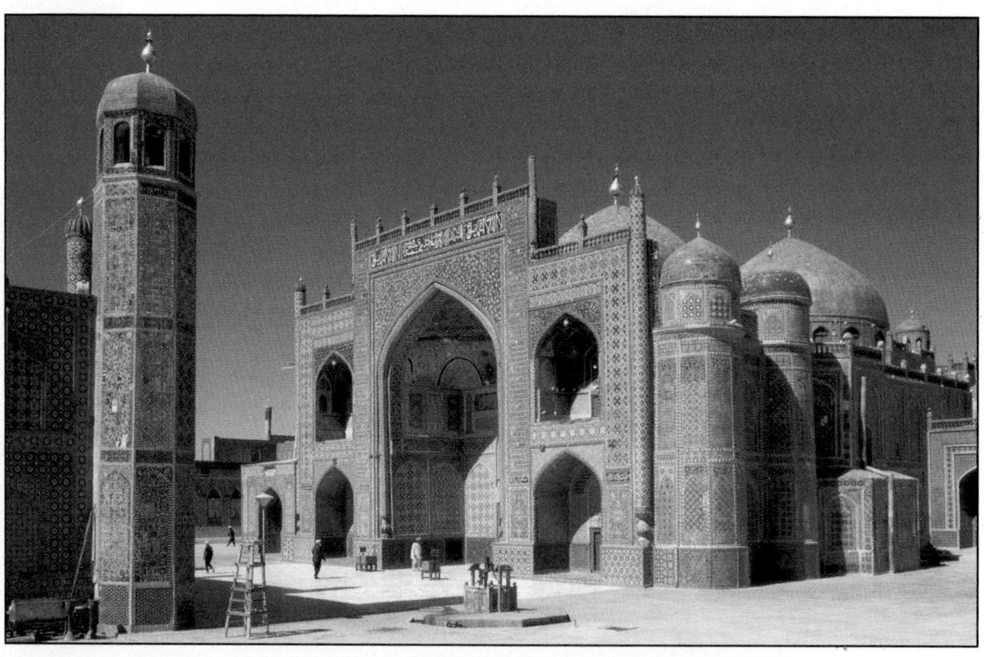

Muslims built beautiful buildings throughout Southwest Asia.

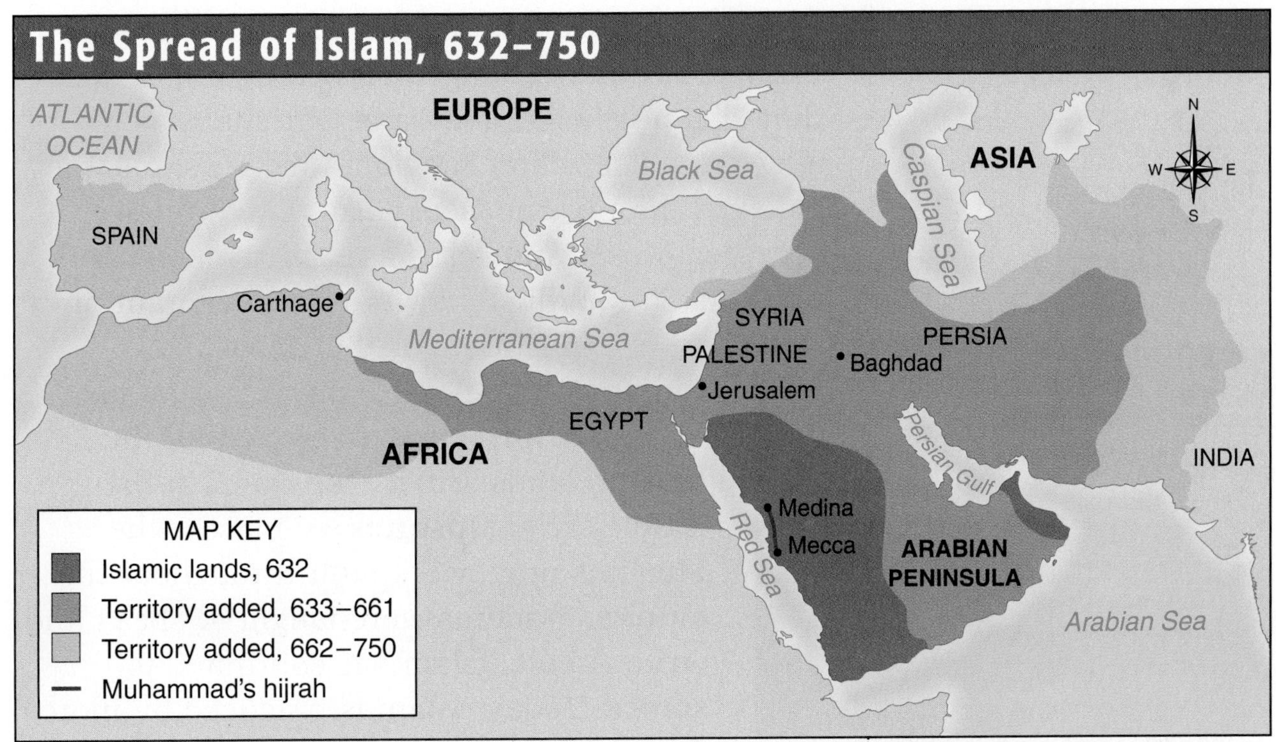

Islam began in the Arabian Peninsula around 630. Between what years did Islam spread to Palestine and Jerusalem?

first pillar is to believe there is only one God and that Muhammad is his **prophet**, or inspired teacher. The second pillar is to pray five times a day. Muslims must turn toward Mecca during prayer. Muslims in Mecca turn toward the Kaaba.

The third pillar is to help the poor. The fourth pillar is to **fast**, or not eat food for a period of time. This is done during the daylight hours of one month every year. The fifth pillar is to make a **hajj**, or trip to Mecca. The Qur'an says that Muslims should do this once during their life if at all possible.

Muslims making a hajj

The Spread of Islam

Muhammad said that Muslims had a duty to spread Islam. After Muhammad's death, Muslims spread the religion throughout Arabia. Within a few years, Muslim armies conquered Palestine, Syria, Persia, and Egypt. Muslims spread across North Africa and into Spain. They also moved into India and central Asia.

Many of the conquered people welcomed Islam. But others changed their religion because they had no choice. Jews and Christians were allowed to keep their religion. Like Muslims, they believed in only one God. Also, Muhammad accepted Moses and Jesus as earlier messengers of Allah. So the Muslims were more tolerant of Jews and Christians. But Jews and Christians did have to pay a special tax.

Muslims in Mecca face the Kaaba when they pray.

Arab culture spread throughout the Muslim lands. Cities were built in the Arabic style. **Mosques**, or places where Muslims pray, were built throughout the empire. Students were taught to speak and write Arabic. Islam has continued to spread. Today, Islam is practiced by more than a billion people around the world.

Lesson 1 Review

Choose words from the list that best complete the paragraphs. One word will not be used.

Word List

hajj
fast
Medina
Mecca
Kaaba

Muhammad was born in __1__ in Arabia. Muslims believe that an angel appeared to Muhammad and gave him a message from Allah. Some people did not agree with the message and wanted Muhammad killed. Muhammad went to __2__ in 622. That marked the first year in the Islamic calendar. Later, Muhammad destroyed the idols at the __3__ in Mecca.

The Qur'an teaches Muslims the Five Pillars of Islam. One pillar is to make a __4__ to Mecca. After Muhammad's death, Islam continued to spread. Today, Islam is practiced around the world.

LESSON 2

Empire in Southwest Asia

Before You Read

- How can religion affect government?
- Why are scientific discoveries important to civilizations?

In Chapter 7, you learned that Alexander the Great conquered the Persian Empire. After Alexander the Great died, Persia fell under the control of several different groups. The Sassanids rose to power around A.D. 200. The Sassanid Dynasty lasted 400 years. After the fall of Rome in 476, the Byzantine Empire and the Sassanid Dynasty were two of the most powerful kingdoms in the world.

This image shows a Sassanid king in battle.

New Words

treason
relic
caliph
caliphate
bazaar
converted
calligraphy
Arabic numerals

People and Places

Sassanids
Heraclius
Mu'awiyah
Damascus
Umayyads
Abbasids
Harun al-Rashid
Baghdad
Iraq

This container holds parts of the relic of the cross.

The Sassanids

The Sassanids made Zoroastrianism the official religion of Persia. To practice any other religion was **treason**.

The Sassanids attacked the Byzantine Empire. They captured Syria, Palestine, and Egypt. In 619, the Sassanids burned down a Christian church in Jerusalem. They also captured a **relic** of the cross on which, many people believe, Jesus died. That angered Heraclius, the Byzantine emperor. He raised a new army and defeated the Sassanids in 628. Heraclius won back lands, as well as the relic of the cross.

The fighting, however, weakened both sides. A few years later, Muslim Arabs from the Arabian Peninsula attacked the Sassanids. In 642, the last Sassanid king died. The Arabs also captured the Byzantine lands of Syria, Palestine, and Egypt.

The Umayyads captured lands once held by the Byzantines and the Sassanids. Which two cities on this map were ruled by both the Byzantines and the Umayyads?

The Umayyad Caliphate

In 661, Mu'awiyah became the leader of the Muslims. He was named **caliph**, or head of the Islamic communities. His rule began the

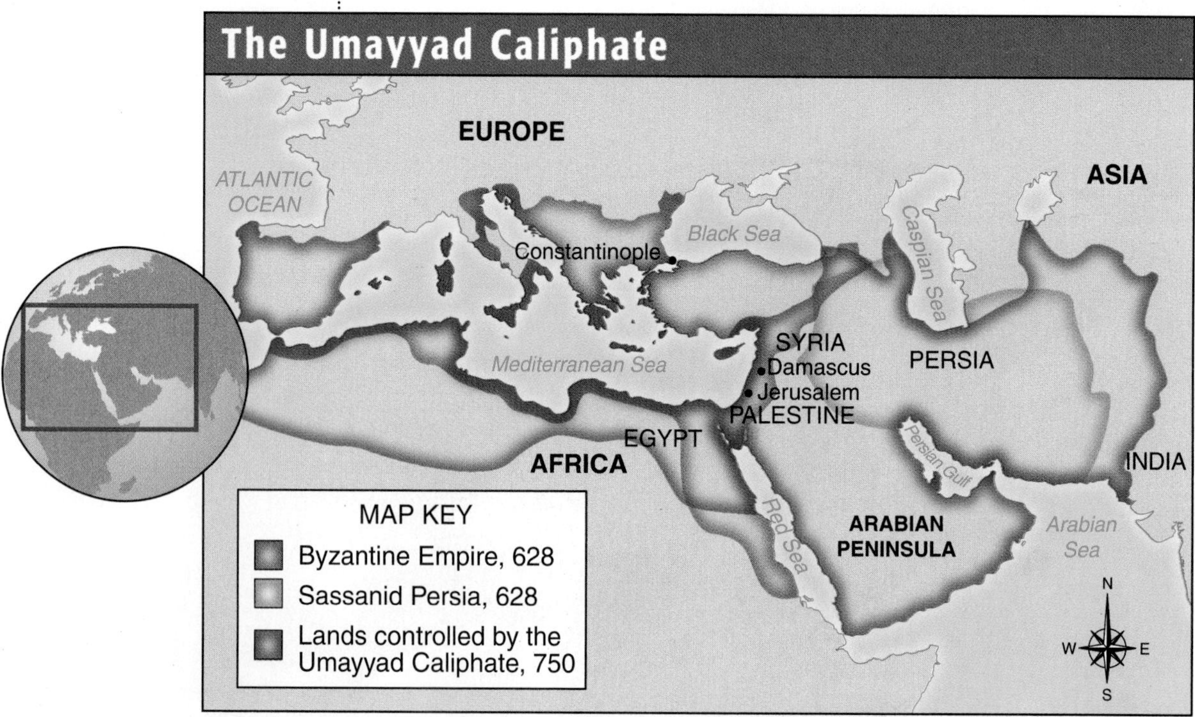

Umayyad **Caliphate**. Mu'awiyah made the Syrian city of Damascus his capital. It became a center of trade in Asia, Europe, and Africa. Merchants from all over Southwest Asia came to the **bazaar**, or market, in Damascus.

Umayyad artifact

The Umayyad Caliphate lasted less than 100 years. Arab victories continued during that period. Arabs won control of North Africa, most of Spain, Persia, and lands as far east as India. They had their only failure when they tried to capture Constantinople.

The Umayyads were poor governors. They lived a rich style of life, while the common people had nothing. The Umayyads didn't treat Muslims equally. Many non-Arabs had **converted** to Islam. But the Umayyads favored Arab Muslims. In 750, the Umayyads were replaced by the Abbasids. The Abbasids promised to treat all Muslims fairly.

The Golden Age of Harun al-Rashid

Harun al-Rashid ruled the Abbasids from 786 to 809. Charlemagne ruled the Holy Roman Empire around the same time. The two leaders admired each other. They exchanged gifts to help encourage peace. Harun al-Rashid even gave Charlemagne an elephant as a gift.

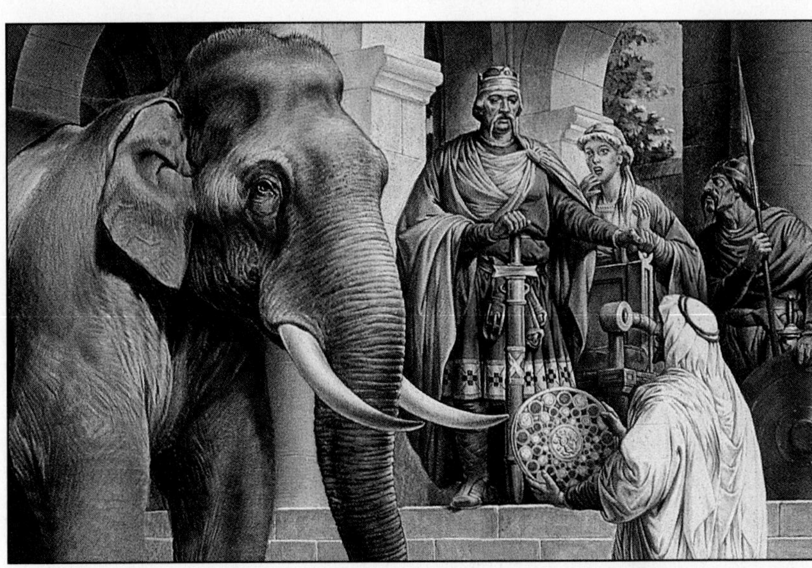
Charlemagne received an elephant from Harun al-Rashid.

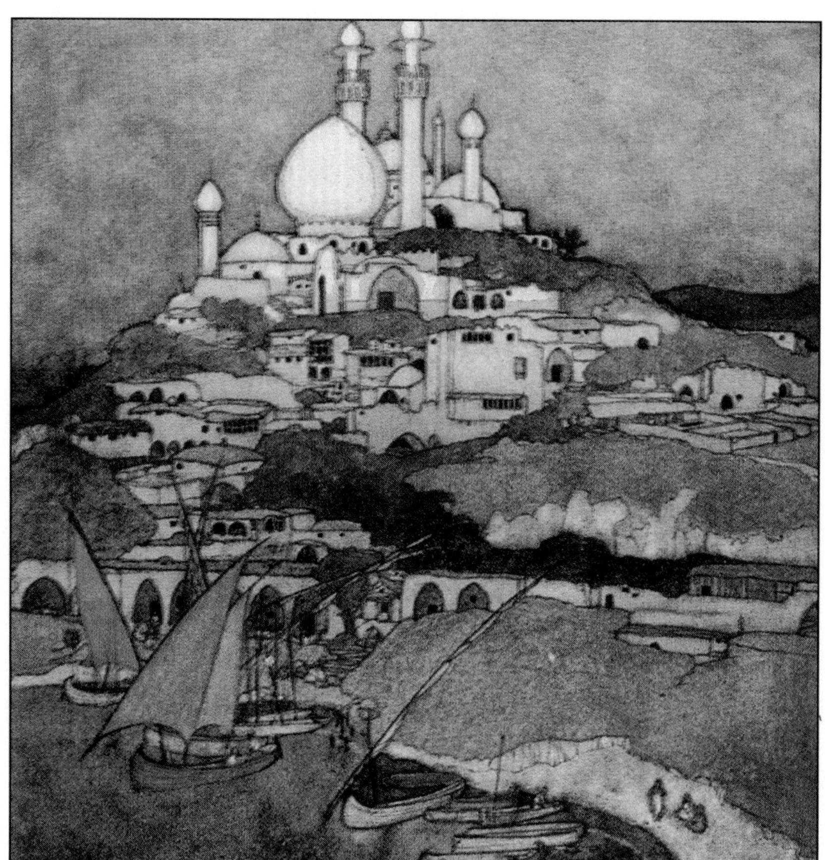

Ancient Baghdad was filled with magnificent buildings.

Harun al-Rashid's capital was the new city of Baghdad. It took four years and 100,000 workers to build the city on the banks of the Tigris River. Like Damascus before it, Baghdad soon became a center for trade. Baghdad was filled with magnificent buildings and gardens. Today, Baghdad is the capital city of Iraq.

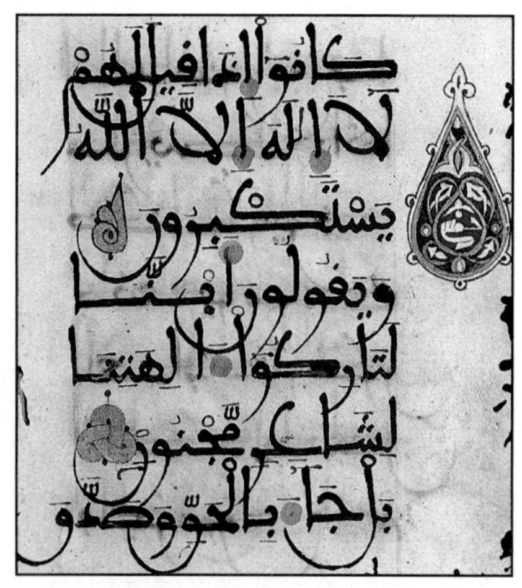

Arabic calligraphy

The Abbasid Caliphate

The Abbasid Caliphate lasted 500 years. It was a time of much development. Muslim artists used designs and beautiful writing, called **calligraphy**, to decorate books and buildings. All writing was done in Arabic, which became the language for Muslim leaders. People from conquered lands such as Egypt gave up their old languages and learned Arabic. Sharing one language helped unite all Muslims.

Baghdad had many clean hospitals, and Muslim doctors during this time were among the world's most advanced. The doctors had to pass a difficult test before they could practice medicine. Muslim doctors were the first to add sugar to medicine. The sweet taste made people more willing to take medicine. Muslim doctors showed how a disease could be passed from one person to another. Muslim doctors also wrote books on different diseases and how to treat them.

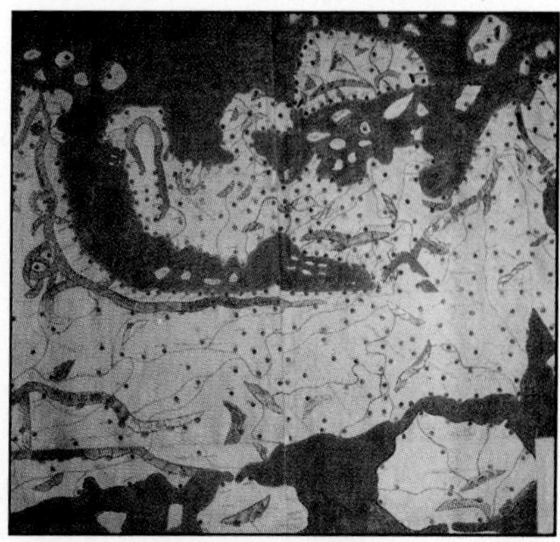
Muslim map

Muslim scientists discovered that the earth was round. They also proved that the earth was about 25,000 miles around. Muslims made some of the most correct maps of the time. They also learned the movements of the moon and planets.

From India, Muslims learned to use the numbers 1 through 9. These numbers became known as **Arabic numerals**. They took the place of Roman numerals (I, II, III, IV, and so on), which were more difficult to use.

Lesson 2 Review

Choose words from the list that best complete the paragraphs. One word will not be used.

The Byzantine Empire and the __1__ Dynasty were two of the most powerful kindoms after the fall of Rome. Arabs then took over the Sassanid Dynasty. Their leader, Mu'awiyah, became __2__ of the Umayyad Caliphate in 661. Soon, Muslims controlled land from Spain to India.

In 750, the Abbasids took over. They promised to treat all Muslims fairly. Their capital was __3__. The Abbasids used a form of writing called __4__. They made major advances in art, science, math, and medicine.

Word List

Damascus
Sassanid
Baghdad
caliph
calligraphy

Chapter 12: Using What You've Learned

Summary

- Muhammad was born in Mecca in A.D. 570. As an adult, he began teaching a new religion, Islam. Followers of Islam are called Muslims.
- Islam spread throughout North Africa, Spain, India, and central Asia.
- After the fall of Rome, the Sassanid Dynasty in Persia was one of the world's most powerful kingdoms.
- The Umayyad Caliphate began when Arab Muslims captured Sassanid Persia.
- In 750, the Abbasid rulers took control. Under the Abbasid Caliphate, Arab culture made advances in art, science, medicine, and mathematics.

Find Out More!

After reading Chapter 12, you're ready to go online. **Explore Zone**, **Quiz Time**, and **Amazing Facts** bring this chapter of world history alive.

Visit www.exploreSV.com and type in the chapter code **Ch12**.

Vocabulary

Number your paper from 1 to 6. Write the word or words from the list that best complete each sentence. One word will not be used.

1. The holy book of Islam is called the ____.
2. Places where Muslims pray are called ____.
3. Muslims believe that Muhammad is a ____, or inspired teacher.
4. The head of the Islamic communities was called a ____.
5. Muslim artists decorated books and buildings with designs and writing called ____.
6. The numbers 1 through 9 are called ____.

Word List

prophet
Arabic numerals
caliph
mosques
bazaar
Qur'an
calligraphy

Comprehension

Number your paper from 1 to 5. Write one or more sentences to answer each question below.

1. At first, why did the people of Mecca not accept Muhammad's message?
2. What are the Five Pillars of Islam?
3. How did Islam spread to other countries?
4. What did Heraclius gain when he defeated the Sassanids?
5. What were two scientific discoveries made during the Abbasid Caliphate?

Critical Thinking

Main Idea **Number your paper from 1 to 4. Write the sentence that is the main idea in each group.**

1. Some people lived in Arabia as bedouins, or nomads.
   For most of early history, very few people lived in Arabia.
   Some people settled in the few places in Arabia with water.
2. Arab culture spread throughout Muslim lands.
   Cities in the Muslim empire were built in the Arabic style.
   Students were taught to speak and write Arabic.
3. Mu'awiyah made Damascus the capital of his lands.
   Merchants from all over Southwest Asia came to the bazaar in Damascus.
   Damascus was an important city in Southwest Asia.
4. The Umayyads were poor governors.
   The Umayyad leaders were rich, while the common people had nothing.
   The Umayyads did not treat all Muslims equally.

Writing

Write a paragraph telling how the Umayyad and the Abbasid rulers of Persia were alike and how they were different.

Skill Builder: Reading a Physical Map

A **physical map** shows what the land in an area looks like. This kind of map shows the features of the land. Some features are bodies of water, mountains, hills, and deserts.

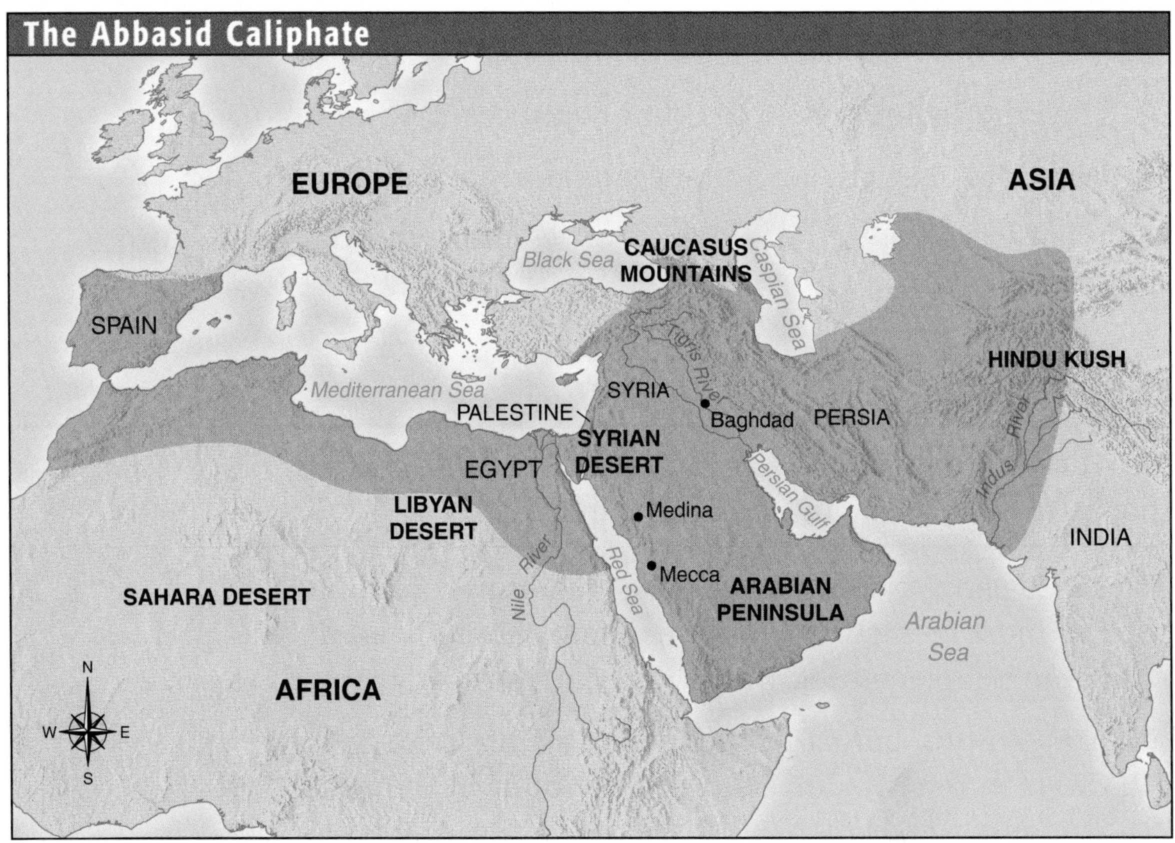

Number your paper from 1 to 5. Answer each question with a complete sentence.

1. What mountains are located in the Abbasid Caliphate?
2. What deserts are located in this empire?
3. What three bodies of water surround the Arabian Peninsula?
4. The Mediterranean Sea is what direction from the Syrian Desert?
5. Baghdad is located on what river?

LESSON 1

China Unites

Before You Read

- Why might a ruler allow people to practice different religions?
- Do art and poetry make a civilization better?

When the Han Dynasty ended in A.D. 220, China was divided into small states. For more than 350 years, China remained divided. Then, in 581, the Sui Dynasty united China once more. This dynasty didn't last long, but it left an important mark on Chinese history.

The Sui had only two emperors. Both were harsh rulers. They made people pay high taxes. They made them work hard on **public works** projects. The first ruler, Wen Ti, made the people rebuild the Great Wall of China. The second ruler, Yang, made them dig the first **Grand Canal**. The canal connected the Huang He in the North to the Yangtze River in the South. This made it easier to trade goods throughout the kingdom.

New Words

public works
Grand Canal
opera
movable type
gunpowder

People and Places

Sui
Wen Ti
Yang
Yangtze River
Tang
T'ai Tsung
Empress Wu
Li Po
Song

The Grand Canal is still used today.

Tang China, c. 900

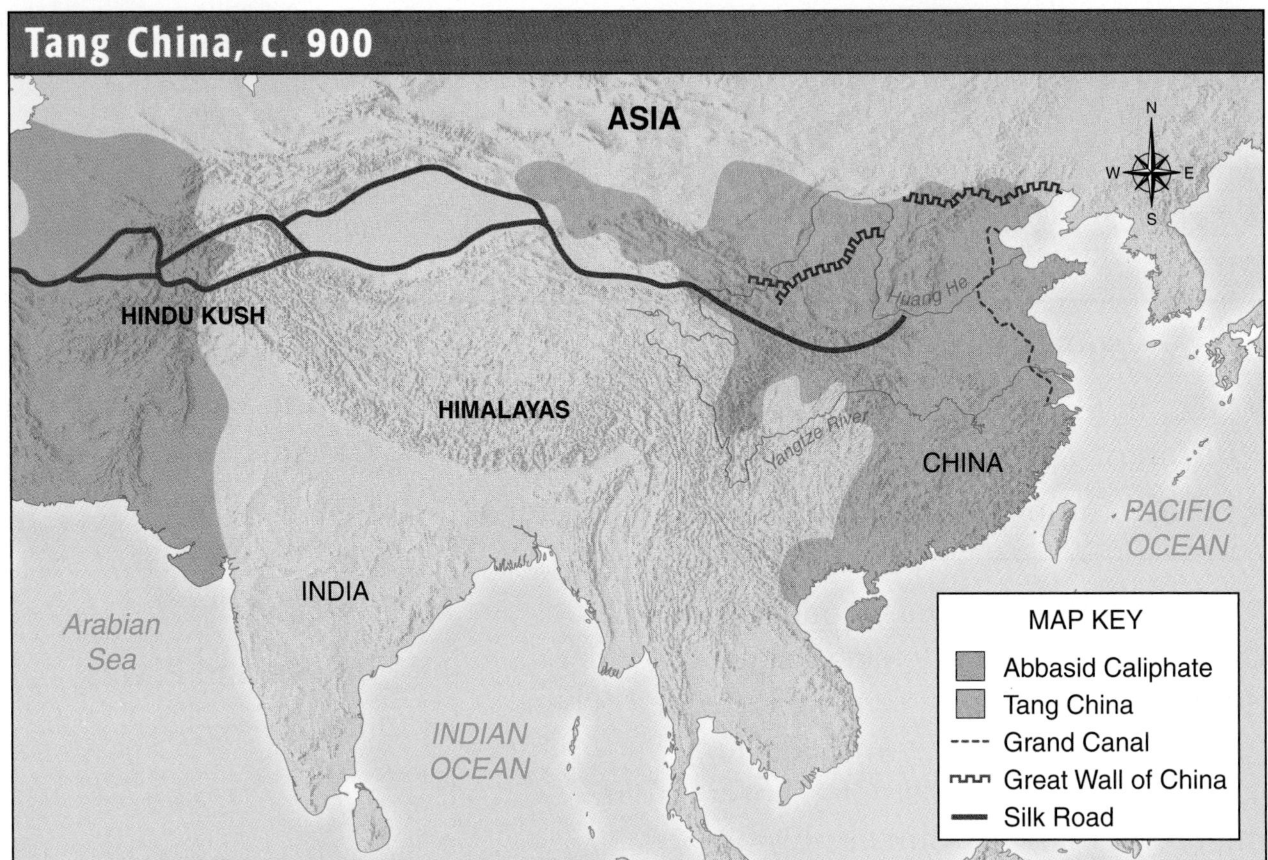

The Tang Dynasty ruled much of East Asia. What trade route connected the Tang Dynasty with the Abbasid Caliphate?

Two Tang Rulers

The Tang Dynasty replaced the Sui Dynasty in 617. The Tang kept the Mandate of Heaven for almost 300 years. China became powerful and wealthy under the Tang.

One Tang emperor, T'ai Tsung, ruled from 627 to 649. T'ai Tsung made China safe by defeating enemies. He added new lands to China. T'ai Tsung worked to make life better for the Chinese. He lowered taxes for peasants. T'ai Tsung chose strong leaders. He believed it was better to have good leaders than good laws.

T'ai Tsung accepted new ideas. Buddhism spread into China during the Tang Dynasty. Christianity, Zoroastrianism, and Islam were introduced to China through trade with the West. The local beliefs in Confucianism and Daoism also grew during the Tang Dynasty.

T'ai Tsung

One of only a few female rulers in Chinese history was the Tang ruler Empress Wu. She came to power when her husband died in 690. She ruled for 15 years. Empress Wu was a stern ruler. She had many of her enemies killed. She taxed the peasants heavily. Empress Wu also wanted to spread Buddhism throughout China. She favored Buddhism because, unlike other religions, it allowed women to be rulers.

Empress Wu

Art Under the Tang

Art and culture grew under the Tang. Poetry, for example, became popular. It was a sign of learning. Many people wrote poems. One of China's greatest poets was Li Po, who wrote about ordinary people and about nature.

Nature was a powerful force in Chinese art. One of Li Po's short poems was titled "Waterfall at Lu-Shan." It shows how Li Po felt about nature.

**"Sunlight streams on the river stones.
From high above, the river steadily plunges–
three thousand feet of sparkling water–
the Milky Way pouring down from heaven."**

Chinese music and dance also developed. The Chinese created new musical instruments. They invented new dances. People began to sing poems and often sang several poems together. This was the beginning of Chinese **opera**. Poems were often sung in houses that served tea. The custom of drinking tea grew under the Tang.

Court ladies of the Tang Dynasty

The Five Dynasties

The Tang Dynasty fell in 907. For the next 53 years, China had no central government. This time is known as the Five Dynasties. There were five small dynasties that came to power and fell during these years. Although there was no strong dynasty, China made progress in several areas.

Printing blocks

Tea became an important trading good. Also, artists improved porcelain by making it harder and thinner. Around 940, the Chinese made the first attempts to print books instead of copying them by hand. Also, the first paper money was introduced in China during this time. China had few metals to make coins. Paper money made it easier for merchants to do business.

The Song Dynasty

The Song Dynasty took control of China and ruled from 960 to 1279. The Song ruled a smaller area than the Tang did. But the Song kept tight control over the money coming in from taxes and trade. By 1000, the Song government was making three times more money than the Tang had made at the height of its dynasty.

Under the Song, the Chinese were the first to use **movable type** in printing. They cut Chinese symbols on blocks of wood. The blocks could be moved to make new sentences. Printing led to more books. More books led to more education for more people.

This painting was made during the Song Dynasty.

Another new idea was the use of **gunpowder** in weapons. The Chinese had used gunpowder to make fireworks. In weapons, they used it to destroy enemy walls.

The Chinese also developed the compass, a tool for telling direction. Like compasses today, the early Chinese compass had a needle that always pointed north. The Chinese used the compass on ships when traveling long distances.

Art continued to develop under the Song. Some artists changed from using color to using black and white. This captured a special feeling in their paintings. The trees, mountains, and rivers almost seemed to move. If there were any people in a painting, they were small, suggesting that nature is more important than people.

Painting from the Song Dynasty

Lesson 1 Review

Choose words from the list that best complete the paragraphs. One word will not be used.

Word List

compass
movable type
opera
Empress Wu
Grand Canal

Under the Sui Dynasty, the people rebuilt the Great Wall of China and built the __1__. The Tang Dynasty leader, T'ai Tsung, lowered taxes for the peasants. He believed that good government was based on good leaders. __2__ was one of only a few female rulers in Chinese history.

The Chinese made progress during the Five Dynasties, although there was no central government. They continued that progress under the Song Dynasty. They were the first to use __3__ to print books. They used gunpowder in weapons. The Chinese also invented the __4__ to help tell direction.

LESSON 2

Korea and Japan

New Words

mainland
ally
influence
archipelago
Shinto
shrines
Taika reforms
reforms

People and Places

Korean Peninsula
Japan
Korea
Koguryo
Manchuria
Paekche
Silla
Koryo
Kotoku
Nara

Before You Read

- How might living on an island affect a culture?
- Why do some cultures adopt foreign ideas?

The Korean Peninsula extends south from northeastern China. It is located between two larger neighbors—China and Japan. Around 108 B.C., the Han Dynasty of China conquered lands in Korea. Chinese culture spread to the peninsula. But three Korean kingdoms developed, which fought against the Chinese rule.

The Three Kingdoms

The Kingdom of Koguryo controlled northern Korea. It also controlled a part of Manchuria, an

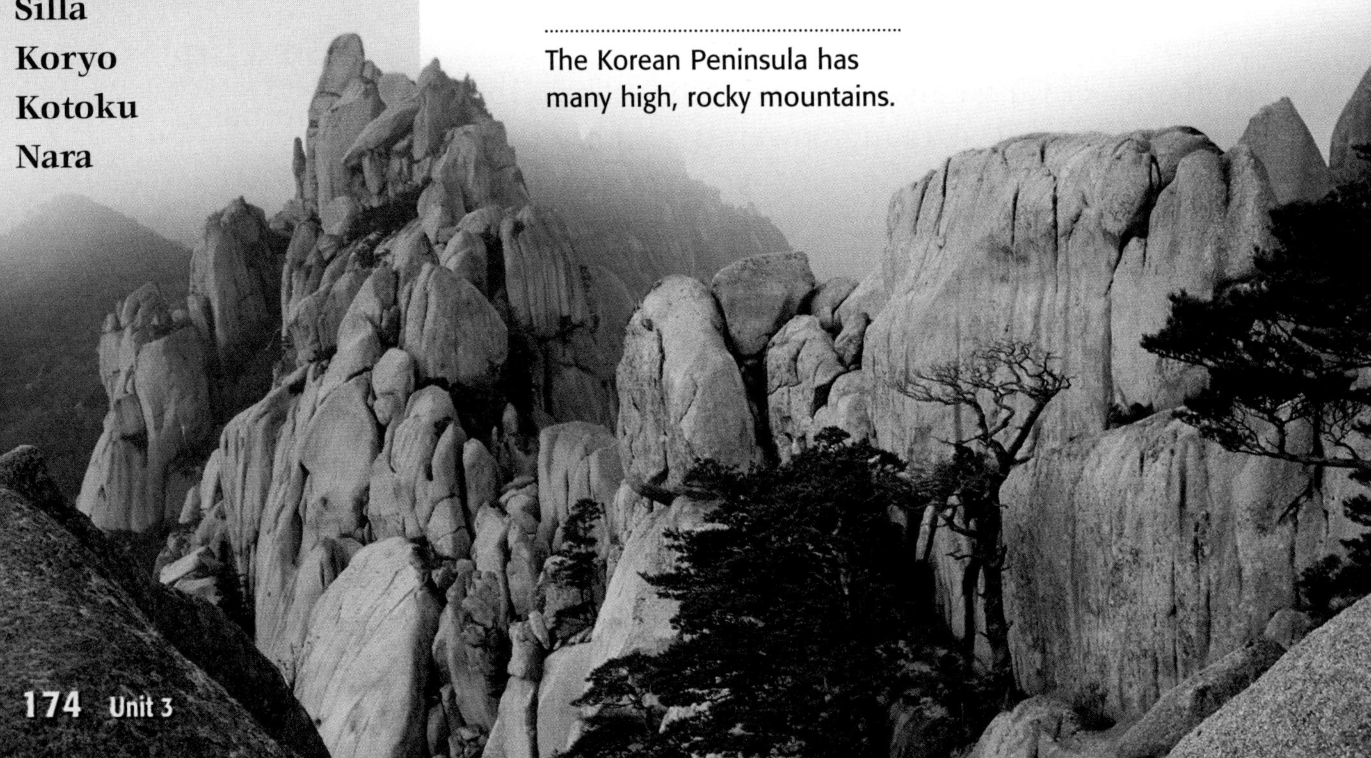

The Korean Peninsula has many high, rocky mountains.

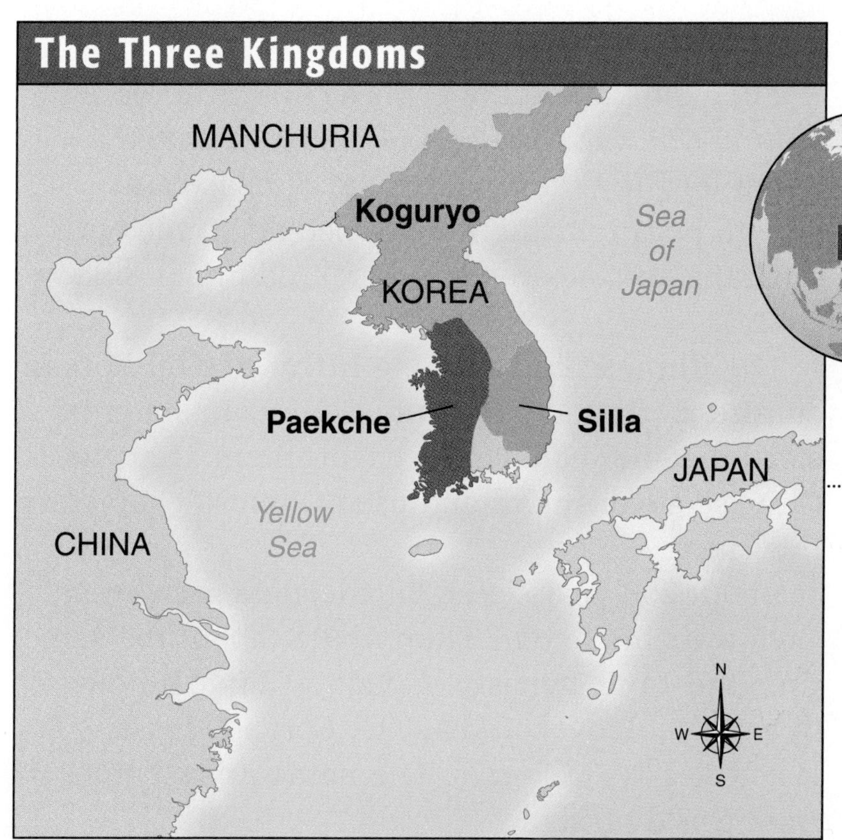

The Korean Peninsula is located between China and Japan. Which of Korea's Three Kingdoms was closest to Japan?

area on the **mainland** of Asia. The Kingdom of Paekche held the southwest corner of the peninsula. The Kingdom of Silla held the southeast corner. This time in Korean history is known as the Three Kingdoms period.

In A.D. 342, China attacked Koguryo. After several years of fighting, the Koreans kept the Chinese from taking over. Still, Chinese culture remained. The Koreans accepted Buddhism in 372. They also accepted Chinese ways in art, philosophy, and trading practices.

Around 610, the Chinese under the Sui Dynasty attacked Koguryo with a huge army. The Koreans once more held back the Chinese. Later, the Tang emperor T'ai Tsung tried three times to defeat Koguryo. Each time he failed.

Then in 668, the Chinese made the Kingdom of Silla an **ally**, or wartime friend. Silla joined with the Chinese in an attack on Koguryo and Paekche. Koguryo and Paekche were caught between the two armies and were defeated.

Earrings from Korea's Three Kingdoms period

United Under Silla

Then Silla drove the Chinese out of Korea. By around 670, the Kingdom of Silla had united Korea for the first time. A time of peace and growth began for the Korean people. Trade with the Tang and Japan even increased under Silla control.

The Chinese had a strong **influence** on Korean culture. Both Buddhism and Confucianism grew steadily. Silla modeled its government after the Chinese government and used Chinese characters in writing.

Bronze dragon from early Koryo Dynasty

About 200 years later, Silla leaders grew weak. Civil wars broke out. Then in 918, about the same time the Tang Dynasty ended in China, a new dynasty took over Korea. The Koryo Dynasty lasted nearly 500 years. The name *Korea* comes from this dynasty.

Early Japan

Japan is east of Korea. It is an **archipelago**, or chain of islands. It has more than 3,000 islands. Most are small, but a few are very large. In its early history, Japan was protected by the sea. No foreign army could invade and conquer it.

We know little about the early history of Japan. Scientists have found no written records before the fifth century A.D. Koreans came to Japan at that time. They brought Chinese writing with them. The Japanese then used Chinese characters to write their own language.

The Japanese adopted many other parts of Chinese culture. They studied Chinese art and wore Chinese clothing. They used Chinese ideas about government and copied the Chinese calendar. In 552, Buddhism was introduced into Japan. Many Japanese quickly accepted Buddhism, although they had their own native religion, **Shinto**. The people had no trouble practicing both religions.

Coast of Japan

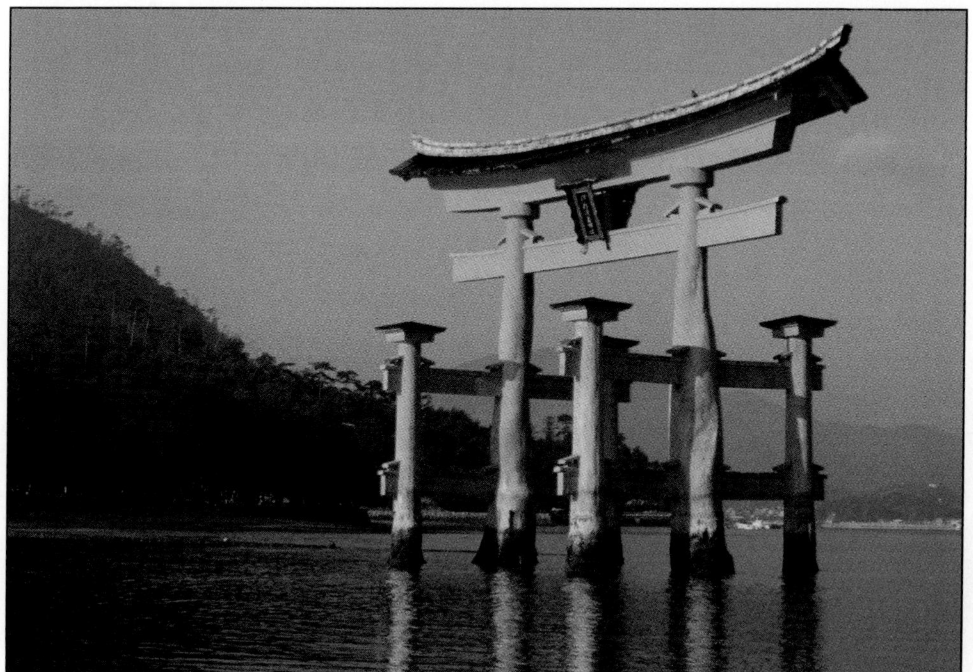

This gate stands in front of a modern Shinto shrine.

The Shinto Religion

The word *Shinto* means "the way of the gods." No one knows who started the religion. Shinto has no holy books like the Torah, the Bible, or the Qur'an.

Early Shinto **shrines** were plain buildings made from wood. They were built to honor a part of nature, such as a waterfall, some trees, or a large rock. Most Shinto gods come from nature. The most important is the sun goddess. The Japanese thought that all their emperors were related to the sun goddess. The belief that the emperor was a god lasted until the mid-1900s.

Statue of an ancient Japanese warrior

Changes in Government

For a long time, Japan had no central government. It was divided into small states run by local clans. The Japanese did have an emperor. Although thought of as a god, the emperor was not a true leader of the government. Then, in 645, the Emperor Kotoku announced the **Taika reforms**. These **reforms** changed government in Japan.

Confucian teachers wrote the reforms. Confucianism taught that a strong central government was important. The teachers used the Tang Dynasty as a model for the reforms.

Buddhist temple in Nara, Japan

The Taika reforms made the emperor the true ruler of Japan. The power of the clan leaders was limited. The emperor ruled by the Mandate of Heaven and had total power. Unlike the Chinese emperor, however, a Japanese emperor could not lose the Mandate of Heaven.

With the Taika reforms, a central government was formed. All land came under the control of the emperor. In 710, the Japanese built a new capital at Nara. Nara looked like a small Chinese city. It had Buddhist temples and Chinese art. In time, the Japanese changed the Chinese ideas into a culture of their own.

Lesson 2 Review

Choose words from the list that best complete the paragraphs. One word will not be used.

Word List

Koguryo
Silla
Shinto
ally
Taika reforms

The Koreans came under Chinese rule during the Han Dynasty. Then three kingdoms developed. Two of these kingdoms, __1__ and Paekche, fell when both China and Silla attacked. Then __2__ fought China and won control of Korea for more than 200 years.

Japan is an archipelago. The native religion of Japan was __3__. In 645, Emperor Kotoku began the __4__, which created a strong central government in Japan. The Japanese believed their emperors were gods. The emperors could not lose the Mandate of Heaven.

LESSON 3

Southeast Asia

Before You Read

- How did China influence its neighbors?
- What might neighboring lands like and dislike about China?

China was so large and powerful that it influenced all of its neighbors. China's neighbors wanted to learn about Chinese inventions. They liked Chinese culture and art. They also liked Chinese writing and laws. But they did not want the Chinese to control their lives. That was why the Koreans fought the Chinese. It was also why Vietnam, China's southern neighbor, spent around 1,000 years fighting China.

New Words

delta
guerrilla tactics
location

People and Places

Vietnam
Red River Delta
Annam
Trung Trac
Trung Nhi
Indonesia
Sriwijaya
Sumatra
Strait of Melaka
Borobudur
Java
Prambanan

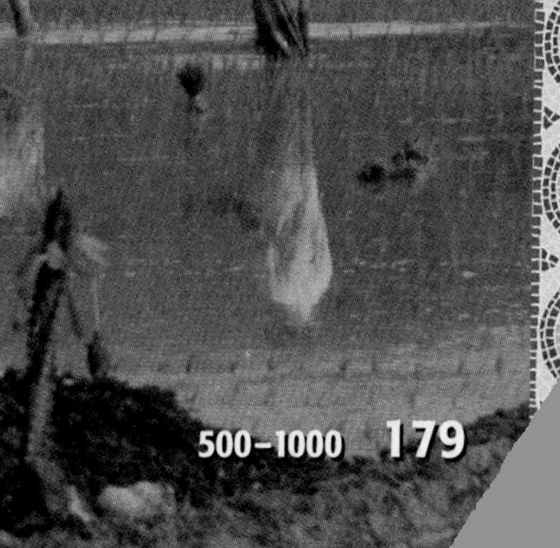

Vietnamese farmers plant rice in wet fields.

Early Vietnamese History

More than 2,000 years ago, the Vietnamese grew rice in the rich soil of the Red River **Delta**. In 111 B.C., the Han army of China took over lands in Vietnam. At that time the land was called Annam. At first, the Chinese were kind rulers, allowing the local people to keep their customs. But then China began taxing the Vietnamese people and putting them to work for China. The Vietnamese didn't like this. They wanted to rule themselves.

In A.D. 40, the Vietnamese fought for their independence. Trung Trac and her sister Trung Nhi led the fight. Their armies defeated the Chinese, and they ruled as queens for three years. But stronger armies came back to conquer Vietnam. The Trung sisters drowned themselves rather than let the Chinese capture them. The Trung sisters became great heroes to the Vietnamese. They are still a symbol that Vietnam is free from foreign rule.

Vietnamese statue of a Hindu god

The Trung sisters led a fight for Vietnamese independence in A.D. 40.

The Vietnamese continued to fight against China. Vietnam finally won its freedom in A.D. 938. The Vietnamese used **guerrilla tactics**. They hid in jungles. They made surprise attacks at night. Then they slipped back into the jungle.

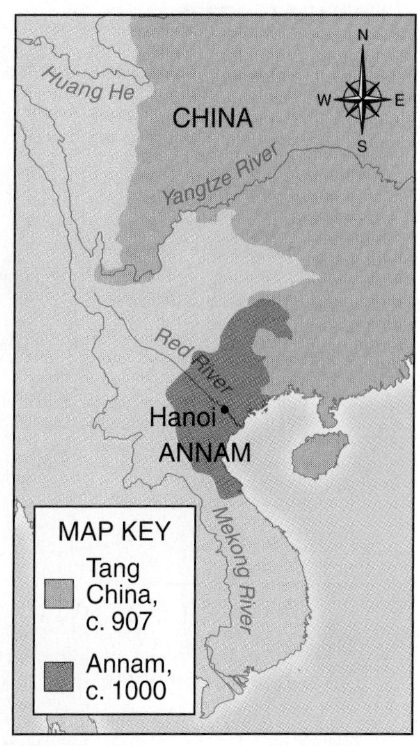

Annam

Chinese Influence in Vietnam

The Chinese influenced the Vietnamese people and culture. The Chinese had roads, harbors, and waterways built in Vietnam. Every year, peasants were forced to give several days of free work to the government on these projects.

The Chinese trained a few Vietnamese as local officials. The Chinese taught the officials how to use the examination system. They shared the ideas of Confucius. They shared the Chinese language with the officials.

The Chinese also brought Buddhism to Vietnam. As in Japan, many Vietnamese began practicing Buddhism along with their own beliefs.

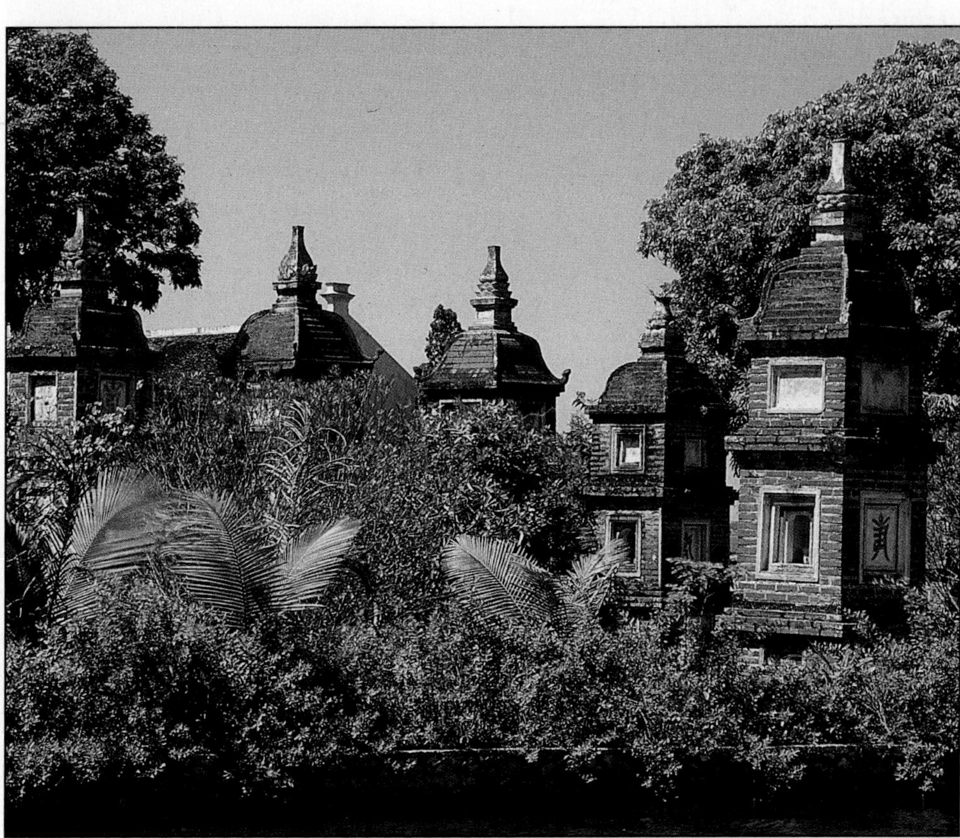
This Buddhist temple was built in Vietnam in the 500s.

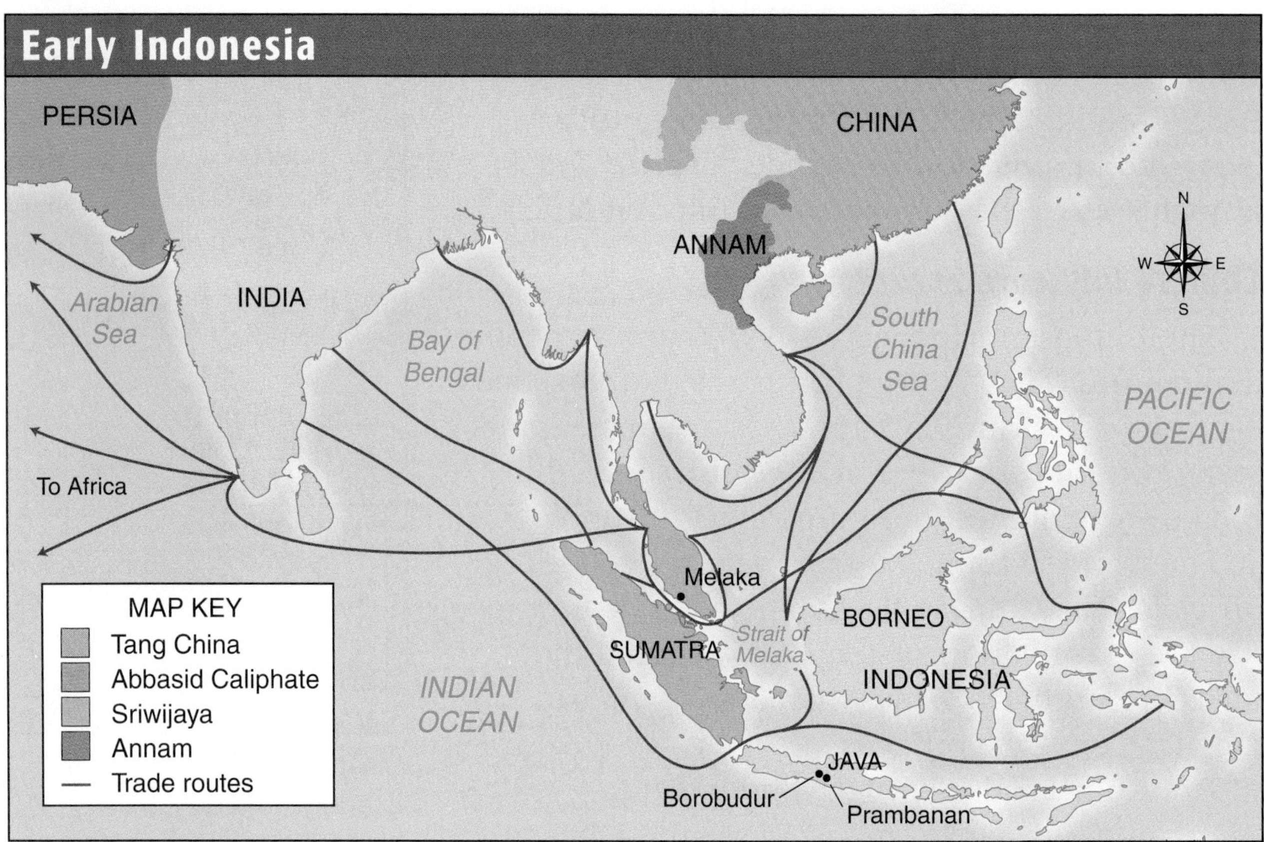

Valuable trade routes ran through the Strait of Melaka. Which kingdom controlled this strait?

Early History of Indonesia

Indonesia is a vast archipelago. Its more than 13,000 islands stretch 3,000 miles from the Indian Ocean to the Pacific Ocean. Long ago, traders from all parts of Asia came to Indonesia for its spices. These spices were used to flavor food. They also were used to make medicines.

One early Indonesian kingdom was Sriwijaya. It began in the seventh century on the island of Sumatra. Sriwijaya grew strong because of its **location**. It controlled the Strait of Melaka. Traders used this narrow waterway whenever they sailed from Arabia, Persia, or India to China.

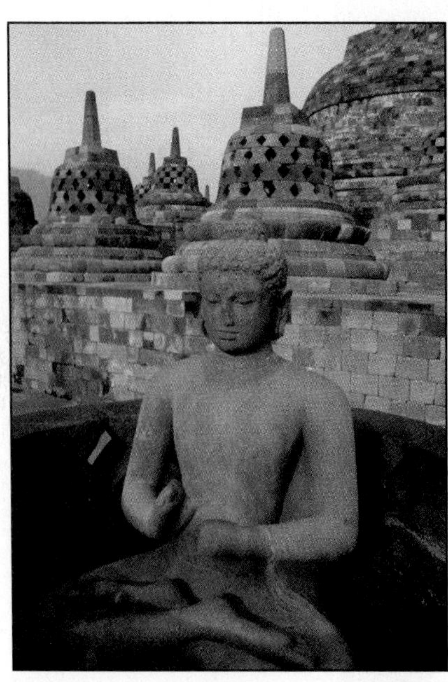

Statue at Borobudur

Religion in Indonesia

Trading brought many different cultures to Indonesia. Buddhism and Hinduism came from China and India. Around A.D. 800, Buddhist Indonesians built the monument called

Borobudur on the island of Java. Borobudur is the largest Buddhist monument in the world. Carvings on its eight levels show the Eightfold Path to enlightenment.

About the same time, Hindu Indonesians also built great temples on the island of Java. One temple was located on the plains of Prambanan. It was built to honor the god Shiva and stood 152 feet tall.

Both Buddhism and Hinduism spread throughout Indonesia. Like other people in Southeast Asia, the Indonesians successfully blended the new religions with their native beliefs.

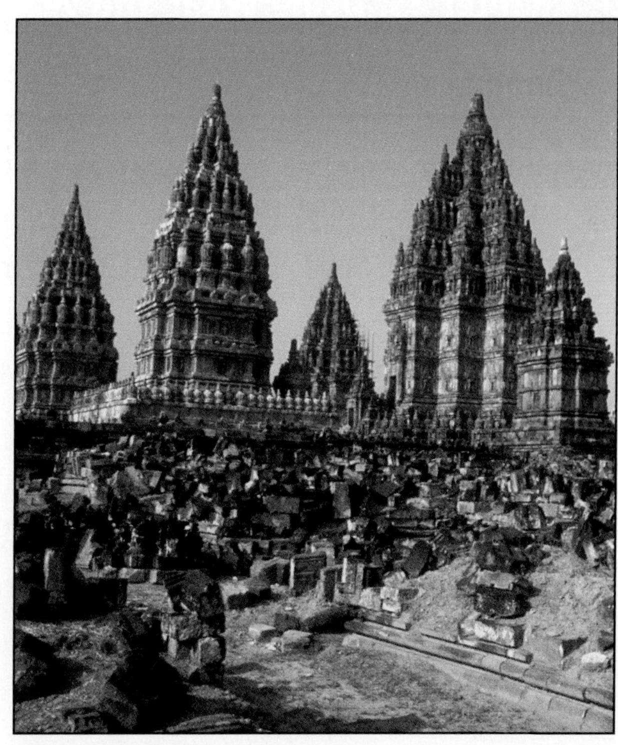

Hindu temple at Prambanan

Lesson 3 Review

Choose words from the list that best complete the paragraphs. One word will not be used.

The Vietnamese fought against China for 1,000 years. The __1__ sisters defeated the Chinese for a short time. The Vietnamese kept fighting. They used __2__ against the Chinese. Vietnam finally won its freedom in 938.

Many traders came to the islands of Indonesia for its spices. One early Indonesian kingdom was __3__. Its location gave Indonesia contact with traders from Arabia, Persia, India, and China. Trading brought different cultures to Indonesia. Hinduism and Buddhism spread. The Buddhist monument __4__ has eight levels. It is the largest Buddhist monument in the world.

Word List

guerrilla tactics
Melaka
Sriwijaya
Borobudur
Trung

Chapter 13: Using What You've Learned

Summary

- The Sui Dynasty united China. China became powerful under the next dynasty, the Tang.
- Under the Song Dynasty, the Chinese invented many things.
- The Kingdom of Silla drove the Chinese out of Korea in 670.
- The first religion of Japan was Shinto. Shinto shrines were built to honor nature.
- Vietnam, or Annam, fought for around 1,000 years against China's rule.
- Trade brought many cultures to Indonesia.

Find Out More!

After reading Chapter 13, you're ready to go online. **Explore Zone, Quiz Time,** and **Amazing Facts** bring this chapter of world history alive.

Visit www.exploreSV.com and type in the chapter code **Ch13**.

Vocabulary

Number your paper from 1 to 5. Write the letter of the correct answer.

1. The Chinese developed the _____, a tool for telling direction.

a. compass **b.** opera **c.** porcelain **d.** movable type

2. In 668, the Chinese made Silla an _____, or wartime friend.

a. icon **b.** idol **c.** ally **d.** artifact

3. Japan is a chain of islands called an _____.

a. empire **b.** archipelago **c.** avenue **d.** aqueduct

4. The _____ changed government in Japan.

a. Grand Canal **b.** Trung sisters **c.** Empress Wu **d.** Taika reforms

5. The Vietnamese fought against the Chinese by using _____.

a. deltas **b.** bedouins **c.** guerrilla tactics **d.** public works

Comprehension

Number your paper from 1 to 5. Write the word or words from the list that best complete the paragraph. One word will not be used.

The __1__ Dynasty had only two emperors. These emperors made the Chinese people work hard on __2__, such as the Great Wall and the Grand Canal. In 617, the __3__ Dynasty came to power. This dynasty kept the Mandate of Heaven for almost 300 years. Then in 960, the __4__ Dynasty took control of China. During this dynasty, the Chinese started using __5__ in weapons.

Word List

public works
movable type
Sui
gunpowder
Song
Tang

Critical Thinking

Categories Number your paper from 1 to 5. Read the words in each group below. Think about how they are alike. Write the best title for each group.

Korea Indonesia China Vietnam Japan

1. built the Grand Canal
   first to use movable type
   first to use paper money
2. Kingdom of Koguryo
   Kingdom of Paekche
   Kingdom of Silla
3. Shinto religion
   small states run by local clans
   Taika reforms
4. Red River Delta
   Annam
   Trung sisters
5. spices
   island of Sumatra
   Borobudur

Writing

Nature was a popular subject for poetry during the Tang Dynasty. Write your own short poem about nature.

LESSON 1

Kingdom of Ghana

New Words

Sahel
evaporate
monopoly
jihad

People and Places

Soninke
Senegal River
Niger River
Ghana
Kumbi
Al-Bakir
Wangara
Almoravids

Before Your Read

- Why might a desert make trade difficult?
- How might a kingdom's location bring it wealth?

There are no written histories from the early West African civilizations. Instead of writing, West Africans used stories and songs to pass their history from one generation to the next. Arab travelers reached West Africa in the eighth century. They were the first to write about people in West Africa.

The Camel and the Desert

The Sahara Desert stretches across North Africa. It is so large, so dry, and so hot that traveling across it was nearly impossible. In ancient times, a few traders from Egypt made the

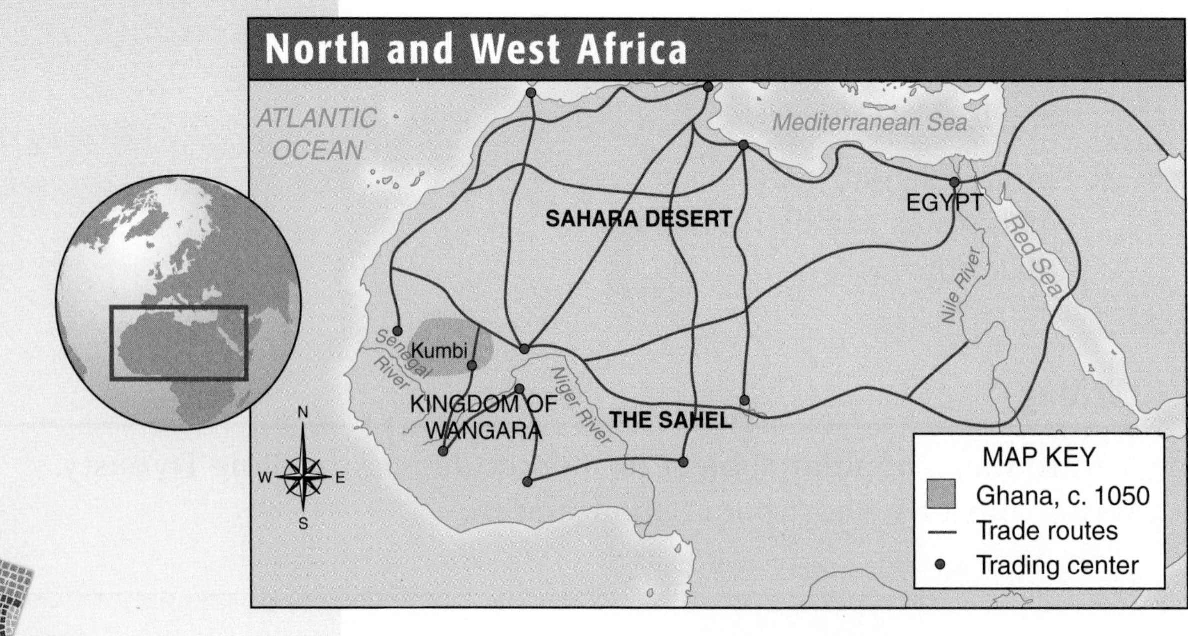

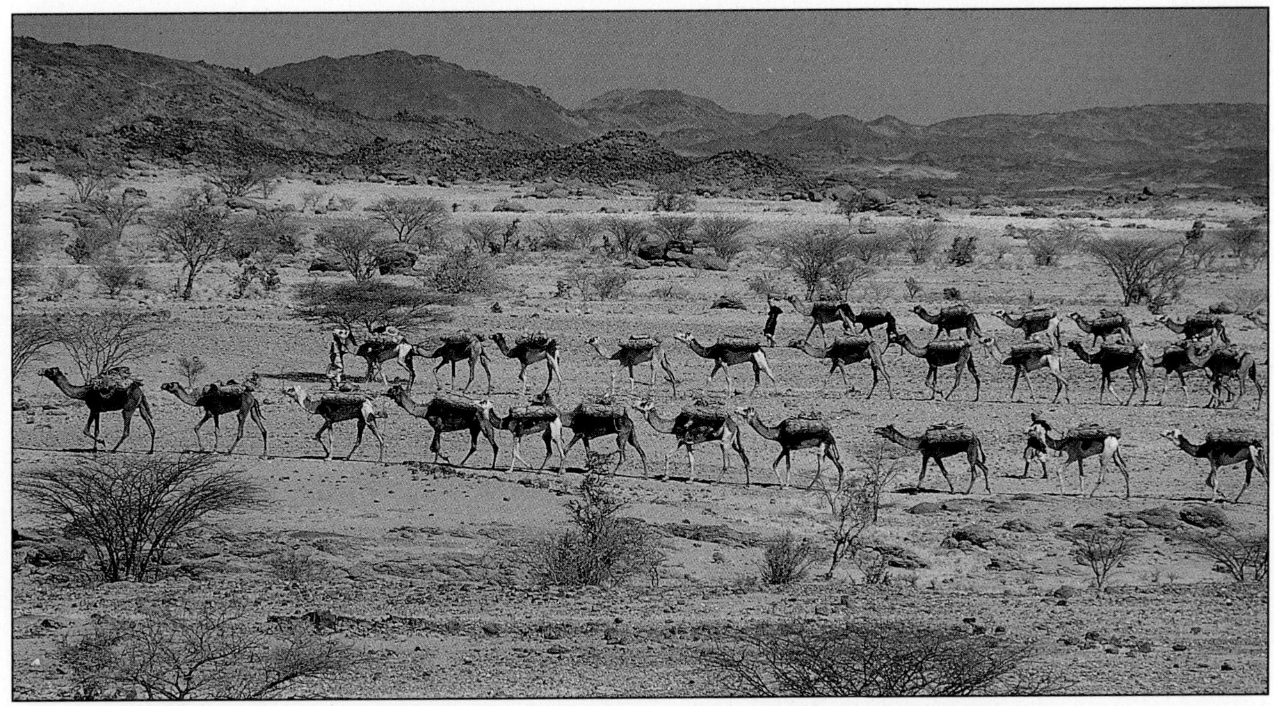

After crossing the Sahara Desert, traders came to the dry grasslands of the Sahel.

trip to West Africa. They brought back gold, ivory, and other valuable goods. But the trip was too long and hard to make it a regular trade route.

Around 750, traders from North Africa began to use camels to cross the Sahara Desert. The camels could carry heavy loads a long distance. They could walk over rough sand easily. The use of camels brought great changes to the **Sahel**, the region south of the Sahara Desert. The Sahel was a hot region of dry grasslands. It became an important trading area for goods going across the Sahara Desert.

The Kingdom of Ghana

Around 400, people called the Soninke developed a kingdom between the Senegal River and the Niger River. By 700, the Soninke had taken over much of the West African Sahel. The leaders of the Soninke were called *Ghana*, which means "war chief." Later, their kingdom became known as Ghana. The Soninke set up a capital at Kumbi, a city on the edge of the Sahara Desert.

The kings of Ghana came from the female side of the family. When a king died, his son was not the next king. Instead, the son of the king's sister took over the throne.

The Kingdom of Ghana reached its greatest power around 1000. The Muslim traveler Al-Bakir wrote a book in 1067 called *Glimpses of Ghana*. He was greatly impressed by Ghana.

Voices In History

"[The king] is the master of a large empire . . . . The king of Ghana can put two hundred thousand warriors in the field . . . . [He is guarded by ten soldiers] holding shields and gold-mounted swords . . . . On his right hand are the sons of the princes . . . with gold [braided] into their hair."

West African Trade

Ghana's location made it a perfect center for trade. The traders coming from North Africa and the Mediterranean Sea wanted gold. Gold was plentiful in a kingdom south of Ghana called Wangara. The people of Wangara needed salt,

salt is still gathered by digging holes and letting the water evaporate.

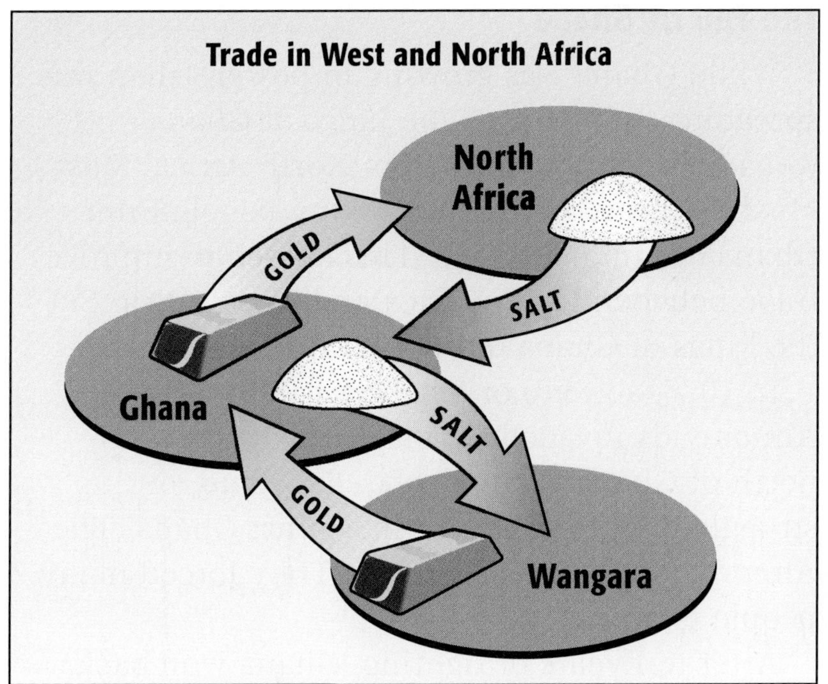

which was gathered in North Africa. The Arabs of North Africa gathered salt by digging holes in the ground where there was salt. They filled the holes with water. Then they let the water **evaporate**, or dry up. A ring of salt was left behind. After doing this many times, a solid block of salt was created.

Along with salt, Arabs brought metals, cloth, and weapons to Ghana. In exchange, the Arabs got gold, ivory, nuts, animal skins, and slaves. The slaves worked in the homes of rich Arabs.

Ghana's location between Wangara and North Africa gave Ghana a **monopoly** over gold trade. The king owned all the gold. He could decide when to sell and when to wait for a better price.

The king of Ghana made money by taxing each load of goods coming into Ghana or going out. In addition, the Arabs and the people of Wangara paid a tribute to the king of Ghana. The king used the tax money to raise a huge army. The army kept West Africa peaceful. It also kept the trade routes safe.

The Fall of Ghana

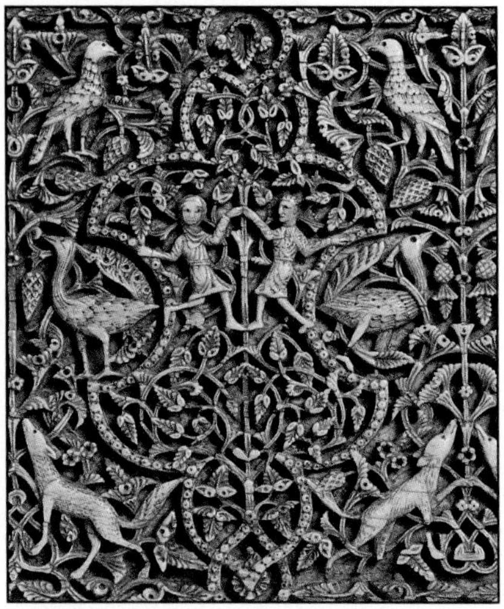

While Ghana was growing in power, Islam was spreading into Africa. The kings of Ghana welcomed the Muslims from North Africa. Most Muslims came as teachers. Many people from Ghana became Muslims. This helped to improve trade between North Africa and West Africa. But the kings of Ghana did not become Muslims.

In 1075, a group of Muslims called the Almoravids invaded Ghana. They came from north of Ghana. They declared a **jihad**, or struggle to protect the faith, against Ghana. The Almoravids destroyed Kumbi. They forced many people to accept Islam.

After ten years of fighting, Ghana won back its land. But the power of the king was broken. Ghana never gained back its power.

Muslim art

Lesson 1 Review

Choose words from the list that best complete the paragraphs. One word will not be used.

Word List

Wangara
Sahara
monopoly
jihad
Sahel

Around 750, traders began to use camels to cross the __1__ Desert. Camels allowed them to carry heavy loads a long distance. The use of camels brought changes to the region south of the desert called the __2__.

Ghana began around 400. Ghana got gold from a kingdom south of Ghana. From the North Africans, Ghana got salt. The kings of Ghana grew rich by taxing all goods passing through the kingdom. Ghana had a __3__ on the gold trade. Muslims from the North declared a __4__ on Ghana in 1075.

LESSON 2

The Bantu Migrations

Before You Read

- What causes groups to move to new areas?
- What can one culture share with another culture?

A little more than 2,000 years ago, many people from West Africa began to move. They headed south and east. They traveled to the rain forests of the Congo River. They also traveled to the **highlands** of East Africa.

The mass movement of these people is called the **Bantu migrations**. The West Africans spoke Bantu languages but left no written history. It has been difficult for scientists to learn why and how the West Africans moved.

New Words

highlands
Bantu migrations
tones
Swahili
overpopulation
elders

People and Places

Congo River

West Africans traveled to the highlands of East Africa.

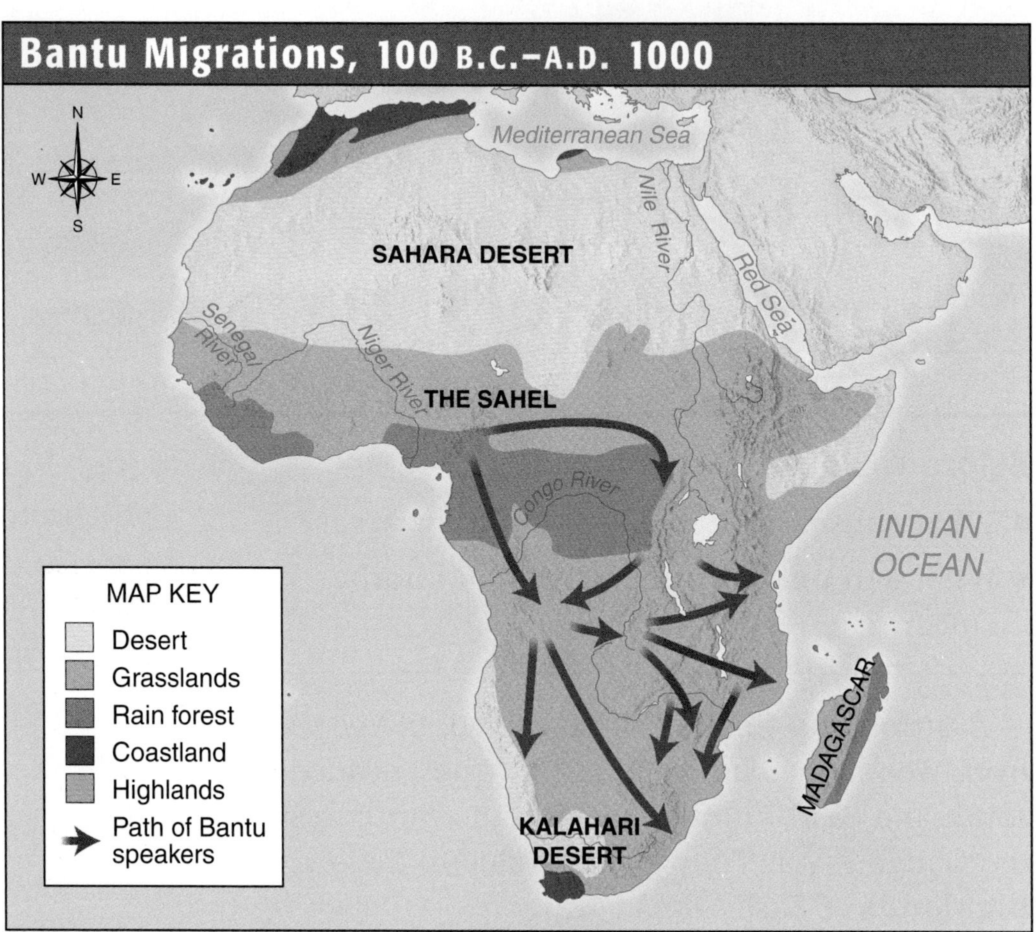

The Bantu people traveled over many different types of land. What type of land was around the northern part of the Congo River?

The Bantu Languages

As the West Africans moved, they met other African groups. Some of these people adopted the Bantu languages. Others mixed Bantu with their own language. Bantu spread easily. Today, hundreds of languages in Africa have Bantu words. The word *Bantu*, which means "the people," is in nearly all modern African languages.

Many Africans today speak in the same way the first West Africans spoke. They use **tones** to give a word its meaning. That means one word can have several meanings, depending on how the word is spoken. If a word is spoken with a high voice, it has one meaning. If it is spoken with a low voice, it has a different meaning. The only major Bantu language that does not use tones is **Swahili**.

Causes for the Bantu Migrations

The Bantu migrations took place over a very long period of time—from about 100 B.C. to A.D. 1000. No one really knows why the West Africans left their homes. The reasons probably varied with different groups in different times.

Some West Africans might have left because there were too many people in their own area. Most West Africans at that time were farmers or herders. They needed open land to grow crops or raise animals. **Overpopulation** might have forced them to seek new lands. Drought or war also might have forced the West Africans to move.

A modern Bantu person from South Africa

How They Moved

The Bantu migrations did not happen all at once. Most people believe the West Africans traveled as families or clans. Some families may have left hundreds of years after another family. Families traveled over the deserts, grasslands, and rain forests of Africa.

The Bantu people lived in huts made of dried grass.

African making iron tools

The West Africans were highly skilled and had strong iron tools. They had learned how to use iron long before many other people. They had plows that could easily prepare new lands for farming. As they moved, they could farm and find food rather easily.

Some West Africans went farther and faster than others. The herders, for example, could keep moving while their animals grazed along the way. It was easier for them to leave an old spot and move to a new one. Farmers had to wait to harvest their crops before they could move.

Southern Africa and Eastern Africa

The West Africans shared more than their language with the people of southern and eastern Africa. They also shared their knowledge. They taught the people in other areas how to use iron. They also taught them how to plant crops such as yams and bananas.

The people of southern and eastern Africa learned new ways of farming from the West Africans.

More food led to an increase in population. More and more villages developed in southern and eastern Africa. Some villages joined together to form larger communities. Trade became more important.

As people settled in larger communities, they needed a government. Some communities grew and became states under the rule of a king. Others organized their villages under the leadership of a chief. Still others were led by a group of **elders**.

The Bantu migrations lasted more than 1,000 years. They changed southern and eastern Africa forever. They changed the languages people spoke and the tools people used.

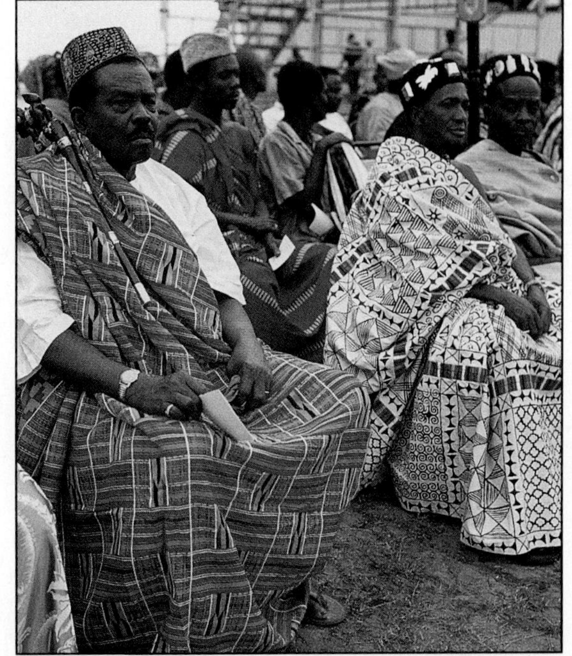

African elders

Lesson 2 Review

Choose words from the list that best complete the paragraphs. One word will not be used.

During the Bantu migrations, many people moved away from West Africa. The Bantu languages of West Africa spread throughout the continent. In most Bantu languages, the meaning of a word depends on its __1__. One of the reasons for the migrations might have been __2__.

The West Africans knew how to use __3__. They shared their language and knowledge with the local people. The Bantu migrations led to more organized communities. Older people called __4__ ruled some villages.

Word List

iron
overpopulation
elders
highlands
tone

Chapter 14: Using What You've Learned

Summary

- Around 750, North African traders began to use camels to cross the Sahara Desert. The Sahel became an important trading area.
- The Kingdom of Ghana developed in West Africa. The kings of Ghana taxed all goods traded in the kingdom and grew rich.
- In 1075, the Almoravids invaded Ghana. After ten years of fighting, Ghana won back its land. It never gained back its power, however.
- From around 100 B.C. to A.D. 1000, the Bantu people slowly moved from West Africa to southern and eastern Africa.
- Many people in southern and eastern Africa adopted Bantu languages. They also learned farming and iron working skills from the Bantu.

Find Out More!

After reading Chapter 14, you're ready to go online. **Explore Zone**, **Quiz Time**, and **Amazing Facts** bring this chapter of world history alive.

Visit www.exploreSV.com and type in the chapter code **Ch14**.

Vocabulary

Number your paper from 1 to 5. Write the word or words from the list that best complete the paragraphs. One word will not be used.

The __1__ was south of the Sahara Desert. It became an important trading area for goods going across the desert. Ghana's location between Wangara and North Africa gave it a __2__ over the gold trade.

Around 2,000 years ago, the people of West Africa began a mass movement called the __3__. Most of the Bantu languages use __4__, such as a high or a low voice, to give a word its meaning. One possible reason for the mass movement was __5__, or too many people living in an area.

Word List

Bantu migrations
Sahel
overpopulation
tones
jihad
monopoly

Comprehension

Number your paper from 1 to 5. Write **True** for each sentence that is true. Write **False** for each sentence that is false.

1. West Africans used stories and songs to pass their history from one generation to the next.
2. The Sahara Desert was easy for traders to cross.
3. The kings of Ghana welcomed Muslims from North Africa.
4. The West Africans learned how to use iron long before many other people did.
5. After the Bantu migrations, some communities in southern and eastern Africa were led by elders.

Critical Thinking

Sequencing Number your paper from 1 to 5. Write the sentences below in the correct order.

By about 1000, the Bantu migrations had ended.

Traders from North Africa began to use camels to cross the Sahara Desert.

The Soninke developed a kingdom between the Senegal River and the Niger River around 400.

The Bantu migrations began.

In 1075, the Almoravids invaded Ghana and declared a jihad against the kingdom.

Writing

Write a paragraph explaining how goods were traded in West Africa.

Skill Builder: Reading a Flow Chart

A **flow chart** shows facts in their correct order. This flow chart shows how the Arabs of North Africa gathered salt. They traded this salt for other goods.

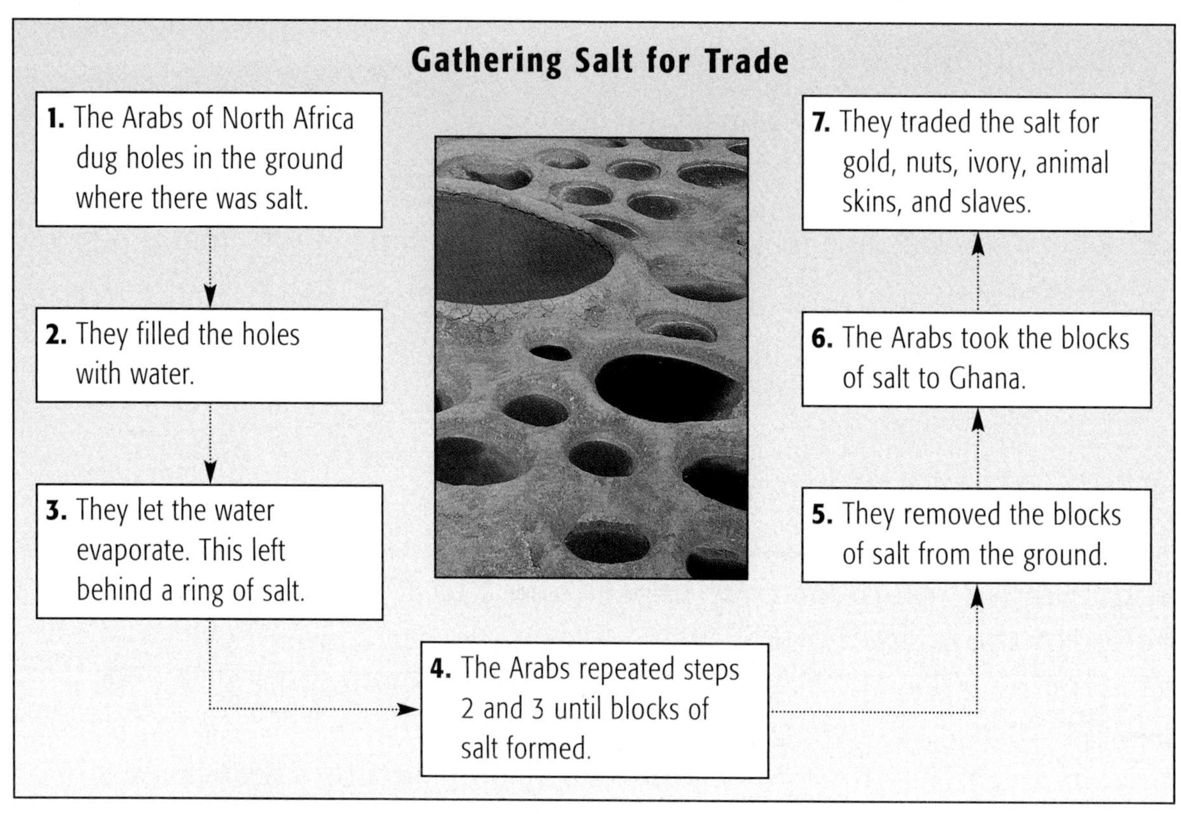

Gathering Salt for Trade
1. The Arabs of North Africa dug holes in the ground where there was salt.
2. They filled the holes with water.
3. They let the water evaporate. This left behind a ring of salt.
4. The Arabs repeated steps 2 and 3 until blocks of salt formed.
5. They removed the blocks of salt from the ground.
6. The Arabs took the blocks of salt to Ghana.
7. They traded the salt for gold, nuts, ivory, animal skins, and slaves.

Number your paper from 1 to 5. Write the letter of the correct answer.

1. In Step 1, the Arabs dug holes in the ground where there was ______.
   a. water **b.** salt **c.** gold
2. In Step 2, the holes were filled with ______.
   a. water **b.** nuts **c.** ivory
3. After the water evaporated, a ring of ______ was left behind.
   a. gold **b.** animal skins **c.** salt
4. To form blocks of salt, the Arabs repeated steps ______.
   a. 1 and 2 **b.** 2 and 3 **c.** 5 and 6
5. Step 6 was to bring the blocks of salt to ______ for trade.
   a. North Africa **b.** Ghana **c.** Wangara

LESSON 1

Classic Maya

Before You Read

- Why did the Maya plant crops on raised fields?
- Why does the end of some cultures remain a mystery?

New Words
Classic Maya
glyphs
mathematicians
smelt

People and Places
Tikal
Toltec
Tula
Pacal
Palenque
Lady Zac-Kuk

The Maya settled on the Yucatan Peninsula in Central America around 200 B.C. Their civilization was at its height between A.D. 300 and A.D. 900. This time is called the **Classic Maya**.

The Maya were remarkable people. They drained water from marshes. They built raised areas to plant crops. They even built terraces on hillsides to gain more area for planting. The Maya also built cities, designed temples, and studied the stars.

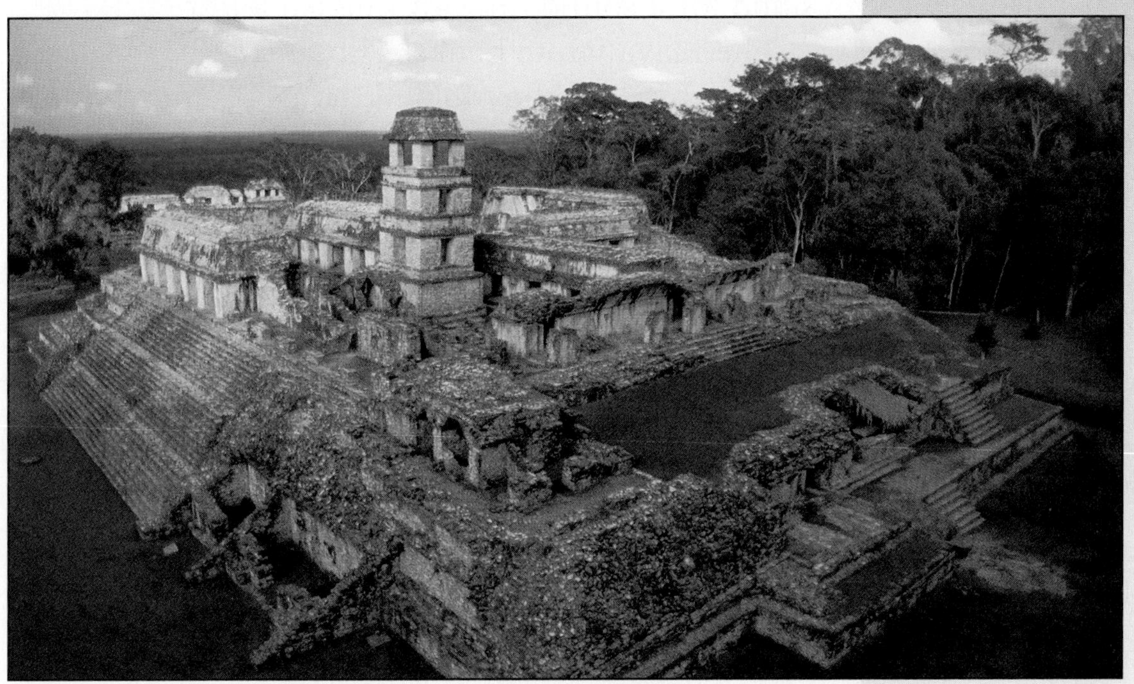

These ruins are in the Mayan city of Palenque.

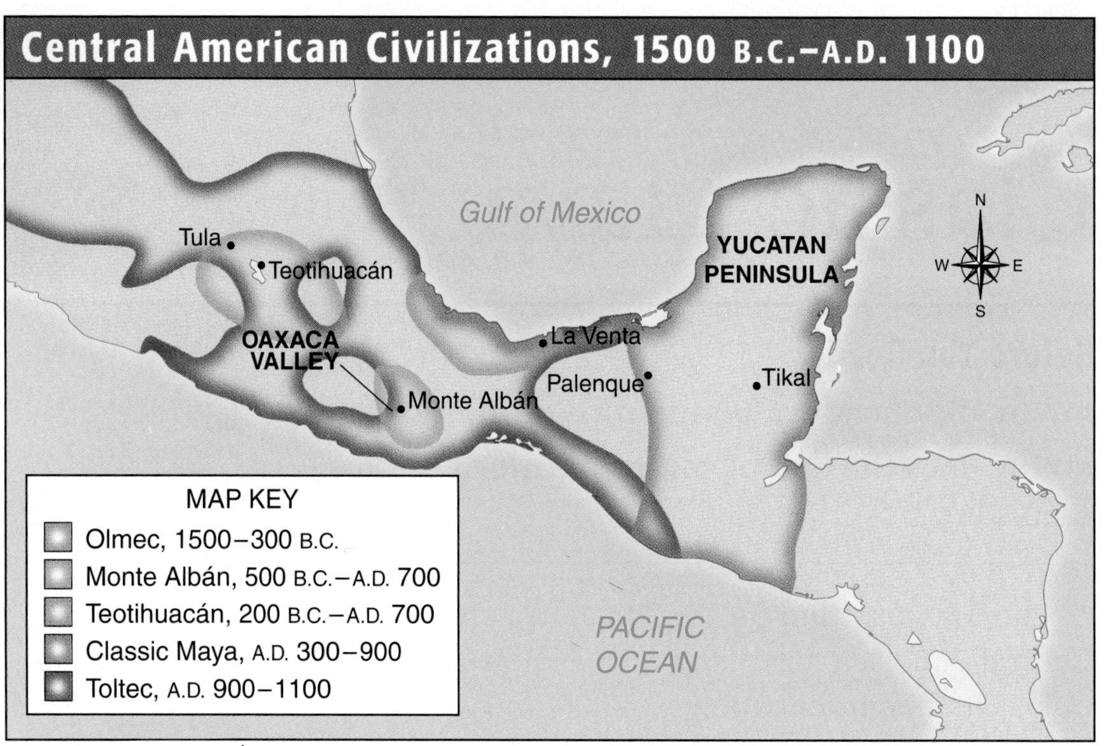

This map shows the early Central American civilizations between 1500 B.C. and A.D. 1100. Which group lived in the Yucatan Peninsula?

Mayan Writing

The Maya created their own form of writing. They used pictures, sometimes mixing animals and people. The Maya also used several hundred characters called **glyphs**. Each glyph stood for something. It could stand for an idea. Or it could stand for a sound, like an English letter.

The Maya wrote books. They made paper using tree bark. Then they folded the pages together to create a book. The books opened like a fan. Only four of these books remain.

The Maya wrote stories about their gods. They believed the god Heart-of-Sky created Earth because he was lonely. This is explained in one Mayan book, *The Book of Creation*.

"And so Heart-of-Sky thinks,
'Who is there to speak my name?
Who is there to praise me?'
. . . Heart-of-Sky only says the word 'Earth,'
and the earth rises, like a mist from the sea."

Other Mayan Advances

The Maya were skilled architects. They built many cities, which became active centers for trade and religious services. The largest city was Tikal. Tikal had two massive stone temples next to a huge plaza. The temples looked like pyramids with flat tops.

The Maya were also **mathematicians**. Like the Gupta in India, they came up with the idea of zero. The Mayan number system was based on 20 rather than 10.

The Maya studied the stars and the night sky. They knew the movement of the sun, moon, and stars. They created two calendars. One showed when ceremonies should be held. The other was a yearly calendar. Both were as correct as any calendar today.

The Maya studied the stars from this building.

Each Mayan city had its own ruler and its own way of life. People living near mountains used precious stones to make knives and jewelry. People who lived on plains grew cotton and made pottery. Those along the coast traded salt.

This wall painting was found in the ruins of a Mayan city.

Did You Know?

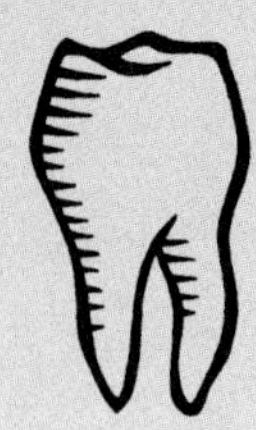

Sparkling Teeth

Teeth were important to the Mayan people. They chewed with them, of course. But they also decorated them. Some Maya had jewels put into their teeth. First, a hole was drilled in a tooth. Then, a jewel was fit into the hole. The jewel could be a piece of gold, or it could be a shiny red, green, or blue stone. Getting a jewel put in wasn't easy. One slip, and the tooth could be destroyed.

The Fall of the Maya

Something unexpected happened in the late 800s. The Maya simply stopped building temples and deserted their cities. In just a few years, nearly the entire Mayan civilization was gone. The age called the Classic Maya was over.

As with other early civilizations, it is not clear what happened to the Maya. Some say the Mayan cities fought wars against one another. Those who lived were perhaps too few and too weak to save the cities. Perhaps overpopulation caused the fall of the Maya because the food supply could not feed all the people. Diseases also might have killed the Mayan people.

The Toltec

After 700, a group called the Toltec began building an empire in what is now Mexico. They were skilled stone builders. In fact, the word *Toltec* means "master builders." Little is known about the Toltec. Around 900, they settled in Tula. This city was near the ancient city of Teotihuacán. There they built a capital city. They collected tribute from nearby tribes. The Toltec knew how to **smelt**, or melt, metals. Like the Maya, they studied the stars.

The Toltec built massive temples. These temples honored their gods. Like the people of Teotihuacán, the Toltec believed in human sacrifice. The Toltec believed such sacrifice was necessary to keep their gods alive and happy.

Toltec armies conquered much of Mexico. Around A.D. 1000, they took over what was left of the Maya in the Yucatan. The Toltec spread their influence throughout Central America. But during the 1100s, the Toltec began losing control of their empire. In time, invading groups, such as the Aztec, replaced the powerful Toltec.

King Pacal (603–683)

People In History

The young boy Pacal was named the Mayan king of Palenque, a Mayan city, in 609. But since he was only six years old, Pacal didn't have a strong claim to the throne. His mother, Lady Zac-Kuk, came from a family of rulers. She herself had ruled for more than ten years. She believed Pacal should be the next leader. So when he was 12 years old, she officially turned the kingdom over to him.

Pacal turned out to be a great leader. He ruled until his death at age 80. He improved the city of Palenque. He had a beautiful temple built there. It was called the Temple of the Inscriptions. Inside the temple, one hallway displayed the names of past kings. When Pacal died, he was buried deep inside this temple. Archaeologists discovered his tomb in 1952.

Lesson 1 Review

Choose words from the list that best complete the paragraphs. One word will not be used.

In Mayan history, the period from around 300 to 900 is called the __1__ Maya. The Maya created a form of writing that used pictures and __2__ to make words and sentences. The largest Mayan city was __3__. The Mayan number system was based on 20. The Maya created calendars. The Mayan king Pacal improved the city of Palenque. No one knows why the Maya __4__ their cities.

The Toltec settled in Tula. They began building a large empire in modern-day Mexico. The Toltec Empire lasted until the 1100s.

Word List

smelt
Tikal
deserted
Classic
glyphs

LESSON 2

South America and North America

New Words

ceramics
lagoons
lost wax method
fibers

People and Places

Nazca
Moche
Chimu
Moche River
Chan Chan
Anasazi
Mogollon
Hohokam
Inuit

Before You Read

- How do scientists learn about cultures that did not have a written language?
- How did climate affect what early people ate and how they lived?

Civilizations in South America continued to develop and grow. The story of the Nazca began around 200 B.C., the Moche appeared around A.D. 100, and the Chimu rule began around A.D. 1000. In North America, more groups settled and developed their own ways of life.

The Nazca made this huge spider. The full spider can only be seen from the sky.

The Nazca

The Nazca lived on the coast of modern-day Peru, near the ancient city of Caral. Little is known about these early South Americans. Archaeologists do know that the Nazca were experts at making pots. They used many colors to decorate their pots with birds and other animals.

The Nazca are best known for the huge shapes they carved into the ground. They did this by cutting away the dark soil on the top. The lighter soil below then showed the shapes. But the figures were so huge that the whole shape could not be seen from the ground. These shapes could only be seen from the sky. It is still a mystery why the Nazca made these figures. The Nazca lived in Peru until around A.D. 800.

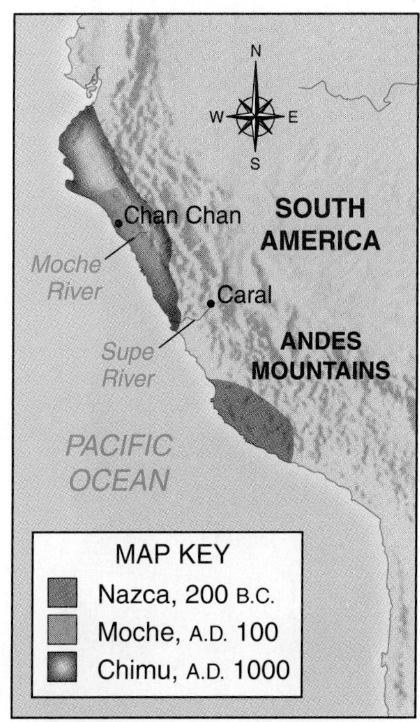

Early Civilizations in South America

The Moche

Around A.D. 100, the Moche also settled on the coast of Peru, north of the Nazca. They settled in the Moche River valley, which was rich with clay and metals. With these materials, the Moche crafted works of art. They were most famous for their **ceramics**. The Moche made ceramics by heating clay. They shaped the heated clay into pots, bottles, and other kinds of pottery. The Moche often shaped their pottery to look like people or animals. Moche artists also worked with gold, copper, and silver.

Like other South American groups, the Moche had no written language. But the decorations on their pots tell us how they lived. The decorations show scenes from daily life. Some decorations show religious ceremonies. Others show that the Moche had a class system. Priests and warriors were at the top. Artists came next. Farmers and fishermen followed. Servants and slaves were at the lowest level.

Moche ceramic bottle in the shape of a deer-man

The Chimu

The Chimu built their capital at Chan Chan in the Moche River valley about 300 years after the Moche civilization ended. Chan Chan was one of the largest cities in the Americas at the time. Chan Chan had pyramids made from bricks. It had parks and **lagoons**.

Chimu gold vase

The Chimu used the **lost wax method** to make gold objects. First, they carved wax into a certain shape. Then, they covered the wax shape with clay. Once the clay was hard, they heated it so that the wax inside would melt. Then, they drained the wax and poured in liquid gold. When the gold hardened, they broke the clay. What was left was a solid gold object.

North American Cultures

In what is now the United States, several different cultures developed during this time. By 500, these people lived in small villages. Those in warmer climates grew corn, squash, beans, and other crops. The North American groups also learned how to store food and to make pottery.

The Anasazi lived in caves and rock cliffs of the southwestern United States.

Each group did something special. The Anasazi used the **fibers**, or long threads, of plants to weave beautiful baskets. Around 750, they began to live in caves and rock structures of the desert.

The Mogollon produced new forms of ceramics. They made black and white bowls. They also painted designs and pictures that told a story on their pottery.

Mogollon bowl

The Hohokam lived in a very dry area, so they built a series of canals. The Hohokam used these canals to bring water to their fields. Some of the canals were 10 feet deep and more than 10 miles long.

In the far north, the Inuit began to move into the Arctic region around 1050. They lived in small villages. They survived by hunting large animals and by fishing.

Lesson 2 Review

Choose words from the list that best complete the paragraph. One word will not be used.

Several civilizations developed in the Americas. The Nazca from South America carved mysterious figures into the ground that can be seen only from the sky. The Moche made __1__ by heating clay and shaping it into pots. They decorated these pots with scenes from daily life. The Moche had a __2__ system. The Chimu built their capital at Chan Chan. It had parks and __3__. The Chimu used the lost wax method to make gold objects. The Anasazi from North America used plant __4__ to make baskets. The Mogollon made ceramics, and the Hohokam built canals. The Inuit lived in the far north.

Word List

fibers
lagoons
ceremonies
class
ceramics

Chapter 15: Using What You've Learned

Summary

- The Classic Maya period in Central America lasted from A.D. 300 to A.D. 900. The Maya created a complex writing system and were excellent mathematicians.
- The Toltec were master builders. They spread their influence throughout Central America.
- Three ancient civilizations formed in Peru. The Nazca carved huge shapes into the ground. The Moche made fine pottery. The Chimu made objects out of gold.
- Four civilizations also developed in North America. The Anasazi were known for their baskets. The Mogollon made black and white ceramics. The Hohokam built canals. The Inuit lived in the Arctic region.

Find Out More!

After reading Chapter 15, you're ready to go online. **Explore Zone**, **Quiz Time**, and **Amazing Facts** bring this chapter of world history alive.

Visit www.exploreSV.com and type in the chapter code **Ch15**.

Vocabulary

Number your paper from 1 to 6. Finish the sentences from Group A with words from Group B. Write the letter of the correct answer.

Group A

1. Mayan writing used characters called _____ to stand for ideas or sounds.
2. Mayan _____ used a number system based on 20.
3. The Toltec knew how to _____, or melt, metals.
4. The Moche heated clay to make _____.
5. The Chimu capital of Chan Chan had parks and _____.
6. The Anasazi wove baskets using the _____ of plants.

Group B

a. fibers
b. glyphs
c. ceramics
d. lagoons
e. mathematicians
f. smelt

Comprehension

Number your paper from 1 to 4. Write the letter of the correct answer.

1. Where did the Maya live?
   a. South America
   b. Africa
   c. Europe
   d. Central America

2. Which group built an empire after A.D. 700 in what is now Mexico?
   a. Moche
   b. Anasazi
   c. Toltec
   d. Hohokam

3. What are the Nazca best known for?
   a. their calendars
   b. their stories
   c. their number system
   d. their huge carvings in the ground

4. What did the Mogollon people produce?
   a. black and white bowls
   b. a series of canals
   c. pyramids made from bricks
   d. beautiful baskets

Critical Thinking

Cause and Effect Number your paper from 1 to 4. Read the causes in the left column. Then choose the correct effect from the right column. Write the letter of the correct effect.

Cause

1. The Maya built terraces on hillsides, so
2. According to the Maya, the god Heart-of-Sky was lonely, so
3. The Toltec wanted their gods to stay alive and happy, so
4. The Hohokam lived in a very dry area, so

Effect

a. he created Earth.

b. they built a series of canals.

c. they would have more area for planting.

d. they sacrificed humans.

Writing

Write a paragraph telling why the Maya might have left their cities.

UNIT 4

Change and Growth Around the World

1000–1500

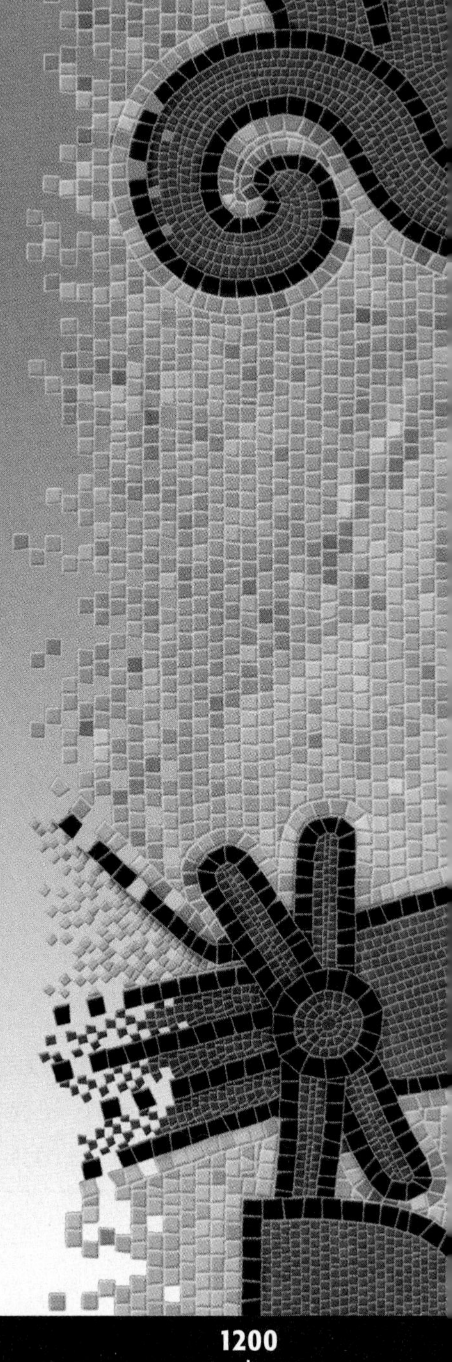

The world faced great changes between the years 1000 and 1500. For some, this was a time of suffering. Religious wars killed thousands of people. A mysterious disease destroyed whole villages. For others, this was a time of learning and wealth. The first universities developed. Increased trading brought great riches.

This unit tells how the world changed during these 500 years. Some groups brought about changes by spreading their religion and conquering new lands. Other groups fought change by protecting their lands from invaders.

A.D. 1000 1100 1200

A.D. 1113
The Khmer Empire in Southeast Asia begins building Angkor Wat.

A.D. 1230
The Kingdom of Mali rises to power in West Africa.

1300 | 1400 | 1500 | A.D.

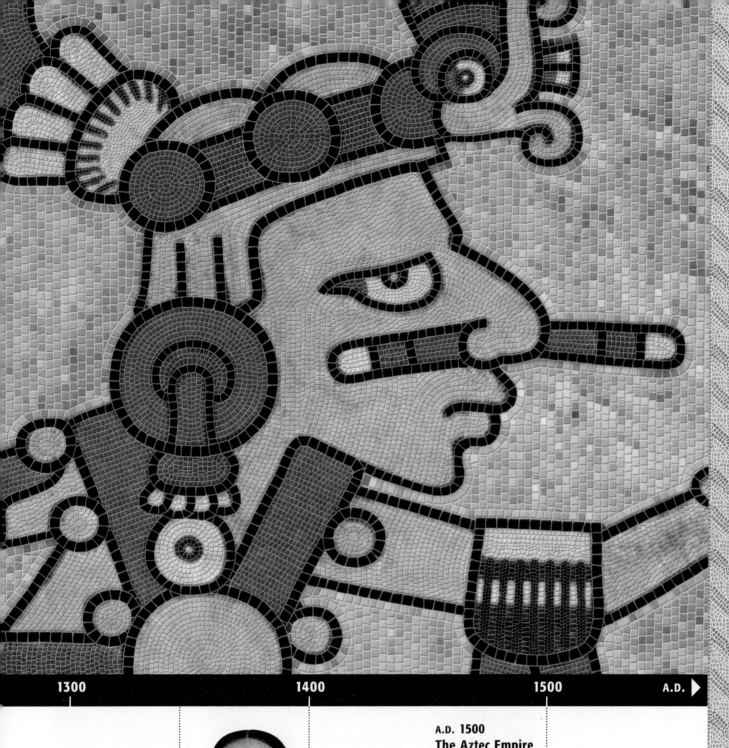

A.D. 1347
Rats spread a deadly disease, killing one third of the people in Europe.

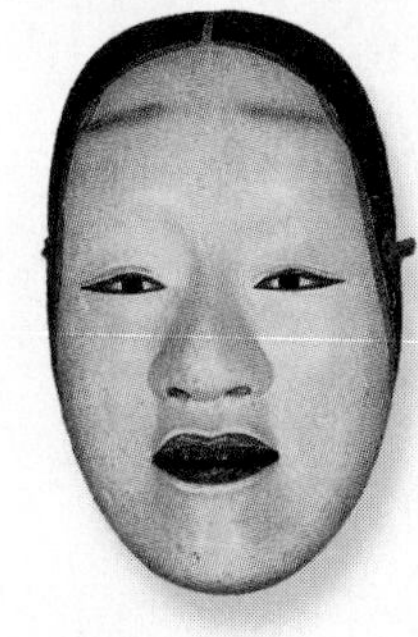

A.D. 1400
The Japanese enjoy a new type of drama.

A.D. 1500
The Aztec Empire in Central America is at its height.

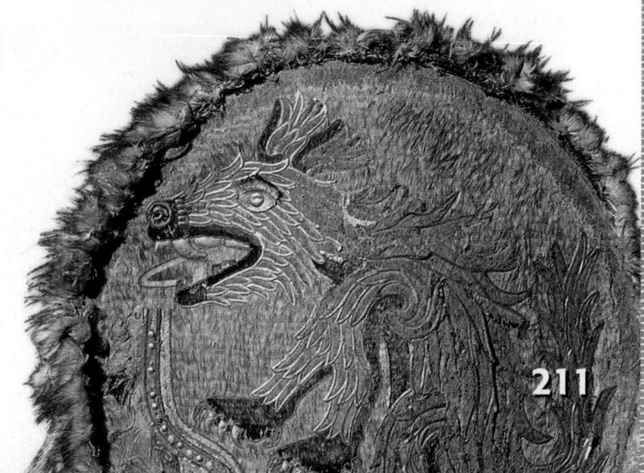

LESSON 1

The Crusades

New Words

Holy Land
crusade
truce
Moors
Reconquista

People and Places

Seljuk Turks
Alexius
Urban II
Saladin
Frederick I
Philip II
Richard I
Cordoba
Spain
Granada

Before You Read

- Why might two religious groups go to war?
- What might Christians and Muslims learn from one another?

Europe's late Middle Ages, from around 1000 to 1500, were a time of change. For nearly 200 years, European Christians and Arab Muslims fought one another in a series of wars. The wars were hurtful to both groups. But the two groups learned from each other. Europeans, for example, were surprised by the Muslim advances in science and medicine. The contact with the Muslim world helped bring Europe out of the Dark Ages.

Muslim doctors used advances in science and medicine to help patients.

A Call for Help

Pope Urban II asks knights to launch a crusade to free the Holy Land.

Christians and Muslims fought for control of Palestine, the land where Jesus lived and died. Christians called Palestine the **Holy Land**. After the Roman Empire fell, Palestine was ruled by the Byzantines and then by the Arabs. For hundreds of years, Christians went to Palestine to pray. The Arabs welcomed the Christians. They let Christians visit holy places in Jerusalem.

Then a new Muslim group rose to power, the Seljuk Turks. In 1071, the Turks defeated a Byzantine army. Later, the Turks captured Jerusalem. It looked as though they might conquer Constantinople, so the Byzantine Emperor Alexius asked Pope Urban II for help.

Urban II agreed to help Alexius. He was looking for a way to unite Europeans and thought a common cause would help. In 1095, Urban II asked knights to launch a **crusade**, or holy war, against the Turks. He said it was their Christian duty to free the Holy Land from Muslim rule.

In return, Urban II promised to forgive the knights' sins. He also promised them lands in Palestine. The Christian knights were eager to fight and win lands.

Crusaders set sail for Jerusalem.

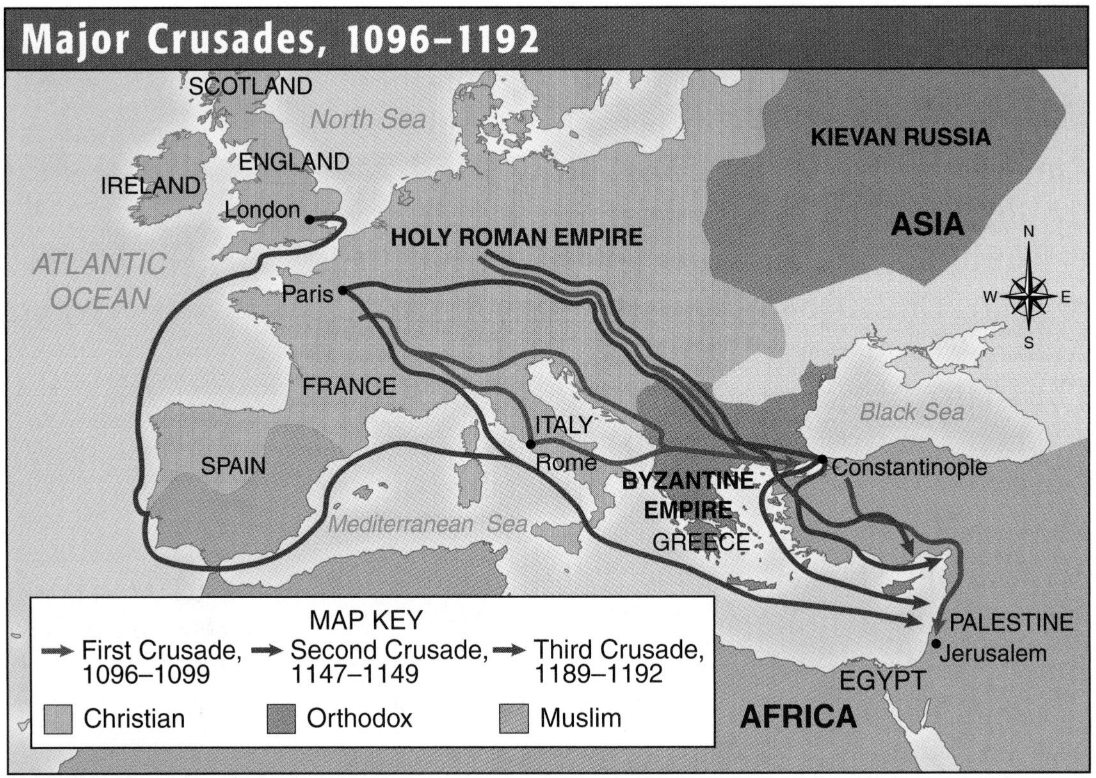

The Crusaders crossed through Christian, Orthodox, and Muslim lands. Were Muslim lands north or south of Christian lands?

The First Crusade

The First Crusade lasted from 1096 to 1099. The Crusaders traveled a difficult journey from France to Jerusalem. Many died from hunger and disease along the way. But the Crusaders reached Jerusalem in 1099. There, the Crusaders fought a long battle with the Turks and drove them from the city. The Crusaders killed many Muslims as well as Christians and Jews living in Jerusalem.

Leaders of the First Crusade

More Crusades

Many Crusaders decided to go home. Others stayed behind and divided the Holy Land into small states. The Christians ruled the Holy Land for almost 100 years. But the Christians began to fight among themselves, while the Muslim armies grew stronger. In 1144, Muslims defeated one of the Christian states.

European rulers and the pope launched the Second Crusade in 1147. Two European armies joined forces and tried to defeat the Turks. The

Turks won the battle, and the Crusaders returned home in 1149.

A new Muslim leader, Saladin, gained control of Jerusalem in 1187. Emperor Frederick I of the Holy Roman Empire, King Philip II of France, and King Richard I of England led the Third Crusade in 1189. Frederick died on the way to Jerusalem. Philip returned home before reaching the Holy Land. Richard and his army continued on and fought Saladin.

Saladin

Richard became known as Richard the Lion-Hearted for his bravery. But the Crusaders could not capture Jerusalem. In the end, Richard and Saladin reached a **truce** and agreed to stop fighting. Saladin allowed Christians to visit Jerusalem. He also allowed them to keep some of their states.

After Saladin died, the truce ended. Europeans tried again to win back Jerusalem and failed. They launched more crusades. One was the Children's Crusade. In 1212, an army of about 50,000 European children began their march to the Holy Land. Along the way, most got sick, died, or were sold into slavery. In 1291, Muslims captured the last Christian state in the Holy Land, ending the deadly Crusades.

Results of the Crusades

Many thousands of Muslims and Christians died in the Crusades. Thousands of Jews, caught in the middle, also died. After all the fighting, the Holy Land remained under Muslim control. The Crusades left both Muslims and Christians angry. Neither group trusted the other.

A Christian and Muslim playing chess

On the other hand, the Crusades brought some good changes to Europe, too. Europeans admired parts of Muslim culture. The Europeans learned about advances in science and medicine. They also began to trade for new products, such as sugar, silk, lemons, and spices.

The Crusades also sparked European interest in the rest of the world. This curiosity led to more exploration.

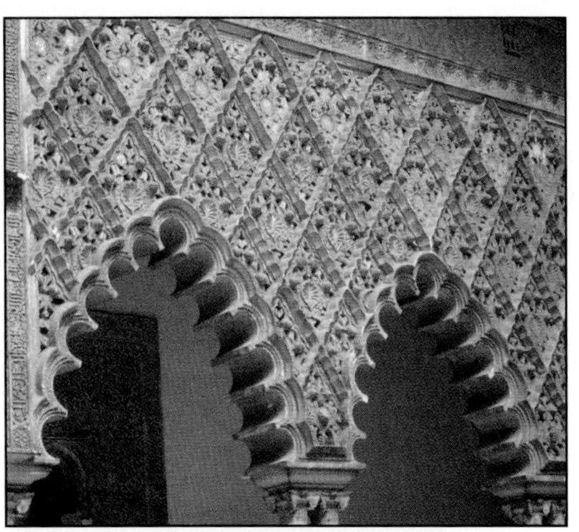
The Moors built beautiful mosques in Spain.

Muslims in Spain

The Christians were able to defeat one Muslim group, the **Moors**. The Moors had set up the Caliphate of Cordoba. In 1000, they controlled most of Spain. When the Moors fought among themselves, the Christians attacked, winning back most of the Spanish lands.

By 1450, the Moors held only Granada in southern Spain. Then the Spanish Christians began the **Reconquista** to win back Granada. In 1492, they drove the Moors out of Spain completely.

Lesson 1 Review

Choose words from the list that best complete the paragraphs. One word will not be used.

Word List

truce
crusade
Reconquista
Alexius
Saladin

Christians and Muslims fought for control of Palestine. In 1095, Pope Urban II urged European knights to launch a __1__ to free the Holy Land. The First Crusade captured Jerusalem in 1099. The Muslims fought back. In 1187, __2__ gained control of Jerusalem. During the Third Crusade, Saladin and Richard I of England reached a __3__. In time, the Muslims defeated the Christians.

Thousands of Muslims, Christians, and Jews were killed during the Crusades. The Christians had one victory against the Muslims. The Spanish Christians began the __4__, which successfully pushed the Moors out of Spain in 1492.

LESSON 2

Life in the Late Middle Ages

Before You Read

- Why might people move from the country into a town?
- How might a deadly disease be spread?

During the late Middle Ages, Europeans became better farmers. There was often a **surplus**, or extra amount, of food. Fewer people needed to be farmers, so more people moved into towns. In towns, workers began to **specialize**. One worker might make shoes, while another worker might make candles or bread.

This worker specialized in making leather.

New Words

surplus
specialize
bartered
guilds
apprentice
journeyman
masterpiece
cathedrals
plague
Black Death

People and Places

Bologna
Oxford
Cambridge
Salerno
Salamanca
Paris
Thomas Aquinas
Henry of Knighton
Norwich

Towns were crowded during the late Middle Ages.

Town Life

Town life in the Middle Ages was rather grim. The streets were narrow and often muddy. People tossed their garbage into the streets. Wooden houses were packed tightly together inside the town walls. Fire was always a danger. There were no fire departments or police departments.

Merchants earned money in towns.

Still, most people liked town life better than country life. Town life was more free than life on a manor, especially for serfs. Sometimes a serf would run away. If the serf didn't get caught for a year and a day, he was legally free.

Also, people could make money in towns. On a manor, no one had any money. Instead, they **bartered**, or traded one good for another. For example, a person might trade firewood for a pair of shoes. In towns, merchants and traders could grow rich.

Crafters Join Together

Workers who specialized began forming **guilds**. There was a guild for almost every craft. Only the best workers could join. The guild set the price for its goods. It also limited the number of goods that could be made. In this way, guilds kept control over their products.

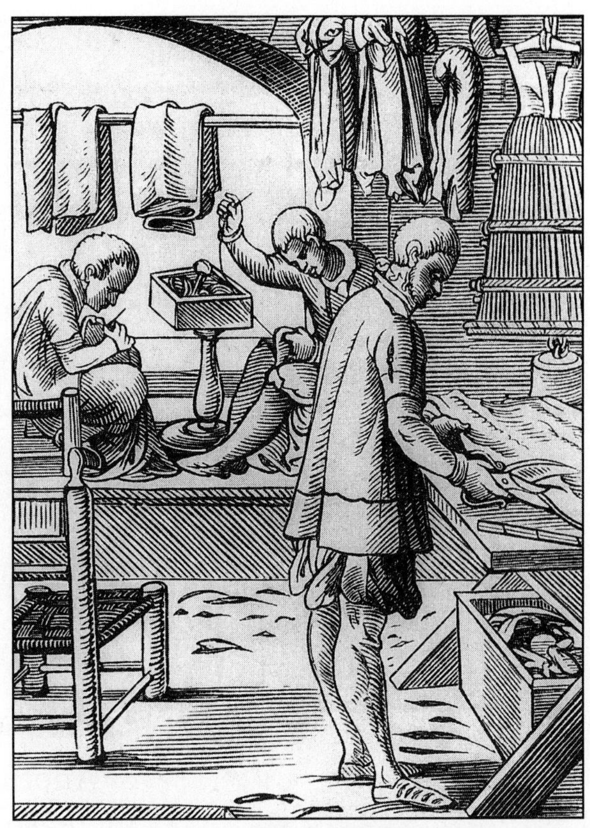

These workers are making clothes.

A young man wanting to join a guild first worked as an **apprentice**. He learned the trade from a skilled worker. He did not get paid. He did, however, get a room, clothing, and food. After a few years, he became a **journeyman**, who was paid. Finally, he became a master by showing he had mastered the skill. He did this by producing what was called a "**masterpiece**."

Universities

Life in towns was very different from life on the feudal manor. The towns needed people with more education. Governments, for example, needed educated people to help keep records. Universities began developing from around 1100 to 1300.

Unlike schools of the early Middle Ages, the universities taught more than religion. Students learned a variety of subjects. One of the first universities was in Bologna, Italy. In England, universities began at Oxford and Cambridge. Spain had a medical school in Salerno and a university in Salamanca. The French city of Paris developed a university, too.

Perhaps the most famous teacher from the Middle Ages was Thomas Aquinas. Aquinas wrote about philosophy and religion. Some beliefs, he wrote, could be understood by reason. Others could only be understood by faith. Aquinas developed many of his ideas from studying the ancient Greek philosophers.

A university in the Middle Ages

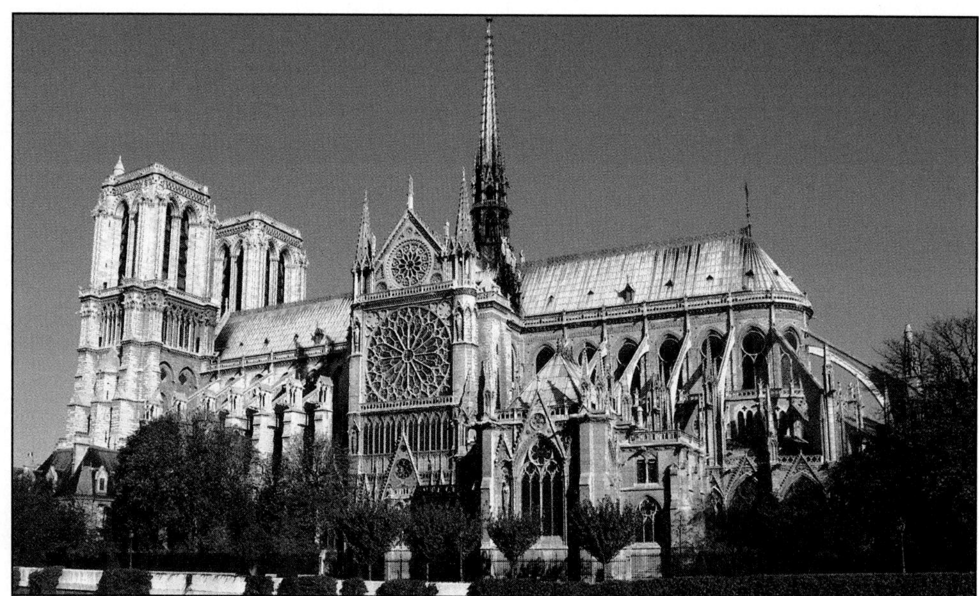
This cathedral in France was completed in the 13th century.

Cathedrals

Another change in the late Middle Ages was the increased building of **cathedrals**. Some of these magnificent churches took more than 100 years to build. The cathedral was always the highest building in a town, showing how important religion was in people's lives.

Stained glass window

Many cathedrals had stained glass windows. The windows were made with small pieces of colored glass held together with metal. Many of the windows showed stories from the Bible.

The Black Death

In 1347, a **plague** struck Europe. It killed one person out of every three. Known as the **Black Death**, it was carried by fleas that lived in the fur of rats. The plague began in China. It spread to Southwest Asia, Russia, and Europe along the trade routes.

People at the time had no idea what caused the plague. They were afraid and began blaming people they did not understand. Some people thought Jews were causing the plague. Many Jews were killed as a result.

Henry of Knighton, an English writer, described what the Black Death was like.

"Many villages . . . have now become quite [empty]. No one is left in the houses, for the people are dead. . . . And truly, many of these [villages] will now forever be empty."

The Black Death lasted in Europe from 1347 to 1351. It killed the rich and the poor, the young and the old. Norwich, a town in England, had a population of about 70,000 people before the plague. After the Black Death, it had fewer than 13,000 people. Some people stopped plowing their fields. They stopped caring for their animals. One man even wrote, "This is the end of the world."

But it was not the end of the world. In time, Europe recovered. It suffered other plagues. But none were as deadly as the Black Death.

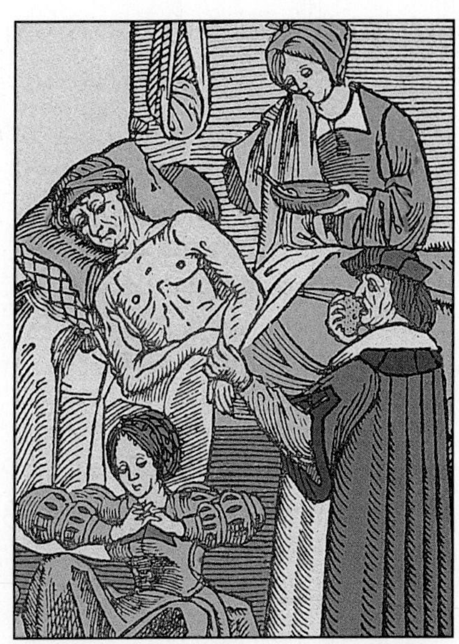

A man dying from the Black Death

Lesson 2 Review

Choose words from the list that best complete the paragraphs. One word will not be used.

Better farming in the late Middle Ages allowed more people to move into towns. Workers began to __1__, or do only one craft. They formed __2__ to control their craft. Universities opened to improve education. Stained glass windows in __3__ often showed stories from the Bible.

In 1347, a plague struck Europe. The __4__ killed one third of Europe's population. The plague ended in 1351.

Word List

cathedrals
specialize
masterpiece
Black Death
guilds

Chapter 16: Using What You've Learned

Summary

- For almost 200 years, Christian crusaders and Muslims fought for control of the Holy Land. This period was called the Crusades.
- Surplus food allowed people to move into villages and towns in Europe's late Middle Ages. Town life offered people freedom and a chance to make money.
- Workers began to specialize by making just one product. They also started guilds to keep control over their products and to train new workers.
- A plague called the Black Death began in China and spread along trade routes to Europe. Between 1347 and 1351, the plague killed one third of the population of Europe.

Find Out More!

After reading Chapter 16, you're ready to go online. **Explore Zone, Quiz Time,** and **Amazing Facts** bring this chapter of world history alive.

Visit www.exploreSV.com and type in the chapter code **Ch16**.

Vocabulary

Number your paper from 1 to 5. Write the word or words from the list that best complete each sentence. One word will not be used.

1. The Third Crusade ended in a ______ when Richard I and Saladin agreed to stop fighting.
2. In the ______, the Spanish Christians fought to win back Granada from the Moors.
3. As Europeans became better farmers, there was often a ______ of food.
4. The people on manors ______, or traded one good for another.
5. The ______ was carried by fleas that lived in the fur of rats.

Word List

Holy Land
surplus
Reconquista
Black Death
bartered
truce

Comprehension

Number your paper from 1 to 5. Write **True** for each sentence that is true. Write **False** for each sentence that is false.

1. In 1095, Urban II asked knights to start a crusade against the Turks.
2. Saladin is called the Lion-Hearted for his bravery in the Crusades.
3. The Moors set up the Caliphate of Cordoba.
4. Thomas Aquinas's writings about philosophy and religion were based on the ideas of ancient Greek philosophers.
5. Henry of Knighton wrote a book describing the great cathedrals of Europe.

Critical Thinking

Points of View Number your paper from 1 to 5. Read each sentence below. Write **Christian** if the point of view is from a Christian in the late Middle Ages. If the point of view is from a Muslim in the late Middle Ages, write **Muslim**.

1. We call Palestine our Holy Land.
2. After the First Crusade, we ruled Palestine for almost 100 years.
3. Saladin is the best leader that my people have ever had.
4. I do not trust the pope and his followers.
5. We have traveled far to fight in the Crusades.

Writing

Write a paragraph explaining the three steps a young man would have to take to become a member of a guild during the Middle Ages.

Skill Builder: Reading a Line Graph

A **line graph** shows how something has changed over time. The line graph below shows how the population of England changed from 1348 to 1375. During this time, crop failures, wars, and plagues caused the population of England to fall.

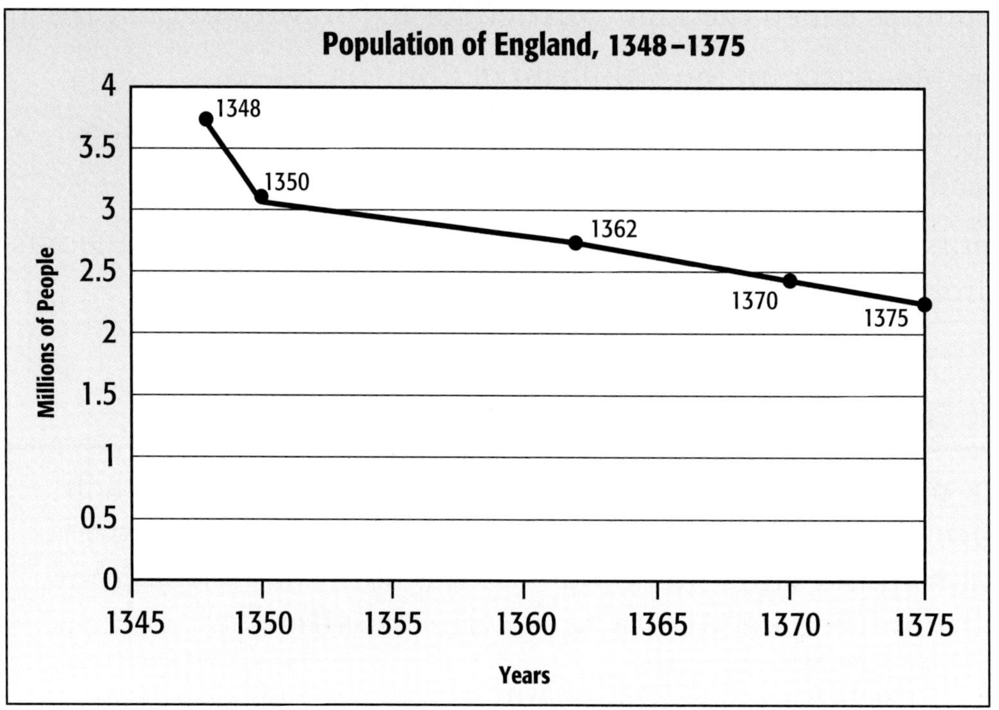

Number your paper from 1 to 5. Write the letter of the correct answer.

1. In 1348, England's population was just below _____ people.
   a. 3 million **b.** 3.5 million **c.** 4 million
2. Between 1348 and 1350, the population of England _____.
   a. fell **b.** stayed the same **c.** rose
3. In _____, the population was almost 2.5 million people.
   a. 1350 **b.** 1362 **c.** 1370
4. The line graph shows that many people _____ in England during this time.
   a. were born **b.** died **c.** moved into towns
5. By 1375, the population was just more than _____ people.
   a. 1.5 million **b.** 2 million **c.** 2.5 million

LESSON 1

The Mongol Empire

Before You Read

- What makes a group of people skilled warriors?
- How could a traveling writer change the way one culture thinks of another?

By the 1100s, the Song Dynasty of China was one of the most advanced civilizations in the world. But it constantly faced pressure from the **Mongols**. The Mongols were nomads to the north and west of China. They raised sheep, cattle, and horses on open plains called the **steppe**. The steppe was a rough land with little rain and few trees. The Mongols lived in wool tents called **yurts**. They became skilled horse riders as they moved from place to place.

The people of the Song Dynasty enjoyed festivals before the Mongols invaded.

New Words

Mongols
steppe
yurts
siege warfare
surrender
catapults
mercy
conquest
bathhouses

People and Places

Genghis Khan
Kublai Khan
Yuan
Beijing
Marco Polo

The Conquering Mongols

Mongol warrior

The Chinese built the Great Wall of China to keep out invaders such as the Mongols. But the Mongols found weak spots in the wall. In the early 13th century, they began attacking China. A Chinese soldier on foot had little chance against a Mongol warrior on a horse. Under the leadership of Genghis Khan, the Mongols quickly captured the countryside. They had trouble, however, taking over cities. The walls around the cities forced the Mongols to find new ways to fight.

The Mongols began using **siege warfare**. They surrounded a city and waited. They would not allow people to go in or out of the city. After a while, the city ran out of food and water. Finally, the people had to **surrender**.

The Mongols also developed **catapults**. These huge slings tossed bombs over high city walls. The Mongols also built special ladders to help them climb over the walls.

Mongols attacking a Chinese city

When Genghis Khan took over a city, he showed little **mercy**. His army sometimes killed everyone inside the city.

Genghis Khan died in 1227, but the Mongols continued to conquer new lands. In 1279, Genghis Khan's grandson, Kublai Khan, completed the **conquest** of China by defeating the Song forces in the south. He began a new dynasty in a united China. He called the dynasty the Yuan, which meant "original."

The Yuan Dynasty ruled China for more than 100 years. Kublai Khan built his capital in the modern-day city of Beijing. He built a huge palace there. The walls were covered with gold and silver. One hall was large enough to hold 6,000 people.

The Mongols also defeated the Abbasid Caliphate and conquered lands in Central Asia,

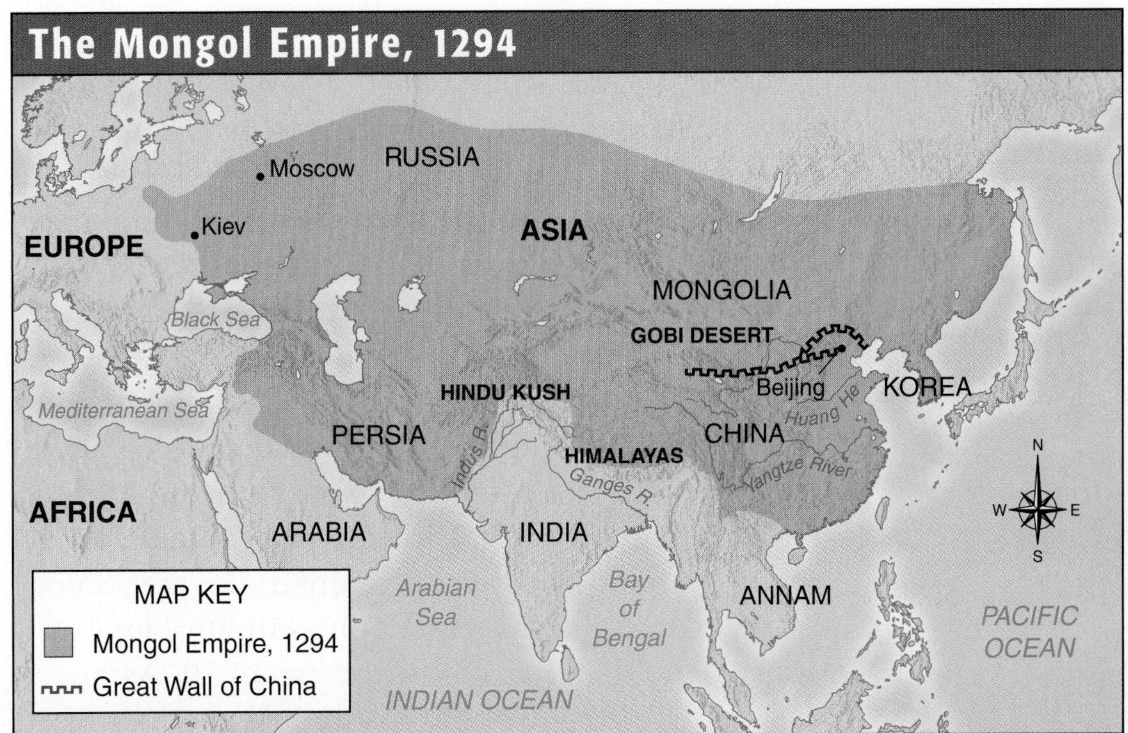

The Mongols ruled the biggest empire in history. What desert was a part of the Mongol Empire?

Russia, and Persia. Stretching from eastern Europe all the way to the Pacific Ocean, the Mongols ruled the biggest empire in history.

The Mongol Government

Kublai Khan was kinder and more educated than earlier Mongol rulers. Kublai Khan knew he needed to keep peace within his empire if it was to stay together. He tried to govern well and improve life in the empire. Under his rule, the Mongols built new roads. They dug new canals and improved the Grand Canal. They also built **bathhouses** that were heated by coal.

Problems remained, however, between the Mongols and the Chinese. Kublai Khan did not treat the Chinese fairly. Only Mongols and a few select outsiders were allowed to take important positions in government. The Chinese were forced to pay taxes and to do the difficult work on building projects.

Kublai Khan

A Visitor from Europe

During Kublai Khan's rule, a young Italian traveler named Marco Polo arrived in China. Marco Polo lived in China for 17 years. He was impressed by all that he saw. He called the palace in Beijing "the greatest palace that ever was." Marco Polo wrote a book about his journeys. It was called *The Travels of Marco Polo*.

Marco Polo

His book was very popular in Europe. Still, many Europeans didn't believe Marco Polo. They couldn't believe China had so many beautiful cities with good roads and working canals. To them, Marco Polo's stories seemed like fairy tales. Some even called his book "The Million Lies." Marco Polo died in 1324 at the age of 70. As he was dying, he said, "I have only told the half of what I saw!" Later travelers proved that Marco Polo had told the truth about China's greatness.

Kublai Khan died in 1294. During the following years, several weak leaders ruled the vast Mongol Empire. In 1368, Chinese peasants led a successful revolt and brought an end to the Yuan Dynasty.

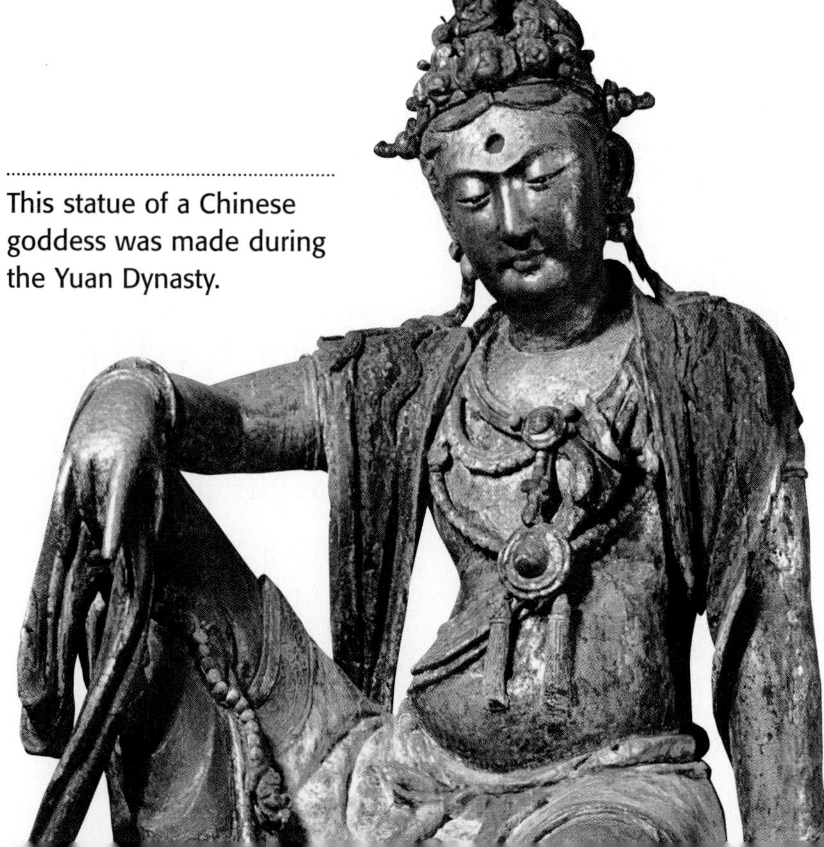

This statue of a Chinese goddess was made during the Yuan Dynasty.

Genghis Khan (c. 1162–1227)

People In History

The Mongol leader Genghis Khan is one of the most well-known rulers in history. Genghis Khan was actually his title, not his name. The term *Genghis Khan* means "top ruler." He was born with the name Temujin around 1162. An enemy killed his father when Temujin was just 12 years old. The tribe leaders thought Temujin was too young to take his father's place. They left him and his mother to die.

Somehow the boy and his mother lived. Then, one by one, Temujin defeated his enemies. By 1206, he was the leader of all the Mongol tribes. That was when he earned the title Genghis Khan. He then raised a great army and began a massive conquest. He is remembered for his cruel treatment of those he captured. But he is also remembered for his skill in war.

Lesson 1 Review

Choose words from the list that best complete the paragraphs. One word will not be used.

Word List

Yuan
steppe
siege warfare
Marco Polo
Beijing

The Mongols moved from place to place across the Asian __1__. The Mongols easily defeated Chinese armies in the countryside. But they had to find new ways to conquer cities. They became experts at __2__.

Genghis Khan was a cruel leader. His grandson, Kublai Khan, began the __3__ Dynasty. He made improvements in China, but he did not treat the Chinese fairly. Mongol rule in China lasted more than 100 years. Europeans learned about Mongol China from __4__. He wrote stories about his travels in China.

LESSON 2

Islam Comes to India

New Words

devout
infidels
plunder
dominion
sultanates
sultans
sack

People and Places

Mahmud of Ghazni
Muhammad Ghuri
Delhi
Amir Khusro
Jalalud-Din
Timur

Before You Read

- How might the spread of Islam have changed India?
- What are some differences between Hindu and Muslim beliefs?

In Chapter 10, you read that the Huns brought an end to the Golden Age of the Gupta by 550. Then in 711, Arab Muslims reached India. For 300 years, the Indians stopped the Muslims from spreading beyond the Indus River. Then, around 1000, a Muslim Turk named Mahmud of Ghazni

Hindu and Muslim Lands, c. 1000

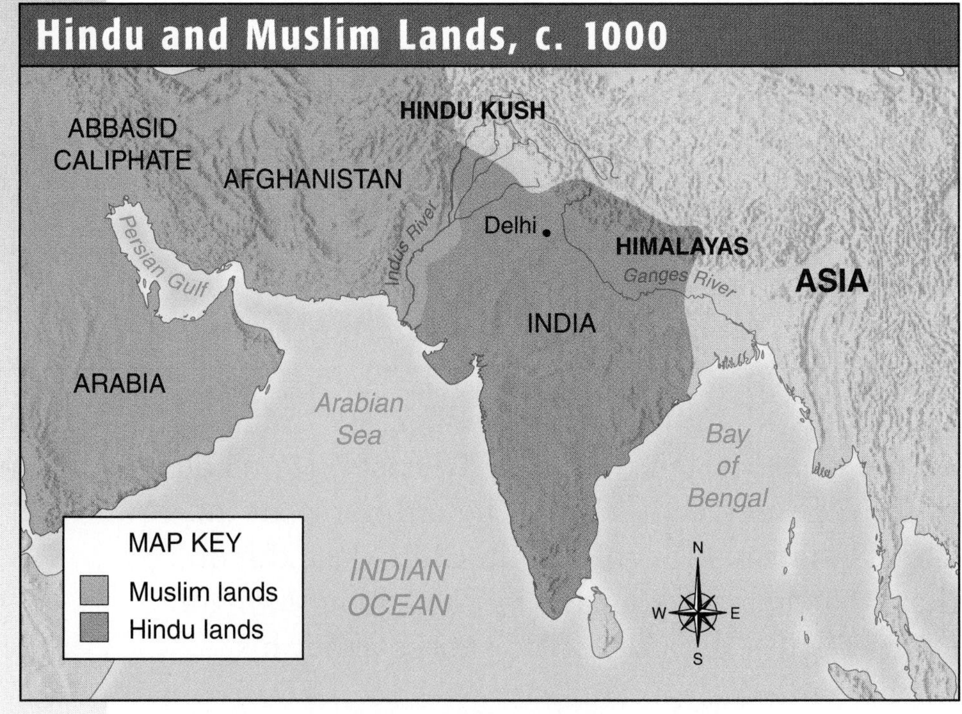

began new attacks on India. His efforts were successful, and Islam spread into the Indian subcontinent.

Mahmud was a **devout** Muslim. He saw the Hindus as **infidels**. Mahmud did not like the way Indians divided people into castes. He believed all people were equal in the eyes of Allah. He also disliked the way Hindus prayed to idols. Mahmud felt he had a duty to conquer India and spread the Muslim religion.

Muslims Conquer India

In 1000, India was divided into small Hindu states that often argued with one another. The Muslim Turks easily conquered northern India. The Hindus only allowed members of the warrior class to fight, but the Turks accepted anyone as a soldier.

At first, the Turks wanted to **plunder** India. They stole gold and jewelry from Indian cities. They took riches from Hindu temples before destroying them. When the hot monsoon season arrived, Mahmud went into the cooler mountains and waited to attack again the next year. In all, Mahmud launched 17 raids into India.

Hindu woman

Muslim and Hindu Beliefs

Islam	Hinduism
■ The Qur'an is the holy book of Islam.	■ The Vedas are the holy books of Hinduism.
■ Muslims believe there is only one God, Allah. Muhammad is a prophet of Allah.	■ Hindus believe in many gods. Two gods are Shiva and Vishnu.
■ Islam teaches that all people are equal.	■ Hindus follow a caste system and believe in reincarnation.

Muslim children

A Delhi sultan

Muslims Stay in India

The raids continued after Mahmud's death. Muslim Turks struck deeper and deeper into India. Another leader, Muhammad Ghuri, led his army south to the Ganges River valley. His soldiers carried away what they could and destroyed the rest.

In time, the Turks learned the value of India. They discovered its rich spices and its importance to trade. The Muslim Turks stopped raiding India and began to stay there. By 1206, much of India was under Muslim **dominion**.

The Delhi Sultanate

The Turks divided India into independent Muslim kingdoms. These kingdoms were called **sultanates**. The most powerful was the Delhi Sultanate, centered in the city of Delhi. The Delhi Sultanate lasted from 1210 to 1526.

The Delhi **sultans** were harsh conquerers. They often were cruel to the Hindus. The Muslims of the Delhi Sultanate were even cruel

This picture is from a book of Amir Khusro's poems.

to one another. Often a sultan was murdered by someone wanting to become the next sultan.

Amir Khusro was a court poet born in 1253. He served under six Delhi sultans. Khusro wrote poems for the sultans. He described how a sultan named Jalalud-Din ruined Hindu temples.

Voices In History

> **"Jalalud-Din went again to the temples and ordered their destruction. There were two [large] bronze idols of the Brahma. These were broken into pieces and the fragments were [scattered]."**

In time, the Muslims of the Delhi Sultanate became less cruel. They improved prisons and built hospitals, bridges, and dams. Many sultans welcomed Muslim artists and teachers into their courts. Delhi became a center of Islamic culture. Beautiful buildings were made that combined both Islamic and Indian styles.

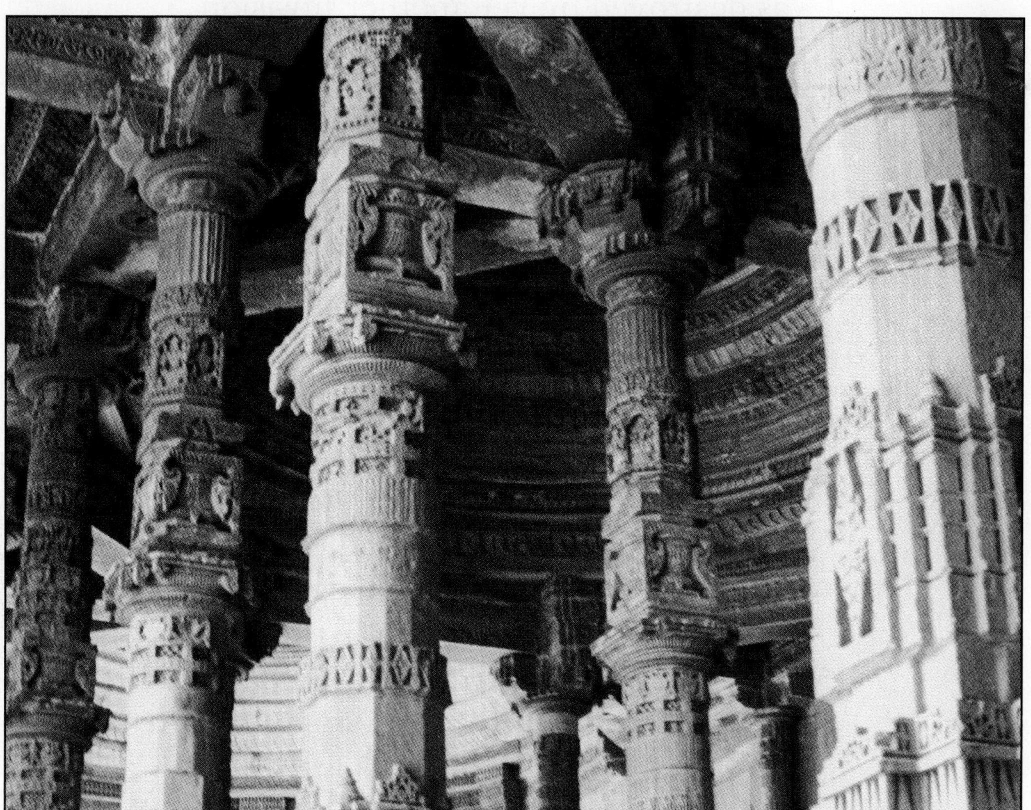

These carved columns show the style of building under the Delhi Sultanate.

Timur

Timur Invades India

The Delhi Sultanate was the largest kingdom in India. Even the powerful Mongols did not defeat it. But the sultanate could never conquer all of India. By the 1350s, the sultanate began to break into smaller states. In 1398, a Muslim warrior named Timur, or Tamerlane, invaded India.

Timur claimed to be a relative of Genghis Khan. Timur led his army from central Asia into India. He killed tens of thousands of people.

His four-month invasion ended with the **sack** of Delhi. The city was completely destroyed. The people either fled or were killed. One man wrote that "not even a bird was left to fly" over the city.

The sack of Delhi greatly weakened the sultanate. Delhi regained some control, but it was never the same. Muslim and Hindu rulers took over parts of India. In 1526, the Delhi Sultanate was destroyed by yet another invasion.

Lesson 2 Review

Choose words from the list that best complete the paragraphs. One word will not be used.

Word List

Timur
devout
Delhi
infidels
dominion

Around 1000, Muslim Turks invaded India. Their leader was Mahmud of Ghazni. He saw the Hindus as __1__ and wanted to conquer them. The Turks defeated the Hindus and developed several Muslim states. The biggest state was the __2__ Sultanate.

By 1206, much of India was under Muslim __3__. In time, Muslim and Hindu cultures influenced one another. Buildings combined the Islamic and Indian styles. The Delhi Sultanate began to weaken. In 1398, __4__ sacked the city of Delhi. The sultanate ended in 1526.

LESSON 3

New Ideas in Japan

Before You Read

- How did the geography of Japan help protect it from invaders?
- Why might a country have a feudal system?

New Words

shogun
shogunate
daimyo
samurai
Bushido
seppuku
defend
kamikaze
haiku
Noh drama

People and Places

Minamoto Yoritomo
Kamakura
Kyushu
Ashikaga
Kyoto

The Taika reforms of the seventh century gave Japan a central government. But they never gave Japan the full control shown by governments in China. By the 1100s, the power of the Japanese emperor was weak. Nobles fought one another. Robbers attacked people traveling through forests. Pirates attacked ships at sea. Many people ignored the laws and refused to pay taxes.

Then in 1192, a new leader named Minamoto Yoritomo came to power. He forced the emperor to make him **shogun**, or top general.

Minamoto Yoritomo was the first shogun of Japan.

Samurai armor

The emperor was still the head ruler, but Yoritomo controlled the army, money, and laws of Japan. Yoritomo could punish criminals and spend tax money. He could appoint government officials and make laws. Yoritomo's rule, and later the rule of his family, became known as the Kamakura **Shogunate**.

The Feudal System in Japan

Japan developed a feudal system similar to the one in Europe. The emperor was at the top of the system but had little real power. Next came the shogun. The **daimyo**, or powerful landowners, were below the shogun. The **samurai**, or warriors, were next. The peasants were below the samurai. The samurai received land from a daimyo. In return, the samurai were loyal to the daimyo and promised to fight for them.

The samurai lived by a strict code of honor called **Bushido**. Samurai had to be brave and loyal. For samurai, nothing was worse than losing

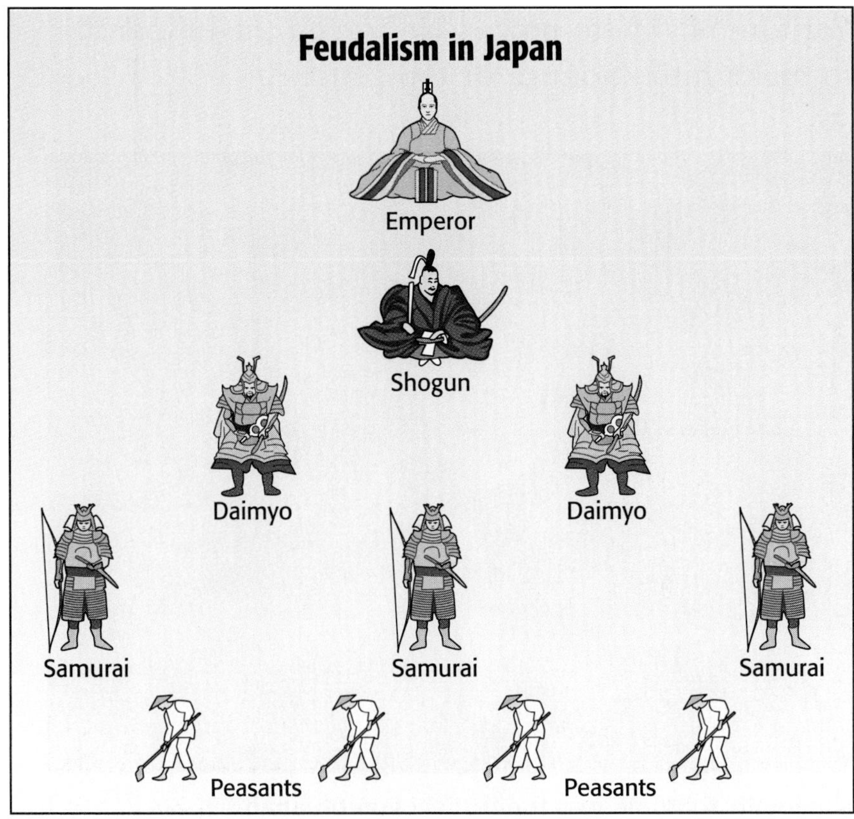

honor. If they lost their honor, samurai might kill themselves in a practice called **seppuku**. By doing so, they believed they regained their honor.

The Mongols Attack Japan

The sea had long protected Japan from attack. But the Mongols did not fear the sea. In 1266, Kublai Khan sent a message to the Japanese. He said he wanted to add Japan to his empire. The Japanese joined together to **defend** their country.

In 1274, a Mongol army landed on the Japanese island of Kyushu. The samurai fought off the Mongols. Then a strong storm came and sank many of the Mongol ships. The Japanese believed that their gods had sent the winds that defeated the Mongols. In Japanese, holy winds are called **kamikaze**.

In 1291, the Mongols attacked again. Kublai Khan sent an even bigger army to Japan. The Mongols brought their best weapons. But the Japanese built a wall to keep the Mongols from landing. Once again, a storm came. Strong winds sank many of the Mongol ships, along with most of the Mongol army.

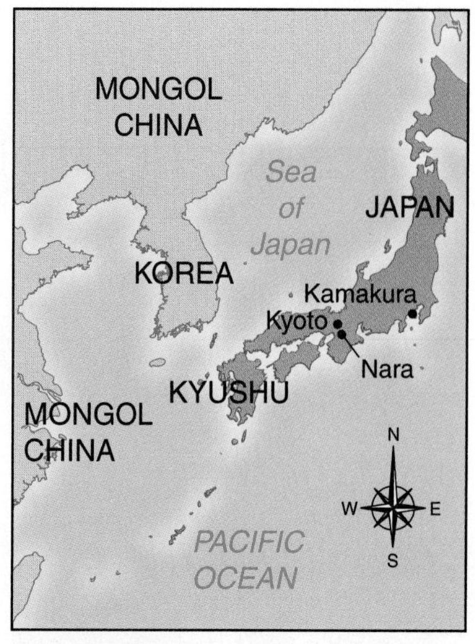

Feudal Japan

This painting shows the winds that defeated the Mongols.

The victory over the Mongols was costly. The Japanese spent a lot of money defending their country. The Kamakura Shogunate weakened, and by 1333, it had ended.

Haiku poem with illustration

Art Under the Ashikaga Shogunate

After several years of civil war, the Ashikaga Shogunate took control in 1394. They made Kyoto their capital city. The new shoguns controlled the city. During the Ashikaga Shogunate, the Japanese developed several new forms of art.

The Japanese created their own form of poetry called **haiku**. The haiku poems had just three lines. The first line had five syllables. The second line had seven syllables. The third line had five syllables. Haiku poets tried to capture one thought or idea. Often it was about nature or a person's role in the world.

The **Noh drama** was a type of theater. The actors wore masks and costumes and made slow and graceful movements. A chorus sang poetry to music.

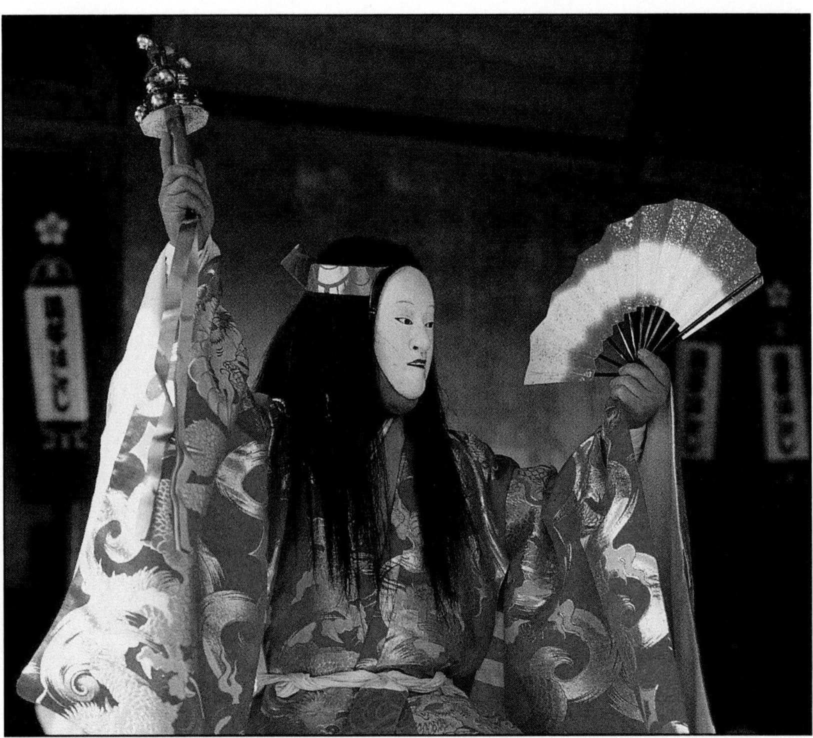

This modern actor is performing Noh drama.

The Japanese also made flower arranging into an art form. Priests, nobles, samurai, and young women all studied the art. They learned how to cut and place flowers to best appreciate the flower's beauty.

The Japanese made an art out of serving tea. It became a special event called a tea ceremony. The tea was served in a peaceful surrounding. There were no loud noises. People sipped their tea and spoke in soft voices.

Another Japanese art was landscape gardening. Some landscape gardens were made with plants, bridges, waterfalls, and ponds. Others simply had small and large rocks placed on sand. The sand was raked into certain patterns. With either type of garden, everything had to be in its proper place.

Modern Japanese rock garden

Lesson 3 Review

Choose words from the list that best complete the paragraphs. One word will not be used.

In 1192, Minamoto Yoritomo forced the emperor to make him shogun of Japan. Japan developed a feudal system. Powerful landowners were called __1__. Japanese warriors were called __2__. The warriors lived by a strict code of honor.

The Mongols attacked Japan twice. Both times the Japanese defeated the Mongols. The Japanese believed their gods sent the __3__, or holy winds, to defeat the Mongols.

The Ashikaga Shogunate took control of Japan in 1394. The Japanese developed new forms of art, such as __4__ poetry and the Noh drama.

Word List

seppuku
haiku
kamikaze
samurai
daimyo

LESSON 4

Kingdoms of Southeast Asia

New Words

Sanskrit
evacuated
declined

People and Places

Ly Thai
Champa
Khmer Empire
Angkor Wat
Bach Dang River
Le Loi
Nguyen Trai
Majapahit

Before You Read

- How might a country's culture influence nearby countries?
- Why might one group fight for freedom from another group?

The Vietnamese won their freedom from China in 938. In 1010, Ly Thai started the Ly Dynasty in northern Vietnam, known as Annam. Ly kings developed a strong central government. They collected taxes. They built dikes and canals to bring water to farmlands. The Ly kings were heavily influenced by China. They accepted

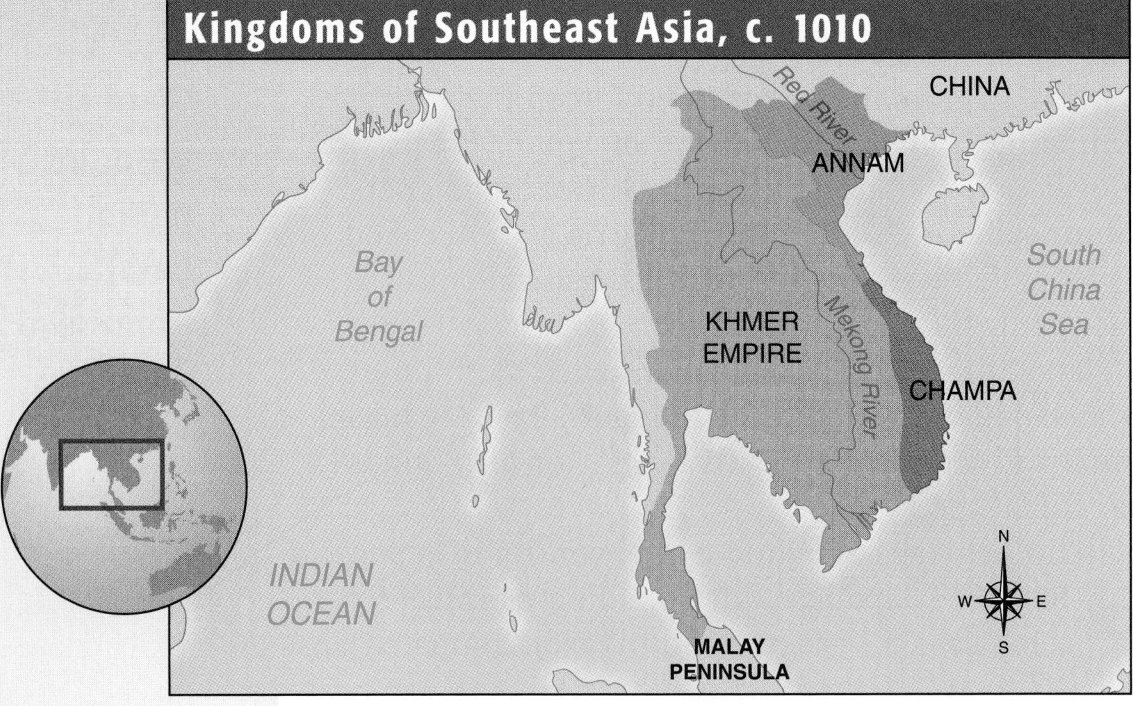

Angkor Wat was built as a Hindu temple. Buddhist temples were later added to the religious center.

Buddhism, the religion of China. Buddhist leaders helped the Ly kings rule Annam.

Wars with Neighbors

During their rule, Ly kings often had to fight China to keep Annam's freedom. They also fought the Kingdom of Champa to their south and the Khmer Empire to the west. Both Champa and the Khmer Empire were influenced by India. Their people practiced Hinduism and spoke an Indian language called **Sanskrit**.

Bas-relief from Angkor Wat

The Khmer Empire controlled a large piece of land west of Annam and Champa. Around 1113, the Khmer king ordered the building of a massive Hindu temple, known as Angkor Wat. It took thousands of people about 30 years to build Angkor Wat. When they finished, it was the largest religious center in the world.

In time, the culture of Annam began to influence the Khmer Empire. The people of the Khmer Empire even added Buddhist temples to the religious center at Angkor Wat.

The Tran Dynasty

In 1225, the Tran Dynasty replaced the Ly Dynasty. The Tran remained in power for 175 years. Tran rulers improved education and helped farmers. But the Tran are most known for defeating the Mongols. Three times, armies of Kublai Khan invaded Annam. Each time, the Vietnamese **evacuated** the capital city. When the Mongols arrived, they found an empty city. Then the Vietnamese attacked. They used guerrilla tactics to drive the Mongols away.

On the third attack, the Mongols sent a huge fleet of ships up the Bach Dang River. The Vietnamese drove iron stakes in the bottom of the river. They waited until the tide went out and the river dropped. Then the Vietnamese attacked. The Mongols tried to flee. But the iron stakes trapped their ships. The Vietnamese then shot fire arrows into the ships and burned much of the Mongol fleet.

Le Loi

The Tran Dynasty fell in 1400. In 1407, China gained control over Annam once more. The

The Vietnamese defeated the Mongols at a battle on the Bach Dang River.

Chinese ruled harshly. A Vietnamese man named Le Loi refused to work for the Chinese. He wanted the Chinese to leave Annam. He raised an army and fought the Chinese. In 1427, after ten years of fighting, the Vietnamese drove the Chinese out. The following year, Le Loi began the Le Dynasty.

Le Loi was a hero to the Vietnamese people. Legends developed about him. One legend says that a turtle gave Le Loi a huge sword. Le Loi used the sword to defeat the Chinese. After the war, Le Loi was sailing in a lake when the same turtle appeared. Le Loi thought that the gods must have given him the sword to win freedom. Now that Annam was free, it was time to give the sword back. So Le Loi returned the sword to the turtle. Then Le Loi gave the lake a new name—Lake of the Returned Sword. That is still the name of the lake today.

Nguyen Trai

Le Loi did not defeat China alone. One of his partners, Nguyen Trai, was given a high position in the Le Dynasty government. Nguyen Trai was a brave soldier and also a poet. Although he held a high office under Le Loi, he did not want fame or power. His poems tell how he longed for a more simple life.

Voices In History

"[Now] with half my life gone by,
Why should I bother with fame and gain?
Do I really need wealth and position?
Since rice with vegetable and plain water are more than enough."

In 1471, the Vietnamese conquered Champa. The Khmer Empire **declined**, and in time, the Vietnamese gained control of some Khmer lands, too. Rulers of the Le Dynasty stayed in power over the next 300 years.

Did You Know?

Cut Out the Knives

Today, many Asian people eat with chopsticks. This custom began in China long ago when there was a low supply of cooking fuel. To use less fuel, the Chinese people cut food into little pieces. The food cooked faster that way. Food was then served in bite-sized amounts, so knives were not needed at meals anymore. Chopsticks took their place. Today, chopsticks are mostly made of wood, but they can also be made of ivory, jade, silver, or even gold.

Islam Comes to Indonesia

You have read that the Buddhist kingdom of Sriwijaya was centered on the Indonesian island of Sumatra. Sriwijaya lasted until the 1200s. In the 1300s, the Hindu kingdom of Majapahit controlled much of Indonesia. It was centered on the island of Java.

A mosque in Indonesia

Then, in the late 1300s, Arab traders began arriving in Indonesia. They brought the teachings of Islam to the Indonesians. The Arab traders told the people about Muhammad and the Qur'an. Indonesians along the coast began to convert to Islam. Islam spread throughout the islands of Indonesia. In time, Islam became the most popular religion in Indonesia.

Lesson 4 Review

Choose words from the list that best complete the paragraphs. One word will not be used.

Word List

evacuated
Angkor Wat
Le Loi
Champa
Sanskrit

The Ly Dynasty continued fighting wars with China. It also fought against __1__ and the Khmer Empire. The Khmer Empire built a massive religious center known as __2__.

When the Mongols attacked Annam, Tran leaders __3__ the capital city. When the Mongols arrived, the city was empty.

China took over Vietnam in 1407. __4__ and Nguyen Trai worked together to defeat China. Le Loi began the Le Dynasty.

In Indonesia, Islam replaced Buddhism and Hinduism. Islam became the most popular religion in Indonesia.

Chapter 17: Using What You've Learned

Summary

- The Mongols were fierce warriors who conquered much of Asia. In 1279, they started the Yuan Dynasty in China.
- Muslim Turks led by Mahmud entered India around 1000. By 1206, much of India was under Muslim control.
- In 1192, Yoritomo became the first shogun of Japan. Like western Europe, Japan had a feudal system.
- The Vietnamese fought to keep their freedom from China. They extended their empire by defeating Champa and the Khmer Empire.
- In the late 1300s, Arab traders brought Islam to Indonesia. In time, Islam became more popular than Hinduism and Buddhism in Indonesia.

Find Out More!

After reading Chapter 17, you're ready to go online. **Explore Zone**, **Quiz Time**, and **Amazing Facts** bring this chapter of world history alive.

Visit www.exploreSV.com and type in the chapter code **Ch17**.

Vocabulary

Number your paper from 1 to 6. Write the word from the list that best completes each analogy. One word will not be used.

1. Bedouins were to Arabia as _____ were to the area north and west of China.
2. Short is to tall as _____ is to attack.
3. A defeat is to a loss as a _____ is to a win.
4. Emperors are to empires as sultans are to _____.
5. A lord was to western Europe's feudal system as a _____ was to Japan's feudal system.
6. Less is to more as _____ is to increased.

Word List

declined
Mongols
sultanates
conquest
daimyo
seppuku
surrender

Comprehension

Number your paper from 1 to 5. Write the word or words from the list that best complete each sentence. One word will not be used.

1. Kublai Khan started the _____ in China.
2. The most powerful Muslim kingdom in India was the _____.
3. Mahmud did not like the way Indians divided people into _____.
4. The _____ was at the top of the feudal system in Japan.
5. Le Loi was a hero to the _____ people.

Word List

infidels
Yuan Dynasty
castes
Vietnamese
Delhi Sultanate
emperor

Critical Thinking

Main Idea Number your paper from 1 to 4. Write the sentence that is the main idea in each group.

1. The Turks destroyed Hindu temples in India.
   The Turks plundered India.
   The Turks stole gold from Indian cities.
2. Many Delhi sultans welcomed Muslim artists and teachers into their courts.
   Many buildings in Delhi combined Islamic and Indian styles.
   Delhi became a center of Islamic culture.
3. Samurai lived by a strict code.
   Samurai had to be brave and loyal.
   For samurai, nothing was worse than losing honor.
4. Arab traders taught Indonesians about Islam.
   Islam spread throughout Indonesia.
   Indonesians along the coast began to convert to Islam.

Writing

Write a haiku poem about something that is important to you.

LESSON 1

West African Kingdoms

Before You Read

- What changes might traders bring to an area?
- How might a king show other countries that his kingdom is rich and powerful?

New Words

mansa
madrasas
resisted

People and Places

Mali
Sundiata
Mansa Musa
Ibn Battuta
Timbuktu
Leo Africanus
Songhai
Sonni Ali
Gao
Askia Mohammad
Morocco

There were three ancient West African kingdoms. The first was Ghana. After it fell, the West African kingdom of Mali rose to power. Mali began as a province of Ghana. The last king of Ghana tried to weaken Mali by killing its leaders.

One leader named Sundiata survived and raised an army in Mali. First, he took over other provinces of Ghana. Then, he conquered neighboring lands. By about 1230, he had created the Kingdom of Mali. It was twice the size of the Kingdom of Ghana. Sundiata accepted Islam and made Mali a Muslim kingdom. Sundiata ruled from 1230 to 1255 as **mansa**, or emperor, of Mali.

There are many mosques in modern-day West Africa.

The Kingdom of Mali

The decline of Ghana led to a slow down in trade. When Mali rose to power, the old caravan routes opened again. Arab traders came to the Sahel once more. Mali had taken over the gold fields of Ghana. It began trading slaves again as well. But Sundiata did not want to depend on trade alone. The land of Mali was rich. He urged people to farm. They grew crops such as grains, peanuts, and cotton.

Ibn Battuta

The Kingdom of Mali was at its height in the early 1300s under Mansa Musa. Mali had a strong Islamic government. The laws of Islam gave the people a sense of justice. Anyone who broke the law was quickly punished. Mali was a kingdom of law and order. A famous Arab traveler, Ibn Battuta, wrote about the Kingdom of Mali in 1352.

"There is complete [safety] in their country. Neither traveler nor [citizen] in it has anything to fear from robbers or men of violence."

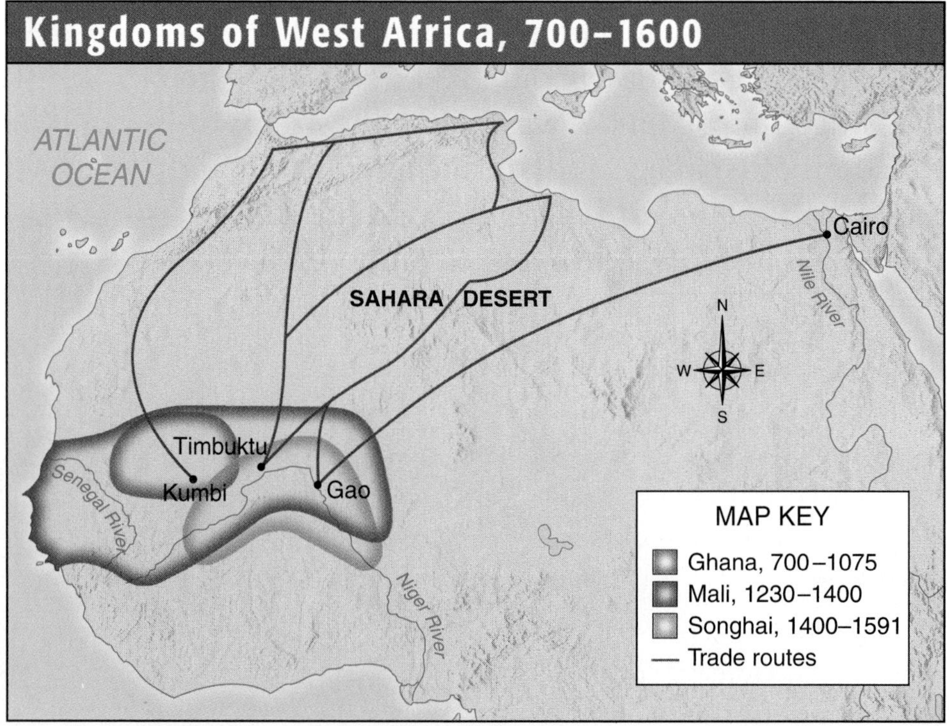

From 700–1600, West Africa was ruled by three different kingdoms. Along what river was the Kingdom of Songhai located?

Timbuktu was a center of trade and learning.

The City of Timbuktu

The Mali city of Timbuktu became a center of trade and learning. The city began as a camp along the Niger River. Nomads founded the camp around 1100. Traders crossing the Sahara Desert began arriving at Timbuktu. Other people came to the city by canoe. They sailed up the Niger River. By the 14th century, Timbuktu had grown into a major trade city. At its peak, Timbuktu might have had as many as 100,000 people. It was the center of the Kingdom of Mali.

Timbuktu also became a major place for Islamic learning. It was a meeting place for the great thinkers of the time. It had huge libraries and beautiful mosques. The city also had **madrasas**, or Islamic universities. A writer named Leo Africanus praised Timbuktu for its many "doctors, judges, priests, and other learned" people.

Statue from Mali

A mosque in Timbuktu

The Kingdom of Songhai

Mali was so large that it was difficult to rule. After Mansa Musa's death, the kingdom began to weaken. Local leaders **resisted** the emperor. In the 1400s, civil war broke out. Then the Kingdom of Songhai took control. It was the third and last of the ancient West African kingdoms.

Sonni Ali was the first Songhai ruler. His capital city was Gao on the Niger River. In 1468, Sonni Ali took over Timbuktu and other Mali cities. Sonni Ali ruled for 35 years. He built a strong army with soldiers both on foot and on horses. He also used a navy on the Niger River.

After Sonni Ali died in 1492, Askia Mohammad became the second Songhai leader. He expanded the empire and trade. He passed fair tax laws. He treated enemies with justice and tolerance. He also encouraged his people to accept Islam.

The Kingdom of Songhai ended in 1591. Morocco, a North African country, sent an army across the Sahara Desert and defeated the Songhai army. But the Moroccans could not hold the empire together. The age of ancient West African kingdoms was over.

This painting shows a busy day at a market in Timbuktu during the Kindgom of Songhai.

Mansa Musa (unknown–1332)

People In History

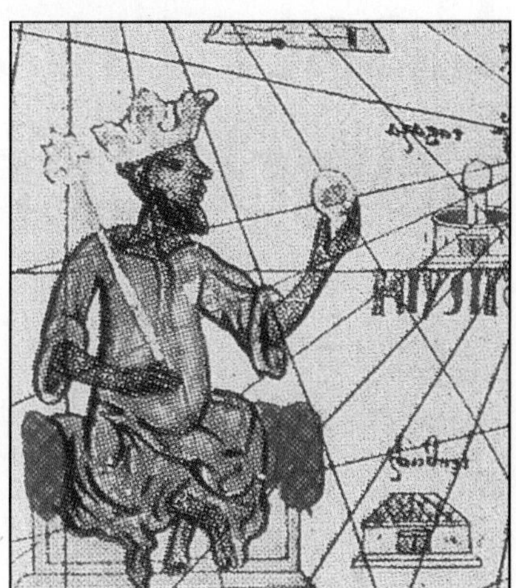

The most famous emperor of the West African kingdoms was Mansa Musa of Mali. He was a strong leader who encouraged education and the arts. He was also a devout Muslim.

Mansa Musa began his hajj, or journey to Mecca, in 1324. It was perhaps the most famous hajj in history. Some people think Mansa Musa took as many as 80,000 people with him. He took soldiers, government officials, his wives, and 500 slaves. He also took an incredible amount of gold. One hundred camels each carried 300 pounds of gold. Every slave carried a golden rod.

As he traveled, Mansa Musa began giving the gold away. He gave so much away that the value of gold dropped in the areas he traveled. Mansa Musa's incredible hajj made him famous as far away as Europe. People learned of the great wealth and power of Mali.

Lesson 1 Review

Choose words from the list that best complete the paragraph. One word will not be used.

Word List
Sonni Ali
Sundiata
Songhai
Mansa Musa
Timbuktu

Mali began as a province of Ghana. __1__ led an army that captured other provinces. He then set up the Kingdom of Mali. The city of __2__ was a major center for trade and learning on the Niger River. The most famous leader of Mali was __3__. He became known for giving away gold during his hajj to Mecca. The last ancient West African kingdom was __4__. It continued to rule West Africa until 1591.

LESSON 2

Eastern and Southern Africa

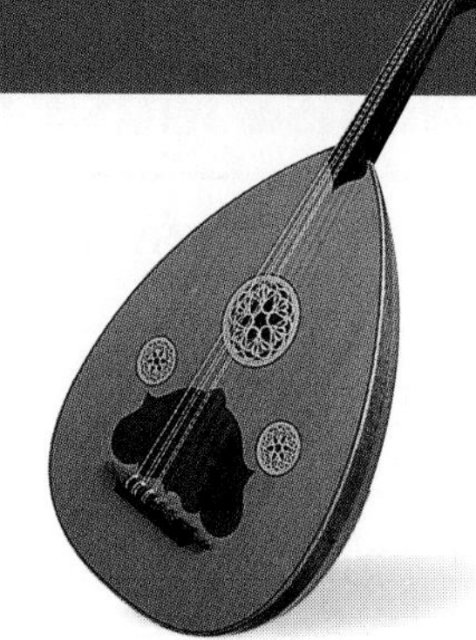

New Words

commodity
oral
mortar

People and Places

Mogadishu
Kilwa
Malindi
Mombasa
Zanzibar
Zambezi River
Great Zimbabwe

Before You Read

- What trade goods might bring riches to a region?
- What can be learned about a people by studying the ruins of their cities?

Between 700 and 1591, West Africa was ruled by three great kingdoms. In East Africa, however, there were no large kingdoms. Instead, East Africa had smaller city-states.

Around 1000, Bantu-speaking people settled along the coast of the Indian Ocean. Merchants from India, Arabia, and Persia also settled there. Arab culture changed East Africa. The Swahili language developed. It was a mixture of Bantu and Arabic. The Swahili culture was also a mixture of Bantu and Arab cultures.

This modern hunter lives in eastern Africa.

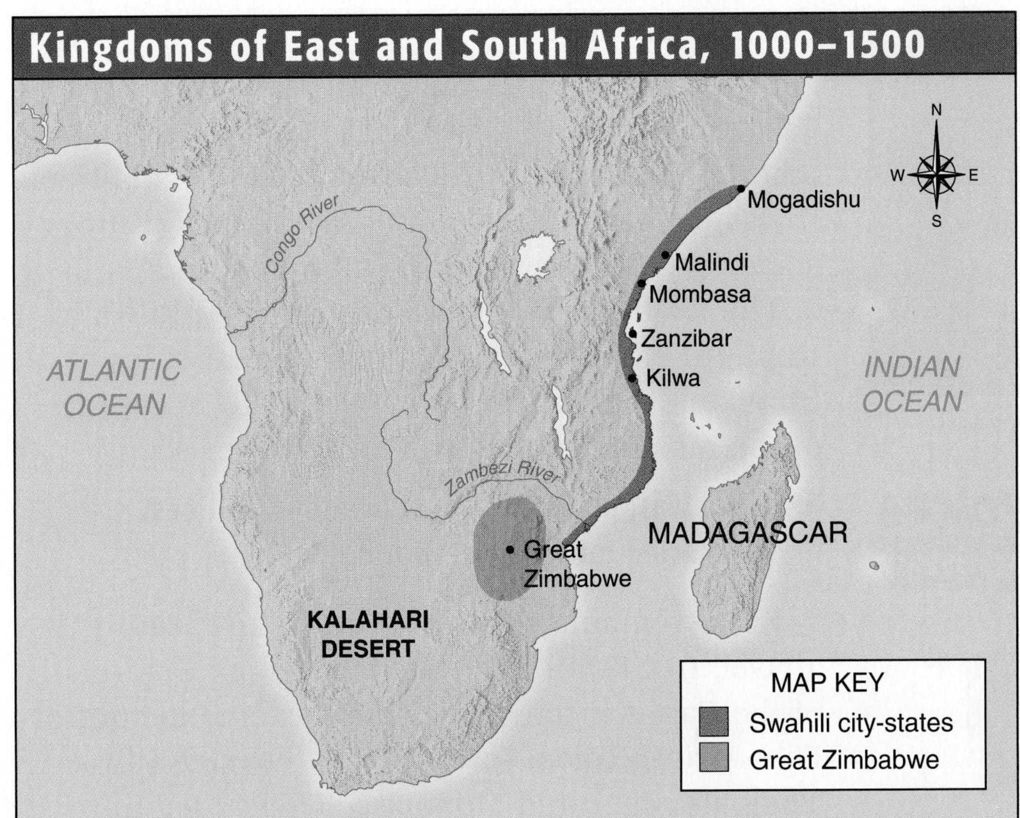

Several city-states developed along the east coast of Africa. Which city-state was the farthest south?

East African Trade

The Swahili city-states were port cities. They stretched from Mogadishu in the north to Kilwa in the south. Malindi, Mombasa, and Zanzibar were three other important city-states. Each one had its own laws, government, tax system, and rulers. The city-states often competed fiercely against one another. Each city-state wanted to control as much trade as possible.

One valuable **commodity** was ivory. Ivory was made from the tusks of African elephants. It was soft, so it could be carved easily. But it was also strong, so it could last a long time.

Gold was another valuable commodity. Like West Africa, East Africa had rich gold fields.

Another African commodity was iron. Traders from as far away as China bought African iron. In return, the East Africans bought cotton cloth, jewelry, spices, and Chinese porcelain.

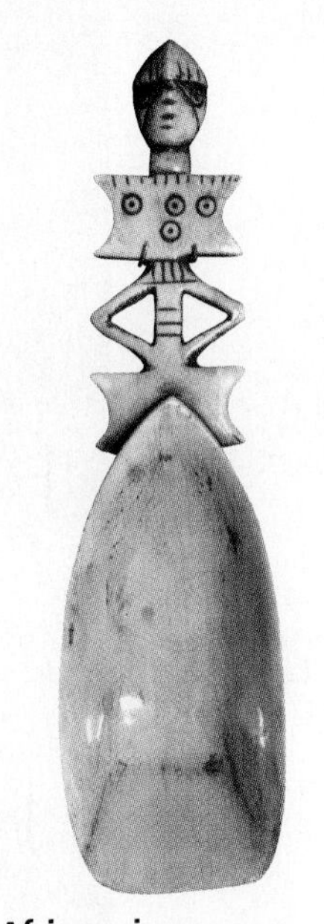

African ivory spoon

Ruins of a mosque in Kilwa

The City of Kilwa

Kilwa was perhaps the most powerful city in East Africa. It was closer to the gold fields than other cities, so it controlled most of the gold trade. It also collected taxes on the sale of gold. Kilwa leaders built grand palaces, mosques, and parks.

The Arab traveler Ibn Battuta visited Kilwa in 1331. He had already been to the great cities of China and India. Still, he thought Kilwa was one of the most amazing cities he had ever seen.

Voices In History

"[Kilwa was] one of the most beautiful and best constructed towns in the world."

Kilwa remained powerful until Europeans arrived in 1497. They were amazed by the wealth of the East African cities. They wanted to control East African trade. In 1505, they burned Kilwa. They also captured Mombasa. This ended the great trading days of the East African city-states. Swahili culture, however, survived.

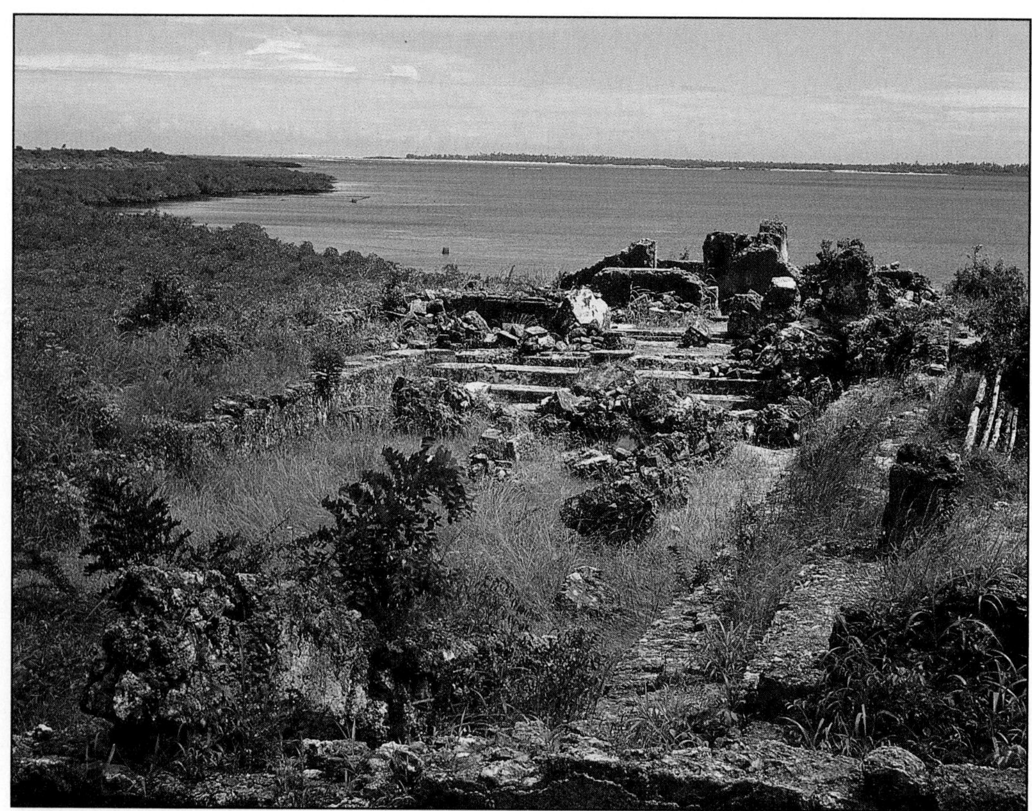
Kilwa was once an active trading city. Today, there are only ruins.

Great Zimbabwe

Far to the south of the city-states, a kingdom developed near the Zambezi River. It was called Great Zimbabwe. The people of Great Zimbabwe lived near gold fields.

Little is known about Great Zimbabwe culture. The people left no written record. Also, they left no **oral** traditions. They did, however, leave behind ruins in the form of stone walls. The stone ruins of Great Zimbabwe show that the stones were cut perfectly. The stones fit together without the use of any **mortar**, or cement. The skill of the stonework gave the city its name. The word *Zimbabwe* means "house of rock."

At one point, Great Zimbabwe might have had as many as 20,000 people. Then, about 1600, the culture disappeared. Without a written record, the full story of Great Zimbabwe remains a mystery.

Stones without mortar

Stone ruins of Great Zimbabwe

Lesson 2 Review

Choose words from the list that best complete the paragraphs. One word will not be used.

Swahili city-states developed along the coast of East Africa. The Swahili language was a mixture of Bantu and __1__. The East African city-states competed with one another for trade. One East African trade good was __2__. One of the most powerful Swahili city-states was __3__. It controlled much of the gold trade.

Less is known about the history of southern Africa during this time. There are stone ruins of a city called __4__. The stones of that city fit together without the use of mortar.

Word List

ivory
Great Zimbabwe
Kilwa
porcelain
Arabic

Chapter 18: Using What You've Learned

Summary

- Sundiata created the Kingdom of Mali in 1230. The Mali city of Timbuktu was once a great center for trade and Islamic learning.
- The last of the ancient West African kingdoms was Songhai. In 1591, Songhai was defeated by Morocco.
- Mansa Musa led a hajj to Mecca in 1324. The amount of gold he gave away on the journey made him famous.
- City-states developed on the east coast of Africa. Kilwa was perhaps the most powerful city in East Africa.
- The rise and fall of Great Zimbabwe, a kingdom in southern Africa, remains a mystery.

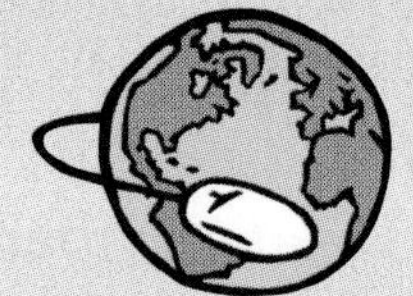

Find Out More!

After reading Chapter 18, you're ready to go online. **Explore Zone**, **Quiz Time**, and **Amazing Facts** bring this chapter of world history alive.

Visit www.exploreSV.com and type in the chapter code **Ch18**.

Vocabulary

Number your paper from 1 to 4. Write the letter of the correct answer.

1. In the African kingdom of Mali, a **mansa** was ____.

a. a trade center **c.** a journey
b. an emperor **d.** an infidel

2. **Madrasas** are Islamic ____.

a. beliefs **c.** mosques
b. universities **d.** villages

3. A valuable **commodity** in East African trade was ____.

a. language **c.** government
b. wood **d.** ivory

4. The walls of Great Zimbabwe were built without **mortar**, or ____.

a. dirt **c.** cement
b. sand **d.** glue

Comprehension

Number your paper from 1 to 6. Write one or more sentences to answer each question below.

1. Why did Mali's leader, Sundiata, urge his people to farm?
2. Why did Mali weaken after Mansa Musa's death?
3. What did Askia Mohammad do as leader of Songhai?
4. What two cultures was the Swahili culture a mixture of?
5. How did Europeans end the great trading days of the East African city-states?
6. Why is so little known about the people of Great Zimbabwe?

Critical Thinking

Fact or Opinion Number your paper from 1 to 5. For each fact, write **Fact**. Write **Opinion** for each opinion. You should find two sentences that are opinions.

1. The Kingdom of Mali was more important than the Kingdom of Ghana.
2. The people of Mali followed the laws of Islam.
3. Each Swahili city-state had its own laws, government, tax system, and rulers.
4. Kilwa controlled most of the gold trade in East Africa.
5. The people of Great Zimbabwe were the most skilled stoneworkers in Africa.

Writing

Write a short paragraph explaining why Timbuktu became a major center of learning in Mali.

Skill Builder: Reading a Bar Graph

A **bar graph** uses bars of different lengths to show facts. The bar graph below shows the greatest population of African kingdoms at the peak of their civilizations.

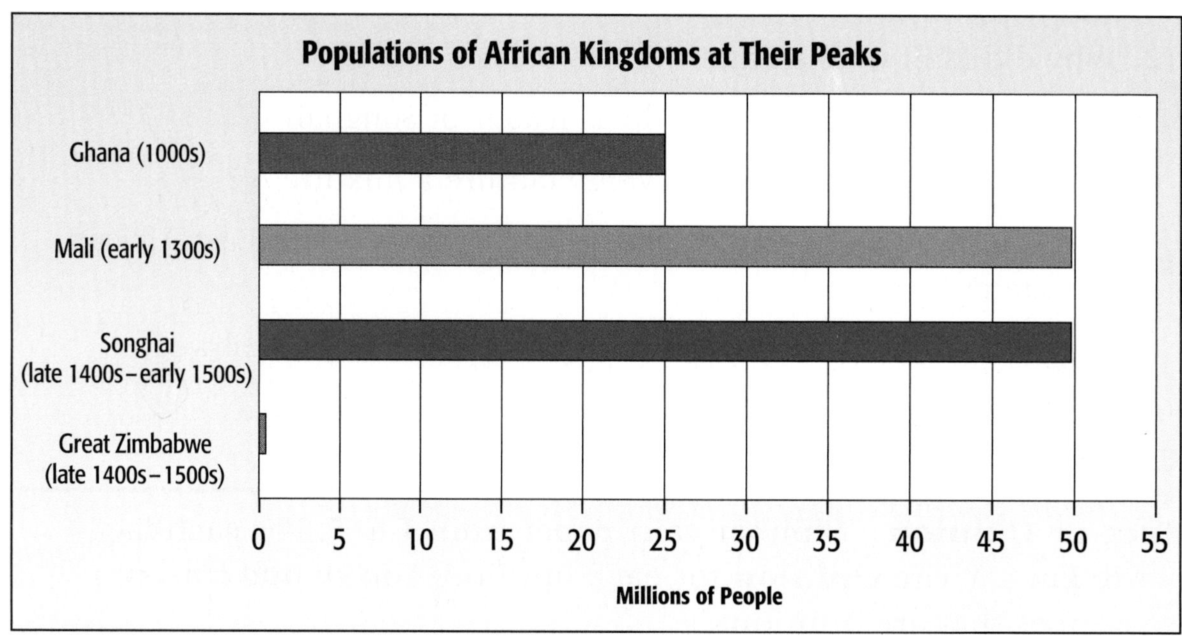

Number your paper from 1 to 4. Write the letter of the correct answer.

1. How many people might have lived in Ghana in the 1000s?
   a. 20,000 **b.** 25 million **c.** 50 million
2. About how many people lived in Mali when it was at its peak?
   a. 20,000 **b.** 25 million **c.** 50 million
3. When did Songhai have around 50 million people?
   a. 1000s **b.** early 1300s **c.** late 1400s to early 1500s
4. Which of these kingdoms had the smallest population at its peak?
   a. Ghana **b.** Mali **c.** Great Zimbabwe

LESSON 1

The Aztec and the Inca

Before Your Read

- How do most civilizations choose where to build their cities?
- How might people communicate without using language?

The Toltec built a huge empire in Central America from around 700 to 1100. Then around 1200, their empire fell to the Aztec. These warlike people had wandered in northern Mexico for centuries. Then the Aztec moved into central Mexico and conquered the Toltec, as well as many other groups. The Aztec then created the most powerful empire in North America.

New Words

causeways
chinampas
quipu

People and Places

Aztec
Lake Texcoco
Tenochtitlán
Inca
Andes Mountains
Cuzco
Machu Picchu

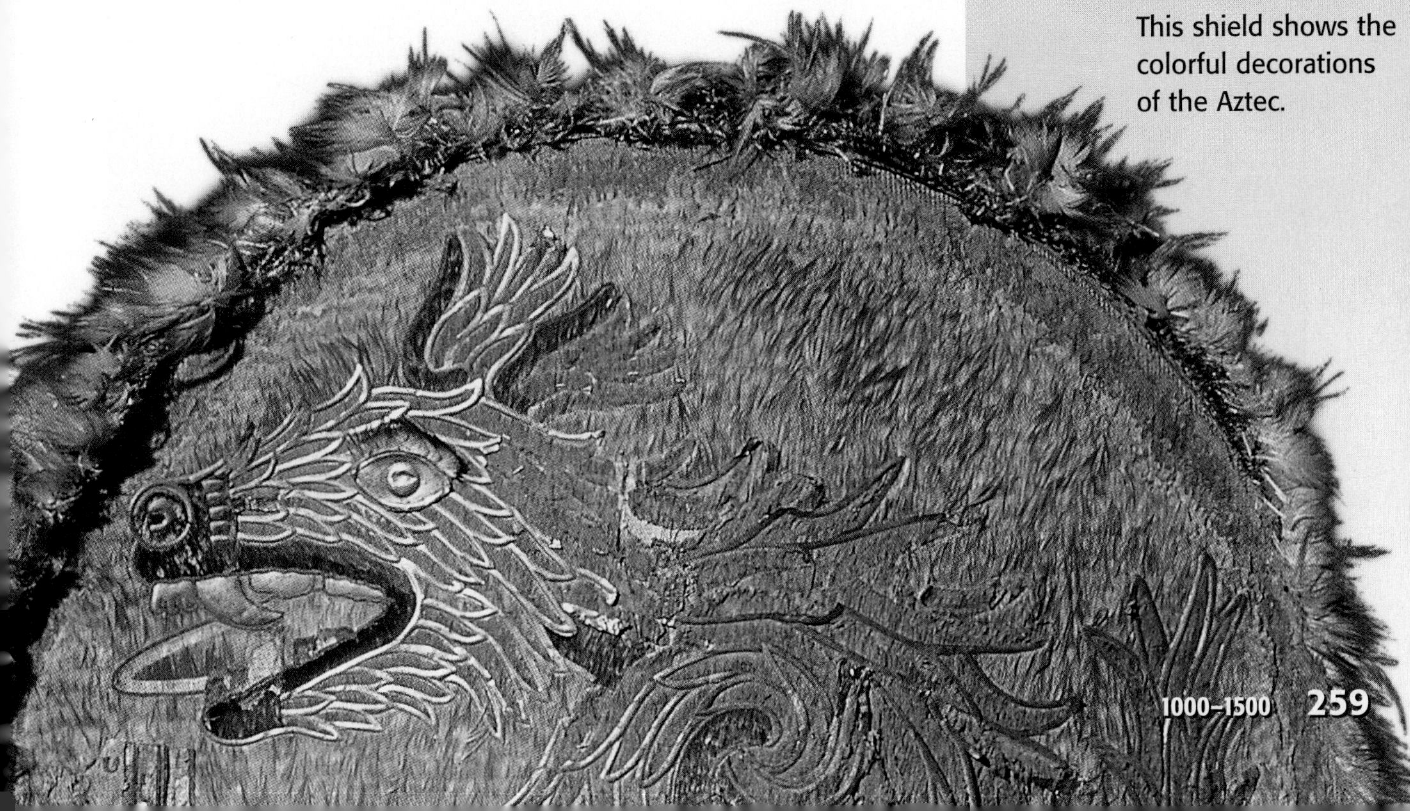

This shield shows the colorful decorations of the Aztec.

Mexican flag

Looking for a Sign

The Aztec searched for a place to build their capital city. Legend says that one of their gods told them to look for a sign. They were to look for an eagle sitting on a cactus, holding a snake in its mouth. Where they saw that sign, they were to build their capital city. The Aztec found this spot on an island in Lake Texcoco. The Aztec built their capital on that island in 1325. They named the city Tenochtitlán. Today, the flag of Mexico shows an eagle sitting on a cactus, holding a snake in its mouth.

The Aztec had another reason for building Tenochtitlán on an island. The water protected them from their enemies. The island also gave them a safe place from which to launch their own attacks.

The Island City

The Aztec turned the island into a great city. It had a large main square. Tenochtitlán also had parks, a zoo, temples, gardens, canals, a library,

The Aztec capital city, Tenochtitlán, was built on an island in Lake Texcoco.

and thousands of houses. Aztec rulers lived in a huge palace with enough room for the royal family and 3,000 servants. To get in and out of the city, the Aztec built **causeways**, or roads over water. They also built canals.

Up to 250,000 people might have lived in Tenochtitlán. To help feed them all, the Aztec built **chinampas**. These were floating gardens in the shallow parts of the lake. On the chinampas, Aztec farmers planted corn and many other crops.

The Aztec Way of Life

War was a way of life for the Aztec. Boys were taught to fight at an early age. The Aztec conquered many neighboring groups. At its height, the empire covered most of modern-day Mexico. In total, about 15 million people lived under Aztec rule.

Human sacrifice was also a part of their lives. The Aztec believed that the sun god demanded such sacrifices. Without the sacrifices, the world would come to an end. For the Aztec, the sun god controlled life and death. One Aztec poet wrote about the power of the sun god.

Voices In History

"He [laughs at] us.
As he wishes, so he wills.
He places us in the palm of his hand,
He rolls us about;
Like pebbles we roll, we spin . . .
We make him laugh."

The Inca

In South America, the Inca lived on the western slopes of the Andes Mountains. They began around 1100 as one small group among many. For about 300 years, they fought a series of wars with neighbors. By the 1400s, the Inca had set up a vast empire.

Did You Know?

Chocolate Money

The next time you eat chocolate, think of the Maya and the Aztec. The Maya first learned how to roast cacao beans. They then ground up the beans and made a chocolate drink. There was no sugar, so they added hot peppers for spice. The Aztec kings valued chocolate so much that they drank it from a golden cup. The Aztec even used the cacao beans as money. An Aztec could buy nearly anything with enough cacao beans.

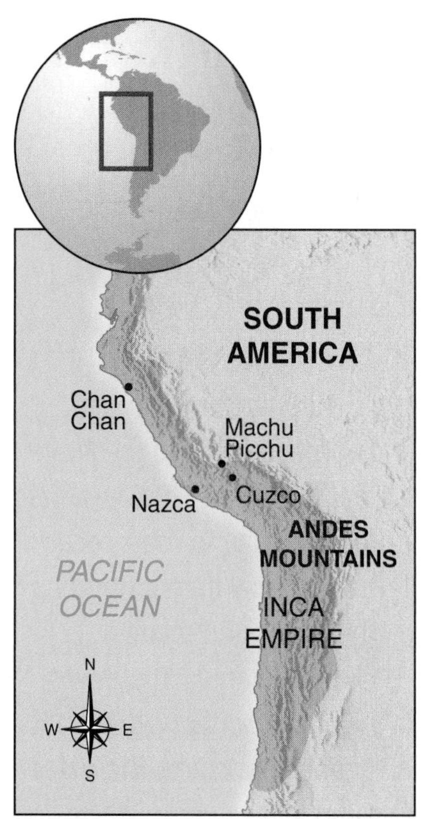

The Inca Empire

The Inca Empire stretched 2,500 miles north to south and 500 miles east to west. The Inca built their capital in the mountains of modern-day Peru. They named it Cuzco. Another famous Inca city was Machu Picchu. Because Machu Picchu was located high in the mountains, Europeans did not discover it until 1911.

An emperor ruled the Inca people. The people believed the emperor came from the sun god. He was treated as if he were a god. The Inca emperor set strict laws. Almost everything in the empire belonged to the emperor. The Inca people had little freedom. But the Inca did take good care of people who became ill or were too old to work.

Roads and Knotted Strings

The Inca built a system of roads to unite their empire. They had no horses and no wheeled carts, so the roads did not have to be very wide. Still, building them wasn't easy. Their land had high mountains and deep canyons. The Inca built rope bridges over the canyons. They carved steps up steep mountain passes. Where they could, the

Today, visitors are impressed by the ancient ruins of Machu Picchu.

Inca made roads with stone. The longest road went the full length of the empire.

The Inca used the roads to send messages from one end of the empire to the other. One runner would run for a few miles. Then a new runner would take over. Using this system, a message could travel more than 100 miles in a day.

The Inca had no written language. The runners had to memorize messages. They used a system of knotted strings called a **quipu**. A quipu was a group of colored strings. The color of the string and the way it was knotted stood for a particular word or number. For example, a certain colored knot could mean danger.

Both the Aztec and the Inca civilizations were at their height around 1500. They continued to grow until Spanish explorers arrived.

Inca quipu

Lesson 1 Review

Choose words from the list that best complete the paragraphs. One word will not be used.

In 1325, the Aztec built Tenochtitlán on an island in Lake Texcoco. They built __1__, which made it easy to get in and out of the capital. To grow more food, the Aztec built __2__, or floating gardens. The Aztec practiced human sacrifice to please the sun god.

The Inca made __3__ their capital city. They built a system of roads to unite the empire. Runners carried messages along the roads. The Inca used a system of knotted strings called a __4__ to communicate because they had no written language.

Word List

quipu
causeways
Peru
Cuzco
chinampas

LESSON 2

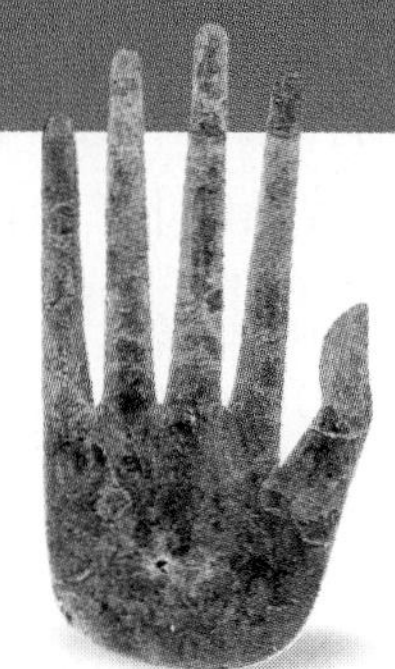

North American Civilizations

New Words
ancestors
pueblos
mesas
burial grounds

People and Places
Navajo
Pueblo Indians
Colorado
Hopi
Zuni
Mound Builders
Hopewell
Ohio River
Mississippians
Mississippi River
Cahokia Mound
Illinois

Before Your Read
- Why might people build their villages into the side of a cliff?
- Why might a group of people be called the Mound Builders?

The Anasazi lived in the southwestern part of what is now the United States. Once nomads, the Anasazi began to settle and farm around 750. The word *Anasazi* is a Navajo word that means "ancient ones." Most people believe the Anasazi were the **ancestors** of the modern Pueblo Indians.

This pueblo in Mesa Verde, Colorado, was built in the 12th century.

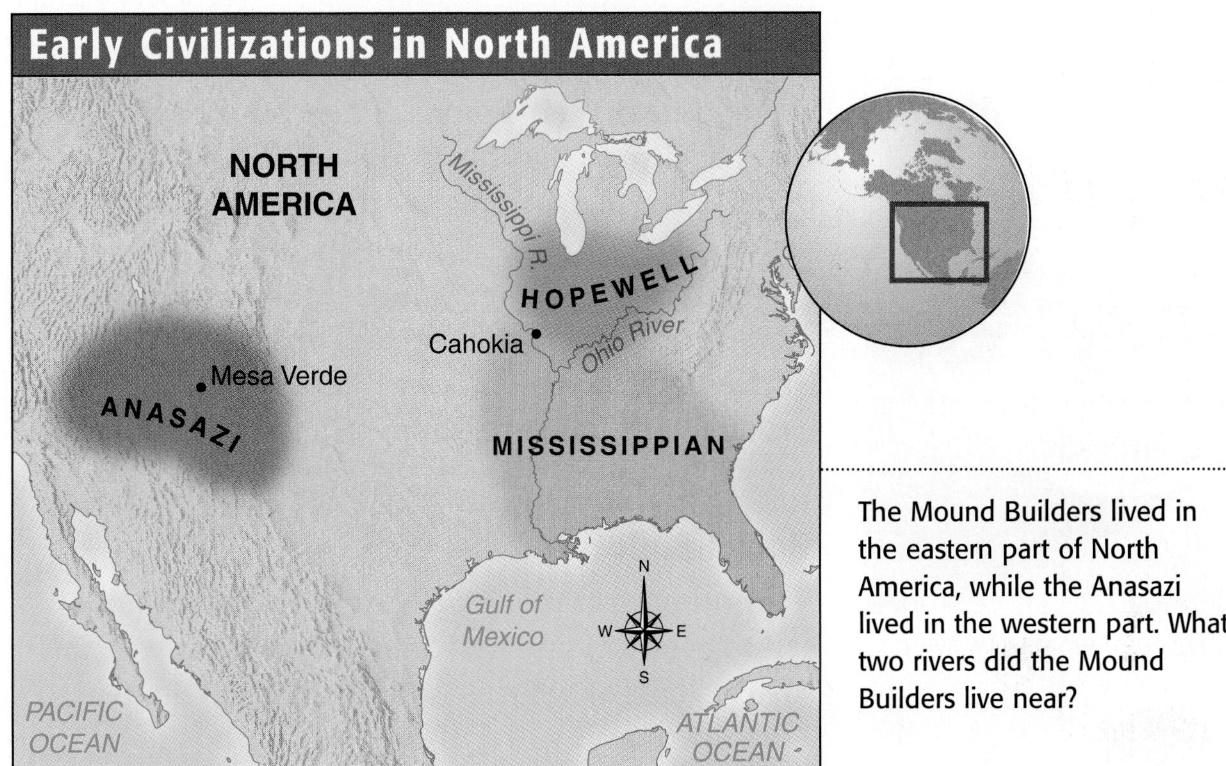

The Mound Builders lived in the eastern part of North America, while the Anasazi lived in the western part. What two rivers did the Mound Builders live near?

The Anasazi

The Anasazi built villages called **pueblos**. They often built them on the top of **mesas**, or flat-topped mountains with steep sides. They also lived in caves that they dug into the sides of cliffs. These homes protected them from the weather and from enemies. Some pueblos were quite large. One pueblo was built in the modern-day state of Colorado. It had 1,800 rooms that held about 3,000 people.

The Anasazi continued their tradition of making beautiful baskets. They began to grow new crops, such as beans. They also made beautiful pottery for cooking and storing food.

The Anasazi civilization declined after 1300. The people began leaving their pueblos. By around 1400, the Anasazi pueblos were empty.

Many scientists believe that the Anasazi people ran out of water. There was a drought from about 1275 to 1300. Overpopulation might have been another cause of the Anasazi decline.

Anasazi frog pin

Modern Hopi woman weaving a basket

Another reason for the Anasazi decline might have been poor health. The Anasazi left their garbage near their homes. This could have brought diseases to the people. Still another cause might have been a neighboring group that drove the Anasazi from their homes.

After leaving their homes, the Anasazi joined other groups such as the Hopi and Zuni. Many Native Americans today still farm land, weave baskets, and make pottery in the same way as the Anasazi.

Mound Builders

Another group of North Americans are known as the Mound Builders. They lived mostly in the eastern half of what is now the United States. They were known for the huge mounds they formed on the ground.

The mounds were built in different shapes and sizes. Some were built in the shape of pyramids. Others were built to look like snakes or birds. Many of these mounds are so large that they can only be seen from the sky.

Several groups built mounds. The Hopewell built mounds in the Ohio River valley. Many

This mound in the Ohio River valley is shaped like a snake.

archaeologists believe that the Hopewells' mounds were **burial grounds**. Another group, the Mississippians, lived along the Mississippi River. Their mounds were foundations for their temples. Other groups might have built mounds as symbols for religious ceremonies or defense.

The Cahokia Mound in the modern-day state of Illinois is one of the largest mounds. Shaped like a pyramid, it is 1,000 feet long, 300 feet wide, and 100 feet high. Scientists believe that 30,000 people might have lived at or near this mound.

The Mound Builders carried dirt in baskets to the place of the mound. The larger mounds must have taken years to build. Scientists have found shark teeth from the Gulf of Mexico in mounds far away from the coast. This could mean that the Mound Builders had contact and traded with other North American groups.

Cahokia Mound

Lesson 2 Review

Choose words from the list that best complete the paragraphs. One word will not be used.

The Anasazi built villages called __1__. They often settled on the top of __2__ to protect themselves from enemies. The Anasazi began to leave their pueblos around 1300. The Anasazi way of life continued in the cultures of many modern Native Americans.

The __3__ lived mostly in the eastern half of the United States. Archaeologists believe that the __4__ used their mounds as burial grounds. Other groups built temples on their mounds.

Word List

Hopewell
Zuni
mesas
Mound Builders
pueblos

Chapter 19: Using What You've Learned

Summary

- The Aztec took control of central Mexico from the Toltec. They built their capital, Tenochtitlán, on an island in Lake Texcoco.
- The Inca built a vast empire in South America. Their capital city, Cuzco, was located in the mountains of modern-day Peru.
- Historians believe the Anasazi were ancestors of the modern-day Pueblo Indians. Around 1300, the Anasazi began to leave their villages and join other groups, such as the Hopi and Zuni.
- Mound Builders lived in the eastern United States. They built huge mounds in the shapes of pyramids, snakes, and birds. These mounds served many purposes.

Find Out More!

After reading Chapter 19, you're ready to go online. **Explore Zone**, **Quiz Time**, and **Amazing Facts** bring this chapter of world history alive.

Visit www.exploreSV.com and type in the chapter code **Ch19**.

Vocabulary

Number your paper from 1 to 6. Finish the sentences from Group A with words from Group B. Write the letter of the correct answer.

Group A

1. The Aztec built _____ so they could get in and out of Tenochtitlán.
2. To grow crops, the Aztec built _____ in the shallow parts of the lake.
3. The Inca kept records by using knotted strings called a _____.
4. The Anasazi built villages called _____.
5. The Anasazi often built their villages on the top of _____.
6. Archaeologists believe that the Hopewell used their mounds as _____.

Group B

a. mesas

b. burial grounds

c. quipu

d. causeways

e. chinampas

f. pueblos

Comprehension

Number your paper from 1 to 5. Write the word or words from the list that best complete the paragraph. One word will not be used.

The Aztec moved into central Mexico around 1200 and conquered the __1__. The Aztec built their capital on an island in __2__. The Inca lived in South America in the __3__ Mountains. The Inca built a system of __4__ to unite their empire. The Aztec and the Inca civilizations grew until __5__ explorers arrived.

Word List

Lake Texcoco
mesas
Toltec
Spanish
roads
Andes

Critical Thinking

Conclusions Number your paper from 1 to 3. Read each pair of sentences below. Then look for a conclusion that follows from these sentences. Write the letter of the correct conclusion.

1. The Anasazi built pueblos on steep, flat-topped mountains. They also lived in caves dug into the sides of cliffs.

2. The Anasazi left their garbage near their homes. This may have given the people diseases.

3. Scientists have found shark teeth in Mound Builder mounds. These mounds are far away from the Gulf of Mexico.

Conclusions

a. Poor health might be one reason for the Anasazi decline.

b. Mound Builders might have traded with other North American groups.

c. Anasazi homes were built to protect the people from enemies and weather.

Writing

Write a paragraph comparing the ways the Inca sent messages within their empire with the ways messages are sent today.

UNIT 5

Global Exchanges

1300–1800

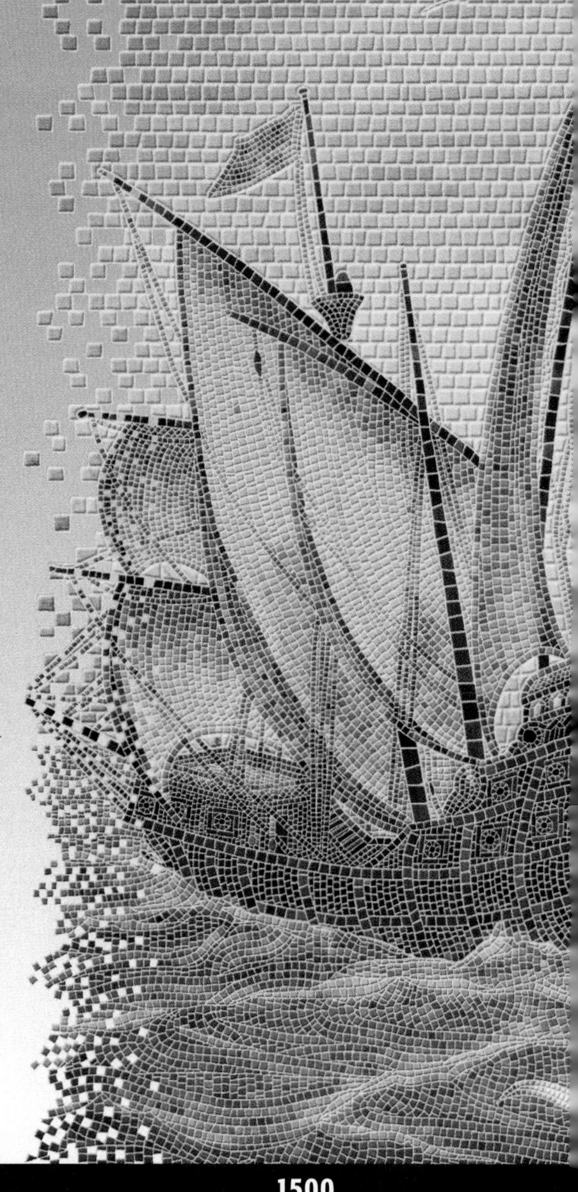

The end of the Middle Ages brought new ideas to Europe. Europeans began to challenge old customs. Feudalism died, and cities grew again. Europeans also began to explore the world and expand trade. This brought distant cultures together for the first time.

This unit shows how the world reacted to European explorations. People in the Americas, Africa, and Asia were very different from Europeans. Sometimes the meeting of cultures was peaceful. Many times it was deadly. Some people welcomed European ideas. Others closed themselves off from world trade. In all cases, the arrival of Europeans to new lands changed the world forever.

A.D. 1300 1400 1500

1300
The Ottoman Empire begins in Southwest Asia.

1368
Ming Dynasty begins.

1521
Spanish forces, led by Hernán Cortés, defeat the Aztec.

1600 | 1700 | 1800 | A.D.

1632
Galileo writes a book about his scientific discoveries.

1701
The Ashanti people unite to build a kingdom in West Africa.

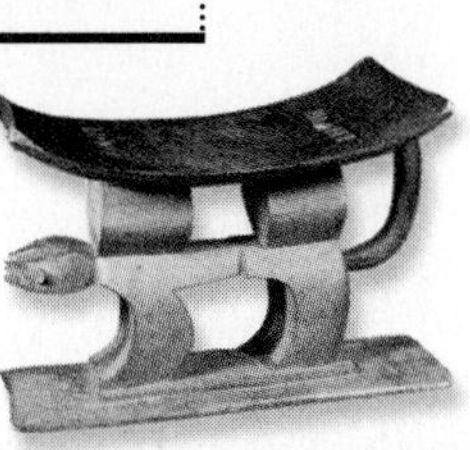

1800
England controls most of India.

LESSON 1

The Renaissance

New Words

Renaissance
scholars
anatomy
architecture
perspective
printing press
humanism
folly

People and Places

Michelangelo Buonarroti
Leonardo da Vinci
Florence
Lorenzo de Medici
Filippo Brunelleschi
Johann Gutenberg
Erasmus
Thomas More
William Shakespeare

Before You Read

- What might Europeans have liked about ancient Greece and Rome?
- Why might artists want to show real life in their works?

By the middle of the 1300s, Europeans started to think in new ways. People wanted to return to the glory of ancient Greece and Rome. They began a movement to advance the arts, the sciences, and philosophy. This time in European history is called the **Renaissance**.

The Renaissance began in Italy. Italians had contact with the rich civilizations of Asia and Africa. From them, Italian traders learned much about ancient Greece and Rome that had been forgotten in Europe. World trade also made Italy a wealthy country. It had more big cities than any other country in Europe. The big cities attracted **scholars** and artists.

Michelangelo's paintings look very lifelike.

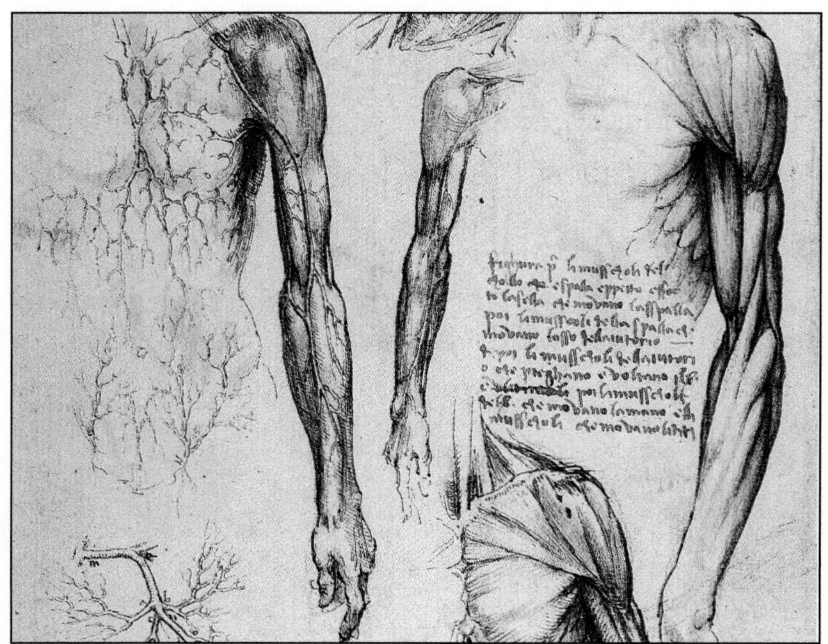

This drawing by Leonardo da Vinci shows his understanding of human anatomy.

The *Mona Lisa*

Renaissance Art

Art in the Middle Ages was almost always religious. The stained glass windows in cathedrals were based on Bible stories. Paintings were also religious. The people in the paintings often did not look real. That was not very important to artists in the Middle Ages.

Renaissance artists were different. They wanted art to show what people really looked like. Michelangelo Buonarroti and Leonardo da Vinci were two Italian artists. They learned **anatomy** by studying human bodies. They wanted to know every bone and muscle so their art could look as real as possible.

The center of the Italian Renaissance was in the city of Florence in northern Italy. City merchants there became wealthy from trade. Some used their money to support artists. One of the richest families in Florence was the Medici family. Lorenzo de Medici helped artists in so many ways that he was called "Lorenzo the Magnificent."

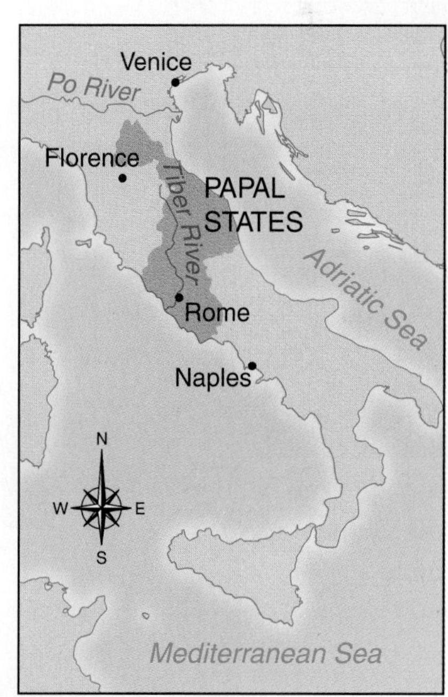

Italy During the Renaissance

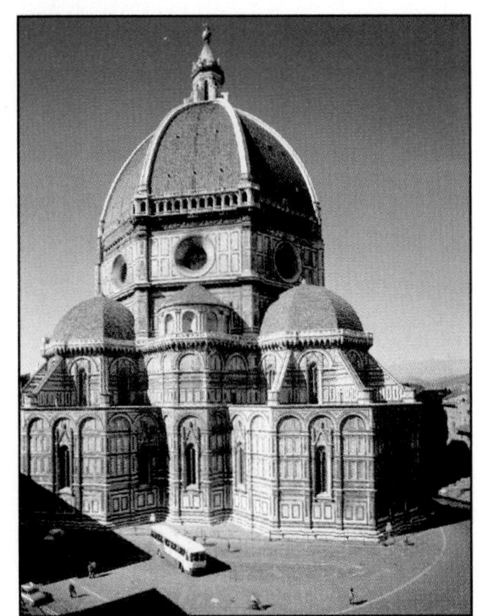
Church dome designed by Brunelleschi in Florence, Italy

Filippo Brunelleschi was an architect who lived in Florence. He studied the way Romans built their temples. Brunelleschi applied his own ideas to the old style. The result was a new kind of **architecture**. He designed small pieces of a building next to larger pieces to show the differences in size. His style of architecture can still be seen today. Brunelleschi also found a way to draw **perspective** on a flat surface.

The Printing Press

One of the greatest inventions in history was the **printing press**. You read in Chapter 13 that the Chinese invented movable type during the Song Dynasty. Around 1456, a German man named Johann Gutenberg used movable type to make a printing press. He used his press to print copies of the Bible.

Within the next 100 years, European printing presses produced millions of books. They printed them in Latin, the language of the church. They also printed them in French, German, English, and Italian.

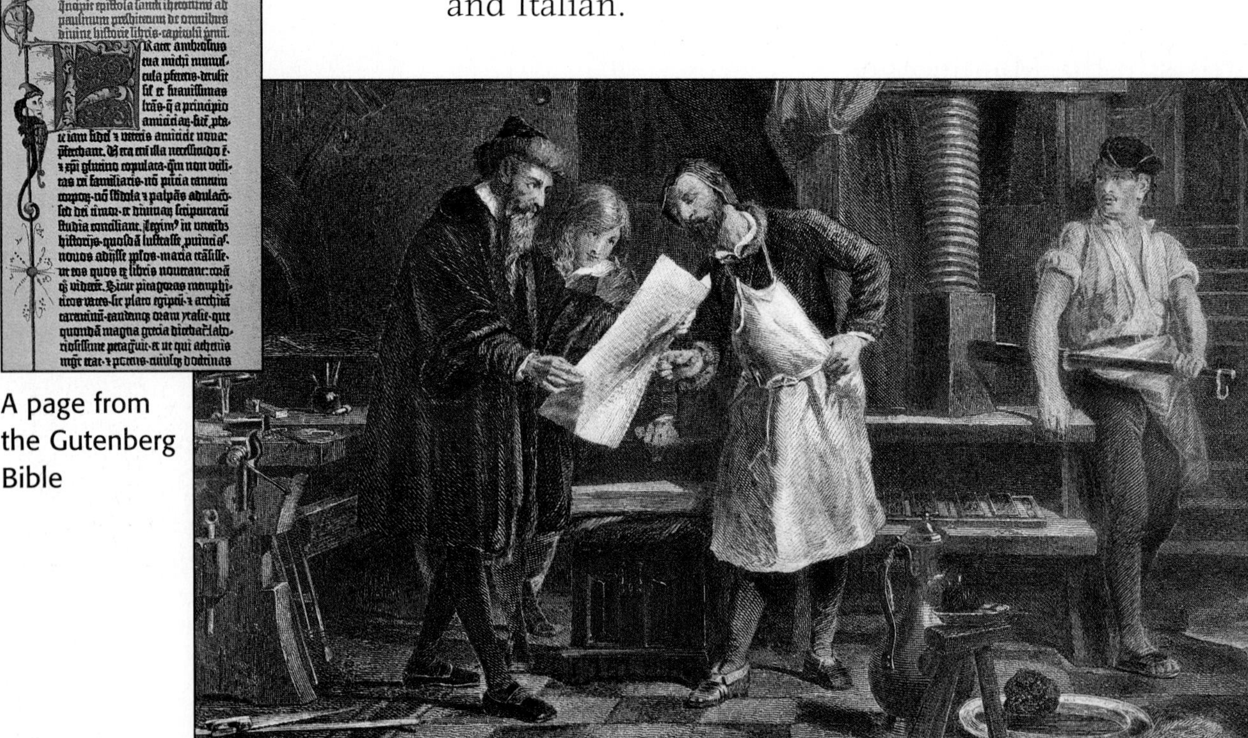
A page from the Gutenberg Bible

Johann Gutenberg shows others how his printing press works.

Before the printing press, all books had to be copied by hand. There were very few books. In the Middle Ages, the church controlled most of the books. But the printing press made books available to many more people. The few common people who knew how to read could read the Bible for themselves for the first time.

Erasmus

Humanism

A new movement called **humanism** grew out of the Renaissance in Italy. In the Middle Ages, life was hard for most people. They looked forward to heaven, where they believed life would be better. Humanists had a different view. They wanted to learn more about life on Earth and less about life in heaven. They wanted to solve "human" problems. To learn more, humanists studied the books of ancient Greece and Rome. They also studied the Bible in its original languages of Hebrew and Greek.

The Renaissance and humanism spread into northern Europe. Erasmus, a Catholic priest, was a Dutch humanist. He wrote of problems he saw in the church in a popular book called *The Praise of Folly*. The book made fun of the **folly**, or foolishness, of the church. Erasmus felt the church had too many ceremonies. He also attacked the church for being too concerned with making money.

Thomas More

An English humanist, Thomas More, had similar ideas. He wrote about problems he saw in the government as well as the church. His book, *Utopia*, compared life in Europe to a perfect, but imaginary, society.

Humanists were not always popular. Their ideas often made government and church officials angry. For example, Thomas More was killed because he would not agree that the king of England was the head of the Catholic Church.

William Shakespeare

William Shakespeare

William Shakespeare lived in England from 1564 to 1616. He wrote hundreds of plays and poems. Many people think Shakespeare was the greatest English writer ever. Many of his sayings have become part of everyday speech. Sayings such as "All the world's a stage" and "All that glitters is not gold" come from Shakespeare.

As a Renaissance writer, Shakespeare wrote plays that are similar to ancient Greek and Roman dramas. The ideas of humanism also made their way into the writings of Shakespeare. His characters are as real today as they were in the 1500s. Even today, his plays are performed around the world. Many of his plays, such as *Romeo and Juliet* and *Hamlet*, have been made into movies.

Lesson 1 Review

Choose words from the list that best complete the paragraphs. One word will not be used.

Word List

anatomy
printing press
folly
humanism
Renaissance

During the 1300s, a new way of thinking began in Italy. The people wanted to return to the glory of ancient Greece and Rome. The __1__ began in Italy and slowly spread through the rest of Europe. Artists of this time studied __2__. They tried to show the real human form. Rich families, such as the Medici family, supported artists.

The __3__ made it possible to print many copies of books. This gave people the power to read and to think for themselves.

The movement called __4__ grew out of the Renaissance. People wanted to think more about this world than the next. These ideas were shown in the writings of Erasmus, Thomas More, and William Shakespeare.

LESSON 2

The Reformation

Before You Read

- Why might someone want to make changes to a religion?
- How can religious practices be changed?

The ideas of the humanists influenced many Europeans. The people began to question some common church practices. Many people felt the church was too strong. In many ways, the church was the most powerful force in Europe. Popes had more power than kings. Some people fought for reform. In the 1500s, the **Reformation** began.

One church practice allowed people to pay monks to be forgiven for their sins.

New Words

Reformation
indulgences
95 Theses
excommunicated
Protestants
Huguenots
divorce
Counter Reformation
Jesuits
Council of Trent
Inquisition

People and Places

Martin Luther
Johann Tetzel
Wittenberg
Leo X
Switzerland
John Calvin
Henry VIII
Catherine of Aragon
Catherine de Medici

Martin Luther posts his complaints on the door of a church.

Martin Luther

The Reformation started with Martin Luther. He was a German monk who disliked certain church practices. He was particularly unhappy about the sale of **indulgences**. A person who sinned could buy an indulgence from the church. The person was then forgiven. To Luther, the sale of indulgences was wrong. He felt it was a way for church leaders to get rich.

In 1517, a monk named Johann Tetzel started selling indulgences. Luther warned people not to buy them, but most people didn't listen. Luther made a list of complaints about the church. On October 31, 1517, he nailed this list to a church door in the German city of Wittenberg. The list became known as the **95 Theses**. Luther knew his list would anger some people. Still, he felt people needed to learn of his complaints. He wrote about his determination to stand by his beliefs.

Voices In History

"These are the [ideas] on which I must stand, and God willing, shall stand even to my death. I do not know how to change or surrender anything in them."

The church acted quickly. Tetzel said, "I will have Luther burned and his ashes scattered on the water!" The church demanded that Luther deny his beliefs. He refused. In 1521, Pope Leo X **excommunicated** Luther. Luther was no longer a member of the Catholic Church.

Pope Leo X

The church then split. Many people supported Luther's protest of the Catholic Church. They were called **Protestants**. The Protestants developed a church of their own. Luther encouraged them to speak German, not Latin, in their church services. He also translated the Bible from Latin into German. Protestant church members could read the Bible for themselves. In time, this group became known as Lutherans.

The Protestant Movement Spreads

The Protestant movement soon spread. In Switzerland, John Calvin began to speak out against the Catholic Church. But he disagreed with Luther on several issues, too. Calvin's beliefs became known as Calvinism. In France, Protestants were known as **Huguenots**.

In England, King Henry VIII was a loyal Catholic and even spoke out against Martin Luther. But he had his own problem with the church. Henry wanted a **divorce** from Catherine of Aragon. The Catholic Church did not allow divorce. So in 1534, Henry made himself the head of a separate church, the Church of England.

Unlike the Catholic Church, the Church of England allowed divorces. But it was like the Catholic Church in most other ways. The Church of England became known as the Anglican Church.

King Henry VIII

The Protestant Movement began in Wittenberg. What form of Protestantism was practiced in Scotland?

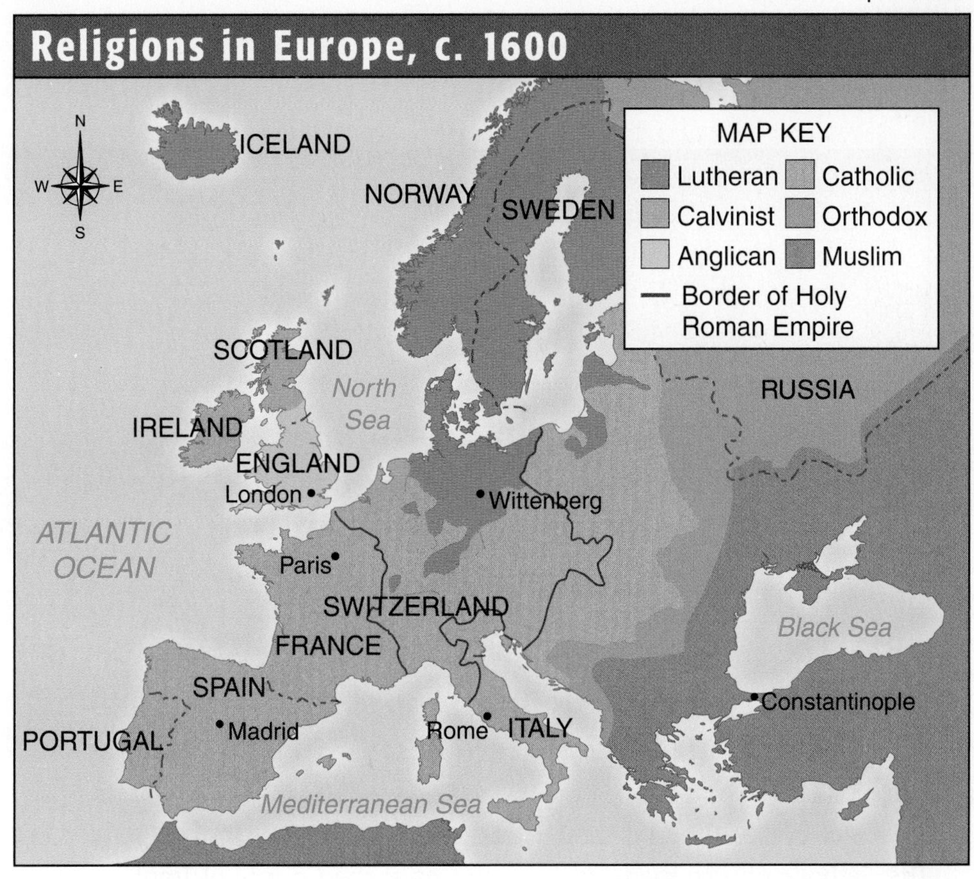

The Counter Reformation

The Catholic Church launched a **Counter Reformation** in the 1530s. The Counter Reformation was meant to slow the spread of the Protestant Reformation. New groups, such as the **Jesuits**, worked to strengthen the Catholic Church. Jesuit priests helped the poor and spread the Catholic faith.

Jesuit priest

During the Counter Reformation, the Catholic Church made reforms of its own. It tried to clearly state its beliefs. At a meeting called the **Council of Trent**, for example, the church ended the sale of indulgences. But it still did not accept the ideas of Luther, Calvin, and the other Protestants.

The Catholic Church had used a special court called the **Inquisition** since the Middle Ages. Throughout the Reformation, the church brought people to this court to test their religious beliefs. If a person did not agree with the Catholic beliefs, that person could be killed. This court was especially powerful in Spain.

The Catholic Church made several reforms at the Council of Trent.

Catherine de Medici (1519–1589)

People In History

Catherine de Medici was born in Italy in 1519. She was a member of the powerful Medici family of Florence. Her parents died when she was only one year old. She was raised by Catholic nuns. In 1533, she married a man who later became King Henry II of France. In 1560, her son Charles became king of France. But he was a weak king. Catherine was the real ruler of France.

Catherine, a Catholic, tried to get along with the French Protestants called Huguenots. But when war broke out between the two groups, she no longer tolerated the Huguenots. In 1572, on a Catholic holiday called St. Bartholomew's Day, she ordered Catholics to kill Huguenots. Catholics killed thousands of Huguenots in a surprise attack. Pope Gregory XIII had a special medal made to honor the event.

Lesson 2 Review

Choose words from the list that best complete the paragraphs. One word will not be used.

In the 1500s, many Europeans began to protest the Catholic Church. These Protestants were led by men such as Martin Luther and __1__. The Reformation split Europe into two religious groups, Protestant and Catholic. Pope Leo X __2__ Martin Luther for challenging church beliefs.

Henry VIII split with the Catholic Church when the pope would not grant him a divorce. He began the __3__ Church in England. The Catholic Church began a __4__ to slow the Protestant Reformation. The Catholic Church made some reforms and used a court to test people's religious beliefs.

Word List

excommunicated
Anglican
Counter Reformation
Johann Tetzel
John Calvin

Chapter 20: Using What You've Learned

Summary

- The Renaissance began in Italy in the mid-1300s. This was a time for new ideas in many fields, including art and philosophy.
- The printing press gave more people access to new ideas, like humanism. Humanists wanted to solve human, rather than religious, problems.
- The Reformation began when Martin Luther nailed a list of complaints to a church door in the German city of Wittenberg. Soon, others protested against the Catholic Church, starting the Protestant movement.
- The Catholic Church responded to the Protestant movement with the Counter Reformation.
- The Catholic Church had a court called the Inquisition. The Inquisition punished anyone who did not agree with the Catholic Church.

Find Out More!

After reading Chapter 20, you're ready to go online. **Explore Zone**, **Quiz Time**, and **Amazing Facts** bring this chapter of world history alive.

Visit www.exploreSV.com and type in the chapter code **Ch20**.

Vocabulary

Number your paper from 1 to 5. Write the word or words from the list that best complete the paragraphs. One word will not be used.

Europeans began to explore the arts, the sciences, and philosophy. This time in Europe was called the __1__. Artists and __2__ moved to the cities. Some artists learned __3__ by studying human bodies.

The __4__ was started by Martin Luther. Luther's list of complaints about the practices of the Catholic Church is called the __5__.

Word List

95 Theses
Renaissance
Reformation
anatomy
scholars
indulgences

Comprehension

Number your paper from 1 to 5. Read each sentence below. Then write the name of the person who might have said each sentence. One name from the list will not be used.

1. "I found a way to draw perspective on a flat surface."
2. "The Catholic Church has too many ceremonies."
3. "All the world's a stage."
4. "I am a loyal Catholic, but I want a divorce from Catherine of Aragon."
5. "My son is a weak king, so I am the real ruler of France!"

Word List

Erasmus

William Shakespeare

Catherine de Medici

Pope Leo X

Henry VIII

Filippo Brunelleschi

Critical Thinking

Sequencing Number your paper from 1 to 5. Write the sentences below in the correct order.

The printing press was invented by Johann Gutenberg around 1456.

In 1521, the pope excommunicated Martin Luther from the Catholic Church.

The Church of England was started by Henry VIII in 1534.

The Renaissance began in Italy.

Johann Tetzel started selling indulgences.

Writing

Write a paragraph describing how art made before the Renaissance was different from art made during the Renaissance.

Skill Builder: Reading a Circle Graph

A **circle graph** shows how something is divided into parts. The parts add up to 100 percent, or 100%. The circle graph below tells about the followers of religions in Europe today. The main religions of Europe in 1600 are also the main religions of Europe today.

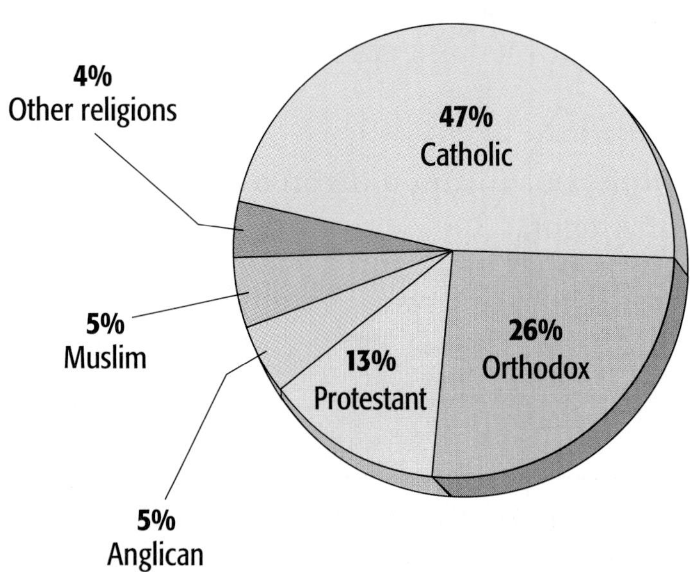

Number your paper from 1 to 5. Choose a word or number to finish each sentence. One word or number will not be used.

Protestants **5** **4** **26** **47** **Catholic**

1. Followers of the Orthodox religion make up _____ percent of the followers of religions in Europe today.
2. _____ make up 13 percent of the followers of religions in Europe today.
3. The religion with the largest number of followers in Europe today is _____.
4. Anglicans and Muslims each make up _____ percent of the followers of religions in Europe today.
5. Other religions make up _____ percent of the followers of religions in Europe today.

LESSON 1

Scientific Revolution

Before You Read

- What makes people accept or question what they are taught?
- How are scientific discoveries made?

New Words

authority
Scientific Revolution
scientific method
hypothesis
revolve
house arrest

People and Places

Nicholas Copernicus
Galileo
Isaac Newton
René Descartes

Suppose that you had a ten-pound ball and a one-pound ball. If you climbed to the top of a high bridge and dropped both balls at the same time, which ball would fall faster?

You might think that the ten-pound ball would fall faster because it is heavier. Europeans in the Middle Ages thought this. They were sure that the ten-pound ball would fall ten times faster. They believed this because the ancient Greek philosopher Aristotle said so. Aristotle was an **authority**. In the Middle Ages, an authority was not questioned.

The Greek philosopher Aristotle was Alexander the Great's teacher.

Scientist at work

But Aristotle did not have the right answer. The truth is that the ten-pound ball and the one-pound ball would fall at the same speed. They would hit the water at the same time.

The Renaissance brought change to the way people thought. Scientists in Europe began to ask hard questions. They began to question authority. They made many new discoveries about the world, bringing about a time known as the **Scientific Revolution**.

The Scientific Method

During this time, scientists developed the **scientific method**. Testing ideas was part of the scientific method. Scientists no longer believed something was true just because someone said so. They wanted to prove it for themselves.

The scientific method has five steps. First, ask a hard question or state a problem. Second, make a good guess about the answer. This guess is based on what you already know. It is called the **hypothesis**. Third, test your guess. At this point, you would actually drop the balls off the bridge. Fourth, write down what happened. Fifth, decide if your hypothesis was right. In order to be right, another scientist should be able to do the same test and get the same result. Modern scientists still use the scientific method.

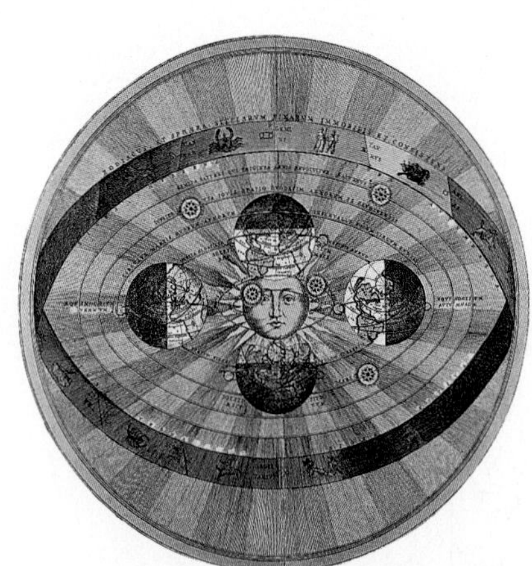
Copernicus's model of the universe

Copernicus and Galileo

The Catholic Church was a strong authority in the Middle Ages. The church said Earth was at the center of the universe. The sun and the planets moved around Earth. For most people, there was no reason to question this. The idea made sense.

Then in 1543, Nicholas Copernicus developed a new idea. He said that Earth and all the planets **revolve** around the sun. But Copernicus did not have the instruments he needed to prove this.

In the early 1600s, an Italian scientist named Galileo showed that Copernicus was right. He built a telescope to study the stars and planets. He saw things no one had seen before. He saw mountains, valleys, and craters on the moon. Galileo saw rings around Saturn and moons revolving around Jupiter. His studies convinced him that Earth did indeed revolve around the sun.

Galileo saw craters on the moon.

In 1632, Galileo wrote a book about his discoveries. The book seemed to support the ideas of Copernicus. Church leaders were angry with Galileo because they still believed that Earth was at the center of the universe. The church called Galileo before the Inquisition.

After many tough questions, Galileo finally weakened. He was forced to deny his discoveries and say that Earth did not move around the sun. The church still didn't trust Galileo. Galileo spent the rest of his life under **house arrest**.

Although he denied his discoveries, Galileo had written down the things he saw through his telescope. Many of his ideas influenced modern scientists. In fact, it was Galileo who proved that all objects fall at the same speed.

Galileo used his telescope to study the night sky.

Isaac Newton discovered that gravity causes an apple to fall from a tree.

Isaac Newton

In the late 1600s, Isaac Newton studied the works of Copernicus, Galileo, and other scientists. There was one question that the earlier scientists had not answered. If Earth was spinning around the sun, why didn't things fly into space? Newton, an English scientist, found the answer. He discovered the law of gravity. Gravity is an invisible force that pulls one object toward another. A larger object always pulls a smaller object toward it.

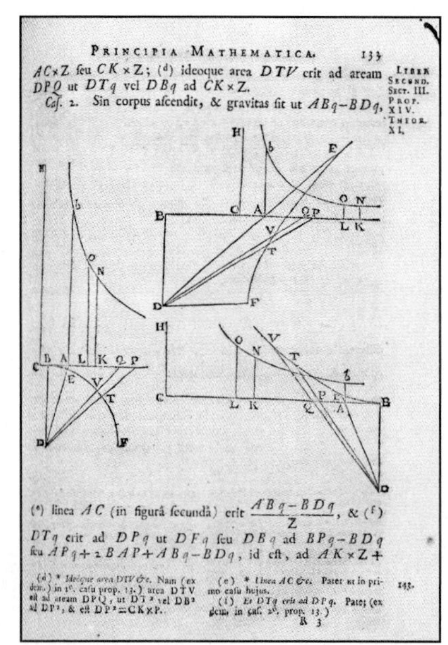

PRINCIPIA MATHEMATICA. 133

$AC \times Z$ seu $CK \times Z$; (d) ideoque area DTV erit ad aream DPQ ut DTq vel DBq ad $CK \times Z$. LIBER SECUND. SECT. III. PROP. XIV. THEOR. XI.

Cas. 2. Sin corpus ascendit, & gravitas sit ut $ABq - BDq$, (e) linea AC (in figurâ secundâ) erit $\frac{ABq - BDq}{Z}$, & (f) DTq erit ad DPq ut DFq seu DBq ad $BPq - BDq$ seu $APq + 2BAP + ABq - BDq$, id est, ad $AK \times Z +$

(d) * Ideoque area DTV &c. Nam (ex dem.) in 1°. casu prop. 13.) area DTV est ad aream DPQ, ut DT^2 vel DB^2 ad DP^2, & est $DP^2 = CK \times P$.

(e) * Linea AC &c. Patet ut in primo casu hujus.

(f) Et DTq erit ad DPq. Patet (ex dem. in cas. 2°. prop. 13.)

243.

R 3

A page from a book by Isaac Newton

Newton's law of gravity explained why an apple falls from a tree to the ground. It also explained how the planets move through space. They are held in their position by the gravity of the sun. In the same way, the moon is held in place by the gravity of Earth.

Newton compared the universe to a watch. Newton said things in nature run by a clear set of laws, just like a watch. Newton died in 1727 at the age of 85. His work changed the study of science. His discoveries gave clear laws that explained how objects move. Scientists today use his ideas when developing anything from basketballs to airplanes.

René Descartes

René Descartes was a French philosopher and mathematician. He was famous for questioning authority. He felt that only the most basic truths could be accepted without proof. For example, he even questioned whether he was real.

In the end, he decided that he was real just because he could think. He once said, "I think, therefore, I am."

The Scientific Revolution gave Europeans a better understanding of the world they lived in. The ideas of these scientists forever changed the way people looked at the world.

René Descartes

Lesson 1 Review

Choose words from the list that best complete the paragraphs. One word will not be used.

Scientists during the Renaissance began to question __1__. They no longer accepted the ideas of people such as Aristotle. Instead, they examined problems by using the __2__. One part of this was to make an educated guess called a __3__. Another part was to test the guess.

Copernicus believed the planets moved around the sun. Galileo proved him right by studying the stars and planets with a telescope. Newton discovered __4__, which explained why planets stay in their position. Descartes questioned everything, even whether he was real.

Word List

scientific method
gravity
hypothesis
authority
revolve

LESSON 2

Nationalism and Absolutism

New Words

nationalism
monarchs
absolutism
cardinal
reign
monarchy
Spanish Armada
divine right
Parliament

People and Places

Netherlands
Poland
Louis XIII
Richelieu
Louis XIV
Versailles
Peter the Great
Baltic Sea
St. Petersburg
Elizabeth I
James I
Charles I
Charles II

Before You Read

- What makes people feel loyal to a nation?
- Why might a country not want an absolute ruler?

Both the Reformation and the Scientific Revolution weakened the power of the Catholic Church. Kings and queens gained more power. With a strong ruler, people began to feel as if they were part of their country. Under feudalism, people's loyalty was to a noble. But in the 1500s, people's loyalty switched to something much larger—the nation. This change was the start of **nationalism**.

The French palace at Versailles has a large Hall of Mirrors.

The Age of Kings

During the Middle Ages, nobles and the pope limited the power of rulers. But by 1600, **monarchs** had gained power. In many countries, the monarch's power was almost total. Many nations united under a powerful monarch. This **absolutism** was especially strong in France and Russia.

It was not true for all nations. In England, the power of the monarch was never absolute. The Netherlands, Switzerland, and Poland all put limits on the ruler's power. Still, this was an age when powerful rulers built strong nations.

King Louis XIV

Absolutism in France

The French king Louis XIII came to power in 1617. He was often ill and chose **Cardinal** Richelieu to run the country. Richelieu said his duty was to increase the king's power. To do this, Richelieu weakened the power of the Huguenots and the nobles. His goal was to unite France under "one faith, one law, one king."

When Louis XIII died in 1643, Louis XIV became king. He ruled France for 72 years, the longest **reign** in French history. During his long reign, Louis XIV became the absolute ruler of France.

Louis XIV built a strong central government. He placed the army under his control and brought the nobles into his government. Louis XIV also built a massive palace at Versailles. All nobles had to spend time there. That way, Louis XIV could watch them.

The palace at Versailles was an expensive project. But Louis XIV spent the money because he wanted to show the world the power of the French **monarchy**. Versailles became a model. Many European kings and queens wanted a palace as beautiful as the one in Versailles.

A fountain at the palace at Versailles

Kings in France and Russia gained absolute power during the 17th century. The city of St. Petersburg is in which of these nations?

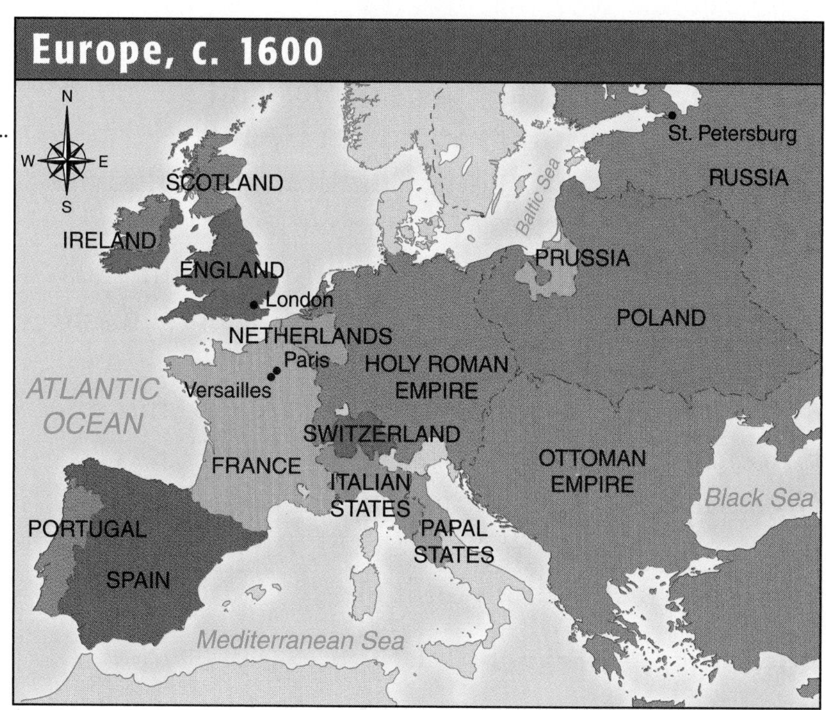

Peter the Great

Absolutism in Russia

Peter the Great became the king of Russia in 1682. He believed in absolute power. Peter wanted Russia to be more like the nations of western Europe. He used his power to make it happen. He forced Russians to shave their beards and to dress like western Europeans. He asked foreign scholars and artists to visit Russia. Peter built a new capital on the coast of the Baltic Sea, nearer to western Europe. He named it St. Petersburg.

Queen Elizabeth I

England Rejects Absolutism

Elizabeth I was the daughter of King Henry VIII. She became the queen of England in 1558. Elizabeth was a wise ruler. The people loved her. She ruled a strong and united England for 45 years. Her navy sank the mighty **Spanish Armada** in 1588.

Elizabeth spoke several languages. She also loved the arts. Great writers, including William Shakespeare, lived during her reign. Elizabeth died in 1603. Her long rule became known as the Elizabethan Age.

Elizabeth had no children. Her cousin James I became king in 1603. He believed in the **divine right** of kings. This was like the Mandate of Heaven in China. James believed that God had chosen him to rule. He wanted to be the absolute ruler of England.

His son, Charles I, also believed in the divine right and absolute power of rulers. Members of England's **Parliament** did not agree with him. When Charles I asked for money to fight a war, the Parliament refused.

In 1642, this argument led to civil war. It was a fight against absolutism. In the end, Parliament won. Charles I was killed. For several years, England had no monarch at all. By 1660, English people wanted a monarch again. Charles II then became king. His power, however, was limited. The monarchs of England would never have absolute power like rulers in France and Russia.

King Charles I

Lesson 2 Review

Choose words from the list that best complete the paragraphs. One word will not be used.

In France and Russia, kings held __1__ power. The French king Louis XIV came to power in 1643. He built the palace at __2__. In Russia, Peter the Great used his power to make Russians look and act more like western Europeans.

Elizabeth I ruled England for 45 years. Her navy defeated the __3__ in 1588. England then rejected the idea of absolutism. __4__ would not give Charles I the money he wanted to fight a war. England entered a civil war. One result of the war was a limit on the monarch's power.

Word List

Versailles
absolute
Parliament
Spanish Armada
monarchy

LESSON 3

Exploring New Lands

New Words

journal
Northwest Passage

People and Places

Portugal
Bartolomeu Dias
Cape of Good Hope
Vasco da Gama
Ferdinand
Isabella
Christopher Columbus
Caribbean Sea
East Indies
Amerigo Vespucci
Ferdinand Magellan
Philippine Islands
John Cabot
Jacques Cartier
St. Lawrence River

Before You Read

- Why did Europeans want to trade with Asia?
- Why might Europeans want to find an all-water trade route?

In the late Middle Ages, Europeans began buying silk, spices, and jewels from Asia. The goods were traded over long land routes. They were bought and sold at several stops before they arrived in Europe. At each stop, prices went up. When the goods reached the Mediterranean Sea, the Italians raised prices even more and sold the goods to the rest of Europe.

European explorers searched for an all-water route to Asia.

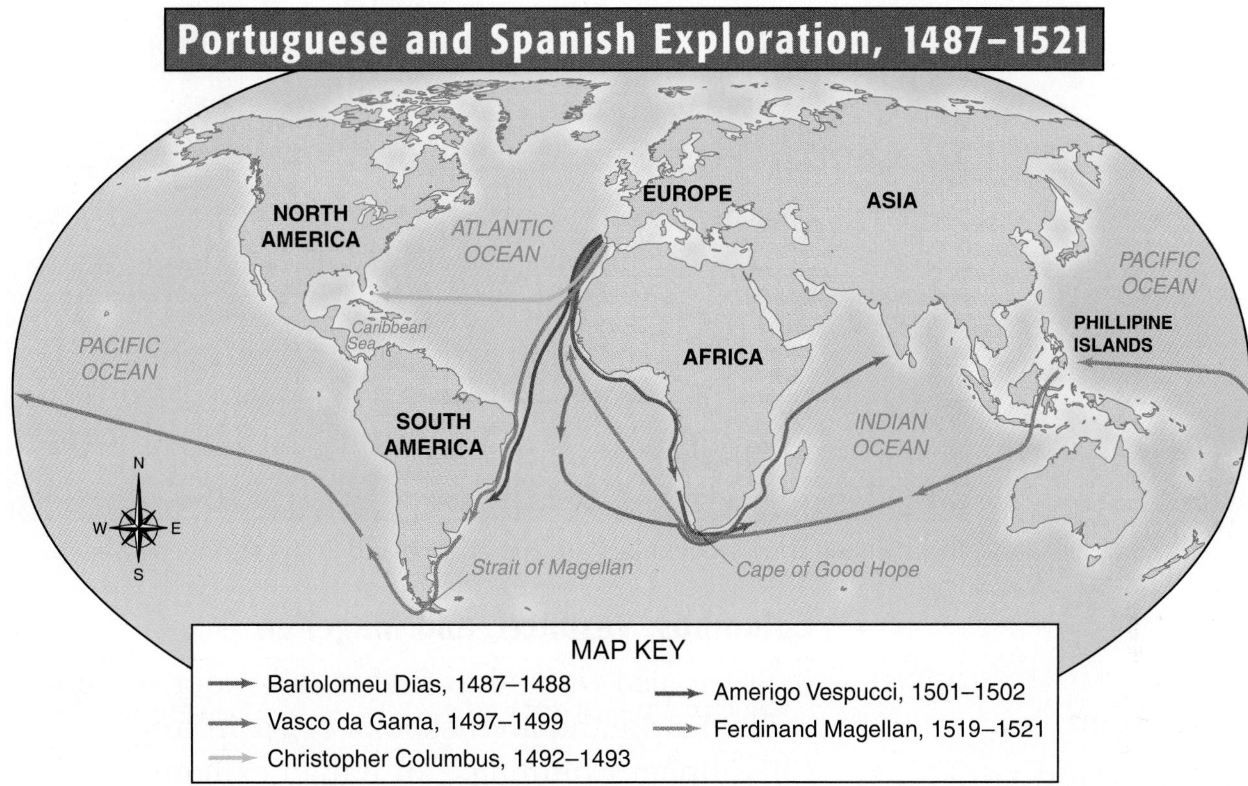

This map shows Portuguese and Spanish explorers from 1487–1521. Which explorer traveled up the east coast of Africa?

The rest of Europe wanted to find a better way to travel between Europe and Asia. They needed an all-water route so that goods wouldn't have to stop in so many places. With an all-water route, the goods wouldn't be so expensive.

Explorers from Portugal

The Portuguese were the first European explorers. The Portuguese looked for a new way to get to Asia. They first began to explore Africa. They thought that perhaps they could get to Asia by sailing around Africa.

In 1487, Bartolomeu Dias sailed around the southern tip of Africa. He found a way to reach Asia by sea. The king of Portugal was happy and hopeful when he heard the news. He renamed the tip of Africa the Cape of Good Hope. Vasco da Gama, another Portuguese explorer, traveled further. He sailed up the east coast of Africa in 1497. The next year, he sailed to India. The Portuguese had found an all-water route to Asia.

Vasco da Gama

This painting shows Columbus arriving at an island in the Caribbean Sea.

Columbus, Vespucci, and Magellan

Spain also wanted to find an all-water route to India. Ferdinand and Isabella of Spain hired Christopher Columbus, an Italian explorer. Columbus believed he could reach Asia by sailing west across the Atlantic Ocean.

In August 1492, Columbus sailed west from Spain with three small ships—the *Niña*, the *Pinta*, and the *Santa María*. On October 12, he reached an island in the Caribbean Sea. He thought he was on an island in the East Indies, off the coast of Asia. He called the people there Indians.

The people living on the Caribbean island came to the shore to greet Columbus. Columbus wrote in his **journal** what the people were like.

"As I saw that they were very friendly to us, and [saw] that they could be much more easily converted to [Christianity] by gentle means than by force, I presented them with some red caps and strings of beads . . . . They were much delighted and became wonderfully attached to us."

Columbus returned to Spain thinking he had found a shorter route to Asia. He made three more trips to the Caribbean islands. He never knew that he had not reached Asia.

An explorer named Amerigo Vespucci crossed the Atlantic Ocean after Columbus. But he did not think he was in Asia. He called the continent a New World. For Europe, it was a new world. The land became known as the Americas, after Amerigo Vespucci.

In 1519, Ferdinand Magellan sailed west across the Atlantic Ocean with five ships. Like Columbus, he hoped to reach Asia. He sailed around the tip of South America and across the vast Pacific Ocean. The trip took more than three years. Magellan died in the Philippine Islands, but his crew kept sailing. Only one ship made it back to Europe. But that ship was the first to sail around the world.

Ferdinand Magellan

Europe Builds Colonies

Several European explorers went on voyages in the 1500s and 1600s. By 1700, Europeans had built new empires around the world.

The Portuguese took over the east coast of South America. They also set up colonies in Africa. Spanish explorers conquered most of Central America and much of South America.

Europe began building colonies around the world. Which European nation controlled Central America?

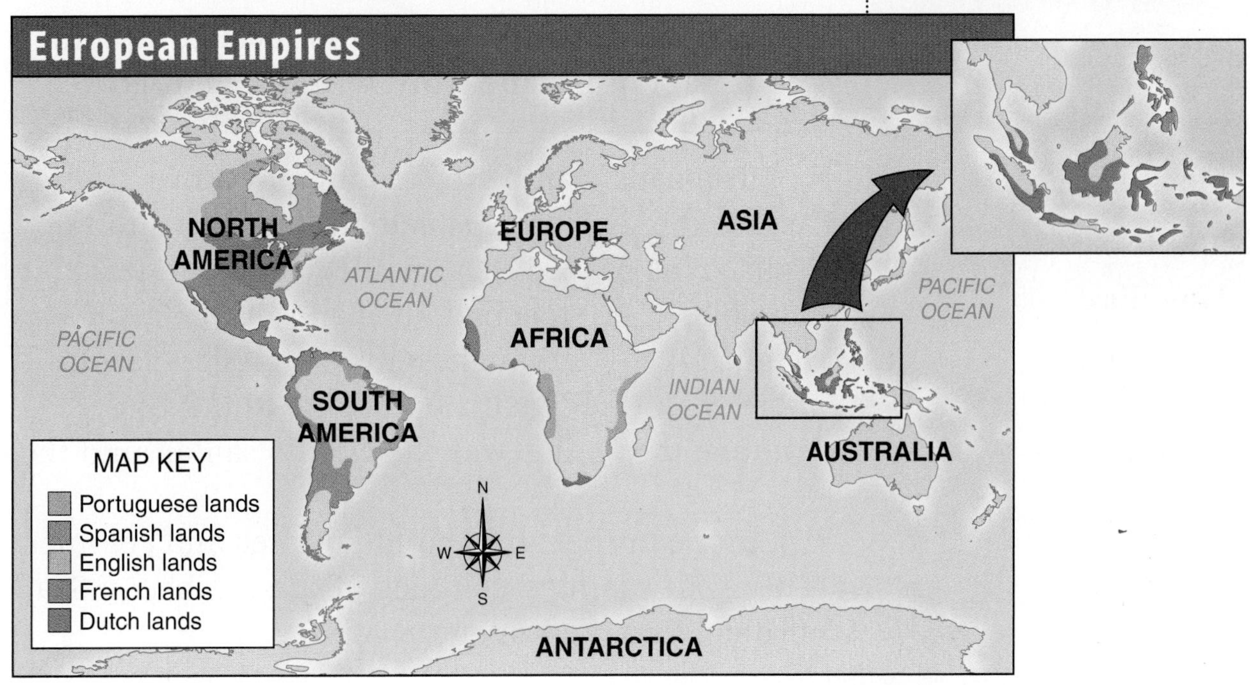

The English and the French sent explorers to North America. They were looking for a **Northwest Passage** to India. John Cabot was an Italian captain of an English ship. In 1497, he explored the coast of North America and claimed land for England. In 1534, Jacques Cartier from France sailed up the St. Lawrence River. He claimed land for France.

Jacques Cartier arriving in North America

Dutch explorers claimed smaller areas of land along the east coast of South America. They also set up colonies in the Caribbean Sea, in Indonesia, and in South Africa.

Several European countries extended their power and influence around the world. But often that power brought terrible changes to people already living in those lands.

Lesson 3 Review

Choose words from the list that best complete the paragraphs. One word will not be used.

Word List

Spanish
Magellan
Columbus
Portuguese
Dutch

Europeans wanted to find an all-water route to Asia. __1__ explorers sailed around Africa to India. This proved that an all-water route was possible. __2__ reached an island in the Caribbean Sea in 1492. He thought he was in Asia. It took more than three years, but a ship under the command of __3__ was the first to sail around the world.

Europeans began to build empires and colonies. The __4__ claimed colonies in the Caribbean Sea, in Indonesia, and in South Africa.

Chapter 21: Using What You've Learned

Summary

- During the Scientific Revolution, scientists questioned authority. They used the scientific method to test their new ideas.
- Galileo and Copernicus studied the stars and planets. Newton discovered the law of gravity. Descartes questioned the nature of life itself.
- Nationalism grew in Europe during the 1500s. Rulers in France and Russia had absolute power.
- In England, Parliament and the king fought over who should have more power. After a civil war in England, monarchs never again had absolute power.
- In the 15th century, European explorers searched for an all-water route to Asia. They landed in what they called the New World.

Find Out More!

After reading Chapter 21, you're ready to go online. **Explore Zone**, **Quiz Time**, and **Amazing Facts** bring this chapter of world history alive.

Visit www.exploreSV.com and type in the chapter code **Ch21**.

Vocabulary

Number your paper from 1 to 5. Write the word or words from the list that best complete each analogy. One word will not be used.

1. Fact is to truth as _____ is to guess.
2. Dynasty was to China as _____ was to France.
3. Mandate of Heaven was to China as _____ was to James I of England.
4. Senate is to the Roman Republic as _____ is to England.
5. A letter is to a note as a _____ is to a diary.

Word List

divine right
Parliament
hypothesis
monarchy
journal
house arrest

Comprehension

Number your paper from 1 to 6. Write one or more sentences to answer each question below.

1. What was the Scientific Revolution?
2. What happened when Galileo was called before the Inquisition?
3. What is the law of gravity?
4. How did Peter the Great change Russia?
5. What caused a civil war in England in 1642?
6. Why did Europeans want to find an all-water route to Asia?

Critical Thinking

Categories Number your paper from 1 to 4. Read the words in each group below. Think about how they are alike. Write the best title for each group.

Scientific Method **Elizabethan Age** **Louis XIV** **Portuguese**

1. state a problem
   make a guess
   test the guess
2. ruled France for 72 years
   strong central government
   Palace at Versailles
3. Queen Elizabeth I
   strong and united England
   navy sank Spanish Armada
4. found all-water route to Asia
   took over east coast of South America
   set up colonies in Africa

Writing

Write a paragraph explaining how a person could use the scientific method to find the answer to the following question: Does a paper clip float or sink when placed in water?

LESSON 1

The Spanish in the Americas

Before You Read

- Why did explorers come to the Americas?
- How did Spanish explorers defeat the Aztec and the Inca?

Christopher Columbus made four voyages to the Americas. On each voyage, he claimed more lands for Spain and brought Spanish settlers. In 1496, he founded the first Spanish town, Santo Domingo, on the island of Hispaniola.

Cortés Looks for Gold

The Spanish took over Cuba in 1514. Five years later, they heard a **rumor** that the Aztec had gold. The Spanish governor of Cuba told Hernán Cortés to find it. Cortés was a **conquistador**, or Spanish conqueror. In 1519, he set sail with 11 ships and 508 soldiers. He brought horses and guns.

New Words

rumor
conquistador
hostage
immunity
smallpox
advantage
Columbian Exchange

People and Places

Santo Domingo
Hispaniola
Cuba
Hernán Cortés
Moctezuma
Francisco Pizarro
Atahualpa

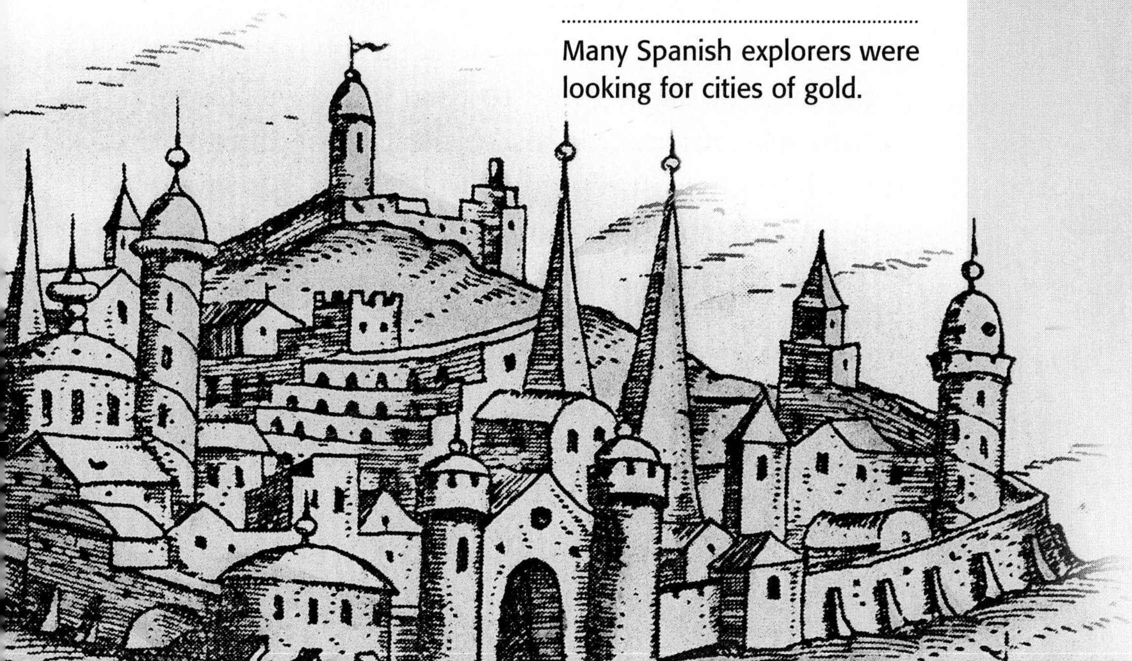

Many Spanish explorers were looking for cities of gold.

In 1519, Cortés met Moctezuma in Tenochtitlán.

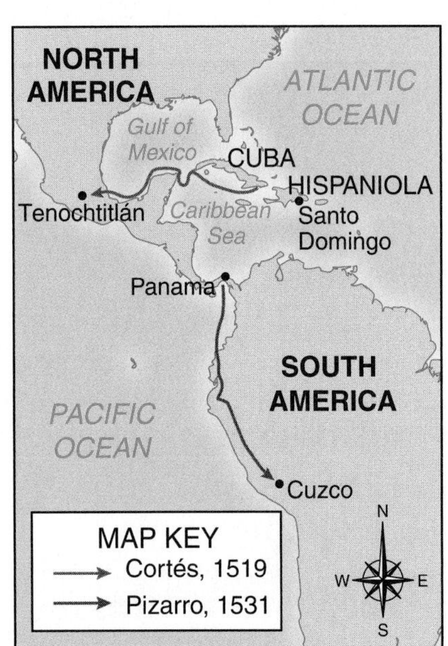

Routes of Cortés and Pizarro

Cortés and his men landed on the coast of Mexico. The Aztec had ruled this land for more than 300 years. Messengers told Moctezuma, the Aztec ruler, that white strangers had arrived.

Moctezuma could have ordered an attack on the Spanish invaders. If the Aztec had attacked, they might easily have defeated the Spanish. The Aztec had far more soldiers.

But Moctezuma did not order an attack. He thought Cortés was a god. According to legend, Quetzalcoatl, an Aztec god, was supposed to return that year. So the Aztec treated Cortés as if he were Quetzalcoatl.

The End of the Aztec

Many of the Spanish soldiers were nervous about the Aztec. They had no idea what they might face. Some wanted to turn back, but Cortés said no. He burned all his ships. His soldiers had no choice but to stay and follow him. On the way to the Aztec, the Spanish defeated several smaller Native American groups. These groups decided to join Cortés. For a long time, the Aztec had forced the groups to give the Aztec money and humans for sacrifice, so the groups wanted to help Cortés.

Quetzalcoatl

Moctezuma welcomed Cortés with gifts of gold. He opened the gates to the city of Tenochtitlán. "Welcome," said Moctezuma as Cortés marched in. "We have been waiting for you. This is your home."

Moctezuma

Moctezuma soon discovered his mistake. Cortés was not a god, but a conqueror. Cortés took Moctezuma **hostage**. The Aztec king was now a Spanish prisoner. Later, fighting broke out between the Aztec and the Spanish. During the fighting, Moctezuma was killed, but the Spanish were driven out of Tenochtitlán.

Cortés came back to conquer the Aztec. He brought fresh supplies, guns, and more Native American allies. This time, he defeated the Aztec. In August 1521, the Aztec surrendered. One Aztec poet wrote about the defeat.

> **"Where shall we go now, oh my friends? The smoke is rising, the fog is spreading, the waters on the lake are red. Cry, oh cry, for we have lost the Aztec nation."**

Pizarro and the Inca

Ten years later, the Inca Empire in South America also fell to a Spanish conquistador. Francisco Pizarro also heard rumors of gold.

In 1531, Pizarro set sail for Peru with fewer than 200 men. High in the Andes Mountains, he met Atahualpa, the Inca ruler. Fighting soon broke out. A civil war had weakened the Inca. The Inca were not as strong as they once had been. The Spanish easily defeated the Inca.

Pizarro taking Atahualpa prisoner

The Spanish made Atahualpa a prisoner. Then the king found out that Pizarro wanted gold. So he offered a deal. If he would give Pizarro enough gold to fill a room, Pizarro would let him go. Atahualpa kept his promise. But Pizarro killed him anyway. It was the end of the Inca Empire.

Native Americans had no immunity against diseases such as smallpox.

Why the Spanish Won

How did a few hundred Spanish soldiers defeat these empires so easily? One reason was the diseases Europeans brought with them. Native Americans had no **immunity** against some of the European diseases. Their bodies had no natural defense against diseases such as **smallpox**.

The plague in Europe during the Middle Ages killed about one person out of every three. The European diseases that were carried to the Americas were even more deadly. About nine out of every ten Native Americans were killed by European diseases.

Another reason the Spanish won was that they arrived at just the right time. Many Native American groups had come to hate the Aztec. They were happy to join the Spanish.

Also, civil war had weakened the Inca just before Pizarro arrived. Had Pizarro tried to attack

The Spanish conquered much of North America and South America by 1780. What river ran through Spanish lands in North America?

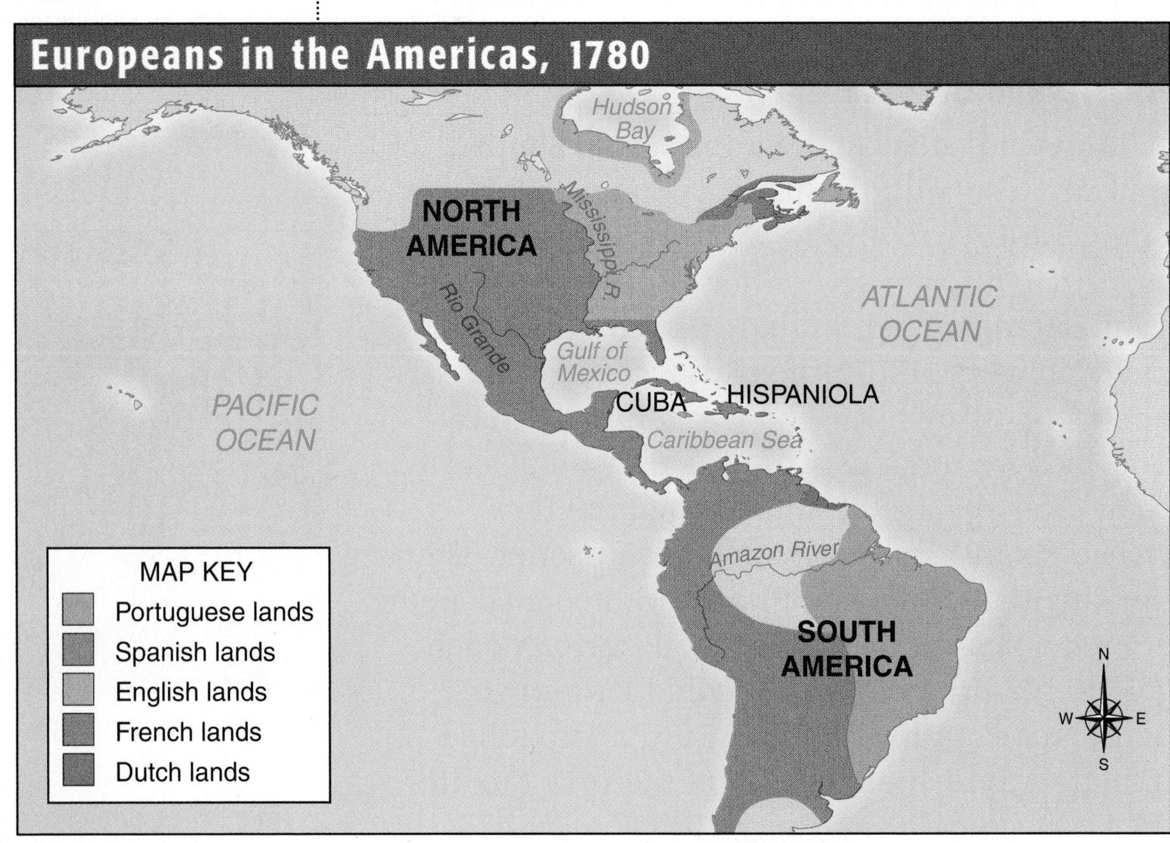

a few years earlier, the Inca might easily have defeated the Spanish.

The Spanish had another **advantage**. The Aztec and Inca had never seen guns and horses. They didn't know how to defend themselves against powerful weapons and fast horses.

Columbian Exchange

When Columbus landed in the Americas in 1492, a global exchange of goods and ideas known as the **Columbian Exchange** began. American goods such as corn, chocolate, potatoes, and silver were brought across the Atlantic Ocean. European and Asian goods such as sugar, tea, and coffee were brought to the Americas.

Silver became popular in China.

People, plants, animals, and diseases began crossing the Atlantic Ocean. Europeans, Africans, Asians, and Americans were all affected by the Columbian Exchange.

Lesson 1 Review

Choose words from the list that best complete the paragraphs. One word will not be used.

In 1519, Cortés set sail from Cuba to look for gold. He was a __1__. The Aztec ruler, __2__, thought Cortés was a god. Aztec legend said a god would be coming that year. Cortés defeated the Aztec in 1521. Pizarro set sail for Peru in 1531. He defeated the Inca Empire and killed their leader, __3__.

The Spanish brought new diseases to the Americas. The Native Americans had no __4__ against these diseases. The Columbian Exchange was a worldwide exchange of goods between the Americas and the rest of the world.

Word List

immunity
conquistador
Moctezuma
rumor
Atahualpa

LESSON 2

Europeans in North America

New Words

establish
abandoned
cash crop
indentured servants
Separatists
Pilgrims
Quakers
paradise
treaties
frontier

People and Places

Roanoke Island
Jamestown
Plymouth
Peter Minuit
13 colonies
Sieur de la Salle
Canada
New France

Before You Read

- Why might Europeans have wanted to set up colonies on another continent?
- How might Native Americans have felt about Europeans in the Americas?

John Cabot's voyage in 1497 gave England a claim to land in North America. It was almost 100 years, however, before they acted on that claim. The English saw Spain growing wealthy from American silver. It was only then that the English began to **establish** colonies. The first English colony was on Roanoke Island off the coast of modern-day North Carolina in 1585.

A supply ship arrived at Roanoke a few years later. The sailors found the colony **abandoned**.

No one knows what happened to the early settlers of Roanoke.

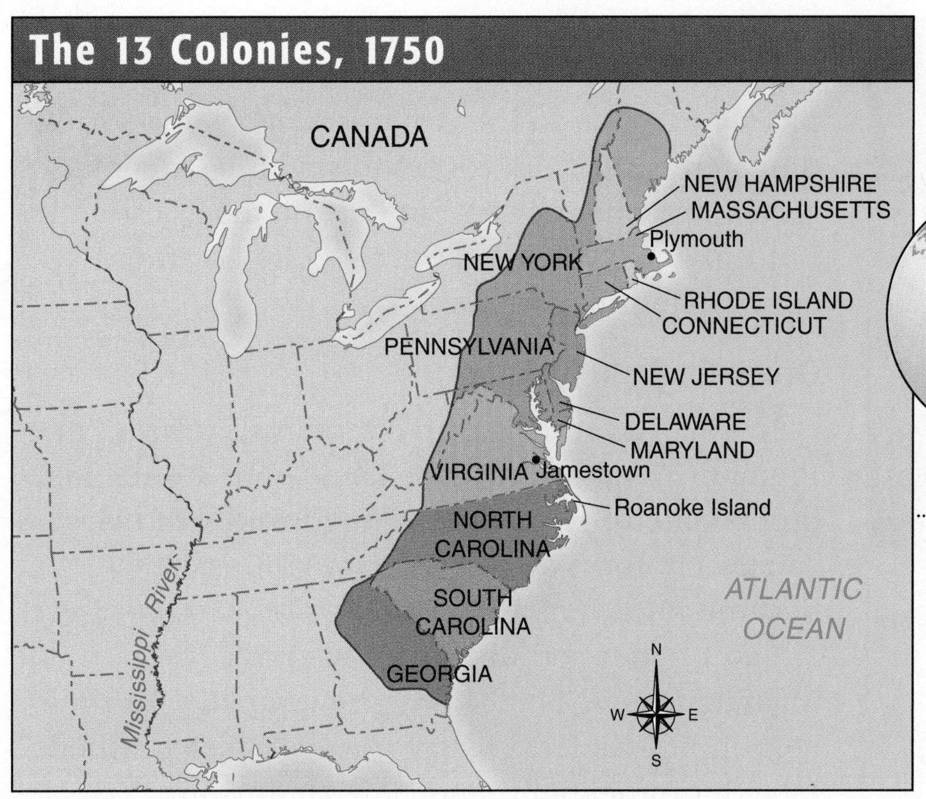

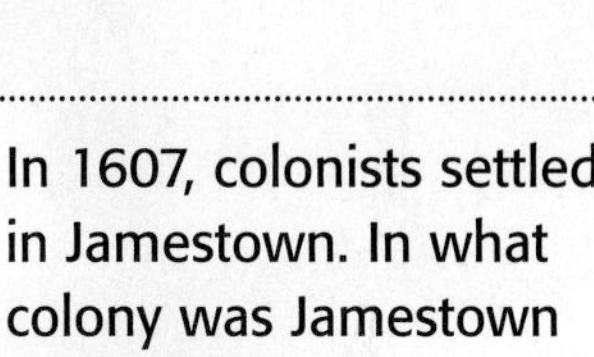

In 1607, colonists settled in Jamestown. In what colony was Jamestown located?

There was not a single person left. The sailors only found some letters carved on a tree. No one knows what happened to the early settlers.

The English Return

The English did not return to the Americas until 1607. They settled in Jamestown, Virginia. The colonists came to find gold. Instead, they found cold and disease. Most of the colonists died in the winter. Native Americans saved many of the colonists by giving them food.

The Jamestown colonists soon learned to grow tobacco. This **cash crop** helped save the colony. Tobacco grew easily in the soil of Virginia. Europeans liked smoking, so demand for tobacco grew rapidly. Demand also grew for workers to plant and harvest the tobacco crops. The colonists turned to Africa for these workers. The first African slaves arrived in Virginia in 1619.

Tobacco grew easily in Virginia.

Pilgrims

Other workers came as **indentured servants**. They were often poor. They did not have the money to come to the Americas on their own. So they agreed to work for up to seven years. Like slaves, they usually worked in the tobacco fields. But unlike slaves, they were free to go after a certain amount of time.

Other English Colonies

In 1620, another group of colonists arrived in Plymouth, Massachusetts. They were a religious group called **Separatists**. They wanted to live separately from other religious groups. They became known as **Pilgrims**.

Later, other settlers began to arrive in Massachusetts. The colony grew rapidly. In time, certain people left to start new colonies in Rhode Island, Connecticut, and New Hampshire.

The English were not the only colonists. Dutch settlers founded New Netherlands. In 1624, Peter Minuit paid Native Americans 24 dollars for the island of Manhattan. He called it New Amsterdam. Later, the English took over the colony and renamed it New York. Colonists from Sweden settled in Delaware, but they also lost their colony to the English.

Other colonies were started for religious reasons. English Catholics founded Maryland. **Quakers**, an English Protestant group who believed in peace, founded Pennsylvania. The founders tried to attract more settlers. They wrote to people back in England that North America was a **paradise**, or perfect place. Many people came because they liked the promise of cheap land and personal freedom.

Quakers in Pennsylvania

King Charles II's brother gave two friends land to start the colony of New Jersey. King Charles II gave colonists land that became North Carolina and South Carolina. The last English colony was

Europeans in North America, 1750

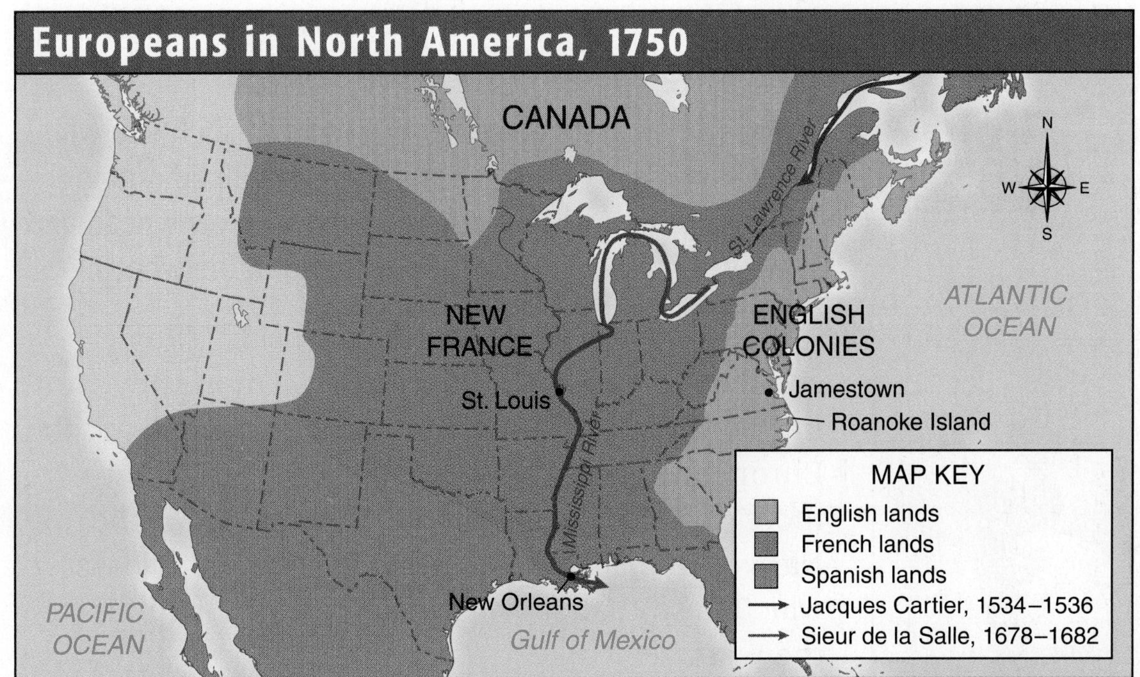

The French explorers Cartier and la Salle both sailed along rivers. Along which river did Cartier sail?

founded in Georgia in 1733. These English lands made up the 13 colonies.

The French in America

The French explorer Jacques Cartier came to North America in 1534. He claimed the area around the St. Lawrence River for France. Another French explorer, Sieur de la Salle, came to North America in 1682. He sailed down the Mississippi River to the Gulf of Mexico. By the 1700s, the French had claimed a huge area of land from the Gulf of Mexico to Canada. They called the land New France.

Native Americans

In the beginning, there was some friendly trade between Europeans and Native Americans. But the issue of land quickly began causing trouble.

The English began settling farther west. As they did so, they forced Native Americans west as well. The English often signed **treaties** with Native Americans. They would promise not to take more land, and then take it anyway.

Sieur de la Salle

One Native American leader told a French explorer his concerns in 1633.

Voices In History

"You will build a house that is a fortress, then you will build another house . . . and then we will be nothing but dogs that sleep outdoors. You will grow wheat, and we will no longer look for our [food] in the woods."

The Native Americans fought back. They attacked forts along the **frontier**. Often they won. In the end, however, they could not hold back the Europeans. There were too many settlers with more powerful weapons. By 1780, most of the Native Americans had either died from disease or war. Those that survived had been pushed far to the west.

Native American woman and girl

Lesson 2 Review

Choose words from the list that best complete the paragraphs. One word will not be used.

Word List

frontier
New France
treaty
cash crop
Roanoke

The English set up their first colony on __1__ Island. The English settled in Jamestown in 1607. The Jamestown colonists learned to grow tobacco, a __2__. More colonies developed along the east coast of North America.

The French also claimed lands in North America. They gained lands around rivers in the north and south. Their land was called __3__.

The English took Native American lands as they settled farther west. Native Americans attacked the forts along the __4__, but they could not hold back the Europeans.

Chapter 22: Using What You've Learned

Summary

- Spanish explorers such as Cortés and Pizarro came to the Americas looking for gold. Their conquests ended the Aztec and Inca empires.
- The Columbian Exchange began when Columbus landed in the Americas in 1492.
- The first English colony on Roanoke Island failed. The second colony at Jamestown, Virginia survived by growing and selling tobacco.
- In 1620, the Pilgrims arrived at Plymouth, Massachusetts. Soon, England had 13 colonies in the Americas.
- The English colonists came into conflict with the Native Americans. By 1780, most Native Americans had either died or had been forced to move west.

Find Out More!

After reading Chapter 22, you're ready to go online. **Explore Zone**, **Quiz Time**, and **Amazing Facts** bring this chapter of world history alive.

Visit www.exploreSV.com and type in the chapter code **Ch22**.

Vocabulary

Number your paper from 1 to 5. Write the word or words from the list that best complete each sentence. One word will not be used.

1. A Spanish conqueror was called a _____.
2. Native Americans had no _____ against European diseases.
3. A farm crop grown to be sold or traded is called a _____.
4. The _____ were an English Protestant group that believed in peace.
5. The English signed _____ with the Native Americans promising they would not take any more land.

Word List

immunity
treaties
hostage
conquistador
cash crop
Quakers

Comprehension

Number your paper from 1 to 4. Write the letter of the correct answer.

1. Who defeated the Aztec?

a. Hernán Cortés
b. Christopher Columbus
c. Francisco Pizarro
d. John Cabot

2. In what year did the Columbian Exchange begin?

a. 1514
b. 1496
c. 1492
d. 1531

3. Which religious group settled in Plymouth, Massachusetts?

a. Catholics
b. Separatists
c. Quakers
d. Huguenots

4. What was the land from the Gulf of Mexico to Canada called?

a. New Spain
b. New Netherlands
c. New France
d. New Amsterdam

Critical Thinking

Points of View Number your paper from 1 to 6. Read each sentence below. Write **European** if the point of view is from a 16th century European. If the point of view is from a 16th century Native American, write **Native American**.

1. Cortés might be our god, Quetzalcoatl.

2. The Spanish have a right to take the gold in the Americas.

3. We have never seen guns and horses before.

4. African slaves are needed to help grow tobacco in Virginia.

5. We would like cheap land and personal freedom.

6. We are worried that all of our land will be taken from us.

Writing

Write a paragraph telling how the Inca Empire came to an end.

Skill Builder: Reading a Resource Map

A **resource map** uses symbols to show where different resources can be found. The map key tells what each symbol means. The resource map below shows where some resources could be found in the 13 colonies.

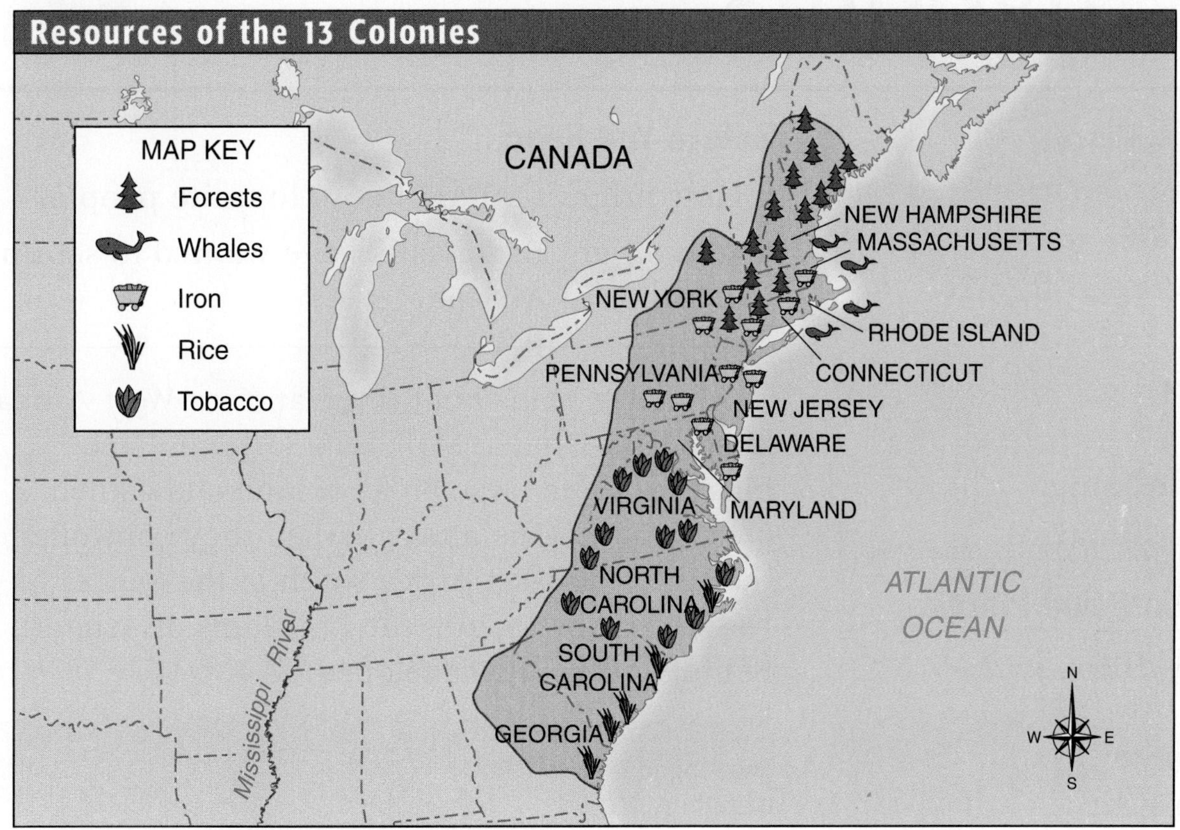

Number your paper from 1 to 5. Answer each question with a complete sentence.

1. What five resources are shown on the map?
2. What symbol is used to show forests?
3. Colonists from which colonies were most likely to hunt whales?
4. What are three colonies where iron could be found?
5. Which two resources could be found in North Carolina and South Carolina?

LESSON 1

Life in African Kingdoms

New Words

confederation
golden stool
extended family
talking drums
oba
ehi
manikongo
missionaries

People and Places

Ashanti
Benin
Kongo
Kumasi
Osei Tutu
Okomfo Anokye
Angola
Nzinga Nkuwu
Afonso I

Before You Read

- How might a ruler choose to unite people?
- Why might Europeans have wanted to set up colonies in Africa?

You have read about three ancient West African kingdoms—Ghana, Mali, and Songhai. Each kingdom ruled large areas of land and gained great wealth. One after another, they controlled the region of West Africa south of the Sahara Desert. Farther south, the kingdoms of Ashanti, Benin, and Kongo developed.

The Kingdom of Ashanti united in 1701.

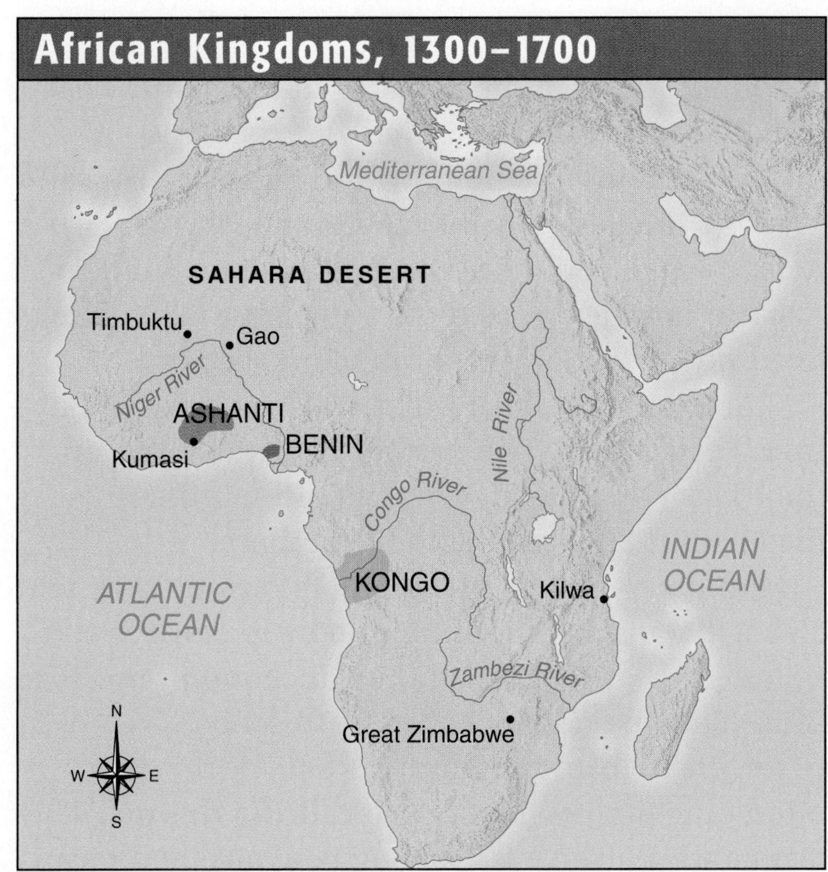

This map shows three African kingdoms that developed between 1300 and 1700. All three kingdoms were located near what ocean?

The Golden Stool

In 1701, the Ashanti people united to build a kingdom with Kumasi as their capital. The Kingdom of Ashanti was a **confederation**. A confederation is a group of smaller states under one government. The states controlled local affairs and kept local customs.

Osei Tutu was king of the Ashanti. His friend, a priest named Okomfo Anokye, wanted a symbol to keep the many states of the confederation united. The Ashanti believed that Anokye had magical powers. They thought he had brought a **golden stool** down from heaven. The golden stool became the sign that united the Ashanti people. Anokye wanted to make sure everyone knew that the confederation was united. The states all agreed that the golden stool represented a united Ashanti people.

Ashanti golden stool

Ashanti Culture

Family life was important to the Ashanti. They usually lived in an **extended family**. This included the mother, father, and children, as well as aunts, uncles, cousins, and grandparents. Ashanti men could have more than one wife. So Ashanti families were often very large. The family lived in a series of huts around a courtyard.

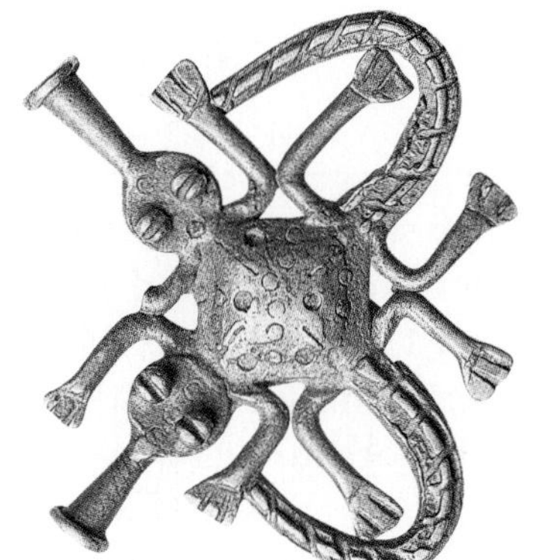

Ashanti brass weight

The Ashanti believed that children got souls from their father. The mother gave the children their flesh and blood. The Ashanti felt that this made children closer to their mothers.

Mothers taught their daughters how to cook and clean. They also taught them how to work in the fields. Fathers controlled the education of their sons. They paid for them to go to school.

An uncle from the mother's side of the family often taught boys how to use **talking drums**. The drums were used for learning language and for spreading news.

The Ashanti believed that animals and plants had souls. The Ashanti believed in different gods. The greatest of these was Nyame, but there were lower gods as well.

The Kingdom of Benin

Bronze head from Benin

The Kingdom of Benin was located in what is now the nation of Nigeria. It was founded before 1300. It reached its greatest power between the 14th and 17th centuries.

The king was called the **oba**. The people believed that the oba came from the gods. He had total power. The obas raised a powerful army and conquered nearby villages. They also built strong wooden walls around the capital city of Benin.

Like the Ashanti, the Benin people believed in different gods. The god who created the world was considered the greatest. But there were lesser gods, too. People had their own personal god called an **ehi**. The ehi helped a person decide what to do in life. Then the ehi stayed with that person as a helpful guide until death.

The Kingdom of Kongo

The Kingdom of Kongo began in the 14th century. It was centered in what is now northern Angola. A king, called the **manikongo**, ruled the Kingdom of Kongo. Kongo grew large enough to be divided into six provinces.

The Portuguese first visited Kongo in 1482. Nzinga Nkuwu, the manikongo, liked Portuguese culture. In 1491, more Portuguese arrived. They included soldiers and **missionaries**. The soldiers helped end local battles. The missionaries converted many people, including Nzinga Nkuwu, to Christianity.

Afonso I, the next manikongo, was raised as a Christian. He wanted his people to become Christians. But the people were not easily converted. They did not like the way the Portuguese treated many Kongo people.

Kongo statue

These Europeans are kneeling in front of the king of Kongo.

Some Portuguese came to bring Christianity to the African people. But many Portuguese were in the kingdom only to make money. They did this by buying and selling slaves. Many of the African kingdoms had used slaves for centuries. But the Portuguese took the Africans from Africa and sold them to people in Europe and the Americas. This caused trouble in the kingdom.

A manikongo becoming a Christian

After the death of Afonso, civil wars broke out. In 1665, a Portuguese army defeated the army of Kongo. Portugal then ruled the Kingdom of Kongo.

Lesson 1 Review

Choose words from the list that best complete the paragraphs. One word will not be used.

Word List

ehi
oba
confederation
manikongo
extended

In the late 17th century, the Ashanti states united to form a __1__. Okomfo Anokye used the golden stool as a symbol of a united Ashanti people. The Ashanti lived in large __2__ families. They believed that animals and plants had souls.

The Kingdom of Benin was founded before 1300. The people of Benin believed that everyone had a personal god. This __3__ helped guide a person through life.

The people of Kongo first welcomed the Portuguese. The __4__ Afonso I wanted all his people to become Christians. But the Portuguese were cruel to the Africans. This led to civil wars and defeat by the Portuguese.

LESSON 2

The Slave Trade

Before You Read

- Which ancient cultures have had slaves?
- How might trade occur between three continents?

New Words

status
plantations
Middle Passage
triangular trade
manufactured goods

People and Places

Olaudah Equiano
West Indies

Slavery has existed since the beginning of history. The Egyptians used slaves to build the pyramids. The Greeks and Romans had slaves, too. In Asia, Africa, and the Americas, rulers and rich people often owned slaves. Slaves were usually prisoners of war. Sometimes people who committed a crime became slaves.

Slaves and Slavery

Religion did not stop slavery. Both Christianity and Islam allowed slavery. In some cultures, slaves had rights, but in others, slaves had none. Some slaves could earn money and buy their freedom but others could not.

The Egyptians used slaves to build the pyramids.

Did You Know?

What's in a Name?

Many Africans believed that you didn't exist until you had a name. They held special ceremonies for naming babies.

Many African names described a baby's place in the family or what the baby looked like. For example, one name was *Idowu*. It meant "born after twins." Another name was *Dada*. It meant "born with lots of hair." At the naming ceremony, the baby's foot was touched to the ground. This showed his or her first step was "in the right direction."

Once the slave trade began, many Africans could not keep the names they were given at the naming ceremony. If they became slaves, they were often given new names.

Slavery had long existed in Africa. African kings such as Mansa Musa had slaves. A king's **status**, or place in society, often depended on how many slaves he had. But slaves in Africa had some rights. They could work and earn money. Slaves could even buy their freedom.

Europeans in Africa

Early Portuguese explorers began the European slave trade. They brought African slaves from West Africa to Portugal. Slavery was not in high demand in Europe. But it was in the Americas.

European settlers in North America and South America wanted slaves. In the Caribbean islands, the Spanish had large sugar **plantations**. English settlers raised tobacco. Settlers in the southern English colonies had large cotton plantations. The settlers wanted workers to plant and harvest these crops. At first, settlers used Native Americans as slaves. But many Native Americans had died from European diseases. The settlers turned to Africa.

Africans first were sent to the west coast of Africa. Some were sent as prisoners. Others were stolen from their homes. On the west coast, these

This painting shows a sugar plantation in the Caribbean islands. The plantation owner's house is on top of a hill with the slave houses below.

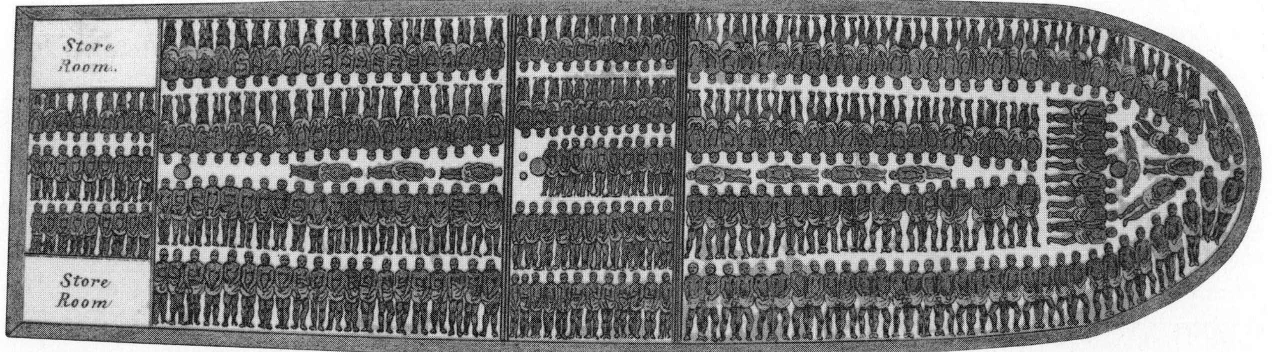

African slaves were packed tightly into ships going from Africa to the Americas.

slaves were sold to traders. Next, they were crowded into ships and sent to the Americas. The trip from Africa to the Americas was called the **Middle Passage**. The voyage was brutal. Slaves were chained together and poorly fed. As many as one out of five died during the Middle Passage.

In the 1750s, Olaudah Equiano was captured from West Africa when he was just 11 years old. He later wrote about what it was like.

"One day, when all our people were gone out to their work as usual, and only I and my dear sister were left to mind the house, two men and a woman got over our walls. In a moment [they] seized us both and, without giving us time to cry out . . . they [covered] our mouths, and ran off with us into the nearest wood."

The Slave Market

At first, the Europeans got slaves from lands in the Kingdom of Kongo. African kings sold the slaves to the Europeans. In return, the kings received cloth, metal goods, guns, and horses. Slowly, the slave trade moved north. The Kingdoms of Benin and Ashanti developed a large slave market. By the late 1700s, much of the African west coast was involved in the slave trade. In all, about ten million Africans were sold into slavery and sent to the Americas.

The slave trade was a key part of a system known as the **triangular trade**. European ships sailed to West Africa carrying **manufactured goods**. These goods, as well as horses, were traded for slaves and gold. The slaves were shipped to American islands known as the West Indies or to the American colonies.

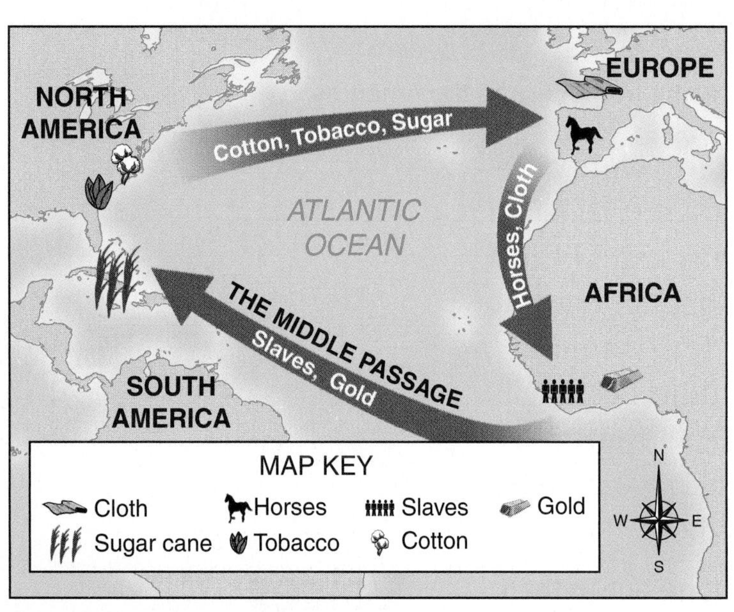

Triangular Trade

Money from the sale of slaves and gold allowed Europeans to buy cotton, tobacco, sugar, and other American goods. Finally, these goods were shipped to Europe.

The slave trade brought huge amounts of money to Europe. Europeans also used money from the slave trade to pay for the artistic and scientific advances during the Renaissance and the Scientific Revolution.

Lesson 2 Review

Choose words from the list that best complete the paragraphs. One word will not be used.

Word List

plantations
Portuguese
triangular trade
status
Middle Passage

Slavery has existed throughout much of world history. Even world religions accepted it. The __1__ began the European slave trade. Settlers in the Americas wanted slaves to work their sugar, tobacco, and cotton __2__.

Africans were taken from their homes and crowded into ships. The __3__ was the brutal trip from Africa to the Americas. Many Africans died along the way. The slave trade was one part of the system of __4__.

Chapter 23: Using What You've Learned

Summary

- The Kingdoms of Ashanti, Benin, and Kongo developed in Africa between 1300 and 1700.
- Many people in the Kingdom of Kongo welcomed the Portuguese when they first arrived in 1482. Over time, the Portuguese began to sell the Kongo people as slaves.
- The need for workers in the American colonies made the slave trade grow in the 1700s. The slave trade was part of a system called the triangular trade.

Find Out More!

After reading Chapter 23, you're ready to go online. **Explore Zone**, **Quiz Time**, and **Amazing Facts** bring this chapter of world history alive.

Visit www.exploreSV.com and type in the chapter code **Ch23**.

Vocabulary

Number your paper from 1 to 5. Write the letter of the correct answer.

1. A **confederation** is a group of smaller states under one ____.

a. religious leader
b. trade route
c. extended family
d. government

2. In the Ashanti culture, **talking drums** were used to ____.

a. spread news
b. make money
c. honor gods
d. control animals

3. In the Kingdom of Benin, the **oba** was the ____.

a. priest
b. god
c. king
d. capital city

4. **Plantations** are large ____.

a. kingdoms
b. markets
c. schools
d. farms

5. Many slaves died during the **Middle Passage** from Africa to ____.

a. Asia
b. the Americas
c. Europe
d. Australia

Comprehension

Number your paper from 1 to 5. Read each sentence below. Then write the name of the person or people who might have said each sentence. One name from the list will not be used.

1. "The golden stool is a symbol that unites us."
2. "We each have a personal god called an ehi."
3. "We have come to Kongo to convert people to Christianity."
4. "Money from the slave trade lets us buy American goods."
5. "I was captured when I was 11 years old and was later sold into slavery."

Word List

Benin people
Ashanti people
Afonso I
Europeans
Olaudah Equiano
missionaries

Critical Thinking

Cause and Effect Number your paper from 1 to 5. Read the causes in the left column. Then choose the correct effect from the right column. Write the letter of the correct effect.

Cause

1. Family life was important to the Ashanti, so
2. The Benin people believed their king came from the gods, so
3. The Kingdom of Kongo grew very large, so
4. Many Native Americans had died from European diseases, so
5. African kings sold slaves to the Europeans, so

Effect

a. the king had total power.
b. they lived in extended families.
c. European settlers looked to Africa for slaves.
d. it was divided into six provinces.
e. they received cloth, metal goods, guns, and horses.

Writing

Write a paragraph describing family life in the Ashanti culture.

LESSON 1

Islamic Empires

Before You Read

- Why would a group want to change the name of a city it conquered?
- How might all-water trade routes have affected empires in central Asia?

After the Mongols, two new empires developed in Southwest Asia. The Ottoman Empire began with a Turk named Osman around 1300. It grew to become one of the greatest empires in world history.

The empire of Safavid Persia began around 1500. It united many warring groups to build a large and powerful empire.

Both empires had the same religion, Islam. But they each belonged to a different **sect** of Islam. Their different beliefs often led to war. Both empires also wanted to control Southwest Asia.

The Blue Mosque is one of the most famous Ottoman buildings.

New Words

sect
Janissaries
elite
military
Shi'ite
Sunnite
shah
foreigners

People and Places

Ottoman Empire
Osman
Safavid Persia
Turkey
Istanbul
Bayezid II
Selim I
Suleyman
Sinan
Shah Abbas I
Isfahan
Iran
Afghanistan

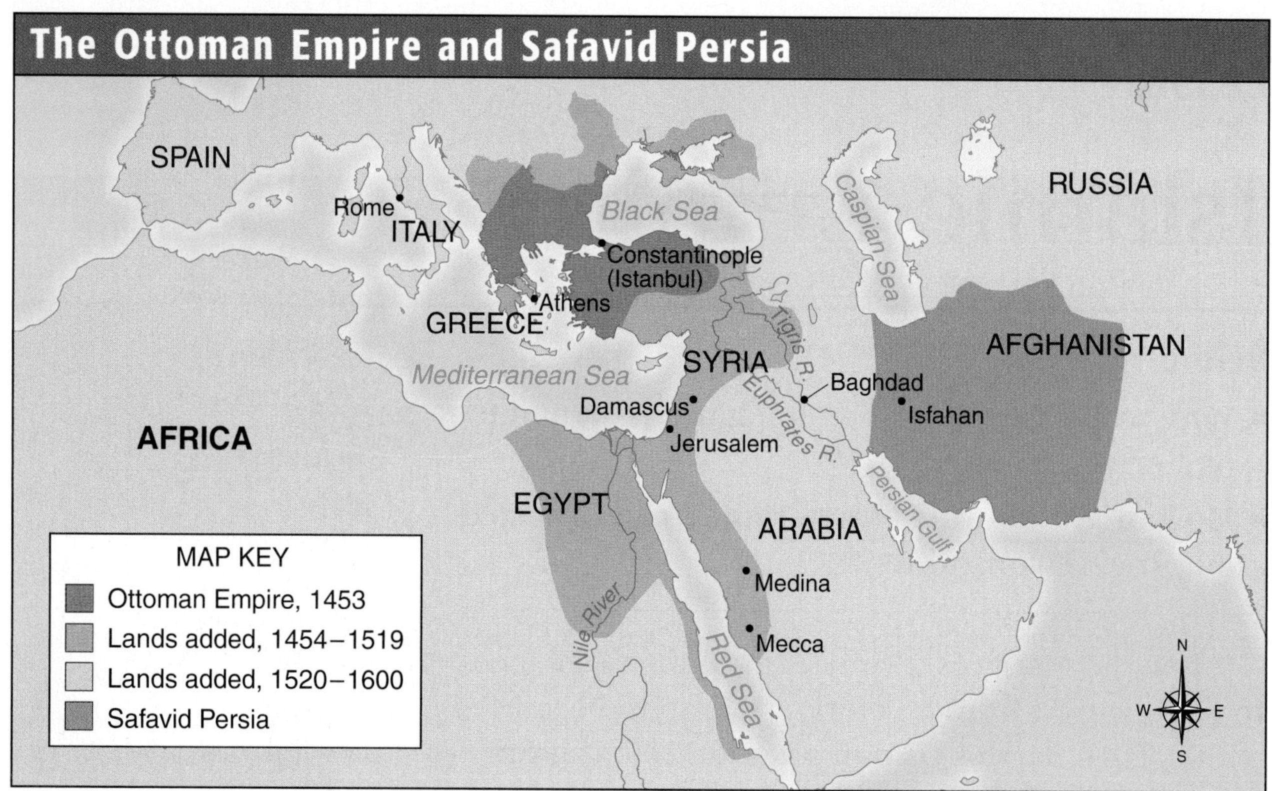

The Ottoman Empire grew during the 15th and 16th centuries. Name one city it conquered between 1520 and 1600.

The Growth of the Ottoman Empire

During the time of Osman, the Ottomans controlled only a small part of what is today the country of Turkey. Over the next 200 years, the empire grew greatly. The Ottomans took over Egypt. They won lands in North Africa and Arabia. They also conquered the Byzantine capital, Constantinople, in 1453.

The Ottomans changed the name of Constantinople to Istanbul and made it the capital of the Ottoman Empire. The Ottomans also conquered lands to the north, including parts of western Europe.

Ottoman Janissaries

The powerful Ottoman army had soldiers called **Janissaries**. In the beginning, these soldiers were mostly Christian slaves. The Ottomans put the Janissaries through a tough training program. They forced the Janissaries to convert to Islam. The Janissaries became the **elite** soldiers in the Ottoman army. The sultans gave the best

Janissaries important jobs in the government. Over time, the Janissaries gained so much power they even threatened the sultan.

The Golden Age of the Ottoman Empire

The Ottoman Empire had its Golden Age between 1481 and 1566. Sultan Bayezid II built a powerful navy. His son, Selim I, won control of the holy cities of Mecca and Medina. He also gained a monopoly over all trade routes between Asia and Europe. The Ottomans grew rich by taxing the goods traded across Asia. The Ottoman monopoly was one reason Europeans searched for an all-water route to Asia.

Suleyman the Magnificent

Selim's son Suleyman became sultan in 1520 and ruled for 46 years. He was known as Suleyman the Magnificent. Suleyman captured several European cities. He fought three wars against Persia. He also built roads and mosques within the empire.

Suleyman also reformed the laws of the Ottoman Empire. He improved the government and **military**, and he united the many territories of the Ottoman Empire.

Suleyman believed the whole world was his gift from God. He wrote about his own greatness.

> "Slave of God, master of the world, I am Suleyman and my name is read in all the prayers in all the cities of Islam. I am the Shah of Baghdad and Iraq, Caesar of all the lands of Rome, and Sultan of Egypt."

Life Under the Ottomans

The Ottomans were great architects. One architect named Sinan designed more than 300 buildings. The Blue Mosque in Istanbul, built in the 17th century, is one of the most famous Ottoman buildings. It was designed by one of Sinan's students.

Did You Know?

Good Clean Fun

You might take long showers. But you probably don't spend as much time bathing as the Ottomans did. Turkish baths were like Roman baths. They were not just a place to get clean. They were a place to meet friends and talk.

Turkish women especially enjoyed the baths. They were not allowed to meet openly on the streets. So they went to the bathhouses. They brought picnic lunches. Some brought musical instruments. Many women even brought their pets. Only at the end of the day would they pack up and return home.

People of the Ottoman Empire enjoyed music and dance.

The Ottomans loved entertainment. They had puppet shows that told stories of warrior heroes. The whole city of Istanbul closed down in the spring for the Tulip Festival. Turtles with candles on their backs lit up the tulip gardens at night. Music and dancing were also popular.

Suleyman the Magnificent died in 1566. By the 1600s, the Ottoman Empire was weakening. Europeans began using the all-water trade routes. The Ottomans no longer could tax the goods traveling through the empire. Although weakened, the Ottoman Empire lasted until 1923.

Safavid Persia

The empire of Safavid Persia was east of the Ottoman Empire. The Safavids often fought with the Ottomans about religion. The Safavids were **Shi'ite** Muslims. They believed only relatives of Muhammad could lead the Muslim people. The Ottomans were **Sunnite** Muslims who believed that any man could lead the Muslims. For 200 years, Safavid Persians and Ottomans fought about who were the true followers of Muhammad.

The height of Safavid Persia came during the rule of **Shah** Abbas I in the late 1500s. He made his capital at Isfahan in what is today the country of Iran. Abbas turned Isfahan into one of the most beautiful cities in Persia.

Shah Abbas welcomed **foreigners**, especially Europeans. Persia became a center for trade and the exchange of ideas. All forms of art grew under the Safavids. They became famous for their Persian carpets. Even the Ottomans wanted Persian carpets.

After Abbas died in 1629, the empire of Safavid Persia began to decline. Weaker leaders followed Abbas. Enemies began to take land from the empire. In 1722, an army from Afghanistan captured Isfahan and ended the Safavid Empire in Persia.

Persian carpet

Lesson 1 Review

Choose words from the list that best complete the paragraphs. One word will not be used.

The Ottoman Empire was one of the greatest empires in history. In 1453, the Ottomans captured Constantinople and renamed it __1__. The Ottomans made slaves into Janissaries, or __2__ soldiers. Suleyman fought three wars against the Persians.

The Safavids were __3__ Muslims. Under Shah Abbas, the Safavids built a magnificent capital city in __4__. The Safavids gained world fame for their beautiful Persian carpets.

Word List

Sunnite
Shi'ite
Istanbul
elite
Isfahan

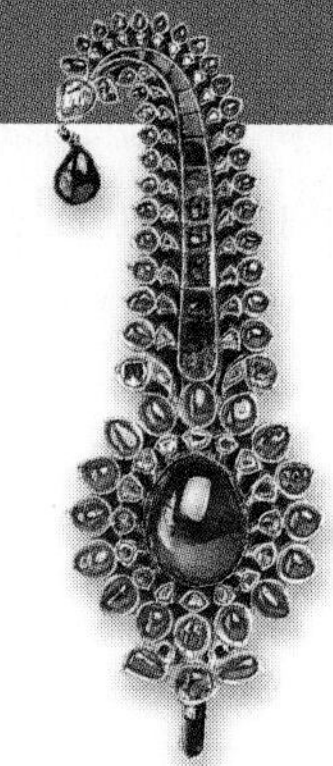

LESSON 2

Mughal Empire in India

New Words
civil servants
suttee
textiles

People and Places
Babur
Mughal
Akbar
Jahangir
Shah Jahan
Mumtaz Mahal
Aurangzeb
Goa
Bombay
Calcutta
Madras

Before You Read

- How might a ruler who believes in one religion successfully govern people who believe in a different religion?
- Why do people build beautiful buildings?

In Chapter 17, you read that the Delhi Sultanate in India ended in 1526. It was conquered by an attacker from the north. That attacker was Babur, a Muslim warrior from central Asia. Babur's ancestors included the Mongol leaders Genghis Khan and Timur. Babur made Delhi his capital and began the Mughal Empire in India. He died just five years after his victory, but the Mughal Empire continued.

This painting shows life at the Mughal court.

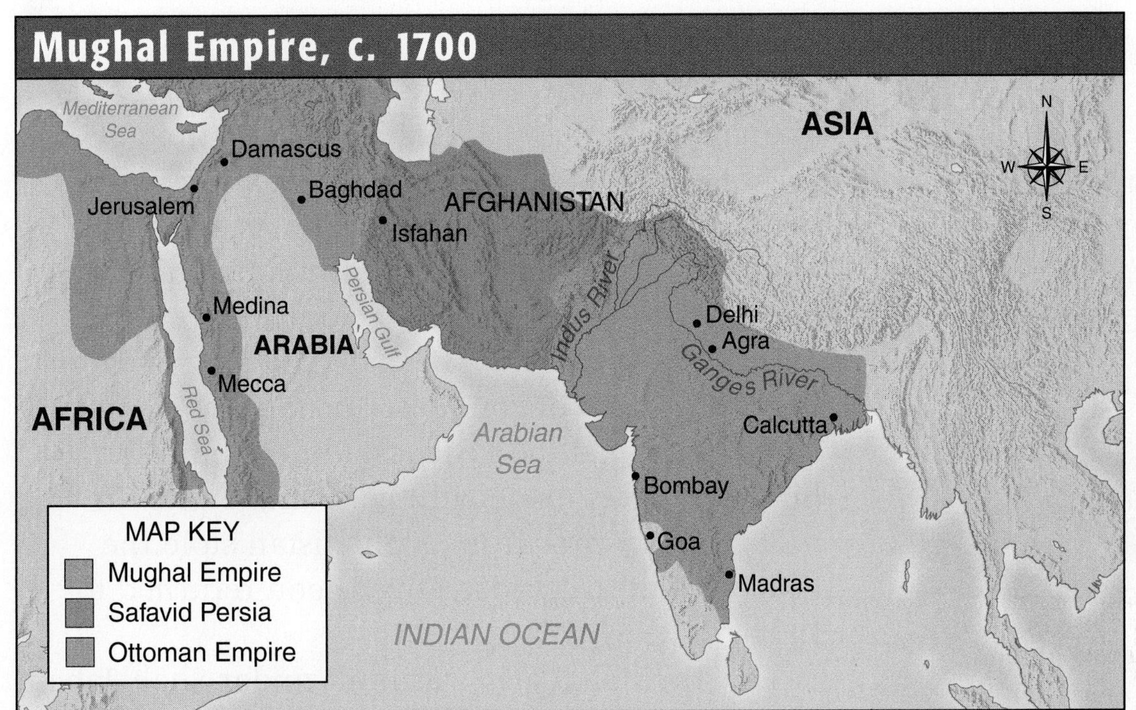

By 1700, the Mughals ruled almost all of the Indian subcontinent. Which city in the Mughal Empire was the farthest south?

The Rule of Akbar

In 1556, Akbar, Babur's grandson, became ruler of the Mughal Empire. Akbar was just 13 years old, but he was a great warrior. He defeated a Hindu army and gained control of northern India. Akbar set up a good government. He used **civil servants** to carry out his orders.

Many historians consider Akbar one of the greatest rulers in history. One reason was his tolerance. Many Muslim leaders tried to destroy the Hindus, but Akbar was kind to them. Akbar even married a Hindu princess.

Akbar tried to end the custom of suttee.

Akbar also worked to make India a better place for women and children. He tried to end the Hindu custom **suttee**. This custom called for widows to throw themselves into a funeral fire after their husbands died.

Akbar never learned to read, but he enjoyed learning new things. He had other people read to him. He also invited great thinkers to visit him. He even tried to create a new religion that would make everyone happy. It was a mix of several religions, but very few people accepted it.

The Mughals after Akbar

Peacock Throne

The rulers who followed Akbar were not as tolerant. Still, the Mughals had a long time of peace and growth. Jahangir, Akbar's son, helped to encourage all forms of art. The art of the Mughals was a mixture of Hindu, Muslim, and Persian art.

In 1628, Shah Jahan became the Mughal ruler. He fought wars of conquest and won new lands. Shah Jahan had the Peacock Throne built for himself. It was made with gold and jewels. In 1739, a conqueror from Afghanistan stole the Peacock Throne. It has never been returned to India.

The Taj Mahal also was built under Shah Jahan in the mid-17th century. It was a tomb for his wife, Mumtaz Mahal. Made with white marble, the Taj Mahal took 22 years and more than 20,000 workers to build. Many people think that the Taj Mahal is the most beautiful building in the world.

The Rule of Aurangzeb

When Shah Jahan grew old, his sons fought about who would be the next shah. One son,

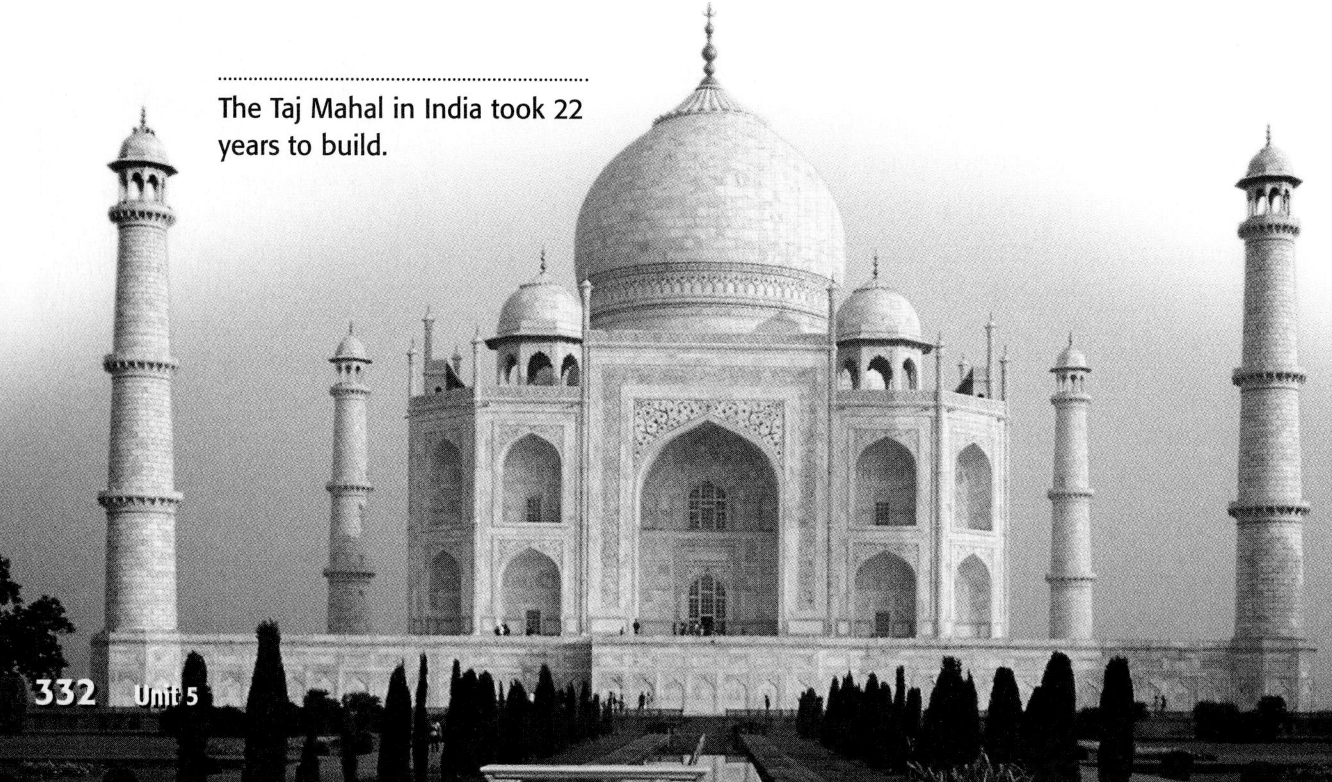

The Taj Mahal in India took 22 years to build.

Aurangzeb, killed his three brothers and then threw his father in jail. Shah Jahan could see the Taj Mahal from the window of his cell.

Aurangzeb, like the other Mughals, was a Muslim ruler. But unlike Akbar, he was not tolerant of the Hindus. Most of the people in India were still Hindu. Aurangzeb had the Hindu temples destroyed. He raised their taxes. He passed laws against many of the things Hindus enjoyed. These laws caused much trouble. Still, Aurangzeb stayed in power and ruled for 50 years. The Mughal Empire weakened soon after his death in 1707.

Shah Jahan

Europeans and Trade

During Mughal rule, European explorers began arriving in India. They came to trade for spices and cloth. Under Shah Jahan, the Mughal Empire gained control of most of India, but not all. The Portuguese controlled the city of Goa. They made it their port for trade in India.

In the 1600s, other Europeans arrived in India. The Dutch and English drove out the Portuguese. Indian **textiles** were popular in England. English factories wanted more and more Indian cloth. Queen Elizabeth I asked for permission from the Mughal emperor to set up the British East India Company in India. The Mughal emperor agreed, and trading between England and India increased. In return, the Indians got gold and silver, as well as tin and other metals. They used these items, especially silver, to trade with the Chinese.

This British prince in India is greeted by an elephant salute.

Slowly, the power of the English grew in India. They built trading posts in the cities of Bombay, then Calcutta and Madras. There was little the Mughals could do. English soldiers had better guns. The Mughals were skilled at horseback, but they had no navy to fight the English at sea. By the year 1800, England controlled most of India.

People In History

Mumtaz Mahal (1593–1631)

Mumtaz Mahal was born in 1593 with the name Arjumand Banu. In 1612, she married Shah Jahan. It was a Mughal custom for ladies to receive a new name when they married. Arjumand Banu became Mumtaz Mahal, which meant "High One of the Palace." Shah Jahan and Mumtaz Mahal loved each other very much. They were together all the time. She even went with him into battle.

Shah Jahan often asked Mumtaz Mahal for her advice. She told him to be kind to the poor and the weak. She became well known throughout the Mughal Empire for her kindness.

Mumtaz Mahal had 14 children. She died giving birth to the last child. Her death deeply saddened Shah Jahan. He decided to build the Taj Mahal as a symbol of their eternal love and Mumtaz Mahal's beauty. Today, both Mumtaz Mahal and Shah Jahan's graves are under the floor of the Taj Majal.

Lesson 2 Review

Choose words from the list that best complete the paragraphs. One word will not be used.

Word List

Taj Mahal
textile
Babur
England
civil servants

An attack by __1__ ended the Delhi Sultanate in 1526. Akbar extended Mughal control over northern India. He used __2__ to carry out his orders. Akbar tried to treat people fairly.

Shah Jahan became ruler in 1628. He built the __3__ to honor his wife, Mumtaz Mahal. He expanded Mughal control over most of India.

During Mughal rule, European explorers began to set up trading companies in India. The Mugal Empire weakened after 1707. By 1800, __4__ controlled most of India.

LESSON 3

Ming and Qing Dynasties

Before You Read

- Why might a country not want to trade with foreigners?
- How can people show respect to a ruler?

In 1368, a Chinese peasant led a revolt against the Yuan Dynasty. His army defeated the Mongols and began the Ming Dynasty. The word *Ming* means "bright." The Ming Dynasty lasted until 1644. Zhu Yuanzhang was only the third peasant to be emperor. He became known as the Hongwu Emperor.

The emperor passed laws to help peasants. He kept their taxes low and stored food to help them in times of hunger. He also helped the peasants by fixing dikes to control spring floods.

New Words

- self-sufficient
- expeditions
- novel
- Forbidden City
- forbidden
- kowtow
- stable
- inland

People and Places

- Ming
- Hongwu Emperor
- Manchuria
- Qing

This painting was made during the Ming Dynasty in China.

Trade and Agriculture

The Hongwu Emperor believed that farming was more important than trade. He wanted all villages to be **self-sufficient**. He believed villagers should grow and make the things they needed. China had all it needed and did not need to rely on trade with foreigners.

By the early 1400s, however, Ming rulers sent seven great **expeditions** to faraway places. Chinese ships traveled to India and East Africa. At the time, China had the best ships in the world. They could carry up to 500 sailors.

Chinese expedition ship

Then, in 1433, the expeditions suddenly stopped. Perhaps the Mongols threatened to attack again. Maybe the expeditions cost too much money. Or perhaps the Chinese simply did not want to expand. Unlike the Europeans, the Chinese were not searching for an all-water trade route. Their expeditions were to show their wealth and power. Whatever the reasons, the Chinese sent no more expeditions.

Advances of the Ming

Instead of sending expeditions, the Ming emperors made many advances within their borders. The Ming improved their porcelain by adding more colors. New kinds of writing also developed under Ming rule. The most important advance in writing was the **novel**. Novels were written in the language the people spoke. Many people could enjoy them. Other forms of writing were written in classic Chinese. Only nobles and scholars could read them.

Chinese porcelain from the 18th century

The Ming wrote encyclopedias and dictionaries. They also made it easier to write the Chinese language. The number of characters in the language went from 540 to 214.

The Great Wall of China had not always been kept up. The Ming repaired it and added new sections. They redesigned the watch towers and added cannons. The Great Wall of China that stands today is largely the result of Ming efforts.

The Ming encouraged trade within China and with Japan and Korea. Ming China had all it needed to make some of the most advanced manufactured goods in the world.

Statue of a Ming official

The Forbidden City

The Ming made Beijing their capital. There they built one of the largest palaces in the world. It was completed in 1420 after 14 years of building. It stretched two miles around, much larger than the French palace of Versailles. It was called the **Forbidden City**. It was **forbidden** because very few people were allowed inside.

Only the emperor, his wives, and his officials lived inside. Foreign leaders were allowed inside, but they had to bring gifts and **kowtow**, or bow deeply, before the emperor. This was done to show respect to the Chinese emperor.

For a long time, Ming rule remained **stable**. The people were happy. They were one of the most advanced civilizations in the world. The Ming rulers felt little need to explore Europe or any other continent.

Very few people were allowed inside the Ming palace called the Forbidden City.

Manchu warrior

When Europeans came to China in the early 16th century, the Ming were not very interested. They only wanted two items that Europeans gained from the Columbian Exchange. The Chinese wanted silver to make into coins. They also wanted American crops such as corn, potatoes, and peanuts.

The Coming of the Manchu

The Ming tried hard to defend the empire from invaders. They didn't want China to be taken over by outsiders ever again. The Ming fought long wars with the Mongols in the north. The Japanese, to the east, attacked Chinese port cities. The Ming moved these cities **inland**, but that hurt trade. Also, the Ming emperors began to neglect the peasants. This led to a revolt that weakened the Ming even more.

Northeast of China, in an area called Manchuria, the people watched and waited. They knew that a weak China would be easy to defeat.

The Qing Dynasty ended the Ming Dynasty and added lands to China. Were these lands mostly to the north or south of Ming China?

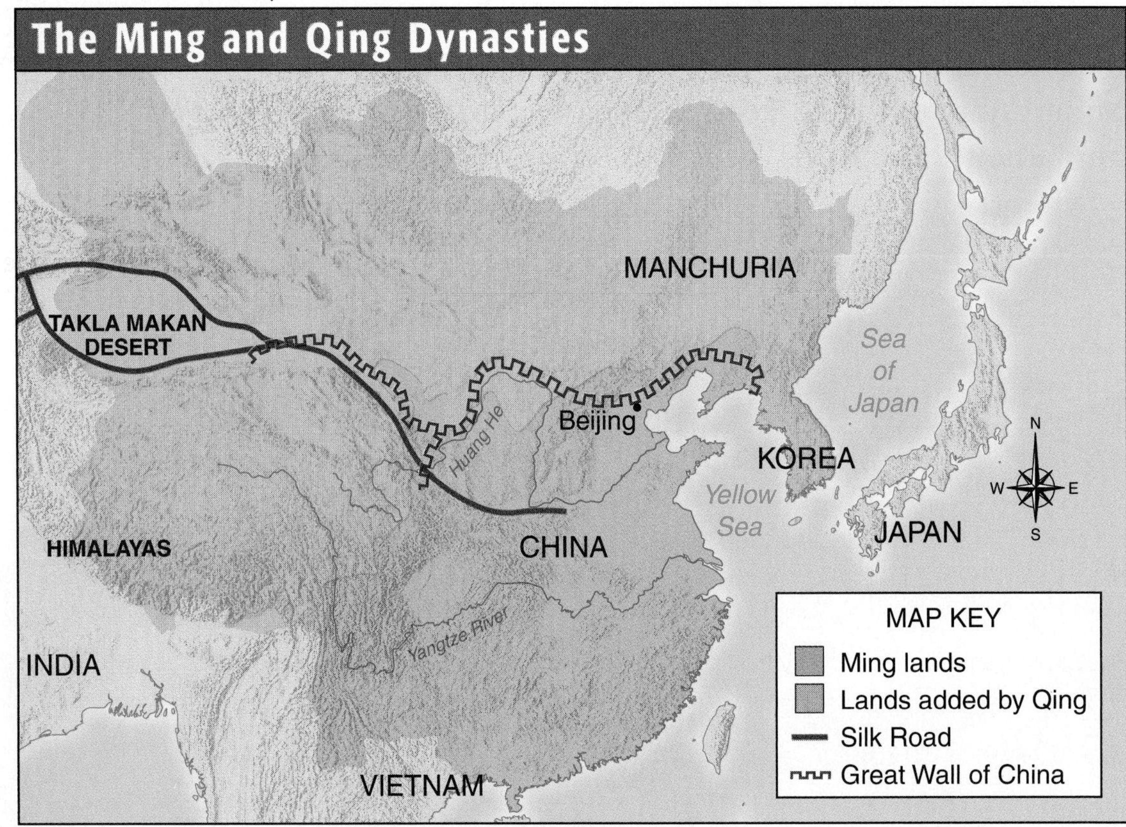

In 1644, a Manchu army broke through the gates of the Forbidden City, ending the Ming Dynasty. The Manchu called their new dynasty the Qing. The word *Qing* means "pure."

Chinese culture had long been a way of life in Manchuria. So the Manchu behaved much like the Chinese. Only their language was different. Even so, the Manchu, like the Mongols, were a foreign power. China was once again ruled by outsiders.

The Manchu passed laws to keep themselves apart from the Chinese. For example, a Manchu person could not marry a Chinese person. The Manchu also forced Chinese men to wear their hair in a long braid. This was a constant sign that they were under Manchu control.

The Manchu wore their hair in a long braid.

Lesson 3 Review

Choose words from the list that best complete the paragraphs. One word will not be used.

The Hongwu Emperor began the Ming Dynasty. He did many things to help the __1__. He kept their taxes low and tried to improve their lives. The emperor believed Chinese villages should be __2__. They did not need foreign trade. In 1433, the Chinese stopped sending expeditions to other parts of the world.

The Chinese began writing __3__ during the Ming Dynasty. The Ming built the Forbidden City. They also made writing Chinese easier and improved the Great Wall of China. In 1644, the __4__ took over the Forbidden City. They set up the Qing Dynasty.

Word List

self-sufficient
Manchu
kowtow
peasants
novels

LESSON 4

Japanese Isolationism

New Words

isolationism
policy
kabuki
troupe
riverbed

People and Places

Tokugawa Ieyasu
Edo
Tokyo
Nagasaki
Okuni

Before You Read

- How might skilled Japanese warriors have felt about foreigners with guns?
- What might the Japanese shoguns have thought about Christianity?

In the 1500s, the Ashikaga Shogunate controlled Japan, but civil wars were being fought in the countryside. Local army leaders fought one another for about 100 years. One of these army leaders, Tokugawa Ieyasu, defeated his enemies in a large battle in 1600.

In 1603, the emperor made Ieyasu the shogun. This began the Tokugawa Shogunate. It lasted until 1867.

This painting shows all of the shoguns of the Tokugawa period.

The city of Edo grew under the Tokugawa Shogunate.

Life Under the Tokugawa

Ieyasu moved the capital from Kyoto to Edo. He turned the small village into a large, well-guarded town. Edo later became Tokyo, the modern-day capital of Japan.

Ieyasu then developed a plan to control the daimyo, or landowners. He made them promise loyalty to him. He forced them to live part of every year in Edo. When a daimyo went home, the shogun kept his family hostage. He let them go only after the daimyo returned to Edo.

In Tokugawa Japan, the samurai were in the highest social class. Next were the farmers and then the craftspeople. In the lowest social class were the merchants. The Japanese, like the Chinese, did not want to rely on trade with outsiders.

Before the Tokugawa shoguns came to power, people could move from one class to another. The Tokugawa shoguns, however, wanted to keep everyone in their place. They thought this would help them stay in power. The Tokugawa shoguns made it much harder to change classes.

Tokugawa Japan

The Portuguese arrived in Japan in the mid-1500s.

A Tokugawa shogun

Isolationism

When the Portuguese arrived in Japan in the mid-1500s, they introduced guns and Christianity. Many samurai did not like guns. They trained many years to be skilled warriors. They felt the guns did not require the same amount of training. The Tokugawa shoguns disliked Christianity. They did not want people to feel loyal to a power other than the shogunate.

The Tokugawa shoguns wanted to control the terms of any trading. They allowed trade with China, Korea, and the Dutch. They even accepted ideas from the Scientific Revolution. But the Tokugawa shoguns knew that if they did not control trade, they might lose power. The Tokugawa shoguns came to believe in **isolationism**.

They forced the foreign Christians to leave Japan. They killed many Japanese Christians who refused to give up their new religion.

The **policy** of isolationism meant no trading ships were built in Japan. Also, no one could leave the country. If someone did, he or she could never come back. Most foreign traders were not allowed to visit. Only the Dutch were allowed to send one ship a year to the port of Nagasaki.

The Art of Kabuki

Japan continued developing new art forms. **Kabuki** was a play that used song and dance. The actors dressed in colorful costumes and fancy makeup. They moved in ways that made the story seem larger than life. Often the audience was involved in the play, too.

According to legend, kabuki began in 1603. A woman named Okuni created a **troupe**, or theater group, with some other women. Okuni dressed as a man. She and her troupe put on a performance in a dry **riverbed** in Kyoto. People loved her troupe. Kabuki theater had begun.

Okuni

Kabuki became a popular form of theater in 17th century Japan.

The Class System and Kabuki

Modern kabuki actor

It was mostly the common people who enjoyed kabuki. The upper classes didn't like it. Many of them still preferred the Noh drama of the 15th century. The upper classes called the kabuki actors "beggars of the riverbed." One reason they didn't like the new style was that kabuki often made fun of the upper classes.

The Tokugawa shoguns kept a close watch on kabuki. They did not want the plays to cause social trouble. They did not allow women to perform on stage. They said kabuki could only be performed in poorer areas of large cities. They also tried to control what could be said or done on stage. They passed a law against showing anything about life in present-day Japan, so writers had to set their plays far back in history.

Lesson 4 Review

Choose words from the list that best complete the paragraphs. One word will not be used.

Word List

hostage
troupe
Tokugawa
kabuki
isolationism

The __1__ Shogunate lasted from 1603 to 1867. Tokugawa Ieyasu didn't trust the daimyo. He made them swear loyalty to him. When they left Edo to go home, Ieyasu held their families __2__ until they returned.

In Tokugawa Japan, the samurai were in the highest class of society. Merchants were in the lowest. The Tokugawa shoguns believed in __3__. During their rule, Japan was cut off from the rest of the world. A new form of art called __4__ developed, which often made fun of the upper classes.

Chapter 24: Using What You've Learned

Summary

- The Ottoman Empire ruled much of Southwest Asia. The Safavids controlled Persia. The Ottomans and the Safavids often fought about religion.
- In 1556, Akbar became ruler of the Mughal Empire in India. He tried to make India a better place by practicing tolerance. The Mughal Empire was a time of peace and growth in India.
- The Ming Dynasty began in China in 1368. The Chinese built the Forbidden City and rebuilt the Great Wall during this time. The Manchu overthrew the Ming in 1644.
- The Tokugawa Shogunate began in Japan in 1603. The shoguns tried to limit foreign influence.

Find Out More!

After reading Chapter 24, you're ready to go online. **Explore Zone**, **Quiz Time**, and **Amazing Facts** bring this chapter of world history alive.

Visit www.exploreSV.com and type in the chapter code **Ch24**.

Vocabulary

Number your paper from 1 to 6. Write the word or words from the list that best complete the paragraphs. One word will not be used.

The Ottoman Empire and Safavid Persia each belonged to a different __1__ of Islam. Their different beliefs often led to war. The Ottoman army had soldiers called __2__ who went through a tough training program to become __3__ soldiers.

During the Ming Dynasty, the rulers of China sent seven __4__ to faraway places to show their wealth and power. A palace called the __5__ was built in Beijing. Few people were allowed inside. Foreign leaders who were allowed inside had to __6__, or bow deeply, to the emperor.

Word List

troupe
kowtow
Janissaries
expeditions
Forbidden City
sect
elite

Comprehension

Number your paper from 1 to 5. Write the word or words from the list that best complete each sentence. One word will not be used.

1. The Safavids were _____ Muslims.
2. The Taj Mahal was built during the rule of _____.
3. Elizabeth I set up the _____.
4. The Manchu started the _____ Dynasty in China in 1644.
5. The Tokugawa shoguns believed in _____.

Word List

Qing
self-sufficient
Shi'ite
isolationism
Shah Jahan
British East India Company

Critical Thinking

Main Idea Number your paper from 1 to 4. Write the sentence that is the main idea in each group.

1. The Ottomans took over Egypt.
The Ottoman Empire grew greatly.
The Ottomans conquered North Africa and Arabia.
2. The Ottoman Empire had its Golden Age from 1481 to 1566.
The Ottomans grew rich in the late 1400s by taxing goods traded across Asia.
Suleyman the Magnificent built roads and mosques in the 1500s.
3. Akbar set up a good government in the Mughal Empire.
Many historians think Akbar was a great ruler.
Akbar was tolerant toward Hindus.
4. The upper classes of Japan did not like kabuki.
Kabuki often made fun of the upper classes.
The shoguns kept a close watch on kabuki.

Writing

Write a paragraph explaining the causes of isolationism in Japan and the effect isolationism had on trade.

Skill Builder: Reading a Population Map

A **population map** shows the number of people living in different places. The map key of a population map uses colors or patterns to show different numbers of people. This map shows how many people per square mile were living in the Ottoman, Persian, and Mughal empires at their heights.

Population of Asian Empires at Their Heights

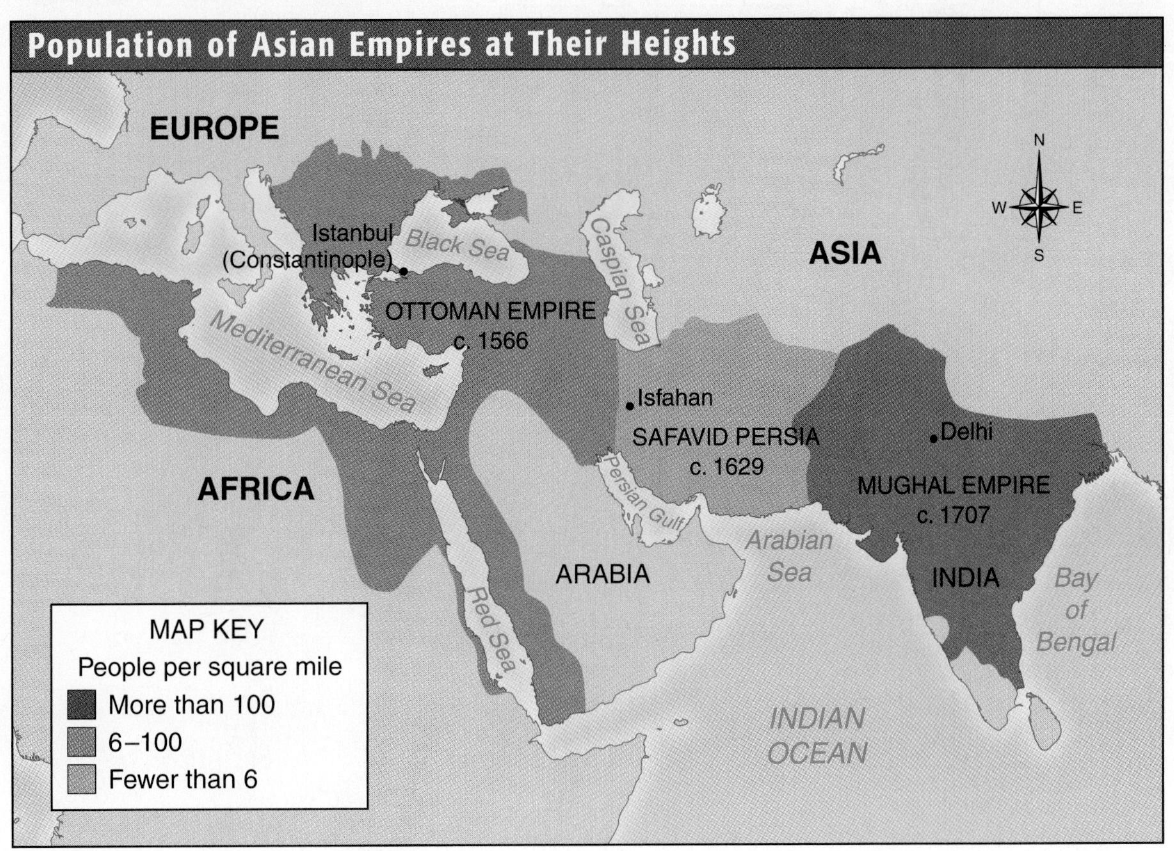

Number your paper from 1 to 5. Answer each question with a complete sentence.

1. What color shows fewer than 6 people per square mile?
2. How many people per square mile lived in the Mughal Empire at its height?
3. Which empire had 6 to 100 people per square mile?
4. Which empire had the fewest people per square mile?
5. At its height, each of these empires had about the same amount of land, but not the same population. What are some things that can effect population?

UNIT 6

Revolutions, New Nations, and Growing Empires

1750–1914

In the Americas and in France, the spirit of independence was strong during the 18th, 19th, and early 20th centuries. In many European countries, the power of rulers fell as the power of the citizens rose. In Africa and Asia, Europeans began adding lands to their empires.

This unit tells the story of how the world changed once Europeans began settling in lands across the globe. Some people fought for freedom and a better life. Some fought to control foreign lands. Others fought just to keep their cultures alive.

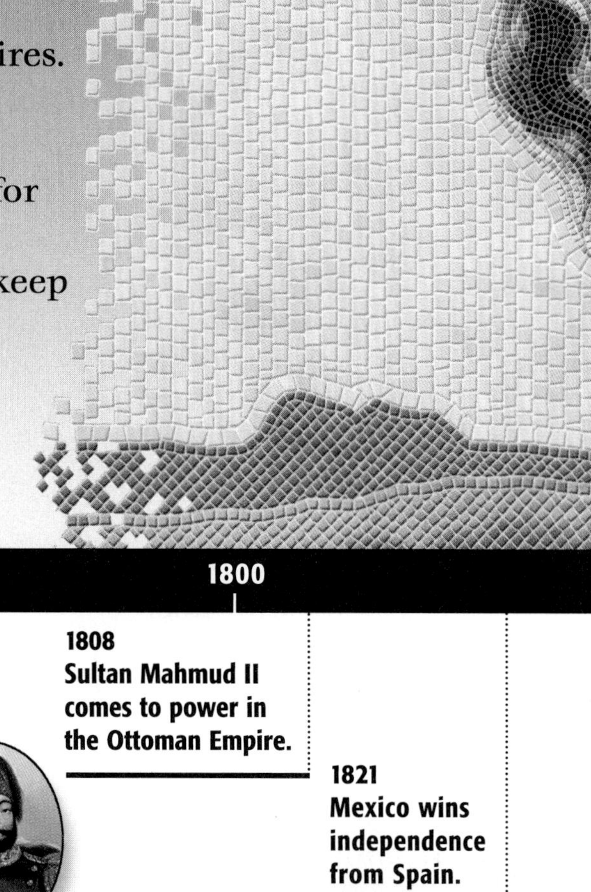

A.D. 1750 1800

1776
The 13 colonies declare independence from Great Britain.

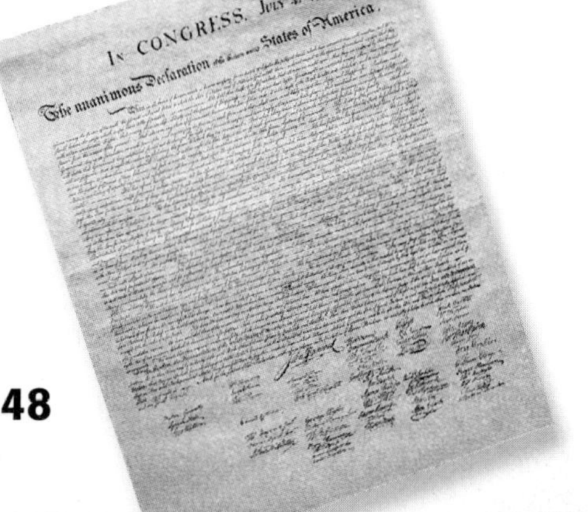

1808
Sultan Mahmud II comes to power in the Ottoman Empire.

1821
Mexico wins independence from Spain.

1850 | 1900 | A.D.

1854
After a visit from a United States military officer, Japan agrees to trade with Americans.

1871
Led by Otto von Bismarck, the German states are united.

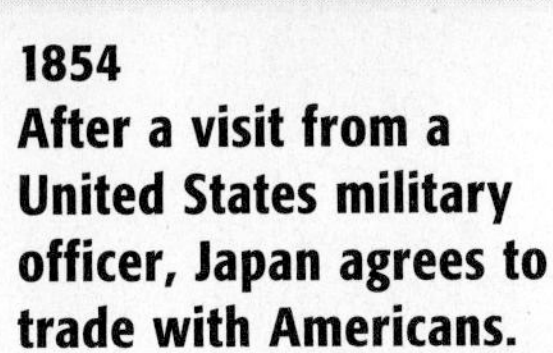

1879
Thomas Edison invents the electric light bulb.

LESSON 1

The American Revolution

New Words

Stamp Act
representation
repeal
quarter
boycott
minutemen
Declaration of Independence
Constitution

People and Places

Scotland
Wales
Great Britain
Boston Harbor
Massachusetts
Lexington
Concord
Thomas Jefferson
George Washington
Saratoga
New York
Charleston
South Carolina
Yorktown
Virginia

Before You Read

- Why might colonists want independence?
- How might colonists gain independence?

England shared an island with Scotland and Wales. In 1707, they formed one kingdom, known as Great Britain. The Kingdom of Great Britain continued to rule the 13 American colonies. But Great Britain was 3,000 miles away from the colonies. By the mid-1700s, most colonists had never seen Great Britain. They were loyal to Great Britain, but many colonists began to think of themselves as more American than British.

The French and Indian War

Great Britain and France had been fighting a series of wars during the 18th century. In 1754,

As people settled in the colonies, they began to think of themselves as Americans.

France and Great Britian fought one another in North America.

their fighting moved to North America, where both countries claimed lands. The fighting in North America became known as the French and Indian War. The French and some Native American groups fought on one side. The British, the American colonists, and other Native American groups fought on the other.

The British won the war in 1763. The French lost almost all of their lands in North America. It was an expensive victory for the British. The British wanted the colonists to pay part of that cost, but the colonists felt they had already paid enough since many had fought and died in the war. Also, the British had left soldiers in the colonies in case there was more trouble. The colonists felt threatened.

Colonists had to have a stamp such as this on certain goods.

The Road to War

Starting in 1764, the British Parliament passed several laws that angered American colonists. The laws were meant to raise money from the colonies. The 1765 **Stamp Act** taxed newspapers, playing cards, and many other goods. It required colonists to have a special stamp for these goods.

Boston Tea Party

The colonists protested. They did not want to be taxed without **representation**. There were no American colonists in the British Parliament. Colonists had no voice in deciding what laws were passed. They felt they should not be taxed by Parliament. The protest forced Parliament to **repeal** the Stamp Act.

The British passed more laws that upset the colonists. The colonists had to **quarter** British soldiers in their homes, providing them beds and meals. The British also passed a law saying that the colonists could only buy tea from the British East India Company. The colonists then refused to buy tea.

One night in 1773, some colonists sneaked onto a British ship that was anchored in Boston Harbor. They dressed as Native Americans and dumped boxes of tea into the water. Historians call this event the Boston Tea Party.

Parliament punished the colonists for their actions. It closed Boston Harbor. It limited the power of Massachusetts to rule itself. The colonists acted quickly. They urged people to **boycott**, or refuse to buy, British goods.

The Fight Begins

In 1775, a British army attacked Lexington and Concord in Massachusetts. The American Revolution began. Volunteer soldiers, called **minutemen**, had stored guns in those two towns.

Minutemen could be ready to fight in a minute.

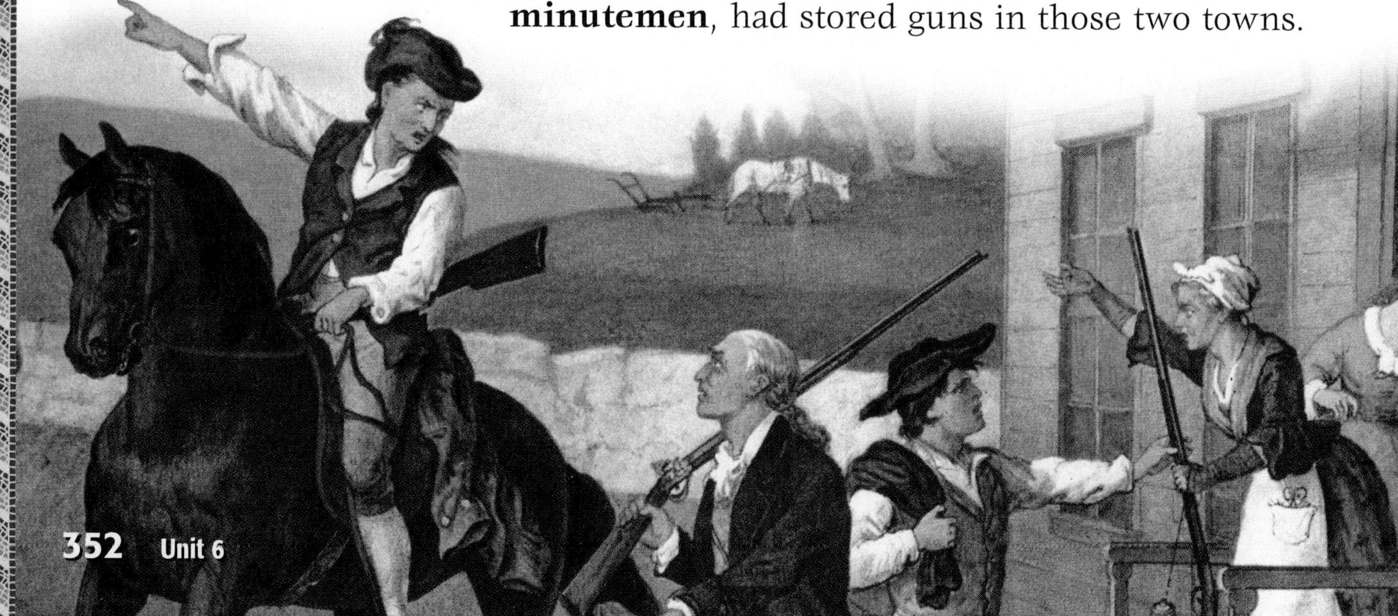

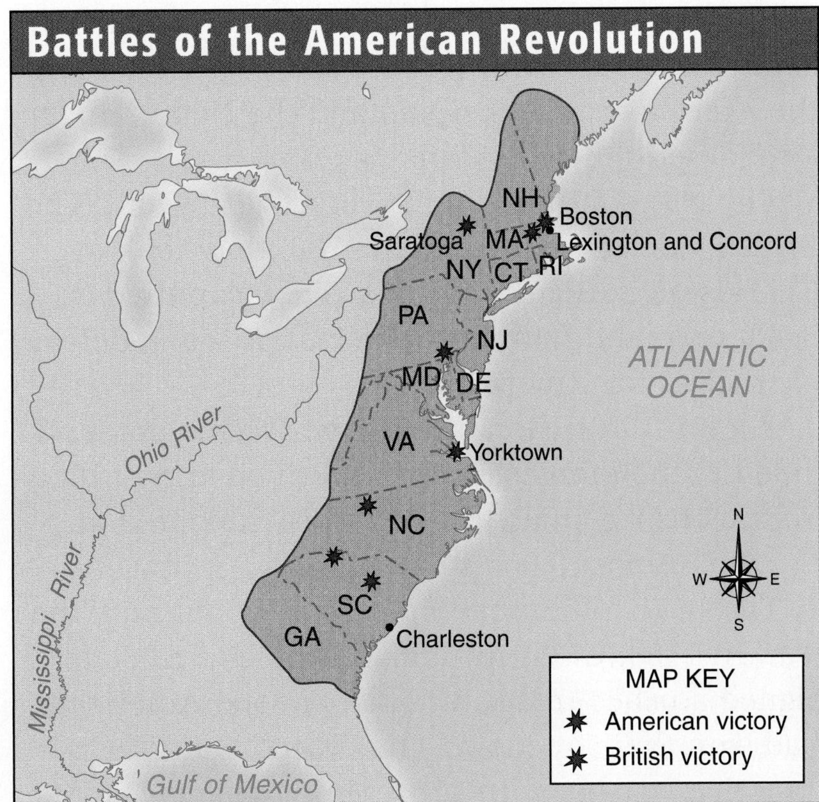

The American Revolution began with battles in Lexington and Concord. Did the Americans or the British win these battles?

The minutemen earned their name because they were ready to fight in a minute. The mighty British army easily defeated the minutemen at Lexington and Concord. But the colonists were more determined than ever.

On July 4, 1776, the colonists officially broke away from Great Britain. Thomas Jefferson, with help from others, wrote the **Declaration of Independence**. In it, he wrote some powerful ideas. He wrote that people had certain rights that no one, not even a king, could take away.

"We hold these Truths to be self-evident, that all men are created equal, that they are endowed by their Creator with certain unalienable Rights, that among these are Life, Liberty, and the pursuit of Happiness."

War and Peace

General George Washington led the American forces. They faced a strong British military and lost many early battles. By 1777, the American cause looked almost hopeless.

General George Washington

The Americans won their first major battle at Saratoga in New York. France then agreed to help the Americans. Later, Spain and the Netherlands also joined the Americans.

The war continued for several more years. The British won more battles. In 1780, they took over Charleston in South Carolina. They captured 5,400 men and four ships. It was the worst defeat of the war for Americans.

Then in 1781, General George Washington and allied French forces trapped a British army unit at Yorktown, Virginia. The British surrendered an army of almost 8,000 soldiers.

The British then had no chance of winning the war. In 1783, Great Britain and the United States signed a peace treaty in Paris, France. Americans had won their freedom. The United States of America was born. In 1787, United States leaders wrote the **Constitution**. In 1789, Washington became the new country's first president.

Lesson 1 Review

Choose words from the list that best complete the paragraph. One word will not be used.

Word List

Declaration of Independence
boycott
representation
minutemen
Stamp Act

For many years, Great Britain ruled the American colonies peacefully. The British defeated the French in the French and Indian War. The British then wanted colonists to help pay for the war. The colonists protested tax laws such as the __1__. They said there should be no taxes without __2__ in Parliament. Colonists began to __3__ British goods. They even threw British tea into Boston Harbor. War began in 1775. One year later, Thomas Jefferson wrote the __4__. The colonists won their freedom in 1783.

LESSON 2

The French Revolution

Before You Read

- How might one country's revolution affect other people living under an absolute ruler?
- How might a strong military leader fail?

Helping the Americans win independence was costly to the French. In addition, France had been ruled by kings who spent large amounts of money on grand palaces and expensive furniture. After years of heavy spending by French kings, the country had little money left.

Many French people were upset with their weak king, Louis XVI. Inspired by the successful American Revolution, the French people began thinking of revolution, too.

New Words

Estates General
National Assembly
adjourn
Bastille
Reign of Terror
guillotine

People and Places

Louis XVI
Marie Antoinette
Napoleon Bonaparte
Corsica
Prussia
Austria
Elba
Waterloo
Belgium
St. Helena

French kings spent large amounts of money on expensive furniture.

The Estates General

The **Estates General** was a French assembly of three estates, or classes. The First Estate was made up of church leaders who paid no taxes. The Second Estate was made up of nobles who also paid no taxes. The Third Estate was for everyone else. Its members included rich merchants as well as poor peasants. The Third Estate paid all the taxes. Each estate met separately and got one vote each. The two votes from the First and Second Estates always counted more than the one vote of the Third Estate. Yet the Third Estate represented about 97 percent of the French people.

King Louis XVI

In 1789, Louis XVI called for the Estates General to meet to discuss France's money troubles. The Third Estate refused to separate for voting. They said that the Estates General represented all the French people, so they should all vote as individuals. Louis XVI sent members of the Third Estate out of the meeting.

Members of the Third Estate established their own **National Assembly**. A few priests and nobles joined them. The members gathered at an indoor tennis court. There they promised not to **adjourn** until the laws of France were changed.

Members of the National Assembly met in an indoor tennis court.

Revolution Begins

Over the next few months, fear spread across France. Most people didn't know what would happen next. They feared the king might use force to break up the National Assembly.

On July 14, 1789, an angry crowd stormed the **Bastille**, a royal prison. Many of the king's weapons were stored in the Bastille. It was also a symbol of the king's absolute authority. The crowd destroyed the Bastille. The French Revolution had begun.

The attack on the Bastille

The National Assembly passed new laws. It called an end to the old estates. It declared that all people were free and equal. It took lands away from the church and sold the land to raise money. It also took away the king's absolute power. He, too, would have to obey the laws.

The Reign of Terror

By 1791, many thought the revolution was almost over. King Louis XVI publicly agreed to the new laws that limited his power. Secretly, however, he planned for other countries to invade France and stop the revolution. Louis XVI and his family tried to escape from France. They dressed as servants, but someone recognized the family. They were then sent to a jail in Paris.

Louis XVI at the guillotine

Soon, new leaders took charge of the revolution. They introduced many more changes. They set up the French Republic. They also declared war on anyone who stood against them. This part of the French Revolution is called the **Reign of Terror**.

In 1792, the leaders of the French Republic put Louis XVI on trial. He was found guilty. He and his wife, Marie Antoinette, were killed by the **guillotine**. This machine dropped a heavy blade on the neck of its victims.

Napoleon Bonaparte

By 1793, most nations in Europe were at war with France. These countries still had monarchs and did not like what the French had done to Louis XVI. The leaders of the French Republic punished anyone they thought was not loyal. More than 40,000 people died during the Reign of Terror. Many died on the guillotine.

In 1794, yet another group of French leaders took power. They used the guillotine to kill those who had started the Reign of Terror.

The Age of Napoleon

By 1795, the revolution was over. In 1799, Napoleon Bonaparte, a military leader, took over the government. This began a new period in France called the Age of Napoleon.

Napoleon Bonaparte was born on the island of Corsica in the Mediterranean Sea. He supported the ideas of the French Revolution. Napoleon set up a code of laws that are still used in France today. The code encouraged religious tolerance.

In 1812, Napoleon had almost all of Europe under his control. What states were against Napoleon in 1812?

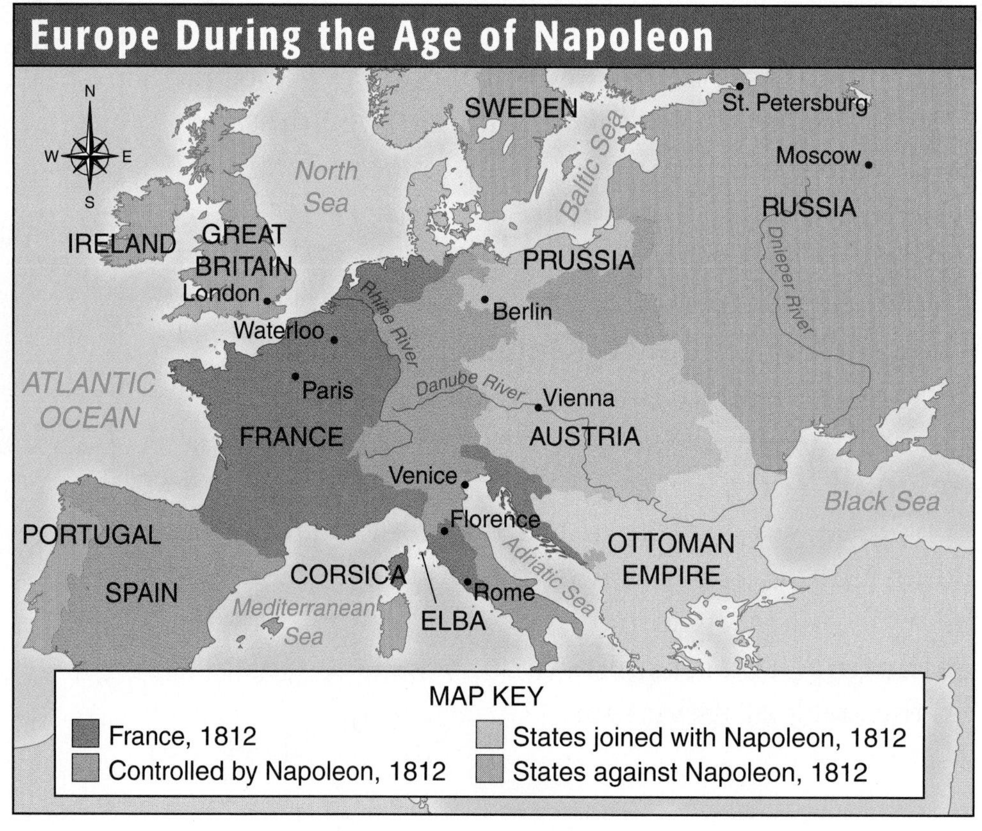

Napoleon wanted to rule all of Europe. In 1804, he crowned himself emperor. He led his army in battles from Spain to Russia.

The fall of Napoleon began when he invaded Russia with 600,000 soldiers in 1812. They were not prepared for the extremely cold weather. When Napoleon left Russia, he had only a few thousand soldiers left in his army. Russia then attacked France. Great Britain, Prussia, and Austria joined Russia in a battle against Napoleon.

In 1814, Napoleon's enemies sent him to the island of Elba in the Mediterranean Sea. He escaped to fight one last battle in Waterloo, Belgium. He lost the Battle of Waterloo in 1815. He gave up his power, and the monarchy was brought back to France. Napoleon was sent to the distant island of St. Helena off the coast of Africa. He died there in 1821.

Battle of Waterloo

Lesson 2 Review

Choose words from the list that best complete the paragraphs. One word will not be used.

Word List
- Elba
- Waterloo
- Estates General
- guillotine
- adjourn

Under Louis XVI, France was troubled by a lack of money. Louis XVI called a meeting of the __1__ to find a solution. But the Third Estate created its own National Assembly. Leaders promised not to __2__ until the laws were changed.

During the Reign of Terror, many people, including the king and queen of France, were killed by the __3__. Napoleon came to power in France after the Reign of Terror. His fall came after an unsuccessful invasion of Russia. Napoleon lost his final battle at __4__.

LESSON 3

Revolution in Latin America

New Words

peninsulares
creoles
haciendas
mestizos
mulattoes
liberator

People and Places

Latin America
Iberian Peninsula
Toussaint-Louverture
Saint Domingue
Haiti
Miguel Hidalgo
Don Pedro
Jose de San Martin
Simón Bolívar
Argentina
Chile
Venezuela
Colombia
Ecuador
Panama
Bolivia

Before You Read

- Why might people from a nation's lower classes support revolution?
- How might a colony gain independence peacefully?

In the 1700s, Spain and Portugal gained control of most of the lands in Mexico, Central America, and South America. These lands became known as Latin America.

The Spanish and the Portuguese kept tight control over the people living in Latin America. They put strict controls on trade, forcing Latin Americans to trade only with Spain or Portugal. Inspired by the American Revolution and the French Revolution, Latin Americans began to want freedom, too.

This hacienda was located in Colombia, South America.

The Class System

A class system had developed in the Latin American colonies. The **peninsulares** were at the top of the class system. They were people born in Spain or Portugal, on Europe's Iberian Peninsula. They held all the important jobs in the government, church, and army.

Next were the **creoles**. They were people who were born in Latin America but had European ancestors. The creoles often owned **haciendas**, or Latin American plantations.

By the 1700s, most people in Latin America were neither peninsulares nor creoles. Below these two upper classes were the **mestizos** and **mulattoes**. Mestizos had European and Native American ancestors. Mulattoes had European and African ancestors.

Below the mestizo and mulatto class were the Native Americans and the Africans. Most Native Americans were free, but very poor. They worked for the creoles on the haciendas. Some Africans were free, but most were slaves. They were forced to work on the haciendas.

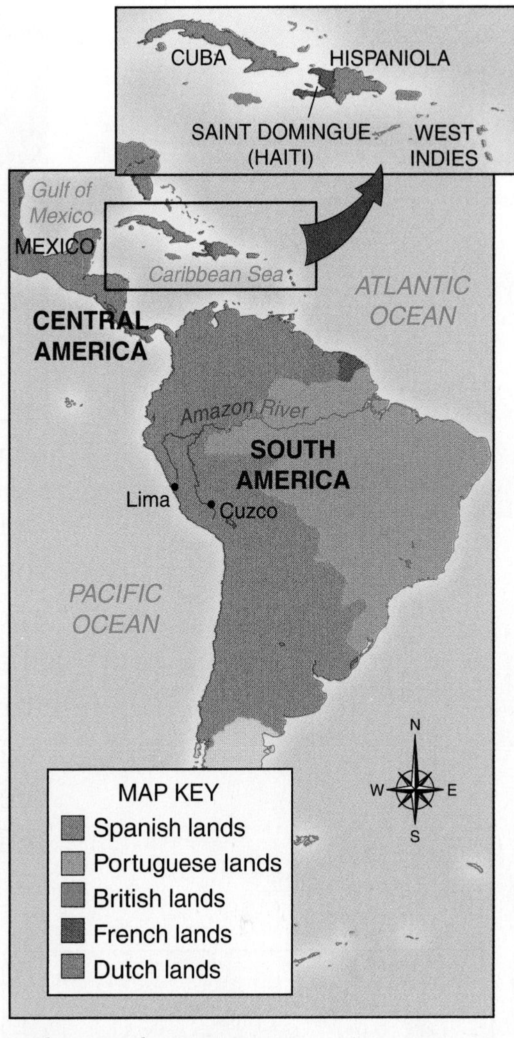

Latin America, 1784

Although many creoles were wealthy, they were unhappy with the peninsulares. The peninsulares kept the creoles from getting certain jobs. So the creoles were ready for a revolution. The mestizos and mulattoes also wanted change.

Revolutions Begin

Toussaint-Louverture led the first Latin American revolution. He was a slave in the French colony, Saint Domingue. In 1791, he began a fight for freedom. Napoleon sent a French army to defeat the colonists, but the French could not stop the revolution. In 1804, Saint Domingue won its independence and took the name Haiti. Haiti was the first independent country in Latin America.

Toussaint-Louverture

Father Miguel Hidalgo led the Mexican Revolution.

In 1810, Father Miguel Hidalgo began a revolution in Mexico. He led Native Americans and mestizos in a fight to win independence from Spain. He also fought for the return of Native American lands and an end to slavery.

Hidalgo was killed by the Spanish in 1811, but the revolution continued. Mexico won its independence in 1821.

Independence for Brazil

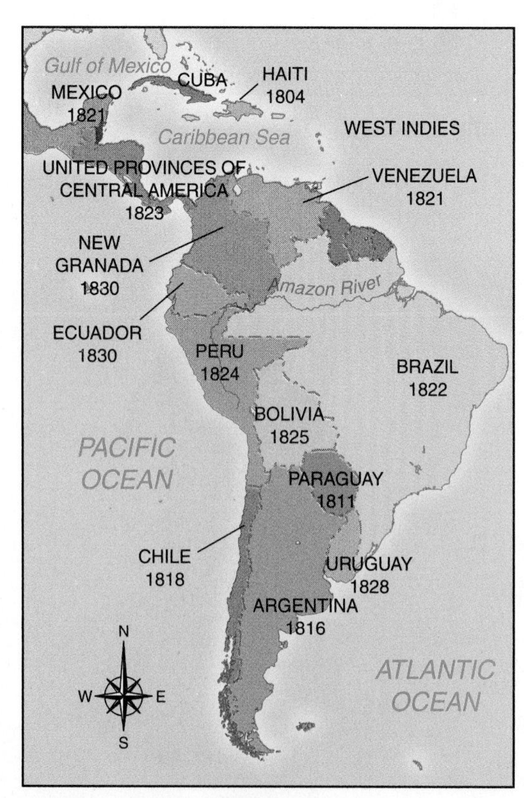

Latin America, 1830

In 1807, Napoleon's army entered Portugal. The king of Portugal fled to his colony in Brazil. After the fall of Napoleon, the king returned to Portugal. He left his son Don Pedro to rule Brazil.

The people of Brazil wanted freedom from Portugal. On September 7, 1822, Don Pedro declared Brazil an independent country. There was no fighting. Portugal let Brazil gain freedom peacefully.

More Latin American countries began seeking independence. Jose de San Martin led creoles in a fight for the independence of modern-day Argentina. He also won independence for Chile. Other nations won independence under the leadership of Simón Bolívar. By 1830, the Spanish Empire in Latin America had been divided into several independent countries.

Simón Bolívar (1783–1830)

People In History

Simón Bolívar was born in Venezuela in 1783. Although he was a rich creole, he spent his life trying to free South Americans from Spanish rule. Known as "The **Liberator**," Bolívar became one of the most famous heroes of Latin America.

Bolívar began his fight in 1810. He lost several battles in the beginning. But in 1821, he won an important victory against a strong Spanish army. As a result, he freed what became the nations of Colombia, Venezuela, Ecuador, and Panama.

Bolívar freed much of northern South America. Meanwhile, Jose de San Martin was working to free the south. The two revolutionaries held a secret meeting in 1822. San Martin turned his army over to Bolívar. Bolívar used the combined army to free Peru in 1824. In 1825, the southeastern part of Peru became a separate state. It was named Bolivia in honor of Simón Bolívar.

Lesson 3 Review

Choose words from the list that best complete the paragraphs. One word will not be used.

The colonies in Latin America developed a class system. In the highest class were the __1__, or people born in Spain or Portugal. Next came the creoles. Below the upper two classes were the people of mixed ancestors. The __2__ had European and Native American ancestors. The mulattoes had European and African ancestors.

__3__ led the first Latin American revolution and freed Haiti. Mexico won its independence in 1821. __4__, known as "The Liberator," led many more Latin American countries to independence.

Word List

creoles
Simón Bolívar
peninsulares
Toussaint-Louverture
mestizos

Chapter 25: Using What You've Learned

Summary

- Angered by new tax laws, the American colonists wanted independence from England.
- The American Revolution began in 1775 at Lexington and Concord in Massachusetts. In 1776, the American colonists issued the Declaration of Independence.
- In France, the Third Estate formed the National Assembly to try to change the laws. An angry crowd stormed the Bastille on July 14, 1789, beginning the French Revolution.
- In 1799, Napoleon Bonaparte took over the government of France. He also tried to invade Russia, beginning several years of warfare. He was defeated in 1815 at the Battle of Waterloo.
- Inspired by the American and French revolutions, Latin American colonies won their independence from European powers.

Find Out More!

After reading Chapter 25, you're ready to go online. **Explore Zone, Quiz Time,** and **Amazing Facts** bring this chapter of world history alive.

Visit www.exploreSV.com and type in the chapter code **Ch25**.

Vocabulary

Number your paper from 1 to 5. Write the word or words from the list that best complete each analogy. One word will not be used.

1. Pass is to give out as _____ is to take back.
2. Refuse is to accept as _____ is to buy.
3. Parliament was to Great Britain as the _____ was to France.
4. Start is to begin as _____ is to stop.
5. The First Estate was to the class system of France as the _____ were to the class system of Latin America.

Word List

quarter
repeal
adjourn
peninsulares
boycott
National Assembly

Comprehension

Number your paper from 1 to 5. Write the word or words from the list that best complete the paragraphs. One word will not be used.

The fighting in North America in 1754 between Great Britain and France was called the __1__. The __2__ won the war in 1763. The __3__ lost almost all of their lands in North America.

In 1765, the British Parliament passed the __4__. This law taxed goods, such as newspapers and playing cards, in the 13 American colonies. The American colonists protested. They did not want to be taxed without __5__ in Parliament.

Word List

representation

French and Indian War

Stamp Act

British

minutemen

French

Critical Thinking

Fact or Opinion Number your paper from 1 to 5. For each fact, write **Fact**. Write **Opinion** for each opinion. You should find two sentences that are opinions.

1. In the Estates General, the votes of the First and Second Estates counted more than the votes of the Third Estate.
2. The crowd of angry French people should not have stormed the Bastille.
3. Napoleon should not have tried to invade Russia.
4. The first independent country in Latin America was Haiti.
5. Many Latin American nations won their independence under the leadership of Simón Bolívar.

Writing

Write a paragraph explaining the class system that developed in the Latin American colonies.

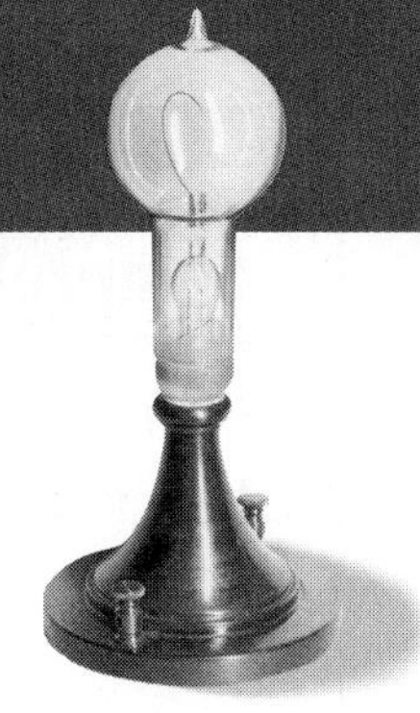

LESSON 1

New Inventions

New Words

- Industrial Revolution
- industrialization
- industry
- flying shuttle
- spinning jenny
- cotton gin
- technology
- transportation
- steamboat
- telegraph
- internal combustion engine

People and Places

- Thomas Newcomen
- James Watt
- John Kay
- James Hargreaves
- Eli Whitney
- Robert Fulton
- Hudson River
- Richard Trevithick
- George Stephenson
- Alexander Graham Bell
- Thomas Edison
- Gottlieb Daimler

Before You Read

- Why do people invent new things?
- How might new sources of power change people's lives?

You have read how early humans used stone tools during the Stone Age. As time passed, people began improving tools. They used new materials, such as bronze and iron.

The **Industrial Revolution** is the time in which people started using machines instead of tools. It was not a revolution like those in the United States, France, and Latin America. It did not occur quickly or with a battle. Still, it was a revolution. It changed the way most people lived.

Before the Industrial Revolution, farmers had to plant seeds by hand.

The Industrial Revolution Begins

There was no single day on which the Industrial Revolution began. It started slowly over hundreds of years. People from many countries played a part in it. Most historians agree that **industrialization** began in the 18th century.

The Industrial Revolution began in Great Britain. Most of the early inventors were English or Scottish. In the 19th century, the Industrial Revolution reached France, Germany, the United States, and Japan. More countries joined the Industrial Revolution in the 20th century.

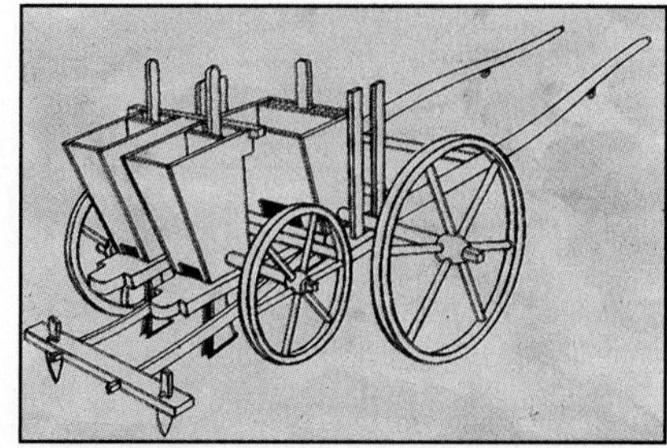

In the 1800s, machines such as this seed drill were invented to plant seeds.

A New Source of Power

Before the Industrial Revolution, there were only three sources of power. Farmers used big animals such as horses and oxen to pull plows. Flowing rivers turned water wheels. Human strength provided the third source of power.

In 1712, Thomas Newcomen built the first steam engine. His steam engine pumped water out of mines. In 1769, James Watt built a better steam engine. The world gained a great new source of power—steam.

James Watt's steam engine provided a new source of power.

Did You Know?

Save the Whales

Whaling was big business in the 19th century. People used whale oil for heating, making soap, and oiling machines. Every year, more and more whaling boats brought back millions of gallons of whale oil. In 1833, there were 392 whaling boats in the United States. In 1849, there were 735. Other countries also had whaling boats. If this had continued, all the whales in the world might soon have been killed.

But the Industrial Revolution saved the whales. In 1849, a Canadian doctor discovered a way to make kerosene, a kind of fuel. Kerosene was better and much cheaper than whale oil. Fewer people killed whales. By 1876, there were just 39 American whaling boats.

The spinning jenny allowed a person to spin many threads at once.

The Textile Industry

The Industrial Revolution brought great changes to the textile **industry**. Making cloth was slow work, but new machines made it much faster. In 1733, John Kay invented the **flying shuttle**. It made weaving easier. Another invention made yarn more quickly. In 1770, James Hargreaves invented the **spinning jenny**. It allowed a person to spin many threads at once.

In 1793, Eli Whitney invented the **cotton gin**. This machine cleaned cotton much faster than people could do by hand. The cotton gin helped the southern United States produce large amounts of cotton. New **technology** made it easier, faster, and cheaper to produce cloth.

The Transportation Industry

Getting cloth and other goods to buyers was still difficult. In the early 1800s, Great Britain began building better roads and more canals for **transportation**. Goods could then move throughout the kingdom, but the goods moved slowly.

In 1807, Robert Fulton developed a new use for the steam engine. He put a steam engine on a boat and sailed up the Hudson River in the United States. His **steamboat** changed water transportation. By the 1840s, steamboats could cross the Atlantic Ocean.

Robert Fulton's steamboat

Some people began to wonder whether steam could provide power for transportation on land. In 1801, Richard Trevithick built a steam engine for hauling coal on tracks. Then George Stephenson put the steam engine on wheels, creating the world's first railroad train. Called *Rocket*, Stephenson's steam-powered train traveled 14 miles per hour. By 1830, Great Britain had a railroad track with a railroad train.

By the 1860s, England and Scotland had thousands of miles of railroad track. Other nations, including the United States, did, too. As the trains improved and were made faster, the railroad brought huge changes. It cut the time and cost for moving goods and people from one place to another.

George Stephenson's *Rocket* was the world's first railroad train.

Thomas Edison holding his electric light bulb

Other Inventions

The **telegraph** was in use by the 1840s. It sent messages over wires in just seconds. In 1876, Alexander Graham Bell sent a human voice over wires and invented the telephone.

In the mid-1800s, oil became a new source of power. People used it to heat their homes. Factories used it to run machines. In 1879, Thomas Edison invented the electric light bulb. It helped replace oil lamps with electric lights. Edison's light bulb could stay lit for two days.

One new product made from oil was gasoline. Several Europeans developed the **internal combustion engine**, which ran on gasoline. In the 1880s, Gottlieb Daimler improved the engine by making it lighter in weight. By the early 20th century, a few people were using the internal combustion engine to drive cars and fly planes.

Lesson 1 Review

Choose words from the list that best complete the paragraphs. One word will not be used.

Word List

steamboat
spinning jenny
telephone
railroad
cotton gin

During the Industrial Revolution, workers began using machines. The textile industry had great changes. Eli Whitney's __1__ made it much faster and easier to clean cotton.

Robert Fulton's __2__ improved water transportation. George Stephenson's *Rocket* was the world's first __3__ train.

Alexander Graham Bell invented the __4__. Thomas Edison invented the first electric light bulb. The development of the internal combustion engine led to cars and planes.

LESSON 2

Effects of the Industrial Revolution

Before You Read

- How might the Industrial Revolution have made people's lives worse?
- How might people improve their working conditions?

New Words

standard of living
leisure
urbanization
child labor
labor unions
strike
communism

People and Places

London
Robert Owen
Karl Marx

Many of the inventions of the Industrial Revolution improved people's **standard of living**, or how well people lived. New farm machines made it easier to produce food. New medicines meant people lived longer. Many people lived more comfortable lives. They traveled farther and faster. They also had more time for **leisure**.

But the Industrial Revolution did not bring all people a higher standard of living. For some, life got worse. Many people began working in dangerous mines, mills, and factories.

These women are working in a textile factory.

Industrial city in England

Growing Cities

During the Middle Ages, Europeans began moving into towns. But even in the 18th century, most Europeans lived on farms. The Industrial Revolution created a need for more people to work in the cities. By the late 19th century, more Europeans lived in cities than in the countryside.

This shift to the cities is called **urbanization**. In 1800, about 20 cities in Europe had more than 100,000 people. By 1850, three cities had more than a million. By 1914, more than 150 cities had that many people.

At first, the cities could not handle so many people. The cities didn't have enough housing or drinking water. Streets were dark and dangerous at night. Fire was a constant danger, and most cities had no police. No one picked up the garbage. People in cities often died from diseases.

During the 1800s, many Europeans moved into the cities. By 1850, which were the three largest cities in Europe?

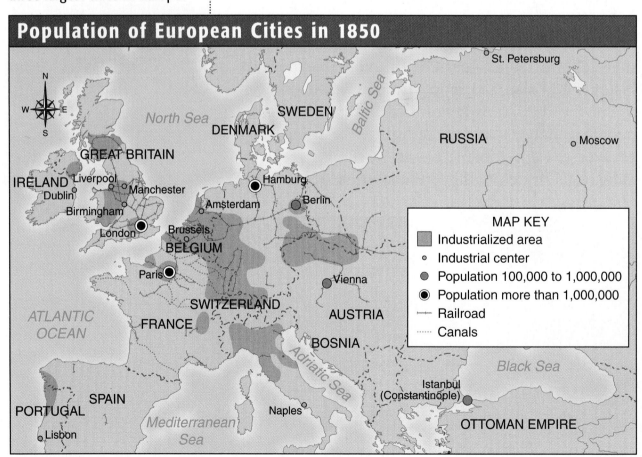

Population of European Cities in 1850

MAP KEY
- Industrialized area
- Industrial center
- Population 100,000 to 1,000,000
- Population more than 1,000,000
- Railroad
- Canals

Men, women, and children worked long hours processing coal.

By 1900, conditions had improved in most cities. City officials provided better housing. They passed laws to reduce the danger of fire. They provided safer drinking water. They put up street lights and hired police officers and garbage collectors.

Hard Work

In the early 19th century, working conditions in Great Britain were hard and dangerous. Factories were often dirty and unsafe. Many workers got hurt when working with machines. When a worker was hurt, factory owners usually did nothing to help the worker. There were no laws to protect workers.

Children often worked in dangerous factories.

Factory owners hired many children. Their small hands were perfect for certain kinds of work. In addition, owners could get them to work long hours for little pay. In 1835, half of the textile workers in England were under the age of 14. Many worked 12 to 15 hours a day.

Men, women, girls, and boys worked in coal mines. As in factories, the working hours were long, and the pay was low.

Mine owners didn't even allow the workers to take a lunch break. One young girl reported about a typical day at work.

Voices In History

"I go to [the mine] at five o'clock in the morning and come out at five in the evening. I get my breakfast . . . and milk. I take my [lunch] with me, a cake, and eat it as I go. I do not stop or rest at any time for [eating]. I get nothing else [to eat] until I get home."

One textile-mill owner, Robert Owen, tried to help workers. He paid his workers well. He did not hire any children under the age of 11. Owen built schools and new houses for his workers. He wanted to prove he could make money without being unkind to workers.

Working for Change

Soon others tried to help workers. Writers wrote stories telling about life in dirty industrial cities. Church leaders and others spoke out when they

These British workers are on strike.

learned what was happening. They fought to change working conditions. The British Parliament passed a series of laws. These laws reduced **child labor**. They protected women in the workplace. They limited the number of hours a worker could work.

Some workers formed **labor unions**. These groups fought for higher pay and better working conditions. Labor unions could go on **strike**, or refuse to work. They hoped this would force owners to meet their demands. By 1900, labor unions in Great Britain had two million members.

A German man named Karl Marx thought that as long as owners ran the mines and factories, nothing would get better. He called for a worker revolution. He urged workers to throw out the owners and take over the factories. They could then own and operate the factories themselves. Marx's ideas became known as **communism**.

Karl Marx

Lesson 2 Review

Choose words from the list that best complete the paragraphs. One word will not be used.

The inventions of the Industrial Revolution improved many people's __1__. During the 1800s, millions of people moved from the country to the city. This __2__ caused serious problems.

Cities grew rapidly. By 1900, life in cities had improved, but work in the factories, mills, and mines was dirty and often dangerous. It was particularly hard for children. New laws helped workers. Some workers joined __3__.

Karl Marx wanted workers to own the factories they worked in. His ideas became known as __4__.

Word List

urbanization
strike
labor unions
communism
standard of living

Chapter 26: Using What You've Learned

Summary

- The Industrial Revolution changed the way people worked. They used machines instead of tools. Two new sources of power were steam and oil.
- Inventions in the textile industry increased production. Inventions in transportation allowed people and goods to move from place to place more quickly.
- The Industrial Revolution caused a great population shift from the countryside to the city. The size and number of cities grew rapidly during the 19th century.
- Working conditions during the early 1800s were grim. A reform movement led to new laws to protect workers, especially women and children. Workers joined labor unions to help their cause.

Find Out More!

After reading Chapter 26, you're ready to go online. **Explore Zone**, **Quiz Time**, and **Amazing Facts** bring this chapter of world history alive.

Visit www.exploreSV.com and type in the chapter code **Ch26**.

Vocabulary

Number your paper from 1 to 5. Finish the sentences from Group A with words from Group B. Write the letter of the correct answer.

Group A

1. The _____ allowed a person to spin many threads at once.
2. The _____ changed water transportation.
3. The _____ sent messages over wires in just seconds.
4. The shift of people moving from the countryside to the cities is called _____.
5. When workers go on _____, they refuse to work.

Group B

a. steamboat
b. telegraph
c. strike
d. spinning jenny
e. urbanization

Comprehension

Number your paper from 1 to 5. Read each sentence below. Then write the name of the person who might have said each sentence. One name from the list will not be used.

1. "My steamboat sailed up the Hudson River."
2. "I invented the telephone in 1876."
3. "My electric light bulbs replaced oil lamps."
4. "I built new houses for my workers."
5. "Workers, take over the factories!"

Word List

Robert Owen
Karl Marx
Robert Fulton
Alexander Graham Bell
Thomas Edison
James Watt

Critical Thinking

Cause and Effect Number your paper from 1 to 5. Read the causes in the left column. Then choose the correct effect from the right column. Write the letter of the correct effect.

Cause	Effect
1. The cotton gin cleaned cotton quickly, so	**a.** factory owners hired many children.
2. The United States had thousands of miles of railroad track, so	**b.** cotton production increased.
3. The Industrial Revolution made it easier to produce food, so	**c.** the time and cost for moving goods and people decreased.
4. Many people moved to cities, so	**d.** some people had more time for leisure.
5. Children would work long hours for little pay, so	**e.** cities did not have enough housing or drinking water.

Writing

Imagine that you owned a factory during the Industrial Revolution. Write a paragraph describing how you might improve conditions for your workers.

Skill Builder: Reading a Double Line Graph

A **double line graph** compares facts by using two different lines. The graph below shows how many miles of railroad tracks were in Great Britain and the United States in the mid- to late 1800s. The blue line shows the length of railroad tracks in the United States. The red line shows the length of railroad tracks in Great Britain.

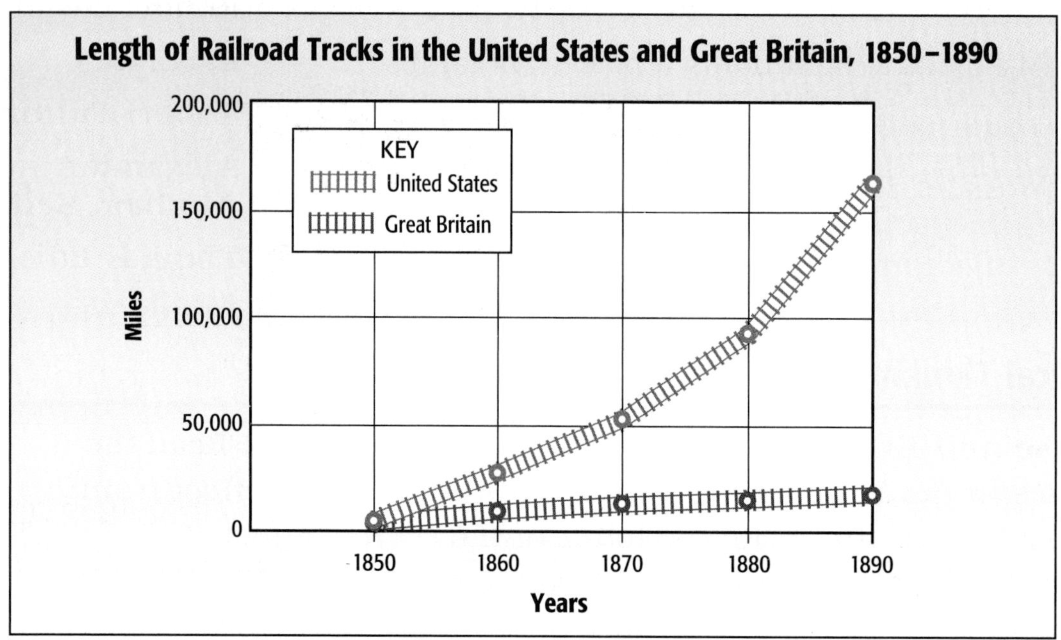

Number your paper from 1 to 4. Write the date or words that finish each sentence.

1. The length of railroad tracks in Great Britain and the United States were almost the same in ______.

   1850 1870 1890

2. The United States had about ______ miles of railroad tracks in 1870.

   10,000 50,000 100,000

3. From 1850 to 1890, the length of railroad tracks in Great Britain ______.

   decreased increased slightly increased greatly

4. The length of railroad tracks in the United States grew the most between ______.

   1860 and 1870 1870 and 1880 1880 and 1890

LESSON 1

Reform and Growth in Europe

Before You Read

- How might nationalism change the citizens of a country?
- Why might a nation want to give its colony more freedom?

After the Age of Napoleon, Europeans were tired of war. In 1814, a group of European leaders held a meeting called the **Congress of Vienna** in Austria. They created new states around France to separate it from its enemies. The Congress of Vienna brought peace to Europe.

Nationalism grew strong in Europe. In the early 1800s, there were many Italian-speaking states. There were also several German-speaking states. Many Italians wanted a united Italy, and many Germans wanted a united Germany.

The Congress of Vienna brought peace to Europe.

New Words

Congress of Vienna
unification
chancellor
kaiser
self-rule
Aborigines
Maori

People and Places

Vienna
Germany
Camillo di Cavour
Sardinia
Napoleon III
Giuseppe Garibaldi
Kingdom of the Two Sicilies
Venice
William I
Otto von Bismarck
Northwest Territories
British Columbia
James Cook
Victoria
New Zealand

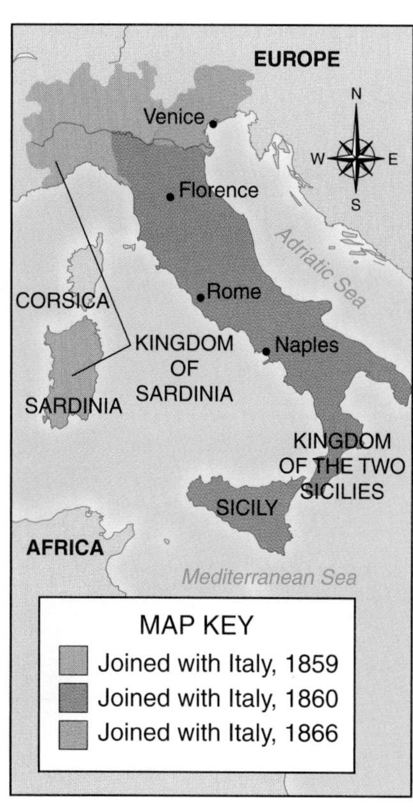

Unification of Italy

Italy United

The Kingdom of Austria ruled the many Italian-speaking states of the Italian Peninsula. Then in 1852, Camillo di Cavour became head of an Italian state called the Kingdom of Sardinia. His lands included the island of Sardinia and northwest Italy. In 1859, he fought Austria with support from Napoleon III of France. Austria was losing the war. Then Napoleon III made peace with Austria. The Italians were forced to continue fighting alone.

By 1860, Cavour had united several Italian states, but **unification** was not complete. The same year, Giuseppe Garibaldi and his army conquered the Kingdom of the Two Sicilies for Italy. Later, Italian states around the cities of Rome and Venice joined Italy as well. In 1870, all of Italy was united.

Germany United

Germany also had been a collection of many states. The strongest state was Prussia. In 1862, King William I of Prussia made Otto von Bismarck

Garibaldi's army became known as "Red Shirts."

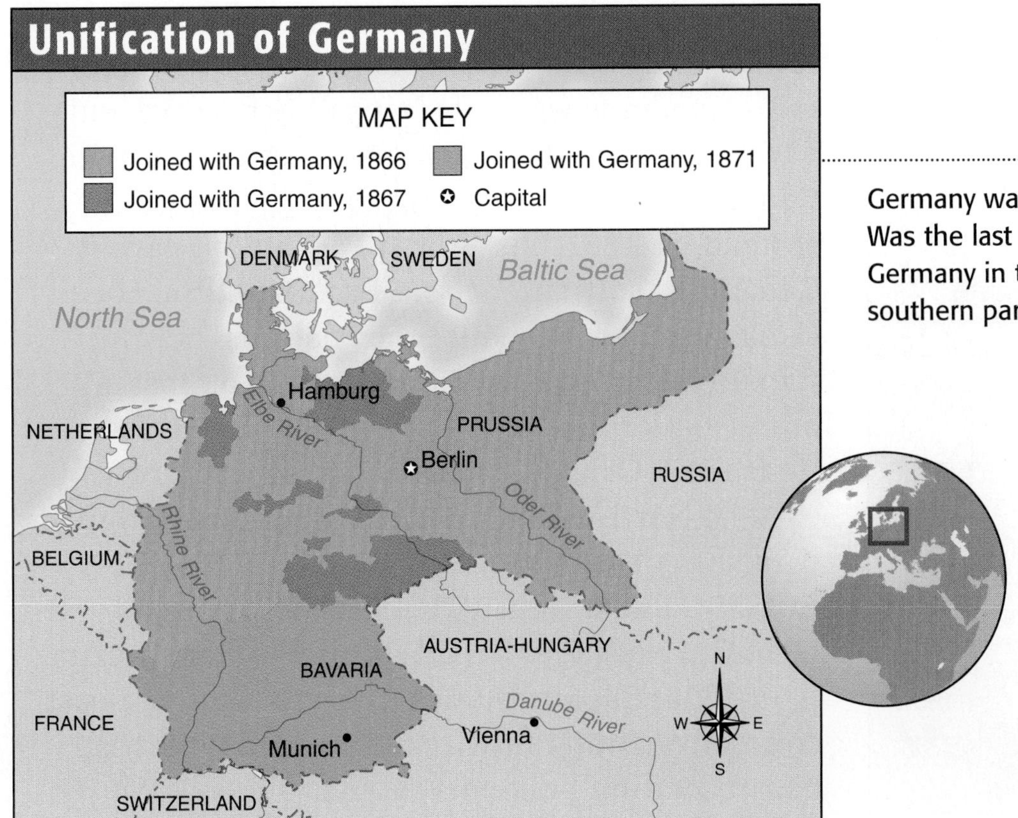

Germany was unified in 1871. Was the last section to join with Germany in the northern or southern part of the empire?

his **chancellor**. Bismarck said that the world was ruled "not by speeches and decisions" but by "iron and blood." He became known as the Iron Chancellor.

Bismarck defeated Austria and added several German states to Prussia. Then in 1870, Prussia defeated France. This brought even more lands to Prussia. In 1871, Prussia became the German Empire. Prussia united all the German states, except Austria, under the rule of the **kaiser**, or German head of government. The German Empire soon became one of the most powerful nations in Europe.

Otto von Bismarck

Growth of the British Empire

Great Britain's empire had grown so large that some people said, "The sun never sets on the British Empire." They meant that the sun was always shining some place in the world over land ruled by the British.

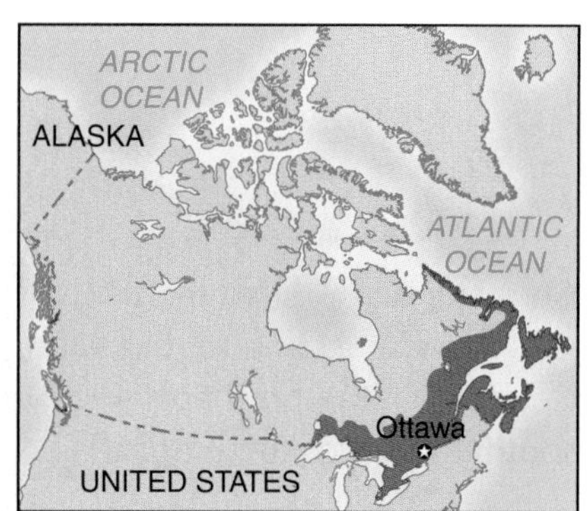

Canada in 1867

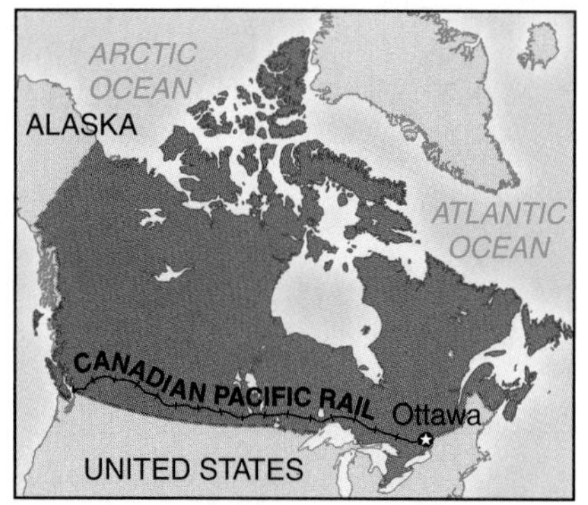

Canada in 1905

After the French and Indian War, Great Britain ruled Canada. But nationalism was growing there, too. Canadians were not happy with British rule.

Great Britain did not want to fight a war with Canada the way it did with the 13 colonies. Instead, in 1867, the British Parliament gave Canadians **self-rule**. Great Britain still managed Canada's relations with other nations, but the Canadians could rule themselves in almost all other matters.

In 1867, Canada consisted of four provinces in eastern North America. Then it began to grow. It gained the Northwest Territories in 1869 and British Columbia in 1871. In 1885, a railroad connected eastern Canada with western Canada.

In 1770, Captain James Cook claimed the east coast of Australia for Great Britain. The British began sending prisoners to Australia in 1788. Then in 1851, gold was found in Australia, and

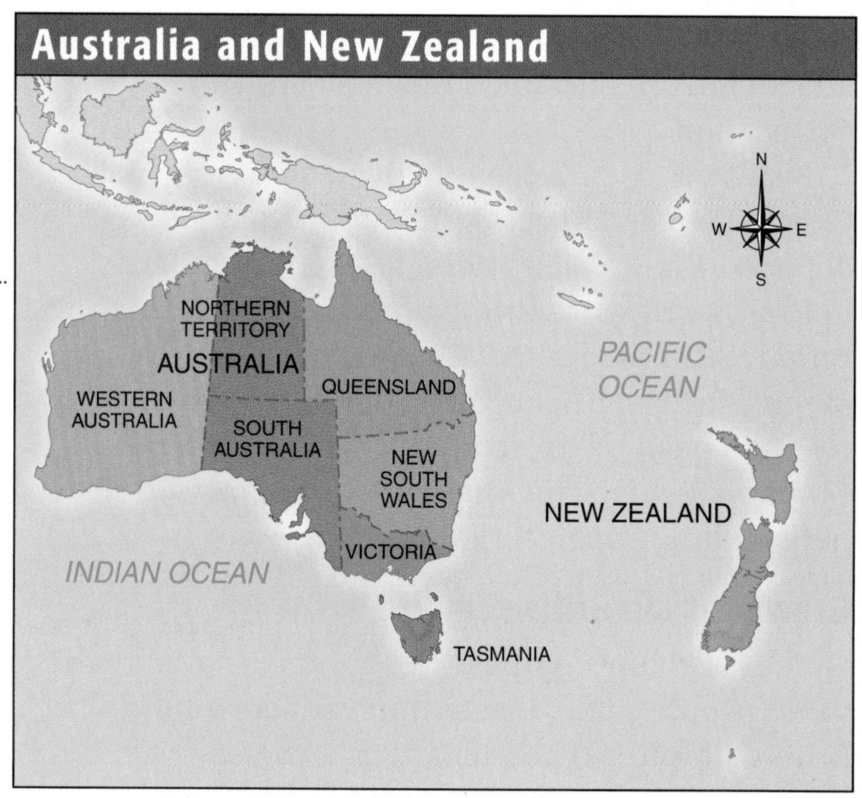

The British gained control of Australia and New Zealand in the 1800s. Including Tasmania, how many colonies did the British set up in Australia?

many British people rushed there. Like the Native Americans in the United States, the **Aborigines** were pushed farther and farther west. Many Aborigines also died from European diseases.

The British set up several colonies in Australia. One colony, Victoria, was formed in 1851. It was named after Queen Victoria of England. The Australian colonies were given self-rule in 1850 and were unified in 1901.

The **Maori**, who lived in New Zealand, signed a treaty with Great Britain in 1840. This gave the British control of New Zealand. British settlers soon began arriving on the islands of New Zealand. The British and the Maori often fought for land during the 1860s and 1870s.

In 1907, New Zealand joined the British Empire. Like Canada and Australia, it had self-rule, but was part of the Kingdom of Great Britain.

Maori chief

Lesson 1 Review

Choose words from the list that best complete the paragraphs. One word will not be used.

After the Age of Napoleon, European leaders met at the __1__. They brought peace to Europe. But nationalism was strong. Camillo di Cavour and Giuseppe Garibaldi won a struggle to unite Italy. Otto von Bismarck led the fight for the __2__ of German states.

In 1867, the British Parliament gave Canadians __3__. Canadians could rule themselves in almost all matters. The Australian colonies were unified in 1901. The __4__ people of New Zealand signed a treaty with the British. Canada, Australia, and New Zealand all had self-ruling governments under the Kingdom of Great Britain.

Word List

unification
self-rule
Aborigine
Maori
Congress of Vienna

LESSON 2

Reform and Growth in the United States

New Words

expansion
manifest destiny
immigrants
Trail of Tears
Missouri Compromise
abolitionists
Emancipation Proclamation

People and Places

Louisiana
Rocky Mountains
Cherokee
Maine
Missouri
Harriet Beecher Stowe
Harriet Tubman
Abraham Lincoln

Before You Read

- How does a nation gain more land?
- What people could not enjoy the ideas expressed in the Declaration of Independence?

The United States started as 13 states along the eastern coast of North America. It soon grew toward the west. In the 1783 treaty with Great Britain, the United States gained land from the Atlantic Ocean to the Mississippi River. Then during the 1800s, the country gained lands all the way to the Pacific Ocean.

This **expansion** created problems. Many Americans didn't want slavery to spread to the new lands. But many others did. The issue of the expansion of slavery lead to a civil war.

Many families traveled west during the 1800s.

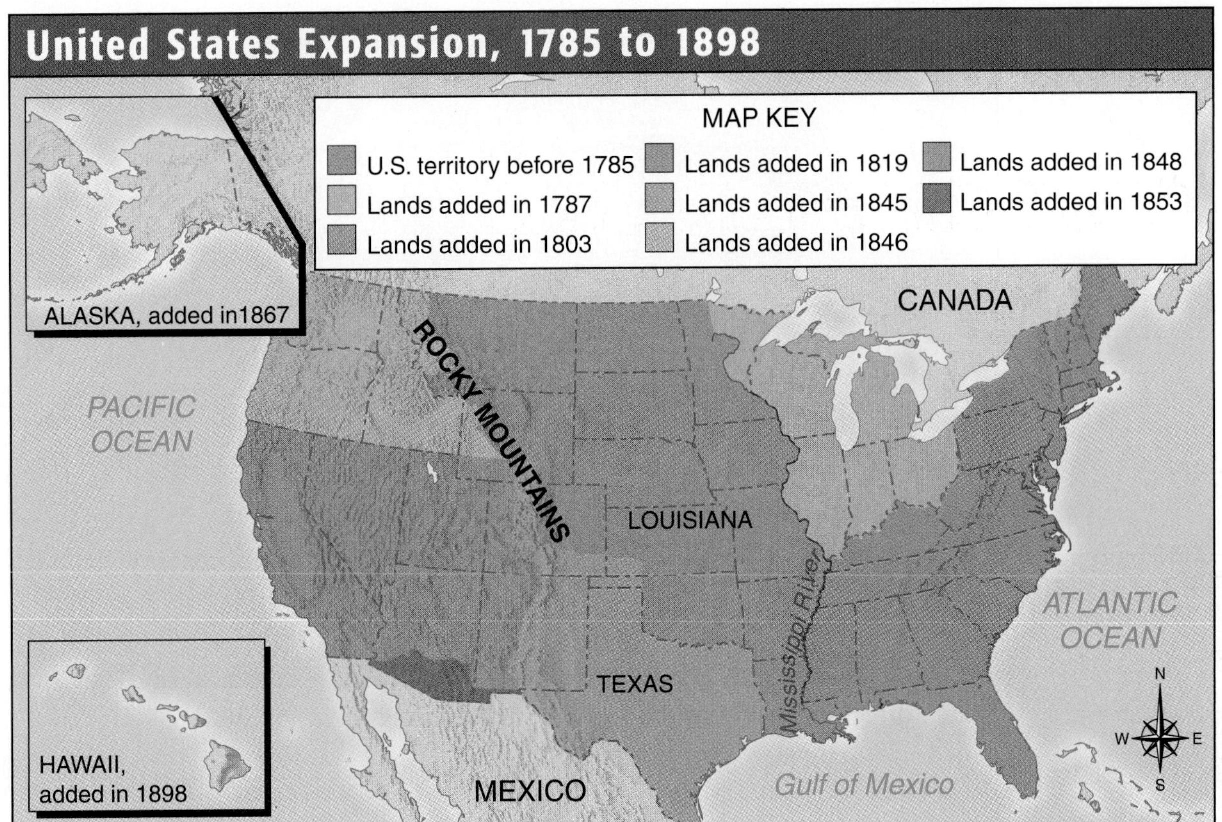

The United States began as 13 states along the Atlantic Ocean. What ocean had the United States reached by 1846?

Manifest Destiny

Most Americans believed in **manifest destiny**. They thought their clear goal was to move west. The United States began gaining land west of the Mississippi River.

First, the United States claimed land to the northwest in 1787. Then in 1803, President Thomas Jefferson bought a large area called Louisiana from France. This purchase doubled the size of the United States. Louisiana extended from the Mississippi River to the Rocky Mountains and from the Gulf of Mexico to Canada.

In 1836, Americans living in Texas broke away from Mexico. In 1845, Texas joined the United States, which led to war with Mexico. The United States won the war and gained even more land from Mexico. This land became part of the southwestern United States. Smaller pieces of land were also added to the United States between 1819 and 1898.

Many immigrants came to the United States during the mid-1800s.

All this land attracted more settlers. Chinese, German, and Irish **immigrants** came in large numbers during the 1840s and 1850s. Later in the 19th century, immigrants from southern and eastern Europe also came to the United States.

Native Americans were forced to move as Americans and immigrants settled. In 1838, the United States Army began to force about 17,000 Cherokee to leave their homes and move west. About 4,000 Cherokee died along the way. The Cherokee called the trip the **Trail of Tears**.

The Trail of Tears

The Road to War

In the early 1800s, many people began to question slavery. Most northern states had passed laws against slavery. In the South, people defended slavery. Still, no one wanted war. So the two sides worked out a series of agreements.

One of these agreements was the **Missouri Compromise** of 1820. It let Maine join the United States as a free state and Missouri join as a slave state. This kept a balance of free and slave states.

But the agreement did not last. Slave owners wanted the right to own slaves in any state, while **abolitionists** fought to put an end to slavery. In 1852, Harriet Beecher Stowe wrote *Uncle Tom's Cabin*. Her novel created great anger against slavery. People in the North began to learn how slavery broke up families. In 1858, one slave reported that she was separated from her parents and never saw them again.

Voices In History

> "My birthplace was in Chester, South Carolina. A very little of my life was spent there. I was raised in Alabama. When I was about four or five years old, I remember that I was loaded on a wagon with a lot more people . . . . Whatever [happened to] my mother and father I didn't know."

A group of abolitionists called the Underground Railroad helped slaves in the South escape to freedom in the North. From 1861 to 1865, the Underground Railroad helped around 1,000 slaves a year. One of its leaders, Harriet Tubman, was a former slave. She helped hundreds of slaves escape.

Harriet Tubman (far left) helped hundreds of slaves escape to freedom.

The Civil War

Abraham Lincoln

Abraham Lincoln was elected president in 1860. Lincoln was against the expansion of slavery to new lands. One by one, the southern states left the Union. In April 1861, the Civil War began.

The Civil War lasted four years, and more than 500,000 people died. The North got stronger. The South got weaker. In 1865, the South surrendered.

The Civil War ended slavery in the United States. President Lincoln had already taken the first step. In 1863, he issued the **Emancipation Proclamation**. It freed slaves living in the South.

After the war, Americans changed their Constitution. One change freed all slaves. The second change made African Americans full citizens. The third change gave African American men the right to vote. Still, it took many years for these changes to take effect.

Lesson 2 Review

Choose words from the list that best complete the paragraphs. One word will not be used.

Word List

Mexico
Trail of Tears
Emancipation Proclamation
Canada
manifest destiny

During the 1800s, the United States grew in size. Americans felt they had a __1__ to expand west. They gained a huge area of land called Louisiana. In a war with __2__, they won much of what is now the southwestern United States. Millions of Americans and immigrants moved into these lands. Native Americans were forced west. The Cherokee called the trip the __3__.

The Civil War began in 1861. The North won the war after four years. In 1863, President Lincoln issued the __4__. Changes to the Constitution ended slavery and gave African Americans more rights.

LESSON 3

Nationalism Comes to Aging Empires

Before You Read

- What might happen when an empire weakens?
- How might the growing German Empire have affected Austria?

In the late 19th century, there were three great empires in Eastern Europe and Southwest Asia. They were Austria-Hungary, the Ottoman Empire, and Russia. These empires covered a large amount of territory. But by the 1900s, they were losing strength. A few rulers made some reforms, but the aging empires began to fall in the early 20th century.

Eastern Europe and Southwest Asia, c. 1900

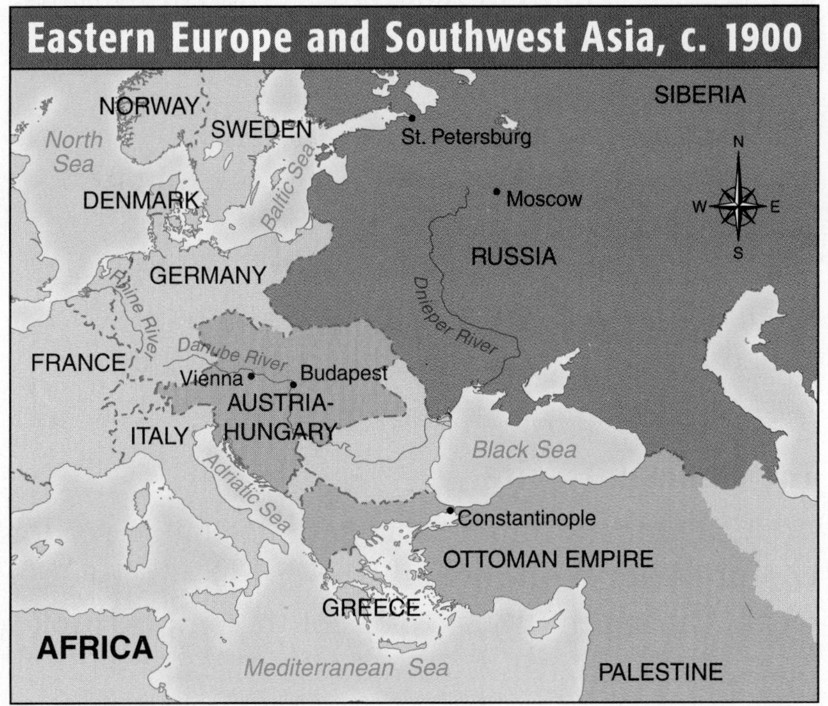

New Words

nationalities
economy
barren
czar
pogroms

People and Places

Austria-Hungary
Hungarians
Franz Josef
Serbs
Czechs
Mahmud II
Siberia
Alexander II
Crimea
Florence Nightingale

Austrian soldiers stopped a Hungarian revolution in 1848.

Austria-Hungary

The 19th century was an age of nationalism. People in Europe didn't want to be ruled by outsiders. In western Europe, this united people and created nations. It was a problem, however, for Austria. Austria was a German-speaking nation, but there were people from many **nationalities** within the empire. Each nationality felt the spirit of nationalism and tried to revolt against Austria.

Emperor Franz Josef

One large group in Austria was the Hungarians. Austria stopped a Hungarian revolution in 1848. To strengthen his empire, Emperor Franz Josef gave the Hungarians self-rule and made Hungary a partner with Austria. So in 1867, the empire became known as Austria-Hungary.

Other nationalities within Austria wanted independence. Groups such as the Serbs and the Czechs tried to gain independence, but they did not succeed.

The Ottoman Empire

The Ottoman Empire had been losing power for centuries. Its **economy** and government were weak. During the 1800s, parts of the empire broke away. Greece, for example, gained independence in 1829. Many people began to call the Ottoman Empire the "Sick Man of Europe."

Sultan Mahmud II

Sultan Mahmud II tried to reform the empire. He ruled from 1808 to 1839. Mahmud tried to restore a strong central government. He also introduced several other reforms. But he could not keep the empire together. Slowly, the Ottoman Empire lost lands to Austria, Russia, Great Britain, and France. Other groups broke away from the empire and became independent. By 1913, the Ottoman Empire controlled only a small fraction of the vast land it had ruled in thc 16th century.

Russia

Russia continued to expand during the 19th century. The Russians built a vast empire that stretched from Europe in the west to the Pacific Ocean in the east. Much of that land, called Siberia, was cold and **barren**. From 1891 to 1905, the Russians built a long railroad across Siberia. They hoped it would encourage settlement and development.

The Russians built a railroad across the cold lands of Siberia.

Czar Alexander II

Russia was slow, however, to accept industrial development. In 1861, **Czar** Alexander II tried to bring reform to Russia. He stopped the use of serfs and tried to create local governments. But Alexander II was assassinated in 1881, and Russia returned to many of its old ways.

Like most large empires, Russia had many nationalities within its borders. The Russians often used force to control them. **Pogroms**, or riots against Jews, became common. In 1881, more than 100 Jewish villages were destroyed. The Jewish people were killed or forced to leave.

The Crimean War

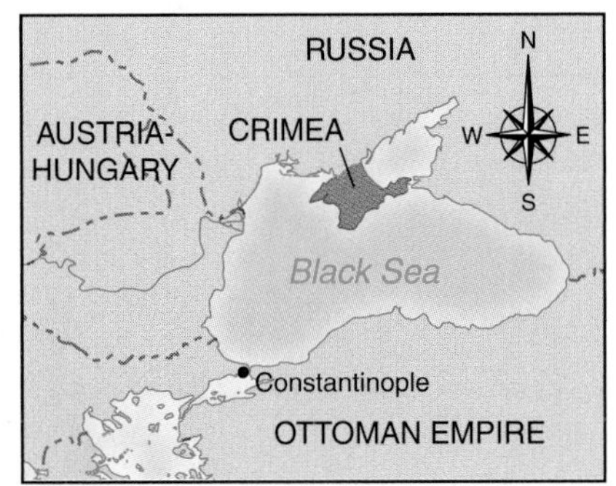

Crimea

The Russians, who supported the Orthodox Church, claimed control over certain holy sites in Palestine. But at the time, Palestine was controlled by the Ottoman Empire. The French, who supported the Catholic Church, did not want the Russians to control Palestine. So in 1854, France, Great Britain, and the Ottoman Empire went to war against Russia.

Most of the fighting took place on Crimea, a Russian peninsula in the Black Sea. Many thousands of soldiers from both sides were killed. Russia was defeated in 1856.

France, Great Britain, and the Ottoman Empire fought Russia in the Crimean War.

Florence Nightingale (1820–1910)

People In History

Florence Nightingale was a British nurse during the Crimean War. Sick and wounded soldiers called her "The Lady with the Lamp."

Nightingale shocked her wealthy parents when she told them she wanted to be a nurse. They didn't think it was a proper job for a well-educated woman. But Nightingale became a nurse anyway. In 1854, she went to a hospital in Crimea.

At first, even the doctors didn't want her, but she was determined to stay. She found soldiers dying from dirty conditions. Nightingale and 38 other nurses cleaned up the hospital. They gave the soldiers care. As a result, the death rate dropped sharply. Florence Nightingale's heroic deeds inspired thousands more women to become nurses.

Lesson 3 Review

Choose words from the list that best complete the paragraphs. One word will not be used.

Austria, a German-speaking nation, had many __1__ within its borders. The different groups began causing trouble for Austria. In 1867, one of these groups, the Hungarians, joined Austria to form an empire called Austria-Hungary.

The __2__ Empire had become weak. It had lost many of its lands. Russia expanded east across Asia but remained weak in many ways. Czar __3__ made some reforms, but he was assassinated. The Russians lost the __4__ War. Florence Nightingale saved the lives of many soldiers during that war.

Word List

Crimean
Alexander II
Ottoman
Mahmud II
nationalities

Chapter 27: Using What You've Learned

Summary

- The spread of nationalism continued in Europe. Italy united under Guiseppe Garibaldi. Germany united under Otto von Bismarck.
- Canada, Australia, and New Zealand gained self-rule, but remained part of the British Empire.
- The expansion of the United States during the 1800s and the issue of slavery were some causes of the Civil War. During the war, President Abraham Lincoln issued the Emancipation Proclamation.
- The struggles for independence fought by the different nationalities living in Austria-Hungary, the Ottoman Empire, and Russia weakened these three empires. Russia was defeated in the Crimean War in 1856.

Find Out More!

After reading Chapter 27, you're ready to go online. **Explore Zone**, **Quiz Time**, and **Amazing Facts** bring this chapter of world history alive.

Visit www.exploreSV.com and type in the chapter code **Ch27**.

Vocabulary

Number your paper from 1 to 5. Write the word or words from the list that best complete each sentence. One word will not be used.

1. In 1871, the German states were united under the rule of the _____.

2. Canadians were given _____ by the British Parliament.

3. The Cherokee were forced to move west in the trip called the _____.

4. The _____ fought to end slavery.

5. More than 100 Jewish villages in Russia were destroyed during the _____, or riots against the Jews.

Word List

self-rule
aborigines
pogroms
Trail of Tears
kaiser
abolitionists

Comprehension

Number your paper from 1 to 5. Write one or more sentences to answer each question below.

1. Why did people say, "The sun never sets on the British Empire"?
2. How did European settlers treat the Aborigines and the Maori?
3. What was the Missouri Compromise?
4. Who was Harriet Beecher Stowe?
5. What caused the Crimean War?

Critical Thinking

Categories Number your paper from 1 to 5. Read the words in each group below. Think about how they are alike. Write the best title for each group.

Manifest Destiny **Russia** **Abraham Lincoln** **Australia** **Congress of Vienna**

1. meeting of European leaders
   created new states around France
   brought peace to Europe
2. James Cook
   Aborigines
   Victoria colony
3. Northwest Territory
   Louisiana Purchase
   Texas
4. elected president in 1860
   against expansion of slavery
   Emancipation Proclamation
5. Siberia
   pogroms
   Alexander II

Writing

Write a short newspaper article about how the United States changed its Constitution after the Civil War. Give your article a title.

LESSON 1

Imperialism in Africa

New Words

imperialism
colonize
political
protectorate

People and Places

Suez Canal
Libya
Somalia
Liberia
Zulu
Boers
Shaka Zulu

Before You Read

- Why might Europeans want to rule Africa?
- How might European rule have affected native people in African colonies?

Western European nations continued adding colonies to their empires. Such empire building and control of foreign lands is called **imperialism**. In the late 19th century, Europeans saw an opportunity to **colonize** the entire continent of Africa.

Business leaders wanted to be able to use the many raw materials in Africa. Missionaries wanted to spread Christianity. **Political** leaders

This settlement in West Africa is divided among European powers.

In 1869, the Suez Canal was completed.

believed owning African colonies would add power and glory to their nations. France, Italy, Great Britain, Germany, Portugal, Belgium, and Spain all took control of parts of Africa.

North Africa

The Ottoman Empire had ruled North Africa since the 1400s. By the 1800s, the empire had grown weak. The French and then the British moved into North Africa. The French took over land along the Mediterranean coast. Later, they controlled much of central and western Africa. The French held the largest European empire in Africa. In 1869, the French finished building the Suez Canal in Egypt. It linked the Mediterranean Sea to the Red Sea.

In 1875, the British bought the canal. The canal made sailing from Europe to India much faster than before. Great Britian held much control over Egypt. Later, in 1914, Great Britian declared that Egypt was a **protectorate**. Egypt was under Great Britian's control and protection. In the south, the British took over an area called Sudan. They also established a protectorate over Zanzibar in 1890. This island off the coast of eastern Africa was a key trading post.

Zanzibar sultans with a British official

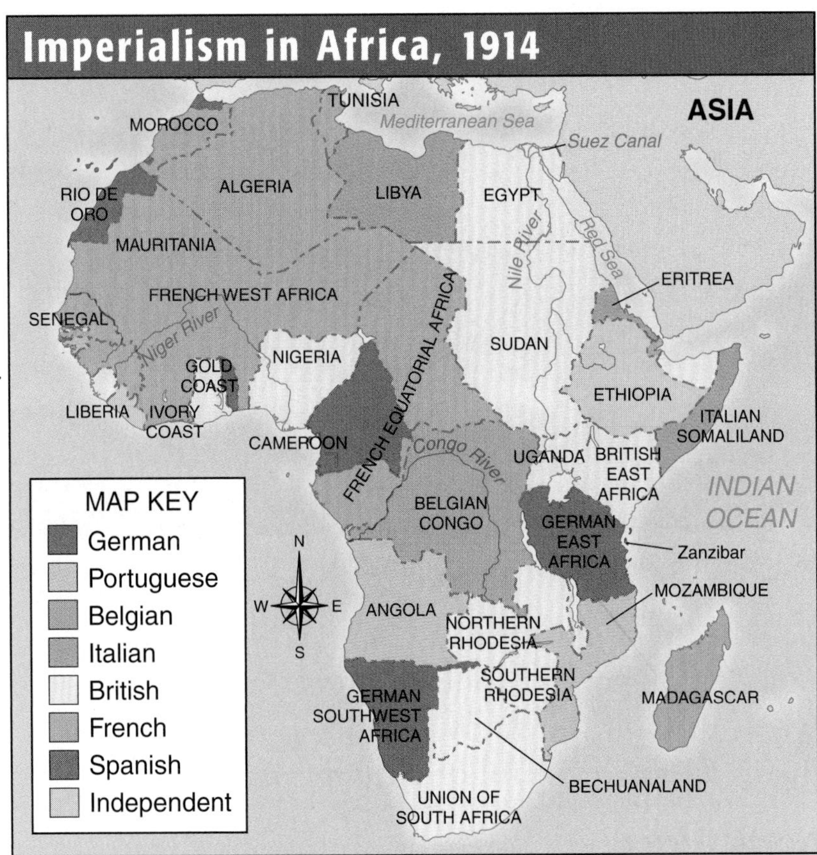

By 1914, European powers controlled almost all of Africa. Which European power controlled Egypt?

The Scramble for Africa

In the 1870s, a race for the rest of Africa began. Europeans divided the continent into several colonies. Italy took over Libya and part of Somalia. Germany gained territory in central, southern, and eastern Africa. Spain gained lands in the northwest. Belgium established a large colony in the Congo River region. Only two nations stayed independent—Liberia and Ethiopia.

The land was divided without thinking about existing borders between different African ethnic groups. Groups with different languages and customs were often placed into one colony. Often, imperialist rulers were cruel to Africans.

Some Africans, such as the Zulu, fought against European imperialism. The Zulu had built a strong empire in southern Africa. They fought early Dutch settlers called the Boers. Led by Shaka Zulu, the Zulu kept the Dutch from settling.

Shaka Zulu

But the Zulu were unable to defeat the British. In 1910, the British united the Boer colonies in South Africa and gained control of the region's rich natural resources, such as gold and silver.

Gold mine in South Africa in late 1800s

Effects of Imperialism

Europeans felt that imperialism was good for Africa. Europeans ended the slave trade in some areas. They built cities, roads, and railroads. They also brought new medicines and opened schools.

But many native Africans felt imperialism was bad for Africa. Europeans often mistreated Africans. Villages and families were broken apart. Europeans stole lands and natural resources.

The Europeans wanted Africans to change their way of life and become more European. But most Africans did not accept European ways. In time, feelings of nationalism began to grow within the African colonies.

Lesson 1 Review

Choose words from the list that best complete the paragraphs. One word will not be used.

The act of building an empire in foreign lands is called __1__. Europeans colonized Africa during the 1800s. The French built the __2__ Canal in Egypt. It connected the Mediterranean Sea to the Red Sea. Great Britain later took over the canal and turned Egypt into a __3__.

The __4__ fought the Boers and the British in South Africa. In the end, the British won control of the lands. Europeans built roads and schools, but they treated Africans poorly.

Word List

protectorate
colonize
Suez
Zulu
imperialism

LESSON 2

Imperialism in Asia

New Words

poverty
opium
addictive
sphere of influence
sphere
Taiping Rebellion
Meiji Restoration

People and Places

Nanking
Hong Kong
Hong Xi Uquan
Laos
Cambodia
French Indochina
Burma
William McKinley
Hawaiian Islands
Guam
Matthew Perry

Before You Read

- Why might countries fight about trade in a region?
- Why might imperialism lead to a spirit of nationalism in a region?

The European race for colonies was not limited to Africa. Europeans wanted colonies in Asia, too. Europeans needed more natural resources for their growing industries. They wanted more trade with Asia. They also thought having colonies in Asia would bring glory to their nations.

Imperialism in India

The British East India Company began in the 17th century. It gained control over much of India. Then in 1858, the British government turned India into a colony.

The British unified India. They made English the official language because Indians spoke many

These European soldiers are guarding a Chinese city.

different languages. English gave educated Indians a common language. The British also built many dams, roads, and hospitals.

On the other hand, improvements such as hospitals led to a rapid growth in population. Often there was not enough food. There was massive **poverty**. The British also hurt the Indian cloth industry. Indians had made cloth by hand. Mills in England made cloth by machine, so they could sell their cloth at cheaper prices. Most people bought the cheaper English cloth. Also, as in Africa, the imperial leaders were often cruel.

British prince visiting India

In 1857, Indians led a revolt against British rule. The fighting did not spread throughout the subcontinent, but it was costly to both sides. Many British and Indians died. The British ended the revolt but began giving Indian officials more power. Still, Indians wanted self-rule like Canada and Australia. In 1885, Hindu leaders formed the Indian National Congress. In 1906, Muslim leaders formed the Muslim League. These groups began to work for Indian independence.

Imperialism in China

During the 1700s, the British bought huge amounts of tea from China, but the Chinese didn't want to buy British goods. They had little need for foreign goods. So the British began selling **opium** to the Chinese. Opium is an **addictive** drug. Once a person starts using it, it is difficult to stop. The British sold more and more opium to the Chinese.

Opium is made from poppies.

The Qing leaders tried to stop the opium trade. One Chinese official asked Queen Victoria of Great Britain to stop the opium trade.

"Let us suppose that foreigners came from another country, and brought opium into England, and [encouraged] the people of your country to smoke it. Would not you . . . look upon such [a process] with anger?"

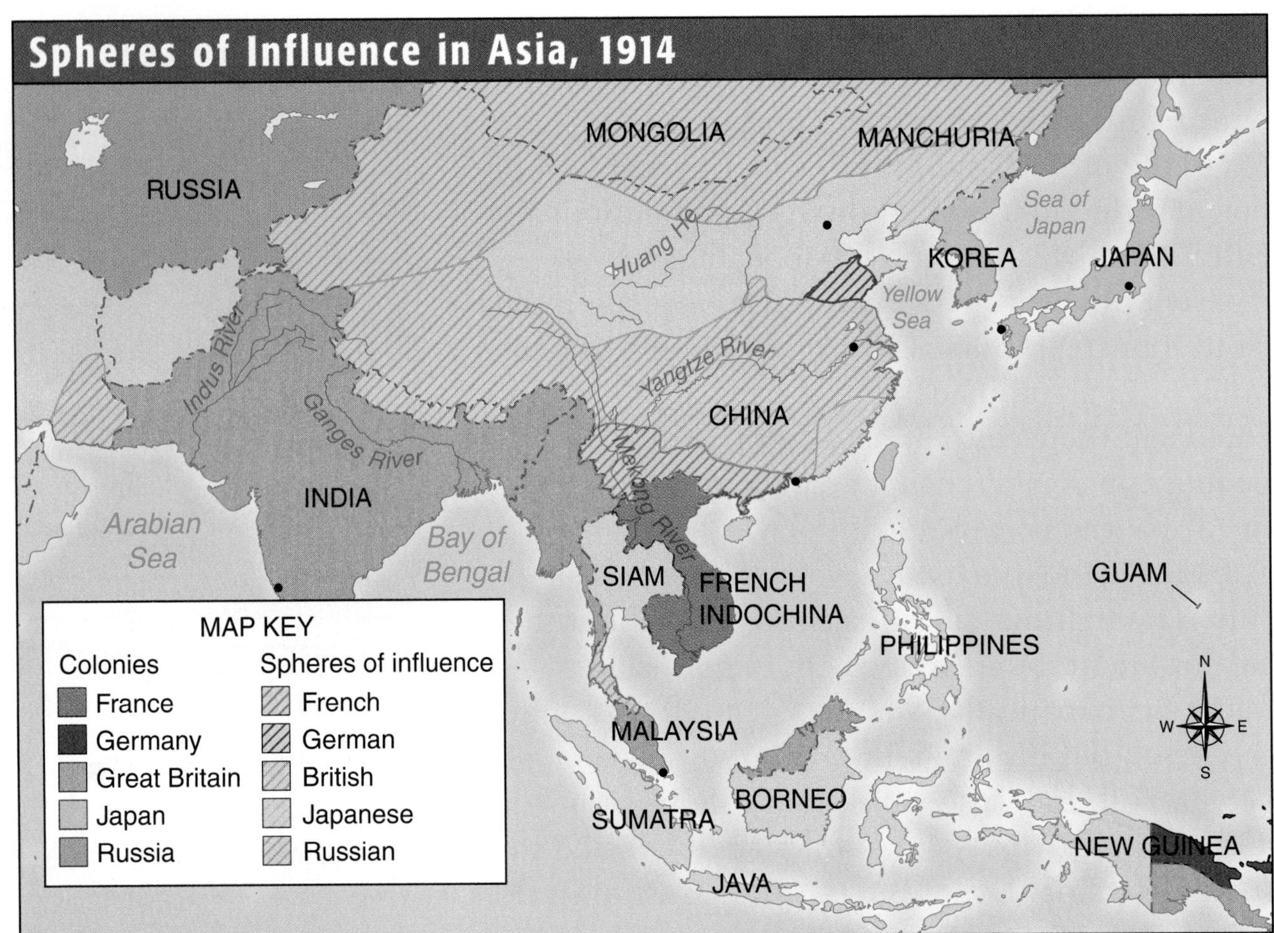

Many European nations had colonies in Asia and spheres of influence in China. Which nation's sphere of influence included the city of Nanking?

Great Britain continued to sell opium to China. In 1839, war broke out between the two countries. Using better weapons, the British defeated the Chinese. The Opium War ended with the Treaty of Nanking in 1842. The British forced China to open up more port cities. The Chinese gave Great Britain control of the port city of Hong Kong.

European nations and Japan moved into China. They did not set up colonies or protectorates. But each nation set up its own **sphere of influence**. Within its own **sphere**, the foreign nation had special trading rights.

Many foreign powers controlled the Chinese economy. The Qing Dynasty had grown weak. Hong Xi Uquan began calling for reform. He and his followers led the **Taiping Rebellion** against the Qing Dynasty.

The Qing fought back. The Taiping Rebellion was the deadliest war of the 19th century. Millions of people were killed. Foreign powers helped end the rebellion in 1864. The fighting greatly weakened the Qing Dynasty.

Imperialism in Southeast Asia and the Pacific

In Southeast Asia, the French took over Vietnam, Laos, and Cambodia and called the region French Indochina. The British took over Burma.

The United States was not a big colonial power. Many Americans remembered they had once been a colony. Still, in 1898, they defeated the Spanish in the Spanish-American War. As a result, they freed the Philippines from Spanish rule.

President William McKinley then decided to take over the Philippines. This made the United States a colonial power. Also in 1898, the United States took control of the Hawaiian Islands and Guam.

The New Japan

In the early 1800s, the Japanese were unhappy with the weak Tokugawa Shogunate. Many Japanese people wanted change. They began to encourage nationalism.

The Philippine army fought against United States control.

Did You Know?

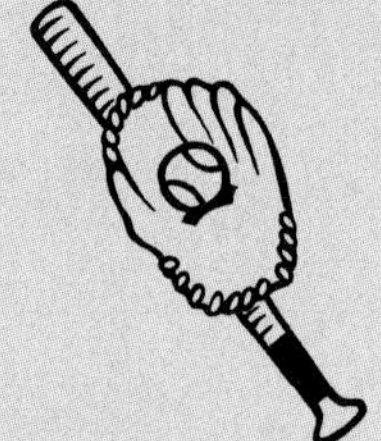

Play Ball

During the Meiji Restoration, Japan was open to new ideas, such as baseball. Horace Wilson brought the sport to the Japanese in the 1870s. He was an American teacher in Tokyo. Soon, the Japanese had teams and leagues. American teams came to play Japanese teams. Baseball became the most popular team sport in Japan. It still is today.

In 1853, the United States sent military officer Matthew Perry to Japan. He asked the Japanese to trade with the United States. Some Japanese wanted to keep their policy of isolationism. Others wanted to open the country up to contact with western nations. The next year, Perry returned, bringing guns, clocks, and even a train engine as gifts. The Japanese agreed to trade with the Americans.

In 1868, the Japanese ended the rule of shoguns. They put an emperor back on the throne. This was called the **Meiji Restoration**. The Japanese then adopted many western European customs. They built a modern army and navy. They became a strong industrial power.

Matthew Perry arrived in Japan in 1853.

Lesson 2 Review

Choose words from the list that best complete the paragraphs. One word will not be used.

Word List

Meiji Restoration
opium
Queen Victoria
Matthew Perry
sphere of influence

Europeans began seeking colonies in Asia. The British unified India and made English a common language. Their policies also led to hunger and poverty. In China, the British sold __1__. This led to war between Great Britain and China. European nations and Japan each established their own __2__ in China.

In 1863, the United States sent __3__ to Japan to open trade. The Japanese began trading with western countries. The __4__ changed Japan's government and helped make Japan a strong power.

Chapter 28: Using What You've Learned

Summary

- Britain and France continued to practice imperialism in Africa and Asia. The Zulu in South Africa and people in India fought against imperialism, but failed. Indian groups continued to fight for independence.
- The Taiping Rebellion in China was the deadliest war of the 19th century.
- The United States became a colonial power when it took over lands in the Pacific Ocean.
- Japan adopted many western ways and became a world power.

Find Out More!

After reading Chapter 28, you're ready to go online. **Explore Zone**, **Quiz Time**, and **Amazing Facts** bring this chapter of world history alive.

Visit www.exploreSV.com and type in the chapter code **Ch28**.

Vocabulary

Number your paper from 1 to 4. Write the letter of the correct answer.

1. **Imperialism** is control of ____.

   a. drinking water **c.** powerful weapons
   b. foreign lands **d.** religious beliefs

2. A **sphere of influence** was an area of a country in which a foreign nation had ____.

   a. class systems **c.** special trading rights
   b. total control **d.** codes of law

3. The **Taiping Rebellion** was a fight for reform in ____.

   a. India **c.** Cambodia
   b. Burma **d.** China

4. The **Meiji Restoration** ended the rule of ____ in Japan.

   a. shoguns **c.** emperors
   b. presidents **d.** queens

Comprehension

Number your paper from 1 to 6. Write **True** for each sentence that is true. Write **False** for each sentence that is false.

1. Egypt was a protectorate, which meant that the British had no control over the Egyptian government.
2. The British East India Company gained much control over India.
3. The Opium War forced the Chinese to open more of its port cities to Great Britain.
4. The French did not set up any colonies in Southeast Asia.
5. The United States was a colonial power in the Philippines.
6. Matthew Perry asked Japan to not trade with the United States.

Critical Thinking

Points of View Number your paper from 1 to 5. Read each sentence below. Write **European** if the point of view is from someone European. If the point of view is from someone African, write **African**.

1. Africa should be colonized because we need its raw materials for our businesses.
2. African colonies would add power and glory to our nation.
3. We must protect our land from the Boers.
4. African nations should be independent.
5. Many African ethnic groups can be placed into one colony.

Writing

Imperialism caused some good effects and some bad effects in Africa and Asia. Write a paragraph about either Africa or Asia explaining two good effects and two bad effects of imperialism in this region.

Skill Builder: Reading a Political Map

A **political map** shows how areas of land are divided. Some political maps show how land is divided into nations. Lines are used to show the borders between nations. Different colors are used to show different nations. This map shows what nations controlled parts of Asia and Australia in 1914.

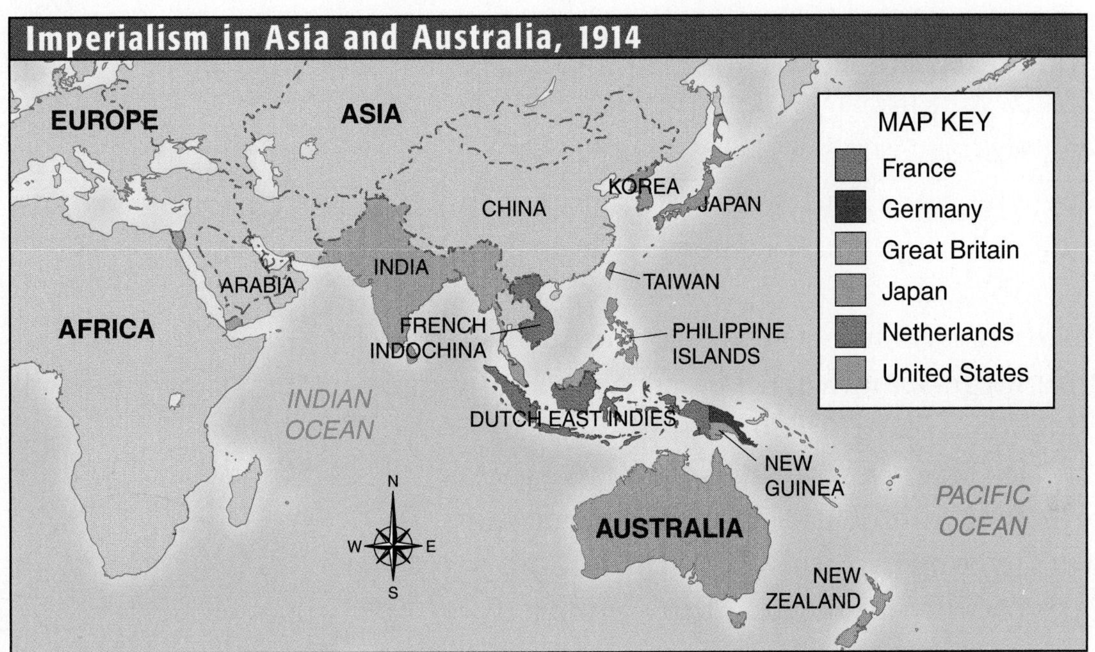

Number your paper from 1 to 5. Answer each question with a complete sentence.

1. What color shows the parts of Asia controlled by France?
2. Which European nation controlled India and Australia?
3. Which European nations controlled land in New Guinea?
4. What country was controlled by Japan?
5. Which nation controlled the Philippine Islands?

UNIT 7

Years of World Wars

1900–1945

You have already read about many wars. But the years between 1900 and 1945 brought the worst wars people had ever seen. World War I and World War II caused more death and damage than all the other wars combined.

This unit tells how the world found itself in these large-scale wars. It also shows how the Industrial Revolution changed the methods of war. New, more deadly weapons brought fear and destruction. Still, between the wars, people around the world had a new appreciation for life. Many people experienced cars, radio, and movies for the first time.

A.D. 1900 1910 1920

1905
Russian workers are killed as they march in St. Petersburg.

1914
World War I begins.

1917
The United States enters World War I.

1918
World War I ends.

1930 | 1940 | 1950 | A.D.

1927
The first talking film, *The Jazz Singer*, is shown.

1935
Led by Mohandas Gandhi, the people of India gain the right to elect their own representatives.

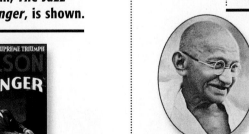

1939
World War II begins.

1945
World War II ends. The United Nations is created to keep peace in the world.

LESSON 1

Causes of World War I

New Words

competition
arms race
alliances
Triple Alliance
Triple Entente
archduke

People and Places

Balkans
Serbia
Franz Ferdinand
Sarajevo

Before You Read

- Why would nationalism make war more likely?
- Why might nations join with other nations?

There was no single cause for the Great War, as World War I was first called. During the early months of 1914, few people thought about war. Europeans were enjoying peaceful times.

Growing Troubles

Imperialism in European nations continued to be strong. Each country was in a **competition** to control more foreign colonies than the others.

Just months before World War I, Europeans enjoyed peaceful times.

The competition led to an **arms race**. When Germany built a strong navy, Great Britain built a stronger navy. Several countries began competing for the strongest military forces.

Nationalism was also strong in Europe. Germany and Italy were unified, powerful nations. They wanted to show their strength. At the same time, other nations tried to stop nationalism within their borders.

Nationalism caused trouble in a region called the Balkans. Austria-Hungary ruled some people in the Balkans, but other groups were free and independent. Serbia became a free country in the Balkans, but the Serbs wanted more land. They wanted to unite all the people of their nationality. Some nations supported the Serbs while others did not.

Serbian soldiers

The Alliance System

Having allies was a sign of strength, so European countries formed **alliances**. Members of an alliance agreed to help one another in times of trouble. The alliances allowed nations to take more risks because they knew they had support.

The Triple Alliance and the Triple Entente were the two major alliances in 1914. Which three countries made up the Triple Alliance?

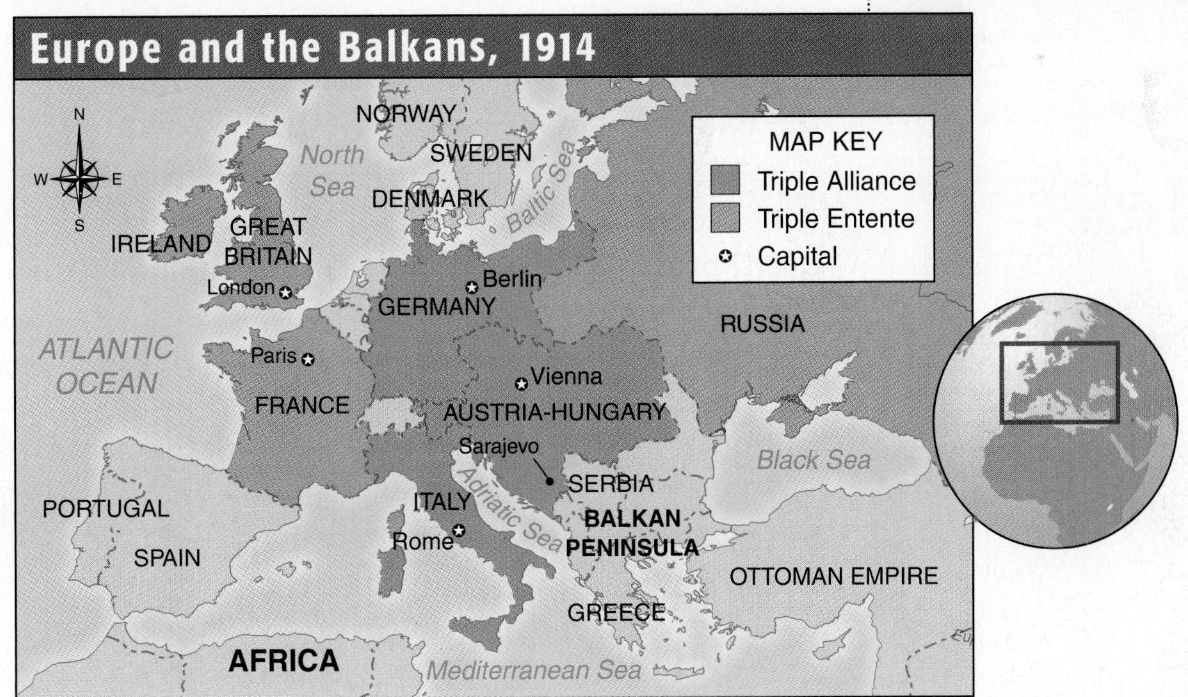

Assassination of Archduke Franz Ferdinand and his wife

By 1914, there were two major alliances. One was the **Triple Alliance**. Its members were Germany, Austria-Hungary, and Italy. The other major alliance was the **Triple Entente**. *Entente* is a French word meaning "understanding." The members of the Triple Entente were France, Great Britain, and Russia.

The Spark that Led to War

On June 14, 1914, Austro-Hungarian **Archduke** Franz Ferdinand and his wife were killed in the Balkans. A Serb man shot them as they drove through the city of Sarajevo. Austria-Hungary demanded justice. It declared war on Serbia on July 28. Germany promised to support Austria-Hungary against Serbia.

At first, no one thought the war would be very big or last very long. But the system of alliances made it a big war. Russia supported the Serbs and got its army ready for war. Germany then got its army ready. On August 1, Germany declared war on Russia. The Great War had begun.

Lesson 1 Review

Choose words from the list that best complete the paragraph. One word will not be used.

Word List

Serbia
Franz Ferdinand
Balkans
arms race
alliances

Few people expected World War I. An __1__ led to stronger militaries across Europe. Nationalism also became a problem. People in the __2__ wanted to be free and to expand their lands. Some nations of Europe joined __3__. Countries became willing to take greater risks. The spark for World War I occurred when Archduke __4__ and his wife were shot and killed in Sarajevo by a Serb man. After that, countries began taking sides, and World War I began.

LESSON 2

Four Years of War

Before You Read

- What would make a war a "world war"?
- Why would it be hard for one country to fight a war in two places?

New Words

neutral
two-front war
trenches
trench warfare
Central Powers
Allies
stalemate
shells
submarine
armistice

People and Places

Marne River
Bulgaria
Gallipoli

Germany did not want France to help Russia, so German troops marched toward France. But the small country of Belgium was between Germany and France. Belgium was a **neutral** country. It did not take sides. On August 4, 1914, the German troops invaded Belgium anyway. For this, Great Britain declared war on Germany. Belgium then joined the fight against Germany.

No Quick Victory

Germany faced enemies on two sides with Russia in the east and France, Belgium, and Great Britian in the west. Germany didn't want to fight a **two-front war**. It hoped to defeat France quickly.

On its way to France, Germany invaded Belgium.

The plan might have worked for Germany. But the Russians moved quickly. The Germans had to move many soldiers to the Eastern Front. That left them too weak to win against France on the Western Front. The French stopped the Germans at the Marne River. The Germans knew then that there would be no quick victory.

Trench warfare in World War I

On the Western Front, both sides built a series of **trenches**. Neither side could move very far. This **trench warfare** continued throughout the war. Fighting in the trenches was difficult. Tens of thousands of soldiers died. For many soldiers, the war made little sense. One soldier wrote about his experience.

Voices In History

"The dead lying on the fields seem to ask, 'Why has this been done to us? Why have you done it, brothers? What purpose has it served?'"

The War Spreads

In the beginning, there were only a few countries at war. Germany and Austria-Hungary were called the **Central Powers** because of their location in central Europe. Great Britain, Russia, France, and Serbia became known as the **Allies**.

British war poster showing Europeans asking for help

Soon other nations joined the war. The Ottoman Empire joined the Central Powers. So did Bulgaria. Italy had been part of the Triple Alliance. But the Italians didn't like the Austro-Hungarians. So in 1915, Italy joined the Allies. Countries as far away as Japan declared war on Germany. Japan wanted to gain German lands in China and the Pacific Ocean. In all, 31 nations took part in World War I.

On the Battlefield

There was a **stalemate** on the Western Front. Neither side could win a clear battle. But there was plenty of movement on the Eastern Front.

World War I was fought between the Central Powers and the Allies. For which side did the Ottoman Empire fight?

The Russians had some early victories. However, the Germans and the Austro-Hungarians soon began to win more battles.

In 1915, the British landed at Gallipoli. They wanted to defeat the Ottomans and take control of the Black Sea. Then they could help the Russians. But the Ottomans defeated the British and forced them to turn back. Gallipoli was one of the worst defeats in British history.

In Southwest Asia, British and Arab forces joined together to defeat the Ottomans. In 1917, the British took control of Jerusalem. There was also fighting in Africa. People living in the colonies fought for the empire that controlled their part of Africa. The Japanese fought the Germans in several battles on islands in the Pacific Ocean. The Japanese easily defeated the Germans.

Women making weapon shells during World War I

Wartime Industry

The Industrial Revolution made new weapons possible. World War I introduced the tank and the machine gun. Both sides used airplanes for the first time. The Germans used a powerful gun called Big Bertha. This cannon fired **shells** many miles away. The new weapons were a big reason that much of World War I was fought in trenches. The soldiers hid in the trenches to protect themselves.

Throughout Europe, factories built the guns and parts necessary to continue the war. Women often took jobs in factories making weapons and shells. Many women also ran farms or took office jobs. Others became nurses in the Western and Eastern Fronts.

The United States Enters the War

One of the new weapons developed during World War I was the **submarine**. The Germans used it to sink ships sailing toward Great Britain. The United States often sent supplies on ships to Great Britain. In early 1917, German submarines began attacking American supply ships and passenger ships. On April 6, 1917, the United States declared war on Germany.

The Russians soon grew tired of war. They began talks for peace with Germany. By the end of 1917, Russia was out of the war. Germany then had a war on only one front. But it was too late.

The submarine was a new and powerful weapon that was developed during World War I.

When the Americans entered the war, the Allies gained a large, fresh group of soldiers.

In the spring of 1918, the Germans launched a massive attack against the Allies. But the Allies were not defeated. By fall, the German military was weak. Germany agreed to an **armistice** on November 11, 1918. The war was over.

World War I lasted from 1914 to 1918. The number of dead from four years of war shocked the world. The Germans and the Russians lost nearly 2 million soldiers each. About 1.4 million French died. The British lost almost 1 million. The Americans lost 115,000 soldiers. Many people who were not in the military also died. Nations around the world suffered losses in the Great War.

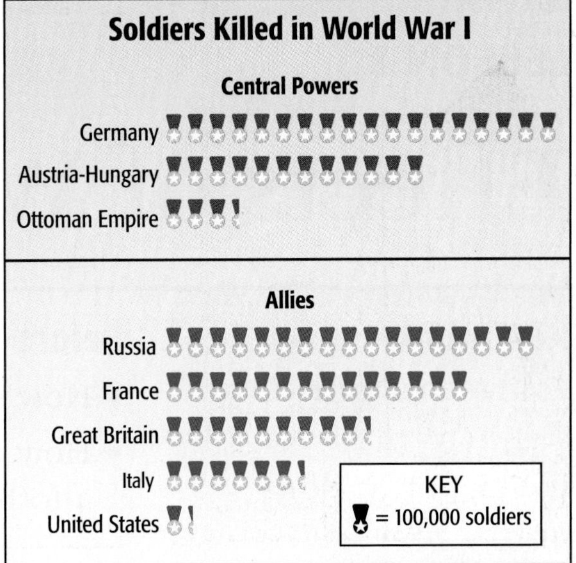

Lesson 2 Review

Choose words from the list that best complete the paragraphs. One word will not be used.

At the start of World War I, Belgium was a __1__ country. The German attack on Belgium brought Great Britain into the war. The Ottoman Empire and Bulgaria joined the __2__ Powers. Italy joined the Allies. The trench warfare on the Western Front turned into a __3__.

World War I introduced many new weapons. Women worked in factories to help produce these new weapons. The German use of the __4__ brought Americans into the war. The Great War ended when Germany agreed to an armistice. By then, millions had died on both sides.

Word List

submarine
neutral
Central
Allies
stalemate

LESSON 3

Effects of World War I

New Words

Fourteen Points
self-determination
League of Nations
buffer zone
reparations
mandates

People and Places

Woodrow Wilson
Rhineland
Finland
Latvia
Lithuania
Estonia
Yugoslavia
Czechoslovakia
Romania

Before You Read

- How did World War I change Europe?
- How might the nations of the world prevent another world war?

The armistice ended World War I. The Allies then had two big questions to answer. How would they prevent future world wars? Who should take responsibility for causing World War I?

The Allies held peace talks at Versailles, France, in 1919. The leaders of Italy, France, and Great Britain, along with President Woodrow Wilson of the United States, led the talks. These leaders were known as the Big Four.

The Big Four met for peace talks in Versailles, France.

This building in France was destroyed during the war.

Wilson's Plan

President Wilson wanted "peace without victory." He presented a gentle peace plan called the **Fourteen Points**. Wilson wanted to end secret deals made between nations. He also wanted neutral ships to be safe at sea even in times of war.

Wilson also addressed nationalism. He wanted all European nationalities treated fairly. Wilson felt that different nationalities should have the right to form their own nations. That right was called **self-determination**.

Woodrow Wilson

The League of Nations

Wilson's 14th point called for the formation of the **League of Nations**. He thought this organization of nations could stop wars before they started. It would keep peace throughout the world.

Most Allied leaders liked the Fourteen Points. The French, however, wanted a more harsh agreement. They wanted to punish Germany. They wanted to make Germany as weak as possible so it would not start another war.

Did You Know?

Worthless Money

In 1918, Germans could pay just over half a mark for a loaf of bread. Within a few years, prices in Germany began to rise. In 1922, the cost of bread jumped to 163 marks. By the end of 1923, a loaf of bread cost 201 billion marks!

As German prices rose higher and higher, the value of German money went down. In 1918, one mark was worth around eight American dollars. In 1923, one mark was worth less than one American cent. Germans would burn their money in the fireplace. It was cheaper to burn the money than to buy logs with it.

Some of the other leaders also wanted a harsher punishment for Germany. For Wilson, the creation of the League of Nations was most important. He was willing to make the agreement harsher if the other leaders would accept the League of Nations. In the end, the leaders accepted the Treaty of Versailles. The treaty laid out a harsh punishment for Germany. It also set up the League of Nations.

A Harsh Treaty

With the Treaty of Versailles, Germany lost all its colonies in Africa and Asia. The treaty cut the size of the German army to 100,000 soldiers. Germany was not allowed to build submarines. Germany also had to return land it won from France in 1871. It was not allowed to put soldiers in an area called the Rhineland. This area was to be a **buffer zone** between Germany and France.

Two parts of the treaty were especially harsh. Germany had to accept total blame for starting the war. They also had to pay for all the damage caused by the war. The payments were called **reparations**. The Allies charged Germany 37 billion dollars in reparations. The Germans tried to pay the full amount, but they could not afford to. The large payments brought serious economic problems to Germany.

The Treaty of Versailles was signed in 1919.

Wilson fought hard for the League of Nations at the peace talks. He then had to present the idea back home in the United States. Wilson tried to convince the United States Senate to join the League of Nations. But the Senate voted against it. Many Americans didn't want to join. They were tired of getting involved in Europe's problems. Wilson was deeply disappointed by this defeat.

The League of Nations met for the first time in 1920. The organization lasted until the 1940s, but it was never a complete success. Without the United States as a member, it did not have the power to keep peace throughout the world.

A New Look for Europe

World War I changed the map of Europe. Land was taken from the German, Austro-Hungarian, and Ottoman empires. Since Russia left the war before it was over, Russia also lost lands. Five new European nations were created from lands lost by Russia. These were Poland, Finland, Latvia, Lithuania, and Estonia.

Compare this map to the map of Europe on page 415. Name three new European countries that were formed after World War I.

Europe After World War I

Kemel Ataturk, first president of Turkey, 1900

Austria and Hungary became separate nations. Yugoslavia and Czechoslovakia were created. Italy, Poland, and Romania gained lands from the old empire of Austria-Hungary.

The Ottoman Empire also ended. Turkey became an independent country. The Ottoman lands in Southwest Asia became **mandates**. A mandate is a territory under the control of another country. Syria became a French mandate, and Iraq and Palestine became British mandates. The Allies promised to give these territories independence in the future.

Many historians think the Treaty of Versailles was too harsh. World War I was not Germany's fault alone. The reparations were far too high. The Allies won the war, but they failed to win peace. Before he died in 1924, Woodrow Wilson warned that another Great War would be likely.

Lesson 3 Review

Choose words from the list that best complete the paragraphs. One word will not be used.

Word List
reparations
mandates
self-determination
Rhineland
Versailles

Wilson hoped his Fourteen Points would bring peace to Europe. He believed all nationalities should have the right of __1__. He also wanted a League of Nations. France wanted harsher punishments for Germany. In the end, the Treaty of __2__ gave a harsh punishment to Germany and created the League of Nations.

Under the treaty, Germans had to accept blame for the war. They also had to pay __3__. New nations were created from lands of the defeated empires. Some territories in Southwest Asia became __4__ with the promise of independence in the future.

Chapter 29: Using What You've Learned

Summary

- The arms race in Europe and conflicts over imperialism and nationalism led to World War I. The killing of Archduke Ferdinand and his wife was the spark that started the war.
- The two sides fighting in the war were the Central Powers and the Allies. Thirty-one nations took part in World War I. The United States entered the war in 1917.
- The Treaty of Versailles was signed in 1919, ending the war. The Germans had to pay harsh reparations to the Allies.
- President Woodrow Wilson created the League of Nations as an attempt to prevent future wars. The United States did not join.

Find Out More!

After reading Chapter 29, you're ready to go online. **Explore Zone**, **Quiz Time**, and **Amazing Facts** bring this chapter of world history alive.

Visit www.exploreSV.com and type in the chapter code **Ch29**.

Vocabulary

Number your paper from 1 to 5. Finish the sentences from Group A with words from Group B. Write the letter of the correct answer.

Group A

1. Each European nation wanted the strongest military force, which caused an _____ in Europe.
2. The members of the _____ were Germany, Austria-Hungary, and Italy.
3. Belgium was called a _____ country because it did not take sides in World War I.
4. The _____ included Great Britain, Russia, France, Serbia, Italy, and the United States.
5. A territory under the control of another country is called a _____.

Group B

a. mandate

b. Triple Alliance

c. arms race

d. neutral

e. Allies

Comprehension

Number your paper from 1 to 5. Write the word or words from the list that best complete the paragraphs. One word will not be used.

Germany had to fight Russia in the east and France and Belgium in the west. This made World War I a __1__. Tanks and other new weapons used in the war caused much of the war to be fought in __2__. The Germans used __3__ to sink ships sailing toward Great Britain. Because some of the ships attacked were American, the United States declared war on Germany.

The leaders of Italy, France, Great Britain, and the United States, also called the __4__, met for peace talks at Versailles, France. President Wilson presented his peace plan called the __5__.

Word List

trenches
stalemate
two-front war
Fourteen Points
submarines
Big Four

Critical Thinking

Sequencing Number your paper from 1 to 5. Write the sentences below in the correct order.

Germany declared war on Russia.

Five new nations were created from lands lost by Russia.

Archduke Franz Ferdinand and his wife were killed.

The United States declared war on Germany.

Germany agreed to an armistice.

Writing

Write a short newspaper article describing how the new weapons used in World War I changed the way wars were fought. Give your article a title.

LESSON 1

Russian Revolution

Before You Read

- In what ways was Russia different from other large European nations?
- What is a Communist government?

In the 18th century, Peter the Great wanted Russia to be a modern nation. Russia made some progress. However, by the start of World War I, Russia was still not as industrialized as western Europe.

The royal Russian family, the Romanovs, held absolute power. Most Russian peasants and factory workers were very poor. They were not happy with the Romanovs.

The Romanovs ruled in Russia from 1894 to 1917.

New Words

marchers
soviets
Duma
abdicate
middle-class
Bolsheviks
Red Army
White Army
revolutionary

People and Places

Romanovs
Nicholas II
Vladimir Lenin
Soviet Union

On Bloody Sunday, Russian soldiers killed hundreds of marchers in St. Petersburg.

Revolution of 1905

Czar Nicholas II

In 1904 and 1905, Russia was fighting Japan for territories in China and Korea. This angered many Russians. They wanted reform, not war. On January 22, 1905, a group of workers marched in the city of St. Petersburg. They had no weapons, but Russian soldiers fired at them. The soldiers killed several hundred **marchers**. This day became known as Bloody Sunday.

The killing sparked a revolution. More workers marched in the streets of St. Petersburg and other Russian cities. They carried red banners as a symbol of the revolution. Many people stopped working, so government and businesses were forced to shut down. Worker councils, known as **soviets**, led the revolution. Finally, the czar promised some reforms. Czar Nicholas II's reforms created a Russian parliament called the **Duma**. This reform satisfied the workers. The revolution calmed.

Revolutions in 1917

The Russians entered World War I in 1914. The Russians did well during the first months of the war but then began losing battles. They had few new weapons. Many of their best officers died. By 1917, most Russian soldiers had left the war and returned to their homes.

The soldiers returned to poor conditions in Russia. There was little food and few goods in the stores. Many people were out of work. Workers led more marches. In early 1917, police and soldiers tried to stop the marchers. But they, too, were angry at the poor conditions. Soon they joined the marchers. Nicholas II was forced to **abdicate**, or give up the throne.

The Russians quickly set up a new government. Doctors, lawyers, and other **middle-class** people ran the government. Workers formed soviets as they had done in 1905.

These men are bringing food to Russian soldiers.

Bolshevik Army poster

The new government continued to fight in World War I although most Russians wanted to end the war. This led to a second revolution in the same year.

On November 7, 1917, the **Bolsheviks** took control of Russia. The Bolsheviks were led by Vladimir Lenin. Lenin was a follower of Karl Marx. The Bolsheviks wanted peace at any cost. They signed a treaty with Germany. Russia gave up huge amounts of land in order to get out of the war.

The Communist Revolution

Lenin set up a government following the ideas of Karl Marx. Marx was the founder of communism. Lenin wanted workers to take over all the factories, farms, shipyards, mines, and railroads. Lenin believed Russia should have a Communist government.

Many Russians supported communism. They had owned nothing under the old system. Under a Communist government, they owned everything. Communism gave poor people some power.

Other Russians did not favor communism. They did not like the idea of all the people sharing power. They and some other groups fought the Bolsheviks in a Russian civil war.

The Communists were known as the **Red Army**. Those who fought against communism were called the **White Army**. It was a bloody and cruel civil war. Many Russians were killed. Czar Nicholas II, his wife, his daughters, and his son were killed by the Red Army. By 1921, the Bolsheviks had won control of Russia. In 1922, Lenin named Russia the Union of Soviet Socialist Republics (USSR), or the Soviet Union.

Red Army parade in 1923

Vladimir Lenin (1870–1924)

When Vladimir Lenin was only 16 years old, his brother, Alexander, was arrested for trying to kill the czar. Alexander was found guilty and hanged.

His brother's death turned Lenin into a **revolutionary**. Lenin was often in trouble with the police. Two years after the 1905 revolution, Lenin left Russia. He stayed away until 1917, when Germans sneaked him back into Russia. The Germans knew that if Lenin came to power, he would pull Russia out of World War I.

Lenin later led the Red Army to victory over the White Army. He established communism as the government of Russia. But Lenin was as cruel as any of the czars before him. "He who is not with us is against us," Lenin said. He ordered the police to kill anyone who was against communism. Lenin died in 1924, only two years after forming the Soviet Union.

Lesson 1 Review

Choose words from the list that best complete the paragraphs. One word will not be used.

At the start of World War I, Russia was not as industrialized as western Europe was. Many people were poor, and the __1__ had absolute power. Bloody Sunday sparked a revolution in 1905. It was led by worker councils called __2__.

Russia had two more revolutions in 1917. During the first one in early 1917, Nicholas II __3__ the throne. The second revolution occurred in November. Lenin and the __4__ took control of Russia. A civil war followed. By 1921, the Red Army had defeated the White Army. Lenin established the Soviet Union in 1922.

Word List

soviets
Romanovs
Duma
Bolsheviks
abdicated

LESSON 2

Life After the Great War

New Words

Roaring Twenties
attitudes
Great Depression
broadcast
stock market
New Deal

People and Places

F. Scott Fitzgerald
Walt Disney

Before You Read

- How might people try to forget a war?
- What happens when businesses can't sell the goods that they make?

The 1920s, known as the **Roaring Twenties**, were a time of wild living for some people. American writer F. Scott Fitzgerald said, "The parties were bigger . . . the pace was faster." It was also a time of new inventions and new **attitudes**, or ways of looking at the world.

The 1930s were quite different. The **Great Depression** ended the good times of the 1920s. Millions of people lost their jobs and homes. People were hungry. Trade greatly slowed. The depression affected every country in the world.

The 1920s were an exciting time for many people.

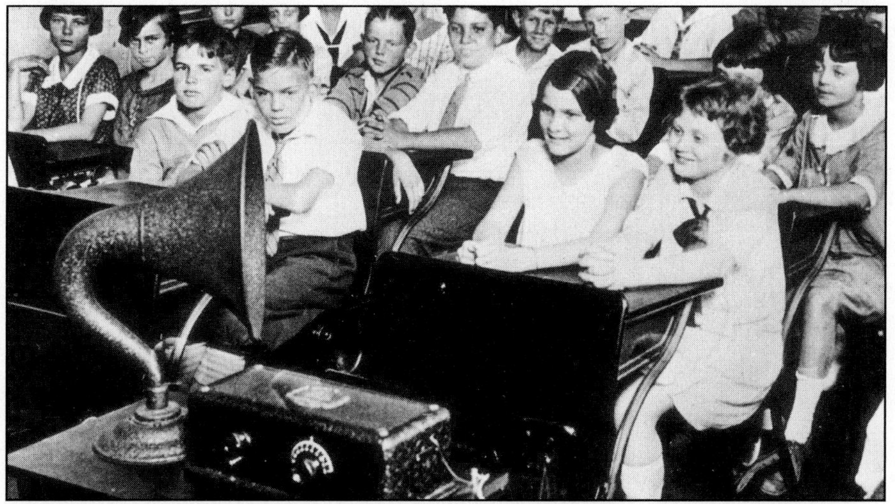

These American children are listening to a radio in their classroom.

New Inventions

The radio, the automobile, and motion pictures all had been invented earlier. But it was during the 1920s that they became part of everyday life. The first American radio station opened in 1920. Within a couple of years, hundreds of stations began to **broadcast**, or send radio signals. Families sat in their homes, listening to music, news, weather reports, and sports.

The automobile greatly changed the way people lived. People could go where they wanted when they wanted. They could visit friends far away. They could drive and see new places.

Young people saw the car as a symbol of fun and freedom. They could drive to the theater and see the latest movie. The first talking film, *The Jazz Singer*, was shown in 1927. A year later, Walt Disney introduced the world to Mickey Mouse in a film called *Steamboat Willie*.

Poster for the film *The Jazz Singer*

New Attitudes

The end of the war brought new attitudes. Around the world, many women earned the right to vote. They took more jobs outside the home. More women went to college and earned higher degrees.

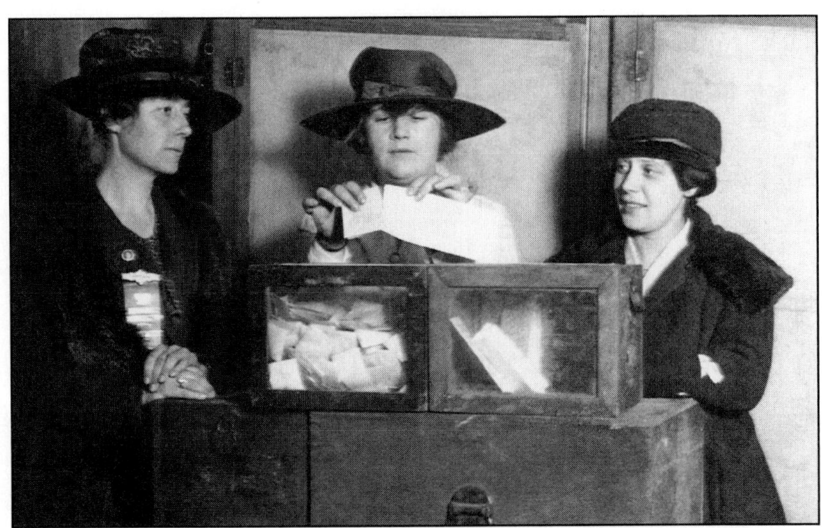

Women in the United States earned the right to vote in 1920.

People had more personal freedom during the Roaring Twenties. Before the war, most people in American cities worked six days a week. By the 1920s, most of them worked only five days a week. That gave them more time to enjoy life. Many Americans enjoyed going to baseball games.

Stock Market Crash

By 1929, the United States was the biggest industrial power in the world. Then in late October, the New York **stock market** crashed. Other markets around the world also crashed.

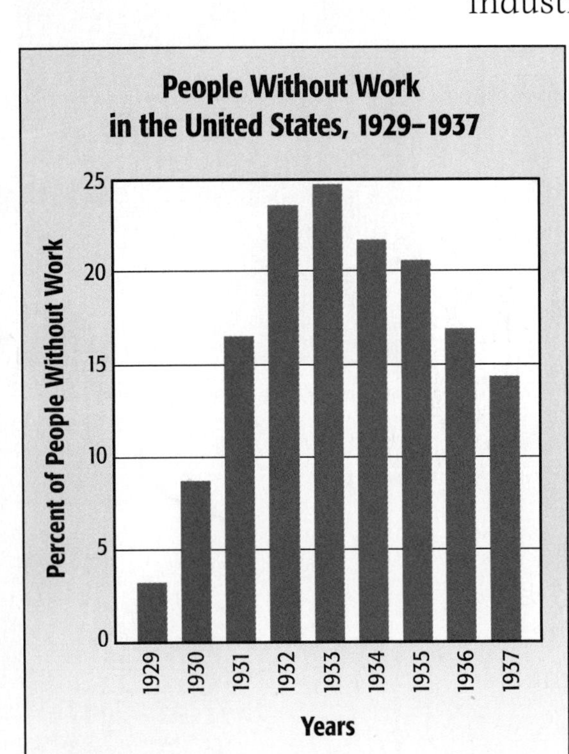

A stock market is a place where people buy shares of stock, or parts of a company. Many people made a lot of money buying and selling stocks during the 1920s. Stock prices kept going up. When the prices came crashing down, many people lost all their money.

The Great Depression

The stock market crash started the Great Depression. This depression lasted until the end of the 1930s. Many people stopped spending money. Businesses couldn't sell the goods they made. Owners had to lay off workers. These workers then had no money to buy goods. This caused even more businesses to lay off more workers.

The Great Depression began in the United States, but it was felt around the world. In 1929, American trade with the rest of the world totalled about 10 billion dollars. By 1933, it had dropped to only 3 billion dollars. The same was true in Europe. Its trade with the rest of the world was at 15 billion dollars in 1929. Five years later, it had dropped to 5 billion dollars.

President Roosevelt giving a radio address

Franklin D. Roosevelt was president of the United States during the Great Depression. He gave weekly radio addresses to encourage American citizens. He introduced a set of programs called the **New Deal**. These programs put people to work. People worked to improve the government and the land.

The New Deal changed the way Americans thought about government. Americans began expecting more from the government.

During the Great Depression, people waited in lines to receive food.

Depression in Latin America, Asia, and Africa

Latin Americans, Asians, and Africans also suffered from the Great Depression. People who lived on farms and grew food for themselves felt little harm. But farmers who raised crops to sell in the United States or Europe were greatly harmed.

Coffee growers in Brazil were hurt by the Great Depression.

In Brazil, coffee was a major crop. By the late 1920s, coffee sales totalled 70% of Brazil's sales to foreign countries. But during the Great Depression, coffee prices dropped sharply. Brazilians made a lot less money. They could not afford to buy foreign goods. Brazilians had to begin making certain products they used to buy from foreigners.

Governments from around the world tried to end the Great Depression. By 1937, things had improved only slightly. It was the start of World War II in 1939 that finally ended the Great Depression.

Lesson 2 Review

Choose words from the list that best complete the paragraphs. One word will not be used.

Word List

Walt Disney
attitudes
stock market
New Deal
broadcast

The 1920s were known as the Roaring Twenties. In 1920, the first radio station began to __1__. The automobile gave people more freedom. New __2__ helped women earn the right to vote.

In 1929, the New York __3__ crashed. This led to the Great Depression. President Franklin D. Roosevelt started the __4__ to help end the Great Depression. Nations around the world were affected by the Great Depression.

LESSON 3

The Rise of Dictators

Before You Read

- How might one person gain total control of a nation?
- Why would an all-powerful ruler want to control what is taught in schools?

Several dictators rose to power in the 1920s and 1930s. A dictator is a person who rules a nation and makes all the laws. Strong dictators took control in the Soviet Union, Italy, Spain, and Germany. In Japan, a group of military rulers took power. Japan's military leaders made all the decisions.

These dictators used the troubles caused by World War I and the Great Depression to gain power. Once in power, they did whatever was necessary to keep it.

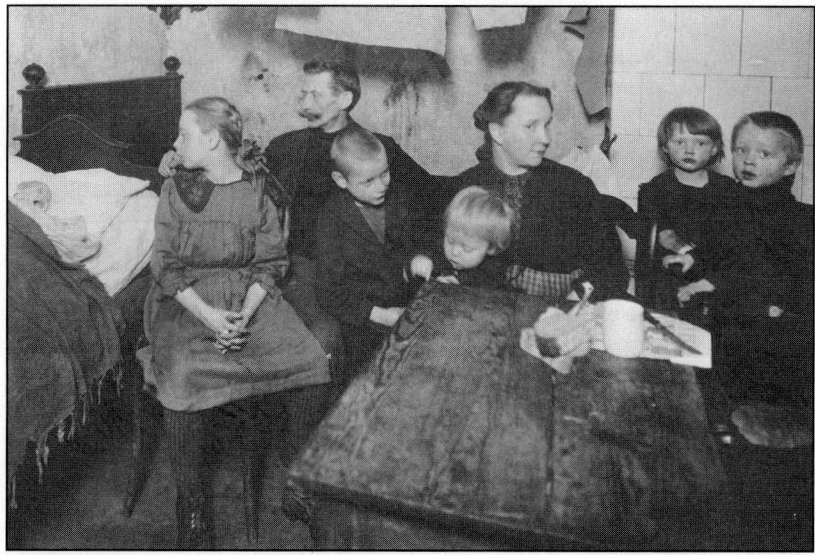

Poverty caused by World War I made it easier for dictators to take power.

New Words

secret police
collective farms
debt
Fascist Party
Nazi Party
overthrow
election

People and Places

Leon Trotsky
Joseph Stalin
Benito Mussolini
Francisco Franco
Weimar Republic
Adolf Hitler
Hideki Tojo

How Dictators Ruled

The dictators wanted total control over their countries. They did not want democracy. Dictators jailed or killed anyone who spoke out against them. They used **secret police** to find and punish enemies. They also decided what should be taught in schools. Students learned that they must always obey their nation's dictator.

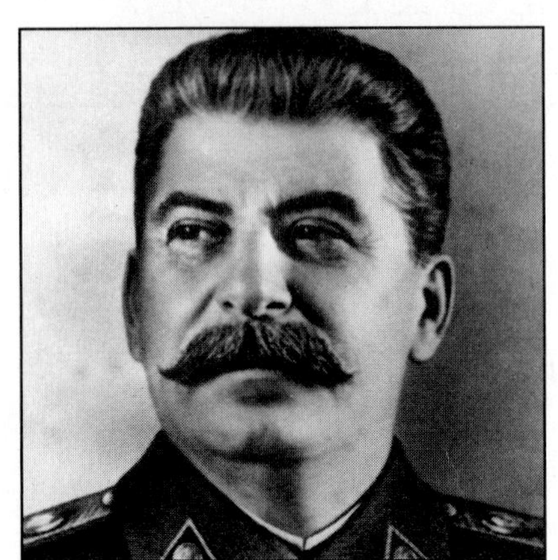

Joseph Stalin

Dictators also controlled the news. In the 1920s and 1930s, they controlled radio stations and newspapers. Dictators let people know only what they wanted them to know.

Dictator in the Soviet Union

After Lenin died in 1924, two men wanted power—Leon Trotsky and Joseph Stalin. Stalin won the support of important Communists. In 1929, Stalin sent Trotsky out of the country. In 1940, Stalin sent men to murder Trotsky.

Stalin was a brutal ruler. He once said that the death of one person was a tragedy. Then he added that the death of a million people was only a number. During his rule, he murdered millions of people. Many were peasants. Stalin forced peasants to work on **collective farms**. Under the rules of communism, peasants owned these

Under Stalin, Soviet peasants worked on collective farms.

Benito Mussolini became the dictator of Italy in 1922.

farms. However, the government actually ran the farms. The peasants had no power.

Stalin did bring some positive changes to the Soviet Union. He built up industries. By 1939, the Soviet Union was a leading industrial nation.

Dictator in Italy

World War I left Italy with many problems. The nation was in **debt**. People lost their jobs. The democratic government was weak. Then in 1919, Benito Mussolini began the **Fascist Party**. Fascists wanted a dictator to control the government. In 1922, Mussolini became the dictator of Italy.

Mussolini promised to make Italy as great as it had been during the Roman Empire. In 1935, Italy invaded the African country of Ethiopia. The League of Nations did little to stop it. Mussolini's success as a dictator encouraged other dictators to take power.

Francisco Franco

Francisco Franco led Fascist forces in Spain. During a Spanish civil war in the late 1930s, Franco destroyed the democratic government. Franco became the dictator of Spain.

Adolf Hitler became the dictator of Germany in 1933.

Dictator in Germany

After World War I, Germany had a democracy called the Weimar Republic. But the republic didn't last very long. Germany had many small political groups. No one group had the support of most of the people.

Adolf Hitler led the **Nazi Party**. The Nazis were similar to the Fascists. They wanted Hitler to be the dictator of Germany. In 1923, Hitler tried to **overthrow** the republic. He failed and was sent to prison. While in jail, he wrote the book *Mein Kampf*, which means "My Struggle."

Voices In History

> **"Those who want to live, let them fight, and those who do not want to fight in this [endless] struggle do not deserve to live . . . . That is how it is!"**

Hitler served only a short time in jail. Most Germans still did not support Hitler, but a growing number did. Hitler made Germans worry about a Communist revolution. He said that if he was ruler, he would not let communism come to Germany. Many Germans were looking for a strong leader. They were hit especially hard by the Great Depression. In 1933, Hitler won an important **election**. He became a strong dictator. Like Mussolini, he promised to return Germany to greatness. He also said he would get back the lands lost from the Treaty of Versailles.

Powerful Rulers in Japan

Japan did not have one all-powerful dictator like Italy, Spain, and Germany had. Instead, the government was controlled by a group of military leaders. The most famous was an army general named Hideki Tojo.

Hideki Tojo

The Great Depression had badly hurt Japan. As an island nation, Japan needed to trade more than most countries. When world trade slowed, the Japanese military blamed the weak democratic government for Japan's troubles. Soon the military took control of the government.

The Japanese had always traded for the raw materials they needed. Under the new military dictators, they just took what they wanted. In 1931, Japan invaded Manchuria. The Chinese province was rich in coal and iron. After this easy victory, Japan began to look for more lands to conquer.

Lesson 3 Review

Choose words from the list that best complete the paragraph. One word will not be used.

Several dictators rose to power during the 1920s and 1930s. __1__ became dictator of the Soviet Union. His rule led to millions of deaths. He forced peasants to work on __2__. In Italy, Mussolini led the __3__ to power. He attacked Ethiopia. The League of Nations did not stop him. Hitler led a group called the __4__. He became the dictator of Germany in 1933. Japan was controlled by a group of military leaders. In 1931, Japan invaded Manchuria to control its coal and iron.

Word List

Fascist Party
Nazi Party
Franco
collective farms
Stalin

LESSON 4

Movements Against Imperialism

New Words

Middle East
Zionism
Balfour Declaration
Mahatma
civil disobedience
partitioned
dispute

People and Places

Mount Zion
Arthur Balfour
Mohandas K. Gandhi
Muhammad Ali Jinnah
Pakistan
Kashmir
Bangladesh

Before You Read

- How might colonies gain their freedom?
- Why might Europeans have wanted Jews to have their own nation?

At the end of World War I, many of Great Britain's colonies began to fight against imperialism. They were tired of being ruled by foreign powers. The British Empire was so large that it could not keep control over the many nationalist movements growing within its empire.

Great Britain in the Middle East

Great Britain controlled several lands in North Africa and Southwest Asia. This region became

Egyptians in Cairo protested British rule.

known as the **Middle East**. Egypt was a protectorate of Great Britain. After several Egyptian revolts, the British gave Egypt independence in 1922. But the British left troops there. They continued to control Egypt's relations with other countries.

After World War I, Palestine became a British mandate. Great Britain would govern Palestine until it could govern itself. Most of the people living in Palestine were Arabs. European Jews also began moving into Palestine in the late 19th century. They began a movement for a Jewish homeland in Palestine. This movement was called **Zionism**. It was named after Mount Zion, the site of King David's palace in ancient Israel.

The British wanted Jewish support during World War I. British official Arthur Balfour wrote a letter supporting the idea of a Jewish homeland. This letter was called the **Balfour Declaration**.

However, the British also supported the creation of an independent Arab state in Palestine. They offered this support because the Arabs had helped the British defeat the Ottomans.

After Hitler came to power, more Jews left Europe and moved to Palestine. This led to struggles with Palestinian Arabs. Fighting continued between Jewish settlers and the Arabs.

Zionist postcard

These Arabs were living in Palestine around 1920.

After gaining independence, India was partitioned. Which religion did most people in West Pakistan and East Pakistan practice?

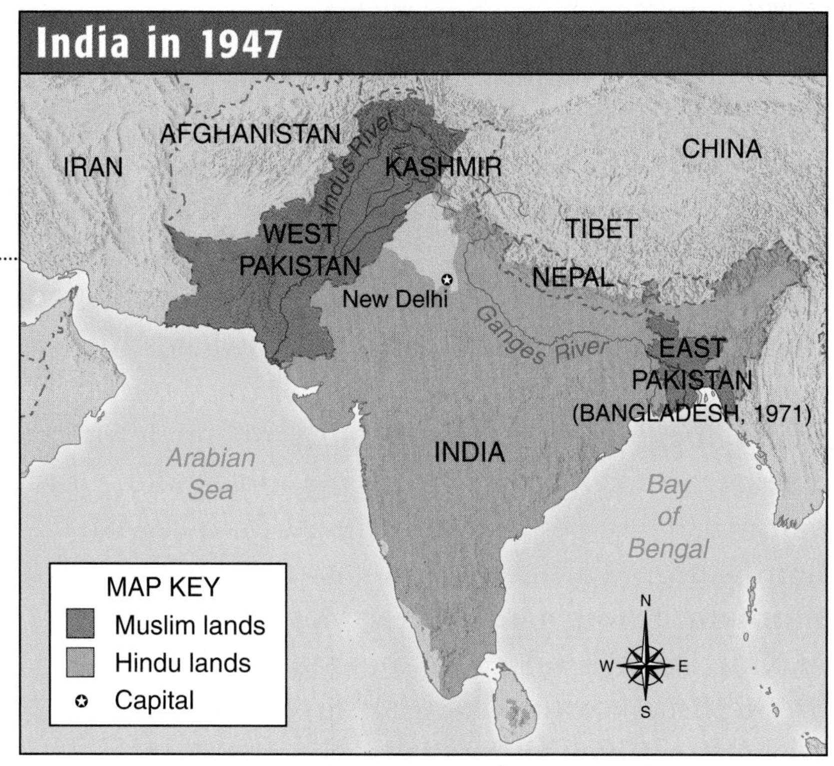

India Gains Independence

India was Great Britain's biggest and richest colony. The Indians, however, wanted independence. After World War I, they actively fought for it. The Indian leader of this struggle for independence was Mohandas K. Gandhi. He was often called the **Mahatma**, or "Great Soul."

Gandhi was against violence. He favored boycotts and **civil disobedience**. Gandhi encouraged people not to buy British goods. He refused to pay taxes to Great Britain. The British put him in jail several times.

Mahatma Gandhi

Gandhi slowly brought change to India. Great Britain gave India a new constitution in 1935. The people of India could elect their own representatives. In 1947, India gained its independence. Gandhi spoke about the struggle for change.

"Almost everything you do will seem insignificant. But it is very important that you do it . . . . You must be the change you want to see in the world."

A Land Divided

Most Indians were Hindus, but millions were Muslims. The leader of the Muslims was Muhammad Ali Jinnah. He once said, "The only thing the Muslim has in common with the Hindu is his slavery to the British."

Shortly after India declared its independence, fighting broke out between Muslims and Hindus. More than 5,000 people died in a single day's fighting. India was then **partitioned**.

The Hindus kept the area that is India today. The Muslims received what became the nation of Pakistan. Millions of Hindus in Pakistan moved to India. Millions of Muslims in India moved to Pakistan. Immediately, the new nations fought over the territory called Kashmir. This land remains in **dispute** even today.

Pakistan itself was divided into East Pakistan and West Pakistan. The northern section of India lay between them. In 1971, East Pakistan became the new nation of Bangladesh.

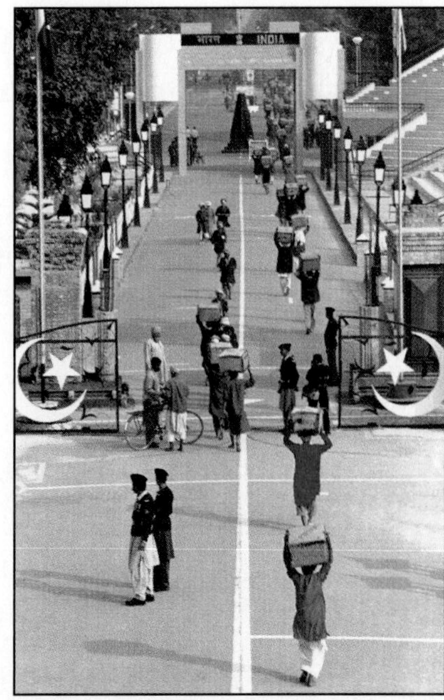

Modern border between India and Pakistan

Lesson 4 Review

Choose words from the list that best complete the paragraphs. One word will not be used.

After World War I, Great Britain granted independence to several colonies in the region known as the __1__. But the British kept control of Palestine. The movement for a Jewish homeland in Palestine was called __2__.

Indians struggled to win independence from Great Britain. Their leader, Mohandas __3__, was against violence. He favored boycotts and __4__. India was partitioned. Hindus controlled what is India today. Muslims controlled Pakistan.

Word List

- Balfour Declaration
- Gandhi
- Zionism
- civil disobedience
- Middle East

Chapter 30: Using What You've Learned

Summary

- By 1921, the Bolsheviks, led by Vladimir Lenin, had won control of Russia. Russia became the Soviet Union.
- During the 1920s, the radio and the automobile became a part of people's everyday lives. People also began to have new attitudes about society.
- The Great Depression was caused by a stock market crash in 1929. The depression affected the whole world, but some countries suffered more than others. The start of World War II ended the Great Depression.
- During the 1920s and 1930s, dictators gained power in Russia, Italy, Spain, and Germany. Military leaders took control of Japan.

Find Out More!

After reading Chapter 30, you're ready to go online. **Explore Zone**, **Quiz Time**, and **Amazing Facts** bring this chapter of world history alive.

Visit www.exploreSV.com and type in the chapter code **Ch30**.

Vocabulary

Number your paper from 1 to 6. Write the word or words from the list that best complete the paragraphs. One word will not be used.

After World War I, many European Jews began a movement for a Jewish homeland in Palestine. This movement was called __1__. The British expressed their support for a Jewish homeland in the __2__.

Indians wanted independence from Great Britain. Their leader, Mohandas K. Gandhi, was also called the __3__. Gandhi used __4__ because he was against violence. Soon after India gained its independence in 1947, India was __5__ into two nations. These nations, now known as India and Pakistan, soon began a __6__ over the territory called Kashmir.

Word List

partitioned
Zionism
civil disobedience
dispute
Balfour Declaration
soviets
Mahatma

Comprehension

Number your paper from 1 to 5. Write the word or words from the list that best complete each sentence. One word will not be used.

1. Lenin set up a _____ government in Russia.
2. The _____ fought against the Communists.
3. People buy parts of a company in a _____.
4. Stalin forced peasants to work on _____.
5. Benito Mussolini was the _____ of Italy.

Word List

White Army
dictator
Communist
election
stock market
collective farms

Critical Thinking

Conclusions Number your paper from 1 to 3. Read each pair of sentences below. Then look for a conclusion that follows from these sentences. Write the letter of the correct conclusion.

1. Most Russian peasants were unhappy with the Romanovs.
   Russian soldiers killed hundreds of workers in a protest march.
2. Coffee was a major crop in Brazil.
   During the Great Depression, coffee prices fell.
3. Many Germans were worried about a Communist revolution.
   Hitler said that he would protect Germany from communism.

Conclusions

a. Brazilians had less money and could not buy foreign goods.

b. Hitler was elected in 1933 as the leader of Germany.

c. A worker's revolution began in Russia.

Writing

Pretend you were living in the 1920s. Write a journal entry explaining how radio, the automobile, and movies might be a part of your everyday life.

Skill Builder: Reading a Political Cartoon

A **political cartoon** is a drawing that shows what an artist thinks about a certain person, event, or issue.

The political cartoon below shows President Franklin D. Roosevelt as a doctor. He is trying to help Uncle Sam, who is a symbol for the United States, recover from the Great Depression. **Remedies** are cures.

Number your paper from 1 to 5. Write 1 to 2 sentences to answer each question.

1. What does the artist use to represent Congress?
2. How do you know that the person in the middle is President Franklin D. Roosevelt?
3. What symbols are used to show that the man sitting down is Uncle Sam?
4. How is President Roosevelt trying to help Uncle Sam?
5. The bottles of medicine on the tables are labeled with the names of New Deal programs. What do you think the artist is trying to say about these programs?

LESSON 1

Causes of World War II

Before You Read

- How might the rise of dictators make another world war more likely?
- Why might a nation want to separate itself from the rest of the world?

New Words

Axis Powers
aggression
demilitarized
prime minister
appeasement
neutrality

People and Places

Sudetenland
Neville Chamberlain
Edouard Daladier
Munich

Before Woodrow Wilson died in 1924, he warned of another Great War. Wilson knew the League of Nations was too weak to keep peace. The League needed the United States, the strongest nation in the world, in order to be effective. Wilson knew the Treaty of Versailles treated Germany too harshly. It created far more anger than peace. Wilson was proven right in 1939 when World War II began.

These United States fighter planes were used in World War II.

German military planes

Similar Causes

There were many causes of World War II. Some of the causes, such as nationalism, were the same causes that led to World War I. Mussolini and Hitler were strong believers in nationalism. They wanted to make their nations powerful. Neither dictator cared how much money or how many lives it took to achieve that power.

An arms race was a cause of World War I. A similar rush to build up the military took place in the 1930s. Germany, Italy, and Japan spent large amounts of money building up their armed forces on land, on sea, and in the air. In 1940, these three nations formed a loose military alliance. They became known as the **Axis Powers**.

Another cause of both wars was imperialism. Before World War I, nations fought to gain new colonies. Imperialism continued during the 1930s. You have read how Italy took over Ethiopia and how Japan conquered Manchuria.

Versailles and the Great Depression

World War II had new causes, too. The Treaty of Versailles pleased few people. It angered the Germans. They were forced to take the blame for World War I and to pay for all the war damages. Even some of the Allies were not happy. The Italians, for example, thought they should have gotten more land from the treaty.

The Great Depression hurt Europe deeply. The continent was just beginning to recover from the war when the depression struck. Millions of people did not have jobs. There were poverty and unhappiness throughout Europe. People grew desperate. They would listen to anyone who offered a solution to their problems. This made it much easier for dictators to seize power.

German money was worth so little that these boys used it to make a kite.

Aggression by the Dictators

Germany, Italy, and Japan grew bolder during the 1930s. The League of Nations did nothing to stop Italy when it invaded Ethiopia. It did not recognize Japan's rule over Manchuria, but it did not force Japan to withdraw. **Aggression**, or the use of force, seemed to be working for Italy and Japan.

Hitler also got bolder. He did not follow the Treaty of Versailles. In 1936, he sent an army into the Rhineland. Under the treaty, this was a **demilitarized** zone. Germany was not allowed to put any soldiers there. But Hitler did put soldiers there, and no one stopped him. Then he broke the treaty once more by taking over Austria.

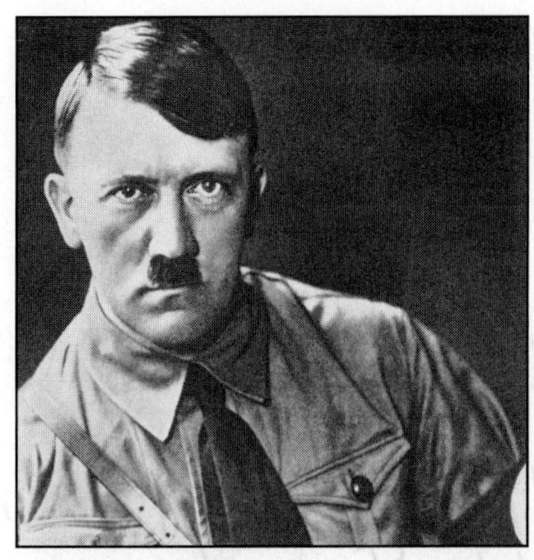

Adolph Hitler

By 1939, Germany and Italy had conquered lands beyond their 1935 borders. Which of these countries took over Poland?

Europe in 1939

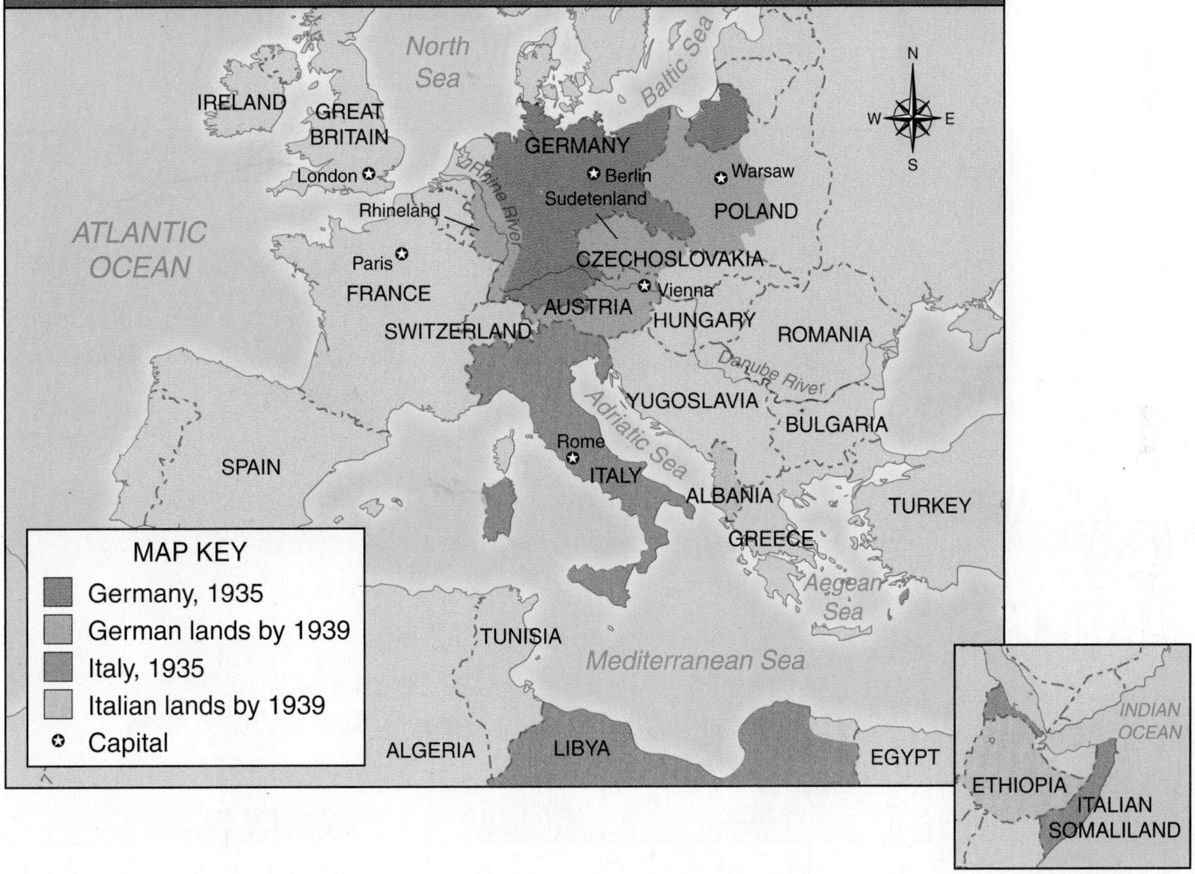

MAP KEY
- Germany, 1935
- German lands by 1939
- Italy, 1935
- Italian lands by 1939
- Capital

The Failure of Appeasement

Neville Chamberlain

Next, Hitler wanted the Sudetenland, which was part of the new nation of Czechoslovakia. The Czechs were ready to fight, but the French and the British were not.

Neville Chamberlain, the British **prime minister**, believed he could make a deal with Hitler. In 1938, he and French official Edouard Daladier met Hitler in Munich, Germany. Hitler promised to stop his aggression if he could just have the Sudetenland. Chamberlain and Daladier agreed to let Hitler have the Sudetenland. This policy of giving Hitler what he wanted in order to avoid war was called **appeasement**.

Chamberlain happily declared that he had won "peace in our time." But Hitler quickly broke the deal by seizing the rest of Czechoslovakia in 1939. The world realized Hitler had lied. The policy of appeasement was over.

MODEL GLIDER

SPECIAL 4 A.M. EDITION

Daily Express

The Daily Express declares that Britain will not be in in a European war this year, or next year either

Mussolini draws up frontier

PEACE!

AGREEMENT SIGNED AT 12.30 a.m. TODAY

German troops march in tomorrow: Then occupation gradually until October 10

FRONTIER GUARANTEED

From SELKIRK PANTON

MUNICH, Friday morning

A PACT of peace was signed in Munich at 12.30 this morning.

WHEN POLAND WILL JOIN

This is what they signed

HE MAY BE SIR NEVILLE

ARE YOU REALLY A GOOD FATHER ?

Premier's wife mobbed

Newspaper page from the day of the agreement

The leaders of Great Britain and France agreed to let Hitler take control of the Sudetenland. They hoped the agreement would avoid a war.

American Isolation

The United States tried to stay neutral. The problems of Europe were not the problems of the United States. Congress passed several laws in support of **neutrality**. Many Americans favored a policy of strict isolation. They did not want to get involved in another European war.

President Franklin Roosevelt knew, however, that the United States might not stay neutral forever. After Japan invaded China in 1937, Roosevelt spoke about the possible effect on Americans.

"Innocent people are being cruelly sacrificed to a greed for power . . . . Let no one imagine that America will escape . . . . There is no escape through mere isolation or neutrality. War is a [disease, and like a disease, war] is spreading."

Lesson 1 Review

Choose words from the list that best complete the paragraphs. One word will not be used.

Word List

Axis Powers
neutrality
appeasement
aggression
demilitarized

World War II shared some similar causes with World War I. These included nationalism, an arms race, and imperialism. Japan, Germany, and Italy formed the __1__. The League of Nations did little to stop the __2__ of dictators from these countries.

The Treaty of Versailles made the Rhineland a __3__ zone. But Hitler put German troops in the Rhineland anyway.

The British and French thought they could avoid a war by following a policy of __4__. But Hitler continued to take more land. The United States tried to stay neutral, as the rest of Europe went to war.

LESSON 2

War Around the World

New Words

non-aggression
blitzkrieg
Maginot Line
D-Day
atomic bomb

People and Places

Denmark
Luxembourg
Norway
Winston Churchill
Moscow
Leningrad
Stalingrad
Pearl Harbor
Midway Island
Sicily
Hiroshima
Nagasaki

Before You Read

- Where might battles of a world war be fought?
- What might cause a neutral nation to join a war?

After taking Czechoslovakia, Hitler then wanted Poland. But he was worried about the Soviet Union. He did not want to fight a two-front war. So he signed a **non-aggression** treaty with Stalin. Hitler and Stalin agreed not to go to war against each other.

The treaty surprised the rest of the world. The Communists and the Nazis were strong enemies. Hitler agreed to the treaty because he was not ready to fight the Poles and the Soviets, though he secretly planned to fight them later. Stalin agreed because his army was not ready for another war. The treaty gave him time to prepare.

For ten months, the German air force attacked Great Britain.

Quick Victories on the Western Front

On September 1, 1939, Hitler ordered an invasion of Poland. Two days later, Great Britain and France declared war on Germany. Other nations joined the Allies. World War II had begun. Over the next six years, more than 70 nations would be involved in the war.

The Germans fought hard and fast. They used planes and tanks. They called this type of fighting **blitzkrieg**. *Blitzkrieg* is a German word for "lightning war." In only a few weeks, Poland surrendered. Hitler then turned west.

The German army gained one quick victory after another. Denmark fell, and so did Luxembourg, the Netherlands, Belgium, and Norway. France built its defenses along a strip of land called the **Maginot Line**. But the Germans flew over or went around the line. France fell to the Germans in June of 1940.

Germany next prepared to conquer Great Britain. Hitler felt certain the British would give up. But Winston Churchill, the prime minister of Great Britain, refused. Hitler tried bombing Great Britain. Day after day, German planes dropped bombs on British cities. British pilots shot down many of the planes. After ten tough months, the British defeated the German air force.

The Eastern Front

It took only two years for Hitler to break his treaty with Stalin. Hitler had always wanted to conquer the Soviet Union. He wanted its vast open spaces and many natural resources. On June 22, 1941, Hitler invaded the Soviet Union. The Soviet Union then joined the Allies.

The Germans quickly captured huge amounts of land. The Soviet army lost millions of soldiers. By December, the Germans reached Moscow and Leningrad.

Did You Know?

Dogs of War

Dogs have been going to war since the beginning of history. They led the Assyrians into battle. During the Middle Ages, they wore armor just like knights did. In World War I, the French and Germans used dogs to find wounded soldiers. The British used dogs to carry messages, and the Italians used dogs to carry food up mountains.

During World War II, thousands of Americans offered their family dogs to the cause. The dogs were named the "K-9 Corps." They took a 12-week training course. Among the best dogs were German shepherds, collies, Dobermans, and giant schnauzers.

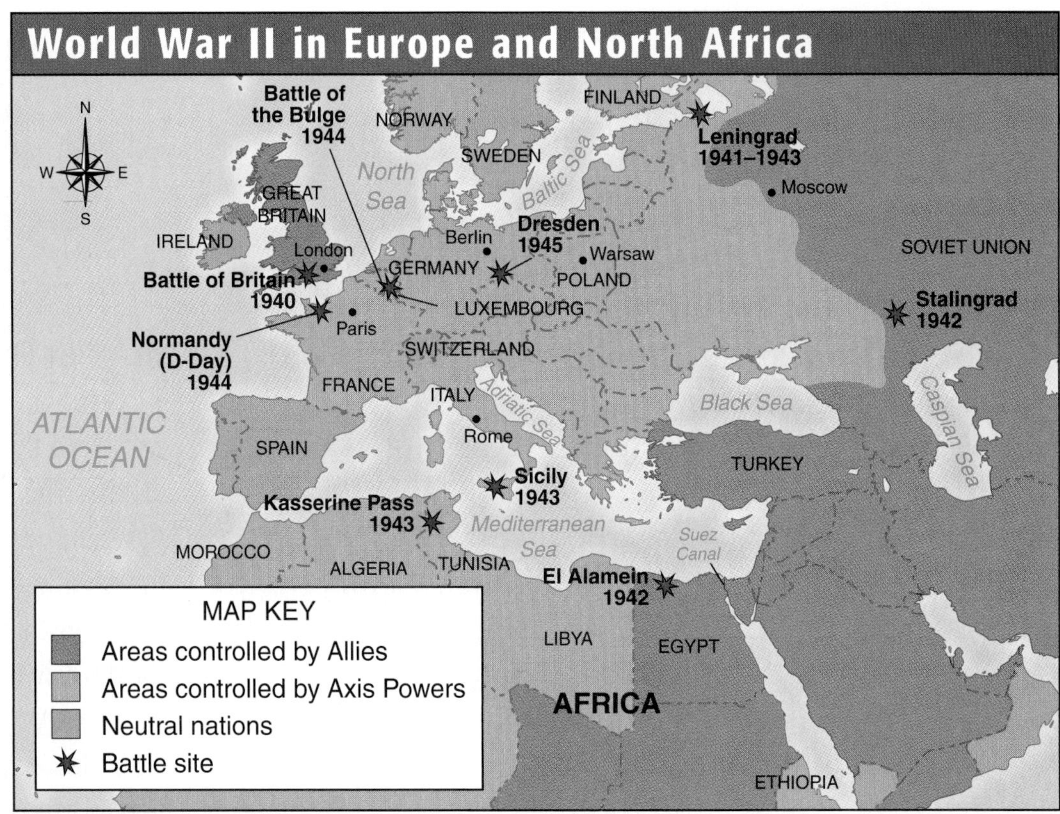

During World War II, the Axis Powers gained control of much of Europe. What Western European nation stayed under Allied control?

But they were not ready for the Soviet winter. Many German soldiers froze to death. Their tanks and weapons didn't work in the extreme cold.

The Soviets then attacked. The Battle of Stalingrad began in August 1942 and lasted five months. Soldiers fought hand to hand. With winter coming, the German commander wanted to pull back, but Hitler did not allow it. On February 2, 1943, the German soldiers in the Soviet Union surrendered. It was a turning point in the war.

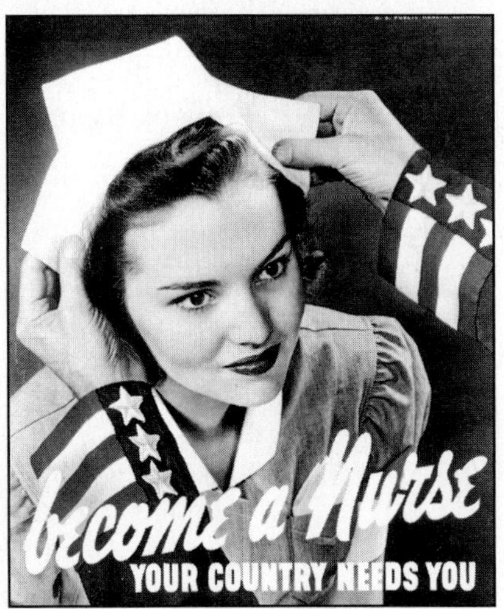

World War II poster

The Pacific Front

As in World War I, the United States tried to stay out of World War II. But the United States wasn't completely neutral. It favored the Allies. It sent military aid to the British.

While the Germans were attacking Europe, the Japanese were attacking territories in the Pacific Ocean. On December 7, 1941, Japan bombed Pearl Harbor in Hawaii. The United States declared war on Japan the next day. Then Hitler and Mussolini declared war on the United States.

In June 1942, the United States defeated the Japanese navy at Midway Island. The Battle of Midway was a turning point in the war in the Pacific. The Japanese held many islands in the Pacific. The United States began to take the islands one at a time.

United States soldiers raise the flag over Iwo Jima, a Pacific island.

War on Three Continents

In North Africa, the Germans and Italians almost gained control of the Suez Canal. They also nearly won the rich oil fields of the Middle East. But British and American troops stopped them. By early 1943, the tide of battle had turned against the Axis Powers.

Next, the Allies conquered the Italian island of Sicily. The Italians forced Mussolini out of office. The new Italian government surrendered to the Allies. Hitler sent fresh troops, but the Allies defeated them and took control of Italy.

From 1941 to 1945, several battles took place on islands in the Pacific Ocean. In what year did the battle of Okinawa take place?

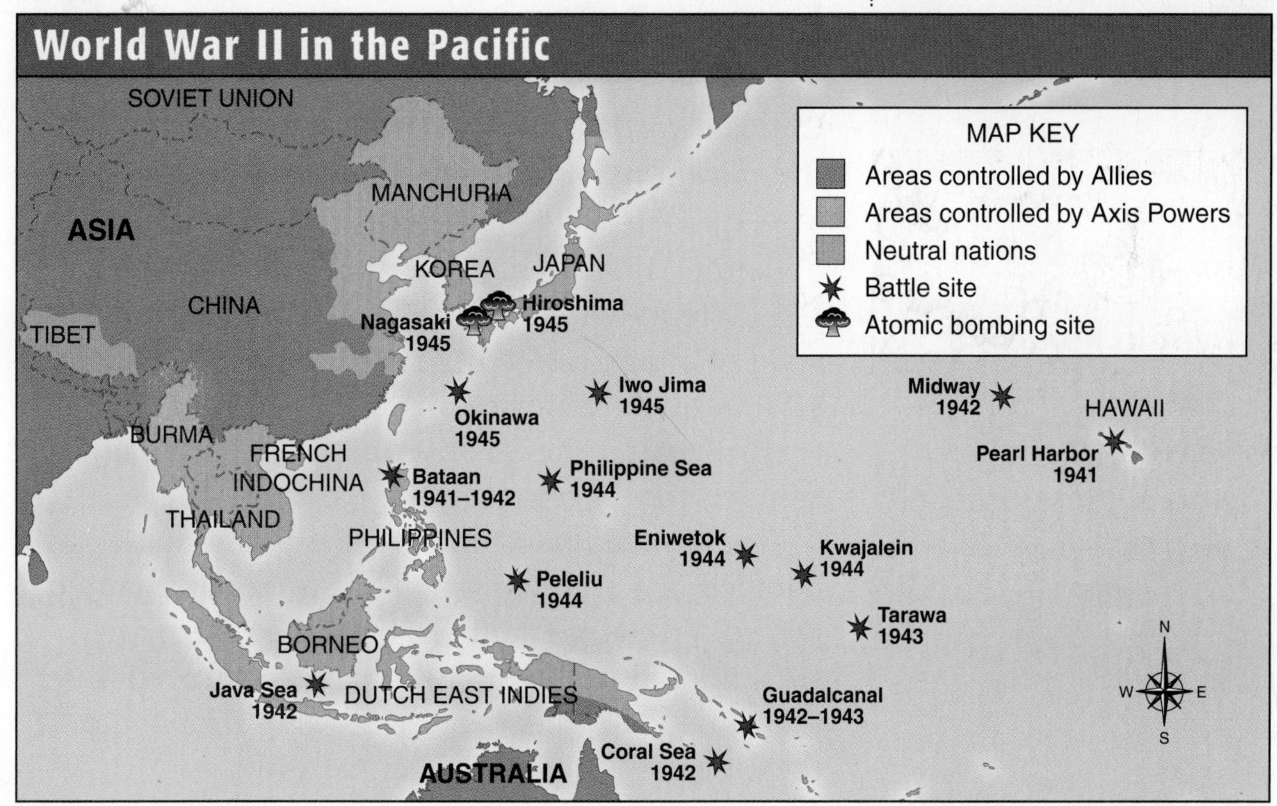

Atomic blast over Hiroshima, Japan

The War Ends

On June 6, 1944, the Allies landed in Normandy, France. The invasion was called **D-Day**. The Germans fought hard, but the Allies had too many soldiers and too many planes. By August, the Allies had freed Paris. Meanwhile, the Soviet army moved in from the east. The Germans were trapped. On May 8, 1945, Germany surrendered. Hitler shot himself to avoid being captured alive.

Japan remained the last undefeated Axis power. American planes bombed Tokyo. The city was in ruins. But the Japanese refused to surrender. Then on August 6, the United States introduced a new, grim weapon and dropped an **atomic bomb** on the city of Hiroshima. About 160,000 people were killed or wounded. Three days later, the United States dropped another atomic bomb on the city of Nagasaki. The Japanese surrendered, and World War II was over.

Lesson 2 Review

Choose words from the list that best complete the paragraphs. One word will not be used.

Word List

atomic bombs
Maginot Line
blitzkrieg
non-aggression
Pearl Harbor

Before Hitler attacked Poland, he signed a __1__ treaty with Stalin. The Germans used a style of attack called __2__. The Germans won several quick victories, but they could not defeat Great Britain. The Soviets and the cold winter stopped the Germans in the east.

The United States entered the war after Japan bombed __3__ in Hawaii. The Americans gained control of many Pacific islands. The Germans surrendered in 1945. The Japanese surrendered the same year after two __4__ were dropped on the cities of Hiroshima and Nagasaki.

LESSON 3

Horrors of World War II

Before You Read

- Why do some people feel they are better than others?
- Why might a nation's citizens fear people of different nationalities during a war?

As the Allies fought in Europe, they began to realize what type of enemy they were fighting. In 1935, the Nazis had passed laws that took away basic rights from Jews. One night in 1938, Hitler ordered the destruction of Jewish property. This night became known as *kristallnacht*, or the "night of the broken glass." After the war started, things grew even worse. The Germans began rounding up and killing Jews in places they had conquered.

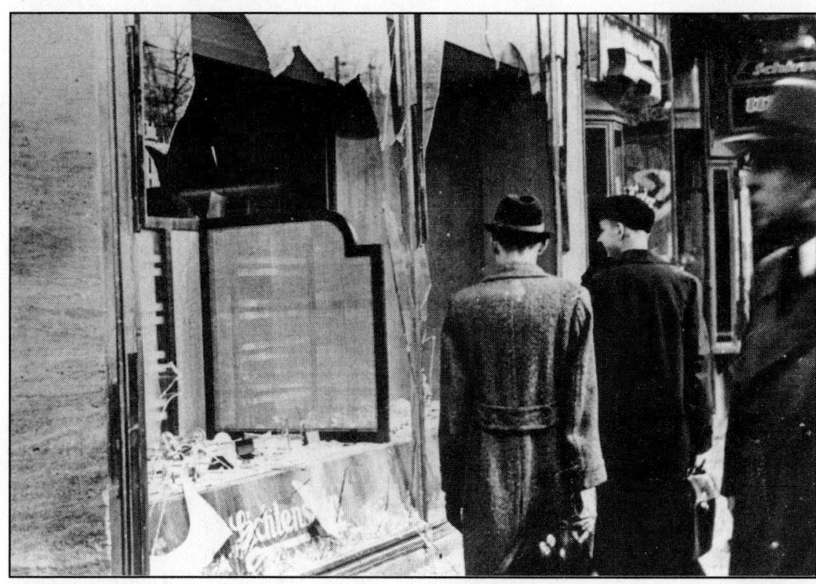

Hitler ordered the destruction of all Jewish property.

New Words

race
racism
anti-Semitism
genocide
concentration camps
Holocaust
disabilities
Nuremberg Trials
internment camps

People and Places

Auschwitz
Anne Frank
Slavs
Gypsies
Nuremberg

Jewish woman and child wearing the Star of David

Hitler's Hatred

Why did Hitler and the Nazis do this? They believed that in order to recover from World War I, the Germans needed to get rid of weak people. Hitler believed the German **race** was better and stronger than all others. This belief that one race is better than another is called **racism**.

Hitler and the Nazis especially hated Jewish people. **Anti-Semitism**, or hatred of Jews, has a long history. You have read about the pogroms in Russia and the killing of Jews during the Black Death. During World War II, Jewish people were forced to wear the symbol of the Star of David on their clothing to identify them at all times.

Hitler promised a "final solution to the Jewish question." He wanted all Jews killed. The goal of destroying an entire people is called **genocide**.

In the summer of 1941, the Nazis began their "final solution." Hitler was determined to meet this goal. During the war, about six million Jews were killed. That was about two out of every three Jews who lived in Europe before the war.

The Nazis murdered thousands of Jews right away. Others were packed into railroad cars and

Many Jews were sent to concentration camps.

shipped to **concentration camps**. One large camp was at Auschwitz in Poland. Without food or water, many prisoners died on the trains.

The concentration camps were slave-labor camps. The Nazis forced strong and healthy Jews to work. They immediately killed all those who couldn't work, including old or sick people as well as young children. When a worker got sick or injured, he or she was killed. Most Jews in concentration camps were killed in gas chambers. Others died from hunger, disease, or torture. This horror became known as the **Holocaust**.

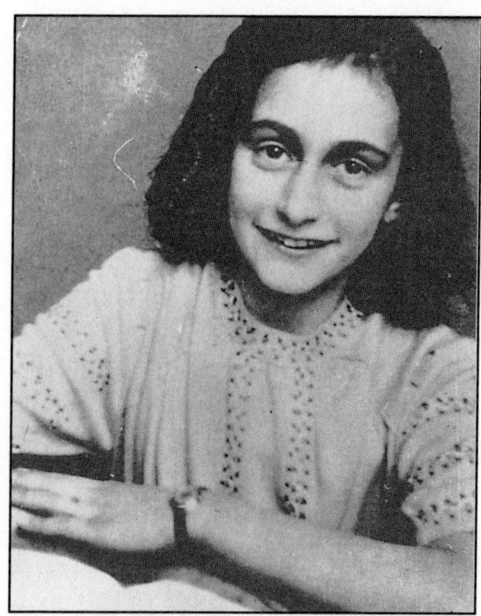
Anne Frank

Many Jews tried to escape. The diary of a girl named Anne Frank tells how Anne and her family hid in a friend's home for more than two years. In time, the Nazis found the Franks' hiding place. The family was sent to a concentration camp. Anne died in the camp in 1945.

Jews were not the only people to suffer. The Nazis also murdered Slavs, Gypsies, people with **disabilities**, and people who did not support the Nazis. After the war, Nazi leaders were brought to trial. They were charged with crimes against the human race. The trial was held in Nuremberg, the German city where the first anti-Semitic laws had been passed. Most of the Nazis brought to trial were found guilty during the **Nuremberg Trials**.

Racism in America

The Holocaust was the worst horror of World War II, but racism was not limited to Europe. After the Japanese bombed Pearl Harbor, many Americans feared the Japanese. They feared Japanese Americans, too. They worried whether Japanese Americans were loyal to the United States or to Japan.

Nuremberg Trials

In early 1942, President Franklin Roosevelt ordered that Japanese Americans be sent to **internment camps**. The camps were like prisons. The had armed guards. About 120,000 Japanese Americans were sent there. Canadians also sent about 26,000 Japanese Canadians to camps. The prisoners had done nothing wrong. Yet their freedom was taken.

Japanese American soldiers

Despite this treatment, 1,500 Japanese American soldiers asked to serve in the United States Army. They fought and won many medals for bravery. In 1988, the United States government officially apologized for sending Japanese Americans to the internment camps. It offered money to those who survived and to their families.

In addition to Japanese Americans, both African Americans and Mexican Americans experienced racism during the 1940s. Both groups were often treated badly. They began fighting for reform.

Lesson 3 Review

Choose words from the list that best complete the paragraphs. One word will not be used.

Word List

Nuremberg Trials
genocide
internment camps
concentration camps
Holocaust

Hitler and the Nazis believed the German race was better than all others. Hitler's "final solution" was __1__. Under his orders, six million Jews died. Some were simply shot. Others were sent to __2__. This horror became known as the __3__.

During World War II, the United States sent about 120,000 Japanese Americans to __4__. The government later apologized for taking away the rights of these American citizens. In the United States, there was also racism against African Americans and Mexican Americans.

LESSON 4

After World War II

Before You Read

- How might people who are not soldiers die during a war?
- What mistakes after World War I might the Allies want to avoid after World War II?

World War II was the deadliest war in history. In World War I, a total of 8.5 million soldiers died. That number doubled to about 17 million in World War II. In the Soviet Union alone, 7.5 million soldiers died. Germany lost 1.8 million soldiers in World War I. It lost 3.5 million soldiers in World War II. The number of American soldiers dead went up from 126,000 in World War I to 400,000 in World War II.

World War II was the deadliest and most damaging war in history.

New Words

civilians
firestorms
displaced persons
orphans
United Nations
General Assembly
Security Council
occupation
superpowers

People and Places

Coventry
Berlin
Dresden
Warsaw
Douglas MacArthur
Eleanor Roosevelt
Theodore Roosevelt

Civilians Dead

Even more **civilians** died in World War II than soldiers. You have read how six million Jews died during the Holocaust. The atomic bombs dropped on the cities of Hiroshima and Nagasaki killed 300,000. Other bombs killed millions of additional civilians as well.

Sometimes whole cities were destroyed. The Germans leveled much of Coventry in England. Allied bombing did the same to Berlin and Dresden in Germany. In Poland, Warsaw was destroyed. Bombings in Japan created **firestorms**. The bombs caused fires in wooden buildings. High winds spread these fires to other buildings.

Warsaw, Poland, after World War II

Millions of civilians also died from disease and hunger. The Soviet Union and China suffered the most. Historians think as many as 19 million Soviets and ten million Chinese died.

In addition, there was a high number of **displaced persons**. These were the people left without a home or a country. Europe had more than 12 million displaced persons. Some were **orphans**, or children whose parents were dead. Some were driven from their homes by the fighting or bombings. Others were prisoners of

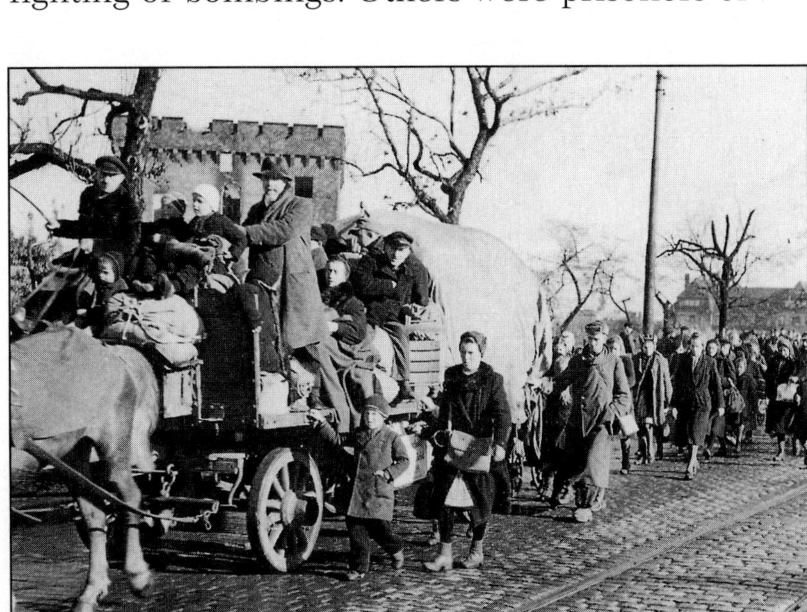

After World War II, many people had no place to live.

Today, the United Nations still works to maintain peace.

war or survivors of concentration camps. New borders for several nations in Europe caused more displaced people.

The United Nations

The League of Nations had failed to keep the peace after World War I. The Allies hoped to do a better job after World War II. In 1945, they created the **United Nations**, also called the UN, to keep the peace. There were two differences between the League of Nations and the UN. First, the United States was a member of the UN. Second, the UN had the power to use military force if necessary.

The United Nations still works to maintain peace. One section of the UN, the **General Assembly**, includes any nation that wants to join. Each member nation, big or small, gets one vote. Another section is the **Security Council**. Its job is to handle threats to peace. The Security Council has five members with permanent seats—China, France, Great Britain, Russia, and the United States. Elected members from ten other nations also serve on the Security Council. Each elected member serves a two-year term.

Many Changes

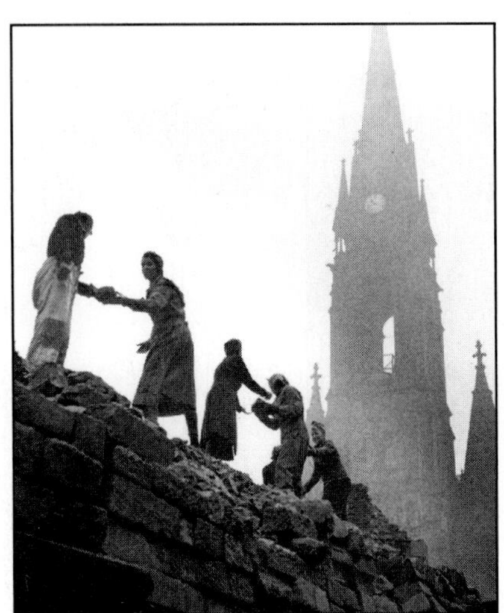
People working to rebuild a damaged city

World War II brought many changes. Japan was put under the rule of General Douglas MacArthur of the United States. He brought democracy to the Japanese. The Japanese got a new constitution. It protected the rights of individuals.

With Mussolini out of power, Italy joined the Allies. After the war, Italy became a republic. It also set up a democracy.

Germany was divided into four zones of military **occupation**. The Soviet Union controlled the zone in eastern Germany. The United States, France, and Great Britain controlled the three zones in western Germany.

After World War II, Great Britain and France were no longer considered great powers. The United States was clearly the world's strongest nation. It had the strongest economy. It also had the only atomic bombs.

The Soviet Union was clearly the second strongest. Despite great losses during the war, it had built up a massive army. People began thinking of the United States and the Soviet Union as the world's two **superpowers**.

Churchill, Roosevelt, and Stalin agreed to divide Germany into zones of occupation.

Eleanor Roosevelt (1884–1962)

People In History

Eleanor Roosevelt was the wife of President Franklin Roosevelt. She was introduced to politics at an early age because her uncle was President Theodore Roosevelt. In 1905, Eleanor married Franklin Roosevelt, who became president of the United States in 1933.

Eleanor brought great changes to the role of First Lady. She traveled around the country to learn the needs of the people. She held press conferences, wrote books, and spoke on the radio.

Eleanor particularly wanted to help the poor and the weak. She fought for new laws to help them. After her husband died in 1945, she worked for the United Nations. She helped to write the *Universal Declaration of Human Rights*. It called for people in all countries to be treated fairly. People often called Eleanor the "First Lady of the World" for her many good deeds.

Lesson 4 Review

Choose words from the list that best complete the paragraphs. One word will not be used.

World War II was the deadliest war in human history. More soldiers and __1__ died in this war than in any other war. Sometimes whole cities were destroyed. In Japan, city bombings created __2__.

After the war, people hoped the __3__ would do a better job than the League of Nations had done. Japan accepted democracy. Germany was divided into four zones of __4__. Great Britain and France lost power. The United States and the Soviet Union became the world's two superpowers.

Word List

occupation
firestorms
civilians
superpowers
United Nations

Chapter 31: Using What You've Learned

Summary

- Germany invaded Poland on September 1, 1939. The Allies declared war on Germany two days later, beginning World War II.
- The Soviet Union joined the Allies after Hitler broke his non-aggression treaty with Stalin. The United States entered the war on the side of the Allies after the Japanese attacked Pearl Harbor in Hawaii.
- World War II ended after the United States dropped atomic bombs on the Japanese cities of Hiroshima and Nagasaki.
- Genocide and racism were two horrors of World War II. Millions of Jews and other people were killed in Nazi concentration camps. The United States also sent 120,000 Japanese Americans to internment camps.

Find Out More!

After reading Chapter 31, you're ready to go online. **Explore Zone**, **Quiz Time**, and **Amazing Facts** bring this chapter of world history alive.

Visit www.exploreSV.com and type in the chapter code **Ch31**.

Vocabulary

Number your paper from 1 to 4. Write the letter of the correct answer.

1. The Axis Powers included Germany, Japan, and _____.

a. France
b. Italy
c. the United States
d. Great Britain

2. The Germans called their type of fighting blitzkrieg, or _____.

a. "non-aggression."
b. "neutrality"
c. "lightning war"
d. "appeasement"

3. D-Day was the Allied invasion of Normandy in _____.

a. Germany
b. the Soviet Union
c. Japan
d. France

4. The UN Security Council has _____ members with permanent seats.

a. five
b. fifteen
c. ten
d. twenty

Comprehension

Number your paper from 1 to 6. Write one or more sentences to answer each question below.

1. How did the Great Depression affect Europe?
2. How did Hitler try to conquer Great Britain?
3. Why was the Battle of Midway important in the war in the Pacific?
4. Why did more civilians than soldiers die in World War II?
5. How was the United Nations different from the League of Nations?
6. Why were the United States and Soviet Union called superpowers?

Critical Thinking

Cause and Effect Number your paper from 1 to 5. Read the causes in the left column. Then choose the correct effect from the right column. Write the letter of the correct effect.

Cause	Effect
1. The Treaty of Versailles treated Germany harshly, so	**a.** Congress passed several laws in support of neutrality.
2. Many Amcricans wanted a policy of strict isolation, so	**b.** Europe had many displaced persons.
3. Hitler did not want to fight a two-front war, so	**c.** Japanese Americans were sent to internment camps.
4. After the attack on Pearl Harbor, many Americans feared Japanese Americans, so	**d.** it created more anger than peace.
5. After World War II, several nations in Europe had new borders, so	**e.** he signed a non-aggression treaty with Stalin.

Writing

Write a paragraph explaining how the causes of World War I and World War II were alike and how they were different.

UNIT 8

Into the 21st Century

1945–Present

Throughout world history there have been some problems that never seem to go away. There are still wars. There is still poverty. But there are also opportunities to improve life.

This unit explains some of the challenges that have faced the world since World War II. There have been smaller wars in many areas of the world. But there also has been great progress. In the late 1900s and early 2000s, medicine, space technology, and communications have improved. New technologies, such as the Internet, have brought people closer together. The advances of this century are the results of the efforts of many past civilizations. Today, the history of our world continues, with each of us playing a part.

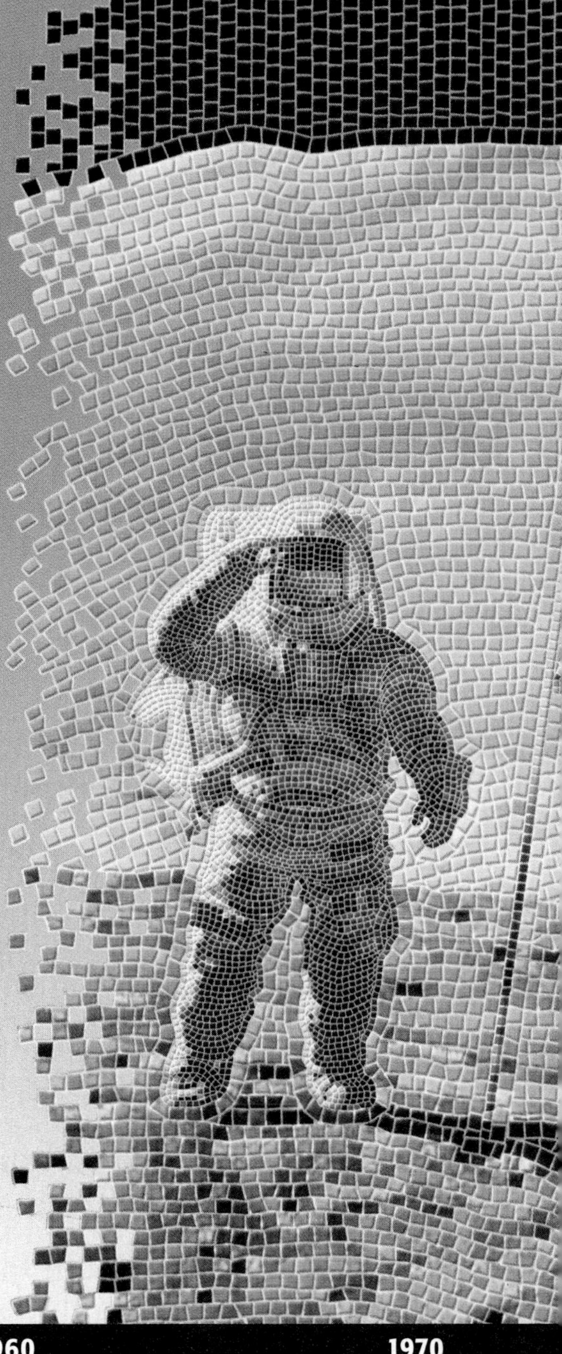

A.D. 1945 1950 1960 1970

1945
Mao Zedong leads the Communists in a civil war in China.

1959
Fidel Castro takes over the island nation of Cuba.

1960
Mali becomes independent from France.

1964
President Lyndon Johnson signs an act giving Americans more equal rights.

1980 | 1990 | 2000 | A.D.

1979
Leaders from Egypt and Israel sign a peace agreement.

1989
The government of East Germany falls, and the Berlin Wall is torn down.

1999
Most European countries agree to use one form of money.

2001
Four airplanes are taken over and used as bombs in the United States.

LESSON 1

The Cold War

New Words
Cold War
nuclear
socialism
capitalism
Iron Curtain
containment
blockade
Berlin Airlift
Berlin Wall
missiles
satellite

People and Places
Budapest
Fidel Castro
John F. Kennedy
Neil Armstrong
Edwin "Buzz" Aldrin

Before You Read

- What are some differences between communism and democracy?
- Why might two countries become enemies?

Soon after World War II, the Soviet Union and the United States became enemies. This new struggle was called the **Cold War**. It was a different kind of war. It was "cold" because neither side declared war. Neither side invaded the other. Still, people were afraid that the Cold War might turn into a regular war between the two superpowers. Since both sides could make atomic bombs, people were also afraid there might be a **nuclear** war.

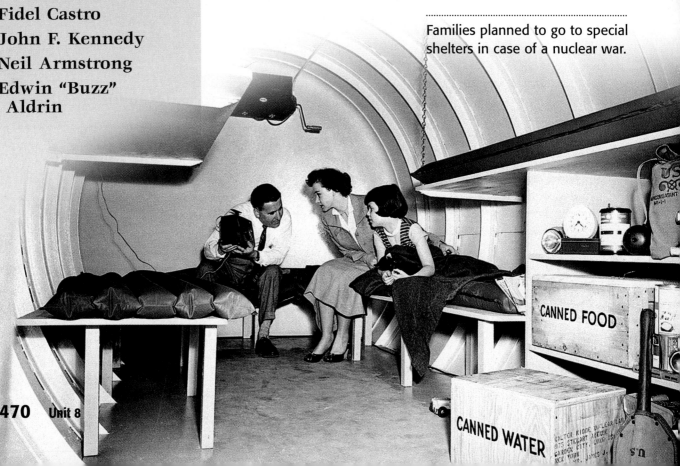

Families planned to go to special shelters in case of a nuclear war.

Different Ideas

The Soviets and the Americans disagreed about many things. A dictator ruled the Soviet Union. An elected president was the head of the United States. The Soviet Union had one political party, the Communist Party. The United States had several political parties. There were Republicans, Democrats, and others.

The two superpowers had different economic systems as well. The Soviet system was called **socialism**. Under socialism, the Soviet government ran all the industries. An individual person had very little power. In the United States, private companies ran most industries. This is called **capitalism**. Each superpower tried to show that its system was the best.

This cartoon shows the world being squeezed by nuclear bombs from Russia and the United States.

Eastern Europe

The Soviet Union wanted to control the countries between itself and Germany. It wanted to protect itself from German invasions. By 1946, the Soviet Union controlled Eastern Europe. Winston Churchill, the prime minister of Great Britain, said that an **Iron Curtain** had fallen across Eastern Europe. This meant that Eastern Europe was separated from Western Europe by different ideas about government and economics.

The United States and the Soviet Union During the Cold War

United States	Soviet Union
■ An elected president was the head of government. ■ The United States had several political parties. ■ Capitalism was the economic system of the United States.	■ A dictator ruled the Soviet Union. ■ The Soviet Union had one political party, the Communist party. ■ Socialism was the economic system of the Soviet Union.

The United States didn't want the Soviets to control any more land. So it adopted a policy of **containment**. The Soviets could keep what they already controlled. But they would not be allowed to spread. The United States and its allies wanted to contain communism.

The Berlin Blockade

In Chapter 31, you read that after World War II, Germany was divided into four zones of occupation. Germany's capital, Berlin, was also divided into four zones, but Berlin was inside the Soviet zone of Germany. Americans had to go through Soviet-controlled East Germany to get to their zone within Berlin.

In June 1948, Stalin ordered a **blockade**. He wanted to see if the United States would stop him. The Soviets blocked all land traffic coming into Berlin from western nations. Germans in West Berlin could not get food and supplies.

The United States and Great Britain did not want to go to war and invade Berlin. Instead, they

After World War II, the city of Berlin was divided into four zones of occupation. Which country controlled East Berlin?

flew over the blockade. For 321 days, the **Berlin Airlift** brought supplies to people in West Berlin. In May 1949, the Soviets lifted the blockade.

American and British planes provided food and supplies to the people of West Berlin.

New alliances formed. Europe was clearly divided into Western Europe and Eastern Europe. In 1949, the Western nations signed a treaty to form the North Atlantic Treaty Organization (NATO). These nations agreed to go to war against a country that attacked any member of NATO. In 1955, the Soviets and other Eastern European nations created an alliance, too. It was called the Warsaw Pact. Each group used the threat of nuclear war to try to keep peace.

The city of Berlin remained divided. Many East Germans tried to escape to the West. In 1961, the East German government built a wall through the city of Berlin. The **Berlin Wall** became a symbol of the Cold War.

The Cold War Spreads

Communism spread throughout the world. Countries such as China and Vietnam came under Communist rule. As communism spread, the Cold War got stronger. Over the next several years, the Cold War caused many struggles.

In 1956, more than 50,000 Polish workers went on strike. They demanded freedom from Communist rule. The Soviets forced them to end the strike. The same year, people in Budapest, Hungary, started a rebellion against communism. Thousands of Hungarians died. The Communists later arrested and killed the leader of the Hungarian rebellion.

In 1959, Communist Fidel Castro took over Cuba. The Soviets put **missiles** in Cuba. This frightened people in the United States, because Cuba was only 90 miles away. In 1962, U.S. President John F. Kennedy demanded that the missiles be removed.

President Kennedy (right) with his brother, Robert Kennedy (left)

Neil Armstrong

The Cuban Missile Crisis was the closest the United States and the Soviet Union came to declaring war on each other. For 13 days, the world waited for nuclear war. The Soviets removed the missiles after the United States agreed not to invade Cuba. Kennedy agreed in private to remove American missiles from Turkey.

The Space Race

The Cold War also led to a space race. The Soviet Union and the United States each wanted to prove that they had more advanced technology. In 1957, the Soviets shocked the world by launching *Sputnik*, the first **satellite**. Soon both countries sent rockets around Earth. They also sent spacecrafts to explore other planets. In July 1969, the United States became the first country to send people to the moon. Neil Armstrong and Edwin "Buzz" Aldrin walked on the moon for two hours and left behind an American flag.

Lesson 1 Review

Choose words from the list that best complete the paragraphs. One word will not be used.

Word List

Iron Curtain
containment
space race
Cold War
blockade

After World War II, the United States and the Soviet Union entered the __1__. It was a struggle to prove which system of government was better.

The United States adopted the policy of __2__. The Soviets tried to control Berlin by using a __3__. An airlift brought supplies to the people of West Berlin. A wall was built to separate the western and eastern parts of the city.

The Cold War created struggles in such places as Poland, Hungary, and Cuba. After the Soviets launched *Sputnik*, the first satellite, a __4__ began.

LESSON 2

Communism in Asia

Before You Read

- Why might some people prefer a Communist form of government?
- Why might the United States have wanted to stop the spread of communism?

The Cold War struggle went far beyond Europe. It was felt in the Americas and in Africa. But, some of the worst struggles of the Cold War were in Asia. There, the Cold War turned "hot."

There were wars in Korea and Vietnam. Americans fought in both wars to stop the spread of communism. The Soviets didn't fight, but they supported the Asian Communists.

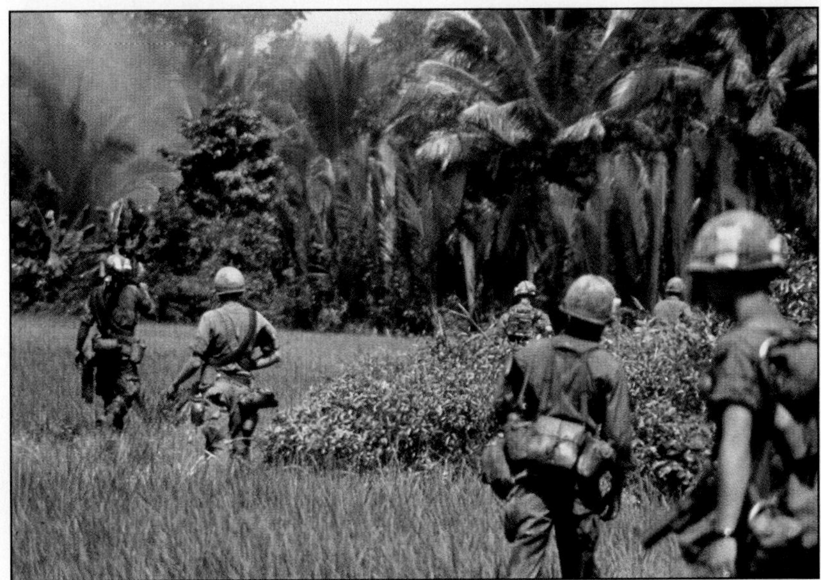

During the Vietnam War, Americans fought to stop the spread of communism.

New Words

Tet Offensive
negotiations
cease-fire
Great Leap Forward
Cultural Revolution
Red Guards
Tiananmen Square Massacre

People and Places

Mao Zedong
Chiang Kai-shek
Taiwan
North Korea
South Korea
Ho Chi Minh
North Vietnam
South Vietnam
Deng Xiaoping

Communism in China

In late 1945, a civil war began in China. Mao Zedong led the Communists, and Chiang Kai-shek led the Nationalists. The bitter war ended in 1949 with a Communist victory. Chiang Kai-shek fled to the Chinese island of Taiwan. China, the largest country in Asia, was under Communist rule.

Mao Zedong became dictator of China as the Chairman of the Communist Party. He said he wanted what was best for the Chinese people.

"We Chinese Communists . . . base all our actions on the highest interests of the broadest masses of the Chinese people and [we believe in] the justice of our cause . . . and are ready at all times to give our lives for the cause."

The Korean War

After World War II, Korea was divided. The Soviets set up a Communist government in North Korea. The Americans set up a non-Communist government in South Korea. In 1950, North Korea

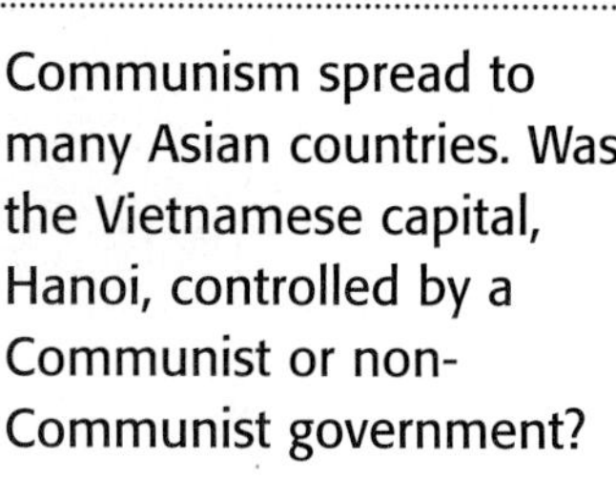

Communism spread to many Asian countries. Was the Vietnamese capital, Hanoi, controlled by a Communist or non-Communist government?

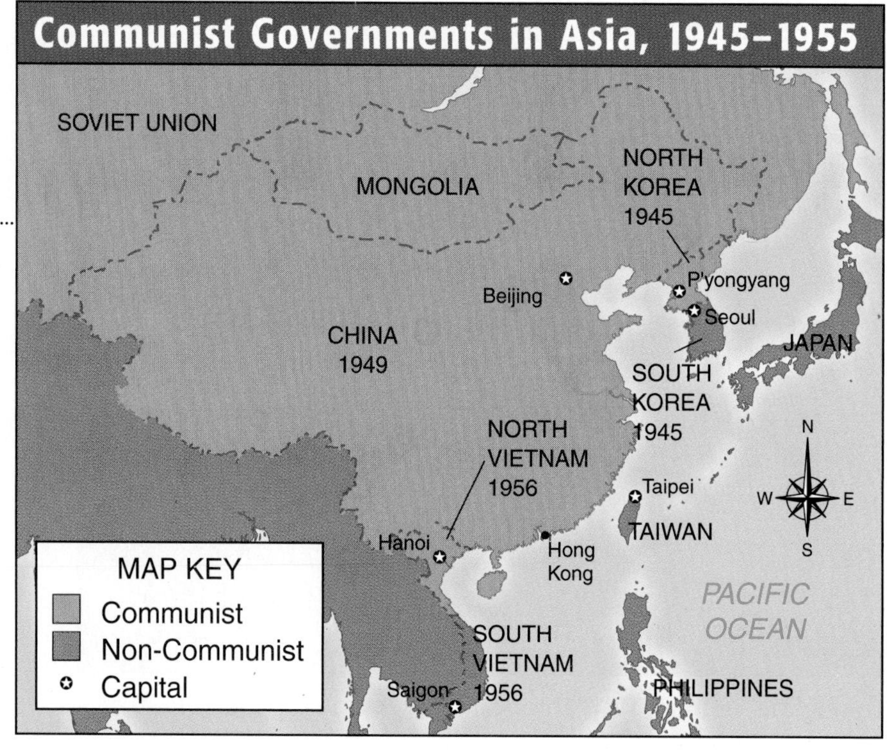

attacked South Korea. The United Nations (UN) responded quickly. The United States led a UN force to fight the North Koreans. They soon pushed the Communists out of South Korea. It looked like an easy victory.

Mao Zedong

Then Mao Zedong sent a huge Chinese army to support the North Koreans. They drove the UN forces back. The Korean War ended in 1953 when both sides agreed to an armistice.

The French in Vietnam

Vietnam had become a French colony in the 1800s. Later, the Japanese occupied Vietnam during World War II. After the war, the French wanted Vietnam back. But in 1945, the Communist leader Ho Chi Minh announced that Vietnam was an independent nation. The French refused to recognize Ho Chi Minh or his government, and war broke out. The Vietnamese defeated the French in 1954.

Many Vietnamese were not Communists. In the treaty that ended the war, Vietnam was divided in half. As in Korea, the Communists controlled the north. The non-Communists controlled the south.

Ho Chi Minh

The Americans in Vietnam

In 1957, the Communists began a second war to unite Vietnam under their rule. The Soviet Union and Communist China supported North Vietnam. The United States supported South Vietnam.

At first, the Communists were winning. Then in 1965, the United States sent in troops. The war grew more deadly with the **Tet Offensive**. The North Vietnamese launched this attack on South Vietnam in 1968.

By 1968, more than 500,000 American soldiers were in Vietnam. More than 58,000 Americans died during the war. In the United States, many people demanded an end to the war.

Soldiers take part in a parade after the Vietnam War

Slowly, the Americans began to leave Vietnam. They also began **negotiations** with the Communists. In 1973, a **cease-fire** agreement was signed. With the Americans out of the Vietnam War, communism continued to spread. In 1975, South Vietnam was defeated. After 30 years, the Communists controlled all of Vietnam.

Changes in China

Mao Zedong brought changes to China. His methods were often brutal. In 1958, Mao began his **Great Leap Forward**. He forced peasants to work on huge collective farms. Mao believed this system would increase food production. But most people hated the collectives. They didn't produce enough food, and many Chinese starved to death.

In 1966, Mao began the **Cultural Revolution**. Millions of young students, or **Red Guards**, joined the fight. Mao ordered them to attack anyone who was not a perfect Communist. Doctors, teachers,

During the Cultural Revolution, millions of young Chinese students supported Mao Zedong.

writers, and others were named "enemies of the state." The Red Guards traveled throughout China, destroying books and ancient art.

The Red Guards got out of control. At last, in 1968, Mao Zedong sent an army to break up the Red Guards. The Cultural Revolution was over.

Mao died in 1976, and Deng Xiaoping soon became the leader of China. He was not as harsh as Mao. Under his leadership, China improved its industries and made many advances.

Then in 1989, Chinese students began to protest against communism. The Chinese government took action. At one protest in Tiananmen Square in Beijing, the government sent tanks in and killed hundreds of protesters. The attack became known as the **Tiananmen Square Massacre**.

During the Tiananmen Square Massacre, this protester tried to stop the tanks.

Lesson 2 Review

Choose words from the list that best complete the paragraphs. One word will not be used.

Communists took control of China in 1949, and __1__ became dictator. The Soviets set up a Communist government in North Korea. The United Nations and the United States prevented the Communists from taking over South Korea.

In 1945, __2__ began a war for Vietnamese independence from France. In a second war, the Communist army forced United States troops to leave Vietnam.

In 1966, Mao Zedong began the __3__. He had to use the Chinese army to restore order. After his death, Deng Xiaoping became the leader of China. In 1989, hundreds of Chinese protesters were killed in the __4__.

Word List

Ho Chi Minh

Mao Zedong

cease-fire

Cultural Revolution

Tiananmen Square Massacre

Chapter 32: Using What You've Learned

Summary

- During the Cold War, the United States and its allies tried to contain communism.
- In 1948, the Soviets blocked all land traffic from western nations into Berlin. The East German government built the Berlin Wall in 1961 to separate West Germany from East Germany.
- Communism spread, causing many struggles in parts of Asia, Eastern Europe, and Cuba.
- In 1949, Communists won a civil war in China. Mao Zedong became the dictator of China.
- North Korea and North Vietnam were controlled by Communist leaders. Wars began when the Communists in both countries tried to take over non-Communist areas.

Find Out More!

After reading Chapter 32, you're ready to go online. **Explore Zone**, **Quiz Time**, and **Amazing Facts** bring this chapter of world history alive.

Visit www.exploreSV.com and type in the chapter code **Ch32**.

Vocabulary

Number your paper from 1 to 5. Finish the sentences from Group A with words from Group B. Write the letter of the correct answer.

Group A

1. The United States adopted a policy of _____ to keep communism from spreading.
2. The Soviets used a _____ to stop all land traffic from western nations into Berlin.
3. Supplies were brought to West Berlin by the _____.
4. During the _____, Chinese peasants were forced to work on collective farms.
5. In 1989, the Chinese government killed hundreds of protesters in the _____.

Group B

a. Berlin Airlift

b. Tiananmen Square Massacre

c. containment

d. blockade

e. Great Leap Forward

Comprehension

Number your paper from 1 to 5. Write **True** for each sentence that is true. Write **False** for each sentence that is false.

1. After World War II, different ideas about government and economics separated Eastern Europe from Western Europe.
2. Members of NATO agreed to go to war against a country that attacked any other member.
3. The Warsaw Pact was made up of the United States and Western European nations.
4. The United States fought in Korea and Vietnam to stop the spread of communism.
5. During the Cultural Revolution, Chinese students were encouraged to study books and ancient art.

Critical Thinking

Points of View Number your paper from 1 to 5. Read each sentence below. Write **Communism** if the point of view is from someone who supports communism. If the point of view is from someone who supports democracy, write **Democracy**.

1. The best person to rule our country is someone who is elected by the people.
2. We should have only one political party.
3. The government should run all the industries in our country.
4. Individuals in our country should have very few rights.
5. Private companies should run most industries in our country.

Writing

Write a paragraph telling how the Korean War and the Vietnam War were alike and how they were different.

Skill Builder: Comparing Circle Graphs

We can learn about the military build up of the Soviet Union and the United States during the Cold War by **comparing circle graphs**.

The circle graphs below show the percent of missile bases and radar systems set up by the United States and the Soviet Union. A **missile** is a rocket that can be aimed to hit a target. **Radar** uses radio to find objects such as missiles.

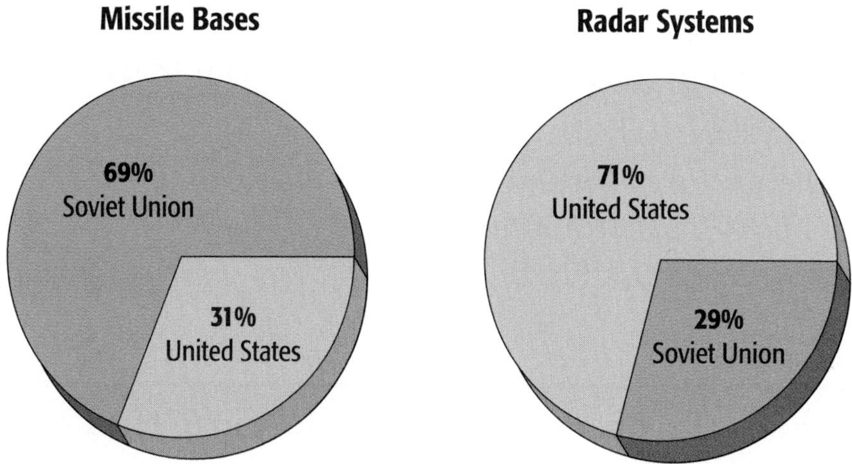

Number your paper from 1 to 5. Write the word or number that best completes each sentence. One word or number will not be used.

more **31** **69** **less**
United States **Soviet Union**

1. During the Cold War, the Soviet Union had _____ percent of the missile bases.
2. The United States had _____ percent of the missile bases.
3. The United States had _____ radar systems than the Soviet Union.
4. The _____ had 29 percent of the radar systems.
5. During the Cold War, the Soviet Union had _____ of a chance of finding missiles with radar than the United States.

LESSON 1

Independence in Asia and Africa

Before You Read

- How did World War II improve chances for colonies to win independence?
- Why might colonial powers be afraid to give independence to the people they controlled?

You have read how India gained independence in 1947. India inspired many other colonies to seek independence. After World War II, many colonies saw a chance to gain independence from their colonial rulers.

In Asia, several paths led to independence. The United States gave freedom to the Philippines in 1946. In 1948, the British gave independence to Burma in Southeast Asia. The Indonesians fought the Dutch for four years and gained independence in 1949. The Vietnamese fought the French and won their independence in 1954.

New Words

uprising
descendants
apartheid
illegal

People and Places

South Africa
Tunisia
Algeria
Gold Coast
Kikuyu
Kenya
Mau Mau
the Congo
Katanga
Mobutu Sese Seko
Zaire
Democratic Republic of the Congo
Kwame Nkrumah

The Vietnamese celebrated after winning independence.

Did You Know?

Happy Kwanzaa!

Kwanzaa is a holiday that is celebrated in the United States but has its roots in Africa. It was created in 1966 by Dr. Maulana Kalenga. The name of the holiday comes from the Swahili word *kwanza*, which means "first fruits."

Kwanzaa is celebrated from December 26 to January 1 every year. In Africa, Kwanzaa is a time to celebrate the year's harvest. In the United States, people gather to sing, dance, eat, and enjoy the company of family and friends.

Africans felt hopeful that they would gain independence after World War II as well. After all, many Africans fought for the Allies and helped in the victory. But in 1950, nearly all of Africa was still controlled by Great Britain, France, Belgium, and Portugal. Only South Africa, Ethiopia, Egypt, and Liberia were independent.

North Africa

The French had three colonies in North Africa. They were Morocco, Tunisia, and Algeria. The French had no plan to give independence to any of them. The French put the leaders of independence movements in jail. However, the North Africans began to use guerrilla tactics.

In Chapter 32, you read how France had fought to keep control of Vietnam. The French were weak from trying to fight battles in Asia and Africa at the same time. In 1956, the French gave Tunisia independence. A year later, they did the same for Morocco.

Algeria was a French province. Many Europeans lived in Algeria and considered it their home. But nine out of ten Algerians were African. They did not want to be part of France. They wanted their own country. From 1954 to 1961, they fought a bitter war for independence. In 1962, the French declared Algeria independent.

South of the Sahara Desert

The British colony of the Gold Coast gained independence in 1957. It took the ancient African name Ghana. In 1960, Great Britain gave Nigeria its independence. Mali gained independence from France the same year. Several smaller colonies in West Africa soon gained independence.

Many of the Europeans living in East Africa wanted to keep things the way they were. They worried what might happen if Africans gained control. In the early 1950s, the Kikuyu people in

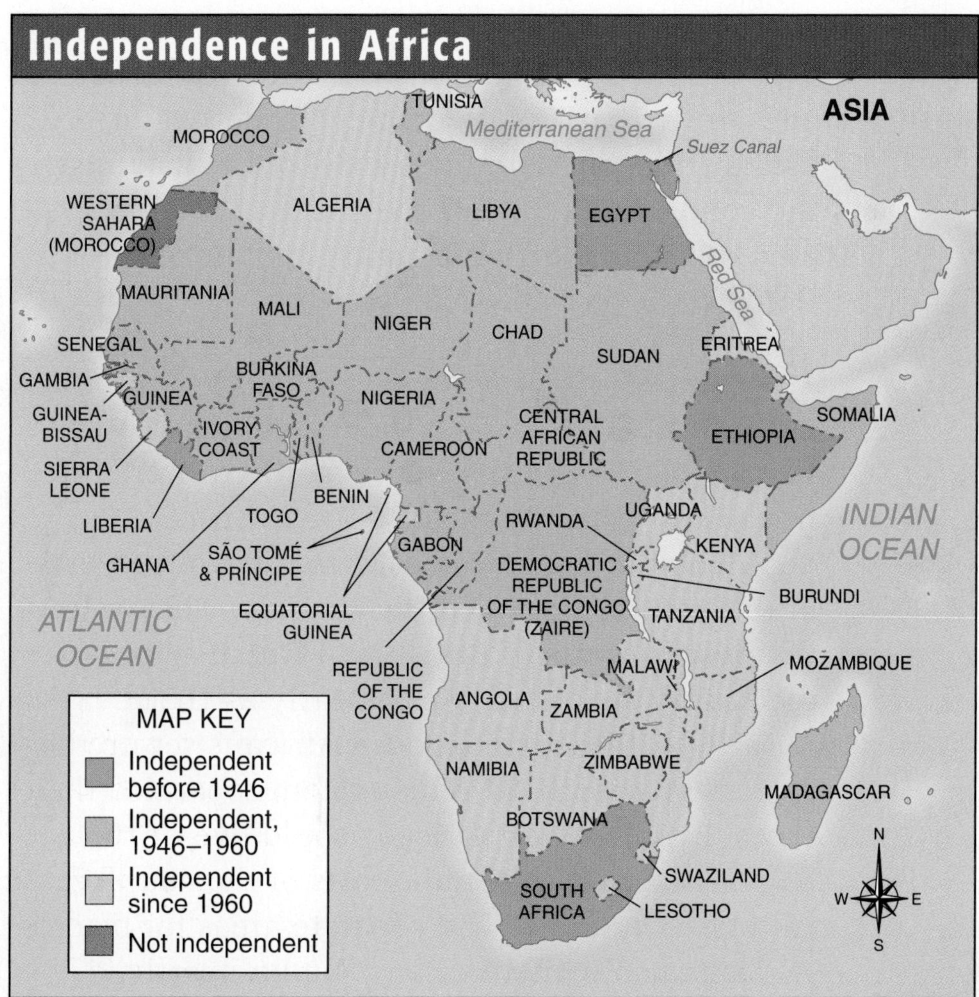

During the 20th century, African countries gained independence from European powers. Did the East African country of Somalia gain independence before or after 1961?

Kenya formed a group called the Mau Mau. This group wanted to drive the Europeans out of Kenya. The Mau Mau led an **uprising** against the British that lasted five years. Around 100 Europeans died. More than 2,000 Africans loyal to the British also died. The British government then took action and killed more than 10,000 Kikuyu. The Kenyans continued to struggle for independence. They held elections in 1963. Later that year, they won their freedom.

The Belgium Congo

The Belgians left the Congo in 1960. They did little to prepare the people for independence. Civil war soon broke out. One part of the Congo was called Katanga. It had rich copper mines. Katanga tried to break away from the Congo.

Belgium and the UN stepped in. After four years of struggle, the Congolese army took control and unified the Congo. Its new leader was a dictator named Mobutu Sese Seko. He renamed the country Zaire. After the death of Seko in 1997, Zaire became the Democratic Republic of the Congo.

Mobutu Sese Seko

South Africa

South Africa had been independent since 1910. But the black Africans who lived there were not free. They made up most of South Africa's population. White Africans, less than 20 percent of the population, ruled the country. They were the **descendants** of British and Dutch settlers who came to South Africa as early as 1652.

In 1948, these white South Africans set up the system of **apartheid**. This system separated the races. By law, black Africans could live or run businesses only in certain parts of the country. All public buildings had separate areas for black Africans and white Africans. Under apartheid, black South Africans couldn't vote or hold public office.

Under apartheid, public buildings were separated for black and white Africans.

Kwame Nkrumah (1909–1972)

People In History

Kwame Nkrumah was the son of a goldsmith. He grew up in the Gold Coast but later went to school in Great Britain and the United States. Nkrumah returned to the Gold Coast in 1947. He immediately led protests and boycotts to win independence for the country. The British arrested Nkrumah in 1950 but released him a year later.

The Gold Coast gained independence in 1957. In 1960, the country changed its name to Ghana. Nkrumah was Ghana's first president. He built up many of Ghana's industries and gained total power.

Nkrumah then made it **illegal** to challenge his power. Ghana's industries began losing money, and the country fell deeply into debt. Many well-educated people left Ghana. In 1966, while Nkrumah was out of the country, army leaders took over his government.

Lesson 1 Review

Choose words from the list that best complete the paragraphs. One word will not be used.

Word List
- Belgium
- Kenya
- apartheid
- France
- uprising

Many Asian countries gained independence in the years following World War II. African countries also struggled for independence. __1__ gave independence to Tunisia and Morocco. After a bitter war, Algeria gained independence, too.

The Mau Mau led a revolt against the British for independence of __2__. A civil war broke out in the Congo after the region gained independence from __3__. In South Africa, the white leaders set up a system of __4__ to separate blacks from whites.

LESSON 2

Results of Colonization

New Words
dictatorship
ethnic strife
self-reliant

People and Places
Ibo
Biafra
Burundi
Rwanda
Sri Lanka

Before You Read

- Why were some people better prepared for independence than others?
- What are the things a new nation needs in order to have a good economy?

You have read how many former colonies around the world gained independence. People celebrated winning their freedom. They danced in the streets or joined hands and sang songs. Many countries made their date of independence a national holiday. But freedom brought huge changes to the former colonies. The new countries faced tough questions. What kind of government would be best? How should the economy be run? What should the country's foreign policy be?

Children in Mali celebrated their first independence day in 1960.

These people are supporting one leader in the Congo civil war.

After Independence

Some new nations were better prepared to answer these questions than others. In India, the British had sent some Indians to school. They also had allowed certain Indians to work in the colonial government. This made it a little easier for Indians to rule themselves.

The people of the Congo were not as well prepared. The Belgians did little to educate Africans in their colony. When the Belgians left Africa, the dictator Mobutu Sese Seko took over. After his death, the people of the Congo were not prepared to run the country. They entered a bitter civil war in 1998.

Choosing Democracy

After gaining independence, many nations tried to establish a democracy. But a democracy is difficult to maintain. A **dictatorship** is perhaps the easiest government to set up. Most often, the person with the most military power takes charge. They can usually do this in only a few hours.

A democracy, on the other hand, is very difficult to create. It needs three main ingredients. First, democracy needs experience. This comes with time. People need to establish democratic traditions. In the United States, for example, it took a long time before true democracy was established. The United States became independent in 1776, but slavery was legal until 1863. Women could not vote until 1920.

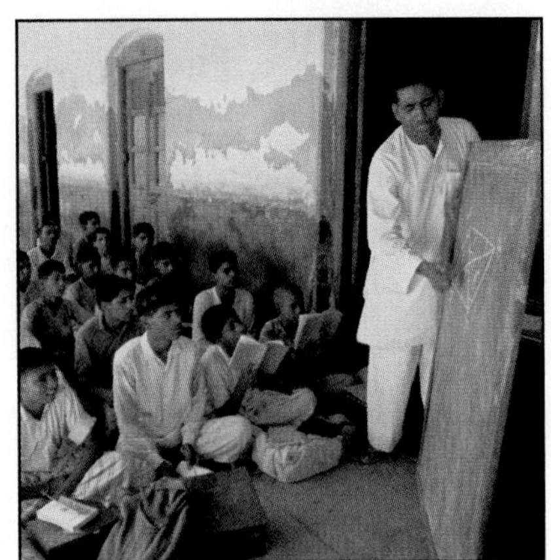

Public education in India

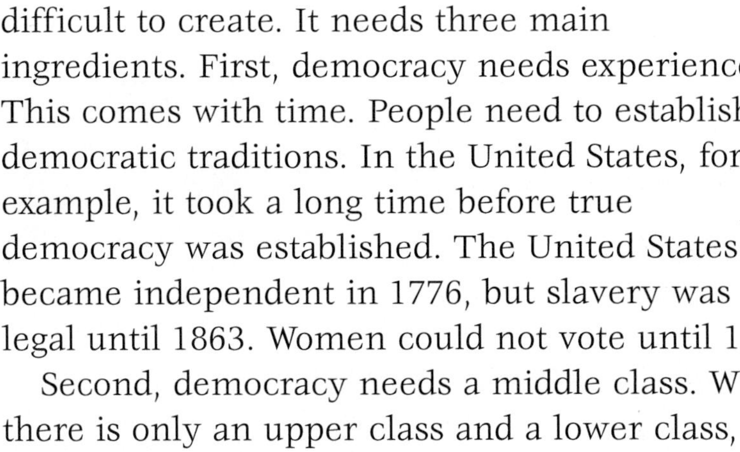

Second, democracy needs a middle class. When there is only an upper class and a lower class, there is often fighting. The upper class might treat the lower class poorly. A democracy needs teachers, business owners, and others who are neither very rich nor very poor.

The third need of a democracy is public education. A democracy must have citizens who can read and think about important issues. Then they can make wise choices when voting. Many former colonies lacked experience, a middle class, and educated citizens. So dictators took over many nations in Latin America, Asia, and Africa.

Ethnic Conflict

Nigerian mother and children

Former colonies faced yet another problem. You read in Chapter 28 how Europeans created colonies that often included people from different ethnic groups. Europeans did not attempt to unite the different ethnic groups. When a colony became independent, the different ethnic groups began to fight one another.

The West African colony of Nigeria declared its independence from Great Britain in 1960. One ethnic group, the Ibo, was very successful. Some of the other ethnic groups wanted their own success. In 1967, a civil war broke out. The Ibo created their own state called Biafra. In 1970, the civil war ended, and Biafra was destroyed. Nearly one million people died.

This kind of **ethnic strife** affected many other new nations. In Africa, it caused war in Burundi and Rwanda. In Asia, ethnic strife also brought trouble to Sri Lanka and Indonesia.

Economic Development

Every former colony faced its own economic challenges. Some new nations had many valuable natural resources. For example, Nigeria had large supplies of oil. Money made from selling oil helped Nigerians recover from their civil war.

Other former colonies did not have many resources. They had relied on the colonial rulers for their goods. They struggled to create successful, independent economies.

In the beginning, most new nations adopted some form of socialism. Their governments developed new industries. They limited foreign trade. They wanted their nations to be **self-reliant**, or economically independent. These new nations felt they had been tied to foreign powers long enough.

Oil drilling is common along the southern coast of Nigeria.

But being self-reliant did not work well in most of the new nations. By the 1980s, the nations became more open to trade. Governments gave up some of their control over industry. People made more of their own economic decisions.

African leaders met in 2001 to talk about trade.

Foreign Policy

The new nations also needed foreign policies. Because the Cold War was the most pressing issue, the nations had basically three choices. They could side with the United States, side with the Soviet Union, or remain neutral. Many new nations tried to remain neutral.

Remaining a neutral nation, however, wasn't easy during the Cold War. If a nation needed something from the United States, it could not simply trade freely. It had to worry that the Soviet Union might think it was taking sides. If a nation traded with the Soviet Union, the United States might think it was becoming a Communist nation.

Lesson 2 Review

Choose words from the list that best complete the paragraphs. One word will not be used.

Word List

middle class
Biafra
ethnic strife
self-reliant
neutral

Some nations were better prepared for independence than others. Dictators quickly took control of some nations. Countries wanting a democracy needed experience, a __1__, and educated citizens.

In Nigeria and other countries in Africa and Asia, __2__ led to civil war. Many new nations wanted to be __3__ but had to open up their economies to the rest of the world. In foreign policy, many new nations tried to remain __4__, but this was not easy during the Cold War.

LESSON 3

Latin America After 1945

Before You Read

- Why do many Latin Americans live in poverty?
- Why is it dangerous for any country to rely on one crop or resource?

New Words

social unrest
coup
one-crop economies
immigrate
illegal immigration

People and Places

Costa Rica
El Salvador
Honduras
Uruguay
Sâo Paulo
Brasilia

As you read in Chapter 25, most countries in Latin America gained independence in the early 1800s. So in the 20th century, Latin Americans did not struggle for independence like many Asians and Africans.

The problem in Latin America was building stable and free nations. From 1945 to the present, Latin Americans have seen revolutions, economic depressions, and **social unrest**.

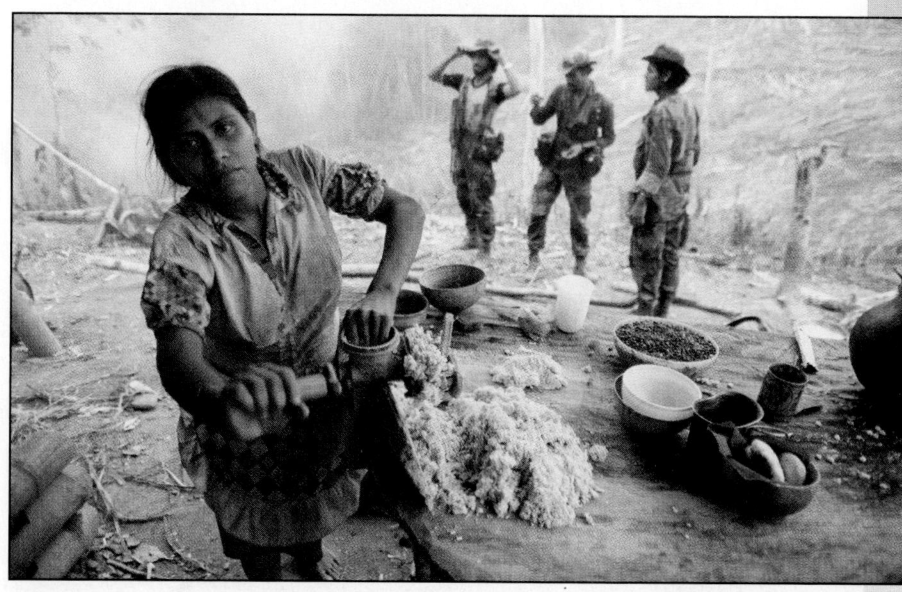

Today, many Latin Americans live among guerrilla soldiers.

Farmers in Mexico

Class Differences

Most Latin American countries had two groups of people. The elite group was made up of a few rich landowners. Many of these people had been in the elite class since colonial times. They passed their land down from one generation to the next.

The second group, made up of peasants, was much larger. These peasants worked for the elite class. They owned no land. They had little or no education, so they could not read or write. They often suffered from disease and hunger.

For centuries, the elite group had been supported by the Catholic Church. But the role of the church began to change in the 1960s. Bishops and priests began fighting for reform. They urged their governments to help the poor.

Unstable Governments

Since the 1980s, most Latin American countries have had some form of democracy. Costa Rica, for example, has had a long and stable democratic tradition. It has a strong economy and a high standard of living.

Democracy is not as stable in other Latin American nations. Latin American countries have

San José, the capital of Costa Rica, is a rich and modern city.

few foreign enemies, so they don't need a big army or navy. However, many of these nations have large militaries. These militaries stay powerful in order to stop revolutions or to overthrow a weak government.

Many Latin American governments face the threat of a military **coup**, or takeover. Soldiers seized control of Brazil in 1964, Chile in 1973, and El Salvador in 1979. Coups have also caused the fall of governments in many other Latin American countries.

Military coup in Chile in 1973

Weak Economies

Much of Latin America is rich in natural resources. Yet most nations there have not developed strong economies. Most nations have developed **one-crop economies**. They depend too much on one crop or mineral.

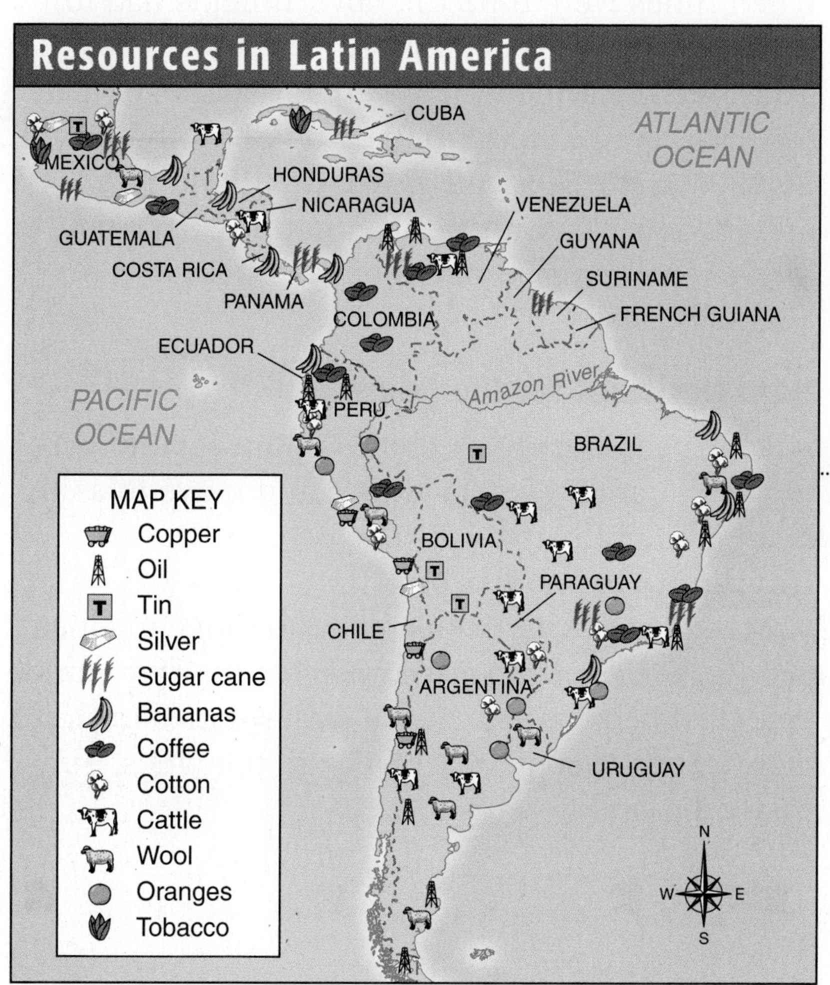

The countries of Latin America are rich in resources. Is copper mined mostly along Latin America's west or east coast?

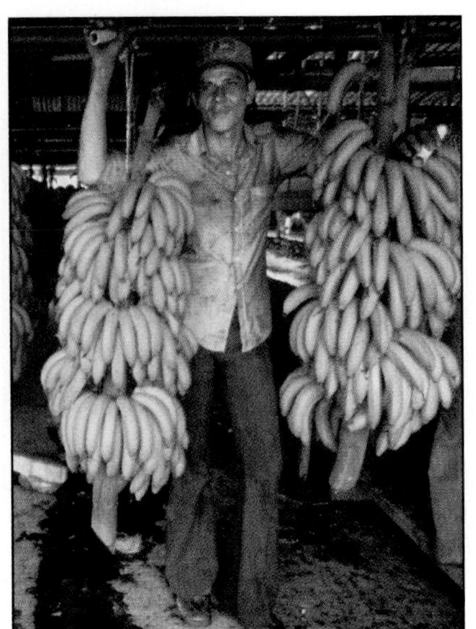
Banana farmer in Honduras

In Colombia, people depend on coffee crops. In Honduras, it is bananas. Wool is the major product of Uruguay, and tin is the major product of Bolivia. Such one-crop economies are rarely strong.

When the price of coffee, bananas, wool, or tin was high, these economies did well. But in poor years, it meant serious trouble. A sudden drop in price destroyed the whole nation's economy. The poor people were hurt most.

Also, Latin Americans looked to the United States for money to build industries. Latin American countries needed the money, yet they wanted to control their own economies. They didn't want to borrow money and then be told how to use it. This often hurt relations between the United States and Latin America.

Another problem for Latin America was debt. When times were difficult, governments had to borrow money. Many Latin American nations went into major debt. In 1970, the nations of Latin America owed other nations around $15 billion. By 1990, their debt had grown to around $420 billion. Some Latin American nations, such as Mexico, have repaid much of their debt to the United States.

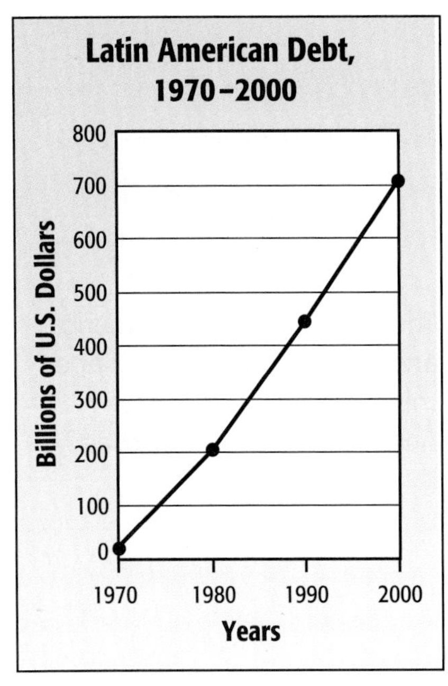

Hard Decisions for the Poor

Poor people had few choices. They could work for a rich landowner, or they could move to a city and look for a better job. They could also **immigrate** to another country.

Many Latin Americans chose to move to cities. Sâo Paulo in Brazil became successful after World War II. It became one of the largest cities in the world. Some people found jobs in the cities, but many did not.

Brazil tried to solve the problem of poverty by building a whole new city in 1960. It was called Brasilia, and it provided many jobs. Today, Brasilia is the capital of Brazil, and about one million people live there. It has a strong economy. The government of Brazil also opened up new lands for settlement.

Many Mexican farm workers came to the United States during World War II. They were needed for the war effort. Later, millions more came in search of jobs.

Many Mexicans came to the United States legally. Others crossed the border illegally. Many people believe that **illegal immigration** hurts the economies of both the United States and Mexico. Both countries continue to work together to solve this problem.

Brasilia, Brazil

Lesson 3 Review

Choose words from the list that best complete the paragraphs. One word will not be used.

A class system has long existed in Latin America. At the top was the rich landowners. At the bottom were the poor peasants. This has made it difficult to build __1__ and free nations.

Military __2__ have overthrown many Latin American governments. Most Latin American countries have __3__ economies. In hard times, they have had to borrow money. This has caused them to go into debt.

Some poor Latin Americans have moved to cities to find better jobs. Others have __4__ to the United States.

Word List

stable
capital
coups
immigrated
one-crop

Chapter 33: Using What You've Learned

Summary

- France gave three of its colonies in North Africa independence. Other African nations, such as Kenya and the Congo, fought for and won independence.
- In South Africa, the white minority set up a system of apartheid to limit the rights of the black majority.
- Former colonies in Africa and Asia struggled to set up stable and free governments. Ethnic strife also affected many of these new nations.
- A strict class system, one-crop economies, debt problems, and dictatorships have hurt the development of Latin America. Many poor people in Latin America have sought better lives in the cities of Latin America or have immigrated to the United States.

Find Out More!

After reading Chapter 33, you're ready to go online. **Explore Zone**, **Quiz Time**, and **Amazing Facts** bring this chapter of world history alive.

Visit www.exploreSV.com and type in the chapter code **Ch33**.

Vocabulary

Number your paper from 1 to 6. Write the word or words from the list that best complete each sentence. One word will not be used.

1. The Mau Mau led an _____ to drive the Europeans out of Kenya.
2. White South Africans set up a system called _____ that separated the races.
3. Economically independent nations are _____.
4. Many Latin American governments have been overthrown by military _____.
5. Colombia has a _____ that depends on coffee.
6. Many Latin Americans _____ to other countries to find better jobs.

Word List

self-reliant
coups
uprising
one-crop economy
immigrate
apartheid
capital

Comprehension

Number your paper from 1 to 6. Write one or more sentences to answer each question below.

1. Why were Africans hopeful that they would gain independence after World War II?
2. Why did civil war break out in the Congo after the Belgians left?
3. What kinds of problems did freedom bring to former colonies?
4. Why is a dictatorship an easy government to set up?
5. Why was it difficult for new nations to remain neutral during the Cold War?
6. Why is illegal immigration a problem between Mexico and the United States?

Critical Thinking

Main Idea Number your paper from 1 to 3. Write the sentence that is the main idea in each group.

1. The Philippines gained independence from the United States in 1946.
   Many colonies gained their independence after World War II.
   The Indonesians gained independence in 1949.
2. Black South Africans were not free because of apartheid.
   Apartheid allowed black South Africans to live only in certain places.
   Under apartheid, black South Africans could not vote.
3. The British had sent some Indians to school.
   Indians were better prepared to rule themselves than people in other former colonies were.
   Certain Indians had worked in the colonial government in India.

Writing

Write a paragraph listing the three main ingredients needed to create a democracy. Explain why each ingredient is important.

LESSON 1

The Fall of Communism

New Words

puppet governments
Solidarity
sit-ins
glasnost
perestroika

People and Places

John Paul II
Mikhail Gorbachev
Ronald Reagan
Erich Honecker
Willy Brandt
Boris Yeltsin
George H. Bush

Before You Read

- Why did the Soviets want to control Eastern Europe?
- What made the Soviet Union a superpower?

You have read how the Soviet Union took over the nations of Eastern Europe after World War II. It had so much control over this area that the governments of Eastern European nations were called **puppet governments**. The Soviets could simply pull the puppet strings, and the governments would do what the Soviets wanted.

Most Eastern Europeans hated this. In Chapter 32, you read how they struggled against the Soviets in the 1950s. The Soviet Union had to use

Workers in Poland protest Communist control.

force to regain control. In the 1980s, Eastern Europeans fought against Soviet control again.

Workers in Poland

Pope John Paul II

Most historians believe that the end of the Soviet Union began in Poland. The Poles had a strong sense of nationalism. They did not want Poland to be a puppet government of the Soviet Union.

In 1980, Polish workers went on strike. They had a non-Communist union called **Solidarity**. Some workers held **sit-ins**. They stayed in buildings so it was harder for the police to stop the protest. Pope John Paul II went to Poland to encourage the workers. It was a long struggle, but Solidarity won many reforms. This began to break the Communist control over Poland.

Changes in the Soviet Union

Meanwhile, there were changes in the Soviet Union. In 1985, Mikhail Gorbachev came to power. He wanted friendlier relations with the United States. Gorbachev and President Ronald Reagan of the United States agreed to destroy some nuclear weapons to soften the tension between the two countries.

United States President Ronald Reagan (left) and Soviet leader Mikhail Gorbachev (right) met in 1985.

Mikhail Gorbachev

Gorbachev made reforms that opened up the Soviet Union to new ideas. He adopted a policy of ***glasnost***, or "openness." Soviets were allowed to speak more freely. They could even vote for people who were not Communists.

To help strengthen the economy, Gorbachev introduced ***perestroika***, or "restructuring." Factories began to produce the consumer goods people wanted. Managers could decide for themselves how to run their business. Gorbachev even encouraged American companies to do business in the Soviet Union.

Fall of the Iron Curtain

In May 1989, Hungarians cut a hole in a wire fence that divided Hungary from Austria and Western Europe. Three months later, they cut a bigger hole. The border was open. Thousands of Eastern Europeans fled to Western Europe.

Many of them were people from East Germany. Erich Honecker, the Communist leader of East Germany, tried to stop them. He asked the Soviets for military help, but Gorbachev refused.

The people of East Germany were more determined than ever. They asked for more reforms. They held protest marches. Every day they worked for changes.

Fallen statue of Communist leader, Vladmir Lenin

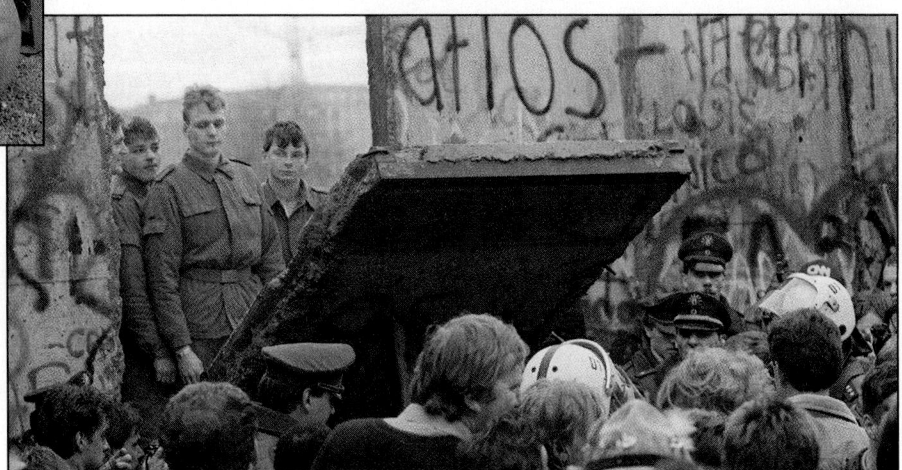

People in West Berlin watch as East German guards open a section of the Berlin Wall.

The Fall of Communism

EAST GERMANY
CZECHOSLOVAKIA
POLAND
HUNGARY
YUGOSLAVIA
ROMANIA
BULGARIA
ESTONIA
LATVIA
LITHUANIA
BELARUS
UKRAINE
MOLDOVA
RUSSIA
GEORGIA
ARMENIA
AZERBAIJAN
KAZAKHSTAN
UZBEKISTAN
TURKMENISTAN
KYRGYZSTAN
TAJIKISTAN
Black Sea
Caspian Sea
N
W
E
S

MAP KEY
Former Communist nations
Border of former Soviet Union

In the late 1980s, Communist governments began to fall. Name one country that was created from the break up of the Soviet Union.

Suddenly, on November 7, 1989, the East German government fell. Two days later, East Germans were told they were free to travel anywhere. Willy Brandt, the former mayor of West Berlin, spoke to a happy crowd of East Germans and West Germans.

> **"I have always been convinced that . . . the division of a city by means of barbed wire and [boundary] lines of death went against the tide of history. Berlin will live and the Wall will tumble."**

The Berlin Wall did tumble in 1989. Joyful Germans hammered at the wall, breaking it into pieces.

End of the Soviet Union

One by one, Communist governments fell. After Hungary and East Germany, the governments of Czechoslovakia and Bulgaria fell. Many Communist governments ended peacefully.

The end of communism was not always peaceful, however. In Romania, a cruel ruler was found guilty of mass murder. He and his wife were shot. These events brought a violent end to communism in Romania.

Finally, the end of communism came for the Soviet Union itself. In August 1991, some Communists tried to overthrow Gorbachev but failed. The Soviet people had tasted freedom. They began to tear down symbols of communism. They destroyed statues of Lenin and other Communist figures.

President Boris Yeltsin (left) and President George H. Bush (right)

In December 1991, the Soviet Union fell. It was replaced by 15 independent nations. The Communists had lost power. Despite Gorbachev's successes, he stepped down as leader. Boris Yeltsin became president of Russia. In 1992, Yeltsin and United States President George H. Bush declared an end to the Cold War.

Lesson 1 Review

Choose words from the list that best complete the paragraphs. One word will not be used.

Word List

Yeltsin
perestroika
sit-ins
Gorbachev
glasnost

For more than forty years, the Soviet Union controlled the puppet governments of Eastern Europe. In 1980, some Polish workers went on strike. Some workers used __1__ to make it harder for the police to break them up.

In the Soviet Union, __2__ made reforms. His policy of __3__ allowed Soviets to speak openly. One by one, Eastern Europeans ended Communist rule. The Berlin Wall fell in 1989. In 1992, President __4__ and President Bush declared an end to the Cold War.

LESSON 2

Tensions in the Middle East

Before You Read

- What might happen when two groups of people feel they have a right to one land?
- Why is oil such a valuable resource today?

In Chapter 30, you read about fighting between Jewish settlers and Arabs in Palestine. In 1947, the British gave up their mandate and let the UN address the Arab-Israeli conflict. The UN divided Palestine into a Jewish state and an Arab state. Jerusalem, a holy city to both Jews and Muslims, was supposed to be an international city. The Palestinian Arabs did not accept the plan, but the Jews did. In 1948, the nation of Israel was created.

The 1948 War

Palestinian Arabs soon attacked Israel. They felt they were fighting for lands that were taken from them. The Israelis felt they were fighting to keep the lands given to them in the UN agreement.

Israelis celebrated on the day their nation was created in 1948.

New Words

refugee
occupied territories
PLO
Yom Kippur
Camp David Accords
intifada
oil reserves
coalition
Operation Desert Storm

People and Places

Sinai Peninsula
Gulf of Aqaba
Jordan
Gaza Strip
Golan Heights
West Bank
Yasir Arafat
Anwar Sadat
Menachem Begin
Jimmy Carter
Lebanon
Kuwait
Saddam Hussein
Saudi Arabia
Golda Meir

Palestinian refugees

The Palestinians had some victories. Within a few months, however, Israeli troops were winning. Both sides agreed to a cease-fire in January 1949. During the fighting, the Israelis captured more land than was given to them in the UN agreement.

The 1948 war created a **refugee** problem. About 400,000 Palestinians fled from their homes in Israel to avoid the fighting. They settled in camps along the Israeli border. The Israeli government would not allow them to return to their homes.

The Six-Day War

The Israeli victory in the 1948 war didn't solve the Arab-Israeli conflict. Israelis began developing a strong army, and Arab-Israeli tensions continued to grow. In 1957, Egypt defeated Israel in a war in the Sinai Peninsula. In 1967, Egypt closed the Gulf of Aqaba to Israel. The Israelis had used the gulf to reach the Indian Ocean. Egypt prepared its army for war.

Yasir Arafat

Israelis believed the Arabs would attack soon. So on June 5, they struck first and attacked the Arab nations of Egypt, Jordan, and Syria. On June 10, after only six days, the war ended in an Israeli victory. The Israelis took over four Arab regions, including the Sinai Peninsula, the Gaza Strip, the Golan Heights, and the West Bank. The regions were called **occupied territories**.

The Six-Day War left many Arabs upset. Many Palestinians no longer believed Arab governments could win back the lands of Palestine. They turned to the Palestinian Liberation Organization (**PLO**), led by Yasir Arafat, for leadership.

War and Peace

In 1973, the Arabs attacked Israel on the Jewish holy day of **Yom Kippur**. The Egyptians and the Syrians led the attack. Other Arab states supported them. The attack caught the Israelis by surprise. But soon they gained control and pushed the Arabs back. The Yom Kippur War ended in a cease-fire agreement after three weeks of fighting.

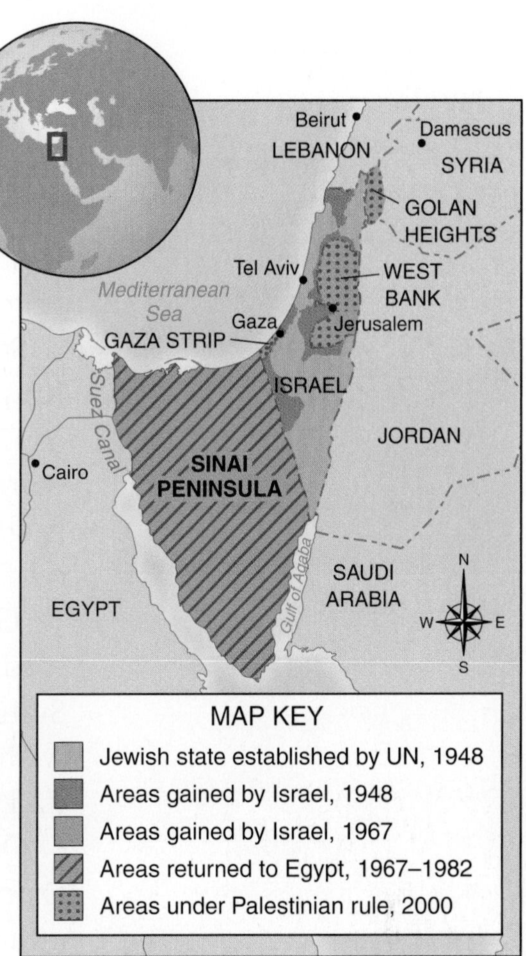

Israel, 1948–2000

In 1977, Egyptian President Anwar Sadat flew to Jerusalem to meet with Israeli Prime Minister Menachem Begin. United States President Jimmy Carter invited the two leaders to Camp David, Maryland, for peace talks. In 1979, Sadat and Begin signed the **Camp David Accords**. The Israelis promised to return the Sinai Peninsula to the Egyptians. The Egyptians said that they would live in peace with the Israelis.

But the Camp David Accords did not end the Arab-Israeli conflict. The agreement did not address the refugee camps or the occupied territories. In 1982, Israel invaded Lebanon because the PLO had launched attacks on Israel from there. In 1987, Palestinians began the **intifada**. During this uprising, many young Palestinian men in Israel threw stones at the Israeli forces. Israel fought harshly against the intifada.

The Camp David Accords were signed in 1979.

The Persian Gulf War

The late 1900s brought conflicts to other countries in the Middle East. The tiny nation of Kuwait is located on the coast of the Persian Gulf. It has massive **oil reserves** in the ground. On August 2, 1990, Iraq invaded Kuwait.

Saddam Hussein

Saddam Hussein, the Iraqi dictator, wanted Kuwait's oil. Iraq had its own oil. But the addition of Kuwait's oil would give Iraq more power over world oil prices. There was a fear that Hussein might even move against Saudi Arabia and its vast oil fields.

The UN demanded that Hussein remove his troops from Kuwait, but he refused. The United States then led a **coalition**. Its goal was the withdrawal of Iraq from Kuwait. This coalition had several Arab members.

On January 18, 1991, the coalition began **Operation Desert Storm**. This was a military attack to drive the Iraqis out of Kuwait. First, the coalition launched air strikes to weaken Iraq. Then ground forces moved in and surrounded Iraqi forces in Kuwait. By the end of February, the Persian Gulf War was over. Kuwait was free once more. But Hussein remained in power.

Iraq invaded Kuwait to gain control of Kuwait's oil fields. How many oil fields are shown in Kuwait?

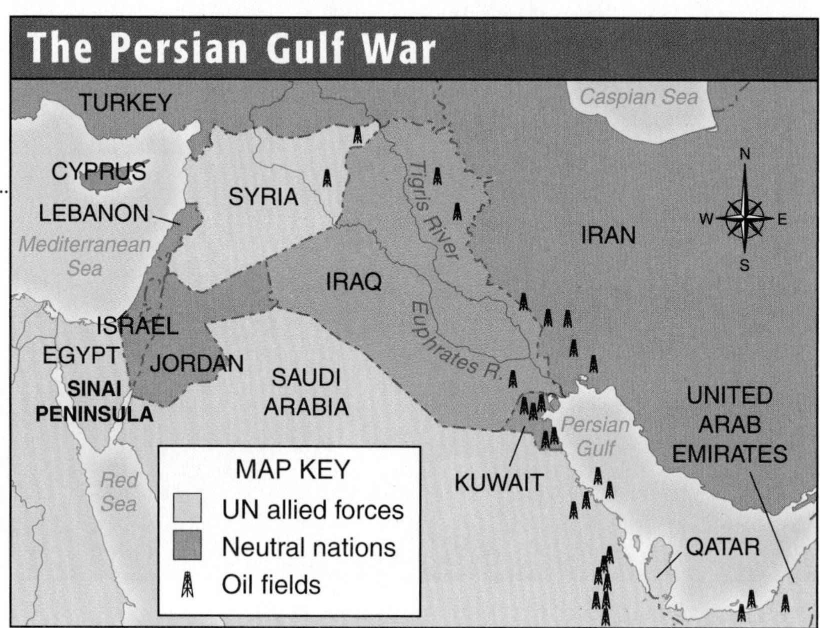

Golda Meir (1898–1978)

People In History

Golda Meir was born in 1898 to a poor family in Russia. In 1906, when Golda was seven years old, she and her family moved to Milwaukee, Wisconsin, to find a better life. Golda went to school and became a teacher. She also became a committed Zionist. In 1921, she and her husband moved to Palestine.

For many years, Golda Meir fought for Zionism. After the creation of Israel in 1948, she was named Israel's minister to the Soviet Union. She also served as labor minister and foreign minister.

In 1969, she was elected to the highest position in Israel. She became prime minister. Some Israelis blamed her when Israel was caught off guard by the Yom Kippur War. In 1974, one year after the Yom Kippur War, Meir stepped down as prime minister. She died in Jerusalem in 1978.

Lesson 2 Review

Choose words from the list that best complete the paragraph. One word will not be used.

The 1948 war in Palestine created many Arab refugees. In the Six-Day War, Israelis took over the __1__ Peninsula, the Golan Heights, the Gaza Strip, and the West Bank. In the __2__ of 1973, Israel was caught off guard by attacks from Egypt and Syria. Egypt and Israel signed the Camp David Accords in 1979. Palestinians in Israel began the __3__ to fight Israeli rule. The United States led an international __4__ to drive Iraq out of Kuwait in the Persian Gulf War.

Word List

coalition
Kuwait
Yom Kippur War
Sinai
intifada

LESSON 3

Changes in Society and Culture

New Words

civil rights
fertilizers
Green Revolution
segregation
sanctions
feminism
discrimination

People and Places

Mumbai
Martin Luther King, Jr.
Lyndon Johnson
Desmond Tutu
Nelson Mandela

Before You Read

- What good things have happened in the world over the last 50 years?
- Why do modern cultures change?

The world was a different place in 2000 than it was in 1900 or even 1970. The 20th century brought change to all parts of the world. You have already read about the results of colonization, imperialism, and wars.

Other forces were at work, too. Populations grew rapidly in most parts of the world. Many nations became more industrialized. People showed a greater concern for **civil rights**.

The number of people living in Tokyo, Japan, grew rapidly in the 20th century.

The Population Explosion

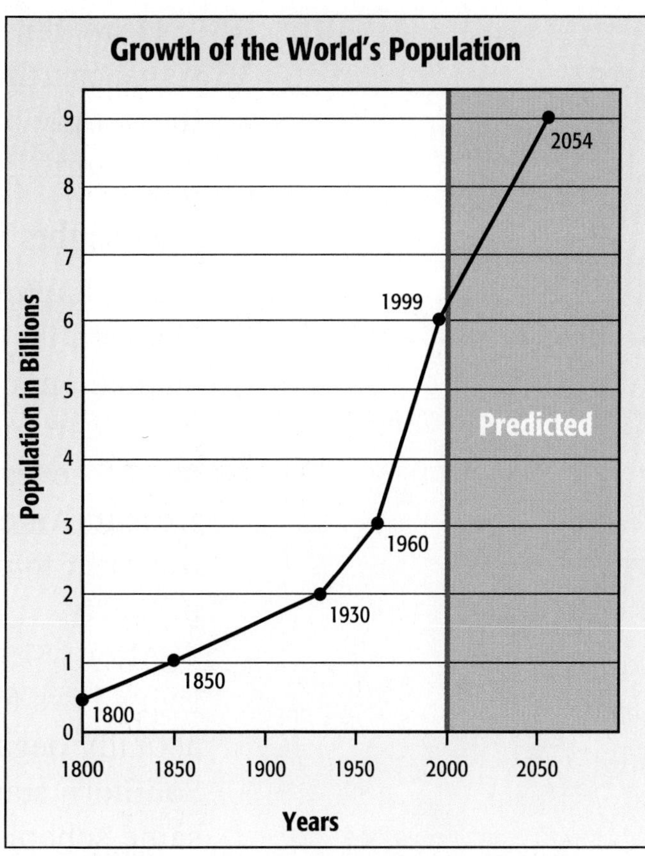

The population of the world is growing quickly. Many people are worried that it is growing faster than the supply of food. For hundreds of years, the population hardly grew at all. From the time of the Roman Empire until 1800, it grew from 250 million people to 500 million. By 1850, it had reached one billion. In 1999, it had reached six billion. The UN predicts the world's population will reach nine billion by 2054.

By the late 20th century, some parts of the world were growing much faster than others. The population of Africa was growing ten times as fast as that of Europe. Asia and Latin America also had much higher growth rates than Europe and the United States.

Some cities have become very crowded. Tokyo, for example, has 26 million people. Mexico City has more than 18 million. Sâo Paulo has nearly 18 million. In 2000, Mumbai (formerly Bombay) in India had 18 million. By 2015, the UN predicts Mumbai will have 26 million people.

The Food Supply

The Green Revolution helped farmers in India.

Can the world support its growing population? More than 200 years ago, people began worrying that the population would soon outgrow the food supply. But industrialization increased the food supply in the 1800s and early 1900s. In the late 1900s, powerful **fertilizers** greatly increased the amount of food farmers could grow. This was called the **Green Revolution**. The Green Revolution worked especially well in places like India.

However, in the early 21st century, there are signs that the population is growing faster than the supply of food. This could be especially harmful to people in poorer nations.

Civil Rights in the United States

In Chapter 27, you read how the United States changed its Constitution after the Civil War. One change ended slavery. Another gave African American men the right to vote. Congress also passed several civil rights laws. The laws gave African Americans specific legal rights, including the right to sue in court and the right to own property.

After 1875, Congress did not pass any more civil rights laws for a long time. African Americans actually began to lose their rights. In some Southern states, they lost the right to attend the same schools as white children. They also lost the right to vote in some states. Then in the 1950s, the civil rights movement began. Its leader was Martin Luther King, Jr.

Martin Luther King, Jr., led the civil rights movement in the United States.

President Lyndon Johnson signed the Civil Rights Act in 1964.

After a hard struggle, African Americans won back their civil rights. President Lyndon Johnson signed the Civil Rights Act of 1964. The next year, he signed the Voting Rights Act. In 1968, he signed yet another civil rights law. These laws ended **segregation**. In the years after, people continued working to provide equal opportunities for all citizens.

Nelson Mandela

The End of Apartheid

In Chapter 33, you learned about apartheid in South Africa. It separated black Africans from white Africans. Many people in the world disagreed with apartheid. But white leaders in South Africa refused to change.

Nations began to increase pressure on South Africa. They began using **sanctions**. They refused to trade with South Africa, which hurt South Africa's economy. Inside South Africa, leaders such as Desmond Tutu and Nelson Mandela fought to end apartheid. All this pressure finally worked. Apartheid ended in 1991.

Other Groups Fight for Civil Rights

Firefighter at work

Other groups fought for and gained rights in the 20th century. In the 1960s, women began a movement called **feminism**. Women in Africa, Asia, the Middle East, Latin America, and the United States all fought to earn the same pay as men for the same work. They also fought for better child care and health care.

Many Mexican farm workers united to get better working conditions on American farms. Native Americans started a movement to improve their lives. They also wanted to restore Native American traditions and culture.

French-speaking Canadians began to demand more rights in the 1960s. Catholics in Northern Ireland also fought for their civil rights.

Americans with disabilities fought for a law that prevents **discrimination** against people with disabilities. In 1990, Congress passed the Americans with Disabilities Act.

Lesson 3 Review

Choose words from the list that best complete the paragraphs. One word will not be used.

Word List

fertilizers
discrimination
feminism
civil rights
sanctions

The world's population is growing so fast that it might reach nine billion by 2054. In the late 1900s, farmers began to use powerful __1__ to increase the amount of food they could grow.

In the United States, African Americans fought to restore and expand their __2__. During the 1960s, women began a movement called __3__ to gain rights equal to those of men. In South Africa, __4__ put in place by many nations helped to end apartheid.

Chapter 34: Using What You've Learned

Summary

- In the 1980s, Eastern Europeans fought against Soviet control. These struggles, along with political and economic reforms, led to the fall of the Soviet Union in 1991.
- Arabs and Israelis fought four major wars in the late 20th century. The Arab-Israeli conflict continues today.
- Iraq invaded Kuwait in 1990. A coalition of nations drove the Iraqis out of Kuwait in Operation Desert Storm.
- The world has changed greatly during the late 20th century. The population in some parts of the world has grown rapidly. Many nations have industrialized.
- African Americans, women, and other people won civil rights in the United States. Apartheid ended in South Africa.

Find Out More!

After reading Chapter 34, you're ready to go online. **Explore Zone**, **Quiz Time**, and **Amazing Facts** bring this chapter of world history alive.

Visit www.exploreSV.com and type in the chapter code **Ch34**.

Vocabulary

Number your paper from 1 to 5. Write the word from the list that best completes the paragraphs. One word will not be used.

The Soviet Union had so much control over Eastern Europe that the governments of these nations were called __1__ governments. In the 1980s, Eastern European nations fought against Soviet control. Polish workers who belonged to a non-Communist union called __2__ went on strike. The workers held __3__ in buildings.

In 1985, Mikhail Gorbachev came to power in the Soviet Union. He adopted a policy of __4__ that opened up the Soviet Union to new ideas. Gorbachev strengthened the economy by introducing __5__.

Word List

sit-ins
perestroika
puppet
discrimination
glasnost
Solidarity

Comprehension

Number your paper from 1 to 5. Write the letter of the correct answer.

1. What nation was created in Palestine in 1948?
   a. Kuwait
   b. Lebanon
   c. Israel
   d. Jordan

2. Who was Israel's minister to the Soviet Union?
   a. Golda Meir
   b. Anwar Sadat
   c. Jimmy Carter
   d. John Paul II

3. What natural resource did Iraq want when it invaded Kuwait?
   a. fresh water
   b. natural gas
   c. coal deposits
   d. oil reserves

4. What movement was led by Martin Luther King, Jr.?
   a. Green Revolution
   b. Operation Desert Storm
   c. Solidarity
   d. civil rights

5. What did other nations use to get South Africa to end apartheid?
   a. segregation
   b. sanctions
   c. discrimination
   d. occupied territories

Critical Thinking

Sequencing Number your paper from 1 to 5. Write the sentences below in the correct order.

The East German government fell in 1989.

The United States and the Soviet Union declared an end to the Cold War.

In 1987, Palestinians began the intifada.

The world's population will probably reach about nine billion.

President Lyndon Johnson signed the Civil Rights Act of 1964.

Writing

Write a brief magazine article describing the end of communism in Eastern Europe. Title your article "The Fall of the Iron Curtain and of the Berlin Wall."

Skill Builder: Reading a Double Bar Graph

A **double bar graph** compares facts by using two different colored bars. This double bar graph shows the supply of oil in the Persian Gulf countries and the United States in 1980, 1990, and 2000.

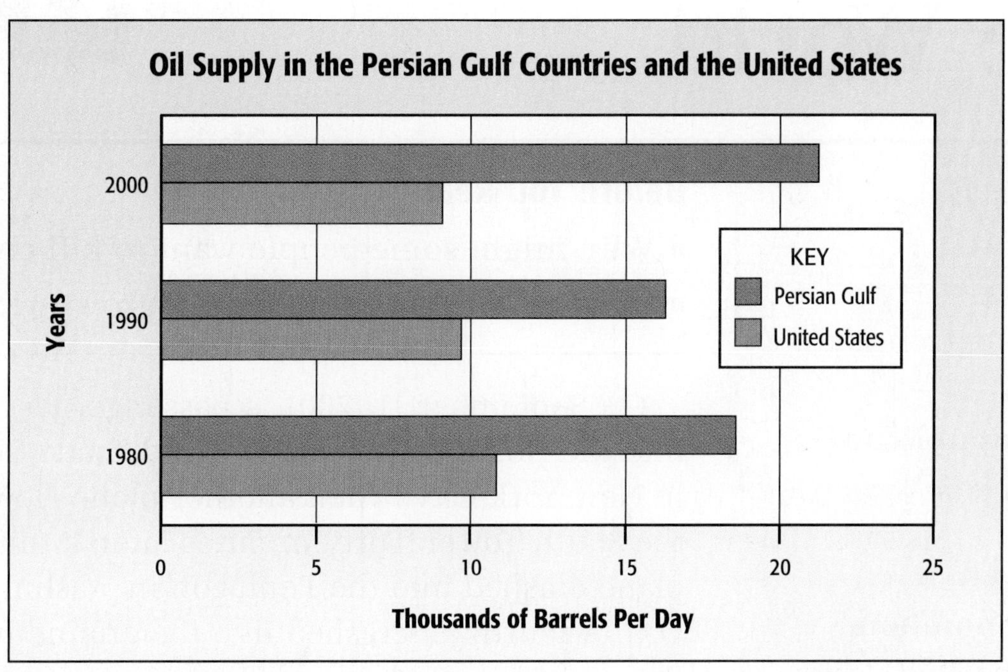

Number your paper from 1 to 5. Write the word or number that best completes each sentence. One word or number will not be used.

increased **decreased** **11** **18** **1990** **2000**

1. The oil supply in the United States was about _____ thousand barrels per day in 1980.

2. The oil supply in the Persian Gulf countries was about _____ thousand barrels per day in 1980.

3. In _____, the United States had its lowest oil supply.

4. Between 1980 and 2000, the oil supply in the United States _____.

5. Between 1980 and 2000, the oil supply in the Persian Gulf countries _____.

LESSON 1

Terrorism Around the World

New Words

terrorism
al Qaeda
Islamic extremists
anthrax
Irish Republican Army
Hamas
Hezbollah
suicide bombers
Japanese Red Army
hijacks

People and Places

New York City
Washington, D.C.
George W. Bush
Northern Ireland
Basques
Oklahoma City

Before You Read

- Why might some people want to kill civilians?
- Why has the fear of an attack grown recently?

On September 11, 2001, a passenger jet crashed into the North Tower of the World Trade Center in New York City. Then another plane flew into the South Tower. Forty minutes later, a third plane crashed into the Pentagon in Washington, D.C. A fourth jet crashed into the ground in Pennsylvania. Both World Trade Center towers fell to the ground. The Pentagon was badly damaged. People watching these events on television could not believe what they were seeing.

Smoke rises from the North Tower of the World Trade Center.

Terrorism Hits the United States

The events of September 11, 2001, were acts of **terrorism**. The terrorists killed around 3,000 people. All the passengers and crew in the four planes died. Most of the people who died, however, were in the buildings that were hit. Several hundred firefighters and police officers also died trying to rescue people trapped inside.

The attack was carried out by 19 members of a group called **al Qaeda**. The group contains many **Islamic extremists** who believe the Qur'an tells them to fight and kill people who are not Muslim. These 19 men took control of the four planes. Several passengers on United Flight 93 fought the terrorists. As a result, the plane crashed in a field in Pennsylvania instead of into an important building.

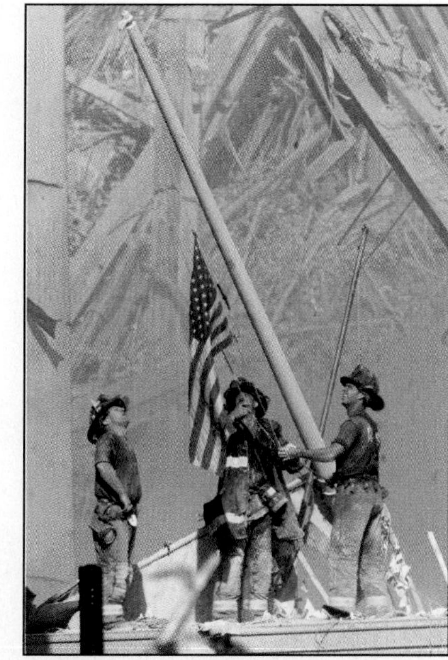

Firemen raise a United States flag over the ruins of the World Trade Center.

On September 20, 2001, President George W. Bush called the terrorist attacks an "act of war." He declared a war on terrorism.

"The enemy of America is not our many Muslim friends; it is not our many Arab friends. Our enemy is a radical network of terrorists and every government that supports them."

Kinds of Terrorism

Terrorism comes in many forms. Later in 2001, the United States faced another threat. Someone mailed **anthrax** in envelopes to newspaper, television, and government offices. The tiniest amount of this germ can be deadly. More than twenty people who handled the envelopes either died or became very sick. Such attacks raised the fear of terrorism for people in the United States and around the world. It was clear that terrorism can strike at any time and in any place.

Mail worker in Argentina wearing a mask for protection from anthrax in 2001

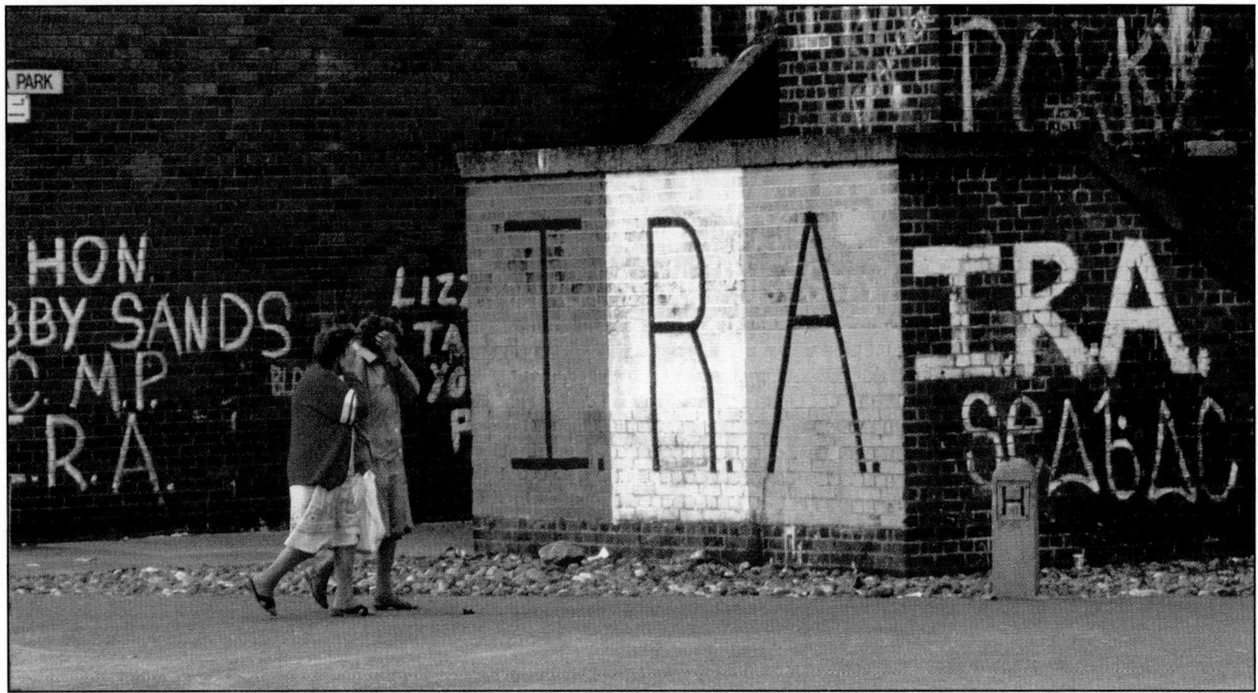

The Irish Republican Army (IRA) is one terrorist group in Northern Ireland.

Terrorism has been around for a very long time. Terrorists come from all parts of the world. Some are highly educated. Others have little or no education. For the most part, however, they tend to be young and male. Terrorists are angry about something and want to make a statement. They hope that by killing some people and scaring the rest, they will get what they want. In modern times, there have been terrorist attacks around the world.

Rescuers respond to a nerve gas attack in a Tokyo subway.

The **Irish Republican Army**, whose members are mostly Catholic, has used terror to try to unify Ireland and drive the British out of Northern Ireland. Protestant groups in Northern Ireland have also made terrorist attacks. In the past 30 years, terrorists have killed hundreds of civilians.

Terrorism has become a major part of the Arab-Israeli conflict. Arab terrorist groups such as **Hamas** and **Hezbollah** have attacked Israel. Members of these groups act as **suicide bombers** by strapping bombs to their bodies. They go into a crowded place and set off the bomb, killing themselves and as many Israeli people as possible. Arabs also experience terrorism from the Israeli soldiers.

In northern Spain, the Basques have used terror to try to win independence. The Basques are a group of people living in Spain and France. In Sri Lanka, terrorists use suicide bombers to kill innocent people. In Japan, the **Japanese Red Army** wants to overthrow the government. It often **hijacks** airplanes. In 1995, terrorists in Japan sprayed nerve gas in Tokyo's subway. The gas killed five people and injured more than 5,500.

In 1995, a bomb blew up a building in Oklahoma City, Oklahoma, leaving 168 people dead. Other terrorist groups have killed innocent people in Peru.

Finding ways to peacefully prevent terrorism is one of the biggest challenges in today's world.

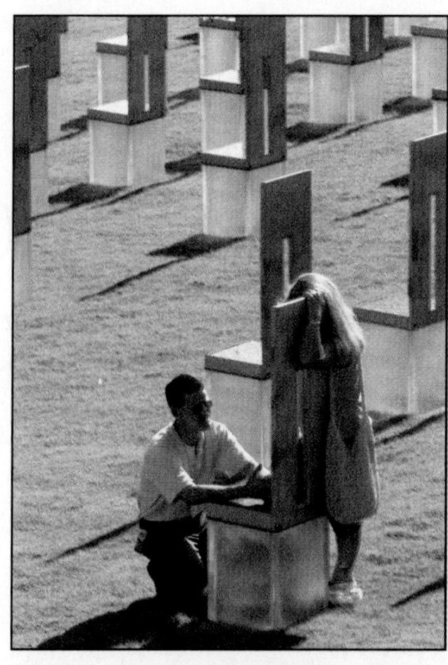

Family members at the Oklahoma City memorial

Lesson 1 Review

Choose words from the list that best complete the paragraphs. One word will not be used.

The events of September 11, 2001, were acts of __1__ against the United States. Two planes crashed into the World Trade Center. Another plane hit the __2__. A fourth plane crashed into the ground in Pennsylvania. The attacks were carried out by members of __3__, a terrorist group of Islamic extremists.

Terrorism has been around for hundreds of years. Terrorists come from all over the world and use many means. Some use germs or gas. Others are __4__ who are willing to kill themselves and others in order to get what they want.

Word List

al Qaeda
suicide bombers
anthrax
Pentagon
terrorism

LESSON 2

Technological Revolution

New Words

technological revolution
Internet
World Wide Web
privacy
X-ray
lasers
hybrids
windmills
solar panels
hydrogen
global village

People and Places

Tim Berners-Lee
Kofi Annan

Before You Read

- How has technology changed the way you learn new things?
- In what ways might technology help bring people closer together?

You have read about many inventions throughout the years of world history. But technology has changed at an amazing rate in the last 100 years. In 1900, no one had a radio or a television. Health care was very simple. In today's world, cars, radios, televisions, and computers are common in many places. You have read about the American and French revolutions. You've also read about the Industrial Revolution. Some people consider our time in history to be a **technological revolution**.

Health workers today often use new technology.

Technology and Communication

Many satellites circle high above Earth in space. These satellites send and receive communication signals. The signals come from radios, televisions, and telephones. Satellites allow you to hear or watch something from thousands of miles away. They allow you to call a friend on the other side of the world.

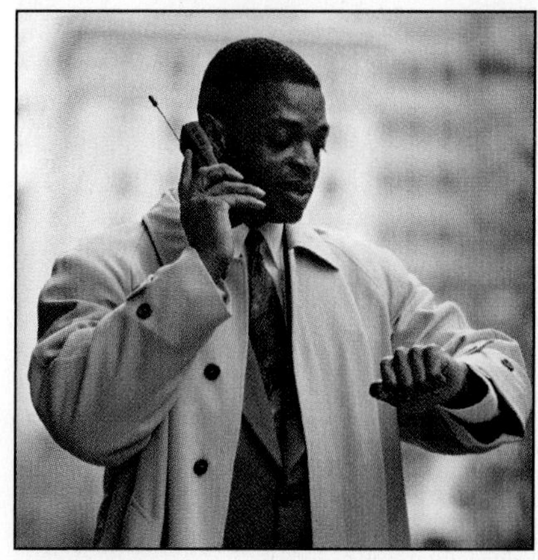

Today, many people use cell phones.

The **Internet** connects computers around the world. In the early years, only universities and the government used the Internet. Then in 1990, an American named Tim Berners-Lee invented the **World Wide Web** (WWW).

The Web made the Internet available to more people. Teachers and students can do research on the Internet. People can shop using the Internet. New businesses sell all sorts of things on the Internet. One founder of an Internet business said, "I wouldn't be surprised if history records Tim Berners-Lee as the second Gutenberg." You might remember that Gutenberg invented the printing press in the 15th century.

With a computer and the Internet, you can send e-mail messages to anyone who has a computer. It just takes an instant. It has become easier than ever to communicate with people around the world.

One issue that concerns many people is **privacy**. Computers store a lot of information about people. Who can get this information? Can you lose some of your privacy on the Internet? Could someone even use this information to harm you? These are some of the difficult questions that the Internet causes us to ask.

Students working with computers

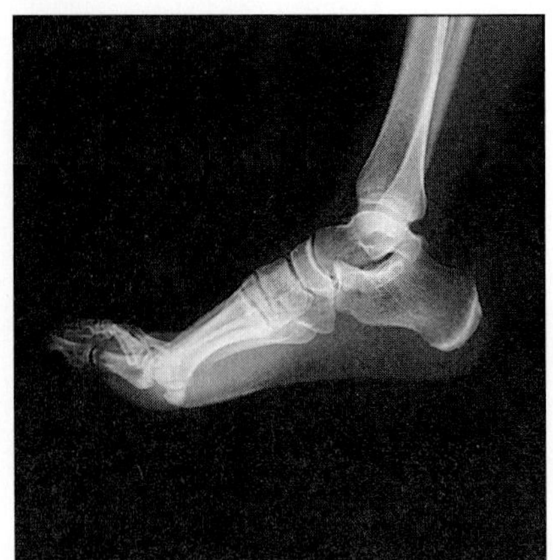
X-ray of a foot, 1960

Technology and Medicine

Doctors today can do amazing things. They can replace certain parts of the body, such as hip and knee joints. They can take out a damaged heart and put in a different one. The doctors of just 100 years ago would be shocked by what doctors today can do.

Technology has produced machines that let doctors see inside the body. **X-ray** machines were developed in the 1890s. But they showed only the bones. Newer machines show muscles and many other parts of the body. Doctors also use **lasers**. A laser is a machine that creates a special beam of light. Doctors use lasers to break up dangerous blood clots and heal wounds. They also use them to improve vision. Doctors continue to find more ways to use lasers to help people.

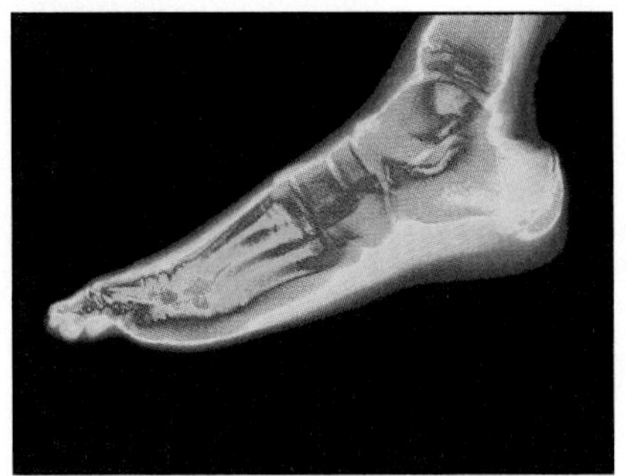
Modern medical image of a foot, 1997

Technology and Energy

Technology has helped to reduce our need for fuels, such as gas and oil. For example, new automobiles have been developed that run on electricity instead of gasoline. **Hybrids** are cars that run on both gas and electricity. They do not use as much gas as regular cars.

Hybrid cars run on both gas and electricity.

Technology has helped make energy from the wind and sun. Modern **windmills** help produce energy from the wind. The windmills have light blades shaped to catch the most wind. Special **solar panels** produce energy from the sun. But solar energy is still expensive.

Perhaps the best hope for cheap and clean energy is **hydrogen**. Hydrogen is found in water, so there is an almost endless supply of hydrogen. More than 70 percent of Earth is covered by water.

When hydrogen burns, it turns into water vapor. It does not harm the environment. Some scientists think hydrogen soon will be used to fuel cars and heat buildings. There are many possible sources of clean, cheap energy. But scientists are still working to find the best one.

New technologies are often expensive. Few people have bought hybrid cars because they cost more than regular cars. New light bulbs have been developed that use much less electricity and last much longer. But they cost more than regular light bulbs. As new technologies are improved, they usually get less expensive. Scientists are working hard to make these new technologies available at lower prices.

Modern windmills help produce energy from the wind.

Did You Know?

A Perfect Fit

New technologies often end up in uses that their inventors never imagined. For example, in the 1950s, around 10,000 shoe-fitting X-ray boxes were in shoe stores all around the United States. Children would try on a shoe and place their feet in the box. The X-rays were beamed onto the foot. They produced an image of the foot inside the shoe. Salespeople could show parents just how well a shoe was going to fit.

There was only one problem. X-rays can actually be harmful. By 1970, the shoe-fitting X-ray boxes were banned in 33 states. Today, they are only in museums.

A Global Village

Some people think all this new technology has turned the world into a **global village**. It has made the world seem as small as a village.

But not everyone is part of this global village. Many of the world's poorer people do not have the newest technology. In 2002, UN Secretary-General Kofi Annan spoke about this problem.

Voices In History

"A technological revolution is [changing] society . . . . If harnessed and directed properly, [technology has] the potential to improve all aspects of our [lives]. It can serve as an engine for development in the 21st century, yet the majority of the world's population has yet to benefit from the new technology."

Many people are working to bring computers to poorer countries. They are finding ways to bring technology to more and more people.

Lesson 2 Review

Choose words from the list that best complete the paragraphs. One word will not be used.

Word List

hydrogen
global village
X-ray
World Wide Web
hybrid

Space satellites and computers allow instant communication around the world. Tim Berners-Lee invented the __1__ in 1990. Technology has also improved medicine. Doctors use lasers to break up blood clots. New technology also saves energy. New __2__ cars use less gas than regular cars. Windmills and solar panels produce clean energy. Some day, __3__ might replace oil and gas as the main source of energy for the world.

With the many advances in technology, some people think of the world as a __4__. Not everyone has all the new technology. But many are working to bring technology to more people.

LESSON 3

The Environment

Before You Read

- Why are people worried about the future of our land and water?
- What can people do to help save the earth?

New Words

pollution
smog
acid rain
ozone layer
pesticides
global warming
polar ice caps
deforestation
carbon dioxide
conservation
recycle

People and Places

Mexico City
Los Angeles
Ho Chi Minh City
Rio de Janeiro

In Chapter 1 of this book, you read how the earth is like the stage on which world history is played. You have seen pictures of Earth's many beautiful places. But many scientists believe that Earth is in serious trouble. The air and water is getting dirtier. Many scientists believe the climate is getting warmer. Too many trees are being cut down. Scientists wonder if the world will still be so beautiful and healthy in the future.

Many places on Earth, such as Antarctica, are known for their natural beauty.

On many days, pollution can be seen over the city of Los Angeles, California.

Dirty Air

In many parts of the world, the air is dirty. Humans have caused most of this **pollution**. Their behavior has made the air unclean. Driving automobiles, running factories, and heating buildings are some ways people pollute the air. These acts usually require burning fuels such as gas and oil.

Cars in traffic

The air is the most polluted over large cities, such as Mexico City and Los Angeles. Cars send harmful chemicals into the air as they burn gasoline. The chemicals mix with water in the air to produce **smog**. The air turns brown and is unhealthy to breathe. In some cities, such as Tokyo and Vietnam's Ho Chi Minh City, people wear masks because the air is so dirty.

When pollution mixes with rain, it can form **acid rain**. Acid rain damages plants, lakes, and rivers. It kills fish. In time, acid rain can even destroy buildings. Air pollution has caused a hole in an important layer in the sky. This layer, called the **ozone layer**, helps to protect people on Earth from the sun's harmful rays.

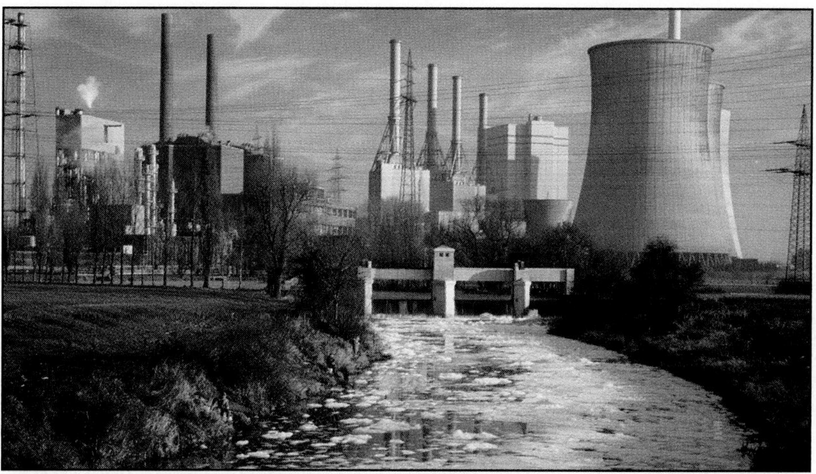
This polluted river flows near a power plant.

Dirty Water

Earth's water is also getting too dirty. When heavy rain falls, chemicals are washed from the land into rivers, lakes, and oceans. The rainwater carries fertilizers and **pesticides** from farms. It washes salt and dirt from roads. Waste products from factories and mines also flow into our water. In 1996, the Environmental Protection Agency (EPA) estimated that 40 percent of American lakes and rivers were polluted. These waters were too dirty for fishing or swimming.

The problem is even worse in poorer countries. These countries often are not able to clean garbage from city streets. In time, this garbage pollutes rivers. People have to drink the polluted water because they have no source of safe water. In the 1990s, this kind of water pollution caused about three million deaths per year.

Polluted water in Jakarta, Indonesia

Global Warming

Many scientists believe another problem facing the earth is **global warming**. The earth seems to be getting warmer every year. Many scientists think burning fuels has caused global warming. Gases, mostly caused by burning fuels, trap the sun's heat near the earth.

Many scientists think global warming is getting worse. Some believe temperatures will rise by as many as six degrees by 2100. That would cause the **polar ice caps** to melt. Cities along coasts, such as New York City, would flood.

Helpful medicines are made from this rain forest plant.

Cutting Down the Forests

In some places, such as Brazil, people are cutting down trees at a rapid pace. The Brazilian government has passed laws to prevent **deforestation**. Still, more than 4,000 square miles of rain forest are destroyed there each year. People cut down the trees to make firewood and lumber. They also cut them down to make room for factories, houses, roads, and farms.

But the trees are a valuable part of the earth. Burning oil and other fuels releases a gas called **carbon dioxide** into the air. Trees take in carbon dioxide and make oxygen for people to breathe. Fewer trees mean more carbon dioxide. Carbon dioxide in the air might also add to global warming.

This rain forest is being cut down to build a road.

Many plants and animals live only in rain forests. If these forests are destroyed, the plants and animals will be gone. There will be no way to know whether those plants could have been used to make valuable medicines.

What People Can Do

Many people are working to improve Earth's environment. Canada, the United States, and other nations have passed laws to clean up the air and water. They have forced automobile makers to make engines that burn fuel more cleanly.

Nations also have worked together. In 1992, more than 150 nations met in Rio de Janeiro in Brazil to talk about the environment. Individuals can help, too. They can practice **conservation**. They can reuse things. They can **recycle** things they no longer need or want. They can reduce waste. Many people around the world are working together to protect the environment.

Recycling helps the environment.

Lesson 3 Review

Choose words from the list that best complete the paragraphs. One word will not be used.

Many human activities require the burning of fuels, such as oil and gas. Burning these creates air pollution. This pollution mixes with rain to form __1__ rain, which can kill fish and plants. Chemicals from factories and farms are washed into rivers and lakes, creating water pollution.

Vast __2__ has reduced the number of trees in the world. Fewer trees leaves more __3__ in the air. Scientists think this contributes to __4__. People around the world are working to solve these problems facing the environment.

Word List

deforestation
carbon dioxide
ozone layer
global warming
acid

LESSON 4

Our World Today

New Words

ethnic cleansing
currency
euro
AIDS
trade barriers
NAFTA

People and Places

Slobodan Milosevic
East Timor
Singapore
Sierra Leone
Mozambique
Zambia
Malawi
Uganda

Before You Read

- What are your greatest hopes and fears for the future of the world?
- What are some problems facing the world today?

This book started with a look at prehistoric people. It then followed the human journey through new ideas, powerful empires, and harmful wars. The story of world history is one of constant change. Today's world can change in an instant. That was made clear by the terrorist attacks of September 11, 2001.

All these changes have brought us to the world we know today. Each region has its own cultures, its own histories, its own successes, and its own challenges.

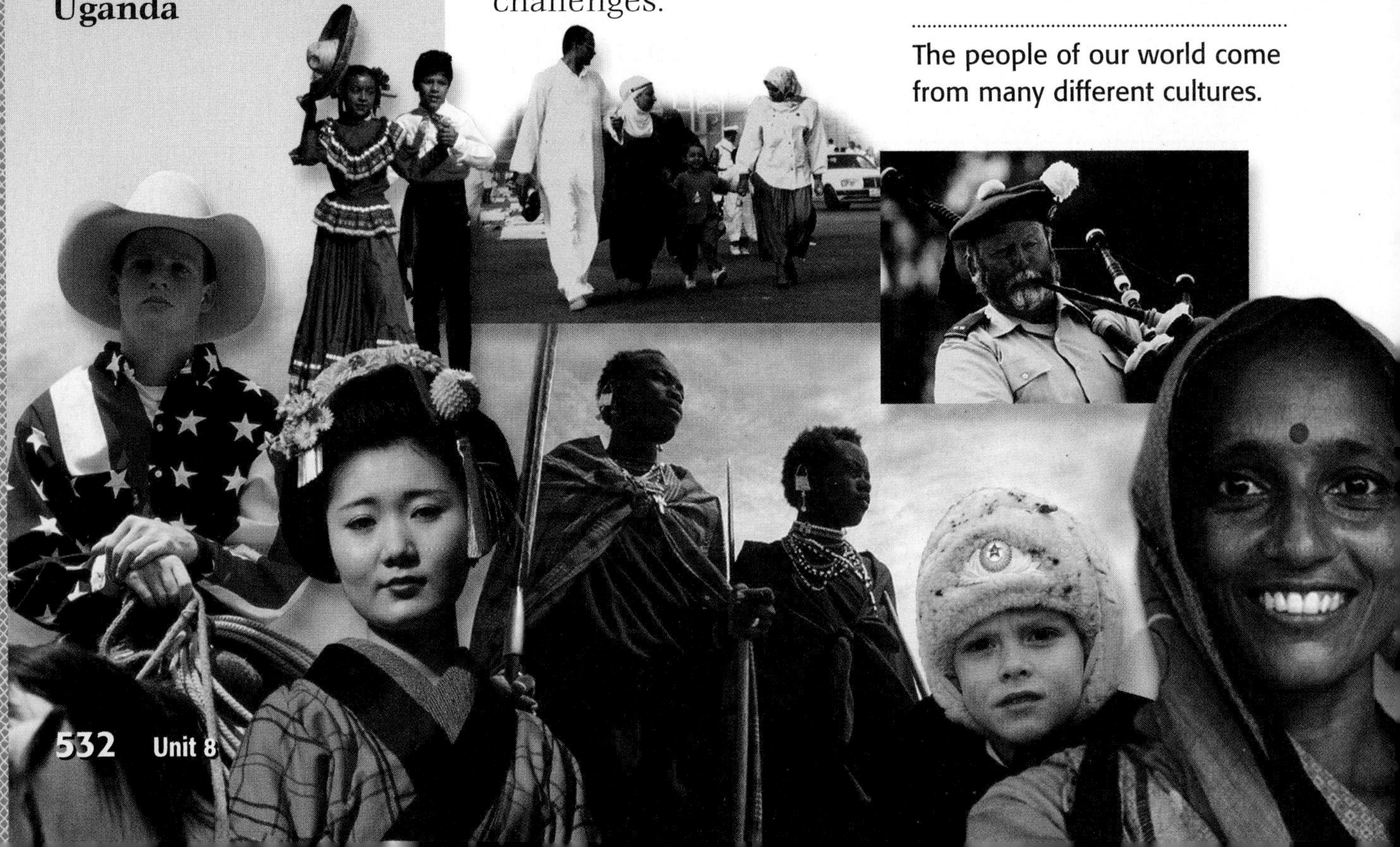

The people of our world come from many different cultures.

Europe Today

In 1990, Slobodan Milosevic, the leader of Serbia, started an effort of **ethnic cleansing**. Milosevic drove non-Serbs out of Serbia. He also killed many of them. In 1999, NATO forces took action against Serbia. Milosevic was removed from power. In 2001, he was arrested and charged with war crimes. He was put on trial in 2002. Yet, ethnic conflict remains a problem in parts of Europe.

Slobodan Milosevic brought to trial in 2000

Another problem for Europe is the issue of unity. Europe has more than 40 countries. Today, there are efforts to unify these countries. Europeans have open trade with one another. In 1999, most of Europe accepted one **currency**, or form of money. It is called the **euro**. Not every country in Europe uses the euro, however. Each country has its own language and customs. Still, Europe's economy is becoming more unified.

Asia Today

Ethnic conflict is also a problem in Asia. India and Pakistan continue to argue about which nation owns the land of Kashmir. Indonesia has had brutal ethnic conflicts. In 1999, the people of East Timor voted to set up their own nation, independent from Indonesia. More than 100,000 people have died in East Timor.

In the Communist nations of China and Vietnam, there is now more economic freedom. People can own their own businesses. The Communist leaders are no longer in power. The city of Hong Kong, which had been controlled by the British, was returned to China in 1997.

Chinese people celebrating Hong Kong's return to China in 1997

Japan is one of the most industrialized nations in today's world. The Japanese make many of the world's finest cars and electronics. Other Asian nations such as Singapore, South Korea, and Taiwan have high standards of living.

Africa Today

A South African woman voting

Africa still struggles with many problems. Nations such as Liberia and Sierra Leone have suffered through civil wars. Droughts have caused famine. The worst drought came in 1992 and 1993. Somalia and Mozambique were two of the hardest-hit nations. The disease **AIDS** has hit Africa especially hard.

But some African countries have improved their quality of life. Democratic elections have taken place in Mali, Zambia, and other nations. In Ghana, Malawi, and Uganda, several economic reforms have been introduced. With stable governments and economic reforms, many African countries can work to solve their problems.

The Americas Today

Most Latin American nations continue to struggle. They have many economic challenges. Their governments are often unstable. Illegal drug trade is also a problem in countries such as Peru and Colombia.

Latin America has made some good changes. Mexico has paid off much of its foreign debt. Education has improved. The middle class is growing larger in much of Latin America.

Citizens of Mexico celebrated the election of President Vicente Fox in 2000.

The United States entered the 21st century as the most powerful nation in the world. That doesn't mean that it is not without problems. The war on terrorism is a big challenge for the United States. Illegal immigration and illegal drugs are also problems.

The International Peace Garden lies on the border between the United States and Canada.

Still, the United States has used its power to improve conditions around the world. It has sent foreign aid to many countries, especially those in Latin America. It has also encouraged other countries to improve their human rights. It has lowered **trade barriers**. The North American Free Trade Agreement (**NAFTA**) took effect in 1994. It called for free trade between Canada, Mexico, and the United States.

Lesson 4 Review

Choose words from the list that best complete the paragraphs. One word will not be used.

Throughout world history, there has always been change. Each region faces its own challenges. Slobodan Milosevic was charged with war crimes for his policy of __1__ in Serbia. Ethnic conflict continues in Asia. Communist governments are lessening their economic controls.

Africa has been hurt by civil wars, droughts, and a disease called __2__. Latin Americans continue to fight economic problems. The United States and its allies are fighting a war on terrorism. Illegal __3__ is a problem. __4__ lowered trade barriers between Canada, Mexico, and the United States.

Word List

famine
NAFTA
AIDS
ethnic cleansing
immigration

Chapter 35: Using What You've Learned

Summary

- On September 11, 2001, the United States suffered the worst terrorist attack in its history. Terrorism comes in many forms and can happen anywhere. Terrorists scare and kill innocent people in order to make a statement.
- Technology has improved medicine, created new forms of energy, and increased our ability to communicate. Many poorer nations do not have access to new technology, however.
- Many scientists believe that the earth is in trouble because the air and water are getting dirtier. They also believe that the earth is getting warmer.
- Today, many nations face serious problems, such as civil war, ethnic conflicts, and unstable governments.

Find Out More!

After reading Chapter 35, you're ready to go online. **Explore Zone**, **Quiz Time**, and **Amazing Facts** bring this chapter of world history alive.

Visit www.exploreSV.com and type in the chapter code **Ch35**.

Vocabulary

Number your paper from 1 to 4. Write the letter of the correct answer.

1. Hybrid cars run on both gas and ____.
   a. X-rays **c.** lasers
   b. electricity **d.** windmills

2. The ____ made the Internet available to more people.
   a. World Wide Web **c.** global village
   b. X-ray **d.** ozone layer

3. The ozone layer protects us from ____.
   a. air pollution **c.** the sun's rays
   b. fertilizers **d.** the polar ice caps

4. The euro is a kind of ____ used in most European countries.
   a. money **c.** language
   b. government **d.** custom

Comprehension

Number your paper from 1 to 6. Write the word or words from the list that best complete the paragraph. One word will not be used.

Acts of __1__ happen throughout the world. In 2001, someone mailed a deadly germ called __2__ in envelopes to many offices in the United States. The __3__ has used terror to try to unify Northern Ireland. Members of Hamas and Hezbollah act as __4__, killing themselves and as many Israeli people as possible. Arabs experience terrorism from __5__. The Japanese Red Army __6__ airplanes to try to overthrow the Japanese government.

Word List

terrorism
hijacks
global warming
Israeli soldiers
Irish Republican Army
suicide bombers
anthrax

Critical Thinking

Conclusions **Number your paper from 1 to 3. Read each pair of sentences below. Then look for a conclusion that follows from these sentences. Write the letter of the correct conclusion.**

1. When hydrogen burns, it turns into water vapor.
   Using hydrogen for fuel does not harm the environment.
2. Rainwater carries fertilizers and pesticides into lakes and rivers.
   Waste products from factories and mines flow into lakes and rivers.
3. Some scientists believe that global warming could cause temperatures to rise by six degrees by 2100.
   This rise in temperature would cause the polar ice caps to melt.

Conclusions

a. Many lakes and rivers are too polluted for fishing and swimming.
b. Hydrogen is a cheap and clean source of energy.
c. Global warming could cause cities along coastlines to flood.

Writing

Choose a region of the world. Write a paragraph describing the recent successes of the region and the challenges the region faces today.

Political Map of the World

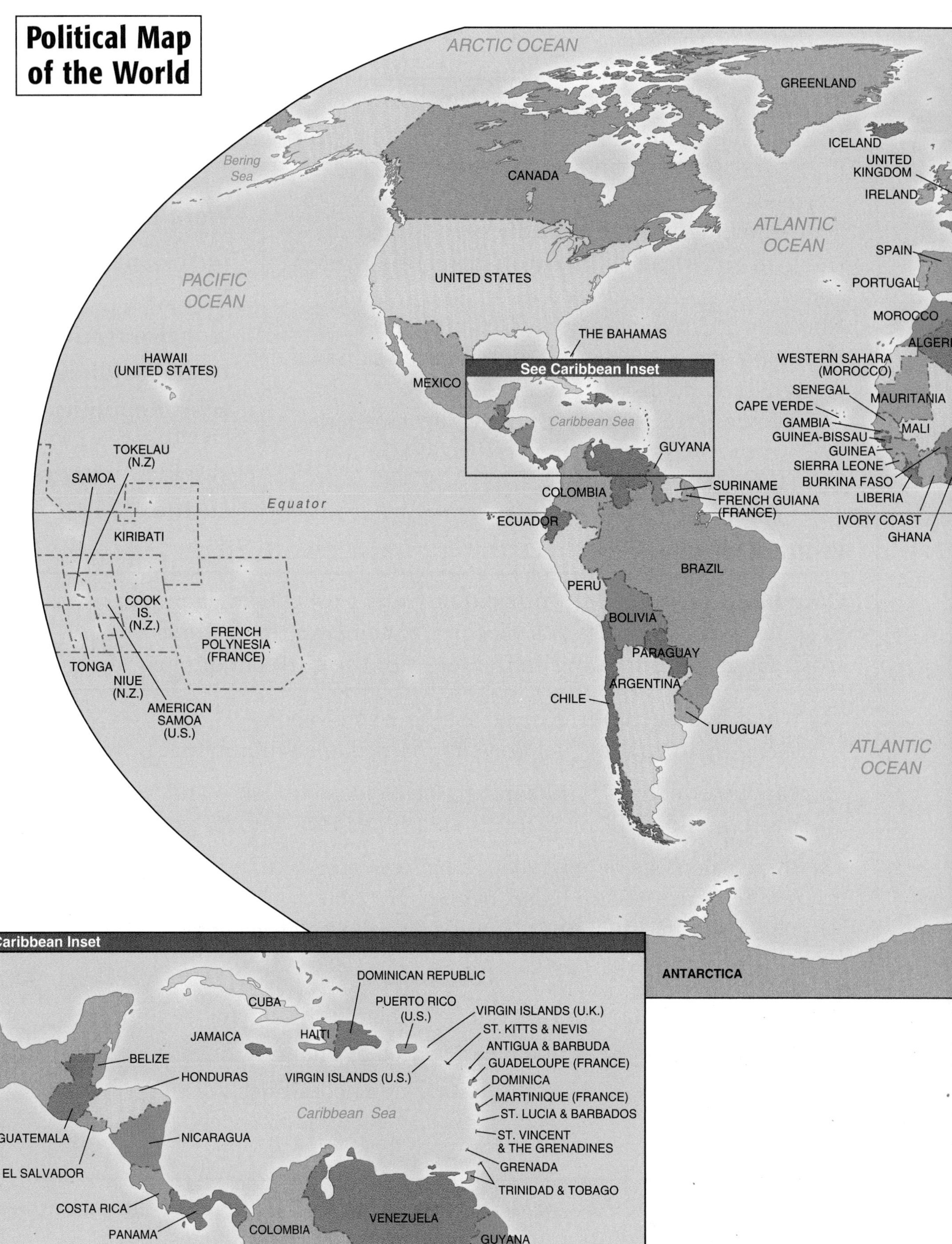

ARCTIC OCEAN
GREENLAND
ICELAND
UNITED KINGDOM
IRELAND
Bering Sea
CANADA
ATLANTIC OCEAN
SPAIN
PORTUGAL
PACIFIC OCEAN
UNITED STATES
MOROCCO
ALGERIA
THE BAHAMAS
HAWAII (UNITED STATES)
See Caribbean Inset
WESTERN SAHARA (MOROCCO)
MEXICO
SENEGAL
MAURITANIA
CAPE VERDE
Caribbean Sea
GAMBIA
MALI
GUINEA-BISSAU
GUINEA
TOKELAU (N.Z)
GUYANA
SIERRA LEONE
SAMOA
SURINAME
BURKINA FASO
COLOMBIA
FRENCH GUIANA (FRANCE)
LIBERIA
Equator
ECUADOR
IVORY COAST
KIRIBATI
GHANA
BRAZIL
PERU
COOK IS. (N.Z.)
BOLIVIA
FRENCH POLYNESIA (FRANCE)
PARAGUAY
TONGA
ARGENTINA
NIUE (N.Z.)
CHILE
AMERICAN SAMOA (U.S.)
URUGUAY
ATLANTIC OCEAN
ANTARCTICA
Caribbean Inset
DOMINICAN REPUBLIC
CUBA
PUERTO RICO (U.S.)
VIRGIN ISLANDS (U.K.)
ST. KITTS & NEVIS
JAMAICA
HAITI
ANTIGUA & BARBUDA
BELIZE
GUADELOUPE (FRANCE)
HONDURAS
VIRGIN ISLANDS (U.S.)
DOMINICA
MARTINIQUE (FRANCE)
Caribbean Sea
ST. LUCIA & BARBADOS
GUATEMALA
NICARAGUA
ST. VINCENT & THE GRENADINES
EL SALVADOR
GRENADA
TRINIDAD & TOBAGO
COSTA RICA
VENEZUELA
PANAMA
COLOMBIA
GUYANA

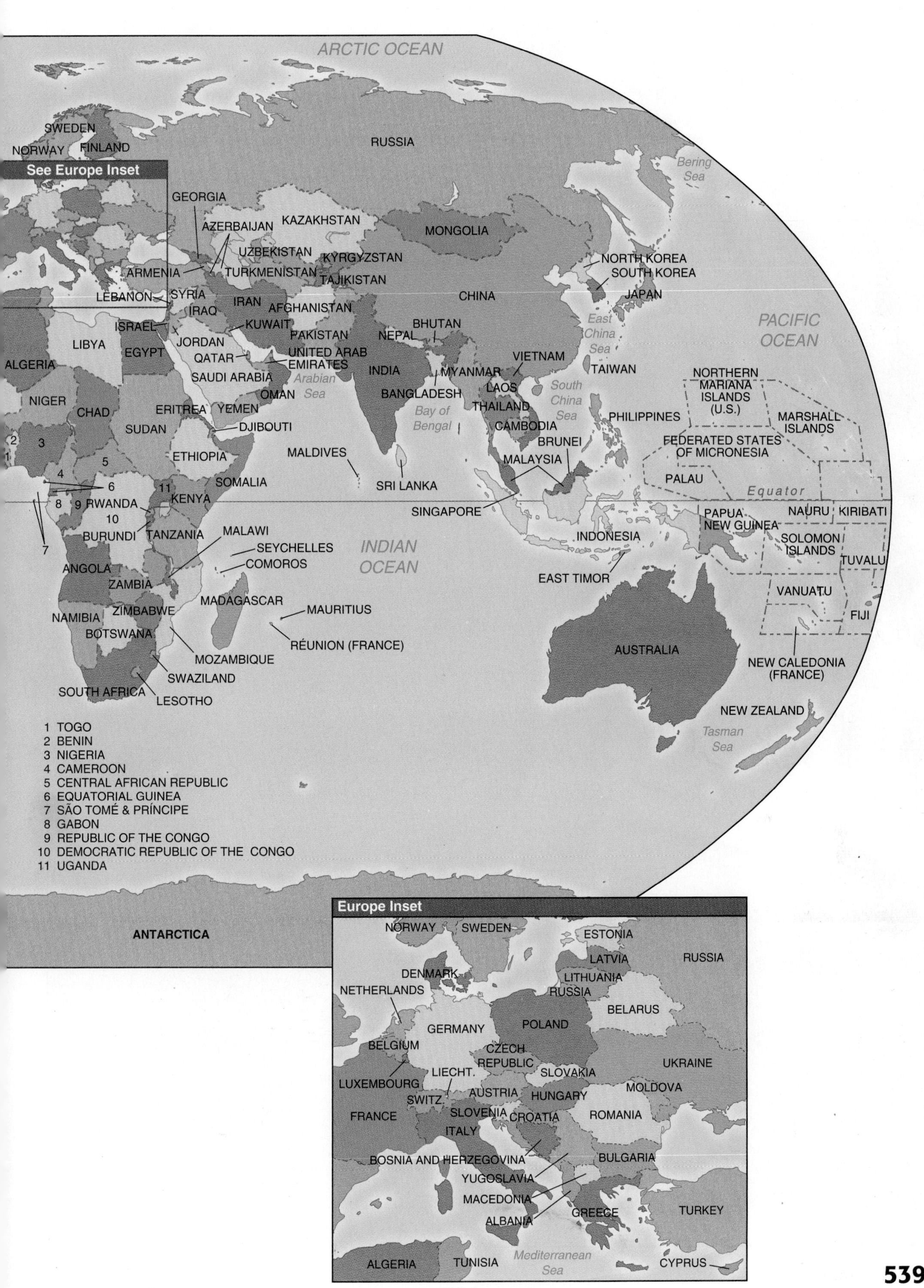
ARCTIC OCEAN
SWEDEN
NORWAY
FINLAND
RUSSIA
See Europe Inset
Bering Sea
GEORGIA
AZERBAIJAN
KAZAKHSTAN
MONGOLIA
UZBEKISTAN
KYRGYZSTAN
ARMENIA
TURKMENISTAN
TAJIKISTAN
NORTH KOREA
SOUTH KOREA
LEBANON
SYRIA
IRAQ
IRAN
AFGHANISTAN
CHINA
JAPAN
ISRAEL
KUWAIT
BHUTAN
East China Sea
PACIFIC OCEAN
LIBYA
EGYPT
JORDAN
PAKISTAN
NEPAL
QATAR
UNITED ARAB EMIRATES
VIETNAM
ALGERIA
INDIA
MYANMAR
TAIWAN
SAUDI ARABIA
Arabian Sea
LAOS
NORTHERN MARIANA ISLANDS (U.S.)
NIGER
OMAN
BANGLADESH
South China Sea
CHAD
ERITREA
YEMEN
Bay of Bengal
THAILAND
PHILIPPINES
MARSHALL ISLANDS
SUDAN
DJIBOUTI
CAMBODIA
FEDERATED STATES OF MICRONESIA
BRUNEI
ETHIOPIA
MALDIVES
MALAYSIA
PALAU
SOMALIA
SRI LANKA
Equator
KENYA
RWANDA
SINGAPORE
PAPUA NEW GUINEA
NAURU
KIRIBATI
BURUNDI
TANZANIA
MALAWI
INDONESIA
SOLOMON ISLANDS
SEYCHELLES
INDIAN OCEAN
COMOROS
TUVALU
ANGOLA
ZAMBIA
EAST TIMOR
VANUATU
MADAGASCAR
ZIMBABWE
MAURITIUS
FIJI
NAMIBIA
BOTSWANA
RÉUNION (FRANCE)
AUSTRALIA
MOZAMBIQUE
NEW CALEDONIA (FRANCE)
SWAZILAND
SOUTH AFRICA
LESOTHO
NEW ZEALAND
Tasman Sea
1 TOGO
2 BENIN
3 NIGERIA
4 CAMEROON
5 CENTRAL AFRICAN REPUBLIC
6 EQUATORIAL GUINEA
7 SÃO TOMÉ & PRÍNCIPE
8 GABON
9 REPUBLIC OF THE CONGO
10 DEMOCRATIC REPUBLIC OF THE CONGO
11 UGANDA
ANTARCTICA
Europe Inset
NORWAY
SWEDEN
ESTONIA
LATVIA
RUSSIA
DENMARK
LITHUANIA
NETHERLANDS
RUSSIA
BELARUS
POLAND
GERMANY
BELGIUM
CZECH REPUBLIC
UKRAINE
LIECHT.
SLOVAKIA
LUXEMBOURG
AUSTRIA
HUNGARY
MOLDOVA
SWITZ.
SLOVENIA
FRANCE
CROATIA
ROMANIA
ITALY
BOSNIA AND HERZEGOVINA
BULGARIA
YUGOSLAVIA
MACEDONIA
GREECE
TURKEY
ALBANIA
ALGERIA
TUNISIA
Mediterranean Sea
CYPRUS

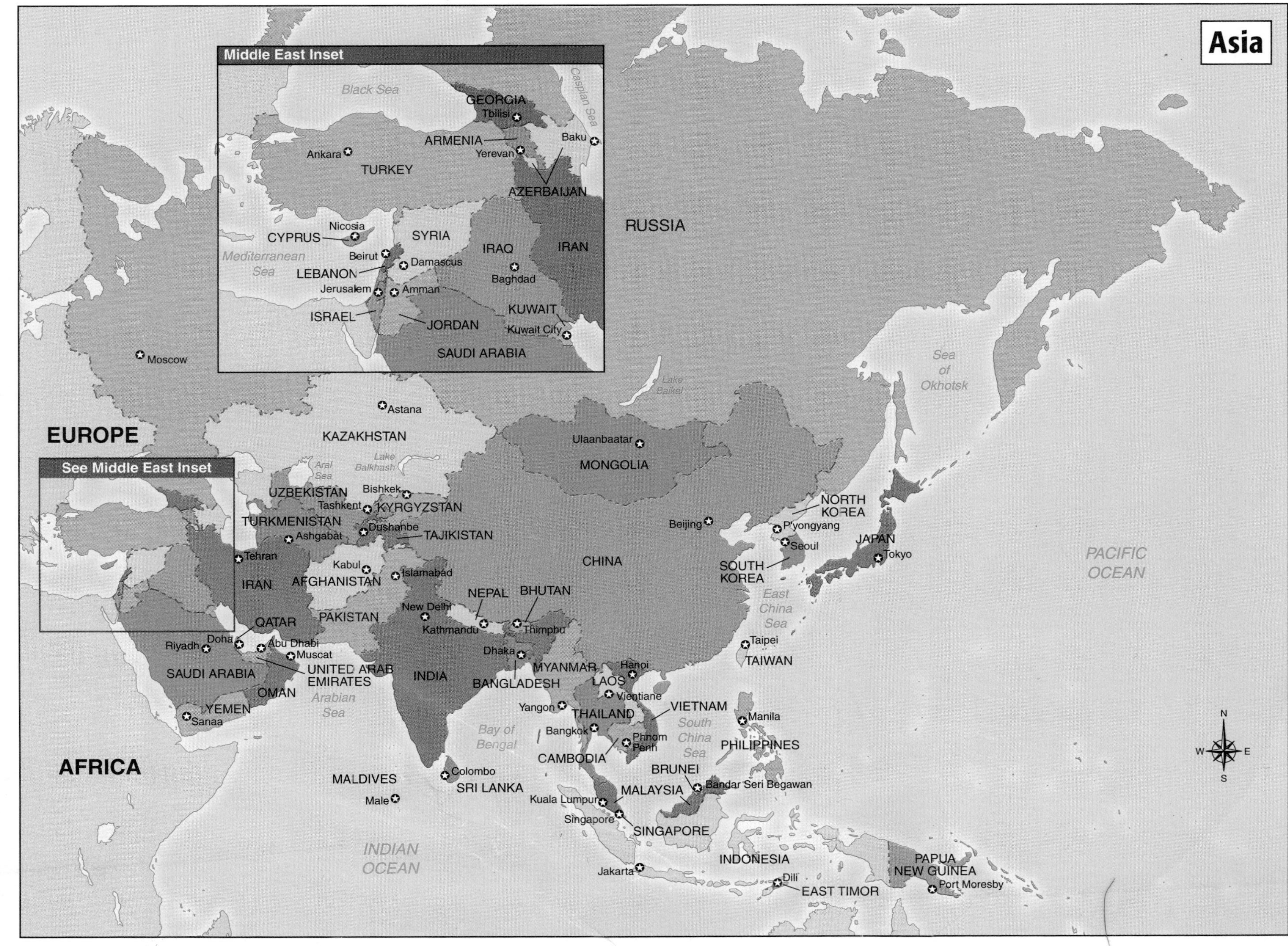

Asia
Middle East Inset
Black Sea
Caspian Sea
GEORGIA
Tbilisi
ARMENIA
Yerevan
Baku
AZERBAIJAN
Ankara
TURKEY
Nicosia
CYPRUS
SYRIA
IRAQ
IRAN
Mediterranean Sea
Beirut
Damascus
LEBANON
Baghdad
Jerusalem
Amman
KUWAIT
ISRAEL
JORDAN
Kuwait City
SAUDI ARABIA
RUSSIA
Moscow
Lake Baikal
Sea of Okhotsk
Astana
EUROPE
KAZAKHSTAN
See Middle East Inset
Aral Sea
Lake Balkhash
Ulaanbaatar
MONGOLIA
UZBEKISTAN
Bishkek
Tashkent
KYRGYZSTAN
NORTH KOREA
TURKMENISTAN
Beijing
P'yongyang
Ashgabat
Dushanbe
TAJIKISTAN
JAPAN
Seoul
Tehran
CHINA
Tokyo
Kabul
Islamabad
SOUTH KOREA
PACIFIC OCEAN
IRAN
AFGHANISTAN
NEPAL
BHUTAN
East China Sea
New Delhi
QATAR
PAKISTAN
Kathmandu
Thimphu
Riyadh
Doha
Abu Dhabi
Dhaka
Taipei
Muscat
MYANMAR
Hanoi
SAUDI ARABIA
UNITED ARAB EMIRATES
INDIA
TAIWAN
BANGLADESH
LAOS
OMAN
Vientiane
Arabian Sea
VIETNAM
YEMEN
Yangon
Sanaa
THAILAND
Manila
Bay of Bengal
South China Sea
Bangkok
Phnom Penh
PHILIPPINES
CAMBODIA
AFRICA
Colombo
BRUNEI
MALDIVES
Bandar Seri Begawan
SRI LANKA
MALAYSIA
Kuala Lumpur
Male
Singapore
SINGAPORE
INDIAN OCEAN
INDONESIA
PAPUA NEW GUINEA
Jakarta
Dili
EAST TIMOR
Port Moresby
N
W
E
S

Africa

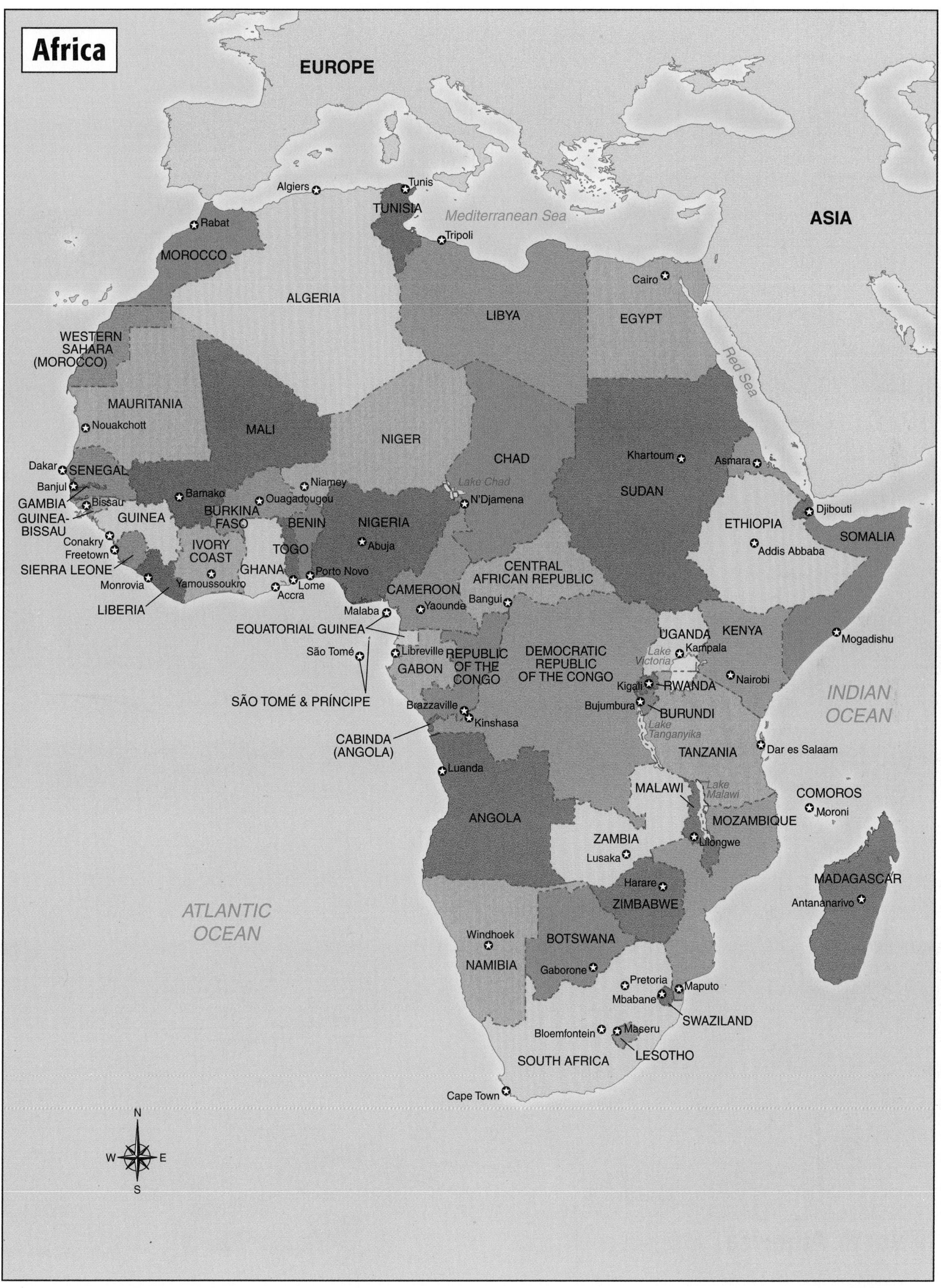
EUROPE
ASIA
Mediterranean Sea
Red Sea
ATLANTIC OCEAN
INDIAN OCEAN
Algiers
Tunis
TUNISIA
Rabat
MOROCCO
Tripoli
ALGERIA
LIBYA
Cairo
EGYPT
WESTERN SAHARA (MOROCCO)
MAURITANIA
Nouakchott
MALI
NIGER
CHAD
Lake Chad
SUDAN
Khartoum
Asmara
Dakar
SENEGAL
Banjul
GAMBIA
Bissau
GUINEA-BISSAU
GUINEA
Bamako
BURKINA FASO
Ouagadougou
Niamey
BENIN
NIGERIA
N'Djamena
Djibouti
ETHIOPIA
Addis Ababa
SOMALIA
Conakry
Freetown
SIERRA LEONE
IVORY COAST
Yamoussoukro
GHANA
TOGO
Abuja
Porto Novo
Lome
Accra
Monrovia
LIBERIA
CENTRAL AFRICAN REPUBLIC
CAMEROON
Yaounde
Bangui
Malaba
EQUATORIAL GUINEA
São Tomé
Libreville
GABON
REPUBLIC OF THE CONGO
DEMOCRATIC REPUBLIC OF THE CONGO
UGANDA
Kampala
Lake Victoria
KENYA
Nairobi
Mogadishu
Kigali
RWANDA
Bujumbura
BURUNDI
SÃO TOMÉ & PRÍNCIPE
Brazzaville
Kinshasa
CABINDA (ANGOLA)
Lake Tanganyika
TANZANIA
Dar es Salaam
Luanda
MALAWI
Lake Malawi
COMOROS
Moroni
ANGOLA
MOZAMBIQUE
Lilongwe
ZAMBIA
Lusaka
Harare
ZIMBABWE
MADAGASCAR
Antananarivo
Windhoek
NAMIBIA
BOTSWANA
Gaborone
Pretoria
Maputo
Mbabane
SWAZILAND
Bloemfontein
Maseru
LESOTHO
SOUTH AFRICA
Cape Town
N
W
E
S

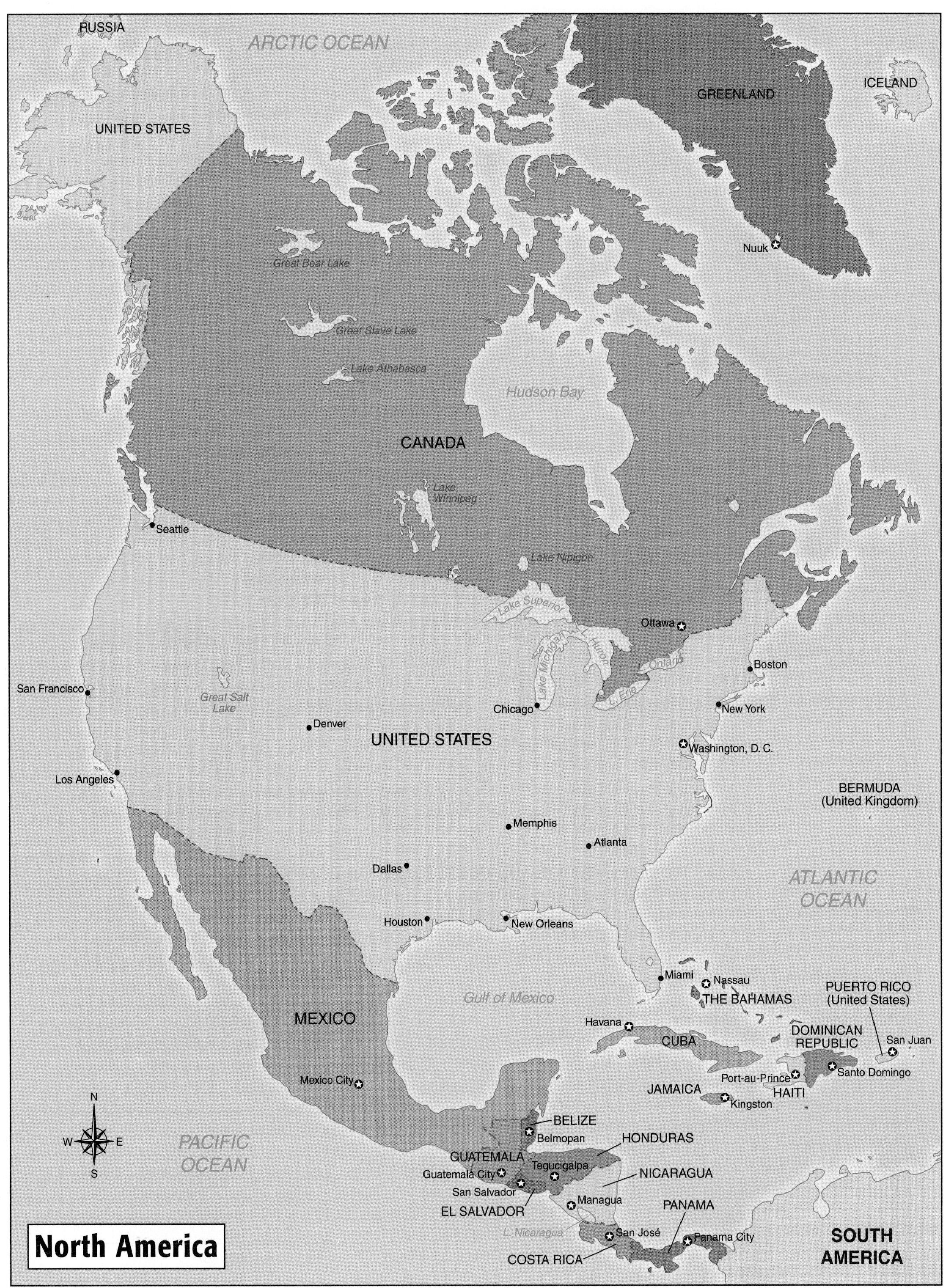

North America

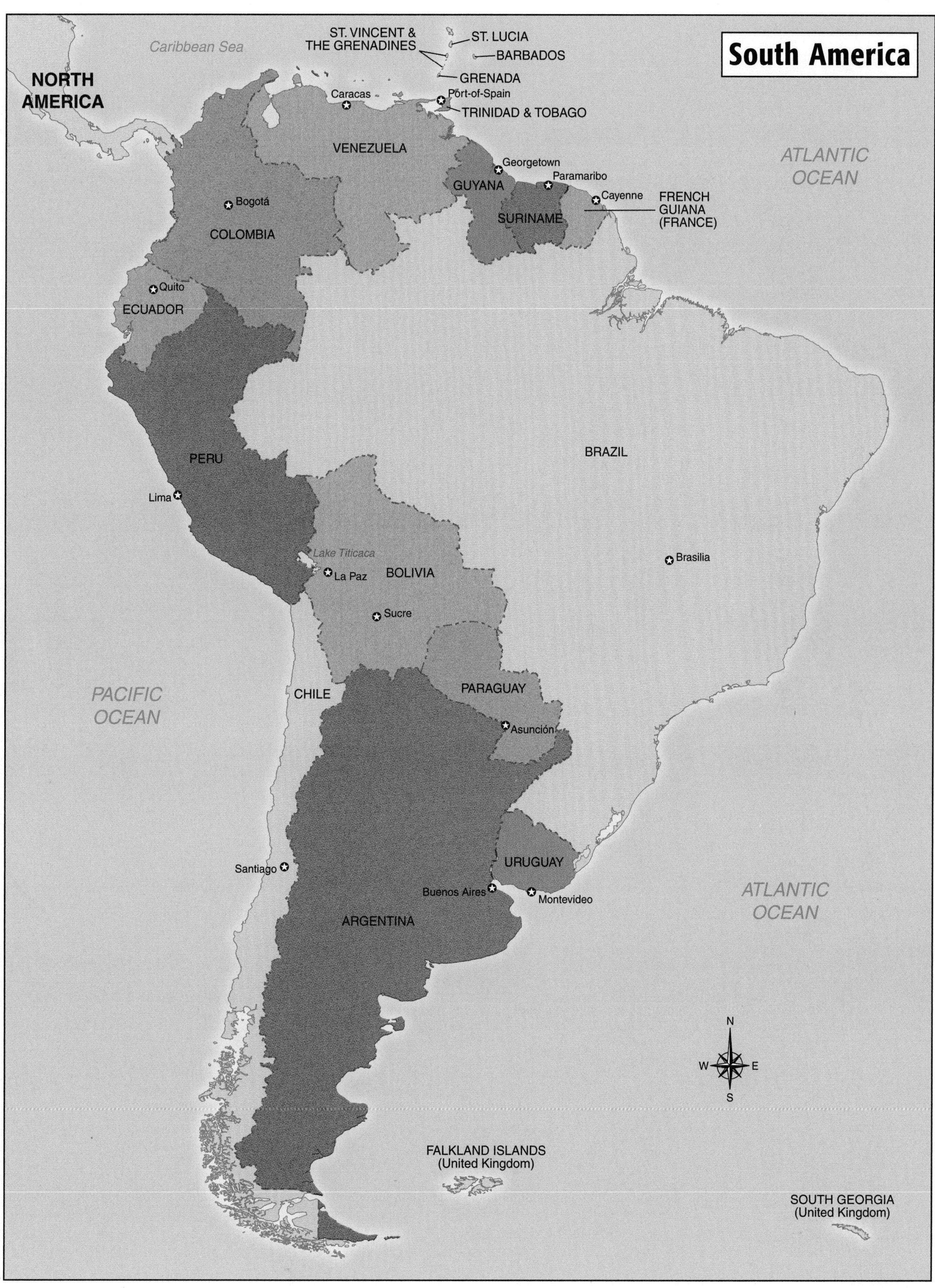
South America
Caribbean Sea
NORTH AMERICA
ST. VINCENT & THE GRENADINES
ST. LUCIA
BARBADOS
GRENADA
Caracas
Port-of-Spain
TRINIDAD & TOBAGO
VENEZUELA
Georgetown
GUYANA
Paramaribo
SURINAME
Cayenne
FRENCH GUIANA (FRANCE)
ATLANTIC OCEAN
Bogotá
COLOMBIA
Quito
ECUADOR
PERU
Lima
BRAZIL
Lake Titicaca
La Paz
BOLIVIA
Sucre
Brasilia
PACIFIC OCEAN
CHILE
PARAGUAY
Asunción
URUGUAY
Santiago
Buenos Aires
Montevideo
ATLANTIC OCEAN
ARGENTINA
N
W
E
S
FALKLAND ISLANDS (United Kingdom)
SOUTH GEORGIA (United Kingdom)

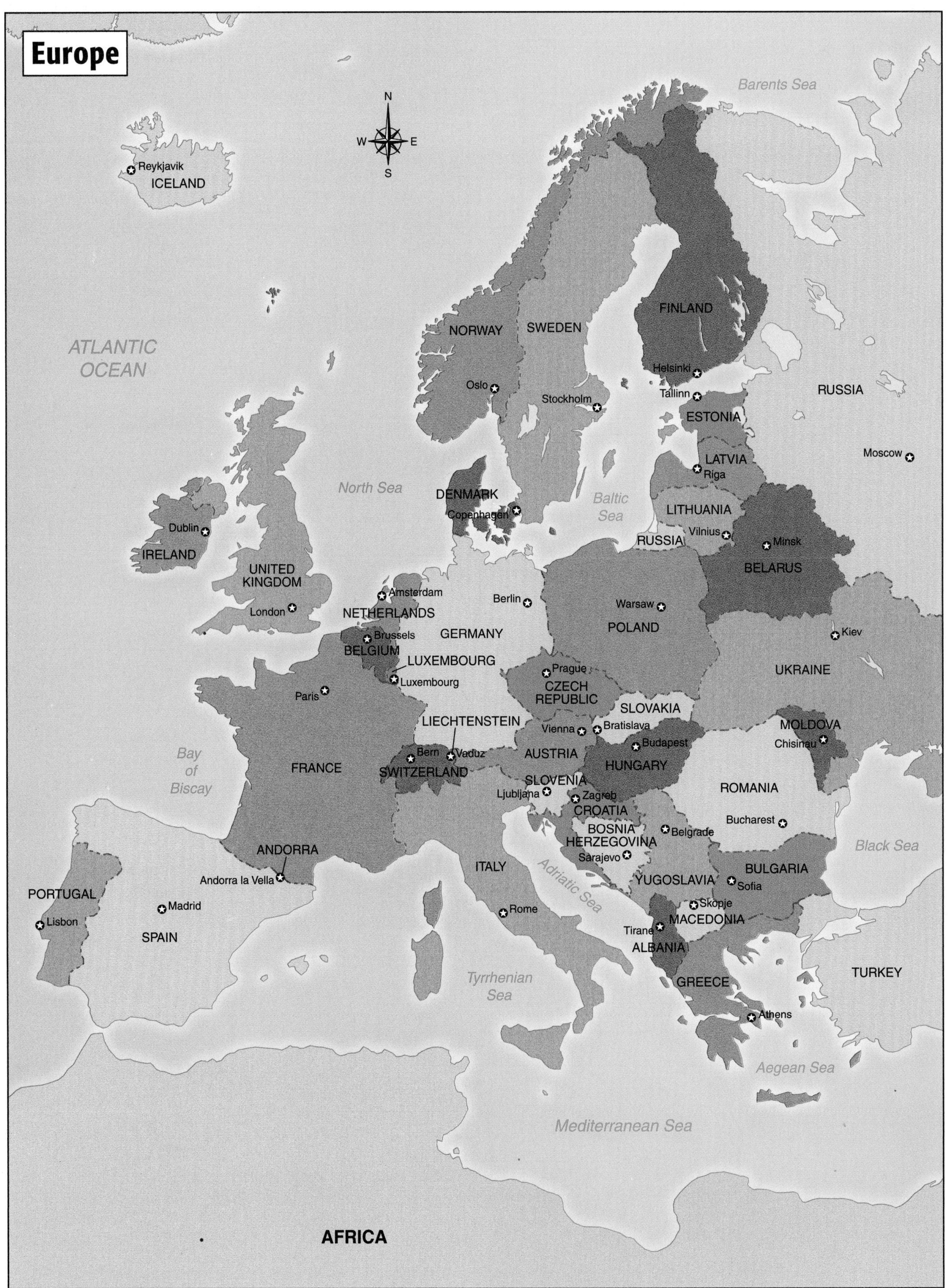

Europe
N
E
S
W
Barents Sea
Reykjavik
ICELAND
FINLAND
NORWAY
SWEDEN
ATLANTIC
OCEAN
Helsinki
Oslo
Stockholm
Tallinn
RUSSIA
ESTONIA
LATVIA
Riga
Moscow
North Sea
DENMARK
Copenhagen
Baltic
Sea
LITHUANIA
Vilnius
RUSSIA
Minsk
Dublin
IRELAND
UNITED
KINGDOM
BELARUS
Amsterdam
Berlin
Warsaw
London
NETHERLANDS
POLAND
Brussels
GERMANY
Kiev
BELGIUM
LUXEMBOURG
Luxembourg
Prague
CZECH
REPUBLIC
UKRAINE
Paris
SLOVAKIA
LIECHTENSTEIN
MOLDOVA
Vienna
Bratislava
Chisinau
Bay
of
Biscay
Bern
Vaduz
Budapest
FRANCE
AUSTRIA
SWITZERLAND
HUNGARY
SLOVENIA
ROMANIA
Ljubljana
Zagreb
CROATIA
BOSNIA
HERZEGOVINA
Belgrade
Bucharest
Black Sea
ANDORRA
Sarajevo
Andorra la Vella
ITALY
Adriatic Sea
YUGOSLAVIA
BULGARIA
Sofia
PORTUGAL
Madrid
Skopje
Rome
MACEDONIA
Lisbon
Tirane
SPAIN
ALBANIA
TURKEY
GREECE
Tyrrhenian
Sea
Athens
Aegean Sea
Mediterranean Sea
AFRICA

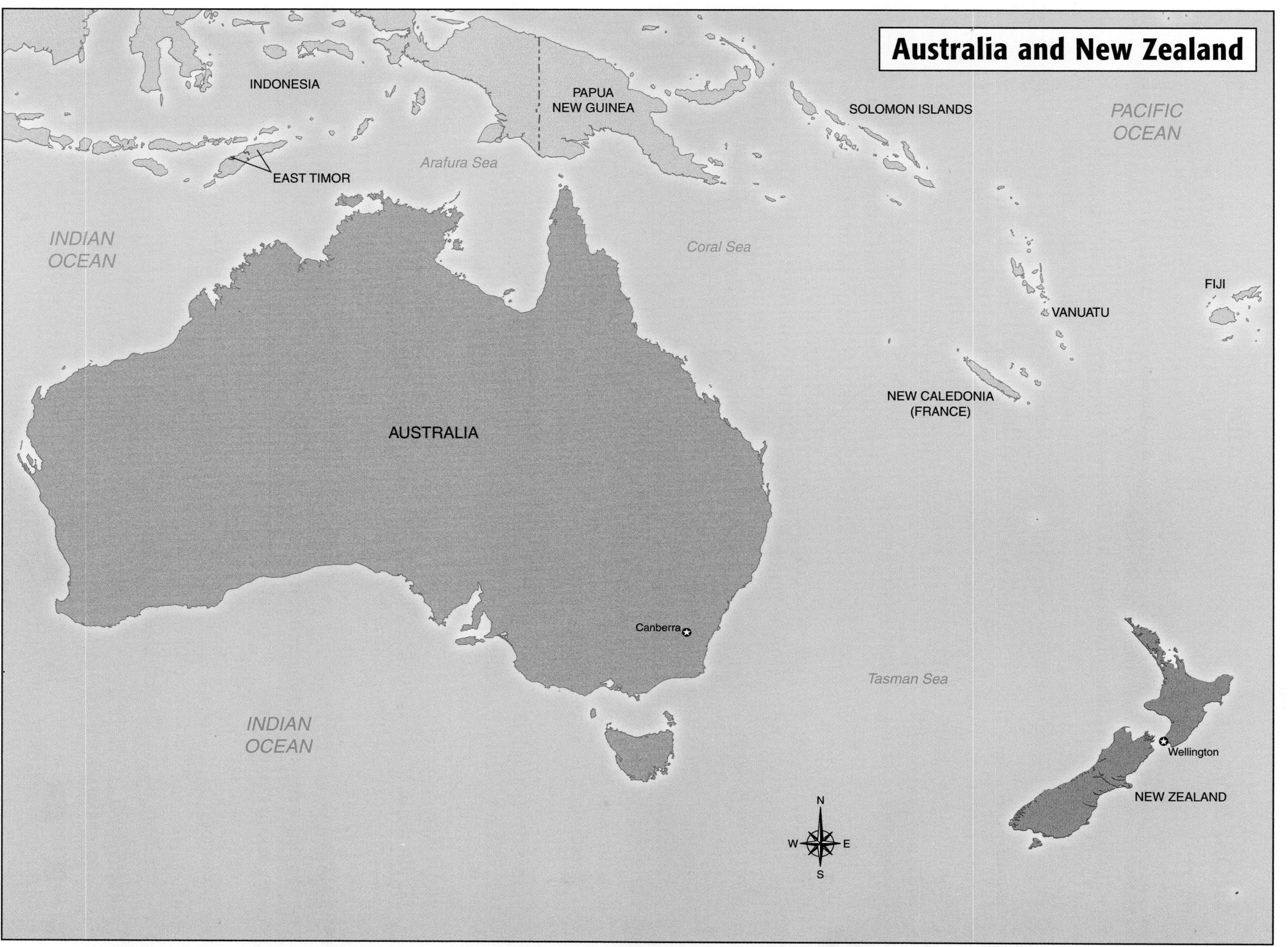
Australia and New Zealand
INDONESIA
PAPUA
NEW GUINEA
SOLOMON ISLANDS
PACIFIC
OCEAN
EAST TIMOR
Arafura Sea
INDIAN
OCEAN
Coral Sea
FIJI
VANUATU
NEW CALEDONIA
(FRANCE)
AUSTRALIA
Canberra
Tasman Sea
INDIAN
OCEAN
Wellington
NEW ZEALAND
N
W
E
S

Glossary

95 Theses (page 278)
The 95 Theses was a list of complaints about the Catholic Church that Martin Luther nailed to a church door in 1517.

A

abandoned (page 306)
Abandoned means left deserted or no longer used.

abdicate (page 427)
To abdicate is to give up one's right to rule.

abolitionists (page 387)
Abolitionists were people who fought to end slavery in the United States.

Aborigines (page 383)
Aborigines are people native to Australia. Their ancestors lived in Australia before Europeans arrived there.

absolutism (page 291)
Absolutism is a system of government in which a ruler has complete power.

acid rain (page 528)
Acid rain is rain that has been changed by pollution in the air.

addictive (page 401)
Something that is addictive is likely to cause a person to want to use it again and again.

adjourn (page 356)
To adjourn is to close a meeting.

advantage (page 305)
An advantage is something that helps a person.

afterlife (page 18)
An afterlife is a life after one's death.

aggression (page 449)
Aggression is the use of force.

ahimsa (page 120)
Ahimsa means never hurting others.

AIDS (page 534)
AIDS is a disease that causes one's body to not be able to fight germs.

al Qaeda (page 519)
Al Qaeda is a group of Islamic extremists who are responsible for many terrorist attacks around the world.

Allah (page 157)
Allah is the Arabic word for God used in the religion Islam.

alliances (page 411)
Alliances are agreements between nations to help one another in times of trouble, such as in a war.

Allies (page 414)
During World War I, the Allies were a group of nations that fought against nations of the Central Powers. During World War II, the Allies fought against nations of the Axis Powers.

ally (page 175)
An ally is a country that helps another country during a war.

anatomy (page 273)
Anatomy is the structure of the body of a human or other animal.

ancestors (page 264)
Ancestors are people of one's family who lived long ago.

anthrax (page 519)
Anthrax is a dangerous germ that can cause death.

anti-Semitism (page 458)
Anti-Semitism is a hatred of Jews.

apartheid (page 486)
Apartheid was a system of laws that kept white South Africans apart from black South Africans.

appeasement (page 450)
Appeasement is a plan to give in to the demands of a nation or leader in order to keep peace.

apprentice (page 219)
An apprentice is a person who learns a trade from a skilled worker.

aqueducts (page 104)
Aqueducts are channels that are used for carrying water.

Arabic numerals (page 165)
Arabic numerals are the numbers 1 through 9.

archaeologists (page 8)
Archaeologists are people who study old bones and objects to learn about the past.

archduke (page 412)
An archduke is an Austrian prince.

archipelago (page 176)
An archipelago is a chain of islands.

architecture (page 274)
Architecture is the style in which buildings are designed and built.

armistice (page 417)
An armistice is an agreement to stop fighting.

arms race (page 411)
An arms race is an attempt by nations to have a better army and navy and better weapons than other nations have.

artifacts (page 68)
Artifacts are objects made by people.

assassinate (page 117)
To assassinate someone is to kill that person. The person killed is usually a leader or someone else important.

atomic bomb (page 456)
An atomic bomb is a powerful weapon that causes a huge explosion.

attitudes (page 430)
Attitudes are ways of looking at the world.

authority (page 285)
An authority is a person with much knowledge or experience and whose opinion or information is often considered to be true.

Axis Powers (page 448)
The Axis Powers were Germany, Italy, Japan, and other nations that fought the Allies during World War II.

B

Balfour Declaration (page 441)
The Balfour Declaration was a letter written by British official Arthur Balfour in which he agreed that Jews should have a homeland in Palestine.

Bantu migrations (page 191)
The Bantu migrations were a mass movement of people from West Africa to the eastern and southern areas of Africa from around 100 B.C. to A.D.S 1000.

barbarians (page 140)
Barbarians were Germans and other people who entered the lands of the ancient Western Roman Empire by force.

barren (page 391)
Barren means unable to support plant life or animal life.

bartered (page 218)
Bartered means traded one good for another.

basalt (page 57)
Basalt is a kind of rock formed from cooled lava.

bas-reliefs (page 70)
Bas-reliefs are carvings made on a flat surface.

Bastille (page 357)
The Bastille was a royal prison in France.

bathhouses (page 227)
Bathhouses are public places where people can take baths.

bazaar (page 163)
A bazaar is a market of shops.

bedouins (page 156)
Bedouins are people who live in the deserts of Arabia, Syria, or North Africa. They do not have permanent homes.

Berlin Airlift (page 473)
The Berlin Airlift was a series of flights by the United States and Great Britain to deliver food and supplies to West Berlin after the Soviets blocked all land traffic from the west.

Berlin Wall (page 473)
The Berlin Wall was a wall built by the East German government to keep East Germans from escaping to West Berlin. It became a symbol of the Cold War and was torn down in 1989.

Black Death (page 220)
The Black Death was a disease that killed many people during the 14th century. It was carried by fleas that lived on rats.

blitzkrieg (page 453)
Blitzkrieg refers to a type of hard and fast fighting used by the Germans in World War II.

blockade (page 472)
A blockade is a closing off of an area to keep people from going in or out.

Bolsheviks (page 428)
Bolsheviks were Communists who took control of the Russian government in 1917.

boycott (page 352)
To boycott is to refuse to buy or use.

Brahman (page 49)
A Brahman was a priest in the Aryan civilization of ancient India. The Brahman was at the top of the social classes.

bribes (page 111)
Bribes are money given to someone in order to get that person to do something wrong.

broadcast (page 431)
To broadcast is to send radio signals.

bronze (page 42)
Bronze is a hard metal that is a mixture of copper and tin.

Buddhism (page 118)
Buddhism is a religion that is based on the teachings of a man called the Buddha.

buffer zone (page 420)
A buffer zone is an area of land meant to separate enemy nations.

bureaucracy (page 129)
A bureaucracy is a group of government officials.

burial grounds (page 267)
Burial grounds are places in which dead people are buried.

Bushido (page 236)
Bushido was the code of honor followed by Japanese warriors.

C

calendar (page 57)
A calendar is a system that divides a year into months, weeks, and days.

caliph (page 162)
A caliph is the head of the Islamic communities.

caliphate (page 163)
A caliphate is the land ruled by the head of the Islamic communities.

calligraphy (page 164)
Calligraphy is a kind of beautiful writing.

Camp David Accords (page 507)
The Camp David Accords was a peace agreement between Egypt and Israel. It was signed in 1979.

capitalism (page 471)
Capitalism is a system in which private companies own most industries in a nation.

caravans (page 66)
Caravans are groups of people traveling through the desert.

carbon dioxide (page 530)
Carbon dioxide is a gas that is released by burning fuels. It also is released when people and animals breathe out.

cardinal (page 291)
A cardinal is an important official of the Catholic Church.

cash crop (page 307)
A cash crop is a crop grown mainly to sell to or trade with others.

castes (page 49)
Castes are classes of people. Hindus believe that people are born into castes.

catapults (page 226)
Catapults are huge slings used to toss bombs or rocks over high walls during wars.

cathedrals (page 220)
Cathedrals are large, magnificent churches.

Catholic Church (page 152)
The Catholic Church is the Christian church based in western Europe. It is headed by the pope.

causeways (page 261)
Causeways are roads over water.

cease-fire (page 478)
A cease-fire is an agreement between nations to stop fighting.

Central Powers (page 414)
The Central Powers was a group of nations that fought against the Allies in World War I.

ceramics (page 205)
Ceramics are pottery and other objects made by heating clay.

chancellor (page 381)
A chancellor is a person in charge of the government in some countries.

chariots (page 22)
Chariots are two-wheeled carts that are pulled by horses. Long ago people used chariots in battles or in races.

child labor (page 375)
Child labor is the use of children as workers in factories, stores, or other businesses.

chinampas (page 261)
Chinampas were floating gardens made by the Aztec in order to grow crops.

Christianity (page 106)
Christianity is a religion based on the teachings of Jesus.

citadel (page 48)
A citadel is a strong fort built to protect a city.

city-states (page 30)
City-states are towns or cities that rule themselves and the land around them.

civil disobedience (page 442)
Civil disobedience is the act of peacefully refusing to follow a government's laws because someone does not agree with them.

civil rights (page 510)
Civil rights are rights that belong to every citizen.

civil servants (page 331)
Civil servants are people who work for government offices.

civil war (page 127)
A civil war is a war in which people of the same country fight against one another.

civilians (page 462)
Civilians are people who are not in the army, navy, or other military unit.

civilizations (page 13)
Civilizations are large communities that have a written language and a government.

clans (page 10)
Clans are groups of people that live and hunt together in order to have a better chance of surviving.

Classic Maya (page 199)
Classic Maya refers to a time period during which the Mayan civilization was at its height, between A.D. 300 and A.D. 900.

climate (page 7)
The climate is the average weather of a place over several years.

coalition (page 508)
A coalition is a group of nations that have joined together for a purpose.

Code of Hammurabi (page 31)
The Code of Hammurabi is a set of about 282 laws put together by Hammurabi, a king of ancient Babylon.

Cold War (page 470)
The Cold War was a struggle between the United States, the Soviet Union, and other nations about the spread of communism.

collective farms (page 436)
Collective farms are farms run by groups of people.

colonize (page 396)
To colonize is to set up a colony or colonies in a foreign land.

Columbian Exchange (page 305)
The Columbian Exchange is a global exchange of goods and ideas between the Americas and other continents that began when Columbus landed in the Americas in 1492.

commodity (page 253)
A commodity is a good that is bought and sold.

communism (page 375)
Communism is a system in which the government or the whole community owns the land.

competition (page 410)
A competition is a situation in which people, groups, or nations are trying to get the same thing.

concentration camps (page 459)
Concentration camps were prisons where captured Jews and other people were sent by Nazis during World War II.

confederation (page 315)
A confederation is a group of smaller states under one government.

Confucianism (page 132)
Confucianism is a philosophy based on the teachings of a man named Confucius, who was born in China around 550 B.C.

Congress of Vienna (page 379)
The Congress of Vienna was a meeting held in Austria in 1814 to create new states around France after the Age of Napoleon.

conquered (page 77)
Conquered means used force to take control of a place or group of people.

conquest (page 226)
A conquest is the act of taking control of a land by force.

conquistador (page 301)
A conquistador was a Spanish leader or soldier who gained control of parts of the Americas during the 1500s.

conservation (page 531)
Conservation is the act of protecting natural resources, such as trees and water.

Constitution (page 354)
The Constitution is the laws and the plan of government for the United States of America.

consuls (page 90)
Consuls were leaders of the ancient Roman republic. Two consuls led the government at a time.

contact (page 37)
To have contact with a group of people is to have communication with them.

containment (page 472)
Containment is a plan to prevent a nation from spreading its ideas or influence.

continents (page 5)
Continents are very large masses of land. There are seven continents on Earth.

convents (page 149)
Convents are places where nuns live, work, and follow their religion.

converted (page 163)
Converted means changed one's religion.

cotton gin (page 368)
A cotton gin is a machine in 1793 that pulls the seeds from cotton.

Council of Trent (page 280)
The Council of Trent was a meeting during the 1530s at which the Catholic Church made several reforms.

Counter Reformation (page 280)
The Counter Reformation was a movement by the Catholic Church to slow the spread of the Protestant Reformation in the 1530s.

coup (page 495)
A coup is a takeover of a government.

covenant (page 35)
A covenant is a strong agreement.

creoles (page 361)
Creoles were people who were born in Latin America but had European ancestors.

crucified (page 107)
To have crucified someone is to have nailed that person to a cross in order to kill him or her.

crusade (page 213)
A crusade is a holy war.

Cultural Revolution (page 478)
The Cultural Revolution was a period of change in China, led by Mao Zedong, in order to make communism stronger. It lasted from 1966 to 1968.

culture (page 65)
Culture is the ideas, customs, skills, arts, and way of life of a group of people.

cuneiform (page 31)
Cuneiform is a form of writing used by Sumerians and other people of ancient Mesopotamia. The writing used different symbols that were carved on a clay tablet.

currency (page 533)
A currency is a form of money.

czar (page 392)
A czar was a Russian emperor.

D

daimyo (page 236)
Daimyo were powerful Japanese landowners in feudal Japan.

Daoism (page 133)
Daoism is a Chinese religion that teaches people to look to nature to see how to live.

daric (page 78)
A daric was a gold coin of the Persian Empire. The Persians used it to create a money system.

Dark Ages (page 145)
The Dark Ages is another name for the early Middle Ages in western Europe.

D-Day (page 456)
D-Day refers to June 6, 1944, the day the Allies invaded Normandy, France.

debt (page 437)
To be in debt is to owe money.

Declaration of Independence (page 353)
The Declaration of Independence was a letter that said the American colonies were free from British rule.

declined (page 243)
Declined means weakened.

defend (page 237)
To defend is to protect.

deforestation (page 530)
Deforestation is the act of cutting down all the trees in an area.

delta (page 180)
A delta is an area of land where a river leaves soil and sand as it enters a sea.

demilitarized (page 449)
Demilitarized means free from the control of soldiers.

democracy (page 83)
A democracy is a kind of government that is run by the people.

descendants (page 486)
Descendants are an ancestor's children, grandchildren, great-grandchildren, and so on.

devout (page 231)
Devout means very religious.

dictator (page 90)
A dictator is a leader with absolute power.

dictatorship (page 489)
A dictatorship is a government that is headed by a dictator, a person with absolute power.

dikes (page 30)
Dikes are mounds of dirt that are used to stop flooding.

disabilities (page 459)
People with disabilities have a condition that makes them less able to do certain things. Not being able to see, for example, is a disability.

disciples (page 107)
Disciples are people who follow the teachings of another.

discrimination (page 514)
Discrimination is the act of treating people differently for some reason.

displaced persons (page 462)
Displaced persons are people without a home or a country after a war.

dispute (page 443)
A dispute is an argument or fight.

divine right (page 293)
The divine right of kings was a belief that the right to rule comes from God.

divorce (page 279)
A divorce is the ending of a marriage.

domesticate (page 12)
To domesticate wild animals is to tame them for human use.

dominion (page 232)
Dominion means rule.

Duma (page 426)
The Duma was the group of people who made laws for Russia from 1905 to 1917. Today, the Duma is a part of the Russian Parliament.

dynasty (page 42)
A dynasty is a series of rulers from the same family.

E

economy (page 390)
An economy is the management of money in a government, household, or other group.

edict (page 108)
An edict is an order.

Edict of Milan (page 108)
The Edict of Milan was an order by the Roman emperor Constantine in A.D. 313, making it legal to be a Christian.

ehi (page 317)
An ehi was a personal god of a person of the Kingdom of Benin in Africa.

Eightfold Path (page 124)
The Eightfold Path is a series of steps a person must follow in order to find true peace, according to the Buddha.

elders (page 195)
Elders are older people who are leaders in a community.

election (page 438)
An election is a people's act of voting for a leader.

elite (page 326)
Elite means best or most powerful.

Emancipation Proclamation (page 388)
The Emancipation Proclamation was a paper that freed slaves living in the South. Abraham Lincoln wrote the paper in 1863 during the Civil War.

emperor (page 96)
An emperor is a ruler of an empire.

empire (page 23)
An empire exists when one group of people rules over another.

enlightenment (page 124)
Enlightenment is the understanding of the truth and nature of life.

epic (page 82)
Epic means having to do with a long poem or story.

establish (page 306)
To establish is to set up.

Estates General (page 356)
The Estates General was an assembly of three classes of French people between the 1300s and 1700s.

ethnic cleansing (page 533)
Ethnic cleansing is an attempt by one group of people to kill off or drive out another group in the same nation.

ethnic strife (page 491)
Ethnic strife is fighting between groups of people with different cultures and languages within a nation.

euro (page 533)
The euro is a form of money used by most European nations.

evacuated (page 242)
Evacuated means removed all the people from an area.

evaporate (page 189)
To evaporate is to dry up.

examination system (page 128)
The examination system in ancient China was a system in which people had to pass a test in order to become a government official.

excommunicated (page 278)
Excommunicated means banned from the church.

Exodus (page 35)
Exodus is one of the books of the Torah. This book tells how Moses led the Hebrews out of Egypt.

expansion (page 384)
Expansion is the act of becoming larger.

expeditions (page 336)
Expeditions are long trips with special purposes.

extended family (page 316)
An extended family is a large family in which the children, parents, grandparents, cousins, aunts, and uncles all live together or near one another.

F

Fascist Party (page 437)
The Fascist Party was the group of people who took control of the Italian government in 1922. They were led by Benito Mussolini.

fast (page 159)
To fast is to not eat food for a period of time.

feminism (page 514)
Feminism is a movement to help women gain rights equal to those of men.

Fertile Crescent (page 29)
The Fertile Crescent is a region in Southwest Asia that has good land for growing crops. It extends from the Mediterranean Sea to the Persian Gulf.

fertilizers (page 511)
Fertilizers are chemicals and other materials that are added to soil to help crops grow.

feudalism (page 148)
Feudalism was a system of loyalty among lords and knights in western Europe and among daimyo and samurai in Japan during the Middle Ages.

fibers (page 207)
Fibers are the long threads of a plant.

fief (page 148)
A fief was an area of land that a noble gave to a knight in exchange for protection and loyalty during the Middle Ages in western Europe.

firestorms (page 462)
Firestorms are huge fires spread by rushing winds that are actually created by the fire. Exploding bombs can cause firestorms.

Five Pillars of Islam (page 158)
The Five Pillars of Islam are the duties that all followers of the religion Islam must perform.

flying shuttle (page 368)
A flying shuttle is a machine invented in 1733 that makes weaving easier.

folly (page 275)
Folly means foolishness.

forbidden (page 337)
Forbidden means not allowed.

Forbidden City (page 337)
The Forbidden City was the Chinese emperor's palace in Beijing, completed in 1420. Very few people were allowed inside.

foreigners (page 329)
Foreigners are people from another country.

Four Noble Truths (page 124)
The Four Noble Truths are teachings of the Buddha about life and the way things are.

Fourteen Points (page 419)
The Fourteen Points was a plan presented by President Woodrow Wilson of the United States to establish peace between nations after World War I.

frontier (page 310)
The frontier is an area of land not yet explored or settled.

G

General Assembly (page 463)
The General Assembly is the part of the United Nations in which member nations each get one vote.

genocide (page 458)
Genocide is the act of destroying an entire race of people.

glaciers (page 7)
Glaciers are vast sheets of ice.

gladiators (page 104)
Gladiators were slaves or prisoners of war in ancient Rome who fought other men or animals to entertain the public.

glasnost (page 502)
Glasnost is a plan for openness, started by Mikhail Gorbachev in the 1980s to give more freedom to the people of the Soviet Union.

global village (page 526)
A global village is a term used to describe the world as one community, connected by modern technology and fast transportation.

global warming (page 529)
Global warming is the slow warming of Earth due to gases that trap the sun's heat.

glyphs (page 200)
Glyphs are pictures and characters used to stand for sounds or ideas. They are a form of writing.

golden stool (page 315)
The golden stool was a symbol of the united Ashanti people of Africa, who believed the stool had been brought from heaven.

Gospels (page 107)
The Gospels are four books of the Bible that describe the life and teachings of Jesus.

granary (page 48)
A granary is a building used for storing grain.

Grand Canal (page 169)
The Grand Canal is a human-made waterway that connects the Huang He with the Yangtze River in China.

gravity (page 119)
Gravity is the force which pulls objects and people toward Earth.

Great Depression (page 430)
The Great Depression was a period of time in which millions of people did not have jobs and trade greatly slowed. It began in 1929 and lasted throughout the 1930s.

Great Leap Forward (page 478)
The Great Leap Forward was a plan by Mao Zedong to increase industrial development and food production in Communist China. The plan failed, and many Chinese people starved to death.

Green Revolution (page 511)
The Green Revolution is the development of new food crops, fertilizers, and farming methods to greatly increase the food supply.

guerrilla tactics (page 181)
Guerrilla tactics are methods of war, including surprise nighttime attacks.

guilds (page 218)
Guilds are groups of people who do the same kind of work. Guilds in western Europe's Middle Ages kept control over their products and trained new workers.

guillotine (page 357)
A guillotine is an instrument used to kill a person by dropping a heavy blade on the person's neck.

gunpowder (page 173)
Gunpowder is a powder that can explode. It is used to make fireworks and weapons.

H

haciendas (page 361)
Haciendas are large Latin American farms.

haiku (page 238)
Haiku is a form of Japanese poetry. A haiku poem has just three lines. The first and third lines have five syllables. The second line has seven syllables.

hajj (page 159)
A hajj is a journey to Mecca, located in Saudi Arabia. It is a journey that followers of the religion Islam are expected to make during their life if they are able.

Hamas (page 520)
Hamas is a group of Palestinian Muslims who use terror against Israelis.

Hezbollah (page 520)
Hezbollah is a group of Lebanese Muslims who use terror against Israelis.

hieroglyphics (page 18)
Hieroglyphics are pictures and symbols used as a form of writing.

highlands (page 191)
Highlands are lands high above sea level.

hijacks (page 521)
Hijacks means to take control of something by force.

hijrah (page 158)
The hijrah was the journey of Muhammad from Mecca to Medina, two Arabian cities, in A.D. 622.

Hinduism (page 119)
Hinduism is a religion that is based on the ancient religion of the Aryans. It is the main religion of India.

historians (page 41)
Historians are people who study and write about history.

Holocaust (page 459)
The Holocaust was the killing of about six million Jews during World War II.

Holy Land (page 213)
The Holy Land is what Christians called the region of Palestine.

hostage (page 303)
To take someone hostage is to make that person a prisoner until certain demands are met.

house arrest (page 287)
A person who is under house arrest is not allowed to leave his or her home.

Huguenots (page 279)
Huguenots were French Protestants during the 1600s and 1700s.

humanism (page 275)
Humanism was a movement during the Renaissance to learn more about human nature, human problems, and life on Earth.

hybrids (page 524)
Hybrids are cars that run on both gas and electricity.

hydrogen (page 525)
Hydrogen is an element that combines with oxygen to form water. Hydrogen gas is lighter than air.

hypothesis (page 286)
A hypothesis is a guess about what the results of an experiment will be.

I

Ice Age (page 11)
An Ice Age is a very cold period of time that can last many thousands of years. During an Ice Age, ice covers much of the earth.

icons (page 152)
Icons are images important to a religion. People sometimes pray to icons.

idols (page 157)
Idols are statues of gods.

illegal (page 487)
Illegal means against the law.

illegal immigration (page 497)
Illegal immigration is the act of coming to another country without it being legal to do so.

immigrants (page 386)
Immigrants are people who come to another country.

immigrate (page 496)
To immigrate is to come to another country.

immunity (page 304)
Immunity is protection against a disease.

imperialism (page 396)
Imperialism is the idea that a nation should build an empire in foreign lands.

indentured servants (page 308)
Indentured servants were people who agreed to work for a given length of time for someone who paid for their trip to the Americas.

indulgences (page 278)
Indulgences were acts of forgiveness that people could buy from the Catholic Church until the 1530s.

Industrial Revolution (page 366)
The Industrial Revolution was the time during the 18th century in which people started using machines instead of tools.

industrialization (page 367)
Industrialization is the act of setting up businesses and factories to make goods.

industry (page 368)
An industry is all the businesses that make a certain product.

infidels (page 231)
Infidels are people who do not believe in a certain religion.

influence (page 176)
Influence is the effect or power someone has over another.

inland (page 338)
Inland means inside a region, away from the coast or border.

Inquisition (page 280)
The Inquisition was a special church court used during the Middle Ages and the Renaissance. It punished people who did not follow the Catholic beliefs.

internal combustion engine (page 370)
An internal combustion engine is an engine that uses gasoline. It is used in cars and airplanes.

Internet (page 523)
The Internet is a huge system that connects computers around the world.

internment camps (page 460)
Internment camps were prison-like camps to which Japanese Americans and Japanese Canadians were sent during World War II.

intifada (page 507)
The intifada is fighting by Palestinians against Israeli forces.

invaded (page 22)
Invaded means attacked a country or other place in order to gain control of it.

invasions (page 113)
Invasions are attacks into a country or other place in order to gain control of it.

Irish Republican Army (page 520)
The Irish Republican Army is a group that uses terror to try to unify Ireland and drive the British out of Northern Ireland.

Iron Curtain (page 471)
Iron Curtain refers to the separation of Eastern Europe and Western Europe because of differences in ideas about government and economics.

iron ore (page 66)
Iron ore is a material from which iron can be removed and used to make things.

Islam (page 141)
Islam is a religion based on the teachings of Muhammad.

Islamic extremists (page 519)
Islamic extremists are people who believe that the Qur'an tells them to fight and kill people who are not Muslim.

isolationism (page 342)
Isolationism is a nation's plan to avoid getting involved in the decisions, agreements, or problems of other nations.

J

jaguar (page 58)
A jaguar is a large cat that can be found in South America, Central America, and the southern parts of North America.

Janissaries (page 326)
Janissaries were well-trained Islamic soldiers of the Ottoman army.

Japanese Red Army (page 521)
The Japanese Red Army is a group of people who are trying to take over the Japanese government.

Jesuits (page 280)
Jesuits are members of a special group of priests in the Catholic Church.

jihad (page 190)
A jihad is a struggle to protect the Islamic faith against an enemy.

journal (page 296)
A journal is an ongoing record of the events in one's life.

journeyman (page 219)
A journeyman is a person who is skilled enough in a craft to be paid but is not yet a master.

Judaism (page 36)
Judaism is the Jewish religion.

Justinian Code (page 151)
The Justinian Code was a set of laws issued by the Byzantine emperor Justinian. The laws were based on Roman laws.

K

Kaaba (page 158)
The Kaaba is an important Muslim temple in the city of Mecca, located in Saudi Arabia.

kabuki (page 343)
Kabuki was a style of Japanese theater begun around 1603. It used song, dance, and colorful costumes.

kaiser (page 381)
A kaiser was the German head of government between 1871 and 1918.

kamikaze (page 237)
Kamikaze were winds that the Japanese believed were holy.

kowtow (page 337)
To kowtow is to bow deeply by kneeling and touching the ground with one's forehead.

L

labor unions (page 375)
Labor unions are groups of workers who work together to get higher pay or better working conditions.

lagoons (page 206)
Lagoons are shallow ponds connected to lakes or seas.

land bridge (page 54)
A land bridge is an area of land that connects two larger areas of land that are otherwise separated by water.

lasers (page 524)
Lasers are machines that create a special beam of light. Doctors sometimes use lasers to treat patients.

League of Nations (page 419)
The League of Nations was a group of nations that worked for peace after World War I.

legends (page 41)
Legends are stories that have been told since earlier times. Legends might be based on history, but they cannot be proven.

leisure (page 371)
Leisure is free time, or time not spent working at a job.

liberator (page 363)
A liberator is a person who frees a country or a group of people.

location (page 182)
A location is the place where someone or something is.

looted (page 111)
Looted means robbed.

lord (page 148)
A lord was a noble who ruled over land in western Europe during the Middle Ages.

lost wax method (page 206)
The lost wax method was a method used to make gold objects.

M

madrasas (page 249)
Madrasas are Islamic universities.

Maginot Line (page 453)
The Maginot Line was a strip of land along which France attempted to defend itself from Germany in World War II.

Mahatma (page 442)
Mahatma means "Great Soul." The people of India often called Mohandas K. Gandhi the Mahatma.

mainland (page 175)
A mainland is the largest part of a continent.

maize (page 55)
Maize is corn.

Mandate of Heaven (page 43)
The Mandate of Heaven was the right to rule ancient China.

mandates (page 422)
Mandates are territories under the control of other countries.

manifest destiny (page 385)
Manifest destiny is the idea that the United States should rule land from the Atlantic Ocean to the Pacific Ocean.

manikongo (page 317)
A manikongo was a ruler of the Kingdom of Kongo in Africa.

manor (page 148)
A manor was land ruled over by a noble during the Middle Ages.

mansa (page 247)
A mansa was a ruler of ancient Mali in West Africa.

manufactured goods (page 322)
Manufactured goods are goods made by people or machines.

Maori (page 383)
The Maori are people native to New Zealand. Their ancestors lived in New Zealand before Europeans arrived there.

marchers (page 426)
Marchers are people who march in a group, often as a way to speak out against or protest something.

maritime (page 81)
Maritime means living near the sea.

masterpiece (page 219)
A masterpiece is a work done with great skill.

mathematicians (page 201)
Mathematicians are people who study numbers and math.

mayor of the palace (page 141)
The mayor of the palace was an official who held much power in the Merovingian Dynasty of western Europe.

Meiji Restoration (page 404)
The Meiji Restoration was a change in Japan in which people ended the rule of shoguns and gave power back to the emperor. It occurred in 1868.

mercy (page 226)
Mercy is kindness, especially to enemies.

mesas (page 265)
Mesas are flat-topped mountains with steep sides.

Messiah (page 107)
A Messiah, or chosen one, is a person whom others believe will bring peace and freedom.

mestizos (page 361)
Mestizos are Latin American people with European and Native American ancestors.

Middle Ages (page 140)
The Middle Ages was the period of European history between the fall of Rome and the modern world (A.D. 476 to A.D. 1500).

middle-class (page 427)
Middle-class people are neither very rich nor very poor.

Middle East (page 441)
The Middle East is a region that includes lands of Southwest Asia and North Africa.

Middle Passage (page 321)
The Middle Passage was a voyage in which European ships brought slaves from Africa to the Americas.

migration (page 54)
A migration is an act of people moving across a large area.

military (page 327)
The military is the armed forces of a nation.

millet (page 42)
Millet is a kind of grass with small seeds that are used to make cereal.

minutemen (page 352)
Minutemen were volunteer soldiers of the American colonies who could be ready to fight against the British in a minute's time.

missiles (page 473)
Missiles are rockets with bombs in them.

missionaries (page 317)
Missionaries are people who try to spread and teach their religion to people in other countries.

Missouri Compromise (page 386)
The Missouri Compromise was an agreement in 1820 to let Maine join the United States as a free state and Missouri join as a slave state.

monarchs (page 291)
Monarchs are kings and queens.

monarchy (page 291)
A monarchy is a government headed by a king or queen.

monasteries (page 149)
Monasteries are places where monks live, work, and follow their religion.

Mongols (page 225)
Mongols are people who live in a region north and west of China.

monopoly (page 189)
To have a monopoly is to have total control over a good or service.

monsoon (page 46)
A monsoon is a very strong wind that blows across the Indian Ocean and southern Asia. During the winter, the wind brings dry weather. During the summer, it brings heavy rains.

Moors (page 216)
The Moors were a group of Muslims who had taken control of most of Spain in A.D. 1000.

mortar (page 255)
Mortar is a kind of cement.

mosaics (page 151)
Mosaics are pictures made from small pieces of colored stone or glass.

mosques (page 160)
Mosques are places where followers of the religion Islam pray.

movable type (page 172)
Movable type is a method of printing using blocks of wood to make words and sentences on a page.

mulattoes (page 361)
Mulattoes are people with European and African ancestors.

mummies (page 18)
Mummies are dead bodies that have been preserved with salts and chemicals so that they will last.

Muslims (page 141)
Muslims are people who believe in the religion Islam.

myth (page 82)
A myth is a type of legend or story.

N

NAFTA (page 535)
NAFTA stands for North American Free Trade Agreement. It is a plan to encourage trade between the United States, Mexico, and Canada.

National Assembly (page 356)
The National Assembly was a government body of French merchants and peasants that gathered together just before the French Revolution.

nationalism (page 290)
Nationalism is a feeling of loyalty to one's nation.

nationalities (page 390)
Nationalities are groups of people who, within their groups, share a common language, culture, and history.

Nazi Party (page 438)
The Nazi Party was the group of people who, under Adolf Hitler, took control of the German government in 1933.

negotiations (page 478)
Negotiations are discussions meant to bring nations to an agreement.

neutral (page 413)
To be neutral is to refuse to fight or take sides in a war.

neutrality (page 451)
Neutrality is the plan of a nation to not take sides or fight in a war.

New Deal (page 433)
The New Deal was President Franklin D. Roosevelt's plan to end the Great Depression in the United States.

nirvana (page 125)
Nirvana is a state of mind in which there is no desire or greed, only true peace.

Noh drama (page 238)
A Noh drama is a type of Japanese theater in which actors wear masks and costumes and a chorus sings.

nomads (page 10)
Nomads are people who do not have a permanent home. They move when necessary to find food.

non-aggression (page 452)
Non-aggression refers to the act of not fighting or attacking.

Northwest Passage (page 298)
A Northwest Passage was a possible water route from the Atlantic Ocean to the Pacific Ocean through the northern Americas. European explorers hoped to find this passage in order to travel west by water to reach Asia.

novel (page 336)
A novel is a book that tells a long story about imaginary people and events.

nuclear (page 470)
Nuclear means involving atomic bombs.

Nuremberg Trials (page 459)
The Nuremberg Trials were trials held after World War II. In the trials, Nazi leaders were found guilty of crimes against the human race.

O

oba (page 316)
An oba was a king of the Kingdom of Benin in Africa.

obelisks (page 23)
Obelisks were tall stone columns that were built to honor gods.

occupation (page 464)
Occupation is the control of an area by soldiers of another country.

occupied territories (page 506)
Occupied territories are regions that are held by force by another nation.

oil reserves (page 508)
Oil reserves are areas in the ground with great amounts of oil.

one-crop economies (page 495)
Nations with one-crop economies are dependent on the selling of a single crop or mineral.

opera (page 171)
Opera is a kind of art in which a play's words are sung instead of spoken.

Operation Desert Storm (page 508)
Operation Desert Storm was the 1991 attack by the United Nations to drive Iraqis out of Kuwait.

opium (page 401)
Opium is a drug made from a plant called the opium poppy.

oracle bones (page 43)
Oracle bones are animal bones or turtle shells that people in ancient China used to tell about the future or to answer questions. A person would determine the answer from the way the bones cracked or broke after being heated.

oral (page 255)
Oral means spoken.

orphans (page 462)
Orphans are children whose parents are dead.

Orthodox Church (page 152)
The Orthodox Church is the Christian church based in eastern Europe.

overpopulation (page 193)
Overpopulation is too many people living on a land that cannot support them.

overthrow (page 438)
To overthrow is to take over a government.

ozone layer (page 528)
The ozone layer is an important layer in the sky that helps block the sun's harmful rays.

P

Papal States (page 142)
The Papal States were lands belonging to the pope.

papyrus (page 18)
Papyrus is a tall water plant found in northern Africa and southern Europe.

paradise (page 308)
A paradise is a perfect place.

Parliament (page 293)
Parliament is a group of government leaders.

partitioned (page 443)
Partitioned means divided.

patricians (page 90)
Patricians were wealthy people who owned land in ancient Rome.

Pax Romana (page 102)
Pax Romana means "peace of Rome." It was a period of time in which ancient Romans enjoyed much peace, good government, and open trade. It lasted from 27 B.C. to A.D. 180.

peasants (page 127)
Peasants are farmers and workers.

peninsula (page 72)
A peninsula is a large piece of land that is mostly surrounded by water.

peninsulares (page 361)
Peninsulares were people in the highest class in Latin America. They were born in Spain or Portugal.

perestroika (page 502)
Perestroika is a Russian word for restructuring. It refers to economic and other changes made in the Soviet Union during the 1980s.

perspective (page 274)
Perspective is the way objects that are farther away appear smaller than nearby objects.

pesticides (page 529)
Pesticides are chemical poisons used to kill insects.

pharaohs (page 18)
Pharaohs were rulers of ancient Egypt.

philosophy (page 83)
Philosophy is the study of life, ideas, values, and knowledge.

Pilgrims (page 308)
Pilgrims were Separatists who began a colony in Plymouth, Massachusetts, in 1620.

plague (page 220)
A plague is a disease that kills many people very quickly.

plantations (page 320)
Plantations are large farms.

plazas (page 69)
Plazas are big open areas in a city.

plebeians (page 90)
Plebeians were farmers and other common people in ancient Rome.

PLO (page 506)
PLO stands for Palestine Liberation Organization. It is a group of Arabs whose goal is to have their own nation in Palestine.

plunder (page 231)
To plunder is to rob by force.

pogroms (page 392)
Pogroms were riots against Jews in Russia during the 1800s.

polar ice caps (page 530)
Polar ice caps are large areas of ice at the North Pole and South Pole.

policy (page 343)
A policy is a plan or course of action.

political (page 396)
Political people are active with a nation's government.

pollution (page 528)
Pollution is chemicals and wastes in air, in water, or on land.

pope (page 113)
In ancient Rome, the pope was the head of the western Christian church. Today, the pope is the head of the Catholic Church.

population (page 55)
An area's population is all of its people.

porcelain (page 129)
Porcelain is a kind of delicate pottery first made by the ancient Chinese.

poverty (page 401)
Poverty is the condition of being very poor.

prehistoric (page 9)
Prehistoric means before people began recording written history.

prime minister (page 450)
A prime minister is the leader of a government in some nations.

printing press (page 274)
A printing press is a machine that uses ink and movable type to press words onto paper.

privacy (page 523)
Privacy is the ability to not have personal information shared with others.

Promised Land (page 35)
The Promised Land was an area called Canaan. Jews believe that God promised this land to the Hebrews.

prophet (page 159)
A prophet is an inspired teacher of a religion.

protectorate (page 397)
A protectorate is a territory controlled and protected by a stronger nation.

Protestants (page 278)
Protestants are people who believe in Christianity but do not belong to the Catholic Church.

provinces (page 77)
Provinces are regions of a nation or empire.

public works (page 169)
Public works are roads, dams, bridges, and other structures that a government builds for people to use.

pueblos (page 265)
Pueblos are Native American villages in the southwestern United States.

puppet governments (page 500)
Puppet governments are governments that seem independent but are actually controlled by another nation.

pyramids (page 17)
Pyramids are buildings that have four sides shaped like triangles. The sides come together to form a point at the top.

Q

Quakers (page 308)
Quakers were an English Protestant group who believed in peace and founded the colony of Pennsylvania.

quarter (page 352)
To quarter someone is to provide shelter, a bed, and meals for that person.

quipu (page 263)
A quipu was a system of knotted, colored strings used by the Inca to keep records.

Qur'an (page 158)
The Qur'an is the holy book of the religion Islam.

R

race (page 458)
A race is a group of people who share the same ancestors and culture.

racism (page 458)
Racism is the belief that one race, or group of people, is better than another race.

rebirth (page 123)
Rebirth is the act of being born again.

reborn (page 122)
Reborn means born again.

Reconquista (page 216)
In the Reconquista, Spanish Christians fought to drive a group of Muslims called the Moors out of Spain.

recycle (page 531)
To recycle is to turn trash or waste into something new.

Red Army (page 428)
The Red Army was a group of Communists who fought for control of Russia in a Russian civil war in the early 1900s.

Red Guards (page 478)
Red Guards were Chinese students who were ordered by Mao Zedong to attack anyone who was not a perfect Communist.

Reformation (page 277)
The Reformation was a movement during the 1500s to make changes in the practices of the Catholic Church. It resulted in the creation of Protestant churches.

reforms (page 177)
Reforms are changes made in order to improve something.

refugee (page 506)
A refugee is a person who has fled from his or her home or country in order to escape danger.

reign (page 291)
A reign is the time that a king or queen rules.

Reign of Terror (page 357)
The Reign of Terror was a period of the French Revolution during which many people were killed for not supporting changes in France.

reincarnation (page 122)
Reincarnation is the act of a soul being born again in a new body.

relic (page 162)
A relic is a holy object.

religion (page 19)
A religion is a belief in a god or gods.

religious (page 19)
Religious means having to do with religion.

Renaissance (page 272)
The Renaissance was a time in European history in which people advanced the arts, the sciences, and philosophy. It lasted from the mid-1300s until the 1500s.

reparations (page 420)
Reparations are payments of money from a defeated nation to pay for damages suffered by the winning nation or nations.

repeal (page 352)
To repeal a law is to take it back or cancel it.

representation (page 352)
Representation is having someone speak or act for others.

representatives (page 89)
Representatives are leaders who represent the people of a nation or group.

republic (page 89)
A republic is a government in which the leaders are elected by the people.

resisted (page 250)
Resisted means stood against or fought.

resources (page 66)
Resources are materials that can be used to fill a need.

resurrection (page 107)
A resurrection is an act of a dead person coming back to life.

revolt (page 79)
A revolt is a fight or struggle against a ruler or government.

revolutionary (page 429)
A revolutionary is a person who tries to bring about major changes to a government or society.

revolve (page 286)
To revolve around something is to turn in a circle around it.

riverbed (page 343)
A riverbed is the channel in which a river flows or has flowed.

Roaring Twenties (page 430)
The Roaring Twenties refers to the 1920s, which for some was a time of wild living, new inventions, and new ways of looking at the world.

rumor (page 301)
A rumor is a story told by many people without proof that it is true.

S

sack (page 234)
A sack of a city is the act of capturing and robbing a city by force.

sacrifice (page 71)
A sacrifice is an act of killing a person or an animal in order to honor a god.

sagas (page 144)
Sagas are stories of Viking adventures.

sage (page 132)
A sage is a very wise person.

Sahel (page 187)
The Sahel is a hot region of dry grasslands south of the Sahara Desert in Africa.

samurai (page 236)
The samurai were Japanese warriors.

sanctions (page 513)
Sanctions are actions taken by nations to force another nation to agree to do or stop doing something. One sanction might be to stop all trade with that nation.

sanctuary (page 113)
Sanctuary is protection by a church.

Sanskrit (page 241)
Sanskrit was a language spoken by Hindus in ancient India.

satellite (page 474)
A satellite is an object that travels around a planet.

scholars (page 272)
Scholars are people who have achieved high levels of education.

scientific method (page 286)
The scientific method is a series of steps scientists follow in order to test their ideas.

Scientific Revolution (page 286)
The Scientific Revolution was a time in which people made new discoveries about the world and tested their ideas, rather than just follow traditional beliefs. It occurred during the 1500s and 1600s.

secret police (page 436)
Secret police are police who secretly search for people who are against a nation's government.

sect (page 325)
A sect is a religious group that has broken away from a larger religious body.

Security Council (page 463)
The Security Council is the section of the United Nations that deals with threats to peace. It can send soldiers to where there is fighting.

segregation (page 513)
Segregation is the act of keeping groups of people apart.

self-determination (page 419)
Self-determination is the right of the people of a nationality to form their own nation.

self-reliant (page 491)
Self-reliant means economically independent.

self-rule (page 382)
People who have self-rule have the right to run their own government.

self-sufficient (page 336)
Self-sufficient means able to function without help from others.

senate (page 90)
The Roman senate was a group of 300 men who advised the leaders of the ancient republic.

senators (page 94)
Senators are members of a senate.

Separatists (page 308)
Separatists were a group of Protestants in the 1600s who wanted to live separately from other religious groups.

seppuku (page 237)
Seppuku was a practice in which Japanese warriors killed themselves if they lost their honor.

serfs (page 148)
Serfs were people who farmed the land owned by a noble or a knight during the Middle Ages.

shah (page 329)
Shah is the title of former rulers of Safavid Persia and Iran.

shamans (page 58)
Shamans were Olmec priests.

shells (page 416)
Shells are small bombs that are fired from a cannon or other weapon.

Shi'ite (page 328)
Shi'ite Muslims are people who believe that only relatives of Muhammad can lead the Muslims.

Shinto (page 176)
Shinto is an important religion in Japan. Followers of Shinto honor nature.

shogun (page 235)
A shogun was a top general in feudal Japan.

shogunate (page 236)
A shogunate was the rule by the family of a top general in Japan.

shrines (page 177)
Shrines are buildings and other places that are used for worship.

siege warfare (page 226)
Siege warfare is a method used to capture a city or fort, such as blocking any routes of escape or delivery of new supplies.

Silk Road (page 129)
The Silk Road was a trade route that stretched from China to the Mediterranean Sea.

silt (page 16)
Silt is rich soil and other materials that have been brought to an area by moving water.

sit-ins (page 501)
Sit-ins are acts of speaking out against a government or business by refusing to leave a building or other place.

slash-and-burn (page 72)
Slash-and-burn refers to a method in which farmers cut down plants and then burn the fields in order to clear the land.

smallpox (page 304)
Smallpox is a disease that causes chills, high fever, and skin blisters.

smelt (page 202)
To smelt is to melt metals.

smog (page 528)
Smog is a mixture of fog and smoke that hangs in the air. It is caused by air pollution.

social unrest (page 493)
Social unrest refers to the condition of a nation in which the people are angry and wanting change.

socialism (page 471)
Socialism is a system in which the government owns all the industries, businesses, and farms.

solar panels (page 525)
Solar panels are surfaces that change sunlight into electricity.

Solidarity (page 501)
Solidarity was a non-Communist labor union in Poland. The name means many people acting together for a single reason.

soviets (page 426)
Soviets were worker councils in Russia and later the Soviet Union.

Spanish Armada (page 292)
The Spanish Armada was the group of Spanish warships destroyed in battle by England in 1588.

specialize (page 217)
To specialize is to focus on one area of work.

sphere (page 402)
A sphere is a place or range of places.

sphere of influence (page 402)
A sphere of influence is a region in which a nation has some control over the actions or decisions of the people in that region.

spinning jenny (page 368)
A spinning jenny is a machine invented in 1770 that allows a person to spin many threads at once.

stable (page 337)
A stable government is one that is strong and not likely to break down or fall apart.

stalemate (page 414)
A stalemate is a situation in which neither side in a battle is winning.

Stamp Act (page 351)
The Stamp Act was a British law that forced Americans to pay a tax on newspapers, playing cards, and many other printed goods.

standard of living (page 371)
A standard of living is how well people live.

status (page 320)
Status is one's place in society.

steamboat (page 369)
A steamboat is a boat that uses steam in order to move.

steppe (page 225)
A steppe is an open plain.

stock market (page 432)
The stock market is the place where shares of companies are bought and sold.

Stone Age (page 9)
The Stone Age was a period of time when early humans made tools and weapons out of stone. The Stone Age ended around 3500 B.C.

strait (page 53)
A strait is a thin body of water that connects two larger bodies of water.

strike (page 375)
To be on strike is to refuse to work.

stylus (page 31)
A stylus is a pointed tool used for making marks in clay or another material.

subcontinent (page 46)
A subcontinent is a very large area of land that is part of a continent.

submarine (page 416)
A submarine is a ship that can travel underwater.

suicide bombers (page 520)
Suicide bombers are people who are willing to kill themselves in order to kill large numbers of their enemy.

sultanates (page 232)
Sultanates are Muslim kingdoms.

sultans (page 232)
Sultans are Muslim rulers.

Sunnite (page 328)
Sunnite Muslims are people who believe that any man can lead the Muslims.

superpowers (page 464)
Superpowers are nations that have great amounts of influence over other nations in the world.

surplus (page 217)
A surplus is an extra amount.

surrender (page 226)
To surrender is to admit defeat.

suttee (page 331)
Suttee was a Hindu custom which called for widows to throw themselves into a funeral fire after their husbands died.

Swahili (page 192)
Swahili is a Bantu language that is mixed with Arabic.

T

Taika reforms (page 177)
The Taika reforms were changes made to the government of Japan in 645. One change was to make the emperor the true ruler of Japan.

Taiping Rebellion (page 402)
The Taiping Rebellion was a war in the 1800s by the Chinese people against the Qing Dynasty. The rebellion failed, and millions of people were killed.

talking drums (page 316)
Talking drums were drums used by the Ashanti people in Africa in order to learn language and spread news.

technological revolution (page 522)
A technological revolution is a time in which great advances in technology are made.

technology (page 368)
Technology is the use of science to change the ways things are done.

telegraph (page 370)
A telegraph is a machine that sends coded messages over wires or radio.

Ten Commandments (page 36)
The Ten Commandments are laws that tell how people should behave. Jews and Christians believe God gave Moses the Ten Commandments.

terraces (page 71)
Terraces are levels on a hill or pyramid.

terracotta (page 68)
Terracotta is a baked, brown-red clay used to make statues and pottery.

terrorism (page 519)
Terrorism is the act of using force or threats to scare people or a government into doing something.

Tet Offensive (page 477)
The Tet Offensive was a major North Vietnamese attack on South Vietnam in 1968.

textiles (page 333)
Textiles are cloths.

Tiananmen Square Massacre (page 479)
The Tiananmen Square Massacre was the killing of hundreds of Chinese students who spoke out against communism in 1989.

tolerance (page 77)
Tolerance is an act of allowing others to follow their beliefs or customs.

tomb (page 24)
A tomb is a room or grave where a dead person is placed.

tones (page 192)
Tones are vocal sounds or pitches used to change the meaning of a word.

Torah (page 34)
The Torah is a set of five books that contains the Hebrew laws. The Torah forms the first part of the Bible.

trade barriers (page 535)
Trade barriers are acts or laws that limit trade between nations.

Trail of Tears (page 386)
When the Cherokee were forced by the United States Army to move west in 1838, the Cherokee called their trip the Trail of Tears.

transportation (page 368)
Transportation is a system or way of moving people and goods from one place to another.

treason (page 162)
Treason is a crime against one's state or country.

treaties (page 309)
Treaties are signed agreements between two or more groups or nations.

trench warfare (page 414)
Trench warfare is a method of fighting in which soldiers fight from long ditches. Trench warfare was heavily used during World War I.

trenches (page 414)
Trenches are long ditches used to hide and protect soldiers during a war.

triangular trade (page 322)
The triangular trade was a system in which Europeans traded horses and other goods for slaves and gold in Africa; the slaves and gold were sold in the Americas, and Europeans bought American goods.

tribunes (page 91)
Tribunes were leaders that represented the common people in ancient Rome.

tribute (page 77)
Tribute is a kind of tax paid to a ruler or ruling nation.

Triple Alliance (page 412)
The Triple Alliance was a group of three nations—Germany, Austria-Hungary, and Italy. In 1914, these nations agreed to help one another during times of trouble.

Triple Entente (page 412)
The Triple Entente was a group of three nations—France, Great Britain, and Russia. In 1914, these nations agreed to help one another during times of trouble.

triumvirate (page 95)
A triumvirate is a group of three rulers.

troupe (page 343)
A troupe is a group of actors or singers.

truce (page 215)
A truce is an agreement to stop fighting.

two-front war (page 413)
A nation that is fighting a two-front war is fighting battles in two different places.

U

unification (page 380)
Unification is the act of joining two or more states into one nation.

United Nations (page 463)
The United Nations, or UN, is a group of nations that first joined together after World War II in order to keep peace in the world.

untouchables (page 49)
Untouchables are people in ancient India that were below the caste system. Another word for "untouchables" is "outcastes."

uprising (page 485)
An uprising is a fight against a government.

urbanization (page 372)
Urbanization is the shift from people living in the countryside to people living in cities.

V

vassal (page 148)
A vassal was a knight who was given land by a noble in exchange for protection and loyalty during the Middle Ages.

Vedas (page 48)
The Vedas are a set of books containing stories and poems of the Aryan religion in ancient India. Today, the Vedas are an important part of the Hindu religion.

Vikings (page 142)
Vikings traveled from northern Europe to attack other European lands. They were skilled sailors.

W

White Army (page 428)
The White Army was a group who fought against communism in a Russian civil war in the early 1900s.

windmills (page 525)
Windmills are machines that use wind energy to make electricity or do work.

World Wide Web (page 523)
The World Wide Web is a group of Internet sites that are connected to one another. People can do research using the World Wide Web.

X

X-ray (page 524)
X-ray refers to a beam of energy that can pass through one's body. An X-ray machine is used to take pictures of teeth, bones, and organs.

Y

yin and yang (page 131)
Yin and yang is the Chinese philosophy that there are two forces that must be balanced in order for there to be peace. Yin is darkness and weakness. Yang is brightness and strength.

Yom Kippur (page 506)
Yom Kippur is a Jewish holy day that occurs in September or October.

yurts (page 225)
Yurts are Mongol tents made of wool.

Z

ziggurats (page 30)
Ziggurats were temples built by Sumerians in ancient Mesopotamia.

Zionism (page 441)
Zionism was a movement for a Jewish homeland in Palestine.

Zoroastrianism (page 79)
Zoroastrianism is a religion based on the teachings of a man named Zoroaster, who lived in Persia around 600 B.C.

Index

A

B

C

D

E

F

G

L

M

S

T

Photo Credits continued: p.53b ©Ralph A. Clevenger/CORBIS; p.54a Illustration by Greg Harlin-Wood Ronsaville Harlin, Inc.; p.55 ©Robert Holmes/CORBIS; p.56a ©Danny Lehman/CORBIS; p.56b ©Yoshio Tomii/SuperStock; p.57b ©National Geographic Image Collection; p.58a ©Werner Forman Archive, Dallas Museum of Art/Art Resource, NY; p.58b ©Underwood Photo Archives/SuperStock; p.58c ©Reuters NewMedia Inc./CORBIS; p.59 ©Chris Hellier/CORBIS; p.62b ©Charles & Josette Lenars/CORBIS; p.62c ©Stock Montage; p.63a ©Hulton Archive/Getty Images; p.63b ©The Bridgeman Art Library; p.64a ©Archivo Iconografico, S.A./CORBIS; p.64b ©Robert Holmes/CORBIS; p.65a ©Christie's Images/CORBIS; p.66a ©The British Museum; p.66b ©University of Pennsylvania Museum; p.67a ©Sandro Vannini/CORBIS; p.68 ©Werner Forman/Art Resource, NY; p.69a ©Alyx Kellington; p.69b ©Richard A. Cooke/CORBIS; p.70b ©Charles & Josette Lenars/CORBIS; p.71a ©Arte & Immagini srl/CORBIS; p.71b ©SuperStock; p.72 ©Stephanie Maze/CORBIS; p.76a ©The British Museum; p.76b, 77a, 78b ©The Granger Collection; p.79a ©Charles & Josette Lenars/CORBIS; p.79b ©R. Ashworth/Robert Harding Picture Library; p.80 ©Gianni Dagli Orti/CORBIS; p.81a ©Christie's Images/CORBIS; p.81b ©Staffan Widstrand/CORBIS; p.83a ©SuperStock; p.83b ©Foto Marburg/Art Resource, NY; p.85 ©Stock Montage; p.88a ©Villa Giulia, Rome, Italy/ET archive, London/SuperStock; p.88b ©Richard T. Nowitz/CORBIS; p.89b ©Réunion des Musées Nationaux/Art Resource, NY; p.90a ©AKG Berlin/SuperStock; p.90b ©Bettmann/CORBIS; p.92 ©The Granger Collection; p.94a ©Hulton Archive/Getty Images; p..94b ©Landesmuseum, Hanover, Germany/SuperStock; p.95b ©Bettmann/CORBIS; p.96a ©Araldo de Luca/CORBIS; p.96b ©Scala/Art Resource, NY; p.97 ©Sandro Vannini/CORBIS; p.101a ©Scala/Art Resource, NY; p.101b ©The British Museum; p.103a ©Hulton Archive/Getty Images; p.103b ©AKG Berlin/SuperStock; p.104a ©Philadelphia Museum of Art/CORBIS; p.104b ©William A. Allard/Getty Images; p.105 ©Christie's Images/CORBIS; p.106a ©The British Museum; p.107a ©Scala/Art Resource, NY; p.107b ©Bettmann/CORBIS; p.110a,b ©The Bridgeman Art Library; p.111b ©Bettmann/CORBIS; p.112a ©The British Museum; p.112b ©Bettmann/CORBIS; p.113 ©Scala/Art Resource, NY; p.116a ©Burstein Collection/CORBIS; p.116b ©The Bridgeman Art Library; p.117b ©K.L. Kamat; p.118b ©Woodfin Camp; p.119a ©Borromeo/Art Resource, NY; p.119b ©The British Museum; p.120, 121a ©Hulton Archive/Getty Images; p.121b ©Picture Finders Ltd./eStock Photography; p.122b ©Scala/Art Resource, NY; p.123a ©The Granger Collection; p.123b ©Gilles Mermet/Art Resource, NY ; p.124a Courtesy of Kamnuan Chanando; p.126a ©The Lowe Art Museum, The University of Miami/SuperStock; p.126b Drawing by Giacinto Gaudenzi, ©1987 Editoriale Jaca Book spa, Milano, Italy. All Rights Reserved; p.127b ©Snark/Art Resource, NY; p.128a ©Erich Lessing/Art Resource, NY; p.128b ©Giraudon/Art Resource, NY; p.129a ©The Bridgeman Art Library; p.130 ©Giraudon/Art Resource, NY; p.131a ©Burstein Collection/CORBIS; p.131b ©The British Museum/The Art Archive; p.133a ©Giraudon/ Art Resource, NY; p.133b ©Jeremy Woodhouse/DRK Photo; p.138a ©Lee & Lee Communications/Art Resource, NY; p.138b ©Erich Lessing/Art Resource, NY; p.138c ©Scala/Art Resource, NY; p.138d ©Werner Forman/Art Resource, NY; p.139a ©Scala/Art Resource, NY; p.139b ©Boltin Picture Library; p.140a,b ©Giraudon/Art Resource, NY; p.141a ©Réunion des Musées Nationaux/Art Resource, NY; p.141b ©The Granger Collection; p.142a,b ©Bettmann/CORBIS; p.143b ©Wagner Museum, Bayreuth, Germany/ET Archive, London/SuperStock; p.144 ©Charles & Josette Lenars/CORBIS; p.145a ©Erich Lessing/Art Resource, NY; p.145b ©The Pierpont Morgan Library/Art Resource, NY; p.147b,148b ©Scala/Art Resource, NY; p.149 ©David Lees/CORBIS; p.150a ©Scala/Art Resource, NY; p.150b ©Christie's Images/CORBIS; p.151a ©Adam Woolfitt/CORBIS; p.151b ©The Granger Collection; p.153 ©Chris Hellier/CORBIS; p.156a ©The Bridgeman Art Library/Getty Images; p.156b ©Jonathan Blair/CORBIS; p.157a ©Stapleton Collection/CORBIS; p.157b ©Historical Picture Archive/CORBIS; p.158a ©Giraudon/Art Resource, NY; p.158b ©Holton Collection/SuperStock; p.159b ©The Granger Collection; p.160 ©Nabeel Turner/Getty Images; p.161a,b ©Erich Lessing/Art Resource, NY; p.162a ©Werner Forman/Art Resource, NY; p.163a ©The Metropolitan Museum of Art, Samuel D. Lee Fund; p.163b ©Andre Durenceau/National Geographic Image Collection; p.164b ©Réunion des Musées Nationaux/Art Resource, NY; p.165 ©Woodfin Camp; p.169a ©Musée Guimet, Paris, France/Lauros-Giraudon, Paris/SuperStock; p.169b ©Liu Xiasyang/China Stock; p.170b ©The Granger Collection; p.171a ©British Library/The Art Archive; p.171b ©Kurt Scholz/SuperStock; p.172a ©Boltin Picture Library; p.172b ©Burstein Collection/CORBIS; p.173 ©The Granger Collection; p.174a ©Sakamoto Photo Research Laboratory/CORBIS; p.174b ©Chris Lisle/ CORBIS; p.175b ©The Metropolitan Museum of Art, Harris Brisbane Dick Fund, 1943; p.176a ©The Metropolitan Museum of Art, Purchase, The Vincent Astor Foundation Gift, 1999 Benefit Fund, and The Rosenkranz Foundation Inc. Gift, 1999; p.176b ©Joel W. Rogers/CORBIS; p.177a ©Dallas and John Heaton/CORBIS; p.177b ©The Metropolitan Museum of Art, The Harry G.C. Packard Collection of Asian Art, Gift of Harry G.C. Packard and Purchase, Fletcher, Rogers, Harris Brisbane Dick and Louis V. Bell Funds, Joseph Pulitzer Bequest and The Annenberg Fund, Inc. Gift, 1975; p.178 ©Werner Forman/Art Resource, NY; p.179a ©Erich Lessing/Art Resource, NY; p.179b ©Jeremy Horner/CORBIS; p.181b ©Keren Su/Stock Boston; p.182b ©Charles & Josette Lenars/CORBIS; p.183 ©Arvind Garg/CORBIS; p.186a ©Werner Forman/Art Resource, NY; p.187 ©Holton Collection/SuperStock; p.188 ©SuperStock; p.190 ©The Metropolitan Museum of Art, John Stewart Kennedy Fund, 1913 ; p.191a ©Herschel Mair/ Iziko Museums of Cape Town; p.193a ©Charles & Josette Lenars/CORBIS; p.193b ©SuperStock; p.194b ©Peter & David Turnley/CORBIS; p.195,198 ©SuperStock; p.199a ©Richard Heinzen/ SuperStock; p.199b ©Danny Lehman/CORBIS; p.201a ©Charles & Josette Lenars/CORBIS; p.201b ©Peabody Museum of Archaelogy and Ethnology; p.203 ©Scala/Art Resource, NY; p.204a ©Lee Boltin Picture Library; p.204b ©Yann Arthus-Bertrand/CORBIS; p.205b ©Werner Forman/Art Resource, NY; p.206a ©Gianni Dagli Orti/CORBIS; p.206b ©Tom Bean/CORBIS; p.207 ©Werner Forman/Art Resource, NY; p.210a ©Werner Forman/Art Resource, NY; p.210b ©Hidekazu Nishibata/SuperStock; p.210c ©Heini Schneebeli/The Bridgeman Art Library; p.211a ©Tim Flach/Getty Images; p.211b ©The Granger Collection; p.211c ©Victor R. Boswell, Jr./National Geographic Image Collection; p.212a ©Erich Lessing/Art Resource, NY; p.212b ©Archivo Iconografico, S.A. /CORBIS; p.213a ©Giraudon/Art Resource, NY; p.214b ©The Granger Collection; p.215a ©SEF/Art Resource, NY; p.215b ©The Granger Collection; p.216 ©Charles & Josette Lenars/CORBIS; p.217a ©Massimo Listri/CORBIS; p.217b ©Scala/ Art Resource, NY; p.218a ©Stock Montage; p.218b ©Scala/Art Resource, NY; p.219a ©Brown Brothers; p.219b ©The Granger Collection; p.220b ©Kevin Schafer/CORBIS; p.221 ©Stock Montage; p.225a ©Erich Lessing/Art Resource, NY; p.225b ©Snark/Art Resource, NY; p.226a ©Victoria and Albert Museum, London/Art Resource, NY; p.226b ©Werner Forman/Art Resource, NY; p.227b ©ET Archive/ SuperStock; p.228a ©The Granger Collection; p.228b ©Burstein Collection/CORBIS; p.229 ©The Granger Collection; p.230a ©The British Museum; p.231a ©Brian A. Vikander/CORBIS; p.231b ©Majid/ Liaison/ Getty Images; p.232a ©Werner Forman Archive/Art Resource, NY; p.232b ©Freer Gallery of Art, Smithsonian Institution, Washington, D.C.; p.233 ©Shishir Thadani; p.234 ©The Granger Collection; p.235a ©Sakamoto Photo Research Laboratory/CORBIS; p.235b ©Burstein Collection/CORBIS; p.236a ©Scala/Art Resource, NY; p.237b ©Janette Ostier Gallery, Paris, France/Giraudon, Paris/SuperStock; p.238a ©Asian Art & Archaeology, Inc./CORBIS; p.238b ©Steve Vidler/SuperStock; p.239 ©Chris Lisle/CORBIS; p.240a ©Musee Guimet, Paris, France/ Erich Lessing/Art Resource, NY; p.241a ©Hidekazu Nishibata/SuperStock; p.241b ©Dan McCoy/Rainbow/Picture Quest; p.244 ©Jack Fields/CORBIS; p.247a ©The Lowe Art Museum, The University of Miami/SuperStock; p.247b ©Sandro Vannini/CORBIS; p.248a ©James Stanfield/National Geographic Image Collection; p.249a ©Musée des Arts Africains et Océaniens/Dagli Orti/The Art Archive; p.249b ©Heini Schneebeli/The Bridgeman Art Library; p.250a ©Werner Forman/Art Resource, NY; p.250b ©Michael A. Hampshire/National Geographic Image Collection; p.251 ©The Granger Collection; p.252a Courtesy of Dimitri Dalagiorgos; p.252b ©Jeffrey L. Rotman/CORBIS; p.253b ©Charles Lenars/ CORBIS; p.254a,b ©Werner Forman/Art Resource, NY; p.255a ©M.P. Kahl/DRK Photo; p.255b ©Robert Aberman/Barbara Heller/Art Resource, NY; p.259a ©Werner Forman/Art Resource, NY; p.259b ©Victor R. Boswell, Jr./National Geographic Image Collection; p.260b ©Hans Georg Roth/CORBIS; p.260c ©Schalkwijk/Art Resource, NY; p.263,264b ©Werner Forman/Art Resource, NY; p.265b ©Dewitt Jones/ CORBIS; p.266a ©Ray Manley/SuperStock; p.266b ©SuperStock; p.267 ©Richard A. Cooke/CORBIS; p.270a ©Bettmann/CORBIS; p.270b ©Earl & Nazima Kowall/CORBIS; p.270c ©The Granger Collection; p.270d ©Hulton Archive/Getty Images; p.271b ©Bridgeman Art Library; p.271c ©Bettmann/CORBIS; p.272a ©Elio Ciol/CORBIS; p.272b ©Sistine Chapel, Vatican, Rome/Canali Photobank Milan/SuperStock; p.273a ©The Granger Collection; p.274a ©Scala/ Art Resource, NY; p.274b,c ©The Granger Collection; p.275a ©Archivo Iconografico, S.A./CORBIS; p.275b ©SuperStock; p.276 ©Hulton Archive/Getty Images; p.277a ©Elio Ciol/CORBIS; p.277b,278a ©The Granger Collection; p.278b ©Scala/Art Resource, NY; p.279a ©Gianni Dagli Orti/CORBIS; p.280a ©The Granger Collection; p.280b ©Scala/Art Resource, NY; p.281 ©Archivo Iconografico, S.A./CORBIS; p.285a ©Brown Brothers; p.286a,b,287b ©The Granger Collection; p.288b ©Archivo Iconografico, S.A./CORBIS; p.289 ©Silvio Fiore/SuperStock; p.290a ©Robert Holmes/CORBIS; p.290b ©Archivo Iconografico, S.A./CORBIS; p.291a ©Musée du Louvre, Paris/SuperStock; p.291b ©Bill Ross/CORBIS; p.292b ©The Granger Collection; p.292c ©SuperStock; p.293 ©Musée de Louvre, Paris/SuperStock; p.294a ©The Granger Collection; p.294b ©Giraudon/Art Resouce, NY; p.295b ©The Granger Collection; p.296 ©Bettmann/CORBIS; p.297a ©Stefano Bianchetti/ CORBIS; p.298 ©The Granger Collection; p.301a ©Archivo Iconografico, S.A./CORBIS; p.301b ©The Granger Collection; p.302a ©Hulton Archive/Getty Images; p.302c ©The Granger Collection; p.303a ©Archivo Iconografico, S.A./CORBIS; p.303b ©Bettmann/CORBIS; p.304a ©The Granger Collection; p.305 ©The British Museum; p.306a ©Peter Harholdt/CORBIS; p.306b ©The Granger Collection; p.307b ©Hulton Archive/Getty Images; p.308a ©The Granger Collection; p.308b ©Francis G. Mayer/CORBIS; p.309b ©CORBIS; p.310 ©Historical Picture Archive/CORBIS; p.314a ©The British Musuem, London/ Bridgeman Art Library, London/SuperStock; p.315b ©Bridgeman Art Library; p.316a ©Heini Schneebeli/ The Bridgeman Art Library; p.316b ©Giraudon/Art Resouce, NY; p.317a ©Christie's Images/CORBIS; p.317b Courtesy of New York Public Library; p.318a ©CORBIS; p.319a ©The Granger Collection; p.320b ©The Granger Collection; p.321 ©Bettmann/CORBIS; p.325a ©Victoria & Albert Museum, London/Art Resource, NY; p.325b ©Earl & Nazima Kowall/CORBIS; p.326b ©The Granger Collection; p.327 ©Christie's Images/CORBIS; p.328 ©The Granger Collection; p.329 ©Giraudon/Art Resouce, NY; p.330a ©Victoria & Albert Museum, London/Art Resource, NY; p.330b ©British Library/The Art Archive; p.331b ©The Granger Collection; p.332a ©Bettmann/CORBIS; p.333a ©Burstein Collection/CORBIS; p.333b ©Bettmann/CORBIS; p.334 ©Hulton Archive/Getty Images; p.335a ©The Granger Collection; p.335b ©Burstein Collection/CORBIS; p.336b ©Giraudon/Art Resource, NY; p.337a ©The Granger Collection; p.337b ©Keren Su/CORBIS; p.338a ©The Granger Collection; p.339 ©The Huntington Library, Art Collections and Botanical Gardens/SuperStock; p.340a ©Oriental Art Museum Genoa/Dagli Orti/The Art Archive; p.340b ©Asian Art & Archaeology, Inc./CORBIS; p.341a ©Christie's Images/CORBIS; p.342a ©Réunion des Musées Nationaux/Art Resource, NY; p.342b ©Bridgeman Art Library, London/SuperStock; p.343b ©The Granger Collection; p.344 ©Charles & Josette Lenars/CORBIS; p.348a ©The Art Archive; p.348c ©Réunion des Musées Nationaux/Art Resource, NY; p.348d ©Schalkwijic/Art Resource, NY; p.349a Bettmann/ CORBIS; p.349b ©Ancient Art & Architecture Collection Ltd.; p.349c ©Schenectady Museum; Hall of Electrical History Foundation/CORBIS; p.350a ©Lee Snider/CORBIS; p.350b ©Ancient Art & Collection, Ltd.; p.351a ©SuperStock; p.351b ©Bettmann/CORBIS; p.352a ©The Granger Collection; p.352b ©SuperStock; p.354 ©National Gallery of Art, Washington, D.C./SuperStock; p.355a ©Kelly-Mooney Photography/CORBIS; p.355b ©Giraudon/Art Resource, NY; p.356a ©Réunion des Musées Nationaux/Art Resource, NY; p.356b ©Erich Lessing/Art Resource, NY; p.357a ©Réunion des Musées Nationaux/Art Resource, NY; p.357b ©Leonard de Selva/CORBIS; p.358a ©Réunion des Musées Nationaux/Art Resource, NY; p.359 ©Gianni Dagli Orti/CORBIS; p.360a ©Museo Nacional de la Mascara San Luis Potosi Mexico/Mireille Vautier/The Art Archive; p.360b ©Museo 20 de Julio de 1810 Bogota/Dagli Orti/The Art Archive; p.362a ©Schalkwijic/Art Resource, NY; p.363 ©SuperStock; p.366a ©Schenectady Museum; Hall of Electrical History Foundation/CORBIS; p.367a,b,368,369a,b ©The Granger Collection; p.370 ©SuperStock; p.371a ©Schenectady Museum; Hall of Electrical History Foundation/CORBIS; p.371b,372a ©The Granger Collection; p.373a ©Explorer, Paris/SuperStock; p.373b ©Lewis W. Hine/George Eastman House; p.374 ©Hulton Archive/Getty Images; p.375 ©The Granger Collection; p.379a ©Elio Ciol/CORBIS; p.379b ©Maximilianeum Foundation, Munich, Germany/SuperStock; p.380b ©Archivo Iconografico, S.A./CORBIS; p.381b ©Ancient Art & Architecture Collection Ltd.; p.383 ©Hulton-Deutsch Collection/CORBIS; p.384a,b,386b ©The Granger Collection; p.386a Courtesy of Library of Congress; p.389a ©Victoria & Albert Museum, London/Art Resource, NY; p.390a ©Archivo Iconografico, S.A./CORBIS; p.390b ©Kunsthistorisches, Vienna, Austria/ Bridgeman Art Library, London/SuperStock; p.391a ©Réunion des Musées Nationaux/Art Resource, NY; p.391b ©Alinari/Art Resource, NY; p.392a ©The Granger Collection; p.392c,393 ©Bettmann/CORBIS; p.396a ©Werner Forman Archive/Art Resource, NY; p.396b ©The Granger Collection; p.397a ©Bettmann/CORBIS; p.397b Courtesy of the Zanzibar Archives; p.398b ©The Granger Collection; p.399 ©Bettmann/CORBIS; p.400a ©Peter Harholdt/SuperStock; p.400b ©A.K.G., Berlin/SuperStock; p.401a ©Hulton-Deutsch Collection/CORBIS; p.401b ©David Forbert/SuperStock; p.403,404 ©Bettmann/CORBIS; p.408b ©Hulton Archive/Getty Images; p.408c ©The Granger Collection; p.409b ©Bettmann/CORBIS; p.409c ©Wood River Gallery/PictureQuest; p.410b,411a ©Hulton Archive/ Getty Images; p.412 ©Domenica del Corriere/Dagli Orti/The Art Archive; p.413a Courtesy of Julia Hagaman; p.413b ©Bettmann/CORBIS; p.414a ©The Granger Collection; p.414b ©David Pollack/CORBIS; p.416a ©Hulton-Deutsch Collection/ CORBIS; p.416b ©CORBIS; p.418a ©David Lees/CORBIS; p.418b ©Bettmann/CORBIS; p.419a ©Hulton Archive/Getty Images; p.420b ©National Portrait Gallery, Smithsonian Insitution/Art Resource, NY; p.422 ©Hulton-Deutsch Collection/CORBIS; p.425a ©Bridgeman Art Library, London/SuperStock; p.425b ©Scott Swanson Collection/Getty Images; p.426a ©Hulton Archive/Getty Images; p.426b ©Stock Montage/SuperStock; p.427 ©Hulton Archives/Getty Images; p.428a,b ©Scala/Art Resource, NY; p.429 ©The Granger Collection; p.430a ©The Art Archive; p.430b ©The Granger Collection; p.431a ©Hulton Archive/Getty Images; p.432a ©CORBIS; p433b Courtesy of U.S. Information Agency; p.434a ©Hulton Archives/Getty Images; p.435a ©SuperStock; p.435b ©Underwood & Underwood/CORBIS; p.436a ©Hulton Archives/Getty Images; p.436b ©Bettmann/CORBIS; p.437a ©Domenica del Corriere/Dagli Orti/The Art Archive; p.437b,438 ©The Granger Collection; p.439 ©Hulton Archives/Getty Images; p.440a ©Francis G. Mayer/CORBIS; p.440b ©Hulton-Deutsch Collection/CORBIS; p.441a Hayim Shtayer collection, Haifa/photo courtesy of Beth Hatefutsoth, Photo Archive, Tel Aviv; p.441b ©Hulton Archive/ Getty Images; p.442b ©Bettmann/CORBIS; p.443 ©Reuters NewMedia Inc./CORBIS; p.446 ©Stock Montage, Inc.; p.447a,448a ©CORBIS; p.448b ©Hulton Archive/Getty Images; p.449a ©Stock Montage/ SuperStock; p.450a ©AP/Wide World; p.450b ©Hulton Archive/Getty Images; p.450c Courtesy of Imperial War Museum; p.452a Courtesy of Joan Cunningham; p.454b ©AP/Wide World; p.456 ©SuperStock; p.457a ©Bettmann/CORBIS; p.457b,458a ©Hulton Archive/Getty Images; p.459a ©AP/Wide World; p.460 ©The Mariners' Museum/CORBIS; p.461a Courtesy of Alyx Kellington; p.461b ©Anthony Potter Collection/Getty Images; p.462a ©Bettmann/CORBIS; p.462b ©Archiv fur Kunst und Geschichte, Berlin/SuperStock; p.464a ©Hulton Archive/Getty Images; p.465 ©Oscar White/CORBIS; p.468a Courtesy of NASA; p.468b ©Roman Soumar/CORBIS; p.468c ©Jacques M. Chenet/CORBIS; p.468d ©Bettmann/CORBIS; p.468e ©Liaison/Getty Images; p.469a ©CORBIS; p.469c ©Peter Winkler/AP/Wide World; p.469d ©Peter Morgan, Reuters NewMedia Inc./CORBIS; p.470b ©AP/Wide World; p.471a ©James Arthur Wood/CORBIS; p.471b ©The Granger Collection; p.473a ©AP/Wide World; p.473b ©Arthur Rickerby/The Picture Quest; p.474 Courtesy of NASA; p.475a ©Macduff Everton/CORBIS; p.475b ©Hulton Archive/Getty Images; p.477a ©Roman Soumar/CORBIS; p.477b ©Charles Bonnay/The Picture Quest; p.478a,b ©Hulton Archive/Getty Images; p.479 ©Jeff Widener/AP/Wide World; p.483a ©James Marshall/CORBIS; p.483b ©Howard Sochurek/ TimePix; p.486a ©Walter Dhladha/AP/Wide World; p.486b ©Dave G. Houser/CORBIS; p.487 ©Bettmann/CORBIS; p.488a The British Museum; p.488b ©Bettmann/CORBIS; p.489 ©George Mulala/Reuters p.490a ©SuperStock; p.490b ©Terence Spencer/TimePix; p.491 ©James Nelson/Getty Images; p.492 ©AFP/CORBIS; p.493a ©Danny Lehman/CORBIS; p.493b ©Bill Gentile/CORBIS; p.494a ©Dario Lopez-Mills/AP/Wide World; p.494b ©José Fuste Raga/CORBIS; p.495a ©Alberto Bravo/AP/Wide World; p.496a ©Owen Franken/CORBIS; p.497 ©Paolo Fridman/Latin Focus.com; p.500a ©Peter Winkler/AP/Wide World; p.500b ©Bettmann/CORBIS; p.501a © Vittoriano Rastelli/CORBIS; p.501b ©Scott Stewart/AP/Wide World; p.502a ©Kenneth Jarecke/Contact Press Images/PictureQuest; p.502b ©Shepard Sherbell/CORBIS Saba; p.502c ©AFP/CORBIS; p.504 ©David Burnett/Contact Press Images/PictureQuest; p.505d ©David Rubinger/CORBIS; p.506a ©Peter Turnley/CORBIS; p.506b ©AFP/CORBIS; p.507b ©CORBIS; p.508a ©INA/AP/Wide World; p.509 ©Bettmann/CORBIS; p.510c ©Steve Vidler/SuperStock; p.511b © Bagla Pallava/CORBIS Sygma; p.512 Courtesy of UPI Telephoto; p.513a ©Liaison/Getty Images; p.513b ©David Turnley/CORBIS; p.514 ©Jim Zuckerman/CORBIS; p.518b © Peter Morgan, Reuters NewMedia Inc./CORBIS; p.519a ©2001 Thomas E. Franklin/The Record /CORBIS Saba; p.519b ©AFP/CORBIS; p.520a ©Peter Turnley/CORBIS; p.520b ©Tokyo Shimbun/CORBIS Sygma; p.521 © Reuters NewMedia Inc./CORBIS; p.522b ©Peter Beck/CORBIS; p.523b ©Jeff Greenberg/Index Stock Imagery, Inc.; p.524a ©Lester V. Bergman/CORBIS; p.524b ©Pete Saloutos/CORBIS; p.524c ©Reuters NewMedia Inc./CORBIS; p.525 ©Ken Lucas/Visuals Unlimited, Inc.; p.527a ©Lightscapes/CORBIS; p.527b ©Paul A. Souders/CORBIS; p.528a ©Frank Hanna/Visuals Unlimited, Inc.; p.529a ©Premium Stock/CORBIS; p.529b © Jose Fuste Raga/CORBIS p.530a ©Kevin Schafer/CORBIS; p.530b ©Wayne Lawler; Ecoscene/ CORBIS; p.531 ©Jeff Greenberg/PhotoEdit; p.532a ©Adelman/Cohen/Getty Images p.532c ©Ann Purcell /CORBIS; p.532d ©Neema Frederic/CORBIS Sygma; p.532e ©Dewitt Jones/Getty Images; p.532f ©Charles & Josette Lenars/CORBIS; p.532h ©David Turnley/CORBIS; p.533a ©Paul Vreeker/Reuters NewMedia Inc./CORBIS; p.533b ©Mike Fiala/AP/Wide World; p.534a ©David Turnley/CORBIS; p.534b ©R.Kwiotek/Zeitenspeigle/CORBIS Sygma; p.535 ©Tim Hauf/Visuals Unlimited, Inc.

Additional photos by Comstock, Corbis Royalty Free, The Edge of Nowhere, Getty Royalty Free, Hollingsworth Royalty Free, Image Club Graphics, MoviePosters.com, North Wind Pictures Archives, Ragnarok Press, and Snapshots of the Past.